Reforming Justice in Russia, 1864-1996

This work is a study of the Stalin-Era Research and Archives Project of the University of Toronto, funded by the Social Sciences and Humanities Research Council of Canada.

Reforming Justice in Russia, 1864-1996

Power, Culture, and the Limits of Legal Order

edited by

Peter H. Solomon, Jr.

M.E. Sharpe
Armonk, New York
London, England

Library of Congress Cataloging-in-Publication Data

Reforming justice in Russia, 1864–1996: power, culture, and the
limits of legal order / edited by Peter H. Solomon, Jr.
p.   cm.
Includes bibliographical references and index.
ISBN 1-56324-862-X (c: alk. paper)
1. Justice, Administration of—Russia (Federation)—History.
2. Law reform—Russia (Federation)—History.
I. Solomon, Peter H.
KLB470.R44   1997
347.47—dc21   97-11590
CIP
Printed in the United States of America

The paper used in this publication meets the minimum requirements of
American National Standard for Information Sciences—
Permanence of Paper for Printed Library Materials,
ANSI Z 39.48-1984.

BM (c)   10   9   8   7   6   5   4   3   2   1
BM (p)   10   9   8   7   6   5   4   3   2   1

CONTENTS

JUSTICE AND THE RUSSIAN TRANSITION

ACKNOWLEDGMENTS

This book is based upon a set of papers prepared for the conference "Reforming Justice in Russia: An Historical Perspective," which was held at Massey College, University of Toronto, 31 March–2 April 1995. The conference was special in that it provided the first occasion for intensive discussion and collaboration among specialists in law and justice in tsarist Russia and their counterparts working on this subject in the USSR and post-Soviet Russia. Funding for the conference came from the Centre for Russian and East European Studies through its grant from the Andrew Mellon Foundation and from the Stalin-Era Research and Archives Project (SERAP) at the Centre funded by the Social Sciences and Humanities Research Council of Canada. In addition to the contributors to this volume, participants at the conference included: Susan Heuman, Robert Johnson, Joan Neuberger, Ronald Pruessen, Susan Solomon, Olga Solovieva, and Lynne Viola. As commentator for the conference as a whole, Robert Sharlet gave sage advice on the development of this volume.

In preparing this volume for publication, I benefited above all from collaboration with an extraordinarily talented editor, Dr. Edith Klein. As publications officer of SERAP, Edith performed copy-editing and prepared the camera-ready version of the manuscript, for which I am truly grateful. I am also pleased to acknowledge the assistance of Janet Hyer, Gary Wilson, and Brett Young in research, editorial assistance, and conference organization. At M. E. Sharpe, Patricia Kolb and Elizabeth Granda provided firm and patient guidance to bring this volume to the public.

ABOUT THE CONTRIBUTORS

Golfo Alexopoulos is Assistant Professor of History at the University of South Florida in Tampa. She recently received her Ph.D. from the University of Chicago, where she prepared a dissertation on the Soviet disenfranchised, entitled, "Rights and Passage: Marking Outcasts and Making Citizens in Soviet Russia, 1926-1936." The focus of her current research is the practice of amnesty and clemency in Russia.

Girish N. Bhat is Assistant Professor of Russian and European history at the State University of New York, Cortland. He received his Ph.D. in 1994 from the University of California, Berkeley. He is currently at work on a study of the theory and practice of the rule of law in late imperial Russia.

Jane Burbank is Professor of History at the University of Michigan. She is the author of *Intelligentsia and Revolution:Russian Views of Bolshevism, 1917–1992* (Princeton University Press), and is preparing a monograph on Russian legal culture in the early twentieth century.

Todd Foglesong is Adjunct Assistant Professor of Russian and East European Studies at the University of Kansas. He is conducting research on the implementation of judicial reforms in post-Soviet Russia, and completing a manuscript, "Controlling Courts in Russia: The Politics of Judicial Independence and the Faces of Criminal Justice under the Old and New Regimes."

Cathy A. Frierson is Associate Professor in the Department of History at the University of New Hampshire. Her publications include *Peasant Icons: Representations of Rural People in Late Nineteenth Century Russia* and *Aleksandr Nikolaevich Engelgardt's Letters from the Country, 1872-1887* (both Oxford University Press). Her current project is a study of fire and arson in late imperial rural Russia.

Yoram Gorlizki is Lecturer in the Department of Government at the University of Manchester. He is currently completing a book on the politics of the Soviet criminal justice system during 1948-1964.

Lisa Granik is a Graduate Fellow at Yale Law School, whose research explores new directions in legal hermeneutics. Her chapter in this book is part of a larger work examining the potentials and perils of using the legal process to promote social change, and the hermeneutical obstacles in that process.

Eugene Huskey is Professor of Political Science and Director of Russian Studies at Stetson University in DeLand, Florida. Among his works is *Russian Lawyers and the Soviet State* (Princeton University Press, published in English and Russian editions) and numerous articles on Soviet and post-Soviet legal affairs. He has also written on the Russian presidency and on politics in the Central Asian republic of Kyrgyzstan.

Sergei M. Kazantsev is an Associate Professor in the Department of Theory and History of State and Law, St. Petersburg State University. He is the editor-compiler of *Sud priasiazhnykh v Rossii* (Leningrad, 1991) and author of *Istoriia tsarskoi prokuratury* (St. Petersburg, 1993).

Oleg V. Khlevniuk is an editor at the journal *Svobodnaia mysl'*. He is the author of *1937-i: Stalin, NKVD, i sovetskoe obshchestvo* (Moscow, 1992); *Stalin i Ordzhonikidze. Konflikty v Politbiuro v 30-e gody* (Moscow, 1993), published in English under the title, *In Stalin's Shadow: The Career of "Sergo" Ordzhonikidze* (M. E. Sharpe); and *Le cercle du Kremlin: Staline et le Bureau politique dans les années 30: les jeux du pouvoir* (Paris, 1996).

Sarah J. Reynolds is a Fellow at the Davis Center for Russian Studies at Harvard University and an Institute Fellow of the Institute for East European Law of Leiden University, the Netherlands. Her current research focuses on the institutional borrowing in legal reform efforts and on the development of civil and administrative law in the CIS. She is the editor of the journal *Statutes and Decisions: The Laws of the USSR and Its Successor States.*

Gábor T. Rittersporn is Senior Research Fellow at the Centre National de la Recherche Scientifique in Paris. He is the author of *Stalinist Simplifications and Soviet Complications: Social Tensions and Political Conflicts in the USSR, 1933-1953* (1991), and various articles.

Gordon B. Smith is Professor of Government and International Studies at the University of South Carolina. The author of *The Soviet Procuracy and the Supervision of Administration* (Sijthoff and Noordhoff) and *Reforming the Russian Legal System* (Cambridge University Press), he serves on the National Advisory Board of the Rule of Law Consortium, a project designed to assist Russia in the reform of its legal system.

Peter H. Solomon, Jr. is Professor of Political Science and a member of the Centre for Russian and East European Studies and of the Graduate Faculty of the Centre for Criminology, all at the University of Toronto. His most recent book is *Soviet Criminal Justice under Stalin* (Cambridge University Press), and he is pursuing research on judicial reform in post-Soviet Russia.

William G. Wagner is Brown Professor of History at Williams College, Williamstown, Massachusetts. He is the author of *Marriage, Property, and Law in Late Imperial Russia* (Oxford University Press) and of numerous articles and essays on law and legal reform in imperial Russia during the post-reform era. He currently is engaged in a study of women and the Orthodox Church during the nineteenth and early twentieth centuries.

Reforming Justice in Russia, 1864-1996

COURTS AND THEIR REFORM IN RUSSIAN HISTORY

Peter H. Solomon, Jr.

More than once in Russian history the liberalization of politics set in motion a reform of justice and law. Gorbachev's glasnost' and the process of democratization in post-Soviet Russia saw a struggle by jurists in Russia to make their courts independent, powerful, and fair. The judicial reforms that resulted from their efforts reminded observers of the era of the Great Reforms and the adoption by the tsarist leaders of the Judicial Reform of 1864, over whose realization jurists and officials fought for half a century. Between these two eras of reform came the seventy years of Soviet power, during which successive generations of Soviet leaders tried to shape courts and the law to suit their interests and visions. To a considerable degree, they turned back the clock, undoing many of the achievements of the tsarist judicial reform. At the same time, the Soviet experience left a stamp of its own on law and the courts, which made the challenge of judicial reform in the 1990s differ from that of the 1860s.

The contributors to this jointly authored volume explore the attempts to reform or reshape the administration of justice in tsarist, Soviet and post-Soviet Russia. The authors do not try to provide a full or systematic account of the panoply of changes attempted during the century and a half of its purview. Rather they offer a joint exploration of some key issues in the interpretation of that experience. The studies range over a variety of subjects—from the high politics of reform to the way clients and officials reshaped particular initiatives; from civil law disputes to the uses of the criminal sanction; from the role of various courts to alternative forms of complaint and dispute resolution; from the institutions of the law to the types of legal cultures. The authors believe that their adoption of an historical perspective will illuminate the reform of justice in today's Russia. This approach helps them to consider both the cumulative effects of different waves of reforms and the lessons of past reform efforts, as well as to make cross-temporal comparisons.

One of the questions addressed in this book is how the obstacles to the attainment of modern legal order in Russia of 1994 compared with those in Russia of 1864 and 1914. This comparison called for a focus on the difference that the Soviet, and especially Stalinist, experience made for the goal of independent courts. In posing this question, the authors do not assume that there is or should be a universal model for the administration of justice or that Russian reformers of any particular period adhered to the goals that Western observers might consider appropriate. To understand why the outcomes of particular reform initiatives over the 130 years often differed from common Western standards, the authors seek to discover what kinds of legality prevailed in practice, and why, and to probe the aspirations of the reformers themselves. Only in this context can one properly assess the fate of any particular vision of legal order.

Another of the authors' concerns is the realities of political power during the 130 years under consideration, especially the relationship between law and politics. At least until 1992, Russia had an authoritarian political system, in which the ruler—be it Tsar or General Secretary—stood above the law and treated laws as an instrument of rule. The decision in 1864 to create independent courts ran counter to the bases of autocracy and threatened to deprive the ruler of his prerogative to dispense justice. For this reason, if no other, the fifty years of realizing these reforms were marked by tension and by attempts, sometimes successful, to check their impact. For their part Soviet leaders did not even aspire to establishing independent and impartial courts. They gave judges discretion but expected them to implement the policies of the regime and often to heed the advice of authorities in individual cases as well. In contrast, the leaders of post-Soviet Russia were at least formally committed to developing independent courts, but as of 1997 they lacked the resources to realize this goal.

The position of Russia's rulers above the law helped to reinforce a traditional emphasis on the substance of dispute resolution as opposed to the means or procedures employed. This de-emphasis on procedures had a number of consequences. One was a strong and lasting interest in alternatives to the courts, among them a variety of mechanisms for handling of complaints. Another less benign result was the common and expedient use of extra-judicial coercion, especially in the Soviet period.

While the reality of power placed limits on the development of legal order, the real world of courts was also shaped by the attitudes toward the law on the part of different sectors of the population. In the classic study of law in Russian history, Harold Berman argued that before the Bolshevik Revolution Russia had achieved the institutions and forms of law that existed in the West but not their core principles and underlying assumptions.[1] The historians of tsarist justice in this book take this insight further by exploring the actual legal cultures of particular social groups. Thus, in studies of the ways peasants used the *volost'* courts and their resort to such alternatives to the law as arson, the authors develop a portrait of a rural legal culture that was complex and nuanced—"layered" and "fragmented"—one in which the same persons might, on a pragmatic basis, display different legal mentalities at the same time.

In the Soviet period, even the institutions of the law no longer met the Western standards of which Berman wrote. Consequently, the students of Soviet justice in this volume devote more attention to the institutional factors that influenced the nature and quality of justice in Russia. A number of them analyze the development by Soviet leaders during the Stalin and post-Stalin years of new and more reliable ways of ensuring that the courts delivered the results that they desired. In so doing, they detect shifts in the relative weight among the factors limiting the autonomy of the courts (e.g., the influence of local Party officials versus that of the central legal agencies). At the same time, the essays on the Soviet period also demonstrate how from 1930 the special emphasis on criminal law, along with the presence of extra-legal coercion, produced a negative public image of the courts and a diminution in public trust in their capacity to resolve disputes fairly.

Two further issues that receive special attention in this volume are the process of adapting legal institutions imported from the West and the nature of one peculiarly Russian legal institution, the procuracy. Many features of the Judicial Reform of 1864, including trial by jury, were based upon models from England and Western Europe, which in the Russian context took on new features. Thus, the placement of the jury within the context of an inquisitorial pre-trial procedure and a collegial tradition in the courtroom led to a new kind of "consensual justice" that may find replication in the post-Soviet revival of the jury. The tsarist procuracy began as an agency for supervising justice, but in 1864 was converted into a prosecutorial body. The Soviet leaders revived its supervisory functions, which stood as the equal to the prosecutorial ones throughout most of the Soviet period. In post-Soviet Russia legal reformers identified the twin functions of the procuracy and the special power that they produced as a key obstacle to the development of Russian courts.

The essays in this book are arranged in three groups, covering the tsarist, Soviet, and post-Soviet periods, respectively. Here I introduce each group of essays with brief accounts of relevant background—the highlights of the

Judicial Reform of 1864, the development of the Soviet system of justice, and the origins of judicial reform in late Soviet and post-Soviet Russia.

The Judicial Reform of 1864 was sufficiently radical in its aspirations, if not also its achievements, to qualify as revolutionary. To support this character- ization one has only to compare the Reform with the institutions and practices of justice that preceded it.[2] Until 1775 most adjudication in Russia was conducted not by specialized officials or courts but by administrators who performed other functions. In 1775 the Empress Catherine established an intricate system of courts, but it had important limitations. To begin, each of the major free estates—gentry, merchants, and state peasants—had its own structure of courts; but serfs were denied access to the courts and received their justice from the gentry. Moreover, although some of the judgeships were elective, the courts were not independent of political authority. Thus, governors of the provinces had responsibility for supervis- ing the courts, which included protesting unjust decisions to the Senate or Tsar and confirming all death sentences. For their part, most of the judges, many of whom were local notables, had little inclination to stand up to political officials. The typical judge was uneducated in law, depended on his clerks to explain cases, and accepted bribes.

To encourage fulfillment of their laws and decrees, the tsars of pre- Reform Russia gave their courts a pure form of inquisitorial procedure, something that no longer existed in Western Europe. This meant a complete reliance on written documents, to the point where there were no trials as such, only office reviews of relevant documentation. In civil cases, the requirement of providing not only the essence of the case but also references to relevant laws (which were unavailable without writing the capital) made the process complicated, expensive, time consuming, and impractical for most complainants. In the criminal realm inquisitorial procedure helped to create a bias in favor of the prosecution. Trials consisted of office reviews of the written documentation produced by the pre-trial investigations, and judges had little discretion in applying the law. The results of the investiga- tion were unlikely to be challenged, since there were no lawyers present and no oral testimony. To acquit, as well as to convict, required proof, and most cases ended instead in "leaving [the accused] under suspicion," as a result of which he or she often had to move to a new location. The crucially important pre-trial investigation was conducted by police and other administrators. Confessions were encouraged and treated as the best form of evidence; the reputation of the accused (known as "moral evidence") also carried weight along with the material evidence.

Needless to say, since neither civil nor criminal procedure called for the services of lawyers, few were trained. There were no state prosecutors, nor was there a defense bar. To the tsars, lawyers represented a potential threat to their unlimited power.

The Judicial Reform of 1864 changed most of these features of pre-Reform courts and their procedures.[3] First, the system of class courts under the control of the governors was replaced by a new hierarchy of courts open to all citizens, including the former serfs. These courts were designed to be separate from the executive and independent. Consequently, in the higher levels (the district courts and the judicial chambers) judges had life tenure, with removal only for cause. Furthermore, judges gained new discretion in applying the law, including a duty to rely in part upon their conscience, and, at least in the higher courts, the right to interpret the law. To be sure, the Reform statutes included special procedures for cases involving government officials and some political cases as well. The Reform also established two simple courts—the justice of the peace courts and the volost' courts—that were accessible to ordinary persons (townsfolk and peasants), could handle petty disputes without much expense or written documentation, and, in the case of the volost' courts, could apply customary law.

At the same time, the Judicial Reform introduced an overdue modernization of court procedures, moving them away from the pure inquisitorial mode to a mixture of inquisitorial and adversarial elements. In civil and criminal cases alike, the days of the office review were over. A trial was a trial, with the parties, if not also their lawyers, contesting the issues in public before a judge or panel of judges. In the criminal realm in particular, the inquisitorial tradition of compiling a written record was retained, but once introduced at trial that record was subject to challenge, as trials became contests between the sides, open, public, with oral testimony, and representation by lawyers. For the most serious cases trial by jury became an option, with all of the unpredictability of outcome which that institution entailed. The new oral testimony gave impetus to the development of a defense bar. It also required lawyers to prosecute at trial, and, as we shall see, procurators were asked to assume this function.

The development and adoption of this judicial reform was an extraordinary event, possible only in unusual times. The context, of course, was the mounting of a whole series of reforms all emanating from and related to the Emancipation of the serfs. But other ingredients also made the reform process possible. One was the presence of a small cadre of enlightened jurists in high places in the bureaucracy, individuals who promoted and helped write the reform legislation. Second, this group had the advantage of working against the background of a broad consensus that the old system of justice was so bad as to constitute an embarrassment to Russia. Third, the reform was facilitated by the recognition among many of the gentry dispossessed by the Emancipation that the protection of their new property rights required strong law and courts. All of these conditions helped, but the Judicial Reform of 1864 depended equally on the actions of particular persons and on chance.

The 1864 reform produced a judicial system that was bound to challenge the unlimited power of the tsar. No doubt the officials who drafted the reform saw things differently. They assumed that independent courts staffed by legal specialists not only were compatible with autocratic power, but would even strengthen it by ensuring the observance of the tsar's laws. In practice, however, some judicial decisions failed to meet the interests or expectations of the tsar, and it became clear that the law was no longer a reliable instrument of autocratic power. As a result, over the decades of implementing the reform, the tsars and their ministers tried to minimize the loss of imperial prerogatives. They decided to remove more political offenses from the regular courts (and trial by jury) and to introduce special emergency regimes in parts of the country. In addition, they limited the scope of the justice of the peace courts and placed some adjudicatory functions again in the hands of an administrative official, the district land captain. A law in 1885 gave the Minister of Justice the right to ask judges to explain any of their actions and to issue instructions about decisions in cases completed or procedure in future cases. The law also facilitated disciplinary proceedings against judges, increased the grounds for their removal, and allowed for the transfer of judges from one bench or court to another by the Ministry. Through these and other new powers of management, judges in Russia became subject to pressures to conform to the interests of their bureaucratic and political masters. All the same, the bulk of the achievements embodied in the Judicial Reform of 1864 lasted for the five decades preceding World War I, despite serious attempts at counter-reform, and represented an extraordinary innovation, perhaps the most successful of the reforms initiated in the 1860s.[4]

Each of the five chapters of this book dealing with the tsarist period (chapters 2–6) casts new light on the implementation of the Judicial Reform of 1864 and contributes to an assessment of what its fifty years achieved.

William Wagner's study of judicial activism presents one of the previously unknown successes of the Judicial Reform, namely the assertion by judges on the top appellate courts of the right to develop the meaning of the laws through interpretation. The Civil Cassation department proved particularly active when during the 1870s its decisions effectively changed the laws on marital separation by granting to wives the right to choose to live apart from their husbands and receive financial support, if for reasons beyond their control cohabitation had become impossible. As long as the courts found the reasons for separation valid, the separation itself was legal. This example of judicial interpretation, which Wagner tells us was not atypical, suggests that the court system had achieved, at least in the civil realm, not only a good deal of independence from political authority but power as well.

One pre-existing legal institution especially affected by the Judicial Reform of 1864 was the procuracy. According to Sergei Kazantsev, in his essay on that body's history, the reform led to the abandonment of the procuracy's main pre-reform role, the supervision of the legality of public administration (known as "general supervision"), in favor of supervising the courts and conducting criminal prosecutions, an entirely new function for the procuracy. Kazantsev contends that this change was for the better. Not only was the procuracy far more successful and powerful as a prosecutorial body than it had been when attempting to supervise "everything," but also the new functions of the procuracy were more compatible than the old with the goal of strengthening the courts. As we shall see, tsarist experience bequeathed to the Soviet and post-Soviet leaders two models of the procuracy's role, the choice or mixture of which would become an issue of controversy once again.

Perhaps the best known new institution of the Judicial Reform was trial by jury, an institution that the Soviets would reject but their successors in 1992 decide to restore. Ghirish Bhat offers insight into both the design and practice of the jury trial in tsarist Russia, with an emphasis on its procedures. He argues that the criminal process in serious cases before the reform-era courts represented not only a mixture of inquisitorial and adversarial elements, but also a peculiarly Russian style of judicial inquiry, which he calls "consensualism." Despite the presence of the two sides and the conduct of debate, the dominant mode of prescribed discourse, according to Bhat, was non-combative, a part of the common search for truth. Procurators were instructed to avoid one-sidedness and defense counsel excess in pressing their claims. In practice, Bhat's research shows, the judge(s) also took a leading role in deliberations and conferred frequently with counsel about how to proceed; ad hoc and informal arrangements were commonplace.

The development of new institutions was a central aspect of the Judicial Reform of 1864, but for the reform to succeed the emergence of a supportive legal culture was required as well. One of the big questions during the decades before World War I was how to develop an attachment to law among the largest group in the population, the peasantry, which was reputedly backward and attached to custom. Among the liberal intelligentsia of Russia, Jane Burbank tells us, the reigning view was that peasants could become citizens only through knowing and accepting statutory law and using a single unified court system. According to Burbank, however, what really mattered was popular use of any authentic legal institution as the preferred means of resolving conflicts and punishing wrongs. She goes on to show how the volost' courts, especially after their 1889 reform, were not only used by peasants, but even preferred over alternative authorities, for the refereeing of conflicts that mattered, including insults, quarrels, and property disputes. Contrary to the conventional wisdom about the volost' courts (developed largely by urban jurists in Russia), Burbank reveals that in practice they displayed both the formality of legal proceedings and considerable reliance on the laws. She concludes that fifty years of the Judicial Reform led to a significant advance in legal culture among the largest group in the population, something that was eventually lost during the Soviet period. In this respect, post-Soviet legal reforms must unfold in a cultural context more like that of 1864 than 1914.

The volost' courts were not the only place in the legal system where peasants demonstrated an acceptance of law. Peasants also played a major role in the juries of tsarist Russia, constituting by the 1880s the bulk of the jurors everywhere except in the larger cities.[5] But there remained another side of the Russian peasantry that reflected the force of tradition, namely the use of arson as an instrument of dispute resolution. Cathy Frierson explains in her essay that many peasants treated arson not as a crime but as a form of justice, a response to wrongdoing by others. There were, however, clear moral norms. To exercise appropriate revenge peasants had to burn the right buildings and no more; burning the wrong property or harming human beings could and did result in counter-reprisals. Even in the late nineteenth century the peasants in many villages responded directly to burnings they personally saw as unjustified. In this particular area of social relations, peasants distrusted the state. Frierson concludes that peasants overall lived at one and the same time in modern and traditional worlds, and were ready to use both the law, when it seemed effective and convenient, and more traditional modes of conduct, in other situations.

The Revolution of 1917 brought to the seats of power Bolsheviks whose attitudes toward law, courts, and lawyers were ambivalent if not negative.[6] While many of them remained attached to the ideal of a society administered without the cumbersome and biased legal institutions of capitalism, most Bolshevik leaders, especially Vladimir Lenin, quickly accepted the utility of law as an instrument of rule and sought to develop law and courts to serve the new regime. In the early years they took pride in eliminating the vestiges of the tsarist system of class courts and giving the peasantry full access to the new single system of courts. However, the hierarchy of people's courts, provincial (later regional and territorial) courts, and supreme courts of the republics and USSR did not result in equality before the law. For one thing, until the late 1920s the criminal code encouraged judges to give favorable treatment to representatives of the toiling classes, that is workers and peasants. For another, a habit of privileged treatment for representatives of political power (e.g., the Party *nomenklatura*) developed quickly and endured throughout Soviet history. Even the single structure of courts did not last long, as it was supplemented by lay courts (comrades courts and rural lay courts, successors to the volost' courts), arbitration panels for disputes within the state owned economy, and the extra-judicial bodies of the political police.

What progress had been made under the tsars toward the entrenchment of judicial independence was for the most part reversed by the new Soviet regime, and the traditional autocratic subordination of law to political power restored. Judicial appointments involved approvals by Party officials, and terms in office for judges at all levels were of limited duration, thereby making the question of reappointment (at times in the form of renomination for uncontested election) also subject to political vetting. The system of financing courts mainly from local budgets rather than a central one further reinforced the dependence of judges upon politicians in their bailiwicks and helped to assure their cooperation with their political masters. Finally, the strong instrumental conception of law left little place for attachment to the ideal of judicial independence, even though it was declared in the 1936 constitution. Judges were expected at all times to pay heed to the political demands of the moment (expressed in criminal policy or in recommendations from Party officials), while maintaining a public face of impartiality to enhance the court's prestige.

A defining feature of the Bolshevik approach to the administration of justice was the preference for cadres who were loyal over those who were expert. Throughout Soviet history the leaders preferred Party members over non-Party persons for appointments as judge or procurator, and until the mid-1930s saw little virtue in legal education for legal officials. In fact, most legal officials in the 1920s and 1930s lacked even general secondary education, let alone advanced legal training. In the mid-1930s Stalin and his colleagues decided that competency in law did matter after all and planned an expansion of legal education to produce jurists for the courts, but the fulfillment of this new policy came only after World War II. Even then, the norm was to provide secondary education first and then higher legal education by correspondence to the investigators, procurators, and judges of the day; only a small number of well trained jurists became legal officials. This pattern helped to assure that officials who made careers in the legal agencies in the post-war years would not be infected with legal ideals that might threaten their inclination to conform with the expectations of their superiors.

The Soviet administration of justice that developed in the first decade after the Revolution moved away from some of the procedures established by the 1864 Judicial Reform. The most obvious change was the elimination of the jury and its replacement by mixed panels of judge and lay assessors. Although public trials with prosecutions handled by procurators continued, the role of defense counsel at trial weakened. At the same time, pre-trial investigations lost even the remnants of impartiality when the investigators lost their connection with the courts and came in 1928 under the exclusive domain of the procuracy. That body emerged in the Soviet period as the most powerful of the agencies in the justice realm, when it regained the power of general supervision that it had lost in 1864 while retaining its prosecutorial function.

Despite all of the efforts to develop Soviet law and Soviet courts, in the 1920s and early 1930s anti-law views retained currency among some Bolsheviks. Such views favored the simplification of legal procedures and contributed to the readiness to adopt and use alternatives to the courts. Some of these alternatives, such as the various procedures for handling complaints, played a positive role, but this could not be said of the most famous alternative to the courts, namely the use of police bodies to approve extra-legal repression. Stalinist terror in particular went well beyond any extra-judicial coercion of the tsarist years. Not only was it unjust, but it also contributed to the emergence of a condescending attitude toward law on the part of public officials in the USSR and to a decline in the prestige of law among the population at large.

Two of the essays in this book deal with aspects of legal development in the NEP and early Stalin periods; three others focus on the 1930s and 1940s. All five deal, directly or indirectly, with the decline of judicial autonomy and power in the Soviet period.

Both essays on the early period of Soviet law focus upon modes of pursuing complaints outside the courts, especially through the Complaints Bureau of *Rabkrin* (Commissariat of Worker Peasant Inspectorates). Lisa

Granik explores how in the NEP era women tried to use various complaints procedures, including courts, to respond to discrimination and incidents that would now be classified as sexual harassment in the workplace. In her view women in the USSR became active in lodging complaints in the 1920s partly because of the regime's nourishing of a culture of complaint and partly because of the official declarations about gender equality, reflected in developments in family law. Women launched complaints about various forms of rude and disparaging conduct at the workplace, as well as against unjust firings, but did not obtain much satisfaction. In a study of complaints brought against government officials in the 1920s and early 1930s Golfo Alexopoulos highlights the risks run by those pursuing complaints. Despite the regime's encouragement of complaints, it not only failed to assure a good chance of vindication for the complainant but it also failed to prevent complaints from backfiring and leading to reprisals. In reaching this conclusion, Alexopoulos examines complaints brought to both the bureaux of Rabkrin and to the procuracy and courts. Together, the two essays reveal the extent to which in the 1920s dispute resolution, especially relating to complaints against officials and managers, fell outside the courts. Their essays also suggest that it made little difference to the complainant's chances of success whether he or she used a court or another venue. In either case what mattered were factors beyond the control of the complainants and unrelated to the merits of their legal claims, including the political standing of the accused, the degree of publicity, inertia and red tape, and fate.

Oleg Khlevniuk and Gábor Rittersporn in their chapters deal with the implications of the extra-legal repression that unfolded under Stalin for the courts and the legal realm, especially in the 1930s. Khlevniuk argues that Stalin and his Politburo treated law and terror as part of a single policy of repression, with law serving as both a form of coercion and a check on extra-legal repression. He pays particular attention to the use of law and legal institutions as a check on repression and the power of the OGPU/NKVD in 1934-1935 (following collectivization) and in late 1938 and 1939 (following the Great Terror). Rittersporn agrees with Khlevniuk's view of law as part of a larger policy of repression and recognizes the authenticity of the various legal reforms announced in the 1930s. Those measures, Rittersporn argues, accomplished little because the leadership's expedient approach to repression guaranteed that they would sooner or later take actions to undermine any checks that they had earlier imposed. At the same time, through most of the 1930s, Stalin proved unable to pursue a consistent division of labor between the realms of law and terror, as exemplified by his decision to use police bodies (the regional *troiki* of 1935-1936) to pursue various categories of non-political "socially dangerous" persons. While Khlevniuk provides new insights into the role of the Politburo and Stalin in stage-managing all of these developments, Rittersporn offers informed glosses on various aspects of judicial and penal activities before World War II.

In contrast, Peter Solomon focuses upon developments in the administration of justice after World War II, when the separation of the worlds of law and terror was finally secured. The focus of Solomon's study is the development in the late Stalin years and after of a highly centralized, closely monitored corps of legal officials making careers in the legal agencies and by and large conforming with the demands of their political and bureaucratic masters. This was a signal achievement for a regime that had been forced in the pre-war years to tolerate legal officialdom that was largely uneducated, transient, and difficult to control. Solomon pays special attention to the mechanism used by the chiefs of the legal agencies to secure the compliance of officials with their goals, namely the use of statistical indicators of performance. He tells the story of the role of these indicators in the stigmatization of acquittals and reversals on appeal in the late 1940s and early 1950s and of the emergence of a "culture of blame" within the administration of criminal justice. These developments of Stalin's last years outlasted his period of rule by more than three decades.

The first years after Stalin's death are known for the curtailment of extra-judicial coercion, the revival of the procuracy, and the reforms undertaken in substantive law and procedure. Those reforms did not, however, affect the essential features of Soviet justice, including its relationship to political power and the growing bureaucratic pressures facing legal officials.[7] Yoram Gorlizki provides strong evidence in support of this proposition, in his examination of the two attempts by Nikita Sergeevich Khrushchev to reduce interference by local Party officials in criminal cases.[8] The first attempt, announced in a Party resolution in 1954, had little impact not only because of the weak threat of sanctions for offending officials but also because the campaign against interference contradicted the larger Khrushchevian policy of enhancing the role of Party officials in public administration. The second attack on Party interventions, embodied in a reversal of the longstanding rules against prosecution of Party members without clearance from Party officials, coincided with Khrushchev's attack on Party careerists, embodied in the new rules for rotation of members of Party committees. All the same, it did not prove successful in the long run.

While in the Khrushchev era the dependence of judges upon Party officials still represented a major problem, by the 1980s, Todd Foglesong contends, that form of dependence had become overshadowed by the dependence of judges upon the judges of higher courts. He demonstrates the power and impact of higher court judges upon their subordinates through an examination of the mechanisms used to force trial court judges to implement new policies on sentences—the reduction of custodial sentences (from 1982) and the demand in 1986 that judges review evidence in a more rigorous and sceptical fashion. Both of these policies transformed the practice of judges, but only after various kinds of pressure were exerted upon them from above. Foglesong's argument suggests that the collapse of Communist Party power may not prove sufficient to enable judges in post-Soviet Russia to review cases impartially. Even if local political power matters less than it did, the pressures from bureaucratic masters, armed with a variety of carrots and sticks, may still leave their mark.

The Gorbachev years marked the start of a new era of judicial reform in Russia. The beginning was glasnost', the policy of allowing critical discussion of regime policies and practices in public, and already in 1986 a small band of journalists and legal scholars began revealing and attacking some of the more egregious aspects of Soviet justice, including Party interference in cases and the "accusatorial bias" that permeated criminal justice. Their critique had started to swell into a crusade for judicial reform, when in 1988 the reform-minded section of the leadership of the CPSU responded by making reform of law and justice a part of their program for the democratization of the political system. The years 1989 and 1990 witnessed changes in judicial selection and the role of defense counsel and the establishment of a weak form of constitutional supervision. These changes represented, however, only a start along the path of reform, and further reforms from the leadership of the USSR were stymied by the collapse of the power of the CPSU and struggles over the shape of a renewed federation.[9]

Sensing the shift of power to the governments of the republics, in the summer of 1991 a group of reform-minded jurists produced a plan for a judicial reform more radical than anything envisaged in the era of pere-stroika. Their "Conception of Judicial Reform," a document distinguished by its fierce root and branch condemnation of Soviet justice and attack on its structure of power as well, was actually "approved" by the Supreme Soviet of the Russian republic in October 1991. However, attempts to realize its various provisions were to provoke many battles over the next few years between the advocates of reform and their more numerous and powerful opponents in the legal and police bureaucracies.[10] All of the chapters in this volume on post-Soviet judicial reform deal with aspects of this story.

Eugene Huskey begins his overview of post-Soviet judicial reform with a depiction of the bureaucratic politics of reform, including the struggles between a key promoter of the reform package, Sergei Pashin, and opposition in the Procuracy and MVD. Huskey goes on to analyze the various proposals relating to court organization and procedures, including battles over judicial selection, the introduction of the jury, and other means of reducing dependence of judges upon the executive. Huskey's study makes clear that as of the publication of this book many of the reforms envisaged in the Conception had yet to take shape, let alone be implemented, and that the chances for progress in the immediate future have been diminished by the removal of Sergei Pashin from his post at the State Legal Administration.

In his chapter Gordon Smith treats one key initiative of post-Soviet judicial reformers, namely their attack on the most powerful of the agencies involved in the administration of justice, the Procuracy, and especially its general supervisory function. Smith examines the history of this function (see also the essay in this book by Kazantsev) and explains how and why it became so important to reformers. Then he goes on to detail how the leaders of the Procuracy defended their prerogatives between 1991 and 1995 and succeeded in keeping their agency and its functions intact.

Finally, Sarah Reynolds offers a portrait of the reformers' most positive contribution to Russian courts, the revival of the jury. Reynolds shows how the framers of the jury experiment, Sergei Pashin among them, sought explicitly to recreate the Russian jury that existed in the late tsarist period. On a large plane, they hoped through the jury to make the trial once again a real contest between the sides and through citizen participation in juries to democratize the administration of justice. At the same time, the reformers used historical precedents to produce a distinctively Russian jury, marked by an open power of nullification, the right to recommend leniency, and its generous payments to jurors. This last feature of the new Russian juries made them so expensive as to threaten the expansion of the jury beyond nine regions. Reynolds goes on to provide a view of the initial practice of jury trials in 1994-1995, especially in Saratov.

Any attempt to analyze a process like judicial reform over a period of 130 years is likely to bring to the fore the elements of continuity in the story, and our collaborative effort is no exception. If anything, what we have found shows more continuity than we had expected. In the words of one reader of the manuscript (Robert Sharlet), "The replicable patterns of culture, structure, and behavior far outweigh the differences."[11] To be sure, the struggle for law and courts in Russia has been a long one and it is far from complete. Throughout the years under study Russia had a political order that was for the most part inhospitable to law and courts. As a result, the period was marked by spurts of reform, counter-reform, reversals, and finally new reform initiatives. This cyclical pattern prompted the same observer to depict Russian law and courts as "in a state of permanent transition."

At the same time, the exercise pursued by the authors of this book offers an opportunity to illuminate particular situations through comparison, and seek out differences as well as similarities. Most telling are the comparisons between the current, early post-Soviet situation—with its urge to re-form—and two points of time before the Russian Revolution—the early years of realizing the Judicial Reform of 1864 (say 1870) and the judicial system on the eve of World War I (1914), fifty years after that reform's adoption.

Comparing the post-Soviet situation with the early years of the tsarist Judicial Reform, Eugene Huskey found three important differences. The reforms of the 1990s involved fewer new legal institutions. The quality of legal officials was lower (they were less well educated and more "bureau-cratized" than professionalized). And there was a deep public cynicism about the legal enterprise, arguably a natural consequence of the Soviet experience, and more pervasive than what existed in the nineteenth century. None of these obstacles to reform was immutable. As Sharlet suggested, new institutions like the Constitutional Court, the Council of Judges, or the *arbitrazh* courts might well take root and make a difference. Then, too, talent might start to flow into legal officialdom as a spinoff of the attractiveness of private legal practice, and public cynicism might be overcome when people had more positive experiences with the courts. Still, the differences remained real and telling.[12]

Using 1914 as a point of departure yields a different kind of conclusion. The fifty years of Judicial Reform did produce courts that were strong and independent, particularly higher courts in the civil realm. But as long as autocracy remained, criminal courts could not gain full independence. Nor could the regime be stopped from finding ways of ensuring that the cases that mattered found resolution in reliable forums. In short, fifty years of reform brought into focus the limits of change possible under an authoritar-ian government. The big difference in post-Soviet Russia, and the one that may matter most for the future development of law and courts, is the aspiration to building some kind of democracy. For the time being, political institutions are too unstable and democratic procedures too unfamiliar to have much affect on legal reform. In the long run, though, successful consolidation of democratic or proto-democratic beginnings may prove the most important factor in the creation of legal order in Russia. This is, of course, an optimistic scenario, but nonetheless a plausible one. The converse also holds. The more Russia slips back into an authoritarian mode, the more difficult it will prove to realize authentic judicial reform in Russia.

Let us be clear. The optimistic scenario represents a version of Russian political development over many decades. In the near future, other factors, especially the peculiar legacies of the Soviet era, make significant achievements in judicial reform improbable. These legacies include: a cynical and condescending attitude toward law on the part not only of the public but also of officials; and the habit of conducting economic and business activity outside of the law. Both constitute cultural legacies of the USSR that impede the development of strong respected courts.

In short, both power and culture remain critical impediments to the development of legal order in post-Soviet Russia as much as they were in Russia of earlier periods, but they have taken on new forms. The problem of power is no longer one of the authoritarian ruler (tsar or Party leader) treating the law as a mere instrument of rule, but rather of supposedly democratic leaders conducting themselves in a dictatorial manner, ignoring laws, and contradicting even the constitution. The issue of culture is no longer the allegedly harmful influence of the world of the peasants or the provincial backwaters of the Empire but of popular attitudes toward law shaped by the Soviet experience.

Ultimately, any good inquiry, especially a collaborative one, raises more questions than it answers. The contributors to this volume hope that their effort will stimulate readers to see issues of judicial reform in Russia in new ways and open avenues for further study.

Author's note: I would like to thank Jane Burbank, Eugene Huskey, and William Wagner for helpful comments on an earlier draft of this chapter.

Notes

1. Harold J. Berman, *Justice in the U.S.S.R.: An Interpretation of Russian Law*, rev. enlarged ed. (Cambridge, MA, 1963), 217-20.

2. My account of pre-Reform justice is based on Richard Wortman, *The Development of a Russian Legal Consciousness* (Chicago and London, 1976); John Le Donne, "Criminal Investigations Before the Great Reforms," *Russian History* 1, no. 2 (1974): 101-118; and M. A. Cheltsov-Bebutov, *Ocherki po istorii suda i ugolovnogo protsessa v rabovladelcheskikh, feodal'nykh i burzhuaznykh gosudarstvakh* (Moscow, 1957), 688-748. See also Samuel Kutscheroff, "Administration of Justice under Nicholas I of Russia," *American Slavic and East European Review* 7, no. 2 (April 1948): 125-38.

3. On the Judicial Reform of 1864 see Wortman, *Development of a Russian Legal Consciousness*, part III; M. G. Korotkikh, *Samoderzhavie i sudebnaia reforma 1864 goda v Rossii* (Voronezh, 1989); W. Bruce Lincoln, *The Great Reforms: Autocracy, Bureaucracy, and the Politics of Change in Imperial Russia* (Dekalb, IL, 1990), 105-117; and Friedhelm Kaiser, *Die russische Justizreform von 1864: Zur Geschichte der russischen Justiz von Katerina II bis 1917* (Leiden, 1972).

4. William Wagner, "Tsarist Legal Policies at the End of the Nineteenth Century: A Study in Inconsistency," *Slavonic and East European Review* 14, no. 3 (July 1976): 371-94; Theodore Taranovski, "The Aborted Counter-Reform: Muraviev Commission and the Judicial Statues of 1864," *Jahrbucher für Geschichte Osteuropas* 29 (1981): 161-84; B. V. Vilenskii, *Sudebnaia reforma i kontrreforma v Rossii* (Saratov, 1969).

5. Alexandr K. Afanas'ev, "Jurors and Jury Trials in Imperial Russia, 1866-1885," in Ben Eklof, *et al.*, eds., *Russia's Great Reforms, 1855-1881* (Bloomington, IN, 1994), 214-30.

6. This account of how Soviet power affect the courts and law is based on Peter H. Solomon, Jr., *Soviet Criminal Justice under Stalin* (Cambridge and New York, 1996). See also Jane Burbank, "Lenin and Law in Revolutionary Russia," *Slavic Review* 54, no. 1 (Spring 1995): 23-44; John Hazard, *Settling Disputes in Soviet Society* (New York, 1960); Berman, *Justice in the USSR*; Eugene Huskey, *Russian Lawyers and the Soviet State: The Origins and Development of the Soviet Bar* (Princeton, NJ, 1986); and Robert Sharlet, "Stalinism and Soviet Legal Culture," in Robert C. Tucker, ed., *Stalinism: Essays in Historical Interpretation* (New York, 1977), 155-79.

7. Berman, *Justice in the U.S.S.R.*, chapter 2; Gordon B. Smith, *The Soviet Procuracy and the Supervision of Administration* (Alphen aan den Rijn, 1978); Peter H. Solomon, Jr., *Soviet Criminologists and Criminal Policy: Specialists in Policy-making* (New York and London, 1978), chapter 3; John Gorgone, "Soviet Jurists in the Legislative Arena: The Reform of Criminal Procedure, 1956-1958," *Soviet Union* 3, no. 1 (1976): 1-36; George Ginsburgs, "Soviet Court Reform, 1956-1958," in Donald D. Barry, *et al.*, eds., *Soviet Law After Stalin*, III (Leyden, 1979), 77-104; D. D. Barry, "The Specialist in Soviet Policy-Making: The Adoption of a Law," *Soviet Studies* 16 (1964): 152-63.

8. Peter H. Solomon, Jr., "The Case of the Vanishing Acquittal: Informal Norms and the Practice of Soviet Criminal Justice," *Soviet Studies* 39, no. 4 (October 1987): 531-55; Solomon, "Soviet Politicians and Criminal Justice: The Logic of Party Intervention," in James R. Millar, ed., *Cracks in the Monolith: Party Power in the Brezhnev Era* (Armonk, NY, 1992), 3-32.

9. On judicial reform under Gorbachev, see Peter H. Solomon, Jr., "Gorbachev's Legal Revolution," *Canadian Business Law Journal* 17, no. 2 (December 1990): 184-94; Mark Beissinger, "The Party and the Rule of Law," *Columbia Journal of Transnational Law* 28, no. 1 (1990): 41-58; Donald D. Barry, ed., *Toward the "Rule of Law" in Russia? Political and Legal Reform in the Transition Period* (Armonk, NY, and London, 1992), especially essays by Barry, Huskey, and Solomon; Eugene Huskey, "The Administration of Justice: Courts, Procuracy, and the Ministry of Justice," in Eugene Huskey, ed., *Executive Power and Soviet Politics: The Rise and Decline of the Soviet State* (Armonk, NY, and London, 1992), 221-48; Valerii Savitskii, "Democratization in the USSR: Toward the Freedom of the Individual through Law and Courts," *Criminal Law Forum* 2, no. 1 (Autumn 1990): 85-110; and Valerii Savitskii, "Selected Problems of Judicial Reform, Criminal Justice and the Protection of Individual Rights," *ibid.* 2, no. 2 (Winter 1991): 269-92.

10. See "The Conception of Judicial Reform in the RSFSR," *Statutes and Decisions* 30, no. 2 (March-April 1994): 3-92; and Peter H. Solomon, Jr., "The Limits of Legal Order in Post-Soviet Russia," *Post-Soviet Affairs* 11, no. 2 (April-June 1995): 89-114.

11. Robert Sharlet, "Comment," delivered at the Conference "Judicial Reform in Russia, 1864-1994: An Historical Perspective," Toronto, Canada, 2 April 1995.

12. From conference discussions (transcript available from the editor).

2

CIVIL LAW, INDIVIDUAL RIGHTS, AND JUDICIAL ACTIVISM IN LATE IMPERIAL RUSSIA

William G. Wagner

In a polemical essay that appeared in the controversial collection *Vekhi* (*Landmarks*) in 1909, the noted legal theorist Bogdan Kistiakovskii criticized the Russian intelligentsia—and imperial Russian subjects in general—for their inability to appreciate the importance of law for the creation of a just society and a democratic polity.[1] Influential at the time, Kistiakovskii's essay has subsequently been cited frequently as evidence of the inhospitable social and cultural climate in late imperial Russia for the development of either a law-governed state or the rule of law.[2] Among the chief deficiencies in imperial Russia lamented by Kistiakovskii were the lack of public interest in and discussion of the law, the general failure to comprehend the critical role played by law in securing individual freedom, and the inadequacies of the courts created by the 1864 judicial reform. An examination of the public debates over and judicial development of civil law in the post-Emancipation period suggests, however, that in his desire to prick the legal consciousness of the intelligentsia Kistiakovskii underestimated the extent of legal change that had taken place during the last fifty years of the *ancien régime*. So too, consequently, have those scholars who have relied on his analysis.

In fact, as a number of recent studies have shown, public and intra-governmental debate over several important areas of the law occurred almost continuously from the late 1850s onward, albeit at fluctuating levels of intensity. At the heart of many of these debates, moreover, lay precisely the question of the nature of individual freedom and the role of law in securing and expanding it, through both the limitation of discretionary authority and the elimination of existing legal constraints on the actions of individuals.[3] And although the practice of the courts established by the 1864 judicial reform remains largely unstudied, it would appear that the new courts performed more effectively than Kistiakovskii acknowledged, at least in certain key areas of the law. With respect to family, property, and inheritance law, for example, the new judicial system proved capable not only of defining general legal norms and applying them reasonably uniformly to particular cases, but also of adapting the law creatively to changing conditions and attitudes.[4] Public awareness of and concern with the law therefore seem to have been greater, and the impact of the new courts more positive, than Kistiakovskii was willing to concede. Indeed, as the example of marital dissolution demonstrates, while public debate over the law contributed both to the emergence of public politics in post-Emancipation imperial Russia and to the dissemination of new attitudes toward law, judicial practice provided reasonably clear guidelines for planning individual behavior as well as relief from the strains produced by social and economic change.

The statutes of imperial law regulating marital dissolution formed part of a broader set of legal rules intended to project and protect a patriarchal ideal of marriage perceived in both secular and religious terms. Hence imperial law proclaimed the husband to be head of the family and granted him extensive authority over his wife, including the power to control her place of residence and employment. A wife in turn was obligated to live with her husband and to obey him completely.[5] Reflecting the strong influence on the law of religion, and especially of the Orthodox Church, imperial marriage law also assigned to the appropriate authority of each officially recognized faith the power to establish and administer the specific rules governing the conclusion and dissolution of marriages for its adherents, subject to certain general norms.[6]

This latter arrangement placed a majority of the population under the jurisdiction of the Orthodox Church. Holding that "marriage is a sacrament established by God Himself from time immemorial, confirmed by the divine teaching of Christ the Savior, and piously preserved in all Christian religions," the leadership of the church made formal marital dissolution extremely difficult.[7] Hence the church annulled marriages for procedural or similar defects only very rarely, and it permitted divorce only for adultery, prolonged disappearance, sexual incapacity for physical causes arising prior to marriage, and exile to Siberia after conviction of a felony. By making the process cumbersome, complex, and costly, moreover, the church discouraged divorce even when valid grounds for it existed.[8]

Nor did marital separation appear to provide a feasible alternative to divorce. Imperial statutory law prohibited separation except when granted by the Catholic or the Evangelical Lutheran Church. Although this prohibition obviously could not prevent spouses from agreeing informally to separate, it left a wife who lived apart from her husband in a vulnerable position. Not only would any agreement with the husband be unenforceable, but the wife had no legal right to support from her husband, who in turn could impede her ability to support herself through his control over her access to a passport or employment.[9]

Public criticism of these legal arrangements emerged in the 1860s, at the same time as the first in a series of government attempts to reform the law which finally attained partial success in 1914 with the adoption of a bill that allowed wives to obtain separate passports without the consent of their husbands and the courts to recognize and regulate marital separation. During the intervening fifty years an increasing number of imperial Russian subjects were drawn into a debate over reform of the law which represented in part a conscious and dialogic process of defining fundamental public ideals, i.e., the sets of values which serve to legitimize and shape public institutions and to bind a polity together. Through different representations of marriage and explanations of the causes of marital discord, participants in this debate gradually formulated and disputed competing visions of how imperial Russia ought to be structured socially and politically, what its fundamental public values should be, and what the social and political role of law was.[10] In so doing, they helped to create a sphere of public politics which not only influenced the political process in general, but also threatened the political hegemony of the autocracy.[11]

Contrasting sharply with the sporadic character of public discussion of imperial marriage law during the first half of the century, the public debate over the law from the 1860s onward to a large extent reflected the rapid expansion and diversification of publishing and the emergence of professional groups, civic associations, and, ultimately, legal political organizations which took place during this period. In this sense, public debate over marriage law provides merely one example of how these developments generally contributed to the formation of public politics in post-Emancipation imperial Russia. Hence, beginning in the 1860s, the laws governing marital dissolution were discussed frequently if intermittently by the general press, usually in response to particular events or reform proposals. If the "Woman Question" helped to provoke such discussion in the 1860s, for example, in the 1870s proposals for the reform of ecclesiastical courts and particular decisions of the civil courts in cases involving marital separation did so. While the formation in 1882 of a commission to draft a new civil code similarly elicited a flood of criticisms of the law by the general press, after the late 1890s a series of government, ecclesiastical, and Duma proposals to reform the law resulted in almost continuous debate over this issue in the press. Throughout the post-Emancipation period, too, the effects and reform of existing imperial marriage and divorce law and the appropriate locus of jurisdiction over divorce cases were regular topics of debate in specialized juridical and Orthodox religious periodicals and publications, with these debates intensifying and spilling over into medical periodicals and literature after the mid-1890s. The same issues also were addressed frequently at meetings and congresses of the corresponding professional associations and, after the turn of the century, constituted a central concern of philanthropic organizations whose activities focused on the plight especially of urban women. Not surprisingly, the feminist journals and political organizations that emerged after the late 1890s made reform of the law a major objective, while after 1905 moderate and radical political parties likewise pressed for such reform, if generally less insistently.[12]

To a significant extent, in fact, the law of 1914 formally establishing marital separation represented a convergence of these public efforts to change the law with those taking place within the government.[13] This convergence of public and governmental efforts to reform marriage and divorce law demonstrates how by the late imperial period public debate was affecting the tsarist political process and in some cases even the shape of particular policies. On the most general level, the voluminous files of press writings on the law compiled by government officials attest to the extent to which the latter believed that public opinion had come to constitute a force with which they had to contend, to which they felt compelled to respond in some way, and which they often tried to manipulate to their advantage in intra-governmental conflicts. Even while trying to exclude the public from policy formation, in other words, state officials felt constrained to take account of its views.

But state officials did not merely take cognizance of the public debate over the law. Many also participated in it, suggesting that the boundary between state and society was much more porous and interactive than depicted conventionally, both by contemporaries and subsequently by historians. Through their writings on the law and their participation in the meetings of professional societies, for example, a number of tsarist officials and members of the judiciary contributed significantly to the development of the different ideals of marriage which emerged in the course of the public debate over the law. These ideals in turn influenced the officials who drafted, supported, or opposed the various governmental proposals to reform the law. Hence the public and the intra-governmental debates over marriage and divorce law were mutually formative and linked not merely through common ideological orientations and programs of reform, but also through specific individuals. In fact, the development of marriage and family law reveals how in the late imperial period public debate had become an integral part of the political process in Russia—especially after the introduction of legislative bodies in 1906.

The extent of the public debate over marriage and divorce law, and insistent public demands for reform of the law, call into question Kistiakovskii's charge of public indifference to the law. More critical from the perspective of his argument, however, is what this and similar debates over civil law—and over other areas of the law—reveal about public consciousness of and attitudes toward law during the late imperial period. Here conclusions must remain somewhat speculative. Nonetheless, such debates clearly served to disseminate more broadly awareness not only of imperial Russian statutory law and judicial practices, but also of possible alternative legal institutions and arrangements, including those in Western Europe against which members of the educated and upper strata of imperial Russian society tended—both positively and negatively—to measure themselves. Similarly, these debates brought into sharp relief the diversity of legal cultures and arrangements existing within the Russian empire itself and made law—imperial, canon, local, and customary—an important means through which identities were forged and particular interests were defined and promoted. While focusing attention on the law as a means of adjudicating disputes, the ideological and political conflict animating debate over reform of the law also indirectly enhanced the status of law by making it an important medium through which ideological and political goals were pursued and conflicts resolved. But if these political and ideological uses of the law could help to foster habits of conflict resolution essential for the development of *zakonnost'* (legality) and a *pravovoe gosudarstvo* (a law-based state), they also introduced a tension into the legal attitudes expressed particularly by the advocates of these latter ideals. Given the social composition, the multi-ethnic character, and the religious diversity of imperial Russia, the realization of the broader ideological goals of the proponents of legality paradoxically required the use of the didactic and coercive power of law to reshape the values and relationships prevailing among substantial parts of the population.[14] At least in the field of civil law, even for the advocates of legality, law consequently served in part as an instrument of social change based on moral and ideological precepts.[15]

At the same time, however, contrary to Kistiakovskii's claims, these same advocates of legality believed strongly that the law played a critical role in defining, protecting, and expanding individual rights and freedoms, in this instance through the limitation of domestic patriarchal power. Claiming in a pamphlet on marital ethics published in 1896 that existing law enslaved wives to their husbands, for example, one Serafima Argamakova asserted that "[t]he church and school . . . can to a significant extent help to ease the fate of slaves, but only positive law is capable of abolishing slavery."[16] Similarly, at the First (and only) All-Russian Women's Congress in 1908, the radical feminist Mariia Blandova contended that "if a wife is not personally free, if she does not have the right to dispose of her own person," then even her right to separate property could not protect her from an abusive husband and this latter right itself was "no more than a fiction." Hence "the complete arbitrary authority of a husband must be limited by law for the sake . . . of humanity and justice," and to this end "the facilitation of divorce . . . is an urgent need of society."[17] And in an article in 1902 reviewing the provisions on family law in the draft civil code, the noted jurist and Senator in the Civil Cassation Department, Aleksandr Borovikov-skii, argued that the law must establish "clearly and categorically that the marital union is founded on the principle of the equal rights of spouses and that possible disagreements between [the spouses] must be resolved not by the one-sided will of the husband but in accordance with the interests of the family."[18] Again, the facilitation of marital dissolution represented for Borovikovskii an important means for controlling the behavior of a husband and thereby protecting the personal rights and ensuring the equality of his wife.[19]

Public demands for increased access to marital dissolution, therefore, frequently were motivated by the desire to expand and secure the rights of married women perceived as autonomous individuals. Although advocates of such reform generally framed the debate in terms of freeing wives from the oppressiveness of domestic patriarchy and protecting them from abusive and neglectful male behavior, however, they also stressed the liberation of both spouses from marriages that had ceased to be mutually fulfilling and indeed had become unhealthy. In this respect, the facilitation of marital dissolution constituted merely a part of a comprehensive program of legal reform—affecting marriage, property, inheritance, and contract law—intended to create a legal framework through which the affective ideal of the family shared broadly by reformers could be brought to life. Nor, most reformers—and their conservative opponents—assumed, would the effects of such legal reform be limited to the family, given their belief in the formative influence of the family on social and political values and relationships.[20]

Although reflecting a common ideal of the family, however, the specific program of legal reform proposed by different groups varied in significant ways. These differences provide important insights into how each group viewed both law and individual rights. Reflecting their adherence to a form of liberalism that in other historical and cultural contexts has been labeled "social," "communitarian," or "pragmatic," for example, liberals sought through the law to expand the security and autonomy of individual family members while simultaneously limiting this autonomy to ensure the welfare of the family as a whole and the fulfillment of the moral obligations believed to arise naturally from family membership.[21] To protect individual family members, liberals proposed that the authority of husbands and parents be limited by clear legal norms and its exercise subjected to judicial oversight, with the courts having broad power to suspend or even terminate such authority when deemed necessary. At the same time, the obligations owed to other family members by those in authority, and which in the view of liberals largely justified such authority, would become more readily enforceable by the courts and would be extended, especially to include extra-marital children. To ensure the personal autonomy of married women, liberals proposed not only to expand the possibility of marital dissolution, but also to preserve the existing right of wives to control their own property and to reduce the formal power of husbands sharply (and in some cases, to eliminate this power altogether). Nonetheless, the autonomy of wives would remain limited by their family obligations, which Russian liberals—like European liberals generally—normally defined in gendered terms that effectively and often formally preserved the predominant authority of husbands and fathers. Finally, liberals advocated the fundamental reconfigu-ration of property institutions and inheritance rights in order to establish sexual equality with respect to the latter and to increase the control of owners over their property while ensuring that they fulfilled their moral obligations to close family members.[22]

As this program of reform suggests, liberals perceived the rights of family members as deriving partly from their existence as separate individu-als and partly from the reciprocal obligations created by the fact of common family membership. For liberals, the family therefore comprised not merely a collection of individuals, but a moral community that was crucial for the welfare, self-realization, and human fulfillment of its members. The historical vision of liberals, too, stressed the simultaneous autonomy and social connectedness of individuals. Individual autonomy was depicted as developing not from a state of primitive or natural individualism, but through a process that gradually reduced familial constraints on individuals while never eliminating them entirely. Hence individual autonomy was not viewed abstractly, but as operating within a concrete if evolving historical and social context that limited it.[23] This combined natural-moral ideal and historical-sociological explanation of the family justified for liberals the use of law both to foster or ensure the ethical behavior of family members and to protect their rights as individuals.[24] As I have argued elsewhere, if in the conditions of late imperial Russia this combination necessarily reinforced tendencies toward legal positivism, it also implied constraints on state legislative activity from which a concept of the rule of law could be derived.[25]

These same observations apply to the arguments and programs of reform advanced by feminists, at least those feminists who did not advocate some variant of the socialization of the family. With respect to the recasting of the legal framework of the family, as opposed to other areas of political and social life, feminist and liberal proposals for reform essentially coincided, albeit with some important exceptions. Not surprisingly, these exceptions reflected primarily a more radical application of the principles of individual equality and autonomy to the legal position of married women. To ensure both autonomy and full equality for married women, for example, feminists rejected the retention of any residual authority for a husband or priority for the father, refused to accept even a limited and conditional obligation of a wife to reside with her husband, and appeared more willing than most liberals to admit elements of contractualism into the determination of relations between spouses. While agreeing that family membership involuntarily created reciprocal moral obligations between family members, moreover, feminists did not agree that the right of wives to work outside the home therefore should be limited even conditionally, particularly since they believed that in many cases such work enabled women to provide critical support for their families.[26] Whatever their differences with liberals on substantive issues, however, as the above quotes of Argamakova and Blandova indicate, feminists believed just as strongly that law had an important role to play in their liberation.

By contrast, populists (and here I have in view chiefly jurists and legal ethnographers) displayed a more ambiguous attitude with respect to both law and individual rights. On the one hand, despite the difference in the arguments they offered in justification, populists frequently made proposals that substantively were surprisingly similar to those of liberals and feminists. On the other hand, the melding of the affective ideal of the family with an idealization of peasant communalism sometimes produced a more distinctive approach. A number of populists, for example, advocated the creation of family councils through which all adult members would manage the affairs of the family and oversee the use and devolution of property, even that which formally was owned individually. Such populist proposals redistributed authority within the family, notably between men and women, more radically than those of most liberals. But they appeared to provide individual family members with less secure autonomous space by making the protection and even definition of this space to a significant extent dependent on equal participation in the process of decision-making and on the good will arising from mutual affection within the family. The operation of family councils, too, threatened to replace the individual property ownership stressed by liberals and feminists as a guarantee of personal autonomy with a form of family ownership.[27] Despite a mutual concern with individual liberation and self-development, the populist ideal of the family therefore often favored collective over individual interests more than did its liberal and feminist counterparts. It also threatened to subordinate legal guarantees to internal family politics. Perhaps it is precisely in these differences that the insight and limitations of Kistiakovskii's analysis become apparent. Nonetheless, populists still assigned to law an important role in enabling the actualization of the affective ideal of the family which they shared with liberals and feminists.

Just as the affective ideal of the family helped to shape post-Emancipation public debate over imperial civil law, so too did it affect the law itself, as the evolution of the practice of the Civil Cassation Department of the Senate demonstrates. The highest court of appeal for civil cases in the system established by the 1864 judicial reform, the Civil Cassation Department was charged both with making definitive interpretations of the law and with ensuring the uniform application of the law throughout the empire. Holding its decisions to be binding on all lower courts in comparable cases, and the failure to observe its rulings when appropriate to be itself sufficient grounds for setting aside a lower court decision, the Civil Cassation Department exerted a powerful influence over the practical meaning of the law. The extent of this influence, as well as the degree to which public and intra-governmental debate in turn shaped judicial practice, can be seen clearly in the high court's treatment of the question of marital separation.[28] The practice of the Civil Cassation Department on this issue also demonstrates how the activity of the high court helped to construct the institutional prerequisites for the development of the rule of law, however this concept is understood.

As generally, however, when developing the law in this area the Civil Cassation Department was not responding solely to ideological, political, and

juristic debates over the law. These debates in turn, and judicial interpretation of the law, took place in a context of rapid increases in the incidence
both of divorce and of marital separations granted through special administrative procedures. These increases resulted from several causes, including
changes in the law itself, altered social attitudes toward women and the
family, and an expanded access for some women to education and professional occupations. But, given the identity of the overwhelming majority of
people seeking divorce or separation, the principal source of these increases
appears to have been the changes in the economic dynamics and function of
households produced by industrial development and the growth of wage
labor, especially for women.[29] These circumstances not only strained
traditional family relations and often forced or enabled peasant and working-
class women to live more independently, but they also helped to break down
the constraints that previously had induced or compelled women to remain
within a discordant marriage.

These developments confronted the courts with an agonizing dilemma.
Ecclesiastical jurisdiction, of course, excluded divorce from the purview of
the civil courts. But marital separation was another matter. Here, however,
statutory law proscribed marital separation except when granted by the
Catholic or the Evangelical Lutheran Church. Hence, on the one hand, the
conscientious exercise by judges of their role as guardians of the law
produced results that many of them considered unjust, socially harmful, and
contrary both to their own social values and to their professional self-image
of protectors of the "weaker" members of society. On the other hand, the
provision of equitable or effective relief for marital strife appeared to require
contravention of the law that judges had sworn to uphold. As the jurist
David Grimm put it succinctly in the debate in the State Council over the
1914 law on separation, existing statutory law thus "compels [state] authority
either to decline to defend the defenseless or to violate the law."[30]

The Civil Cassation Department at first responded to this dilemma by
preserving the integrity of the law. Hence in a series of decisions from the
late 1860s through the mid-1870s the high court refused to recognize the
legality of marital separation in any circumstances, however compelling.
While the effect of these decisions may not have been to force wives to live
with abusive or negligent husbands, which constituted the basis of the wife's
claim in most such cases, the result was to deprive a wife in these situations
of any legal right to support from her husband and to leave her subordinated
to his authority in such matters as employment and the acquisition of an
internal passport or residence permit.[31]

In a series of decisions in the 1870s, however, the Civil Cassation Department cautiously acknowledged the impracticality and inequity of its initial position, particularly for wives. Groping for a workable doctrine that would preserve the fiction of observing statutory law, the high court gradually formulated the rule that a wife was not obligated to live with her husband, yet retained the right to support from him, if for reasons beyond her control co-residence with him proved impossible.[32] In a landmark decision in 1879, the court also held that spouses could agree to separate as long as the lower courts found the reasons for separation to be valid and the intention of the agreement not to be the permanent dissolution of the marriage.[33] Considerably broadening the application of its doctrine after the mid-1880s, the Civil Cassation Department upheld the right of lower courts to award a separated wife support despite the profession by her husband that he wished to live with her, provided the courts found that the conduct of the husband warranted such action.[34] And in 1906, the high court ruled that a wife who was still living with her husband could sue him for an appropriate level of support and then, if circumstances justified it, leave him.[35]

Although the reasoning of the Civil Cassation Department in these cases was complicated, the affective ideal of the family strongly informed the court's decisions. The net result of these decisions, as the Civil Code Editing Commission approvingly observed, was to allow "under the just demands of life itself . . . so many unavoidable deviations from the law, which seem almost to be new legislative statutes, that in practice [the law] has acquired a meaning incompatible with its literal content."[36] Viewed from this perspective, the 1914 law on marital separation merely formalized and extended the principles of law worked out and propagated by the Civil Cassation Department over the preceding thirty-five years.

A number of influences contributed to the staged retreat of the Civil Cassation Department from its initial position and to its eventual formulation of a doctrine allowing marital separation. The doctrine originally articulated by the high court attracted sharp criticism from both legal commentators and the general press. Lower courts, too, often resisted this doctrine, with many lower court judges arguing that it was unenforceable and left them with no means of dealing with the problems caused by marital discord and break-down. Even members of the high court itself considered the doctrine to be incompatible with their concept of legality and with the affective ideal of the family to which they subscribed. In this regard, the generational change in the composition of the Civil Cassation Department which gradually took place during the 1870s and the early 1880s appears to have played an important role in leading the high court to reverse its position. The education and experience of Senators changed during these years in ways that made them more familiar with both the juridical arguments in favor of marital separation and the human dimension of the cases coming before them.[37]

The reversal by the Civil Cassation Department on its position with respect to marital separation raises the question of the consistency of the high court's practice. Kistiakovskii and other critics of the Civil Cassation Department charged that its decisions were too inconsistent to serve as an adequate foundation for either a law-governed state or the rule of law. While much more research needs to be done on this question, the accusation appears to be ill-founded, at least in the areas of law that I have examined. On most questions, the high court developed its doctrines relatively consistently over time, sometimes in the face of strong criticism by legal commentators and politically motivated critics (of all ideological stripes). As in the case of marital separation, however, in some instances the Civil Cassation Department held to or hedged on a position for a number of years before reversing itself or adopting a firmer stance. The reasons for the court's behavior in such cases are not always apparent. But they would appear to include the persuasiveness or appeal of contrary arguments on especially controversial issues, the crystallization of a consensus among jurists, the changing background of members of the court, and changes in statutory law which altered the practical effects of particular decisions. Having reversed or clarified its position, however, the high court then generally remained consistent with its new doctrine.[38] Such behavior does not seem to be particularly unusual even for a long-established court of final appeal, let alone one operating in the novel context created by the judicial reform.

The novelty of the high court's position, at least for imperial Russia, needs to be stressed. Reflecting both the desire to control the judiciary and its inferior status, prior to the judicial reform judges—especially in the provincial and lower courts—were constrained by formalistic rules of evidence and were required to apply the laws "in accordance with their exact and literal meaning, without any change or expansion." Nor could judicial decisions "be recognized as general laws, obligatory for all, nor serve as the basis for final decisions in similar cases."[39] Where statutory law was unclear, contradictory, or incomplete, cases were referred to the Senate and ultimately to the Minister of Justice and the State Council for resolution through the legislative process. Since judicial decisions were not published, circulated internally, or discussed publicly, as a practical matter they could hardly have served as a source of law in any case, let alone as a guide for planning one's actions.

The new judicial statutes, by contrast, directed judges to decide cases on the basis of their conscience as well as the law. Where the law appeared unclear, contradictory, or incomplete, judges now were to rule in accordance with its "general meaning" (*obshchii smysl*).[40] Instructed to publish for the "guidance" (*rukovodstvo*) of lower courts those of its decisions that explained the exact meaning of the law, the Civil Cassation Department used this charge to assert the obligatory force of its decisions for all lower courts in comparable cases.[41] These decisions, in turn, were published and discussed regularly in official government organs as well as in the special-ized legal journals that began to appear after the late 1850s. The general press, too, commented frequently on decisions of the high court, with most newspapers containing a section devoted to cases heard before both the Civil and the Criminal Cassation Departments, as well as before the local courts. Official and unofficial collections of the decisions of the high court likewise were published regularly, as were unofficial editions of the *Digest of Laws* (*Svod Zakonov*), annotated with relevant rulings of the high court. The textbooks and treatises on imperial civil law that appeared in increasing numbers after the 1880s also invariably discussed the precedents set by the Civil Cassation Department, even when denying their obligatory force. As a result, the rulings of the high court were widely known, especially among judicial personnel and legal practitioners. In short, in the wake of the judicial reform there emerged a juridical infrastructure that granted the courts, and particularly the cassation departments, unprecedented influence over the development of imperial law.

The use of this power by the lower courts and the extent of the influence of the cassation departments on their decisions have yet to be studied. The extensive reference to and reliance on the precedents of the Civil Cassation Department by both litigants and lower court judges seen in the published decisions of the high court, however, suggest that the influence of these precedents was substantial. Secondary sources, too, indicate that the lower courts generally accepted the authority of the Civil Cassation Department and observed its precedents, albeit sometimes grudgingly.[42] In some cases, the practice of the high court also affected the decisions of other government bodies concerned with the administration of law. At a parallel level with the Civil Cassation Department, for example, the First General Meeting and the Second Department of the Senate from the later 1880s onward used the doctrine of marital separation formulated by the high court to justify their own decisions instructing police officials, land captains, and other state officials with administrative authority over the peasantry to allow wives to leave their husbands in cases of abusive or neglectful treatment. This ruling was later extended to the unprivileged strata of the urban population.[43] At the other end of the judicial spectrum, to the extent that after the turn of the century peasant courts utilized imperial law for the resolution of civil cases, they also may have been influenced by high court precedents.[44] To a significant degree embodying the ideal of the family expressed by liberal reformers, the practice of the Civil Cassation Department consequently served both to disseminate the principles contained in this ideal more broadly and to transform them into a source of enforceable rights and obligations. At the same time, the high court's decisions responded to the demands of a much broader circle of the population—in this instance, especially married women—and helped to adapt imperial law to changing social and economic conditions.

Again, it is difficult, and perhaps impossible, to discover the effects of this judicial activism on the legal consciousness of imperial Russian subjects. It is worth noting, however, that the number of cases coming before the civil courts grew rapidly during the post-Emancipation period, suggesting an increased acceptance of the courts as a means of adjudicating disputes. At the least, such growth exposed an ever larger percentage of the population to the ideas embedded in both the processes and the substantive decisions of the new courts.[45]

As the example of marital dissolution indicates, then, by the late imperial period there had emerged a broad public debate over both imperial law in general and the reform of particular laws that directly affected the lives of substantial parts of the population. For women such as Argamakova and Blandova, for example, or for those seeking release from oppressive marital conditions, neither the law nor the issues being debated were abstractions. This debate intersected with those taking place at the same time within the government, the Orthodox Church, and the legal profession, which included the judiciary. The competing ideals worked out in the course of these debates eventually came to shape both state legislation and judicial practice. Among these ideals were legality, a balance between individual autonomy and collective obligation, civil and sexual equality, participatory democracy, and an integral role for law in actualizing each of the others. By demonstrating the feasibility of these ideals through their application to the family, moreover, public debate over the law helped to diffuse more broadly and embed more deeply values that fundamentally challenged those on which the autocratic order rested. In addition, the development after 1864 of a system of establishing and publicizing judicial precedents—particularly those of the Civil Cassation Department—introduced a predictability into the administration at least of civil law which constitutes an essential aspect of the rule of law under any definition of this concept.[46]

Kistiakovskii's harsh assessment of the state of law in late imperial Russia therefore would seem to require qualification. Of course, his essay was polemical and directed primarily at the intelligentsia, many of whose members—to the extent that this elusive group can be defined—exhibited the attitudes toward law that Kistiakovskii was criticizing. Although Kistiakovskii also referred to the public at large, his objective therefore may have diverted his gaze from the substantial debates over the law taking place around him. Subsequent scholars, however, cannot offer a comparable excuse. Kistiakovskii's basis of comparison, moreover, was Western Europe, particularly Germany. Viewed from this perspective, the condition of and public attitudes toward law in imperial Russia indeed appeared to be deficient. But viewed from the perspective of imperial Russia's own past, the environment for the development of a law-governed state or the rule of law appears to have grown substantially more hospitable over the preceding half-century. In this regard, Kistiakovskii's criticisms of the Civil Cassation Department displayed the frequent tendency of academic jurists in imperial Russia to denigrate the practice of the high court as they sparred with it over their relative roles and authority in the novel situation produced by the nearly simultaneous emergence of a legal profession and creation of a new judicial system. Finally, Kistiakovskii's goal was not merely to establish the rule of law in imperial Russia, but more ambitiously to create a liberal society, in part through law. From this perspective, too, the considerable yet limited achievements of the courts—courts seemingly tied to the imperial state—could appear disappointing, particularly given both the hopes originally invested in them by liberals and those raised by the events of 1905-1906. But here perhaps Kistiakovskii overestimated the power of the courts and the law to transform society, especially one as complex and diverse as that in late imperial Russia.

If the image of law and legal consciousness in late imperial Russia drawn by Kistiakovskii appears too bleak, however, the danger of drawing too rosy an image also needs to be avoided. While certainly more effective than their predecessors, the courts established by the 1864 judicial reform were far from perfect and coexisted in constant tension with the state administration and other legal orders that utilized quite different notions of law. Even among advocates of the ideal of legality, itself often imprecisely defined, attitudes toward law were complex and ambiguous and coexisted in tension both with a tendency toward legal instrumentalism and with traditional habits subversive of the ideal of legality.[47] The ideal of legality itself was not universally embraced, even among those elements of society with which this ideal conventionally is associated, and therefore coexisted in tension with other concepts of law and legal order. The working out of these tensions offered not certainties but only possibilities, if perhaps more possibilities than historians over the past few decades have been willing to concede.

In this regard, it can be argued that the possibilities for the development of either a law-governed state or the rule of law were greater in the late imperial period than they are today. Historically, legal systems embodying the rule of law appear to have emerged from the interaction between suitable concepts of law, a political context in which law served as a critical medium through which competing centers of power channelled their conflicts and sought to defend and pursue their interests, and a juridical infrastructure—including personnel and traditions as much as institutions—capable of promoting, institutionalizing, and perpetuating this ideal.[48] From this perspective, the particular correlation of expressed ideas about law, politics, law as an object as well as a medium of politics, the qualities of the juridical profession, and judicial attitudes, attributes, and structures would seem to have been more propitious for the development of the rule of law in the late imperial period than is the case currently in Russia. Concepts of law conducive to the ideal of the rule of law appear to have been more thoroughly assimilated by legal professionals, more widespread generally, and better understood in the earlier period, while the ideal of legality figured more prominently in the programs of political parties and movements and in proposals for legal reform. The quality and sense of autonomy of the legal profession in general and the judiciary in particular declined markedly during the Soviet period and have yet to recover. The post-reform courts more effectively institutionalized the principle of judicial autonomy essential to the rule of law than did the courts bequeathed by the Soviet era to contemporary Russia. While eliminating some serious obstacles to the development of either the rule of law or a law-governed state, most notably the theoretical as well as practical problems posed by tsarist claims to sovereignty, Soviet rule therefore also destroyed or diminished a number of significant advances toward these ideals made during the late imperial period. As a result, their present-day Russian advocates face an even more formidable task than that confronted by their late imperial predecessors.

Notes

1. Bogdan Kistyakovsky, "In the Defense of Law: The Intelligentsia and Legal Consciousness," in Boris Shragin and Alfred Todd, eds., M. Schwartz, trans., *Landmarks: A Collection of Essays on the Russian Intelligentsia—1909* (New York, 1977), 112-37. On Kistiakovskii, see Andrej Walicki, *Legal Philosophies of Russian Liberalism* (Oxford, 1987), 342-403, and Susan Heuman, *Kistiakovsky: The Quest for National and Constitutional Rights in the Last Years of Tsarism* (Cambridge, MA, forthcoming). I am grateful to Susan Heuman for allowing me to read her manuscript prior to its publication.

2. On the distinction between a law-based state (*pravovoe gosudarstvo* or *Rechtsstaat)* and the rule of law, see Harold J. Berman, "The Rule of Law and the Law-Based State (*Rechtsstaat).* With Special Reference to the Soviet Union," in Donald D. Barry, ed., *Toward the "Rule of Law" in Russia? Political and Legal Reform in the Transition Period* (Armonk, NY, 1992), 43-60.

3. Laura Engelstein, *The Keys to Happiness: Sex and the Search for Modernity in Fin-de-Siècle Russia* (Ithaca, NY, 1992) (on criminal law); Thomas C. Owen, *The Corporation under Russian Law, 1800-1917: A Study in Tsarist Economic Policy* (Cambridge, 1991) (on corporate law); William G. Wagner, *Marriage, Property, and Law in Late Imperial Russia* (Oxford, 1994) (on family, property, and inheritance law); Jorg Baberowski, "Das Justizwesen im späten Zarenreich 1864-1914. Zum Problem von Rechtsstaatlichkeit, politischer Justiz und Rüchständigkeit in Rußland," *Zeitschrift für Neuere Rechtsgeschichte* 13, no. 3/4 (1991): 156-72, and *idem*, "Die verhinderte Konstitution: Justiz und Autokratie im späten Zarenreich 1864-1917," in Heinz Mohnhaupt and Dieter Simon, eds., *Vorträge zur Justizforschung. Geschichte und Theorie,* 2 (Frankfurt am Main, 1993), 369-404 (on judicial structures). Indeed, in some cases these debates had begun even earlier, at least within the government, although they were more intermittent and less intense than after the late 1850s.

4. Wagner, *Marriage, Property, and Law*, chapters 5, 9.

5. *Svod Zakonov Rossiiskoi Imperii* (hereafter abbreviated *SZ*), x., pt. 1, arts. 100-108, 2202, and 1-118 in general on marriage. Unless otherwise specified, references are to the 1857 edition. See also xi., pt. 2, *Ust. torg.*, art. 546; xiv., *Ust. o pas.*, arts. 40, 57, 63, 106-9, 124, 171, 176, 238-57, 267 (*Prod.* 1895, *Ust. o vid. na zhit.*, arts. 1, 3, 8-11); and xv. (1845), *Ulozh. o nak.*, arts 2040, 2057, 2064, 2084-6 (1885 ed., arts. 1549, 1566, 1572, 1592).

6. *SZ*, x., pt. 1, arts. 1-99. See also xi., pt. 1, *Ust. dukh. del inost. ispo.* (for non-Orthodox faiths); S. V. Kalashnikov, *Sbornik dukhovnykh i grazhdanskikh zakonov po delam brachnym i o zakonnosti rozhdeniia* (Kharkov, 1891); and V. Ia. Maksimov, *Zakony o razvode pravoslavnago i nepravoslavnago ispovedanii i o razdel'nom zhitel'stve suprugov, s raz"iasneniiami Pravitel'stvuiushchago Senata i tsirkuliarnymi i separatnymi ukazami Sviateishago Synoda* (Moscow, 1909).

7. *Polnoe sobranie postanovlenii i rasporiazhenii po vedomstvu pravoslavnago ispovedaniia Rossiiskoi Imperii. Tsarstvovanie Gosudaria Imperatora Pavla Pervago, 6 noiabria 1796 g.-11 marta 1801 g.* (Petrograd, 1915), 618 (no. 504).

8. *SZ*, x., pt. 1, arts. 45-60. For procedural and other rules, see Maksimov, *Zakony*, 45-111, 427-8; Kalashnikov, *Sbornik*, 10-68, 97-133; S. P. Grigorovskii, *Prichiny i posledstviia razvoda i brakorazvodnyi protsess na sude dukhovnom* (St. Petersburg, 1898); and N. N. Mazurenko, *Rastorzhenie braka i zakon 28 maia* (St. Petersburg, 1905). The Church sometimes relaxed its rules when the Orthodox faith of one of the spouses seemed jeopardized, for example by the conversion of the other spouse to a banned religious sect. As a result of these rules, the incidence of divorce among the Orthodox population remained extremely low throughout the imperial period, despite significant increases after the mid-1860s and again after the turn of the century. See Gregory Freeze, "Bringing Order to the Russian Family: Marriage and Divorce in Imperial Russia, 1760-1860," *Journal of Modern History* 62, no. 4 (1990): 709-746; M. K. Tsaturova, *Russkoe semeinoe pravo xvi-xviii vv.* (Moscow, 1991), 77-98; and Wagner, *Marriage, Property, and Law*, 67-71, 88-100.

9. *SZ*, x., pt. 1, art. 46. Recognizing the problems resulting from such a complete ban on marital separation, the state administration allowed the Third Department of the Imperial Chancellery (1826-1881), and later the State Secretariat (after 1884, the Imperial Chancellery) for the Receipt of Petitions, to issue separate passports to wives in cases of exceptional mistreatment by a husband. See Maksimov, *Zakony*, 375-80, and Wagner, *Marriage, Property, and Law*, 71-72, 88-100.

10. Wagner, *Marriage, Property, and Law*, chapters 3, 4. See also *idem*, "Family Law, the Rule of Law, and Liberalism in Late Imperial Russia," *Jahrbücher für Geschichte Osteuropas* 43, no. 4 (1995): 519-35; *idem*, "The Trojan Mare: Women's Rights and Civil Rights in Late Imperial Russia," in Olga Crisp and Linda Edmondson, eds., *Civil Rights in Imperial Russia* (Oxford, 1989), 65-84; and Engelstein, *Keys to Happiness*.

11. See especially Louise McReynolds, *The News under Russia's Old Regime: The Development of a Mass Circulation Press* (Princeton, NJ, 1991).

12. This and the following several paragraphs summarize parts of the argument in Wagner, *Marriage, Property, and Law*, chapters 2-4. On similar developments with respect to property and inheritance law, see *ibid.*, chapters 7-8. For comparable arguments with respect to public discussion of criminal law, see Engelstein, *Keys to Happiness*.

As this paragraph suggests, the public debate discussed here in the first instance involved primarily the educated and professional strata of society. Even though the social spectrum of participation broadened in the final decades of the imperial period, as both access to the printed word and the forms of possible political activity expanded, members of these social strata continued to claim a preeminent—if not unchallenged—position in public debate over the law. Certainly, although members of these social strata reacted to and extensively discussed the behavior of members of "unprivileged" social groups, they engaged in public debate chiefly with their own number as well as with representatives of the state and the Church.

13. On the urging of the Women's Mutual Philanthropic Society, Octobrist deputies had introduced into the Duma a bill to legalize marital separation at precisely the moment when over a decade of delicate negotiations within the government, and particularly between the Ministry of Justice, the Chief Procuracy of the Holy Synod, and the Synod itself, finally had yielded a comparable proposal. See Wagner, *Marriage, Property, and Law*, 186-95; Linda Edmondson, *Feminism in Russia 1900-1917* (Stanford, 1984), 139-42; and I. V. Gessen, *Razdel'noe zhitel'stvo suprugov. Zakon 12 marta 1914 goda* (St. Petersburg, 1914), which contains the text of the law. The issue of divorce remained unresolved by the time of the

February Revolution and became a source of conflict between the Orthodox Church and both the Provisional Government and, after the October Revolution, the Soviet government.

14. Reformers sometimes acknowledged this use of law. Advocating the limitation of parents' legal authority, for example, the liberal jurist and journalist Mikhail Filippov asserted in 1861 that "parental power has moderated significantly in our society. We have understood that children are not our subjects but our closest friends and collaborators. The backward and routine idea of severe and unlimited parental power remains only among coarse and ignorant people. . . . But we are not speaking of these latter [people]. . . . No, we speak of that leading element of society that has raised itself up to the understanding that even the peasant is a human being and our brother; it is this society that demands that our decrepit law of parental power be abolished." "Vzgliad na russkie grazhdanskie zakony," *Sovremennik*, 1861, No. 86: 260. Using the same reasoning, Filippov also called for the liberation of wives, women in general, and Jews from various forms of arbitrary authority and from legal restrictions on their autonomy. See *ibid.*, No. 85: 523-62; 86: 217-66; and (1862) 92: 5-40, 453-502.

15. This argument is developed more fully in Wagner, "Family Law," and *Marriage, Property, and Law, passim.*

16. S. Argamakova, *K voprosu etiki v sovremennom brake* (Polotsk, 1895), 37.

17. *Trudy pervago vserossiiskago zhenskago s"ezda pri Russkom Zhenskom (Vzaimno-Blagotvoritel'nom) Obshchestve v S.-Peterburge 10-16 dekabria 1908 goda* (St. Petersburg, 1909), 364.

18. A. L. Borovikovskii, "Konstitutsiia sem'i po proektu Grazhdanskago Ulozheniia," *Zhurnal ministerstva iustitsii* (hereafter abbreviated *ZhMIu*), 1902, No. 9: 6.

19. *Ibid.*, 23-26, *idem*, "Brak i razvod po proektu Grazhdanskago Ulozheniia," *ZhMIu*, 1902, No. 8: 23-59; and *idem*, "Novyi zakonoproekt ob uluchshenii polozheniia nezakonnorozhdennykh detei," *ZhMIu*, 1899, No. 8: 31-5.

20. This argument is developed in detail in Wagner, *Marriage, Property, and Law.*

21. On these strands of liberalism, see especially Mark S. Cladis, *A Communitarian Defense of Liberalism: Emile Durkheim and Contemporary Social Theory* (Stanford, 1992); Steven Seidman, *Liberalism and the Origins of European Social Theory* (Berkeley, 1983), 145-200; Steven B. Smith, *Hegel's Critique of Liberalism: Rights in Context* (Chicago, 1989); Donald G. Rohr, *The Origins of Social Liberalism in Germany* (Chicago, 1963); Dieter Langewiesche, "German Liberalism in the Second Empire, 1871-1914," in Konrad H. Jarausch and Larry E. Jones, eds., *In Search of Liberal Germany: Studies in the History of German Liberalism from 1789 to the Present* (New York, 1990), 230-32; Charles W. Anderson, *Pragmatic Liberalism* (Chicago, 1990); David John Manning, *Liberalism* (London, 1976); and Steven Lukes, *Individualism* (Oxford, 1973), 12-14, 22, 38, 71, 73-87. The position of each group discussed in the text necessarily must be presented schematically. For a fuller treatment, see Wagner, *Marriage, Property, and Law.*

22. For examples of such proposals, see Filippov, "Vzgliad"; the articles by Borovikov-skii cited above in note 19; the essays on family, property, and inheritance law in A. Liubavskii, *Iuridicheskiia monografii i izsledovaniia* , 4 vols. (St. Petersburg, 1867, 1875, 1878); I. Orshanskii, "Lichnyia i imushchestvennyia otnosheniia suprugov," in *Izsledovaniia po russkomu pravu semeinomu i nasledstvennomu* (St. Petersburg, 1877), 1-198; K. P.

Zmirlov, "Otmena ili preobrazovanie nashikh zakonov o rodovykh imushchestvakh?", *ZhMIu*, 1898, No. 4: 75-124; P. N. Gussakovskii, "Nasledstvennoe pravo po proektu Grazhdanskago Ulozheniia," *ZhMIu*, 1903, No. 9: 1-52; *Obshchestvo russkikh vrachei v pamiat' N. I. Pirogova. Dnevnik sed 'mogo s "ezda russkikh vrachei* (Kazan, 1899), No. 3: 21-25, and No. 13: 281-87; L. Bertenson, *Fizicheskie povody k prekrashcheniiu brachnago soiuza. Nesposobnost' k brachnomu sozhitiiu. Bolezni. Durnoe ili zhestokoe obrashchenie* (Petrograd, 1917); *Zhurnaly i protokoly Predsobornago Prisutstviia* 4 (St. Petersburg, 1906-7), 112-38 (3rd sect., *zhur.* no. 24), and 37-38, 43-49, 51, 55-57, 63-64 (comb. mtg., 3rd, 6th, and 7th sects., *zhur.* nos. 1-4); *Golos*, 1871, No. 158: 1, and 1872, No. 46: 1-2; *Vestnik Evropy*, 1877, No. 2: 828-30; 1900, No. 2: 812-18; 1903, No. 11: 360-67; and 1912, No. 3: 412-14; "Po brachnomu voprosu," *Nedelia*, 1884, No. 22: 731-33; "Popravki semeistvennago prava," *Nedelia*, 1898, No. 5: 145-49; *Russkie vedomosti*, 1898, No. 299: 2; 1899, No. 333: 2; 1903, No. 97: 2; 1903, No. 103: 2; and 1912, No. 38: 1; *Russkaia mysl'*, 1898, No. 2: 186-88; 1902, No. 12: 428-30; and 1903, No. 1: 38-40; A. S. Izgoev, "Politicheskaia zhizn' v Rossii," *Russkaia mysl'*, 1912, No. 3: 7-8; I. G. [Gessen?], "Davno pora," *Rech'*, 1910, No. 297: 2, and *idem*, "Reforma nasledstvennago prava," *Rech'*, 1911, No. 48: 2.

23. On abstract individualism, see Lukes, *Individualism*, 73-8, 138-40, 146-52.

24. See the proposals in the works cited in note 22 above. In general, see Wagner, *Marriage, Property, and Law*, and *idem*, "Family Law."

25. *Ibid*. This question is complicated by a lack of consensus on the definition of the rule of law. In "The Rule of Law and Its Virtue" (in *The Authority of Law: Essays on Law and Morality* [Oxford, 1979], 210-29), for example, Joseph Raz defines the rule of law as government "by general, open, and relatively stable law," with "*the making of particular laws [being] guided by open and relatively stable general rules*" and with "the law [being] such that people will be able to be guided by it" (p. 213, italics original). Although Raz derives from this definition a number of valuable principles that serve substantially to constrain state legislative activity, within these constraints the state remains free to legislate. Harold Berman, by contrast, argues that within the Western legal tradition the rule of law denotes the limitation of state lawmaking power by "a law that is higher than, or even separate from, the laws that have been promulgated or acknowledged by the state." Embodied in English and American constitutionalism, such a legal order "permits the laws enacted by [the state] to be challenged in the name of some higher legal authority, whether derived from history or from morality" ("The Rule of Law," 43, 46). The concept of law embodied in the proposals of Russian liberals for the reform of family law would appear to meet Raz's criteria for the rule of law, but not those set down by Berman. The historical and moral aspects of this concept of law, however, nonetheless implied limitations on state legislative activity from which the rule of law even as defined by Berman could have been derived. Hence the danger to the autocracy posed by liberal proposals.

26. For example, see *Trudy pervago zhenskago s "ezda*, 9-12, 60-62, 344-48, 359-67, 374-86, 494-95, 512-19, 549-57, 589, 742, 754-60, 768, 825; M. B., "Russkie otgoloski," *Zhenskoe delo*, 1899, No. 8: 77-8; M. Ia. Pergament, "K predpolagaemoi reforme brakorazvodnago protsessa," *Soiuz zhenshchin*, 1908, No. 5/6: 15-18; *Zhenskii vestnik*, 1914, No. 9: 199; and Gosudarstvennyi arkhiv Rossiiskoi Federatsii, *f.* 516, *op.* 1, *d.* 8: 4-28, 53-70. See also Edmondson, *Feminism, passim*.

27. For example, see I. M. Tiutriumov, "Po povodu peresmotra i kodifikatsii grazhdan-skikh zakonov," *Russkoe bogatstvo*, 1884, No. 3: 698-73; and A. M. Evreinova, "Ob uravnenii prav zhenshchin pri nasledovanii (Protokoly grazhdanskago otdeleniia s.-p.-b. iuridicheskago obshchestva. XLI i XLII. Zasedaniia 1 i 15 maia)," *Zhurnal grazhdanskago i ugolovnago prava* (hereafter abbreviated *ZhGiUP*), 1884, No. 3: 149-54, 159. See also R. Wortman, "Property Rights, Populism, and Russian Political Culture," in Crisp and Edmondson, *Civil Rights*, 13-32. For a similar proposal, see K. D. Kavelin, *Sobranie sochinenii K. D. Kavelina*, 4 (St. Petersburg, 1900), 1050-53, 1061-63, 1083, 1107-11, 1183-91, 1216-17, 1241-70, and *idem*, "Russkoe grazhdanskoe ulozhenie," *ZhGiUP*, 1882, No. 9: 1-24, and 1883, No. 1: 33-38, and No. 2: 85-91.

28. On the role and authority of the Civil Cassation Department, see Brian Levin-Stankevich, "Cassation, Judicial Interpretation and the Development of Civil and Criminal Law in Russia, 1864-1917: The Institutional Consequences of the 1864 Court Reform in Russia," unpublished PhD dissertation (State University of New York, Buffalo, 1984), and Wagner, *Marriage, Property, and Law*, 40-52, 206-23, 337-77; but *cf.* Samuel Kucherov, *Courts, Lawyers, and Trials under the Last Three Tsars* (Westport, CT, 1974), 44-48.

29. Wagner, *Marriage, Property, and Law*, 88-100, and Freeze, "Bringing Order." For example, the overwhelming majority of petitions for separation submitted to the Imperial Chancellery between 1890 and 1902 came from women, about 85 percent of whom belonged to unprivileged *sosloviia*. While a social analysis of the people seeking divorce through the Orthodox ecclesiastical process has yet to be done, my perusal of the protocols of the Holy Synod for 1917-18 and of the *opisi* of the archive of the Moscow diocesan consistory for the post-Emancipation period suggests that a substantial majority of these people similarly belonged to unprivileged *sosloviia*, although in the case of divorce the proportion of men and women among successful petitioners appears to have been roughly equal. Rossiiskii gosudarstvennyi istoricheskii arkhiv (hereafter abbreviated RGIA), *f.* 796, *op.* 209, *dd.* 2832-49, and Tsentral'nyi gosudarstvennyi istoricheskii arkhiv goroda Moskvy, *f.* 203.

30. *Gosudarstvennyi Sovet. Stenograficheskii otchet, vos'maia sessiia (1912-1913)* (St. Petersburg, 1913), 1126.

31. *Polnyi Svod Reshenii Grazhdanskago Kassatsionnago Departamenta Pravitel'stvu-iushchago Senata, 1866-1910* (hereafter abbreviated *SRGKD*) (Ekaterinoslav, 1910), 1868, Nos. 461, 526; 1870, Nos. 799, 1145; 1873, No. 1385; and 1875, No. 291.

32. *SRGKD*, 1871, No. 970 (which was a rehearing of 1870, No. 1145); 1872, No. 407; 1873, No. 1666; and 1882, No. 152; for instances where the right was recognized in principle but denied in the particular case, see 1874, No. 1689, and 1876, No. 41; the court reiterated its earlier position in 1875, No. 291.

33. *SRGKD*, 1879, No. 309; the court partially revoked this principle in 1913, No. 95.

34. *SRGKD*, 1886, No. 29, and 1890, No. 18; see also *Resheniia Grazhdanskago Kassatsionnago Departamenta Pravitel'stvuiushchago Senata* (hereafter abbreviated *RGKD*)(St. Petersburg, 1867-1915), 1913, No. 95; for cases where the principle was confirmed but the particular suit denied, see *SRGKD*, 1892, No. 111; 1893, No. 106; and 1908, No. 48.

35. *SRGKD*, 1906, No. 8.

36. RGIA, *f.* 797, *op.* 91-1898, *d.* 53: 34-70, p. 13. The approving tone of the Editing Commission is not surprising, considering that most of its members were or had been members of the Civil Cassation Department.

37. Wagner, *Marriage, Property, and Law*, 211-16.

38. See *ibid.*, chapters 5, 9.

39. *SZ*, i., pt. 1, *Osnov. gos. zak.*, arts. 65, 69, and in general, arts. 47, 52, 54-55, 57, 67-68, 72-73, pt. 2; *Uchrezh. pravit. sen.*, arts. 59, 61, 101-102, 225-28, and ii., pt. 1; *Obshch. gub. uchrezh.*, arts. 281, 744-46.

40. *Sudebnye Ustavy 20 noiabria 1864 g., s izlozheniem razsuzhdenii, na koikh oni osnovany. Chast' pervaia, Ustav Grazhdanskago Sudoproizvodstva* (St. Petersburg, 1866), arts. 9-10, and *Chast' tret'ia, Uchrezhdenie Sudebnykh Ustanovlenii*, arts. 12-13.

41. For the statutory rules, see *ibid.*, arts. 1, 114-19, and *Ustav Grazhdanskago Sudoproizvodstva*, arts. 9-10, 793, 813, 815. For judicial practice, see *SRGKD/RGKD*, 1867, No. 519; 1868, No. 326 (also Nos. 181, 188); 1870, Nos. 1598, 1628; 1872, Nos. 899, 1217; 1874, No. 599; 1876, No. 102 (and related case 1872, No. 1188); 1878, No. 92; 1879, No. 3; 1880, No. 46; 1883, No. 49; 1893, No. 86; 1896, No. 122; and 1914, No. 17 (on the obligatory force of decisions); 1868, No. 326; 1879, Nos. 3, 143; 1882, No. 166; and 1914, No. 59 (on the right of lower courts to interpret decisions of the Civil Cassation Department); 1872, Nos. 974, 1237; 1883, No. 49; and 1884, No. 47 (on the incorrect interpretation and application of high court decisions as grounds for cassation); 1869, No 853; 1872, Nos. 974, 1237; 1878, No. 92; and 1879, No. 3 (on the right of the Civil Cassation Department to review the interpretation and application of its decisions by lower courts); 1868, Nos. 181, 188, 869; 1873, No. 168; 1883, No. 49; 1884, No. 47; 1886, Nos. 42, 106, 107; 1893, No. 86; 1896, No. 122; 1899, No. 105; 1907, No. 102; 1913, No. 36; and 1914, No. 59 (distinguish high court decisions from the decisions of all other courts, including the unpublished decisions of departments within the high court itself);1880, No. 46 and 1887, No. 106; and see also 1870, No. 1628 and 1879, No. 143 (on the Civil Cassation Department altering its decisions). See also the references cited in note 28 above.

Both the charge to judges to base their decisions on conscience as well as law and the lawmaking power of the Cassation Departments at first glance would seem to have striking parallels in the Soviet period. Whereas the Cassation Departments acted as autonomous judicial bodies, however, the "guiding decisions" of the post-1938 USSR Supreme Court were always vetted, and often drafted, by state and Party officials. This effective subordination of the latter court to state and Party authority actually most closely resembles the position of the pre-reform judicial departments of the Senate, whose decisions could be reviewed by the Minister of Justice and referred to the State Council (a legislative body) and the Emperor. Although this question requires further research, the charge to post-reform imperial judges to be guided by their conscience similarly appears to have been intended in large part both to emphasize and ensure the autonomy of the judiciary and to recognize the practical necessity of judicial interpretation of the law, especially in post-Emancipation conditions. Unlike their early Soviet counterparts, imperial judges therefore were not being empowered to judge or disregard statutory law in light of their own conscience, even though they sometimes did so, as the case of marital separation demonstrates. Rather, they were being instructed to follow their conscience when determining the practical meaning of the law in particular cases, in a context where it was acknowledged that statutory law itself was often unclear, contradictory, or incomplete and the circumstances in which the law was being applied were changing. While such subjectivity is inherent in the process of judicial decision-making, the pre-reform judicial statutes sought to proscribe it, whereas the judicial reform gave it broad latitude. Not nearly so much latitude, however, as that received initially by Soviet judges.

42. A. Dumashevskii, "Iuridicheskoe obozrenie," *ZhMIu*, 1868, No. 36: 83-86; Ia. K. Gorodyskii, "Nashi sudy i sudebnye poriadki po dannym revizii 1895 g.," *ZhMIu*, 1901, No. 2: 21, and No.6: 91; N. P. Druzhinin, *Obshchedostupnoe rukovodstvo k izucheniiu zakonov*, 2d ed. (St. Petersburg, 1899), 128-32; G. F. Shershenevich, *Nauka grazhdanskago prava v Rossii* (Kazan, 1893), 232-43; K. Chikhachev, "O iuridicheskoi sile i prakticheskom znachenii reshenii kassatsionnykh departamentov pravitel'stvuiushchago senata," *Zhurnal Iuridicheskago Obshchestva pri Imp. S.-Peterburgskom Universitete*, 1896, No. 7, pt. ii: 40-42, 55-56; G. V. Demchenko, "Sudebnyi pretsedent," *ZhMIu*, 1903, No. 3: 112-13; D. D. Grimm, "K voprosu o poniatii i istochnike obiazatel'nosti iuridicheskikh norm," *ZhMIu*, 1896, No. 6: 153-55; A. L. Borovikovskii, "V sude i o sude. I. 'Zakonnaia sila' kassatsionnykh reshenii," *ZhMIu*, 1896, No. 10: 15-26; V. L. Isachenko, *Voprosy prava i protsessa. Sbornik tsivilisticheskikh statei*, 2 (Petrograd, 1917), 130, 133, 139-41, 155; and V. Nazar'ev, "Sovremennaia glush'. Iz vospominanii mirovogo sud'i," *Vestnik Evropy*, 1879, No. 5: 136, 139-40, 165. Most legal scholars disputed the power claimed by the Civil Cassation Department. For examples, see the works by Dumashevskii, Shershenevich, and Chikhachev just cited; for contrary arguments, see Demchenko, Grimm, Borovikovskii, and Isachenko; see also Wagner, *Marriage, Property, and Law*, 43-44.

43. A. A. Oppengeim, *Ukazatel' voprosov prava razreshennykh Ministerstvom Iustitsii za vremia s kontsa 1885 po 1893 god* (St. Petersburg, 1895), 239-40, no. 92a (1888, No. 18), circulars of the Ministry of Internal Affairs dated from 1902 to 1912 contained in *Gosudarstvennyi Sovet. Sessiia VIII. Kommisiia*, Doklad no. 2 (Harvard Law Library, Special Collections); S. Kozhukov, "O praktike Pravitel'stvuiushchago Senata po voprosu o vydache krest'ianskim zhenam otdel'nyi vid na zhitel'stvo," *ZhMIu*, 1901, No. 3: 158-68; M. B., "Russkie otgoloski," *Zhenskoe delo*, 1899, No. 8: 77-78; and G. S. N., "K voprosu o razdel'nom zhitel'stve suprugov," *Pravo*, 1900, No. 52: 2484-87. These instructions concerned only the issuance of separate passports, however, and did not appear to address the question of support from the husband.

44. On this possibility, see Cathy Frierson, "Crime and Punishment in the Russian Village: Rural Concepts of Criminality at the End of the Nineteenth Century," *Slavic Review* 46, no. 1 (Spring 1987): 57; and I. N. Milogolova, *Sem'ia i semeinyi byt russkoi poreformennoi derevni, 1861-1900 gg. (na materialakh tsentral'nykh gubernii)*, avtoreferat diss. (Moscow, 1988).

45. See the data and citations in Wagner, *Marriage, Property, and Law*, 48-52, 245-52.

46. See note 2 above.

47. On this latter point, see Jane Burbank, "Discipline and Punishment in the Moscow Bar Association," *Russian Review* 54, no. 1 (January 1995): 44-64.

48. This conception of legal development owes much to Harold J. Berman, *Law and Revolution: The Formation of the Western Legal Tradition* (Cambridge, MA, 1983), and *idem, Faith and Order: The Reconciliation of Law and Religion* (Atlanta, GA, 1993); see also Roberto M. Unger, *Law in Modern Society: Toward a Criticism of Social Theory* (New York, 1976).

3

THE JUDICIAL REFORM OF 1864
AND THE PROCURACY IN RUSSIA

Sergei M. Kazantsev

In post-Soviet Russia, when the place and the role of the procurator's office in the system of state power in Russia is once again the subject of controversy, it is worthwhile examining the origins of this institution. In particular, the experience of the Judicial Reform of 1864 may provide today's statesmen with answers to some of the questions under dispute. In the present debate, in both legal scholarship and government circles, there are two concepts of procuracy supervision: one conservative and the other liberal in orientation. The first concept is reflected in the Law on the Procuracy of 1992; the second in the "Conception of Judicial Reform," approved in 1991 by the Russian Supreme Soviet, and in the Russian constitution of 1993. The conservatives consider that the role and the functions of the procurator's office in the "law-based state" should remain virtually unchanged from their Soviet form and include the supervision of legality in public life. The liberals, who prevail in the Presidential administration, argue that in the law-based state the role of the procurator's office should be limited to handling criminal prosecutions.[1]

In the post-Soviet transformation the dispute over the role of the procurator's office is one of the most important issues to be considered in shaping the machinery of government. Naturally, the procuracy's fate depends on the position taken by various supreme bodies. At the same time, the fortunes of not only many officials but also of other state agencies in Russia depend upon the ultimate shape of the procuracy. To be sure, the democratization of bodies such as the police, state security, and the procurator's office, which require a command structure, is difficult. In the case of the procuracy this task is complicated by the absence of a democratic model of the procuracy (as opposed to the courts or legislature). Furthermore, democratic countries offer no uniform mechanism by which legislatures and courts have limited the bureaucratic power of prosecutorial bodies and checked their inevitable authoritarian tendencies.

In Russia, according to a scholar at the Research Institute of the Procuracy, Iu. Korenevskii, "the main issue for debate is whether the future procurator's office should preserve that sphere of its activity called 'general supervision,' that is, whether the procurator's office will continue to be the body vested with the supervision over legality in this country, or will become merely an accusatory authority, the agency of criminal prosecution."[2]

The liberals give a firm answer to this question. The supervisory power of the procurator's office should be relinquished, first, because as a party to a case a procurator should not have the right to supervise the courts, and, second, because the immensity and uncertainty of general supervision either make the procuracy a senseless and ineffective institution, or turn it into an instrument of political struggle, that is, an obedient executor of the will of the leaders in confronting opposition. This conclusion was reached even by the moderate spokesman of judicial reform, Valerii Savitskii.[3]

In contrast, the conservatives contend that the supervisory function of the procuracy lies at the core of its role and shapes its other functions; indeed, to some it even defines the institution. Conservatives do not see any danger or contradiction in the fact that the procuracy should have prosecutorial functions as well as supervisory ones. On the contrary, they consider that the abandonment of procuratorial supervision might result in the decline of legality in Russia, because neither the courts nor any other bodies could substitute for the procuracy in exercising that function, at least at the present stage.

In making their cases, both sides in the dispute over the procuracy refer frequently to both foreign analogues and the lessons of Russian history. Thus, the authors of the "Conception of Judicial Reform in Russia" declared: "As it is known, Peter I set up the post of a fiscal, but Catherine II substituted fiscals for procurators." [4] It is difficult to say where the authors of the "Conception" found this "fact," as they cite no evidence to support this assertion. The second thesis of this part of the "Conception" is no less daring or unfounded: "The Judicial Reform of 1864 essentially changed the institution of the procurator's office, preserving its function of supporting state accusations in court."[5] As we shall see further on, there are two errors in this statement. First, the Judicial Reform did not "preserve" the function of supporting state accusation in court, but introduced it for the first time in Russia. Second, while the Reform made the prosecutorial function central to the procuracy's role, the body had other functions as well. In spite of these errors, the critique of the procuracy developed by the authors of the

"Conception" did represent an appropriate conclusion drawn from the history of the Russian procurator's office.

One critic of this part of the "Conception," V. I. Baskov, who supports the "Soviet" concept of the procurator's supervision, argues that the reformist point of view "interprets the history and purpose of the procuracy's supervision in the Russian Empire in a distorted way."[6] While accusing his opponents of non-historicism, however, he himself shows lack of knowledge of that history. For example, he mistakenly cites the "Basic Principles for the Reform of the Courts" as the "Basic Principles on the Procurator's Office." And he quotes arbitrarily and inaccurately a statement of Nikolai V. Muraviev, who, as the state prosecutor and Minister of Justice, noted in 1889 that the Russian term "procuracy supervision" as the official name of the procurator's office "is now an anachronism." Muraviev considered the term "accusatory authority" to be in wider use and more accurate.[7]

Without assuming the role of arbitrator in today's arguments, I would like to clarify the essence and meaning of the changes experienced by the Russian procurator's office as a result of the Judicial Reform of 1864.[8] To accomplish this, I shall explain first the origins of the Russian procurator's office, so that the reader may understand its evolution up to 1864 and the bases of its reform.

The Pre-reform Procuracy

The procurator's office appeared in Russia during the reign of Peter the Great. It was an entirely new state institution borrowed from Europe. Although some writers have attempted to find an analogy to or forerunner of supervisory authority in pre-Petrine Russia, their arguments are not convincing. In particular, the idea that the *Prikaz* (Department) of Secret Affairs supervised legality is not supported by the evidence.

It is probable that Peter's learning about governance in Europe convinced him of the utility of special supervisory bodies. At first, he borrowed the institution of fiscals which was widespread in Europe of that time. In particular, scholars agree, the tsar took the Fiscal System of Sweden as a model.

The first mention of fiscals in Russia came in an edict (*ukaz*) of Tsar Peter on 2 March 1711 relating to the Senate's duties. The fiscal was entrusted with the duty not only to uncover violations of law by government officials but also to accuse officials directly in the Senate. After some initial difficulty, the office of the Fiscal gave the Tsar positive results. For example, the denunciation by Ober-Fiscal Nesterov in 1717 led to the conviction and execution of the Governor of Siberia, Count Gagarin.

At first Peter planned the post of the "state fiscal" both as the head of the office of fiscal and as the official charged with the delicate task of supervising the Senate itself. When Peter failed to find the right person for the post, he entrusted Guards officers with the function of supervising the Senate, no doubt as a temporary measure.

Why did Peter not look further for the right person for the post of the Fiscal General? Why did he not entrust the Inspector General or the Ober-Secretary of the Senate with these duties? Why did he not accept Henry Fick's proposal for setting up the institution of ombudsman in Russia, following the Swedish model? The design of the procuracy resulted partly by chance. Two events influenced the Tsar's decision: first, his visit to the Paris Parliament in 1717, where a procurator produced a great impression on him; and second, the denunciation and conviction of the Ober-Fiscal Nesterov, for bribe taking. The need to reform the Senate precipitated the final decision on the establishment of the procurator's office. On 18 January 1722, Peter issued his edict on the reform of the Senate, and there we find the first mention of the Procurator General and the Ober-Procurator. Soon after, a special edict was issued on "The Duties of the Procurator General."

Pursuant to this edict, the posts of Procurator of Collegia and Procurator of the *nadvornye* (aulic) courts and, somewhat later, the post of the Ober-Procurator of the Synod, were established. The main function of each of the Procurators was to supervise the activity of the body to which it was attached, i.e., to remind officials of the law and to appeal any unlawful decisions. An objection by a Procurator to a decision automatically superseded its execution. In addition, the fiscals were subordinated to the Procuracy and upon receiving their denunciations Procurators were meant to start criminal cases.

In this way, there appeared in Russia a supervisory institution that, while bearing a French name, did not follow the model of the procurator's office in France. Rather, the Russian procuracy was Peter's creation, one that included elements of the French Procurator's office, the Swedish Ombudsman, and the Swedish and German Fiscals, as well as Russian inventions.

In addition to the name, the hierarchical command structure of the procuracy was borrowed from France, but with a key difference—in France procurators were the servants of law, protecting the interests of the Crown. In Russia they became the servants of the Crown, protecting its laws. Actually, the procurators' main function, in Russia—supervision over compliance with law by the body to which each procurator was attached—

was also borrowed from France, but French procurators were attached to judicial bodies while Russian procurators were mainly attached to administrative ones.

In Russia the fiscals were subordinated to the Procurator General just as fiscals in Sweden were to the Ombudsman (although it should be remembered that fiscal supervision in Sweden was non-governmental). Like the Ombudsman in Sweden, the Procurator General in Russia supervised the execution of edicts, but in Sweden such supervision was confined to the judicial sphere. Both the Procurator General and the Ombudsman were ministers attached to their respective Senates. But while the Ombudsman's duty was to limit aristocratic impulses, however weak, in the interests of the King, the Russian Procurator General was to protect Senators from criminal actions of any kind on the part of Senators, to supervise their spheres of responsibility, and to safeguard the property of the state. To summarize, while in "The Duties of the Procurator General" we can find European parallels, it represents such a mosaic of borrowings as to produce an original Russian picture, whereby the Procurator General helps the Tsar to keep in line all officials.

The death of Peter I and the brief succession of Catherine I resulted in a considerable reduction of the role of the procuracy. Peter I had needed the Procurator General at first to supervise the nobles, but when for a time the monarch fell into dependency on the nobles, the office supervision system then became obsolete. Accordingly, Procurator General P. I. Iaguzhinskii was appointed the ambassador to Poland, but he did succeed in retaining the post of Procurator General. After his departure from Petersburg the process of cutting down the supervisory staff began. In 1727 the institution of fiscals, subordinated to the procurator's office, was abolished; then both the *nadvorny* courts and their procurators were eliminated; and finally the posts of the procurators of collegia were abolished.

The restoration of the various procuratorial posts started in 1730 with the advent to the throne of Anna Ioanovna, who was helped in her accession by the same Iaguzhinskii. But only with the advent to power of Elizabeth Petrovna in 1740 was the procuracy restored once and for all. At that time, the number of procurators increased and their role became more prominent. Procurators performed the tasks of combatting red tape and supervising prisons, but found it difficult to combat bribe taking and other kinds of malfeasance.

The whole system of government in mid-eighteenth-century Russia used bribe taking as the basic source of the income for officials. As a result, the attempts by procurators to combat it met with hostility and incomprehension.

Moreover, legislation was a less significant source of law than legal conscience and custom. Petitions of the period reveal that the established statutory order had little authority: in fact, many officials were unaware of it. Nor could they learn, since the edicts of the Tsar and the Senate were published only occasionally.

Even the procurators knew little about the laws. In 1742 it was discovered, for example, that there was not a single copy of "The Duties of the Procurator General" in the Synod, the Trade Collegium, or the Judicial Department (*Prikaz*).[9] The Senate Office was constantly missing the texts of laws.

In the second quarter of the eighteenth century the significance of the procuracy for the supervision of legality remained minimal, for it was meant to control only the forms and procedures of government. As a result, it mattered little whether the role of the Procurator General in the official hierarchy increased or decreased, or what kind of relations the Procurator General had with the Senate. Even the personal qualities of the people who held the post of Procurator General had little impact on its status. In other words, in the period between Peter I and Catherine II the procuracy represented a superfluous element in the bureaucratic system of autocracy, a sort of fifth wheel in the cart. Officials—central and local alike—tolerated it and even got used to it, but nobody needed it. The procuracy continued to exist mainly because of the authority of its founder—Peter the Great.

Under Catherine II the procuracy gained a variety of administrative and quasi-ministerial functions. This development resulted from the reform first of the Senate in 1763 and then of provincial (*guberniia*) government in 1775. With the liquidation of some collegia the cases previously handed to them were now referred to the Senate, and the Procurator General was put in charge of their distribution to the Senate's different departments. Moreover, the inclusion of Procurator General Viazemskii as a member of the new Council at the Imperial Court (established in 1769) encouraged Governors and Governors General to petition him about decisions of local courts and government bodies. As a result, the Procurator General acquired and combined some of the qualities of a Minister of Internal Affairs and a Minister of Justice. In 1780 the Dispatch Office of State Revenues was placed in the domain of the Procurator General,[10] and the same year he began to supervise "currency transactions."[11] Soon after, he was put in charge of the protection of immigrants,[12] the post-office department,[13] and the bank.[14] As if this were not enough, the Procurator General continued to serve as the head of the Senate Office, the Printing House, and other offices attached to the Senate. Nevertheless, all of this expansion in the duties of the procuracy did not bear on his proper supervisory functions as laid out in "The Duties of the Procurator General," though his position in that field improved as well.

The guberniia reform of 1775 contributed to the further development of the procurator's office, leading to changes in both the structure of the procuracy and its functions. In addition to the new posts of guberniia procurators, the positions of guberniia and district *striapchie* (state attorneys) were also established, to assist the procurator in his relations with the courts. As a result, the procurator's office was for the first time entrusted with managing prosecution on behalf of the state. But this function of procurators and their assistants was insignificant, because of the purely inquisitional system of investigation (procurators and striapchie could not appear in court) and the prevailing theory of formal proofs.

It was under Paul I that the Procurator General obtained the greatest authority. During Paul's reign, the procuracy was called upon, for the first time, to decide about recruitment and material and technical supplies for the army and navy, and to handle financial matters as well. The Procurator General decided these matters on his own or on the approval of the Tsar, without submitting decisions to the Senate. In the field of administration he acted as the Minister of Internal Affairs, by directing Governors General and coordinating the activity of central and local authorities to combat crime, hunger, and disasters. It was he who reported to the Tsar about most peasant revolts. Under Paul I the Procurator General became not just a minister but "acted as a Prime Minister."[15] This elevation of the Procurator General did not, however, result in the triumph of legality. On the contrary, the more executive power was concentrated in the hands of the Procurator General, the more often he was guided not by law but by expediency. At the same time, the supervision of legality became not his main activity, but only one of the functions of ministerial power. Moreover, Paul's commitment to eradicating the evils of bribe taking and bureaucratism with a "white-hot iron" was accompanied by a naive belief in his sacred right to interpret or change the law arbitrarily.

The role of the Procurator General and the procuracy changed fundamentally in 1802 with the establishment of the ministerial system of government. The post of the Procurator General was united with that of the Minister of Justice. The change in the role of the Procurator General resulted not so much from his transformation into one of the Tsar's ministers as from the decline in the role of the Senate, which lost to the new ministries many of its political and administrative functions and became in the main a judicial and supervisory body.

In the first half of the nineteenth century local procuracy offices maintained their structure and functions. To be sure, there were occasional edicts or laws relating to procuracy supervision, but they concerned details. During this period the guberniia procurators paid closest attention to examining the decisions and sentences of judicial and administrative bodies.

Unfortunately, the Code of Laws of the Russian Empire, which came into force in 1835, did not change the position of the procuracy. In the first sixty years of the nineteenth century the tasks and powers of the Procurator General were even more limited than before. Formally nothing had changed, as the Senate continued to deal with supervision, but in fact the Minister of Justice lost his role as "the eye of the sovereign" when the Senate became the top judicial body, and the new supreme state bodies (the Committee of Ministers and the State Council) fell outside of the domain of procuracy supervision. Instead of supervising the government, as Peter the Great intended, the procuracy in the nineteenth century exercised supervision over the courts and local administrative bodies. At the same time, the authority of the local procurators was also reduced. For example, governors and guberniia offices frequently ignored their protests and failed to supply the documents specified by law.

The procuracy continued the struggle against bribe taking, one of the most serious vices of the pre-reform administrative and judicial systems. Tsarina Catherine called upon the procurators to combat "harmful bribes," but few procurators ventured to do so. Moreover, according to gendarme officers, some guberniia procurators themselves succumbed to this sin. Bribe taking in the courts reached such a level in the middle of the nineteenth century that even the Minister of Justice himself bribed an overseer of St. Petersburg District Court. The Minister gave 100 rubles through the director of the department, Topilskii, to speed up the trial of his daughter's case.[16]

The helplessness and ineffectiveness of the procuracy before the reforms was conditioned not only by the vices of autocratic and bureaucratic centralism, but also by the weaknesses of the institution itself. First, the procuracy was subordinated to executive power through the person of a minister. Second, the procuracy did not present a harmonious integral system, for there was no single legislative act defining its structure and activities. Third, the spheres of supervision and the functions of a particular procuracy office were so numerous and vague that fulfillment was unrealistic. In short, the procurator's office, like other bodies of state power during the reigns of Alexander I and Nicholas I, was in a condition of stagnation and in need of radical reorganization.

The Procuracy in the Era of Reform

The performance of the procuracy in the first sixty years of the nineteenth century convinced the designers of the Judicial Reform of 1864 that it was futile to use a bureaucratic agency to improve legality. At the same time, their inclusion in the reform of public trials contested by lawyers required the development of a prosecutorial service. Consequently, they decided to reduce drastically the supervisory function of the procuracy and to make it responsible for criminal prosecutions.

The first proposed changes to the procuracy appeared in the draft "Regulations of Civil Proceedings" (1857), prepared by the Second Department of His Majesty's Private Office. This draft law provided for the replacement of the existing procedure of appeals by procurators with mere resolutions of procurators and striapchie delivered at trial. But this proposal of the Second Department restricting the supervisory functions of the procuracy did not find support in the ministries.

More significant for the role of the procuracy were the new plans to transform the courts and criminal procedure, developed in the various draft laws of 1859-60. They provided for introducing adversarial, public trials, the right of the accused to defense, presumption of innocence, reform of pre-trial investigation, the establishment of a defense Bar, and, finally, a reorganization of the procuracy. In addition to the already existing guberniia procurator, a new special procurator would be placed at every *uezd* (county) and *okrug* (district) court and in each judicial chamber of the Senate; these procurators would perform the new function of criminal prosecution, along with the existing task of supervising the courts.

Between 1857 and 1861 some 14 drafts on different aspects of procedural law were prepared. To coordinate the different approaches and to speed up the process, by the order of the Tsar, "Fundamental Principles of the Transformation of the Courts in Russia" were prepared and passed on 29 September 1862. This Act provided for the post of a procurator at every court and, if needed, an assistant procurator as well. The Procurator General-Minister of Justice exercised supreme supervision with the help of procurators. The functions of the procuracy were reduced in the main to the judicial sphere and consisted of "1) supervision over uniform and exact observance of the law; 2) detection and prosecution of any violation of legality and demand for its elimination; [and] 3) submission to the court of preliminary conclusions in situations stipulated in civil and criminal procedure." The procuracy lost its general supervision function as well as the notorious practice of examining registers of guberniia offices. But the procuracy retained supervision over places of confinement. In short, with the introduction of new adversarial proceedings in courts, the most important function became prosecution.

Published in the Collection of Statutes and Government Decrees, the "Fundamental Provisions" became the subject of wide discussion on, among other things, the role and purpose of the procuracy. Comments on this aspect of the Act showed that it did reflect the views of a majority of Russian lawyers. In practice, none of the participants in the discussion opposed the procuracy's reorganization and none challenged the idea of having procurators prosecute in criminal trials. All agreed that the sphere of supervision should be restricted to the system of justice. Out of 448 persons who offered comments on and proposals to the commission drafting the "Fundamental Provisions," only one—a *striapchii* from Vilenskii Guberniia named Butarovskii—was in favor of preserving the function of general supervision. He proposed to vest in the procuracy "supervision over all local government offices and officials"—this in addition to the duties already set out in the "Fundamental Provisions."[17] While this proposal sounded dissonant at the time, at the end of the nineteenth century and the beginning of the twentieth calls were heard for a return of the function of general supervision to the procurator's office. Thus in 1896 the noted Russian lawyer A. F. Koni wrote: "Abolition . . . of the procuracy's duties concerning supervision over non-judicial matters should be acknowledged as a great error on the part of the drafters of the judicial codes." Koni used a fitting metaphor to describe the reorganization of the procuracy in 1864: "In haste to fill a burning desire to clear an area now overgrown with weeds, for new plantings an oak was felled that stood on guard over the forest."[18]

In the course of the discussion of the "Fundamental Provisions," arguments were made not only to expand the functions of the procuracy but also to limit them further. Some commentators were even ready to abolish the office. The collegium assessor (a civil official in pre-Revolutionary Russia), Serdukov from Mogilev Guberniia, Mstislavskii district, wrote: "In all my writings I have shown the uselessness of procurators and of the former *striapchie*. . . . Now, when there are so many eyes at the trial that not only a law but also the slightest nod of the head will not be missed, they are all the more unnecessary. On the whole with the new organization one can expect absolute truth without procurators and even without the Ministry of Justice. . . ."

The famous criminal law scholar (later outstanding advocate), V. D. Spasovich, criticized procuracy supervision of the courts in the press:

> Since a procurator is just an administrative official, subject to the Minister of Justice, it means that charging him with supervision over courts is tantamount to making courts, which were founded to protect law from violations on the part of both private persons and the administration, subordinate to that same administration. Society does not need any guards other than courts, which depend on nobody and stand under the moral control of public opinion alone. Only judges may supervise courts, higher over lower ones; if supervisors are appointed to watch over these guardians of law, who will watch the supervisors?[19]

Time would show that Spasovich's criticism was not unfounded.

Although Spasovich's point of view was not accepted by other participants in the discussion concerning the "Fundamental Provisions," many of them expressed well-grounded fears that the procuracy might use its powers to protect legality against the law. In particular, the Chairman of Chernigov Criminal Court Chamber, I. Petrunkevich, noted: "The vast authority and the important duties of procurators demand significant actions to prevent arbitrary rule."[20] In order to "protect the society in question from arbitrariness and petty tyranny of procurators," he suggested providing the opportunity for appeal against the procurator's actions in court.[21] But the majority still believed that procurators would use their authority properly and conduct an impartial struggle against law-breakers.

After the publication of the "Fundamental Provisions" of the court reform, specialized commissions started preparing four statutes: the Rules (*ustav*) of Criminal Procedure, the Rules of Civil Procedure, the Statute on the Courts (*Uchrezhdeniia sudebnykkh ustanovlenii*), and Regulations on Punishments Imposed by the Justices of Peace. Adopted on 20 November 1864, these statutes developed the basic principles laid out in the "Fundamental Provisions."

In these new laws, the organization of the procuracy was based on the principle of one-man management and the right of the higher ranking procurators to give their subordinates binding instructions. The Minister of Justice who also served as the Procurator General remained at the head of the procuracy and in charge of the Ober-Procurator's Office of the Senate and the procurators of the judicial chambers (*sudebnaia palata*). In place of the guberniia and district striapchie, the new post of assistant procurator (*tovarishch prokurora*) was established. All procurators and their assistants were appointed by the Tsar on the recommendation of the Minister of Justice. To be appointed a procurator involved meeting educational requirements and some years' experience in the work of courts.

In my view the reformed procuracy represented an improvement over the weak and passive procuracy of the pre-reform period. Prosecuting cases in the new courts gave the procuracy an important function that it could actually perform. The new procuracy not only became a counterweight to the Bar, but also remained a defender of the interests of autocracy, "the eye of the sovereign," within the "judicial republic."

In the second half of the nineteenth and the beginning of the twentieth centuries the development of the procuracy took two main directions: (1) gradual weakening of the guberniia procurator's office—in comparison to procurators of the courts (as the judicial reforms were implemented in different parts of the country) and (2) the intensification of procuracy supervision over the courts and the Bar and increasing predominance within the procuracy of its prosecutorial functions. The effort undertaken to set up a separate system of procuracy supervision over administrative bodies and expand the powers of the "judicial procurator's office" in the field of general supervision based upon the model of the pre-reform guberniia failed because of the pressing need to convert the procuracy into a prosecutorial body. At the same time, the new generation of procurators was largely free of the common vices of its predecessors: bribe taking, incompetence, and irresponsibility.

The judicial reform fundamentally changed the role of the procurator in criminal proceedings: a procurator became an active prosecutor and the central figure in combatting crime, instead of a supervisor (as he used to be everywhere, including in the criminal court). It was universally acknowledged that prosecution had become the main and most important function of the procuracy. This was the activity that the public and lawyers alike identified with the procuracy.

This result was not accidental. The writers of the judicial reform statutes stipulated that prosecution was to become the main function of the procuracy,[22] that a "procurator should act as public prosecutor in all criminal cases and carry them on in all court instances as a representative of government and law."[23] Still, while making procurators responsible for prosecution, legislators preserved their duty to supervise over legality in the judicial sphere; both these duties of "a prosecutor and a limb of the law went together hand in hand."[24] This was especially obvious at the stage of preliminary investigation, when, in bringing a criminal case, a procurator became simultaneously both a party in a court proceeding and a supervisor, directing the investigator's actions. Not surprisingly, the disadvantages of such a paradox above all for investigators were repeatedly condemned in legal literature and in practice.

The combination of prosecutorial and supervisory functions in the single person of the procurator made him master of the proceedings during the preliminary investigation. All inquiries were carried out under the procurator's guidance and sometimes with his participation. In practice, procurators had the temerity to appoint police officers to pursue their inquiries. As a result, the Senate issued a special ruling prohibiting procurators from ordering police chiefs to act on their behalf. Procurators were entitled only to give orders about searches and seizures to officers of the Criminal Investigation Department.[25]

The leading role of a procurator during the preliminary investigation was fixed first of all in Article 281 of the Rules of Criminal Procedure that made the investigator responsible for both carrying out the lawful demands of a procurator or his assistant, and recording which measures had been taken in this regard. In practice, this rule led to controversy and opposing interpretations. The majority of investigators reached the conclusion that they should ignore unlawful demands from a procurator.[26] But there was a disagreement whether investigators were obliged to perform all lawful demands from a procurator or only those that an investigator considered reasonable.

The Rules of Criminal Procedure entitled a procurator to demand supplementary investigation of a case that the investigator thought finished, irrespective of whether he had transferred it to the court or recommended that the case be dropped for absence of a crime or on some other grounds.

The Statute on the Courts also contributed to the dependence of investigators on procurators. Thus, under Article 213 investigators were appointed on recommendations from okrug courts; and the recommendation of a procurator from the court was often enough to shift the investigator to another court.

The dependence of pre-trial inquiry and investigation on procuracy supervision may have been expedient at the stage of preliminary inquiry when the inquisitorial process prevailed, but the extent to which it was necessary when an attorney and a judge examined the evidence is less obvious to the student of the history of the tsarist procuracy.

Certain procurators became well known and gained much authority as public prosecutors in court. The absence of experienced speakers at trials had served as an argument of the opponents of the Judicial Reform. But the first years of the new courts put an end to all of their fears. In society the names of not only defense counsels but also of procurators became well known, among them A. F. Koni, M. F. Gromnitskii, N. V. Muraviev, S. A. Andreevskii, and V. I. Zhukovskii. As A. F. Koni wrote:

> the main features of a newly formed Russian type of prosecutor were—with the exception of a rare but sad tendency to soulless rhetoric—calmness, absence of personal animosity toward the accused, careful elaboration of the prosecution; avoidance of inflaming passions and distorting the evidence, and, finally, what is most important, the complete absence of theatricality in voice, gesture, and carriage in the courtroom. To this add simple language, usually free of mannerisms and of high-flown and 'pitiful' words.[27]

In short, the "fathers" of the Judicial Reform wanted the procurator to appear at trial as "a judge speaking in public."

The judicial statutes would seem to have created close to an ideal type of a state prosecutor, by appropriating the best features of the French procurator and mitigating them in the spirit of Russian pre-reform procuracy, which had combined the functions of "the limb of the law," "the enforcer of punishment," and "the defender of innocence." But after the euphoria of the first post-reform years was over and the swamp of routine started to suck in the new courts, it turned out that—despite the words in the codes, directing procurators and advocates to represent justice and seek truth rather than victory at any cost—prosecutors prosecuted and defenders defended.

With passing years the polarization between the parties at trial became marked, and the procuracy and the Ministry of Justice were largely responsible for it. A negative moral force was exerted on procurators through their participation in investigation and prosecution in political cases. Procurators not only engaged in biased selection of witnesses, and gave distorted and one-sided interpretations of the evidence, but also on some occasions even violated the law. In such cases, a new type of prosecutor, "the speaking policeman," replaced "the speaking judge."

From the moment of its reorganization after 1864 the procuracy became one of the main links in a state machinery to combat the revolutionary movement in the country. Under Article 1034 of the Rules of Criminal Procedure, prosecution of state crimes fell into the domain of the procurators of the Sudebnaia palata, to whom all officials and private persons were to report all relevant information without delay.

In the second half of the nineteenth century the procuracy played an active part in combatting political crimes in the country. At the stage of preliminary investigation the procurators were to supervise the activity of the bodies dealing with conducting the inquiry and investigation, as well as to participate directly in the prosecution. The procuracy not only sanctioned unlawful searches and arrests and the prosecution of persons, but also played the leading part in extrajudicial reprisals against political suspects and dissidents, including exile without trial. At this stage the procuracy collaborated with the police in performing procedural steps specified by law, and assisted them in operational searches.

The judicial rules of 1864 greatly restricted the sphere of the procurator's involvement in civil cases in comparison with the earlier collection of laws. What remained for the procuracy was the task of advising courts, thereby ensuring that settlements were consistent with the laws. In practice, procurators performed even this task poorly. As virtual specialists in criminal prosecution, they had less knowledge of the civil law than the judges of the civil court. Moreover, procurators treated their civil case work formally. As a result, both judges and other participants in the proceedings regarded the procurator's involvement as superfluous.

Still, all things considered, in the history of tsarist procuracy the period after the Judicial Reform of 1864 was the most fruitful and effectual. The noble aims that tsars entrusted to the procurator's office in the eighteenth and the first half of the nineteenth centuries proved unfeasible in practice. From the first days of procuracy supervision the process of its fusion with administration began. It is typical that even in the second half of the eighteenth century, at the time when Procurators General had the most power as a result of development of their administrative command, rather than their supervisory function—a condescending attitude toward law continued in society and state alike.

The complete inadequacy of procuracy supervision was revealed in the first half of the nineteenth century. The tendency toward bureaucratization, typical of that institution in the eighteenth century, increased after the subordination of the procuracy to the executive power in the person of the Minister of Justice. Formally supervision covered almost all spheres of state activity, but in each of them it became more and more empty. In practice, the idealistic dreams of establishing supervision over everyone and everything resulted in neglect and lawlessness.

The foundations of legality in Russia were laid only through the Judicial Reform of the 1860s, which in turn prompted a radical reorganization of the procuracy. It is characteristic that the effort to establish legality accompanied the abolition of general supervision by the procuracy. As a result, the procuracy turned mainly into a prosecutorial body, and it was this kind of procuracy that assumed an honored place in the state apparatus of tsarist Russia. Its activity was the most authoritative in the criminal sphere, where due to the judicial codes of 1864 it succeeded in combining prosecutorial and supervisory functions. In post-reform Russia the procurator became a key figure at all stages of the criminal process.

But it is worth mentioning that the procuracy, as a government body, treated legality from the viewpoint of the struggle against the opponents to the regime. It turned away from law just at the point where it was needed to achieve the highest aims of the regime. Of the institutions of state power the procuracy has always been one of the most reliable and loyal to the regime. This characteristic feature of the procuracy was preserved and developed in the Soviet period and continues to a degree even today. In many ways, the contemporary struggle to develop and implement judicial reforms resembles the era of reform during the reign of Tsar Alexander II. Naturally, to copy historical models blindly—whether domestic or foreign—is both impossible and counterproductive. But one hopes that the designers of the legal reforms in Russia today will pay close attention to the lessons that can be drawn from the history of judicial reform in that country.

Notes

1. For more on the politics of reforming the procuracy in the 1990s, see the chapter in this volume by Gordon Smith, "The Struggle over the Procuracy ."

2. Iu. Korenevskii, "Otmeniat' obshchii nadzor prokuratury—prezhdevremenno," *Rossiiskaia iustitsiia*, 1995, No. 4: 38.

3. V. Savitskii, "Sterzhnevaia funktsiia prokuratury—osushchestvlenie ugolovnogo presledovaniia," *Rossiiskaia iustitsiia*, 1994, No. 10: 24-28.

4. *Kontseptsiia sudebnoi reformy v RSFSR* (Moscow, 1992), 57.

5. *Ibid.*

6. V. I. Baskov, *Prokurorskii nadzor* (Moscow, 1995), 52.

7. N. V. Muraviev, *Prokurorskii nadzor v ego ustroistve i deiatelnosti* (Moscow, 1889), 26.

8. The rest of this chapter is based upon my book, S. M. Kazantsev, *Istoriia tsarskoi prokuratury* (St. Petersburg, 1993). For more details and bibliography please consult it.

9. V. I. Veretennikov, *Ocherki istorii general-prokuratury v Rossii do ekaterininskogo vremeni* (Kharkov, 1915), 371.

10. *Polnoe sobranie zakonov (PSZ)*, Vol. 20, N 15076.

11. *Ibid.*, N 15007.

12. *Ibid.*, N 15668.

13. *Ibid.*, N 15344, 15705.

14. *Ibid.*, N 16838.

15. M. V. Klotchkov, "General-prokurory pri Pavle I," *Zhurnal ministerstvo iustitsii,* 1912, No. 4: 148.

16. N. M. Komakov, "Staryi sud," *Russkaia starina,* 1886, No. 12: 521.

17. *Materialy po sudebnoi reforme v Rossii,* Vol. 21, No. 17 (1865): 60.

18. A. F. Koni, "Dmitrii Alexandrovich Rovinskii," in Koni, *Sobranie sochinenii,* Vol. 5 (Moscow, 1968), 7.

19. V. D. Spasovich, "Sudebnaia reforma," *Sankt-Peterburgskie Vedomosti,* 1863, No. 1-3.

20. *Materialy po sudebnoi reforme v Rossii,* Vol. 22, No. 47 (1866): 462.

21. *Ibid.*

22. *Sudebnye ustavy 20 noiabria 1864 goda s izlozheniem rassuzhdenii, na koikh oni osnovany* (St. Petersburg, 1867), part II, 27-28.

23. *Ibid.*, Part III, 102.

24. *Ibid.*, Part II, 189.

25. *Ustav ugolovnogo sudoproizvodstva. S postateinym materialami, sostavlennymi* M. P. Shramchenko and V. P. Shirkovym (St. Petersburg, 1913), 397-98.

26. P. V. Makalinskii, *Prakticheskoe rukovodstvo dlia sudebnykh sledovatelei,* 6th ed. (St. Petersburg, 1907), 125.

27. A. F. Koni, "Priemy i zadachi prokuratury," in Koni, *Sobranie sochinenii (v 8 tomakh),* Vol. 4 (Moscow, 1987), 124.

4

THE CONSENSUAL DIMENSION OF LATE IMPERIAL RUSSIAN CRIMINAL PROCEDURE: THE EXAMPLE OF TRIAL BY JURY

Girish N. Bhat

In introducing trial by jury as part of the 1864 Judicial Reform, reformers in Russia sought to transform the practice of their courts. The involvement of juries—most fully developed within the adversarial tradition of Anglo-American countries—forced Russia to abandon its pure inquisitorial procedure, marked by office reviews of written documents. Instead, the Reform replaced that procedure with public trials that featured a verbal contest between two attorneys, played out before an audience of judges, jury, and spectators. All the same, Russian jurists proved unwilling to abandon the inquisitorial tradition entirely. As a result, trial by jury led in Russia, as it had in France, to a new and peculiar blend of the two traditions.

This chapter addresses the question of the nature of that blend. Of what did it consist? How should it be understood? The type of adjudication that emerged in Russian jury trials, especially in the 1860s and 1870s, has been characterized as representing a procedural compromise, a "mixed" (*smeshan-nyi*)[1] or "instructional" (*instruktsionnyi*)[2] model of adjudication. According to this view, spelled out most recently by the historian M. G. Korotkikh,[3] the new procedure, in both its pre-trial and trial stages, represented a fusion of the high-handed principles and methods of pre-reform judicial inquiry of the inquisitorial system with a fairer and more even-handed adversarialism. While this interpretation of the Reform's impact on criminal adjudication is accurate, it misses important subtleties and complexities of the new criminal procedure. In contrast, I argue in this study that a model of "consensual" judicial inquiry better captures the essence of Russian jury trial adjudication, including its cultural underpinnings and moral-intellectual wellsprings.[4] For in the actual development of trial by jury, through the early years of the

Reform, judges and attorneys alike displayed a consensual approach to the conduct of trials. To support this argument, I start by examining the main features of the design of the 1864 jury trial system: first, the post-1864 remnants of inquisitorial procedure; second, the components of the new adversarialism; and third, the sources of consensualism in jury trial procedure, including the extension of the collegial style of Russian bureaucratic life into jury procedure. After this, I analyze manifestations of consensualism in actual cases.

The Legacy of Inquisitorial Procedure

Although scholars dispute the "modernization" of Russian law before the imperial era,[5] they agree about the absence of equality in criminal procedure before 1864. Known to contemporary Russians as the "Emperor's justice" (*koronnyi sud, sud koronnago sud'i*), pre-reform criminal "trials" had three main features: presumption of guilt, predominantly written proceedings, and the centrality of "confession" as proof of guilt.[6] The first feature, on which the entire judicial inquiry was based, served the interests of political authority. "The state," as John P. LeDonne put it, "moved peremptorily against the accused, on the assumption that where a crime has been committed there must be a criminal who must be punished, and that it is for the suspect to disprove the allegations raised against him by the prosecution."[7]

The second and third features exemplified the formal system of evidence used in pure inquisitorial procedure everywhere. A court, consisting of a judge and assessors, elected by the nobility and privileged townspeople, based its verdict solely upon an in camera review of an exhaustive written record of all testimony and other evidence from the police investigation. Confession by the suspect loomed especially large. It was described in the 1845 Collection of Criminal Laws (*Ugolovnoe ulozhenie*) to be "the best evidence in the whole world,"[8] a less elegant equivalent to the usual epithet applied to confession in inquisitorial justice: the "queen of proofs."[9] Before the official abolition of judicial torture under Alexander I at the turn of the nineteenth century, the attachment of such high evidentiary value to the confession inevitably produced partially or fully tainted admissions of guilt.

Overall, the inquisitorial system gave adjudication a formal and stultifyingly impersonal quality. Moreover, it entrenched the already rigid hierarchies and social divisions of Russia's "estate" (*soslovie*) system. Under the guise of precise, codified, and theoretically infallible methods of proof flourished a "justice of inequity" that devalued and dehumanized the individual.[10] In some respects, the 1864 Reform preserved the inquisitorial structure of criminal procedure and combined it with the seemingly incompatible jury trial system. In their approach to adjudication, judges continued to honor autocratic authority and favor the interests of the state, despite the 1864 statutes' proclamations about the equality of the sides.

One central feature of the inquisitorial method persisted after 1864 and merits particular attention. The inquisitorial approach to criminal prosecutions inevitably favors the state by entrusting it with the conduct of the pre-trial investigation and, as a result, gives it a big advantage over the accused in the eventual adjudication—whether in an office review or a trial. In fact, the state's leading role in assembling the evidence and data on which the trial was to be based assured that the prosecutor, as the state's representative in post-1864 trials, came to occupy a legal position superior to that of defense counsel. In the reformed criminal procedure, almost all of the evidentiary and administrative preparations for jury trials were completed without the participation or even knowledge of the accused and defense counsel.[11] Furthermore, *even after* the defense attorney was allowed to meet with his client and review the completed file of the case, his resources were limited until the trial itself.

The state's retention of its prerogatives in the pre-trial inquiry was reflected in the authority and responsibilities given to the "judicial investigator" (*sudebnyi sledovatel'*). Created in 1860 in a series of much needed changes to criminal investigative procedures,[12] and consolidated in the 1864 statutes, the judicial investigator came to play a major role in trial by jury. The new office did indeed bring greater equity and accountability to the state's investigative apparatus. Yet despite these improvements and the curtailing of the "paramount importance" of the pre-trial investigation before the Reform,[13] the state's precedence in the preliminary inquiry persisted.[14]

The investigator's wide-ranging duties included questioning of witnesses, preparation of depositions and other pertinent documents, collection of physical evidence, and marshalling of all relevant medical and criminological expertise. His status as an "official member of the court" (*chlen suda*) also vested him with authority during the trial.[15] Despite the reform statutes' stipulation that the investigator approach his task in an impartial spirit, and gather evidence not only against but also in favor of the accused,[16] the investigator usually managed in practice to place the burden of proof on the defendant, even though technically it now fell upon the state.

The statutory affirmation and codification of these differing probative standards lay in Article 751 of the Rules of Criminal Procedure (*Ustav ugolovnago sudoproizvodstva*):

> The conclusions of the state's bill of indictment (*obvinitel'nyi akt*) shall not constitute the only basis of the essential issues in the case. Of equal importance shall be the judicial [pre-trial] investigation, and, *in as much as they develop, supplement, or alter the conclusions in the bill of indictment*, the final courtroom pleadings.[17]

This brief statement provided both a definition of procedural priorities and a statement of the mode of operation for trials.

The official indictment of the accused, based upon the pre-trial preparation of the case by representatives of the state, was treated as the starting point of the trial. This indictment was open to contestation in court but it was taken as "presumptive judicial truth," which the defense had to challenge and overcome in order to win its case. In other words, the trial began with not a tabula rasa but an interpretation of the situation developed during the pre-trial investigation, in which only the state's interests were reflected. Accordingly, the main purpose of the trial was to explore, refine, confirm, or disprove the state's accusations, rather than to *establish* guilt or innocence in an open-ended inquiry. The inquisitorial disinclination to presume innocence endured in this limited form.

Heightening the accused's burden of proof, if only indirectly, were the obstacles encountered by defense attorneys under the reform statutes. Full and equal participation on behalf of the accused, before as well as during the trial, is integral to a legal defender's ability to confront the prosecution on neutral ground. However, Russian attorneys—like their French counterparts until 1896—had to accept severe restrictions on their role in the pre-trial phase. Despite a right to meet his client after the completion of the preliminary investigation and limited access to its results,[18] the defense counsel remained a weak presence in the pre-trial phase. Before and at trial, he became a respondent to the investigator and the procuracy, and conducted his defense in reaction to the state's prior shaping of the inquiry.[19] Much of Russian officialdom's traditional outlook on authority and the law persisted in the operation of the 1864 system, and manifested itself in the weakness of the position of the defense attorney. In practice adversarialism was limited.[20]

A specific and telling instance of enduring inquisitorial structures was one of the routine phases of the pre-trial inquiry, the so-called "administrative session" (*rasporiaditel'noe zasedanie*). After the judicial investigator, assisted by local police officials, had completed his investigation and produced a set of case documents, and after the procurator's office had examined these materials, the "judicial chamber" (*sudebnaia palata*) would review the case to determine whether it should be tried before a jury in the circuit court.[21] After the chamber's approval, but still before the trial, the administrative session would take place. The participating officials were the presiding judge and the other members of the court (judges and investigator), the court secretary, and a procurator; the defense counsel was not invited! To be sure, the administrative sessions dealt only with technical issues, such as the need for special arrangements or guidelines for the case in question. It might be determined, for example, that a trial should be held behind closed doors.[22] Still, the absence of defense counsel from administrative sessions reflected an inquisitorial bias.

Following the administrative session, certain essential case documents (copies of the official bill of indictment, the witness list,[23] the list of medical and criminological experts who had been summoned to testify in court) would be given to the local justice of the peace, who would direct that the accused be brought to appear before him. The justice of the peace would then pass on materials to the defendant (perhaps with his attorney present), and explain that, according to the new code of criminal procedure, the accused had the right to submit (within one week) a specific request for legal representation, and any desired additions to the witness list prepared by the state.[24] The defense attorney, upon assignment to the case, was allowed to consult the state's original, bulky case folder and copy out what materials he deemed necessary. The attorney and the accused were permitted to review and discuss these materials in preparation for the trial.[25] Yet the cumulative effect of these preliminary procedures was to insure that a case's pre-trial disposition continued to reflect a high degree of administrative exclusiveness.

The New Adversarialism

Adversarialism was the second major procedural component of Russian jury trial procedure and the one intended to address the glaring defects of pre-1864 Russian justice. Above all else, the shapers of the new judicial order sought fairness—that is, equity and even-handedness in resolving disputes at law and a fundamental respect for the individual as a subject of the law. Adversarialism presupposes open competition between contending parties, in a formal court setting, with the common aim of determining legal truth and obtaining judicial satisfaction. The state, representing the victim (and society), is opposed, on equal terms, by the legally-empowered defender of the accused. Adversarial[26] procedure is also governed by the presumption of innocence, the overriding importance of orality in adjudication, and an official adherence to rigorous standards of proof in evaluating testimony and material evidence. The jury trial, by virtue of its procedural format and legal-philosophical basis, represents the best aspects of adversarial justice.[27]

Russian legal theorists of the reform era understood how the "accusatory form of justice," as adversarialism was often termed, should be constituted. The new statutes could not "simply limit themselves to the mere structuring of legal representation for the prosecution and defense." Genuine adversarialism also "required that the capacity to present and inquire into evidence be granted to both sides, possessing equal rights in court." As a consequence, "the court would function merely as an impartial settler of disputes" between prosecution and defense.[28] Vital to this conception of adversarialism is the recognition that its essence lies in the actual process and substance of adjudication.

The guidelines for jury trials laid out in the new criminal procedure embodied the reformers' vision of adversarial style of "oral debate" (*sudebnye preniia*). The term *sostiazanie* ("contest, competition"), the root word and concept underlying the Russian equivalent of adversarialism (*sostiazatel'nost'*), appears regularly in the statutes as a characterization of the core of the trial. The two opposing sides (*storony na sude*), represented by the procurator[29] and the defense counsel, advance arguments, present evidence, and examine witnesses in order to determine the legal fate of the defendant. The proceedings are meant to unfold in an atmosphere of orality and openness (*ustnost'*, *glasnost'*), and are to be guided and supervised by the presiding judge, assisted by the other members of the court. The ultimate reference point for all the trial's participants, naturally, is the jury, which must decide on a verdict.

Two statutory provisions capture the adversarial style of procedure envisioned by the reformers. Article 630 of the Statute of Criminal Procedure stipulated the following:

> The two sides at law, the procurator (or civil plaintiff) and the accused (or the defense counsel), shall possess identical rights in the judicial contest [*v sudebnom sostiazanii*]. The following rights are granted to each side:
>   1) to present evidence in support of its testimony,
>   2) to have removed from testimony, with just cause, witnesses and experts; to put questions to them with the permission of the presiding judge; to object to witnesses' testimony and to request that a particular witness be cross-examined in the presence or absence of another witness,
>   3) to make observations and offer explanations concerning all that transpires in court, and

4) to refute the conclusions and views of the opposing side.[30]

In recognition of the defense's need for as many opportunities as possible to press its case in order to neutralize the many presumptive advantages enjoyed by the prosecution, Article 632 of the criminal procedure statute provided that

> In the judicial contest, the right to the last word on the overall substance of the case, as well as on each disputed topic during the trial, always belongs to the accused or to the defense counsel.

A Consensual Design

The system of criminal procedure codified by the Reform represented an attempt to balance distinct and not necessarily compatible adjudicative models. As noted above, the resulting blend has been classified in the Reform's historiography as "mixed" or "instructional." The latter term, denoting a partly inquisitorial, partly adversarial system, refers to a procedural framework in which—despite the roles of counsel and the jury—the judge retains a significant degree of "initiative" in adjudication (*samodeiatel'nost'*) and remains responsible for exposing the "uncondi-tional" and "material" truth of the case.[31]

While recognizing that the jury trial procedure reduces the judge's status to that of one participant in the trial, I argue that trial by jury in the early reform era reflected a distinctively Russian version of criminal justice—one in which adversarial adjudication, still undergirded and shaped by vestiges of inquisitorial procedure, evolved into a consensual mode of decision-making in the courtroom, that is, *consensual justice*. The notion of consensus in adjudication refers to a continuous and shifting interaction among *all* legal actors in the trial. A well-defined and accepted hierarchy of authority can still inform such a process; its indispensable element is the participants' shared understanding of their task. In Russian jury trials the explicit common goal was the attainment of justice (*spravedlivost'*) through the ascertainment of the truth (*istina*). In contrast to the judicial imperatives that animate inquisitorial or adversarial systems, consensual adjudication aims at justice that is *negotiated, agreed,* and *worked out* rather than *gained, rendered,* or *meted out.*

Viewing the Russian jury trial procedure of the 1860s and 1870s as "consensual" affords greater insight into the internal process or *style* of adjudication. The attitudes and patterns of conduct that constitute a procedural style display essential aspects of a society's broader legal culture. While the judicial reformers of the early 1860s intended to create vigorous and authentic "debates" (*preniia*) in trial by jury, they remained wary of full adversarialism. This ambivalence derived from both a lack of experience with adversarial methods and a realization that untrammeled adversarialism English style would entail a transformation of the structure of power in the courtroom at the expense of the judge representing the "imperial element" (*koronnyi element*). In short, the reformers could not ignore the implications of adversarialism for the relationship between law and political authority.

The presence of consensualism in jury trials reflected the reformers' commitment to bring to the courts Russia's civil service tradition of collegialism ("collective decision-making, collaborative administration"). Long before the era of the Great Reform, collegialism had taken root in the Russia of Peter the Great as a theory of bureaucratic administration and basis for the delegation of decision-making authority within the civil service. In the Russian setting, the word "college" (one of numerous Petrine borrowings from European bureaucratic vocabulary) referred to a "board" or "committee." The core principle governing the routine tasks of the various boards and committees of the civil service was the use of pluralistic, decentralized decision-making procedures.

The Petrine-era reformers tried to upgrade Russia's civil service by widening the scope of participation and individual authority in its daily functions. They believed that installing operational curbs against arbitrary bureaucratic power, high-handed administrators, and hidebound time-servers would improve the quality, stature, and effectiveness of the bureaucracy. Even though Peter's colleges were abandoned in the early 1800s with the introduction of ministerial government, the mentality and practices of collegialism persisted in Russian bureaucratic life into the era of the Great Reforms and beyond.[32]

Not surprisingly, the principle of collegialism enshrined in bureaucratic culture influenced aspects of the administration of justice before 1864. For example, the investigation of serious crimes had a collegial flavor. In LeDonne's words,

> . . . [criminal] investigations were conducted by the land captain, the sheriff, or the district inspector. In important cases, however, such as peasant disorders, the appearance of bands of robbers, serious cases of arson, or multiple murders, the law required a *joint investigation* by a "temporary section" of the land court consisting of the captain, the inspector of the district where the crime took place, the county procurator (*striapchii*) and, if necessary, the county doctor and the marshal. This was

a guarantee that greater care would be taken in sifting the evidence; the quality of work was raised *by means of a collegial investigation.*[33]

One central institution of the law, however, had remained untouched by the collegial legacy of the Petrine era: the judiciary. This may have reflected the sorry state of courts and judges, whose inefficiency and corruption were legendary. In any event judicial reformers trying to revitalize Russia's judiciary embraced the hoary principle of collegiality.

A collegial structure was introduced into nearly all the instances or levels of the new, post-1864 court system. According to the Statute on the Court (*Uchrezhdenie Sudebnykh Ustanovlenii*), the circuit courts, where trial by jury was to be employed, would have a minimum of three "members" (*chleny*) when the court was in session (including a presiding judge), and further specified that the judicial investigator possessed official "member" status.[34] To be sure, the court had a chairman who presided over the proceedings, but only as a *primus inter pares* (Article 149). Moreover, the Statute established collegiality as the central principle in the operation of most of the courts, with the exception of the peace courts. According to Article 3,

> The justice of the peace possesses indivisible authority; the congresses of justices of the peace, the circuit courts, the "judicial chambers" [*sudebnye palaty*], and the Senate are collegial institutions.

The panel of professional judges used in the middle and higher courts was referred to by the legal community as the "imperial element" in the judicial process. In order to strengthen its collegiality and introduce broad life experience into deliberations, the reform statutes provided flexible minimum credentials (more rigorous for the chairmen) for joining the court. Jurisprudential experience *was* required at some level of the civil service or judiciary, but the statutory criteria frequently did permit non-jurists to serve as members.[35]

In this way, through pluralizing and diversifying judicial authority and expertise, the reformers sought to make collegiality a guiding principle in the conduct of jury trial proceedings. The reason and justification for introducing collegial organization in courts lay in the reformers' longstanding distrust of any government official's acting alone. Judges as well might display bias or even make mistakes unintentionally.[36] Tempering the opinions and intellectual leanings of one judge with the ideas and perspectives of others seemed to be crucial for the development of fair and respected courts.

Strangely, though, the reformers did not treat the jury as an integral part of collegialism in the courtroom. To be sure, they regarded the jury (the "popular [*narodnyi*] element" in the court) as indispensable and in its deliberations as a kind of "people's collegial institution."[37] But they did not include the jurors as a part of the collegial structure of authority in the courtroom itself.[38]

Having organized the operation of the courts along collegial lines, the judicial reformers then developed procedural rules that included elements of both inquisitorial and adversarial models. But the governing principle in shaping this blend was producing a form of consensual adjudication. Although they did not state this explicitly, there are signs in both the legislation of the reform and later trial transcripts.

How did the design of criminal procedure encourage the emergence of consensualism? As noted earlier, in the summoning and questioning of witnesses and recording their statements for trial, the judicial investigator and the procurator's office functioned on their own, without involvement of defense. This entire process was managed by the state.[39] And, although a distinction did exist between witnesses of the prosecution and of the defense, the rules made the examination of witnesses at trial a part of the *court's* inquiry into the case.

Two statutory articles governing witnesses' trial testimony highlight this underlying purpose in a case's pre-trial disposition. Article 700 of the Rules of Criminal Procedure stipulated:

> The victim or victims of the crime shall be questioned first; next on the stand shall be the witnesses specified by the accuser; and to be questioned last, those individuals called by the defendant.

Article 701 granted the presiding judge the power to alter the structure or sequence of witnesses' testimony as he saw fit, depending on a variety of circumstances. The judge, furthermore, had the right to open the questioning of each witness. In the context of adversarialism, where each side's counsel tried to use particular witnesses to advance its arguments, the reform statutes promoted the commonality of the issues at stake in a trial, and the assurance that these concerns were investigated in an open and informal manner, rather than in a competitive, self-interested one.

This emphasis on the eliciting of testimony in a non-combative fashion, giving all persons connected to the case the chance to be heard, suggests an approach to adjudication that values all potentially relevant concerns, not simply those aspects of the case deemed essential by the prosecution and defense. This non-partisan, universalist attitude extended even to the norms governing the *prosecutor's* approach to his role at trial. According to Article 739,

> In his concluding speech, the procurator should not present the case in a one-sided manner by drawing out from it only the circumstances incriminating the defendant; furthermore, he should exaggerate neither the significance of the incriminating proof and evidence in the case nor the gravity of the offense under examination.

Carrying the implicit logic of Article 739 to its conclusion in practice, Article 740 stated:

> If the procurator is sufficiently impressed by the defense's attempted vindication of the accused, then he is obligated to cease his affirmation of the original bill of indictment, now refuted by the judicial inquiry, and to announce this to the court out of a sense of conscience.

These remarkable provisions enjoined the state's counsel, whose main duty was to win a conviction, to prosecute cases in the spirit of an impartial, even-handed pursuit of the truth. Indeed, by invoking the authority and imperatives of "conscience" (*sovest'*), the rules of procedure encouraged prosecutors to adhere to their personal ethical principles and moral standards. Instead of functioning merely as a combatant in a legal duel, the prosecuting attorney was to participate in a system of adjudication whose highest priority was to *arrive at* justice, not merely determine it. Even the representative of the state had responsibilities in a collective process of finding the truth.[40]

Although the Rules of Criminal Procedure did not oblige defense counsel to act impartially, the statutory definition of his role—entirely without precedent in Russian law—did give him a special place as well in the open, consensually-oriented jury trial format. Thus, Article 744, in a common sense fashion, specified the defender's legal obligations to his client in the culminating stage of the trial:

> In his concluding speech, the defense counsel shall explain all of the circumstances and arguments that either refute or undermine the accusation brought against the defendant.

Article 745 dealt with the tone and style of the defense attorney's concluding remarks:

> The defense counsel shall confine himself to topics bearing directly on the case. He shall be expected to show proper respect to religion, the law, and established authority, and shall not employ expressions of speech deemed insulting to any individual.

Finally, Article 746 stipulated the kinds of legal statutes on which the defender could draw during the trial:

> In cases tried before a jury, the defense attorney, during the pleadings and debates preceding the issuance of a verdict, shall refer only to legal statutes that assist in further defining the exact nature of the offense under examination, or to statutes that might justify leniency from the court in the event of a conviction.

On their face, the latter two Articles can be understood as an enumeration of the legal defender's basic duties and a statement of the professional standards that he was expected to uphold. However, if they are interpreted in the light of the reformers' efforts to integrate the advocate's trial activity into a form of adversarial procedure, they take on new meaning. The distinctive feature of Articles 745 and 746 is the way they limit the resources and status of defense counsel. By confining his unprecedented autonomy in a trial within firm boundaries, the reform statutes softened the potentially harsh edges of unchecked adversarialism and called for the integration of advocates into the consensual and cooperative process of adjudication.

The details of the new criminal procedure show that reformers sought a more complex "mixed" form of adjudication, but one even more complex in its defining features than previously recognized. The 1864 statutes fashioned a procedure that balanced judicial tradition and innovation, encouraged the coexistence of custom and novelty, and blended Russian and imported Western forms. The reformers believed that the new adversarialism would curb the worst excesses of inquisitorialism, while the collegial organization and consensual style of proceedings would prevent the emergence of a raw form of adversarialism and ensure an equitable and disinterested pursuit of the truth.

Consensualism in Practice

In what ways did the consensual style manifest itself in the practice of trials in Russia after 1864? The legal newspaper *Sudebnyi vestnik* published accounts, sometimes even transcripts, of important trials of the period. Some of these may serve to illustrate consensual justice in practice.

The procedural structure and adjudicative nuances that characterized the case of Nikolai Frantsov Orvid, tried in the criminal branch of Moscow circuit court in November 1866, provide a vivid example of how consensualism was practiced. Orvid, the son of a chief commissioned officer, was accused of inflicting injuries on Karl Fol'kman and Petr Reinsen, both originally from Riga, and on Kurland native Emmanuel Vigond. Vigond died from his wounds in a hospital; the other two victims survived.[41]

Orvid's principal defense was two-pronged, and inconsistent in its details and logic. He claimed either that, being heavily intoxicated at the time, he could not have known what he was doing, or that he could not remember the incident clearly because he *must have been* excessively inebriated at the time. As he put it repeatedly during the trial: "I cannot positively acknowledge myself guilty." In effect, then, he pleaded "not guilty," yet his comments throughout the trial created precisely the opposite impression on all those present.[42] The accused's indecisive and weak explanations in his own behalf made defense attorney M. I. Dobrokhotov's task impossible. Ultimately the jury returned a guilty verdict. However, owing to the defendant's lack of serious resistance to the charges and his obvious confusion of mind, the jury also declared him deserving of leniency.[43]

Two features of the courtroom pleadings in this case are noteworthy. First, the questioning and cross-examination of witnesses reflected little rigor or formality. The presiding judge P. M. Shchepkin was the first to question each witness, and he delved into many of the case's substantive issues before either counsel had a chance to pose questions. Next came the deputy procurator D. M. Tikhomirov's turn, and finally advocate Dobrokhotov was permitted his queries.[44] Both the prosecution and defense were given a chance to make their tactical points with the witnesses, but the entire process of taking and exploring testimony was conducted more as a loosely structured inquiry into the details of the affair than as a judicial contest between opponents vying for the jury's support, with the judge serving as a moderator. Naturally the level of involvement by the judge, prosecution, and defense varied from case to case. More often than not, however, the defense counsel played a comparatively minor role in the testimony phase of the trial and spent less time examining witnesses than the judge and procurator.

The second significant aspect of the Orvid case concerns the specific role of the accused during the examination of witnesses. As stipulated by the 1864 statutes, in the event of a "not guilty" plea by the defendant, the judge was directed to pose the following question to the defendant as every witness was about to leave the stand: "Do you object to this witness's testimony?"[45]

The accused thus possessed an acknowledged and continuous right of rebuttal throughout the proceedings, which gave him or her an active and vocal role in the trial equal in many respects to that of both the defense and prosecuting counsel! Within the system of adversarial representation by professionally partisan legal advocates, the reform statutes encouraged an informal "dialogue" between defendant and witnesses. This dialogue represented another dimension of the consensual style. The implicit purpose of the dialogue was to ensure that the judicial investigation resolved all disputed issues in the case and produced an outcome understandable and acceptable to all. In the case in question, however, the defendant Orvid's exercise of the right to confront witnesses benefited him little. Frequently his responses to the judge's repeated queries were incoherent, and sometimes they even reaffirmed the truth of the witness's testimony, even if its substance strengthened the charges against him![46]

The trial of Mavra Egorova Volokhova, also held in the criminal branch of Moscow circuit court, was striking in both the details of the criminal act it adjudicated and the consensual features of the adjudication itself. Brought before the court in February 1867, Volokhova, a peasant in her late twenties, was accused of murdering, with premeditation, her husband Aleksei Vasil'ev Volokhov. The trial was well attended by the public and generated tremendous local interest. The main reason for such attention was the unusually gruesome circumstances of the alleged deed: the body of the accused's husband had been found in their cellar, chopped in two.[47] The trial transcript reveals a clumsy, careless, and incompetent performance by the assistant procurator Gromnitskii (in a case that appeared relatively easy to prosecute at the outset). The defense attorney Urusov took advantage of the prosecution's weaknesses and won an acquittal for his client.[48]

The trial's procedural character paralleled the consensual style and temperament displayed in the Orvid case. To be sure, the presiding judge, identified as Arsenev, functioned throughout as the trial's guiding force. Of particular note, however, was Arsenev's insistence that the participants help to resolve crucial issues as the trial unfolded. Indeed, even before testimony began, the judge sought out the opinions of the two counsels on procedural issues. He conferred with both Gromnitskii and Urusov about the type and sequence of testimony to be elicited from the witnesses, and suggested questioning four individuals on the official witness list, all of whom were neighbors or acquaintances of the Volokhovs. Arsenev proposed that they be asked first about the pre-history of the alleged crime (for example, when they last saw the accused and her husband), and then about the discovery of the body itself. Both the prosecutor and defense attorney warned that this approach would lengthen the trial, but made no objections to it. The transcript indicates that the judge's proposal was eventually adopted.[49]

Arsenev tried to incorporate the contributions—legal arguments, information, and mere opinions—of the trial's non-jurists as well. The defendant Volokhova used her right of comment on the testimony to offer pithy and combative remarks in response to each witness's statement, and helped to advance her defense. During the testimony of medical experts, not only the judges but also jurors (especially the foreman) put questions to witnesses whenever they wished and did so in an informal, unaffected manner. These frequent exchanges were neither restrained nor influenced by the judge, and do not appear to have been governed by any procedural guidelines.[50]

The conduct of the Orvid case shows how Russia's new mixture of adversarial and inquisitorial procedure encouraged the achievement of judicial consensus at trial. The key was that the proceedings did not emphasize a rigorously oppositional, "binary" clash of legal counsel. Rather, it entailed dissent, dispute, confrontation, and resolution of issues through the more or less unfettered participation of all those present—with the exception only of the courtroom spectators. The presiding judge Arsenev treated the realization of this informal consensualism as his responsibility.

A third case illustrating the consensual style of procedure was tried in the criminal branch of Riazan' circuit court in January 1871. One Kostrubo-Karitskii, a colonel, was charged with stealing various valuable financial papers (bank documents and the like) from landowner and army major Peremetko-Galich. Vera Pavlova Dmitrieva, Peremetko-Galich's niece, was accused of "receiving and harboring" the papers, and thereby acting as an accomplice in the theft. In addition, according to a set of charges unrelated to those of financial wrongdoing, Dmitrieva was accused of having an abortion and subsequently abandoning the fetus on the street. Karitskii, alleged to be the father, and several others (a doctor, a medical inspector, and a female friend of Dmitrieva's) were charged with assisting in the abortion and subsequently concealing their knowledge of it.[51] In a prosecutorial performance somewhat reminiscent of Gromnitskii's in the Volokhova trial, the assistant procurator Petrov, armed with an ostensibly solid case, ultimately failed to persuade the jury of the multiple defendants' varying degrees of criminality. The five defense attorneys present in court cast doubt on different aspects of the prosecution's arguments and evidence and gained across-the-board acquittals for their clients. Maudlin and morally-charged appeals to the jurors' sense of conscience in the legal defenders' concluding speeches appear to have been crucial in obtaining the decision.[52] The trial of

Kostrubo-Karitskii and Dmitrieva was, as in the Orvid case, marked by free-flowing, informal exchanges among the participants.

Under the supervision and conscious direction of the judge, Rodzevich, all of those participating in the trial engaged in ad hoc resolution of difficult procedural matters as they arose unpredictably in the course of the testimony. Thus Dmitrieva's attorney Urusov[53] requested that the public, meaning all persons attending the trial in a non-official capacity, be excluded from his client's testimony concerning the abortion. He argued that pursuant to the Rules of Criminal Procedure (Article 620) regarding courtroom propriety and decorum, his client's feminine modesty should be spared such a situation. The painful discomfiture induced in her at the thought of discussing such matters before the general public, he contended, would clearly justify the court's decision to hold this specific segment of the trial "behind closed doors," as the new statutes allowed. Instead of simply consulting with the other members of the court and issuing a ruling, Rodzevich invited a general exchange of views on the subject. Consequently, a lengthy and complicated discussion of the problem ensued among the presiding judge, the other members of the official court, all of the defense attorneys, and the prosecutor; at one point the judge even asked for the opinions *of the other defendants* concerning the issue! Finally, in a consensual fashion, a decision was reached to permit Dmitrieva to testify unencumbered by the public's presence.[54]

This case was complicated by the presence of multiple defendants, each with his or her counsel. The involvement of more than one defendant and attorney often works against a coherent strategy of defense. In this case, however, the blatant display of disunity among the accused also reflected the consensual style of the proceedings. The presence of a free-flowing group discussion in the courtroom encouraged each of the accused and counsel to pursue an independent course of self-vindication. The result was a series of openly self-interested and sometimes acrimonious clashes among the various accused and their attorneys.[55] After all, the interests of the particular accused varied as did the charges and punishments that they faced. Yet the judges actually seem to have encouraged these clashes among the accused, viewing this peculiar form of "adversarialism" as a useful and proper way of arriving at judicial truth, all played out in front of the jury. For a consensus on guilt, however obtained, was the purpose of the exercise. In this particular trial, at least, the outcome had the appearance of a group-negotiated and collectively arbitrated pronouncement on the question of guilt.

This analysis of the criminal procedural law and the court practice of trial by jury after 1864 has revealed that the much praised adversarialism introduced into Russian courts by the Judicial Reform was tempered in more ways than previously recognized. On the one hand, significant elements of the inquisitorial tradition remained in place, such as the dominance of the state over the preliminary investigation and the use of its materials at trial, and the role of the presiding judge and his colleagues of the court in the conduct of the trial proceedings. On the other hand, the resulting blend of the adversarial and inquisitorial procedures was colored in crucial ways by an urge for the achievement of consensus about the truth. At trial, this consensual ideal was realized in a flexible and informal manner of discussion that went well beyond the debates among the sides and sometimes rendered such debate irrelevant. Realization of the consensual ideal was not accidental, but the result of a mimicking in the organization of the courts after 1864 of the collegial style of responsibility that had marked other areas of governmental administration since the Petrine era. In short, while the Judicial Reform of 1864 introduced trial by jury and with it a considerable dose of adversarialism, the adversarial qualities of late tsarist justice were qualified and constrained by other features of procedure and practice.

A final comment. The 1864 jury system, whose emblem is frequently the embattled and heroic Russian defense attorney and orator, was not simply part of an oasis of free-enterprise advocacy and individualistic lawyering in a vast desert landscape of autocratic rigidity and oppressiveness in legal life. Nor did trial by jury inhabit an island bastion of freedom and civil rights in a sea of persistent authoritarian inequities, economic privilege, and unjust social hierarchy. Legal practice was more complicated and nuanced, and interpreting it as part of an evolving cultural system shaped by different and even opposed legal and political heritages is the only way to do justice to law and society in the era of the Great Reforms.

Notes

1. M. G. Korotkikh, *Samoderzhavie i sudebnaia reforma 1864 goda v Rossii* (Voronezh, 1989), 155; John P. LeDonne, "Criminal Investigations before the Great Reforms," *Russian History* 1, no. 2 (1974): 118; see also A. Esmein, *A History of Continental Criminal Procedure* (Boston, 1913), 3-4, for a broad typology of such procedure with particular reference to European legal models.

2. *Sudebnye ustavy 20 noiabria 1864 goda za piat'desiat let*, Vol. I (Petrograd, 1914), 527 ff., 626-27 (hereafter cited as *Za piat'desiat let*).

3. Korotkikh, *Samoderzhavie i sudebnaia reforma*, 155. It should be noted as well that the judge's instructions to the jury were also meant to remind jurors of their right and duty

to be guided ultimately by "conscience" in their deliberations; this component of the jury's task, though not examined specifically here, added another distinctive and complicating dimension to the procedural style of Russian trial by jury.

4. For an array of legal-anthropological perspectives on the strengths and shortcomings of scholars' varied attempts to classify modes of formal dispute settlement, see Simon Roberts, *Order and Dispute* (New York, 1979), 53-79; L. Nader and H. F. Todd, Jr., eds., *The Disputing Process—Law in Ten Societies* (New York, 1978), 8-23; Martin Shapiro, *Courts: A Comparative and Political Analysis* (Chicago, 1981), chapter 1; and Francis G. Snyder, "Anthropology, Dispute Processes and Law: A Critical Introduction," *British Journal of Law & Society* 8, no. 2 (1981), reprinted in P. Sack and J. Aleck, eds., *Law and Anthropology* (New York, 1992), 68-81.

5. Daniel Kaiser's *The Growth of Law in Medieval Russia* (Princeton, NJ, 1980) is rich in its consideration of theoretical frameworks for interpreting the modernity of a given legal system; much more recently, George G. Weickhardt, in "Due Process and Equal Justice in the Muscovite Codes," *The Russian Review* 51 (October 1992): 464, 480, challenges, with specific reference to the *Ulozhenie* of 1649, the widely held view that rejects all possibility of progressive, enlightened judicial attitudes and methods in the pre-1864 Russian legal tradition.

6. LeDonne, "Criminal Investigations," 103.

7. *Ibid.*, 102.

8. M. A. Cheltsov-Bebutov, *Ocherki po istorii suda i ugolovnogo protsessu v rabovladelcheskikh, feodal'nykh i burzhuaznykh sosudarstvakh* (Moscow, 1957), 740.

9. LeDonne, "Criminal Investigations," 102.

10. It should be noted, in the interest of historical balance and perspective, that the civil law system of continental Europe in the late modern period, although it is still characterized from time to time as "inquisitorial" (in specific contrast to the "adversarial" approach), retains only the weakest affiliation with original inquisitorial procedure; the horrendous excesses of the earlier system have long since been eliminated.

11. *Za piat' desiat let*, Vol. I, 628.

12. LeDonne, "Criminal Investigations," 101.

13. *Ibid.*, 107-108, 118.

14. *Sudebnye ustavy 20 noiabria 1864 goda i Ustav ugolovnago sudoproizvodstva* (Statutes of Criminal Procedure), Article 278. The judicial statutes in general will henceforth be cited simply as "*Ustavy.*" The specific laws establishing trial by jury under the 1864 reform were decrees 41475 (Statute on the Courts [*Uchrezhdenie Sudebnykh Ustanovlenii*]) and 41476 (Rules of Criminal Procedure [*Ustav ugolovnago sudoproizvodstva*]). Hereafter, decree 41475 will be cited as *Uchrezh. sud. ust.*, and decree 41476 as *Ust. ugol. sudoproiz.*

15. *Ustavy, Uchrez. sud. ust.*, Article 79; *Ust. ugol. sudoproiz.*, Articles 262-277.

16. *Ustavy, Ust. ugol. sudoproiz.*, Article 265.

17. *Ibid.*, Article 751(italics added). See also Korotkikh, *Samoderzhavie i sudebnaia reforma*, 133.

18. In one instance, perhaps atypical, a defense attorney received the case materials two months before the trial opened; *Tsentral'nyi gosudarstvennyi istoricheskii arkhiv goroda Moskvy* (hereafter cited as TSGIAgM), *f.* 142, *op.* 1, *d.* 1: 8 (1871).

19. For additional perspectives on the powerful impact of the investigator's evidence-gathering capacities, see Richard Weisberg, *The Failure of the Word: The Protagonist as Lawyer in Modern Fiction* (New Haven, CT, 1984), 48-51, and Petr Alekseevich Kropotkin, *In Russian and French Prisons* (New York, 1991), 26-33. Weisberg's literary study stresses the similarities between Russian and continental European traditions of basic prosecutorial method. Kropotkin's idiosyncratic consideration of Russian and French penal practices, although clearly hostile to the 1864 reform, is striking in its emphasis on how evidence-preparation retained many of its in camera qualities during the reform era.

20. Korotkikh, *Samoderzhavie i sudebnaia reforma*, 150; N. V. Cherkasova, *Formirovanie i razvitie advokatury v Rossii* (Moscow, 1987), 53-55. On the question of structural limits on adversarialism, it is interesting and instructive to note some of the continuities in prosecutorial power and praxis from late imperial Russia to the Soviet period. Eugene Huskey's *Russian Lawyers and the Soviet State* (Princeton, NJ, 1986), 210-12, offers a compelling description of prevailing prosecutorial strategy and theory (with I. Braude the leading exponent in question) in the mid- to late-1930s. Braude's formulations and principles, although much more openly and aggressively statist than pre-Revolutionary legal officialdom's outlook, nevertheless call to mind various provisions of the 1864 statutes. In certain respects, the basic attitudes and official approach of the state's "prosecutorial arm" remained intact throughout pre-reform, post-reform, and post-Revolutionary Russian legal development. Genuine, full-fledged adversarialism in criminal procedure, it would seem, consistently faced insuperable obstacles in Russian history, and even during an era of westernizing judicial reform put down roots in only a limited fashion.

21. TSGIAgM, *f.* 142, *op.* 7, *d.* 6: 3 (1870-71).

22. TSGIAgM, *f.* 142, *op.* 1, *d.* 17: 5; the relevant statutory provisions were Articles 547 and 548 of the 1864 Statute of Criminal Procedure.

23. According to Article 557 of the *Ust. ugol. sudoproiz.*, the accused was permitted to request the inclusion of certain persons on the official witness list, which would become final at the conclusion of the Sudebnaia palata's review of the case.

24. *Ustavy, Ust. ugol. sudoproiz.*, Articles 556-558.

25. *Ibid.*, Articles 569-570.

26. "Accusatory" is another appropriate and widely used label for it.

27. It is important to note that adversarialism in law and judicial practice was not unprecedented in Russia at the outset of the 1864 reform. Although incompetent judges, poorly written statutes, and deeply ingrained judicial habits effectively nullified the intentions of the *Svod zakonov* of 1857, the structure of litigation in Russian *civil* procedure by the mid-nineteenth century, as it was codified in the 1857 edition of laws, reflected, in many crucial respects, the principles of adversarialism; see *Za piat'desiat let*, Vol. I, 528-30.

28. *Ibid.*, Vol. I, 626.

29. Although the term "prosecutor" is an accurate description of the *prokuror*'s role, the word "procurator" better reflects the institutional and judicial distinctiveness of this legal office in imperial Russia; both terms will be employed throughout this study.

30. In certain circumstances, a civil case could be litigated in a courtroom context ordinarily encompassing criminal matters; hence the inclusion of the term "civil plaintiff" in this article.

31. *Za piat'desiat let*, Vol. I, 627.

32. A considerable literature exists on topics such as bureaucracy, administration, governance, and the particular question of bureaucratic culture in Russia. Among the most useful studies with respect to the origins and development of collegialism in Russia are: Walter M. Pintner and Don K. Rowney, eds., *Russian Officialdom: The Bureaucratization of Russian Society from the Seventeenth to the Twentieth Century* (Chapel Hill, NC, 1980); Daniel T. Orlovsky, *The Limits of Reform* (Cambridge, MA, 1981); George L. Yaney, *The Systematization of Russian Government: Social Evolution in the Domestic Administration of Imperial Russia, 1711-1905* (Urbana, IL, 1973); Marc Raeff, *Plans for Political Reform in Russia, 1730-1905* (Englewood Cliffs, NJ, 1966); Claes Peterson, *Peter the Great's Administrative and Judicial Reforms: Swedish Antecedents and the Process of Reception* (Stockholm, 1979), especially chapter 4; Erik Amburger, *Die Geschichte der Behörden-organisation Russlands von Peter dem grossen bis 1917* (Leiden, 1966). Max Weber's classic treatise, *On Law in Economy and Society* (New York, 1967), offers a penetrating analysis of the general historical and sociological bearing of collegialism in modern bureaucratic cultures.

33. LeDonne, "Criminal Investigations," 106-107 (italics added).

34. *Ustavy, Uchrezh. sud. ust.*, Articles 77-79, 140. In the numerous trial transcripts examined for this study, no judicial investigator ever appears to have actually sat in as a member of the court *during* a trial.

35. *Ibid.*, Articles 200-211. In a fairly typical example of court membership in the reform's early period, three different ranks of *sovetnik*, or "councillor"—college, court, and titular—served as members in a case. See *Sudebnyi vestnik*, 8 January 1870, No. 7: 4 (hereafter cited as *SV*).

36. *Za piat'desiat let*, Vol. I, 468. Similar reasoning underlay the application of the collegial principle in various European countries; see *Za piat'desiat let*, Vol. I, 471 *ff.* Indeed, one is reminded of the pungent French saying: "*Juge unique, juge inique.*"

37. *Ibid.*, 470.

38. *Ibid.*, 480. In an interesting comparison with collegiality in contemporary European legal systems, with a particular focus on the *koronnyi element* and *koronnaia kollegiia* in trial by jury, the authors of the above-cited article claimed that Russia's judicial reform had surpassed European countries' procedural statutes in maintaining the probity and efficacy of the collegial component in judicial administration; see above, 480 *ff.*

39. For a clear illustration, see TSGIAgM, *f.* 142, *op.* 7, *d.* 6: 7-16 (1870-71).

40. Two additional points of interest in this regard: first, Article 265 of the *Uchrezh-denie sudebnykh ustanovlenii* bound the judicial investigator to a similar kind of impartiality; and second, even the American common law system of criminal procedure, perhaps the most adversarial in the history of Western law, has been modified in this century (in theory at

least) in order to make the role of the prosecutor more neutral. See the reference to a Supreme Court ruling on the issue in the 1930s in Floyd Abrams, "Why Lawyers Lie," *The New York Times Magazine,* 9 October 1994: 54.

41. *SV*, 13 November 1866, No. 86: 468.

42. *Ibid.*

43. *SV*, 16 November 1866, No. 87: 472.

44. *SV*, 13 November 1866, No. 86: 468.

45. *Ibid.*

46. *Ibid.*

47. *SV*, 15 February 1867, No. 37: 146.

48. *SV*, 17 February 1867, No. 39: 155.

49. *SV*, 15 February 1867, No. 37: 146.

50. *SV*, 16 February 1867, No. 38: 150-151.

51. *SV*, 10 February 1871, No. 37: 2.

52. *SV*, 23 February 1871, No. 50: 1-3; 24 February 1871, No. 51: 1-4.

53. Also defense counsel in the Volokhova trial discussed earlier.

54. *SV*, 11 February 1871, No. 38: 1-2.

55. *Ibid.*

5

LEGAL CULTURE, CITIZENSHIP, AND PEASANT JURISPRUDENCE: PERSPECTIVES FROM THE EARLY TWENTIETH CENTURY

Jane Burbank

This chapter explores two subjects ordinarily separated by conventional divisions of historical scholarship, but both critical to the analysis of legal reform in Russia. The first is Russian legal ideology—definitions of law put forward and sustained by Russian intellectuals and historians of Russia, definitions with a particular genesis and a long life. The second is the legal practice of peasant courts in late imperial Russia. Addressing these topics together permits both a contextualization of well-established assumptions about what law was and could be in Russia and a re-evaluation of the long-term effects of the 1860s reforms upon the legal culture of Russian society before 1917. I will describe how Russian ideologies of law obscured, even to interested parties, the expansion of legal consciousness in rural Russia before 1917. And I will suggest a different approach to thinking about law—one that emphasizes historical process and contingency, the intertwining of beliefs and practical outcomes, and the connections between legal practices and the creation of citizenship.

My perspective on legal culture centers on the possibility and process of connecting individuals to the state through participation in legal institutions. The linkage between legal culture and nation-building has been highlighted by theorists concerned with the historical provenance of citizenship in Western Europe.[1] Margaret Somers has argued strongly against the prevalent connection of citizenship with modern capitalist economies and social relations; she rejects as well the static definition of citizenship as a status "granted" by the state. Instead, through a comparative examination of European regional and national practices, she locates citizenship as a process instituted through the intersection of national law and community activism.[2]

Somers's work focuses on early modern England, but the analysis she presents of the critical elements of an incorporating legal culture and its nurturing of citizenship is salient both to the interpretation of Russia's legal history and to ongoing efforts to establish a "law-based state" in the Russian Federation. I will return to the contemporary situation at the end of this article. But there can be no "law-based state" without a state, so I will begin briefly with the state.

A vital and powerful means of organizing human beings and resources in the modern period is the state, and the maintenance and transformation of state organization were crucial to the well-being of societies and individuals on the territories of imperial Russia and the Soviet Union. The state's authority faced strong challenges in Russia since the mid-nineteenth century when reformers of the robust absolutist system based on aristocratic governance[3] set out upon a tortuous path in the direction of more democratic arrangements.[4] In the course of a century the state suffered two devastating and risky near-collapses—in 1917 and 1991—breakdowns that called the very survival of the polity into question. In both cases, large territories and populations fell out of Russian control. What role has "law" both as a projected ideal and a means of governance played in the extended and traumatic evolution of Russian state organization since the mid-nineteenth century era of reforms? Did legal aspirations promote a legal culture? Did legal practices bind subjects more securely to the polity?

Ideologies of law have been conspicuous elements in articulated opposition to Russian governments. That a law-based state was a strong wish of many subjects of the Russian empire in the late imperial period, or that a call for "*pravovoe gosudarstvo*" was an effective slogan of anti-Communist rebellion in the perestroika period, is not in doubt. The idea of legal rule—with its implications of order replacing arbitrariness—has held a strong appeal in educated society for over a century.[5] This commitment to an imagined legal order was a dialectical product of the power of persons on which both bureacratic autocracy and bureaucratic Communism rested; in each potential victim of someone else's apparently legitimated ability to wield personal authority lay dormant a passionate longing for a regulated order that would put rules above individuals.

In both imperial and Soviet periods, however, each potential victim was also a potential exploiter of the existing systems of personalized authority. The participation of all individuals in non-rulebound systems of power had a profound effect upon enactments of legal authority when these oc-curred—laws were interpreted as legitimizing personal authority. Thus, the desire for legality, expressed by many members of the educated classes in

Russia, was not a "legal consciousness" or a "legal culture" based on experience of a law-based state, but an ideological commitment defined in relation to the perceived "arbitrariness" of Russian governance. Fervent advocacy of legality could go hand in hand with the normalized breaking of official rules.[6]

Most scholarship on law in Russia, however, has ignored questions of law's penetration of daily life and habit, and focused instead on ideological statements about legality that emerged from the intellectual life of fin-de-siècle and revolutionary Russia.[7] As I have argued elsewhere, the prevailing discourse on law in Russia has been shaped by the powerful personalities of leading liberal jurists such as Nabokov, Maklakov, Koni, and Gessen. Their ideas and representations of their society have exercised an influence far beyond their times on the framing of discussions about Russia's legal possibilities and failures.[8] A legal culture as they envisioned it would rest upon principles such as a single and uniform court system for all citizens, an end to extra-judicial police and military tribunals, publicity, the jury system, protection of individual rights and civil liberties, public knowledge of the written law, rational codification of the laws, regularity of judicial procedures, and independence of the judiciary. The absence of these conditions or violation of them in Russia both before and after 1917 constituted, for the advocates of liberal reform, tragic setbacks if not doom for the prospects of a law-based state.

If liberal intellectuals of the late imperial period developed their notions of legality in dialectic with autocracy and in accord with what they thought of as European law, other strong-minded intellectuals from the late imperial and early Soviet period developed a different set of legal ideas in dialectic with a different opponent—the bourgeoisie. Lenin, Stuchka, Pashukanis, and others based their conceptions of "Marxist" or "Soviet" legality on a critique of bourgeois law and rejection of the Russian liberals' position. The history of legal ideas in Russia has largely focused on these two positions—of Russian liberalism and Russian Marxism—perpetually set in conflict with each other.[9] This narrowly political way of defining legal ideas reinforces the orientation of scholarly inquiry around the presence or absence of "bourgeois" law, as it was represented by early twentieth-century Russian theorists.

My point in this summary treatment of such literature is to suggest, first, that historical study of law in Russia has been based primarily on conceptions of law presented by Russian intellectuals in the late nineteenth and early twentieth centuries; second, that the spectrum of ideas addressed has not changed significantly since their first articulations; and third, that these ideas were just that—ideas of what law might come to be in Russia, not investigations of the extant legal culture, or its possibilities, in Russia then or now. The tight hold of conventional notions of the law upon scholarly discourse set limits on the study of how Russia's legal systems were engaged by both state officials and state subjects, and on the interpretation of this engagement's significance for the polity. In order to reframe the question of legal culture and to address its connections to the possible development of practices of citizenship, it is necessary to identify and appraise the strong elements of the traditional representation of the problem of the law in Russia.

Three notions emerging from pre-Revolutionary debates continue to shape and misdirect the question of legal culture in Russia. These notions are, first, the idea that a legal culture rests upon citizens' knowledge of the written law; second, that a single, uniform national court system is essential to the construction of a citizenry; and third, that state law, because of its "formality," is antagonistic to the preservation and production of "authentic" ethics. I want to suggest instead that a legal culture rests upon the citizenry's recognition of the legal system as a preferred means of solving conflicts and punishing evil; that this recognition may be and was in Russia nurtured by a differentiated court system; and that effective legal systems permit and contribute to widespread national definitions and redefinitions of ethical behavior. I argue, based on this approach, that the Russian state in 1914 had in the growing legal awareness of its subjects the potential to move toward a law-based state and that, for the same reasons, in the 1990s the potential for a law-based state is weak and can emerge only after a belief-building experience similar to that which took place in imperial Russia after 1864, but sustained for a longer time.

Law vs. Custom in Russian Legal Thought

An enduring assumption of nineteenth-century Russian legal thought was the distinction between formal, written, state law and informal, oral, peasant tradition. This firmly established dichotomy between customary and state law guided the administration's efforts to extend written law to peasants, inspired a highly politicized ethnographic search to uncover the principles of customary law, and informed a lengthy debate over whether "custom" could provide the basis for a new national legal system.[10] The administrative initiative central to this debate was the autocracy's establishment of a separate and distinctive court system for peasants in the aftermath of the Emancipation of 1861—the *volost'* courts. Former serfs from neighboring villages could now take their own minor legal disputes to a local court, presided over by three locally chosen judges, to be decided on the basis of local tradition applied within state rules.

The devotion of nineteenth-century legal specialists and Russian intellectuals generally to the definition of law as a formal, state-generated system of written rules is hardly surprising. For one thing, this conception corresponded to the modern preoccupation with regulation, normality, official institutions, and educational discipline described so evocatively by Foucault and so clearly formative in the European professional culture aspired to by many Russian legal specialists.[11] More important, the context of Russian enthusiasm for written law was, after all, Russia, where the formalization and regularization of institutionalized power was all the more attractive for not having been achieved or internalized even for the educated themselves.[12] Less clear is why the strongly dichotomized notion of written law/oral custom continued to structure the discussion of peasant court behavior *after* several decades of volost' court experience and why the association of Russian peasants with customary law perpetuated itself in scholarship about law in Russia for a century, even in the works of "outsider" historians working in other national contexts.

There are functionalist explanations for the conservatism of this powerful historiographic tradition. Scholars often have difficulty breaking with the dualistic categories such as custom/law and country/city that ground their professional and social claims to superior knowledge, status, and authority. Moreover, Western intellectuals—but less commonly today's Russian *intelligenty*—tend to locate their own ideologies in "people without history," as Eric Wolf unfortunately defined pre-capitalist societies.[13] In Russian historiography, "populist" historians like to keep their peasants separate and better; Marxists want peasants to behave as revolutionaries or backward masses; and liberals want them to be future farmers. These extensions of one's politics onto others are much easier to sustain if rural people's own desires remain in the realm of custom and out of written record. But the power of intellectual prejudice over time is all the more impressive when we note that peasant legal practices in Russia were in fact extensively recorded, collected, and retained in imperial archives in great quantities. Half a century of volost' court practice generated a massive written record. Writing itself and written documentation was very much a part of legal practice for rural people. Nonetheless, their "law" was constructed by most scholars and contemporaries as unwritten.

There are specific lineages of legal studies to be traced that may indicate more precisely how the conceptions of Russian scholars and intellectuals from the late imperial period were sustained through generations of left and liberal positivism almost to the present. One route is the well-maintained road of social democratic historiography, represented by the following description of peasant legal practice in Moshe Lewin's much cited article, "Customary Law and Rural Society in the Postreform Era":

> Peasants in Russia, like their counterparts at comparable historical stages elsewhere, did have customs that could qualify as "juridical," but they did not reason abstractly or produce treatises about them and were never allowed to work out a full-fledged system and live according to its precepts.[14]

This statement contains several unquestioned concepts that could have been enunciated in the nineteenth century—the ideas of customary law and of historical stages, the distinction between abstract reason and reason, and the suggestion that a real juridical system would lie in treatises, have a historical working out, and be a whole system. The statement places Russian peasants in an eternal backwardness or, more fairly, a modern backwardness, since Lewin describes Russian peasants in a social stasis that extends "for the period between the abolition of serfdom and the collectivization of agriculture."[15]

Lewin's approach to peasant studies blends nineteenth-century Marxism's conceptions of progress, relentlessly linked with industrial production and patronizing toward rural agriculturalists, with a very Russian sympathy for a sturdy, state-resisting culture.[16] For many intellectual bearers of the idea of customary law, the qualities of oral tradition were enhanced by the notion of freedom *from* state organization. Enthusiasm for "natural" practices of regulation imbues, for example, Paul Vinogradoff's 1925 description of the origins of formal law:

> In rudimentary unions, in so-called barbaric tribes, even in feudal societies, rules of conduct are usually established, not by direct and general commands, but by the gradual consolidation of opinions and habits. The historical development of law starts with custom. Rules are not imposed from above by legislative authorities but rise from below, from the society which comes to recognize them. The best opportunities for observing the formation and application of custom are presented when primitive societies are living their life before the eyes and under the control of more advanced nations.[17]

Vinogradoff, a mainliner of Russian culture into Western peasant studies, displays here an ambivalence toward modernity—it is associated with "command" from "above"—and a Russian liberal's romantic construction of the social—"from below"—origins of law. I want to emphasize his identification of "custom" with "primitive" as typical of the stage-minded liberalism (and Marxism) of his times, but note, too, the similarity between Vinogradoff's image of an imposing authority and Lewin's absent but implied power that "never allowed" peasants to evolve their own law. These are revealing signs of the hesitancy about state power characteristic of the Russian intelligentsia, and so consequential for the conception and the fate of law in Russia.

A non-Russian specialist might imagine that the distinction Vinogradoff and others describe between primitive custom and state law would have lost its relevance to Russian politics with the establishment of the volost' courts in 1861. But in Russia it was the other way around: Lewin's time frame cited above reflects correctly the chronology of Russian elites' engagement with the peasant "problem."[18] The volost' courts provided the main evidence for the construction of the custom/law dichotomy. This interpretation of the invited participation of rural people in a state-created framework for legal process is revealing of the hierarchical, modernizing, and exclusionary conceptions of society shared by most Russian intellectuals at the time.

By identifying and describing customary law in a series of contrasts to advanced, rational, and written law, Russian advocates of law blinded themselves to the commonalities between peasant and "official" legal practice. For one thing, the projection of informality onto the peasant volost' courts (with its implication that the "real" courts held to rigorous procedures) disregarded the fact that both kinds of courts required ritual representation of the connection between citizens and state authority, expressed through adherence to state-defined procedures. As Cathy Frierson has pointed out in a wonderfully tangible description of volost' court operations, the legal process experienced by peasants was full of formality: the presentation of a complaint, the identification of witnesses, the duplicate copies of summons, and—at the trial itself—the judges seated behind a table covered with green cloth, the regularized order of the inquiry and deliberation, the recording and reading out of the sentence.[19] To be sure these procedural forms could be fulfilled with zest or apathy, and accompanied by unregulated activity—such as drinking vodka (the usual intelligentsia complaint), but to describe the process as therefore informal or unofficial is clearly false. The same or similar deformations of propriety—and sometimes of procedures—could occur in any court.[20] Moreover, it was, and is, the essence of legal process to fill blanks between the rules with human content.

Filling in the blanks was the official job of the volost' court scribe, and when we turn to the questions of writing and written rules, the intellectuals' case against the volost' court becomes even more specious. One of the enabling conditions for establishing a divide between formal law and custom and associating customary law with peasant practice (both outside and within the volost' courts) was an unquestioning esteem for education on the part of Russia's elites. Illiteracy and ignorance were indisputable signs of backwardness to the modernizing intellectuals who created and sustained the volost' court debate.[21] The significant aspect of these charges is their fixed association with peasant courts. Clearly, the "regular" courts also failed to live up to the highest contemporary standards of civilization; uncouth behaviors, illiteracy, and lack of education were evident among both accused and accusers, and even in the jury—that icon of Western progress.[22] But it was the volost' court that, in stark contrast to its recorded procedures, remained associated with unwritten law.

The particular aggravation presented by the volost' court was its empowerment of peasant judges, elected by peasants, with no required education. Complaints about peasant judges were reflected in the reforms of the volost' court in 1889, which gave a Land Captain from the nobility the authority to approve or reject the peasants' choice of judges. The reform legislation recognized the impossibility of finding enough literate peasant judges by making literacy a desirable, but not required, quality of a volost' court judge. The other qualifications for judges described in the 1889 regulations are of interest: judges were to be heads of households over 35 years old, and "respected members of the community," unconvicted of various crimes and unsentenced to serious sentences or punishments, not holders of other volost' offices, and not non-Orthodox sectarians. An intriguing regulation was that, with the exception of persons over sixty years old or those who had already served a full term, peasants were not allowed to refuse appointment to the court. After 1889, peasant judges were to receive a salary.[23]

These regulations, adhered to or not, do not constitute a recipe for unfettered "custom," but an explicit attempt to link the rural population to the law through judges that met the standards of both "the community" and the state. Writing was important to this linkage, even if not a requirement for judging. People were summoned to the volost' court in writing; they affixed their signatures to their testimony and to decisions, or had the presiding judge sign for them; the entire process was recorded by the court's scribe in an official record book. The written record served as the basis for the Land Captain's review of the case, and the magnificently printed case books, when full, were submitted to the Procuracy for retention.[24] The process did not stop there, for, as every student of the appeals process knows, peasants used these and other written records with irrepressible litigious zeal to remedy unsatisfactory outcomes.[25] Thus, the volost' courts, far from legitimating oral custom (even if this is what ethnographers and other observers took from their records), in fact bound the rural population closer than before to the written culture of state law and educated society.

Some might argue that this respect for writing is not the same as knowledge of the written law, which was after all the definition of legal competence for so many Russian observers. But here, too, one can observe the misleading nature of this criterion and the distorting effect it has upon the representation of peasant legal culture. Did non-peasants "know" the written law? Of course not, that was what lawyers and codifications were for. Who, in imperial Russia, apart from a few legal experts really "knew" the majority of written laws that could be applied to their lives? Who "understood" the law codes? Surely knowledge of the law in its literal enormity was not a capacity of the educated population, but it was nonetheless a demand the educated elite placed upon the peasants. The distorting and exclusionary consequences of this claim to superior knowledge—its occlusion of existing legal practice by a large part of the population of imperial Russia—emphasizes the importance of recasting the idea of legal culture, and of shifting its definition away from knowledge to process, away from knowing the law to accepting, using, and respecting legal opportunities.

The Question of a Single Justice For All

Connected with the debates over the volost' court and over legal culture in Russia before the Revolution was the issue of a single court system for all subjects of the state. Participants in this controversy took different sides for different reasons;[26] much of the politics connected with this issue concerned the power of the Land Captains introduced with the volost' court reforms of 1889. But an undercurrent and often a high surf of anxiety arose over the significance of the separate status of the volost' court. Those who wanted to integrate peasants into society regarded the distinctive practice of the volost' courts as obstructing the education of the peasants into national community, while people who defended a paternalistic relationship with rural people wanted to retain the separate courts within a hierarchical discipline of subordination to the Land Captains. For both sides, the volost' court stood for separateness as opposed to equality before the law. (This view has also been perpetuated in our times in scholarship on the peasants: modernizers accept the integrationist view, and Marxists emphasize the repressive nature of tsarist authority in the countryside.[27])

Once again, these measurings of the distance between the operating legal system and a political principle meant that other yardsticks of evaluation could not be used. For one thing, with the 1889 reform, the volost' court was no longer an estate-based court, but rather the first instance for adjudication for permanent rural inhabitants, with the exception of the nobility.[28] This meant that the volost' court was the first legal resort for approximately 80 percent of the population. The call for a unified court system meant a demand to bring the volost' courts into (and up to) the court system that served a minority of the subjects of the empire. Nonetheless, the prevailing discourse focused on the exceptionalism of the volost' courts and the normativity of the other instances and legal structures.

Setting aside the unbegged question of whose courts were the exception and whose the rule, how unconventional was the volost' court? Formality, as I indicated above, was abundant. Moreover, by the late imperial period, the judgments of the volost' courts were reported to participants and superiors as based upon national regulation expressed in the legal codes. A decision reported in the record books would be prefaced as follows: "Having heard the case at hand and listened to the explanations of the sides," followed by a big space for the court to fill in its summary of the decision, "and therefore and under the . . . Statute of the Temporary Rules on the volost' Court and on the basis of the Regulations for Punishments, applicable by the Justices of the Peace"—here another big space for comment followed—"decided [*prigovoril*]," followed by another space for the handwritten sentence.

This representation of the deliberations of the court and its decision as legitimated by national law was accompanied by ceremonies that enforced the connection to superior instances of legal authority. When the decision was announced at court, the right to appeal and procedures for appealing the decision were explained. The case was then signed by the President, the judges, the accuser, and the accused, whose addresses were recorded. One of the duties of the Land Captain was to review this record, to be sure that decisions had been made in accordance with the law, and that they had been carried out.[29]

What I want to emphasize is that the "process" of the volost' court, like that of other instances, was a blend of legal requirements and specific content. The imperial Russian legal system, like those of most modern societies, encompassed several "court" structures: military, commercial, Justices of the Peace, the circuit courts, not to speak of the higher levels of judicial authority.[30] The insistence of reformers on a single system testifies to their own ideologies and the conflicts that configured their commitments—their devotion to the jury system of the circuit courts, their suspicion of administrative procedures, and their low opinion of rural society. It was not intrinsically detrimental to the development of legal culture that the volost' court had distinctive procedures and regulations. It can be argued instead that the establishment of a rural court for peasants based upon authorities that were not exclusively local or national, but that contained both identifications within an accessible ritual, was a powerful, if unintentional, step toward the inclusion of rural people in a law-based state.

Moralism and Antipathy to the State

One of the achievements (or disasters, depending upon your point of view) of the Soviet period of Russian history has been to bind the idea of law securely to state administration. The institutes and faculties of "state and law" reflect this merger, rooted in the first years of Soviet state building and developed through decades of Communist administrative practice.[31] This elision of law and governance is not the same as "rule-of-law" or a "law-based state," but, in Eugene Huskey's formulation, a variant of a "statist" interpretation of what law can be and become.[32] "Socialist legality" was officially defined to reflect this absolute primacy of state directives. In the words of a Soviet historian, socialist legality means the "unconditional and exact observation by all state organs, civil servants, and citizens of Soviet laws and acts of state administration."[33] It is no accident that many of the reformers of the late perestroika period, such as Gorbachev and Sobchak, chose law faculties in their ambitious student years. It is also not surprising that their notions of legal culture even today are relentlessly directed toward formal observance of whatever laws the state produces.

Such strict association of law with obedience to state rules would have been alien to most of the legal theorists of the late imperial period, as well as to their opponents in the radical parties. A strong undercurrent of hostility to formalist understandings of the law runs beneath the surface of contending waves of thinking on the law in the nineteenth century. Andrzej Walicki argues that the "anti-legalism" of Russian thought was generated by European critiques of capitalist development, which were engaged by Russian intellectuals. Both Slavophiles and leftist theorists traced connections between state law and the expansion of European capitalism with its destruction of "authentic" human relations.[34] For intellectuals who advocated return to "Russian" values or varieties of communism, a moral law could not be generated by a state whose goal was progress along the European path.

But intellectual advocates for law in late imperial Russia also took relentlessly anti-statist positions. As Walicki, Gianmaria Ajani, and others have noted, Russian liberals and moderate socialists insisted on locating law in a moral realm that would free it from the state.[35] The association of the imperial state with oppression and arbitrariness, and the corresponding desire of Russian liberal thinkers to place the law outside the state—in society or in a spiritual covenant—were structuring components of legal thinking throughout the late imperial period.

In an article on law in an 1898 volume of an authoritative scholarly encyclopedia, Vladimir D. Nabokov aligns himself with the natural law school as opposed to positive law theory, and firmly associates law with morality: "L[aw] that would not rely upon the strength of morality, would in vain support itself by means of compulsion alone," he writes.[36] He notes that the "majority" of contemporary analysts of law incline toward perspectives that root law in society, and describes with sympathy the idealist position that demands a grounding for law in the "freedom of the human personality."

> Recognizing the unconditional fundamental basis of human freedom, L[aw] has as its goal the agreement of individual freedom (will) with the general freedom (will). The basic rule [*zakon*] of L[aw] is be an individual (i.e., be free), but respect the individuality of other free beings. This is a boundary for L[aw] that it must not overstep.[37]

This and other variants of idealist and psychological-social groundings of the law produced in late imperial Russia reveal deep aversion to state-based explanations of legal development. The state could not be moral, and the law had to be. As I have argued elsewhere, even Lenin argued for a "natural" law resident in society, that would regulate conduct in a future community undistorted by the linked oppressions of capitalism and the state.[38] The deep insult of autocracy to a significant part of its intellectual elite over the course of the nineteenth century was thus countered by anti-statist ideas of law on the part of the offended. By ruling out the state as a constructive social actor, intellectuals blinded themselves to the gradual process of inclusion in a legal system that was going on around them. They chose ways of thinking about the law and about society that avoided integrating the unintended but powerful consequences of the state's legal reforms into their ideas of national well-being and progress.

This aversion to analytical engagement with the consequences of fifty years of state-produced reform gives Russian legal advocacy a profoundly ahistorical cast. Rather than basing their visions of legal progress on recent transformations and their meaning for ongoing change, Russian intellectuals reached into the deep past or into metaphysics—natural law theory or idealism—to find foundations for a legal culture of the future. Even the proponents of a "customary" base for national law who wished to found Russian law on peasant tradition are examples of this distancing of "society," in a peasant mode, from really existing people and their present-day procedures. The "society" that exhibited moral and legal behavior to Russian intellectuals in the early twentieth century was not the one they lived in.[39] Thus, intellectuals of the late imperial period did not take a historical, processual approach to the development of legal culture, and this allowed them to ignore the critical importance of the population's use of existing legal structures to the future of law and of participatory citizenship in Russia.

Legal Culture Based on Practice

If the study of law is to reveal the inclusions and exclusions on which polities are formed—to engage the very issues that Russian intellectuals were loath to confront in the early twentieth century—it is useful to employ a concept of legal culture that is both historical and social. A processual perspective shifts the focus away from society in the abstract and questions the hidden or explicit opposition of society and state. I assume, first, that the construction of a legal culture takes place at the intersection of state rules and their use by subjects or citizens, and second, that the development of a confidence in the legal system as a primary means of "regulation of mutual relations between people" takes place in time and over generations. Belief in law is the consequence of a historical process. As such, it can emerge, take certain forms, be destroyed, be fostered, be set back; legal culture is historically contingent, not absolute. It depends only indirectly on the intentions of state leaders, although the actions of state leaders in the area of law can have multiple and unanticipated consequences.

From this perspective, the legal experience of the late imperial period made important and positive contributions to the emergence of a legal culture in Russia. A major component of this extension of legal consciousness was the experience of rural people in the volost' courts, a jurisdiction that incorporated a large portion of the population into the empire's legal system. The users of the volost' courts were not engaged, as were Russian elites, in an explicit struggle about the legality or arbitrariness of autocratic government—they were not engaged in a struggle for state power—but they were participants in an unremarked process of interaction with state law. Their participation in this arena should not be given a "political" meaning in the sense of "for or against the state," "resistance or accommodation," but rather seen as one inclusionary component of the uneven and incomplete process of national construction in late imperial Russia. The extent to which peasants chose to use the volost' courts to address social problems and the effectiveness of the provision of this court opportunity to the rural areas are important indicators of the possibilities for a law-based state to emerge before 1917.

I make no claim in this account for the autocratic state's intention to create a legal consciousness among peasants. The volost' courts were a by-product of the Emancipation, and a typical Russian resort to self-administration and government on the cheap. The extension of the volost' court system to ex-serfs who would judge themselves was in this respect consistent with the autocracy's casual attitude toward law. But the outcome of this initiative and the sustained support by the state of the volost' courts for half a century was the formation of a legal consciousness—an accepted resort to law—among rural inhabitants of Russia.

The argument that peasants came to perceive the volost' court system as a useful addition to and substitute for other unlegalized institutions—village meetings, councils of elders, the village headman—is based in part upon the vast numbers of disputes brought to these courts in the late imperial period. The volost' courts were the first instance for the majority of the population, but this did not mean that they had to be used. The historical record suggests, however, that the courts were attractive to rural people. Cathy Frierson has identified a consistent pattern of increasing use of the volost' courts from the 1870s to the turn of the century, based on statistics from several provinces.[40] The scale of activity of these courts in the early twentieth century is indicated by the statistics from Moscow province in 1905, where volost' courts processed 47,761 cases in a single year (see Table 5.1).[41]

These numbers—the average volost' court in Moscow province processed 484 cases in 1905[42]—indicate the extensive use of the volost' court system and its supervisory organs. The majority of the cases heard by the Moscow Provincial Office originated in the volost' courts, another testimony to the rural population's demand for official adjudication. The provincial records reveal a high degree of initiative on the part of rural people and suggest that we should not ignore, but rather highlight, the volost' courts as a locus for accumulation of legal experience, construction of legal culture, and connection to the polity.

Table 5.1
**Number of Cases Processed by Instance
Administrative-Judicial Institutions, Moscow Province, 1905**

Legal Instance	Criminal Cases	Civil Cases	Administrative and Supply Cases	Total Cases
Moskovskoe gubernskoe prisutstvie	324	789	1,174	2,287
Uezdnye s"ezdy Moskovskoi gubernii	2,890	5,022	3,189	11,101
Zemskie nachal'niki Moskovskoi gubernii	7,211	3,833	6,898	17,942
Volostnye sudy	21,859	25,902	—	47,761
Total Cases	32,284	35,546	11,261	79,091

Source: *Obzor Moskovskoi gubernii za 1905* (Moscow, 1906).

Another indication of the centrality of volost' court experience to rural life was the content of those "civil" and "criminal" cases heard by the local judges. My survey of records of volost' courts in Moscow, Petersburg, and Novgorod provinces in the early twentieth century suggests that peasants most frequently went to court to solve three kinds of social problems. First, the most common "crime" by far to come before the volost' court was some kind of insult. A rich variety of offenses against personal dignity—verbal, physical, or both—caused peasants to bring each other to justice. Peasants at this time considered it worth both time and money to defend their personal dignity in the courts.[43]

Second, from among the "civil" cases, the major reason that people filed complaints was what officials labeled "all manner of quarrels and suits."[44] These "quarrels and suits" emerge as a significant category from the court records precisely because they were the kinds of cases the state did not consider important. The administration required its representatives to report on the numbers of civil cases in categories such as "violations of land rights," "violations of land inheritance," etc., but the majority of civil cases brought by peasants did not fit these classifications. "All manner of quarrels and suits" included the usual rural headaches: claims about debts, unpaid work, unpaid rent, leaving debris on someone's land, planting trees in the wrong place, ruining equipment, cutting grass, trampling crops, burning someone else's firewood.

A different kind of civil case provided a third common reason for going to the volost' court: this concerned the *allotment* of property, both land and moveables, to individuals and families. Into this category fell both the regulation of inheritance and family divisions and the settling of disputes about control of land and other property. The volost' courts heard many of these cases and acted both in the routine legitimation of property transfers after deaths as well as in the resolution of conflicts over control and ownership.

The centrality of the issues settled in the volost' courts—the defense of individual dignity, disputes over property and labor, the reallocation of property from one family, individual, and, overall, generation to an- other—suggests that the court was a significant arena for local justice. In support of this interpretation, I note that peasants were not obliged to bring most of these cases to court. The majority of "civil" and "criminal" cases that the volost' courts adjudicated—the courts were not particularly concerned with this official distinction—were matters that no one cared about outside the village. No administrator forced suits concerning fruit trees and firewood upon the volost' court, and nothing made it impossible for such issues to have been settled in the village by other institutions, such as the village assembly. But as the voluminous court records of the imperial administration show, peasants took their problems to the volost' instance with zeal, as well as using the threat of a volost' suit to force "out-of-court" resolutions. Bringing a suit involved a fee and time and probably gifts—but nonetheless peasants registered their complaints in droves.

The state's idea of what went on in the local courts and the peasants' use of the courts were quite dissimilar. A list of the rubrics provided by higher judicial authorities to a volost' scribe in Moscow province shows that many of the categories postulated by the state were left blank or filled in with insignificant numbers. For example, in one volost' in 1910, there were no entries for the following civil categories: quarrels over allotments held as household (not communal) property; over the "reinstatement of the violated ownership of immoveable property"; inheritance and divisions of single-household (not communal) property. Among the criminal categories submitted to the same volost', the following rubrics were undersubscribed or not used at all: acts against orderly administration—11 cases out of 115; "a breach of decorum during church services"—no cases; violation of the hunting and fishing regulations—no cases; violation of the passport regulations—no cases; violation of the regulation on construction and transportation—no cases; and, finally, theft, swindling, and fraud—9 out of the 115 criminal cases processed. This record was returned by a volost' that had processed 82 cases about communally held allotments, 128 "miscellaneous suits and quarrels," and 82 cases of personal insults.[45] The poor fit between the rubrics provided for the scribe and the actual case record neatly displays the disjuncture between what the state thought it would get from the volost' courts and what the system of peasant justice in fact accomplished. It also shows that peasants, given a legal institution outside the village, used this opportunity extensively and of their own will to solve conflicts central to the functioning of their communities.

If the volost' courts gave peasants the possibility to defend their individual dignity and to resolve conflicts over work and property—issues central to defining one's place in rural society—then what role did the judicial system play in defining a peasant's place in national life, among the other inhabitants of the empire? Did the volost' courts provide an arena for the enactment or generation of claims to citizenship?

A graphic indicator of peasants' notions of their place in the nation, in the larger, perhaps hypothetical, community, can be found in the records of the volost' court of Tsaritsyno in the Moscow region in 1917. The Provisional Government, stepping into the state structure after the collapse of the monarchy in the February Revolution, as one of its first acts abolished the estate system—the formal division of the population by hereditary status into peasants, nobility, townspeople, and clergy. On 9 March 1917, one week after the February Revolution, the scribe of the Tsaritsyno court, the same person who in his meticulously kept records had relentlessly categorized each accuser, defendant, and witness by her or his estate—as "peasant" so and so, *krest'ianka* Pelagea Nikolaevna Riabinina, *krest'ianin* Ivan Il'ich Levin—now recorded every court participant as "citizen." This title—*grazhdanin, grazhdanka*—remained consistently in use—without a single slip or crossing out throughout 368 cases—from 9 March until the records of this volost' court broke off a year later.[46]

This recorded grasp at citizenship when it was finally offered by the Provisional Government—and the rejection of identification as peasants—points to an important, if inadvertent, consequence of the volost' court system. This system let peasants be peasants (whatever that meant) in their local relations, but—through its record books, through its reports, through the limits set on whom could be judged—it also underlined the disabilities of separateness and exposed caste to judgment. The volost' courts had offered peasants a chance to use and even shape the law on their own terms and to make legal process a respected part of rural life. Peasants resorted to the courts to regulate quarrels over property and work, to legitimize changes in authority, and to defend individual dignity against public assaults, and in this process they learned that to be labeled a peasant was a civil disability. In court, at any rate, the title of "citizen" made sense.

Perhaps the liberal reformers who opposed the separate volost' courts on the grounds that peasants would not grow into citizenship had won in spite of themselves. But this result should not be surprising if we theorize law as a process, rather than a set of rules, and if we acknowledge the lack of correspondence between the intentions of rulers and the interpretations of the ruled. For it was the process of the courts, the possibility of legal judgment rendered by one's peers yet legitimated by the state, that made the volost' courts attractive to rural people and part of their thinking about themselves. Through these courts, peasants acquired a connection to the state, beyond their obligations to pay taxes and provide service. They acquired a possibility to act as members of the nation, citizens in the legal order—as people who participate in the regulatory procedures of their country, who use its institutions, and who regard legal institutions as a means to defend their rights. In this respect the volost' courts were a great, unintended gift of the tsarist administrators to peasants and to the Russian polity, a legal structure that encouraged legal culture.

Citizenship Immediately Redefined

I am not arguing that citizenship, of an extensive or an exclusionary kind, was achieved in Russia in the Revolutionary period. In fact, a weakness of nationalist identity is a striking fact of modern Russian society. I am suggesting that the courts—particularly the local courts—offered that participatory, yet national arena where ideas of citizenship could emerge. This potential was undercut by the new state-making institutions of the Bolsheviks who rejected the concept of citizenship for all after 1917. As Marc Vishniak argued in 1920, the Bolshevik government introduced a legal structure that revived estate-like distinctions among the population.

Vishniak, a socialist revolutionary and graduate of the law faculty of Moscow University, fled to Paris during the Civil War and there began to publish studies of the Bolshevik government. In his work, *Le régime soviétiste*, subtitled *Étude juridique et politique*, he relied upon a critical analysis of the Soviet constitution to make his major point: the principles of Bolshevik government were fundamentally at odds with democracy as, he hoped, Western intellectuals would understand it. It was not accidental that Vishniak focused his reason and passion on the Bolsheviks' constitution, for he had been a member of the commission that prepared the elections for the Constituent Assembly and had suffered through the Assembly's abortive meeting as its secretary. What Vishniak wanted to emphasize above all else in his missive to the West was the Bolsheviks' rejection of the principle of equal rights and duties in favor of legal distinctions based on class. To him, the Bolshevik constitution, with its granting of rights to the formerly exploited classes alone, was not a "higher" kind of justice, but a return to the principles of absolutism.[47]

Addressing a Western audience presumed to share his commitment to progress through equality, Vishniak tried to show that the Bolsheviks, rather than continuing in the direction of the French Revolution, were setting the historical clock back:

> The Great French Revolution declared the unalienable rights of man and of the citizen. This declaration has become the slogan of the new [Soviet] society. However, the creators of these new values wanted to liberate themselves from the prejudices of the French third estate. They have replaced the declaration of the rights of the individual with the declaration of the rights of a collective, of a class. But one can distinguish very clearly in this Bolshevik innovation the traces of the system of the old pre-revolutionary epoch and the methods of the epoch of the police state and of what we call enlightened absolutism.[48]

Vishniak's critique stressed the inequities of Bolshevik electoral laws, with their disenfranchisement of some groups and weighting of the suffrage in favor of city workers and against peasants. (One worker's vote equalled five peasant votes.) He also cited the legalized allocation of material rewards according to hierarchies determined by a social category's usefulness to the state. His book described the Bolsheviks' violation of their own laws— elections to the Soviets were never held within the three month period established by the constitution—their use of extra-legal institutions (the Cheka), and the undemocratic reality of top-down rule by the self-selected members of the Bolshevik Central Committee. Vishniak's major concern was not so much Bolshevik illegality or extra-legality, but the significance of legalizing differential access to political authority and of returning to government based on the administration of unequal estates. His writings underscore the significance of the Bolshevik leaders' choices during the revolutionary hiatus of state authority, when they took upon themselves the tasks of defining through both law and practice the principles of association that would bind people to each other and to the state.[49]

Prospects for a Legal Culture

The explicit choice for basing rights on class, including the weight of one's vote or one's testimony in court or the right to be appointed as a judge, represents a choice for some kinds of national community and against others. One might regard the Bolsheviks' class principles as permitting the same kind of gradual nation-building initiatives as had the autocracy's estate-based courts. But the Soviet legal system turned hierarchies only partly upside down: peasants remained "dark masses" to the makers of the new system, and, most important, rural people were not given the materials or the relatively unsupervised legal opportunities to which they had become accustomed. It was impossible to further a culture of participation and rights in the undersupplied and overly instructed local courts of Soviet Russia.

The choice for legalizing class-based hierarchy may instead have radically undercut the possibilities for a law-based state in Russia. As Douglas Hay has argued in his study of eighteenth-century English law, the efficacy of the law as a disciplining and uniting system depended on its appearance of disinterest in class. Through an extensive practice of majestic ritual, the exercise of mercy, and an ideology of impartial justice, English law incorporated the lower orders into the state, even as it promoted, overall, the interests of the rich.[50] The Bolsheviks' rejection of the ideology of equality before the law deprived the new system of a powerful claim to loyalty, based on inclusive, universal justice.

The ideology of group privilege and group guilt expressed in Soviet law outlasted the formal statement of classless social relations in the 1936 constitution. By that time, the rhetoric, if not the consistent practice, of class hierarchy was well established, as well as the primacy of Party and not judicial institutions. Just as the Stalinist turn toward meritocracy was undercut by the primacy of party loyalty over talent,[51] the significance of the Soviet court system was subverted by every citizen's knowledge that Party bosses were the real dispensers of official justice. The development of the second economy in the post-Stalin period further diminished the relevance of the judicial apparatus to everyday affairs of ordinary citizens. Who would rely on the courts when each individual was caught up in the informal economic web and when the occasional legalized shooting of a publically excoriated boss served only to emphasize the inability of Soviet law to deal with the most notorious operators?[52]

I am not making the argument that corruption itself is to blame, for corruption—in the sense of bribery or irregularities in following procedures or using personal influence—is to some degree part of any legal system. What I want to emphasize is the image of law and legal process in the late Soviet period. The presence of rule-of-law as a *goal* in the political struggles of the late 1980s and early 1990s was a testament to its absence in reality. Law described a wish for order, rather than a familiar aspect of the existing system.

The courts existed, of course, and law schools and law professors and lawyers, and one can hope that with time the powerful dons of Russia will come to understand that enforceable contracts (of the non-lethal variety) and recourse to state-organized adjudication will be more profitable than private understandings and private organization of the means of violence. Perhaps the writers of the Russian constitution will come to see this document as more than a stamp of respectability upon the post-Soviet state. Formal statements or restatements of legal rule, however, will not suffice to make Russia lawful, and discipline from above cannot produce a citizenry. My analysis of both legal ideology and legal practice in the past suggests that a legal culture cannot arise from rules alone, but only after a lengthy experience with judicial institutions, through which people learn that law can serve their interests, both individual and public. The volost' courts of pre-Revolutionary Russia simultaneously enhanced both personal dignity and state authority by linking them in a public, participatory process. A law-based Russian polity of the future would rely upon a similar dialectic between citizens and state authority. Setting this dialectic in motion is just the first, but nonetheless essential step on a long road toward legal culture.

Author's note: I thank Valerie Kivelson, Peter Solomon, and Fred Cooper for their helpful comments on this chapter, and Cathy Frierson for many years of discussions of peasant legal practice. Research for this article was supported by the International Research and Exchanges Board.

Notes

1. See Rogers Brubaker, *Citizenship and Nationhood in France and Germany* (Cambridge, MA, 1992); Margaret Somers, "Law, Community, and Political Culture in the Transition to Democracy," *American Sociological Review* 58, no. 5 (October 1993): 587-620; and Margaret Somers, "Rights, Relationality, and Membership: Rethinking the Making and Meaning of Citizenship," *Law and Social Inquiry* 19, no. 1 (Winter 1994): 63-112.

2. See Somers, "Law, Community, and Political Culture," 588-90.

3. I rely on John LeDonne's interpretation; see his *Absolutism and Ruling Class: The Formation of the Russian Political Order, 1700-1825* (New York, 1991).

4. I am using democracy in the sense of locating the source of political authority in "the people," in contrast to aristocracy or monarchy. The struggle over what democracy might mean for institutions of political control continues to the present, both in Russia and elsewhere.

5. See Gianmaria Ajani's article "The Rise and Fall of the Law-Based State in the Experience of Russian Legal Scholarship: Foreign Patterns and Domestic Style," in Donald D. Barry, ed., *Toward the "Rule of Law" in Russia?: Political and Legal Reform in the Transition Period* (Armonk, NY, 1992), 3-21. Ajani locates the concept of *pravovoe gosudarstvo* in the legal scholarship of the late imperial period, and draws an important distinction between legal ideas and "legal experience" (p. 3).

6. This kind of behavior should be familiar to any one engaged in academic or other transactions in the Russian Federation today. As he did during the last years of perestroika, David Remnick still provides the most thought-provoking and detailed descriptions of how the not-so-new system works: see his "Letter from Moscow: The Tycoon and the Kremlin," *The New Yorker*, 20 & 27 February 1995: 118-139. Another provocative analysis is Lev Timofeev's *Russia's Secret Rulers: How the Government and the Criminal Mafia Exercise their Power* (New York, 1992).

7. Outstanding examples of studies of Russian legal philosophy are Andrzej Walicki, *Legal Philosophies of Russian Liberalism* (Oxford, 1987) and Harold Berman, *Justice in the U.S.S.R.*, rev. ed. (New York, 1963).

8. Jane Burbank, "Discipline and Punish in the Moscow Bar Association," *The Russian Review* 54, no. 1 (January 1995): 45-48. This article focuses on the paternalistic and didactic culture of the Russian bar.

9. See, for examples, *Soviet Legal Philosophy*, trans. Hugh W. Babb, introduction by John N. Hazard (Cambridge, MA, 1951); Piers Bierne, ed. *Revolution in Law: Contributions to the Development of Soviet Legal Theory, 1917-1938* (Armonk, NY, 1990); Richard Pipes, *Legalized Lawlessness: Soviet Revolutionary Justice* (London, 1986); and Leonard Schapiro's introductions to his *The Origin of the Communist Autocracy: Political Opposition in the Soviet State, First Phase 1917-1922*, 2d ed. (Cambridge, MA, 1977).

10. C. A. Frierson, "Rural Justice in Public Opinion: The *Volost'* Court Debate 1861-1912," *Slavonic and East European Review* 64, no. 4 (October 1986): 526-45. On the peasant question in the nineteenth century, see Michael B. Petrovich, "The Peasant in Nineteenth-Century Historiography," in Wayne S. Vucinich, ed., *The Peasant in Nineteenth-*

Century Russia (Stanford, CA, 1968), 191-230, and Cathy Frierson, *Peasant Icons: Representations of Rural People in Late Nineteenth Century Russia* (New York, 1993).

11.   See Michel Foucault, *Discipline and Punish: The Birth of the Prison*, trans. Alan Sheridan (New York, 1979), esp. 298-303.

12.   See the address to the distinctiveness of the Russian context in my article, "Discipline and Punish in the Moscow Bar Association," esp. 58-64.

13.   Eric Wolf, *Europe and the People Without History* (Berkeley, CA, 1982).

14.   Cited from Moshe Lewin, *The Making of the Soviet System: Essays in the Social History of Interwar Russia* (New York, 1985), 72.

15.   That is, for a period of seventy years, depending on when one defines the collectivization of agriculture, a *durée* that approximates the entire existence of the Soviet Union.

16.   See Lewin's *Russian Peasants and Soviet Power: A Study of Collectivization* (London, 1968).

17.   Quoted in Sally Falk Moore, *Law as Process: An Anthropological Approach* (London, 1983), 14. The citation is from Vinogradoff's *Custom and Right* (Oslo, 1925).

18.   Frierson's work *Peasant Icons* is devoted to the exploration of this engagement.

19.   Cathy Frierson, " 'I must always answer to the law . . .': Rules and Response at the Reformed *Volost'* Court," *Slavonic and East European Review* 75, no. 2 (April 1997): 308-334.

20.   The signs of disorderly conduct in the Moscow courts are plentiful in the records of the city's bar association. See my article "Discipline and Punish, in the Moscow Bar Association," 49-57, for examples.

21.   See Frierson, "Rural Justice," and Frierson, *Peasant Icons*, 54-75.

22.   The issue of irregular, un-normalized behavior appears in the debate over the jury system: for a summary, see S. M. Kazantsev, "'Sudebnaia respublika' tsarskoi Rossii," in S. M. Kazantsev, comp., *Sud prisiazhnykh v Rossii: Gromkie ugolovnye protsessy 1864-1917gg.* (Leningrad, 1991), 16-17.

23.   I am relying on Frierson's account of the 1889 regulations in her paper, " 'I must always answer to the law . . . .' "

24.   These books are available in various Russian archives. For the volost' courts of Moscow province they can be found in Tsentral'nyi gosudarstvennyi istoricheskii arkhiv goroda Moskvy [hereafter TsGIAgM].

25.   The masses of peasant complaints in the records of the Senate are one piece of evidence of the peasants' insistence that the law could be made to work for them: see, for many examples, the files in Rossiiskii gosudarstvennyi istoricheskii arkhiv [RGIA], *fond* 1344: Vtoroi (kresti'ianskii) departament Senata.

26.   See Frierson, "Rural Justice."

27. For example, see Frierson's conclusion to her article on the volost' court debate: "the state fell back on to a system of customary law which neither reflected the reality of rural change, nor had the potential to draw the rural inhabitant closer to the national experience" ("Rural Justice," 545). Esther Kingston-Mann's work attempts to break with the modernization ethos; see her "Breaking the Silence: An Introduction," in Esther Kingston-Mann and Timothy Mixter, eds., *Peasant Economy, Culture, and Politics of European Russia 1800-1921*(Princeton, NJ, 1991), 4-19. A recent example of the emphasis on state authority, rather than peasant accomplishment, is A. M. Anfimov's "On the History of the Russian Peasantry at the Beginning of the Twentieth Century," *The Russian Review* 51, no. 3 (July 1992): 396-407.

28. Frierson, " 'I must always answer to the law . . . .' "

29. For examples, see the record books of the Tsaritsynskii volostnoi sud: TsGIAgM, *f.* 74, *op.* 1, *d.* 50 for 1914.

30. See the concise description of the court system in Kazantsev, "'Sudebnaia respublika' tsarskoi Rossii," 4-6.

31. The turn toward administrative law began at least in 1918: see my article, "Lenin and the Law in Revolutionary Russia," *Slavic Review* 54, no. 1 (Spring 1995): 23-44.

32. Eugene Huskey, "A Framework for the Analysis of Soviet Law," *The Russian Review* 50, no. 1 (January 1991): 53-70. See also Eugene Huskey, "From Legal Nihilism to *Pravovoe Gosudarstvo*: Soviet Legal Development, 1917-1990," and Harold J. Berman, "The Rule of Law and the Law-Based State with Special Reference to the Soviet Union," both in Barry, ed., *Toward the "Rule of Law"*, 23-60.

33. A. A. Nelidov, *Istoriia gosudarstvennykh uchrezhdenii SSSR, 1917-1936 gg.* (Moscow, 1962), 130.

34. Walicki, *Legal Philosophies of Russian Liberalism*, 2.

35. *Ibid.*, 5; Ajani, "Rise and Fall of the Law-Based State," 7-13.

36. *Ibid.*, 869. Nabokov expands: "Law—has as its task the regulation of mutual relations between people, living in society, by means of the establishment of rules of behavior ('juridical norms'), supported by coercive [*prinuditel'noe*] action on the part of state or social authority [*vlast'*]." "Coercion" and its association with authority is clearly an important word in this description.

37. *Ibid.*, 870.

38. See my "Lenin and the Law in Revolutionary Russia."

39. This reluctance to take a processual perspective on the development of law in Russia was perhaps connected to intellectuals' fundamental commitment to repairing the gap between Russian and European levels of historical progress. Too close a confrontation with the very recent establishment of Western-style legal institutions in Russia would reveal again the fragility of legal development in Russia and throw open to doubt the Russian intellectuals' own status as equal members of an international elite.

40. Frierson, " 'I must always answer to the law . . . .' "

41. *Obzor Moskovskoi gubernii za 1905* (Moscow, 1906), 79-131.

42. *Ibid.*, 115-31. The judicial instances cited here are described by Eroshkin as those of "pravitel'stvenno-dvorianskii nadzor"—i.e, the hierarchy of supervision established for the volost' courts after 1889 (N. P. Eroshkin, *Istoriia gosudarstvennykh uchrezhdenii Rossii do velikoi oktiabr'skoi sotsialisticheskoi revoliutsii* [Moscow, 1965], 267-68).

43. For example, the records of the volost' court of Nagatino, in Moscow province, in March 1914 showed that insults, beatings, threats, and other assaults against individual dignity accounted for 32 out of 52 criminal cases. The next highest category of crime recorded in Nagatino was property offenses, of which there were only 6: TsGIAgM, *f.* 10, *op.* 1, *d.* 99. I have discussed the case records of the volost' and their significance in my article "A Question of Dignity: Peasant Legal Culture in Late Imperial Russia," *Continuity and Change* 10, no. 3 (1995): 391-404.

44. "*Po vsiakogo roda sporam i iskam.*"

45. TsGIAgM, *f.* 846, *op.*1, *d.* 4: 1-4.

46. TsGIAgM, *f.* 74, *op.* 1, *dd.* 55, 57, 58; see *d.* 55: 6-6o, *d.* 57: 9-10; and *d.* 58: 5-6, for this transition in status.

47. Marc Vishniac, *Le régime soviétiste* (Paris, 1920). On Vishniak's life, see his several autobiographies: *Dan' proshlomu* (New York, 1954); *"Sovremennye zapiski": Vospominaniia redaktora* (n.p.: Indiana University Publications, 1957); *Gody emigratsii 1919-1969: Parizh-N'iu-Iork* (Stanford, CA, 1970).

48. Vishniac, *Le régime soviétiste*, 26.

49. These ideas are developed in several of Vishniak's writings. See Jane Burbank, *Intelligentsia and Revolution: Russian Views of Bolshevism, 1917-1922* (New York, 1986), 85-99.

50. Douglas Hay, "Property, Authority, and the Criminal Law," in Douglas Hay, *et al.*, *Albion's Fatal Tree: Crime and Society in Eighteenth-Century England* (New York, 1975), 17-63. See my discussion in "Lenin and the Law in Revolutionary Russia."

51. On the prioritizing of loyalty over talent, see Roy Medvedev's moving biographical essay, "Meetings and Conversations with Aleksandr Tvardovsky," in Jane Burbank and William G. Rosenberg, eds., *Perestroika and Soviet Culture*, special issue of *Michigan Quarterly Review* 28, no. 4 (Fall 1989): esp. 622-23.

52. A display of the law's impotence even in the face of public outrage was the firing of the popular investigator Telman Gdlyan in 1988, after his five-year inquiry into economic corruption in and between the highest authorities in Central Asia and Moscow. See Timofeev, *Russia's Secret Rulers*, 11.

6

OF RED ROOSTERS, REVENGE, AND THE SEARCH FOR JUSTICE: RURAL ARSON IN EUROPEAN RUSSIA IN THE LATE IMPERIAL ERA

Cathy A. Frierson

Arson in the Russian countryside in the second half of the nineteenth century served as eloquent testimony to the difficulties of bringing statutory law to the majority of the population of the European provinces of the Empire and of developing within that population a respect for and trust in the law. On at least three levels, it served as a reminder of the failure of formal law to reach into village culture and of the richness of alternative conceptualizations of justice that countered official definitions and regulations. First, arson's prevalence throughout the provinces of European Russia made it one of the most obvious examples of pervasive criminality, according to official definitions of crime, in the countryside. Second, the many purposes of arson in the peasants' practice bespoke a moral code of right and wrong that departed from official definitions of crime. Third, the universally acknowledged failure of the police and judicial systems to capture and convict peasant arsonists pointed to the logistical and cultural obstacles the imperial government faced when it tried to penetrate and control the rural population through statutory law and judicial procedure. Throughout the last half-century of imperial rule, arson symbolized the frustration of outsiders—be they police officials or would-be legal reformers—to bring "legal consciousness" to the Russian countryside.

By the term "legal consciousness," I mean the attitude toward the law that educated members of society hoped the peasants would develop in the post-Emancipation period. That attitude included understanding of formal law, trust in statutory law's ability to achieve justice for citizens and to maintain order in society, and respect for the law as the best agent for mediating relationships among citizens and between state and society. *Pravosoznanie* among the peasants in this definition was a major goal of the

Reform judicial institutions of the volost' court, trial by jury, and the Justice of the Peace.[1]

Early reformers envisioned these institutions as schools of legal consciousness where the most basic, but essential, lessons would come through procedure. They believed that consistent judicial procedure would contrast with the caprice and arbitrariness (*proizvol*) of the pre-reform judicial system, as well as with the personal whim of powerful, unconstrained serf owners. Russian reformers shared the faith in proper procedure that Roberto Unger has described as central to the modernist confidence that "formality as rules and formality as ceremony" would serve as "the legal antidote to the subjectivity of values."[2] The chapters by Bhat and Burbank in this volume illustrate the extent to which Reform judicial institutions brought legal procedure to the lower elements of the Russian population and make clear that some of the aspirations of the reformers of the 1860s were being realized by the turn of the century.[3] Arson in the countryside, however, served as a reminder of the partial nature of that success, for when peasants resorted to arson to settle disputes, they rejected legal procedure. In the reality of daily life in the countryside as well as in the public debates about the need to develop legal consciousness among the peasantry, arson represented an alternative to a day in court or before the Justice of the Peace.

Arson in the rural setting was doubly disturbing. When peasants practiced arson against non-peasants, usually gentry landowners or lumber merchants, it signified a threat both to the old social hierarchy and to property and profit as features of the emerging capitalist economy. Arson in the countryside was much more frequently an exclusively peasant affair, however. And for those who reported on it, debated its causes, and sought its remedies, this peasant against peasant arson signified rural lawlessness. Evidence accumulated in the reports that came in to zemstvo insurance bureaux, governors' chancelleries, local newspapers, ethnographic bureaux, and government commissions on the various purposes arson served within the peasant milieu and on the difficulty of making legal solutions an attractive, dependable alternative. It became clear that arson was deeply embedded in rural custom and often played an important role in order and justice as conceptualized by the peasants.[4]

This divergence in definitions of right and wrong and, more importantly, the ends that arson accomplished for the peasant population constituted one of the obstacles blocking the full development of legal consciousness as it was envisioned by modernist reformers in late imperial Russia. Modernist critics within Russian culture were acutely aware of this obstacle. Laura Engelstein has recently identified the formal legal visions of these critics as "three competing yet mutually implicated paradigms: rule of law, police or administration, and disciplinary authority."[5] To understand fully the challenges these critics faced and the elements of their worldview, we should add to Engelstein's list the survival of customary law. They recognized that political solutions at the top would only go part of the way toward realizing the liberal, rule-of-law society they envisioned. It was not only "the failure of constitutionalism" that they feared, but also the failure to bring public and positive law into the countryside and into the consciousness of the majority population of the Empire.

The experience of arson in the countryside provides an additional explanation for the difficulties of bringing a genuine rule of law to Russia at the end of the nineteenth century. Not only peasant conceptualizations of justice and willingness to use arson as a form of dispute resolution stymied would-be reformers. The failure of the judicial and police systems to protect the peasants—the absence of "law and order"—also encouraged the peasants to seek alternative forms of self-protection. Sometimes peasants resorted to arson for no other reason than that they had little faith in the ability of the police or the courts to ensure their safety or because they saw legal due process as unnecessarily time-consuming. Practical considerations were thus sometimes as compelling as concepts of justice in determining the reach of formal law into the villages of late imperial Russia.

Arson as Evidence of Pervasive Criminality in the Russian Countryside

One has only to pick up an issue of the *Kurskie gubernskie vedomosti* (*Kursk Provincial News*) from 1870 to get a quick sense of how pervasive arson was in the imperial countryside. Beginning in April and extending through September, Kursk entered a veritable arson season, with arson fires breaking out daily in peasant courtyards and on gentry estates alike. On 8 May, for example, 25 peasant homesteads burned down in the village of Samo-durovka (4,275 rubles losses); on 17 May in the village of Mikhel'pol'e, arson took a threshing barn and thresher (3,000 rubles losses) on a gentry estate; four peasant houses burned in Shchetinkino on 23 May (1550 rubles losses); on 6 July in the village of Khokhlovo, 11 peasant homesteads, including their grain barns, burned (5,870 rubles losses); 16 peasant homesteads went up in flames in the village of Afanas'evskoe on 13 July (3,305 rubles losses). These were just a few of the many arson fires reported to the provincial governor, who turned the information over both to the Ministry of the Interior and to the editors of the provincial newspaper.[6]

From 1860 to 1910, the Central Statistical Committee of the Ministry of the Interior received statistics on the incidence, causes, and impact of fires in the provinces of European Russia. Those statistics demonstrated the ubiquitous nature of conflagrations across European Russia, and conveyed the prominence of arson in rural daily life. Of the 2,121,839 reported fires between 1860 and 1909, approximately 12 percent were identified conclusively as arson fires.[7] The figure of 12 percent obscures more than it conveys, however. First of all, all observers across the fifty-year period agreed that the number of fires conclusively identified as arson was only a very small percentage of actual arson fires. For reasons that will become clearer below, peasants never reported the majority of arson fires to officials, who were able to investigate and record only those which came to their attention. Second, there was great regional variation in the incidence of reported arson fires, with the Baltic provinces and provinces of the Central Black Earth region having the highest incidence. Some provinces, such as Kursk and Vladimir, regularly reported over 20 percent of their fires as arson fires.

Behind these figures was the reality of burning houses, threshing and storage barns, grain, forest, mills, smithies, and bathhouses. With losses running in the millions of rubles every year, arson became a concern not only in the legal experience, but also the economic existence of the Russian Empire. Often, arson fires were the result of what even the most post-modernist theorist would be hard-pressed to define as anything other than rural lawlessness. A typical case of this kind took place in a village of the Porech'e District, Smolensk Province. A fire broke out on 8 September 1879 for the following reason: following market day and a church festival, the pot house opened and a large number of peasants got drunk. Two in particular, Sergei Fedorov and Semen Semenov, got into a brawl, were arrested, and put in the storeroom of the volost' adminstration offices to sober up. They continued to fight there and shouted threats to burn the place down if they weren't let out. The elder and local policeman didn't pay any attention to them because they had searched them and taken their matches away. Even so, the storeroom burst into flames fifteen minutes later, the volost' offices burned to the ground, as did the village school attached to them.[8]

Similarly, a case brought to trial in 1867 linked drunkenness, hatred, and arson in an episode of lawless behavior. The 21 December 1867 issue of *Sudebnyi vestnik* published the transcript of a jury trial against Anna Ivanovna Belonovskaia, a forty-two-year old peasant woman. In May 1867, Belonovskaia had made it known to her neighbors that she was about to commit a crime. Shortly after that her hay barn went up in smoke, taking the izba and the rest of the outbuildings in her homestead with it. Her neighbors took her directly to the volost' offices where, drunk and belligerent, she boasted loudly that she had started the fire because she hated her husband. The jurors convicted her following testimony from several witnesses who described her as a bad wife and mother and a dissolute troublemaker.[9]

These were the kinds of actions that convinced many educated observers that the Russian village was mired in ignorance, alcoholism, and stubborn resistance to the penetration of law. They were incidents of arson that fully fit the definition of the crime in the formal codes of law. The primary criterion of criminality assigned in the criminal code was intentional damage to or destruction of property. Who set the blaze or why was less important than the fact that property burned. The universal principle governing justice through statutory law was harm done to property. V. V. Esipov's evolutionary history of laws governing arson (1892) traced the increasing focus on property in statutory law at the expense of clan or personal vengeance. In his analysis, these characteristics in the definition of arson and its punishment existed in inverted proportion to each other. The very title of his study, *Property Damage Caused by Fire According to Russian Law*, placed property at the center of the progress of Russian law. It was a sign of the maturation of Russian law that it had shifted its focus away from the individual who committed arson, Esipov declared, to "the abstract concept defining the damage itself of property by fire."[10]

When observers read the constant accounts of arson in the countryside, or considered the statistics published by the Central Statistical Committee, they could only conclude that rural Russia had somehow missed out on the evolution of Russian statutory law. There was ample evidence that not the rule of law but lawlessness prevailed in village life. Furthermore, the very vestigial forces characterizing immature Russian law in Esipov's vision— personal or clan vengeance—seemed to be especially prominent in acts of arson as understood by those who reported on them.

Mad Babas, Red Roosters, Fried Geese, and Self-Help

The case of Anna Ivanovna Belonovskaia described above confirmed the formulaic explanation that arson in the countryside was the product of "*mesti i zloby*," vengeance and spite. Observers believed that as long as arson for revenge had a prominent place in village culture, law and legal consciousness would not. In a culture where legal consciousness prevailed, reformers believed, law must mediate relations between members of the society. Remedies and restitutions for injury and loss must come through judicial decisions governed by accepted laws. In the understanding of educated observers, the disputes settled by arson in the countryside fell under the wide umbrella of "vengeance and spite." Finally, vengeance and spite either obscured or blocked the faculty of reason.

Arson for revenge was most frequently described as a female crime. This pattern of discussion was consistent with the general depiction of peasant women as the most egregiously backward elements of the dark village.[11] In the reporting on and discussion of arson as an indication of the lack of legal consciousness in the village, observers often identified peasant women as the least rational, the most likely to act out of vengeful emotion. Some observers argued that young women were the most frequent arsonists in the village because they were the most helpless. As D. M. Pogodin explained, "Thus it is the young *baba*, most often a young woman, who has not yet been tempered by every kind of hardship and sorrow, completely exhausted by the demands in her family and having consequently lost all reason, who takes vengeance; she sets fire to the house of her father-in-law or husband in a fit of meaningless despair and impotent spite. . . ."[12]

In Anna Belonovskaia's case, arson was the product of hatred and drunkenness—the emotional and physical antonyms of reason and law as solutions to family conflict. More spectacular cases of female arsonists driven by the urge for revenge were current. In a case reported in 1898 to the Tenishev Ethnographic Bureau by a correspondent from Penza Province, a peasant woman in the village of Stepanovka stole one of her neighbor's chickens and sold it for 15 kopeks to a widow in the village. By chance, the chicken's owner happened by the widow's house and recognized her chicken. The widow identified the seller as a neighbor of the victim, who accused the neighbor of the theft. A fight broke out between the two women, during which the thief threatened, "You just wait, I'll get you with your chicken! I'll remember your chicken with a red rooster!"[13] Three days later, all of the adults in the village left their children behind when they went to a spring five versts away to pray for rain, because of a three-week drought. The chicken thief stayed in the village, fired up her stove, gathered hot coals in a basket, swaddled her two young children and went out into her yard. There, she placed the hot coals in the corner closest to the yard of the neighbor from whom she had stolen the chicken. She then dragged her two swaddled children over to the chimney of her neighbor's house, where she left them. The hot coals quickly ignited the litter in her yard, and the fire spread immediately across the street. Within 30 minutes, the whole village was on fire. By the time it died down, six children, including the arsonist's own, had perished, and 120 homesteads had gone up in flames.[14]

It was precisely this kind of arson for revenge, issuing from a petty dispute, so maddeningly disproportionate in its damages, that made the need to replace vengeance with legal consciousness seem desperately urgent. And it was reports such as this that made arson for revenge seem to be a peculiar product of peasant women's short-sightedness, blind passion, and unwillingness to take disputes to any institution of formal justice.

Beatrice Brodsky Farnsworth's article about "litigious" daughters-in-law suggests that this characterization was not entirely accurate, given the frequency with which women took their complaints about family problems to the volost' courts.[15] Indeed, women's complaints before volost' courts showed that they recognized them as one possible remedy for family tension. We have debated the meaning of peasant participation in the volost' courts as evidence of emerging legal consciousness in the sense that reformers used the term. In view of those debates, it seems to me that peasant women's extreme choice of practicing arson for revenge or filing a complaint before the volost' court underscores the role that the volost' courts *could* serve in drawing peasants into the realm of formal law. As Brodsky Farnsworth points out, a dispute over a chicken or a goose was just the kind of case women brought to the volost' court even in its first decade of existence.[16]

Contemporaries were less impressed by peasant women's use of the volost' courts than they were by their use of arson. This was undoubtedly true partly because arson fires were spectacular and newsworthy while appearances before volost' judges were not. In the mind of peasants and local officials alike, the face of the arsonist was often imagined to be female, and the search for culprits following mysterious fires was likely to lead to an unhappy woman in the village. This tendency was striking in the transcripts of a trial published in *Sudebnyi vestnik* in 1867. In this case, Fekla Antonovna Sergeeva, a resident of the village of Zmievka, Riazan Province, came before the Riazan District Court where she was accused of setting seven fires in her village from 21 August to 8 September 1864. *Sudebnyi vestnik* devoted the "Court Chronicle" section of three issues to the transcripts of this case, which serves as an indication of the interest they thought such a case might hold and the messages about juridical practice in the reformed system it could offer.

At the time of the fires, Fekla Antonovna was eighteen years old and in a marriage whose unhappiness was common knowledge in the village. Several witnesses stated that her relations with both her husband and his family were quite bad. Beginning on 21 August, fires broke out in various outbuildings belonging to members of her husband's family. In each case, the fires had broken out in structures where there was no reason to have any fire.

The fires all originated in structures belonging to Sergeeva's in-laws, and several of them had spread. The fire on 8 September, for example, had consumed 18 peasant homesteads, including houses and outbuildings. This generalized damage meant that members of the community beyond Sergeeva's in-laws wanted to identify and punish the culprit.

Their decision to accuse Fekla Antonovna was the result of their perception of her family situation as well as of the fact that several of them had observed her in the vicinity of the fires when they broke out. During the trial, the defense added another reason for their accusation precisely against Fekla: that she was a woman, that they expected the guilty party of such a crime to be female, "and so she committed arson out of female stupidity and impotent spite" in the words of her accusers. Finally, Fekla Antonovna was an outsider in this community, having only recently been married to a young boy in Zmievka for financial reasons. Before that marriage, she had been a stranger. She had remained a stranger for two reasons. First, she was extremely reserved, "rather severe" in her own estimation, "sullen" according to her in-laws. Worse still, having kept entirely to herself while she was with her husband's family, she also took off frequently to return to her mother's home in another village, complaining of leg pain, and seeking treatment there. Immediately before the first of the series of arson fires, her father-in-law had gone twice to retrieve her to do her share of the fieldwork during the harvest. She refused to return the first time, and came the second time only when he brought a horse. Witnesses disagreed about the level of force her father-in-law used.

The prosecution's case rested almost entirely on his definition of Fekla Antonovna's motive, which in turn rested on the most negative portrayal possible of her position in her husband's family. His witnesses stressed the lack of love on all sides, the harsh demands of the father-in-law for his daughter-in-law's labor, and the weakness of the young husband, who never spoke out to protect his wife. The prosecutor contrasted the prosperity of the young girl's natal home with the poverty and constraint of her marital home. He suggested that it was almost inevitable for a young peasant bride in such bad straits to strike back, especially one as sullen and reserved as Fekla Antonovna. "I already said that she is very reserved. With such people, feelings rarely break through, but when they do, they do so strongly."[17] Clearly, the prosecutor was confident that the jurors would draw associations between women and revenge, arson as their preferred method, and the brutalizing effects of peasant family life in arriving at their verdict.

The defense lawyer took the opposite tack. He downplayed the troubles of Fekla Antonovna's marriage, calling them typical of any peasant household. Their very typicality undermined the presumption that they would provoke resentment in a peasant girl, familiar with conditions of village life, sufficient to prompt her to practice arson for revenge not one, but several times. He stressed, further, that her very reserved and undisturbed nature throughout the investigation and trial made it difficult to cast her as one likely to take desperate measures. He recast her visits home as genuine efforts to find medical treatment for a sore on her leg, diagnosed as a "scrofulous ulcer" by the state's doctor after her arrest. The defense lawyer placed most of his weight on bad investigative procedure, calling into question preliminary interrogation of witnesses, examination of the fire sites, and the very objectivity of the chief investigator himself.

When the case was presented to them, the jurors acquitted Fekla Antonovna of all charges of arson, although they agreed that several of the fires had indeed been set. When they read out their decision, the crowd in the courtroom burst into loud applause. Reading the court's transcript, I could not have predicted the jurors' decision, nor would I have predicted that the public would have approved so whole-heartedly of their decision. Fekla Antonovna seems to have been saved by at least three things. The image of the female arsonist was of a desperate, passion-driven, irrational individual. Neither at the time of the fires nor during the investigation and trial did Fekla Antonova display these traits. Instead, she was strikingly self-contained and calm. Second, the nature of the fires themselves made it difficult to characterize them as the act of a desperate individual striking out irrationally and in distress. Their timing and location betrayed careful preparation and persistence. Third, Fekla Antonovna may have enjoyed the sympathy of the jurors, who agreed that arson had occurred, but refused to issue a guilty verdict against her. In this, the outcome of Fekla Antonovna's case was typical of cases of arson brought to trial by jury, which as often as not, ended in acquittal for reasons I will discuss below. Three communities of justice came into conflict in this case: the community of Sergeeva's in-laws and the prosecutor who relied on the association of women, vengeance, and arson to accuse Fekla Antonovna; the community of the jurors who acknowledged arson, but refused to convict the accused arsonist; and the defense lawyer who used the tactics of formal law to protect Fekla Antonovna from the urge for vengeance in her community. We should note here that this case *did* come to court. Fekla Antonovna was fortunate in that fact alone, as another case of arson from Orel Province twenty years later makes clear.

A horse thief, Ivan Tereshin, showed up in the village of Brednikha. When he began to steal from the local peasants, they turned him in to the authorities; he was found guilty and spent time in jail. The community began their struggle with Tereshin, thus, by appealing to formal law and the judicial system to protect them. But Tereshin stole from them again, and their reaction was to beat him nearly to death. During the beating, he warned them, "You'll remember me, yep, you won't forget me! Van'ka knows how to pay people back!" One night soon thereafter, Ivan and his brother set fire to two houses and made off toward another community. The entire village burned to the ground, but the peasants caught the Tereshin brothers. They beat them, tied them up, and threw them into the flames of a bonfire of the brothers' property. When a local official urged them to pull the arsonists out of the flame and leave the case to the local authorities, the peasants replied, "They're headed down that road anyway!"[18]

Here we have fire being used as revenge by both sides in a conflict between outsiders and a community. The Tereshin brothers had violated the community code by stealing within the community, earning reprisals from the local peasants. In vengeance, they then burned the entire village down. But, in response, the community members joined together to fight fire with fire, to exact vengeance in the form they had received it, even to the point of being willing to burn the arsonists alive. This was not the only report of such punishment.[19] Burning alive arsonists who were caught red-handed was one of the most spectacular forms of *samosud* (vigilantism). It conformed to the peasants' usual explanation for preferring self-help to legal procedure: self-help was a more certain way to prevent the arsonist from harming them again. In this instance, the local officials' pleas to leave the arsonists' fate to the authorities and the courts fell on deaf ears. Convinced of the justice of a fiery death as the physical equivalent of moral damnation in hell, the peasants of Brednikha had no inclination to leave this matter to be resolved by the law of the state.

Fighting fire with fire here also reflected the general tendency to adjust the punishment to fit the level of harm done.[20] Because the Tereshin brothers had caused so much evident harm to the residents of Brednikha, the victims were comfortable imposing the maximum penalties on them: burning their property and consigning them to fire themselves. As they reportedly shouted into the Tereshin brothers' faces after they piled up their belongings in front of them to burn, "So whose goods are these? You begged us to pull them out. No, sweethearts, it's not going to turn out the way you want, but the way *we* want: you burned our goods, and so let your goods burn!"[21] The same sense of evening the score by forcing the arsonists to experience the loss they had caused inspired some of the villagers' reaction to the death of their poultry and livestock in the fire. Running around their devastated yards, the peasants grabbed the charred carcasses of geese, piglets, and chickens. Shouting, "So it was you who fried this goose! Then you eat it!," they shoved the animals into the arsonists' mouths or swung them against their mouths, faces, and necks. Taking a cue from their elders, the children of the village surrounded the arsonists and cast burned pieces of wood at them.[22]

In this incident, the question of membership in the community also arises. It seems that peasants were most likely to practice vengeful arson against outsiders, or to use the most violent forms of samosud against those captured arsonists who were themselves outsiders.

Insiders, Outsiders, and Arson

Two cases reported from Novgorod Province to the Tenishev Bureau hinged on the combination of the arson victims' status as outsiders and the community's determination to protect their economic well-being against the profiteering of those outsiders. In the first, a local peasant sold his father's mill to a peasant from another village. The mill had always caused periodic flooding of the village's fields when it was in operation, but as long as a peasant from the village owned it, the community was willing to tolerate this hardship. As soon as an outsider began to operate the mill, however, and the usual flooding resulted, the local peasants demanded that he close the mill down. When he refused, the community got together and torched it.[23]

In a second village in Cherepovets District, a new young priest replaced a familiar old one. The former priest had enjoyed the reputation of being generous to members of the community. The new priest, by contrast, exacted fees for his services that the villagers considered excessive. When they urged him to lower the fees, he replied, "No, fellows, it's not up to you to teach me, but me to teach you, and quickly." The peasants' anger and vengeance escalated from threats, which he ignored, to setting fire to some of his outbuildings, finally to setting fire to his entire homestead, killing his wife, his two children, and an old nurse. The authorities suspected that the peasants had poured kerosene over the house, because it burst into flames from all sides at once.[24] In both of these cases, we see that the old "kto-kogo" (who did what to whom?) question looked different from the perspective of the peasants and those who would impose legal definitions of arson. For in both of these cases, the peasants saw themselves as the primary victims, with the miller and the priest being clear wrongdoers. In this worldview, burning someone else's property did not constitute wrongdoing. On the contrary, for the peasants, fire in these cases equalled justice, all the more easily imposed on the wrongdoers because they were not members of the community.

In the case of multi-ethnic regions, the issue of outsider status and frequency of arson may have been especially acute. Over the three decades for which I have been able to map the reported incidence of arson, the highest percentages of fires attributed to arson were in districts with a large percentage of non-Russians.[25] Narrative accounts of fire and arson also pointed to the role of ethnic outsiders in the practice of arson in the countryside. In his reminiscences of fires in Riazan Province in the late 1840s, D. M. Pogodin recalled that the local people were convinced that the exceptional number of fires in 1847 and 1848 were the handiwork of "nerusskie liudi," non-Russians, especially along the Astrakhan highway.[26] It may also be the case that villages near major highways or riverways were more susceptible to all forms of crime as transient laborers moved through the area, free of any community constraints or sense of identification with their victims.

Arson and Exploitation[27]

For students of Russian history, scenes of peasants moving across the southern provinces of European Russia setting gentry estates ablaze have become icons of peasant resistance and class consciousness during the rebellions of 1905-1907.[28] Within the discourse about fire and arson among contemporaries, this form of arson appeared also, and became especially acute after 1907.[29] During the fifty years beforehand, however, such peasant actions against gentry and merchant neighbors were reported as simply one more manifestation of the peasants' reprisal—leveled against peasants, merchants, and gentry landowners alike—for perceived exploitation and unacceptable profiteering.

The case of the greedy priest in Novgorod Province described above fit into this category of arson. So did an incident in the Saransk District of Penza Province when a poor peasant set fire to a rich peasant's storehouse after the latter refused to give him some grain.[30] In April 1875, *Sudebnyi vestnik* reported a case in which a female arsonist was convicted largely because of her well-known resentment against the victim, who had refused to let her use his barn to store some of her crops.[31] Tavern-keepers and traders were also frequent targets of arson by peasants for the same reason.[32] Forest fires were often ascribed to arson caused by peasants' resentment of the gentry for restricting their access to firewood.[33] Peasants also protested the sale of the forest for profit by attacking felled and stacked timber, sometimes after having received payment for cutting and hauling. Such was a case in the Dorogobuzh District of Smolensk Province when local peasants set fire to 400 sazhens (around 850 meters) of birch in 1887.[34] Similarly, in Sapozhsk District, Riazan Province, over the course of 1901, there were ten major arson fires in the large private forests of one Shuvalov, despite the fact that he had doubled the mounted and foot patrols. Laconic fire reports in local newspapers often suggested that this kind of arson was the cause of major forest blazes.[35] These cases appear time and again throughout local sources, attesting to arson's use in this way to protest the redefinition and delimitation of forests and wood in the post-Emancipation countryside.[36]

When peasants used arson against local landowners, they almost never set fire to the manor house or any other residential structure on the land-owner's estate. Instead, they set fire to the source of their resentment: stores of grain harvested by their hands and held by the gentry for sale at a high price when the market was ripe. These were the most frequent types of fires between peasants and lords. In one two-week period in 1882 in Smolensk Province, for example, out of 13 reported fires, four involved gentry property. In the village of Pridishche in Gzhatsk District, a fire of "unknown causes" on a gentry estate burned a full grain storehouse, with losses of 4,000 rubles. In the village of Lozitskakh in Roslavl District, an arson fire burned a grain merchant's grain storehouse with losses of 5,000 rubles. Near the village of Andreikova in Viaz'ma District, a fire of "unknown cause" on a merchant's estate consumed two storehouses containing grain, hay, and farming implements for losses of 6,500 rubles. "Carelessness" on a noble estate in the outskirts of the town of Roslavl led to a fire which consumed 6,000 rubles of property.[37] While only one of these fires was conclusively identified as an arson fire, "unknown causes" and "carelessness" were often the best that local investigators could come up with, and readers understood that the real cause was probably arson. The local correspondent from Porech'e District reported to *Smolenskii vestnik* in October 1882 that there had recently been a series of suspicious fires on gentry estates. The usual targets were full grain barns in the meadows, far from other structures. There was no doubt among the local gentry that these fires resulted from arson, striking at their wealth following the harvest.[38] Reports from Kursk Province suggest that gentry landowners there had much the same to fear, with the added anxiety that peasants also often set fire to buildings housing agricul-tural machinery.[39]

None of these reports provide a motive; they do not identify any specific complaint by the peasants against the lord. In other sources, we find that such acts of arson often resulted from land disputes between lords and peasants, or labor disputes between peasant laborers and their gentry bosses.[40] One such case from 1871 in Nizhnii Novgorod Province, Vasilii District, resulted in the destruction of a gentrywoman's livestock barn and losses of 3,500 rubles. The accused arsonist was a peasant from a nearby village who was angry that the owner had leased a piece of her land not to him, but to another peasant.[41] A case record from 1884 in the Smolensk Archive explained that a local peasant, Koz'min, was suspected of arson against the landowner Vonlialiarskii because Koz'min resented him for something that had happened between them while he was working on Vonlialiarskii's estate. Koz'min was so offended that he left the job without receiving his pay. Shortly before the fire, furthermore, Koz'min had been spotted near the scene of the blaze, after having publicly declared his hatred of Vonlialiarskii.[42] The consistent pattern of arson fires being set in non-residential structures, and most often in structures where grain was being held for the market, invites the inference that peasants struck precisely these targets because their contents symbolized the exploitation they felt. To peasants arson in this form qualified not as wrongdoing, but as justice served upon those who had wronged them.

Wealthy peasants in the village also feared this form of arson. Anticipating that their homesteads would be targets for arson, kulaks preferred to build them smack in the middle of the village rather than on the end of the street or the village periphery. As long as their residences were in close proximity with other homesteads, they could count on their neighbors' fear of a generalized conflagration to counteract their desire to attack kulak wealth.[43] This strategy did not always save them. In the September 1882 report from *Smolenskii vestnik* cited above, there was also one reported arson fire in Roslavl District directed against peasant houses. In this case four peasant houses valued at 2,400 rubles burned. By contrast, a fire due to "unknown causes" in Sycheva District consumed three peasant houses valued only at 400 rubles. It seems fair to assume that the houses targeted in the arson fire belonged to prosperous peasants.[44]

For those members of educated Russian society who hoped to replace arbitrariness and self-help in peasant culture with respect for and confidence in the law, these various uses of arson to settle differences within the community represented an obstacle and sign of the failure of the law to penetrate the countryside. From the perspective of statutory law, all of these acts of arson were crimes because they met the criteria of criminality assigned in the criminal code. The arsonist had intentionally damaged or destroyed property. For the peasants who practiced arson in these ways, however, there were sometimes other compelling principles that were captured more fully in the notions of justice as *pravda* or fairness, *spravedlivost'*. These principles remind us of the primacy of moral concerns in peasant concepts of justice. These moral concerns rise to the surface in the prohibitions *against* arson that existed within the peasant community.

When was Arson Unacceptable in the Russian Village?

Arson was not always perceived by the peasants of European Russia as a legitimate form of dispute resolution. There were certain community constraints on the use of arson. Once a member of the community violated those constraints, he or she became a wrongdoer in the community's eyes, as well as a sinner. In such cases, peasants were more likely to agree that the action warranted reprisal, either through formal justice or through self-help. In evaluating the acceptability of arson as a means to settle a score, peasants imposed norms consistent with those they imposed on all acts of serious wrongdoing.

As with other actions that were defined universally as criminal in statutory law, but which were susceptible to varying definitions in the peasant milieu, arson varied in its definitions primarily according to three main criteria: the harm it caused to the community, the membership of the victim in the community, and the type of dispute it was being used to settle.[45] The greater identifiable harm arson caused to individuals or to the community, the more likely it was to be declared sinful. Once identified as sinful, it was more likely to be identified as an act requiring a community response.

In that light, an individual act of arson committed against one outbuilding, which consumed only that outbuilding and brought economic loss only to the victim was considered fully legitimate if the community also acknowledged the legitimacy of the arsonist's complaint. This type of deliberately set fire was least likely to be identified as such in official reports, because the community shielded the arsonist, considering it the arsonist's private retaliation against his victim for the offense he perceived. Obviously the arsonist recognized that he had destroyed his victim's property—that was the goal of his action in bringing his victim back onto his level of economic play—but property damage in and of itself did not constitute a violation of community morality in the villages of European Russia. Arson became punishable wrongdoing when it was simultaneously sinful. And to be sinful, it had to cause debilitating hardship and suffering, or to take the life of some of God's creatures.

For that reason, the worst kind of arson fire was one that became a runaway conflagration that consumed many homesteads, including residential structures, livestock barns, and grain storage barns.[46] Even if the arsonist had intended to set only a limited fire in one outbuilding that subsequently spread, he or she was considered guilty of unacceptable, sinful wrongdoing. Despite membership in the community and the intention to commit an act that was implicitly sanctioned by the community, a peasant who was reckless in setting a fire to settle a score was vulnerable to the maximum penalty of death through samosud if caught red-handed. "There's no way for him to be excused, because his enemy's innocent neighbor suffered," the peasants of Novoladozhsk District in St. Petersburg Province explained to a correspondent of the Tenishev Ethnographic Bureau.[47]

Intentionally setting fire to a residential structure, setting an arson fire that led to loss of human life, the death of livestock or poultry, or the burning of an icon were all acts that violated community morality and exceeded the use of arson as an acceptable weapon directed toward positive or sanctioned ends. In some areas, it was also considered a sin and thus a crime to set fire to stored grain if doing so deprived the victim of sustenance.

These prohibitions suggest that peasants distinguished between property as shelter and sustenance and property as commodity. If we look only at the peasants' assault on property as commodity, held by either noble landowners, lumber merchants, or kulaks, we would quickly conclude that they were displaying the kind of "sub-political" consciousness characteristic of the nascent working class in industrializing Britain described by E. P. Thompson.[48] These incidents of arson in rural European Russia share the reflection of "an older moral economy, which taught the immorality of any unfair method of forcing up the price of provisions by profiteering upon the necessities of the people" that Thompson identified.[49]

My emphasis here is on morality. Within the context of our discussion of the search for a law-based society and efforts by reform-minded elements in the state and community of jurists to draw the peasants of European Russia into a modern legal system, we should pause to recognize the power of the moral code of arson in the village. It was this moral code that defined burning the hoarded grain or stacked timber of gentry, merchants, and kulaks as sanctioned justice. Simultaneously, however, it constrained the urge toward vengeance by setting clear limits on the objects of arson as a sanctioned weapon of justice. The prohibitions against setting fire to residential structures and livestock or poultry barns, with the burning of an icon an additional taboo, point to fundamental notions of sanctity attached to physical objects and the degree of harm the community would tolerate. Governed by these taboos, peasants often committed arson not out of irrational vengeance or "blind spite," but according to a code of behaviors that was understood and enforced widely in their communities.[50] Within the context of the discussion in this volume, my point is that the force of moral norms in the use of arson points to the diverging concepts of justice and law in custom and statutes, and among peasants and educated Russians searching for paths to a rule of law.

As Jane Burbank argues in her contribution to this volume, one mark of a legal culture is that it "rests upon the citizenry's recognition of the legal system as a preferred means of solving conflicts and punishing evil . . . ," and that "effective legal systems permit and contribute to widespread national definitions and redefinitions of ethical behavior."[51] Both of these goals required a degree of internalization of the ethical and legal norms expressed in statutory law that arson in the countryside belied. Arson practiced within the peasant community and against neighboring gentry and merchants indicated that local norms held firm and were not yet susceptible to replacement by genuine internalization of "widespread definitions and redefinitions of ethical behavior."

A legal culture might also develop if the state were able to nurture respect through effective external enforcement of those definitions and redefinitions. Viewed in the light of arson fires, however, the Russian judicial system had not succeeded in this area either. For the experience of peasants with the courts in arson cases revealed both divergent definitions of ethical behavior and the frequent failure of the courts to provide peasant plaintiffs the protection they sought through the law.

Arson and the Failure of Legal Procedure

Several of the cases of arson I have described point to the peasants' willingness to give the formal judicial system a try. Fekla Antonovna's fellow villagers took her to court, after all, rather than subjecting her to samosud. The peasants of Brednikha had turned Ivan Tereshin in to the local authorities when he first began to steal from them. The woman who burned down her neighbor's barn when he refused to let her store grain in it was also convicted in a court of law after her community turned her in. Similarly, Brodsky Farnsworth's "litigious daughters-in-law" were plaintiffs, not incendiaries. They were part of the process of developing a legal culture that Burbank emphasizes in her chapter here on the Justice of the Peace and the volost' courts. But the very persistence of arson as both sanctioned justice and serious wrongdoing in the countryside calls into question the maturity of that legal culture by the end of the century.

Divergent concepts of justice among the peasants and in statutory law rose to the surface when arson cases came to trial before peasant jurors. As in the case of Fekla Antonovna described above, jurors often failed to convict accused arsonists, even in the face of compelling evidence.[52] They did so primarily for three reasons. The first was that they refused to sanction the severity of official justice embodied in sentences for arsonists. For all forms of arson, against forest and against residential and non-residential structures alike, punishment involved exile or resettlement in Siberia.[53] For the majority of arson cases in the peasant community or against the property of landowners and timber merchants, such a sentence would seem excessive to peasants. The very goal of most sanctioned acts of arson was to re-establish an equilibrium of sorts in the community, not to excise a member of the community from its body. The second reason was that peasant jurors who viewed some acts of arson as legitimate means of achieving immediate justice might sympathize with the accused.

The third reason was sheer fear of revenge from the arsonist or his or her family. Even in cases of arsonists who had harmed or systematically terrorized a community, this fear often prevented peasant jurors from convicting them or peasant witnesses from testifying against them. The conviction rate of arsonists hovered at around 50 percent, so there was an even chance that the arsonist would return to the community.[54] Arsonists and their victims seemed to be fully aware of this, leading to a phenomenon of arson bullies who often kept whole villages in fear, extorting from the peasants with the threat of the red rooster.[55] Such was the peasant Golubev who tyrannized the village of Kliment'ev generally, and in September 1874, turned to arson as his weapon. On the night of 8 September, on the afternoon of 11 September, and again on the night of 12 September, he set fire to his neighbors' property, causing 10,000 rubles losses before they turned him in to the authorities. When the case came to trial, it turned out that he had decided to set fire to one of his victims' houses after he demanded money from her and found the amount she gave him too small.[56]

Peasants had little confidence in the state's ability to protect them from such arsonists or their relatives, in the event that the court convicted the arsonists themselves. There was little reason to turn to the law or its agents when it did so little to protect them. Furthermore, there was little reason to serve the law by participating in legal proceedings at court when the costs for doing so could be so high. Peasants were not interested in serving the abstract principles of justice embodied in legal procedure; they were interested in the stability and safety of their individual communities and households. They were intimate with arson fires; they knew how little evidence an arsonist left behind and how difficult it could be to build a formal case. Burning an arson bully alive, if he or she were caught red-handed, was a far more effective deterrent against future threat than a day in court. For cases of arson when the arsonist succeeded in setting a fire that remained within the norms of acceptable reprisal in the community, his or her fellow villagers, and even the victims themselves, were unlikely to seek legal redress. The community at large had nothing to gain from formal procedure and much to lose if they were called as witnesses. The victims could choose simply to take note of the message sent by the arsonist or continue a "dialogue" of sorts by striking back through another act of reprisal sanctioned within the community. Practical concerns thus joined divergent conceptions of justice to keep peasants of European Russia distant from faith in legal procedure and the ethical norms it defended.

Conclusion

If we share Jane Burbank's redefinition of legal culture by turning our emphasis "away from knowledge to process, away from knowing the law to accepting, using, and respecting legal opportunities," arson in rural Russia in the late imperial Russia should cause us to pause in our optimistic appraisal of the gains made in developing such a legal culture. We have ample evidence by now that peasants accepted and used legal opportunities on hundreds of thousands of occasions to resolve disputes by the turn of the century. My own work on the volost' court during these years convinces me that judicial reform had made strides in the countryside.[57] But peasants also practiced arson as a form of dispute resolution on hundreds of thousands of occasions by the turn of the century. Furthermore, these acts of arson were usually not manifestations of exceptional group discontent in the form that Russian historians have usually envisioned them. Rather, they were part of rural daily life, they constituted a language of their own, and they often expressed community ethical norms. The very mundane nature of much of rural arson pointed to one of the obstacles to developing fully the legal culture that Burbank has defined.

Many acts of arson within the village community and outside it against merchants and landowners constituted justice for peasants in the most immediate sense of the term. The moral code of the community defined both the legitimacy of arson as a form of dispute resolution and delimited the extent of acceptable attack. This was a sure frustration of the modernist "intention to find the legal antidote to the subjectivity of values."[58] The variability of the peasants' definition of arson as justice or evil, depending upon whether it conformed to the restrictions of the village code, also defied official, imperial law's focus on property damage as the defining and criminal feature of arson. Arson as self-help also continued to be preferable to legal procedure for peasants. Whereas judicial reformers placed great faith in proper procedure as insurance against arbitrariness and tyranny, peasants viewed jury trials of arsonists as costly in time, risky, and most uncertain as the means to eliminate arson bullies from their midst. Finally, the law patently had not and could not reach into village communities to protect them from vengeful arsonists. Arson reminds us of the constraints binding legal reformers in late imperial Russia. They confronted tenacious community concepts of right and fairness in their effort to bring about the internalization of shared ethical norms, while battling simultaneously against the chronic weaknesses of the systems of policing and advocacy that were essential to effective prosecution of arson cases. A genuine legal culture for the peasant majority population of the Russian Empire required a judicial system that broke free of those constraints. Only then could Russia enjoy a law-based society, which was essential to the emergence of a rule of law state.

Author's note: I received support for the research for this chapter from the International Research and Exchanges Board, the Kennan Institute for Advanced Russian Studies, the Russian Research Center at Harvard University, the National Council for Soviet and East European Research, and the University of New Hampshire. Lucy Salyer, J. William Harris, Lynne Viola, and Richard Stites offered comments on earlier drafts.

Notes

1.   Cathy A. Frierson, "Rural Justice in Public Opinion: The Volost' Court Debate, 1861-1912," *Slavonic and East European Review* 64, no. 3 (October 1986), 526-45; Cathy A. Frierson, *Peasant Icons: Representations of Rural People in Late Nineteenth Century Russia* (New York, 1993), 54-75; Jane Burbank, "Law without the State? Peasant Ideas of Justice in Revolutionary Russia," Paper presented at the Twentieth National Convention of the American Association for the Advancement of Slavic Studies, Honolulu, November 1988; Joan Neuberger, "Popular Legal Cultures," in Ben Eklof, John Bushnell, and Larissa Zakharova, eds., *Russia's Great Reforms, 1855-1881* (Bloomington and Indianapolis, IN, 1994), 231-46; in the same volume, Alexander K. Afanas'ev, "Jurors and Jury Trials in Imperial Russia, 1866-1885," 214-30.

2.   Roberto M. Unger, *Law in Modern Society: Toward a Criticism of Social Theory* (New York, 1976), 204-205.

3. I have also described advances made in the volost' court in " 'I must always answer to the law. . .': Rules and Response at the Reformed *Volost' Court*," *Slavonic and East European Review* 75, no. 2 (April 1997): 308-334.

4. Arson as an element of customary law among the Russian peasantry thus illustrated the gap between visions of order and justice between educated, propertied citizens of the Empire and peasants. This gap is similar to that described for the English in Keith Wrightson, "Two concepts of order: justices, constables and jurymen in seventeenth-century England," in John Brewer and John Styles, eds., *An Ungovernable People: The English and their law in the seventeenth and eighteenth centuries* (New Brunswick, NJ, 1980), 21-46.

5. Laura Engelstein, "Reply," *American Historical Review* 98, no. 2 (April 1993): 376.

6. *Kurskie gubernskie vedomosti*, No. 45 (15 June 1870): 3; No. 58 (28 July 1870): 3; No. 64 (18 August 1870): 3.

7. Tsentral'nyi statisticheskii komitet, Ministerstvo Vnutrennikh Del, *Statistika Rossiiskoi imperii*, Volume LXXVI. *Statistika pozharov v Rossiiskoi imperii za 1895-1910 gody. Chast' 1. 63 gubernii Evropeiskoi Rossii* (St. Petersburg, 1912), XIV and XXI.

8. *Gosudarstvennii arkhiv Smolenskoi oblasti* (GASO), *f.* 1, *op.* 5, *d.* 217 (1879): 2.

9. "Sudebnaia khronika," *Sudebnyi vestnik*, No. 273 (21 December 1867): 1123-25.

10. V. V. Esipov, *Povrezhdenie imushchestva ognem po russkomu pravu* (St. Petersburg, 1892), 137. In this centrality of property in the development of law, Russian statutory law resembled that of the English as described by Douglas Hay, "Property, Authority and the Criminal Law," in Douglas Hay, *et al., Albion's Fatal Tree: Crime and Society in Eighteenth-Century England* (New York, 1975), 17-63.

11. For a discussion of this tendency, see my *"Baba*: The Peasant Woman—Virago, Eve, or Victim?" in Frierson, *Peasant Icons*, 161-80.

12. D. M. Pogodin, *Pozhary i podzhogi v provintsii (iz otryvochnykh vospominanii)*, 2d ed. (Moscow, 1879), 6-7.

13. To threaten someone with the red rooster was to threaten to set fire to their property.

14. Russkii etnograficheskii muzei, *fond* 7, *opis'* 1 (hereafter Tenishev Fund), *d.* 1292 (Gorodoshchensk District, Penza Province): 77-79.

15. Beatrice Brodsky Farnsworth, "The Litigious Daughter-in-Law: Family Relations in Rural Russia in the Second Half of the Nineteenth Century," *Slavic Review* 45, no. 1 (Spring 1986): 49-64.

16. *Ibid.*, 51.

17. "Sudebnaia khronika," *Sudebnyi vestnik*, No. 146 (6 July 1867): 535.

18. Tenishev Fund, *d.* 1115: 3 - 7.

19. See also Tenishev Fund, *d.* 1490 (Khvalinsk District, Saratov Province): 8; Tenishev Fund, *d.* 656 (Vasil'-Sursk District, Nizhnii Novgorod Province): 8.

20. See Cathy A. Frierson, "Crime and Punishment in the Russian Village: Rural Concepts of Criminality at the End of the Nineteenth Century," *Slavic Review* 46, no. 1 (Spring 1987): 64-69.

21. Tenishev Fund, *d.* 1115 (Orel District, Orel Province): 6.

22. *Ibid.*: 6-7.

23. Tenishev Fund, *d.* 805 (Cherepovets District, Novgorod Province): 12.

24. *Ibid.*: 16.

25. Tsentral'nyi statisticheskii komitet Ministerstva Vnutrennikh Del, *Vremennik tsentral'nago statisticheskago komiteta Ministerstva Vnutrennikh Del*, No. 13 *Pozhary v rossiiskoi imperii v 1883-1887 god. i svod dannykh za 28 let* (St. Petersburg, 1889), 2-99; Tsentral'nyi statisticheskii komitet Ministerstva Vnutrennikh Del, *Vremennik tsentral'nago statisticheskago komiteta Ministerstva Vnutrennikh Del*, No. 44 *Pozhary v rossiiskoi imperii v 1888-1894 godakh* (St. Petersburg, 1897), 66-74.

26. Pogodin, *Pozhary i podzhogi v provintsii*, 66-67.

27. In this paper, I am not treating the question of arson for profit, a practice that appeared in the villages of European Russia after the introduction of zemstvo insurance programs.

28. Arson is the most dramatic and prominent feature of the peasant rebellions of 1905-1907 in Teodor Shanin's account, *Russia, 1905-07. Revolution as a Moment of Truth.* Volume 2 of *The Roots of Otherness: Russia's Turn of Century* (New Haven, CT, 1986), 79-99. See also Robert Edelman, *Proletarian Peasants: The Revolution of 1905 in Russia's Southwest* (Ithaca, NY, 1987), 86; S. M. Dubrovskii, *Krest'ianskoe dvizhenie v revoliutsii 1905-07 gg.* (Moscow, 1956), 33-73.

29. For two examples of this, see A. S. Ermolov, *Sovremennaia pozharnaia epidemiia v Rossii* (St. Petersburg, 1910) and V. Purishkevich, *Natsional'noe bedstvie Rossii* (St. Petersburg, 1909).

30. Tenishev Fund, *d.* 1393 (Saransk District, Penza Province): 32.

31. "Korrespondentsiia. Rybninsk," *Sudebnyi vestnik*, No. 76 (8 April 1875): 4.

32. Tenishev Fund, *op.* 1, *d.* 977 (Briansk District, Orel Province): 27.

33. Tenishev Fund, *d.* 1711 (Iukhnov District, Smolensk Province): 40; also *d.* 857 (Cherepovets District, Novgorod Province): 1.

34. Tenishev Fund, *d.* 1589 (Dorogobuzh District, Smolensk Province): 33.

35. *Smolenskii vestnik*, No. 119 (8 October 1882): 8.

36. They also appear in the chronology of peasant actions in P. A. Zaionchkovskii, ed., *Krest'ianskoe dvizhenie v Rossii v 1870-1880 gg. Sbornik dokumentov* (Moscow, 1968), 513; A. V. Shapkarin, ed., *Krest'ianskoe dvizhenie v Rossii v 1890-1900 gg. Sbornik dokumentov* (Moscow, 1959), 615, 641.

37. *Smolenskii vestnik*, No. 115 (9 September 1882): 2. For reports of similar fires, see *Smolenskii vestnik*, No. 24 (20 August 1878): 2; No. 36 (1 October 1878): 2; No. 41 (19 October 1878): 2; No. 44 (29 October 1878): 2; No. 97 (18 August 1882): 1-2.

38. *Smolenskii vestnik*, No. 120 (10 October 1882): 1. Similar incidents can be found in L. M. Ivanov, ed., *Krest'ianskoe dvizhenie v Rossii v 1861-1869 gg. Sbornik dokumentov* (Moscow, 1964), 662; Zaionchkovskii, ed. *Krest'ianskoe dvizhenie*, 111-12; A. S. Nifontov, ed., *Krest'ianskoe dvizhenie v Rossii v 1881-1889 gg. Sbornik dokumentov* (Moscow, 1960), 280, 578-79, 791, 808, 813; Shapkarin, ed., *Krest'ianskoe dvizhenie*, 633, 634.

39. See, in particular, "Proisshestviia," *Kurskie gubernskie vedomosti*, No. 55 (17 July 1870): 3; No. 58 (28 July 1870): 3; No. 64 (18 August 1870): 3; No. 92 (24 November 1870): 3.

40. *Trudy mestnykh komitetov o nuzhdakh sel'skokhoziaistvennoi promyshlennosti*. Volume XXXIV. *Riazanskaia guberniia* (St. Petersburg, 1903), 319; also XV. *Kievskaia guberniia* (St. Petersburg, 1903), 213.

41. "Proisshestviia," *Nizhegorodskii listok*, No. 58 (15 June 1871): 3.

42. GASO, *f.* 1, *op.* 5, *d.* 82 (1884): 1-2.

43. P. N. Miasoedov reported to the Roslavl District Committee in Smolensk Province in 1902 that this concern acted as a brake on programs for breaking up crowded village housing as a fire prevention measure because peasants were afraid to build homesteads isolated out in the fields where they would be more vulnerable to arsonists. *Zhurnaly uezdnykh komitetov Smolenskoi gubernii o nuzhdakh sel'skokhoziaistvennoi promyshlennosti. 1902 god* (Smolensk, 1903), 227.

44. See also Shapkarin, ed., *Krest'ianskoe dvizhenie*, 641, where an incident in Poltava Province involving arson against the grain and outbuildings of a kulak is listed.

45. For a discussion of the importance of these consequences in the peasants' appraisal of deeds in the community, see Frierson, "Crime and Punishment in the Russian Village."

46. Several local respondents to the Tenishev Ethnographic Survey in 1897-1898 reported this pattern of evaluating the seriousness of arson among the peasants in their area. See the following: Tenishev Fund, *op.* 1, *d.* 1466 (Skopinsk District, Riazan Province): 36; *d.* 1475 (Novoladozhsk District, St. Petersburg Province): 11; *d.* 656 (Vasil'-Sursk Kistrict, Nizhnii Novgorod Province): 7; *d.* 1115 (Orel District, Orel Province): 2-3.

47. Tenishev Fund, *op.* 1, *d.* 1475 (Novoladozhsk District, St. Petersburg Province): 11.

48. E. P. Thompson, *The Making of the English Working Class* (New York, 1966), 63-65.

49. *Ibid.*, 63.

50. The fact that so many fires identified as arson consumed only one outbuilding, usually a shed or barn, testified to the careful handling of fire by the arsonists. The Russian village was incredibly flammable and capable of going up in flames in under thirty minutes. Most arson fires did not spread, most did not lead to huge conflagrations. This indicates that the typical peasant arsonist was not acting rashly, blinded by passion into careless vengeance, but was acting within an internalized code of community constraint that governed how and where he or she would set a punitive fire.

51.   Burbank, "Legal Culture, Citizenship, and Peasant Jurisprudence: Perspectives from the Early Twentieth Century," 86.

52.   Trials of accused arsonists in the countryside would have come before district court juries made up primarily of peasants, most of whom were from the less prosperous layers of village culture. See Afanas'ev, "Jurors and Jury Trials," 214-30.

53.   *Svod zakonov ugolovnykh*. Chast' pervaia. *Ulozhenie o nakazaniiakh ugolovnykh i ispravitel'nykh* (St. Petersburg, 1885), Articles 1606-1615, pp. 333-35.

54.   *Trudy mestnykh komitetov o nuzhdakh sel'skokhoziaistvennoi promyshlennosti*. Volume XXVIII. *Orlovskaia guberniia* (St. Petersburg, 1903), 760-64; *Trudy mestnykh komitetov o nuzhdakh sel'skokhoziaistvennnoi promyshlennosti*. Volume XXI. *Minskaia guberniia* (St. Petersburg, 1903), 60.

55.   *Trudy mestnykh komitetov o nuzhdakh sel'skokhoziaistvennoi promyshlennosti*. Volume XVI. *Kovenskaia guberniia* (St. Petersburg, 1903), 54; *Trudy mestnykh komitetov o nuzhdakh sel'skokhoziaistvennoi promyshlennosti*. Volume IX. *Voronezhskaia guberniia* (St. Petersburg, 1903), 142.

56.   "Korrespondentsiia. Rybninsk," *Sudebnyi vestnik*, No. 76 (8 April 1875): 4.

57.   This is my argument in " 'I must always answer to the law. . . .' "

58.   Unger, *Law in Modern Society*, 205.

7

THE TRIALS OF THE *PROLETARKA*: SEXUAL HARASSMENT CLAIMS IN THE 1920s

Lisa Granik

Sexual harassment is "the norm, our version of the work ethic," a Russian journalist recently remarked.[1] As this comment suggests, women have long been, and continue to be, the subject of discrimination and sexual harassment in Russia. Scholarly notice of flagrant discrimination against women in the workforce centers primarily on the 1920s, when seesawing female unemployment contrasted sharply with both official and legal proclamations that all citizens had a right and duty to work.[2] But the efforts of many working women in Soviet Russia[3] to address and remedy instances of discrimination and sexual harassment through legal and alternative dispute resolution fora in the mid- to late-1920s have escaped detailed study.

This chapter explores the content, process, and implications of these efforts within the context of Soviet legal attempts to emancipate women and integrate them into the wage labor economy. I argue that ordinary women developed a vocabulary and consciousness to articulate their own views and to appeal to legal institutions in an effort to change the law to incorporate their vision of equality. My analysis depicts a distinction between elite and popular definitions of equality, and illustrates the limitations of using law to promote social change where the rulers are at best ambivalent about according independent power to law, legal, and quasi-legal institutions, and where gender myths are embedded even in legislation designed to create an egalitarian, more gender-neutral society. Finally, in this analysis of Russian women's claims regarding the discriminatory treatment they suffered in the workplace in the 1920s, I demonstrate the limitations of the Soviet commitment to integrate women into the workforce and to deliver legal—or even formal—equality to its female citizens.

Myths and Images of Women and Law

Myths about women and law influenced the early Bolshevik effort to emancipate women after the 1917 Revolution.[4] The dominant image of woman as mother pervaded Russian and Soviet law, policy, and culture.[5] In a society whose literature contains "few references to romantic love and no idealized pair of lovers, the mother . . . [became] an unusually important focus of reference and affection."[6] The mythology of maternity projects a mother-child relationship of "primordial and gravitational force."[7] Nadezhda Krupskaia, Lenin's wife and a major proponent of the new policy toward women, declared that "[w]oman is either a mother or a prospective one. Maternal instincts are strong in her. These instincts are a great power. . . ."[8] One of the most powerful mother symbols and images in Russian culture, and one of great conflict for the Bolsheviks, was that of the *Bogomater'*, the mother of God. Although Soviet Russia was officially an atheist state, this mother image retained resonance. To this day, icons of the Mother and Child have been carried with soldiers, displayed in demonstrations, in the workplace, the home, and the church.

The myth of the mother extended from God (or the Party[9]) to the nation. If the tsar became the *batiushka*, Russia itself (or, as commonly said, herself) came to be thought of as a common mother (*matiushka*). Although Peter did change the country's gender from feminine (*matiushka Rus'* and *rodina*, motherland) to masculine (*otechestvo*, or fatherland) in official language,[10] popular use of feminine tropes continued. This duality in national references allowed the regime to appeal to various unconscious beliefs for its desired purpose. For example, calls to serving the Fatherland reinforce patriarchal power and hark back to female altruism and the myth of female martyrs for the Russian man. Alternatively, proclaiming the power and mission of the Motherland reinforces the mission and myth of motherhood.

Female myths, including the myth of the mother, found expression in the political iconography of the 1920s. Political posters, sculptures, and coins popularized gender images, and their public display played a significant role in political socialization and development of self-definition.[11] Male figures were chosen to personify the Bolshevik regime; the "liberated worker" was a man.[12] When women did appear in political posters extolling the liberation of the worker—posters directed toward both sexes—they were most likely to be in a subordinate position. Women either represented backwardness, the peasantry, or they were passive and subordinate. While the initial focus on the laborer and the official antipathy toward religion increased the mother image's disutility, the image resurfaced by the mid-1920s in realistic posters directed toward a female audience. These images were used extensively, for example, in the campaign to introduce modern child care methods,[13] and reinforced the notion that child care was exclusively a female domain.

There was a clear distinction in the official iconography between propaganda directed toward women and propaganda directed toward men or a mixed audience. Women took a constructive, dynamic, and positive role only in those images intended for a female audience. Literature aimed exclusively at women presented strong, intense, studious, working women, liberated by Soviet law. For example, the frontispiece of a 1928 brochure, "The Working Woman in Industry," depicted a young *proletarka* studying by the light of a factory smokestack.[14] The front covers of *Rabotnitsa* and *Kommunistka* regularly portrayed strong, active women busily contributing to the new society. One poster contrasted the disenfranchised, hungry woman abroad with the healthy Soviet female university student liberated through law.[15] In posters intended for a male or mixed audience, however, women shown in a positive light were engaged in subordinate positions, assisting the male worker. Women could still infer from these images, however, that they had a constructive and affirmative role in shaping their new world.

Other posters, intended again for a "general" (read: male) audience, had a decidedly negative, if implicit, message: women were backward (peasants or village folk healers), or even dangerous. Dangerous women might be prostitutes, who carried disease, or disease itself: one poster urging the boiling of water to ensure its purity warned against the threat of cholera, represented in the form of a grotesque, scarlet, large-breasted female figure.[16] These posters were displayed in schools, in the streets, in public buildings, and in the workplace, to inspire and inculcate the morals, values, and definitions of the New Soviet Man and Woman.

These images and myths of women interacted with myths about law propagated at the same time. Myths about law held that women's emancipation, or formal gender equality, could be established by legal decree. Further, according to the myth, one of the great achievements of Bolshevik power was precisely this establishment of legal equality. Western critics and, more recently, Russian critics[17] argue that even if the Soviet system failed to provide actual equality, it did provide legal, or formal equality. In fact, as I suggest below, gender myths were so embedded in Soviet legislation and legal practice that the notion of formal equality itself was a myth, supported only by official rhetoric and propaganda. Soviet legislation was so engendered that it institutionalized, rather than eradicated, gender inequality.

Early Soviet Legislation and Institutions to Liberate Women

Through law, policy, and socialization, the Bolshevik leaders perpetuated the Russian myth that women (and motherhood) need protection. They organized state and Party agencies to protect working women, mothers, and children. Women needed protection from the hazards on the shop floor and from various sorts of discrimination in hiring, training, promotion, and firing. In fact, as Kollontai argued, women needed protection in order to be liberated.[18] Consequently, much Soviet legislation to promote equality had "the protection of women" as its stated goal. The idea that women were weak, naive, and by nature defenseless was built into the Soviet legislative framework.[19]

Early basic labor legislation reflects the primacy of the myth and image of all women as mothers. Broad proclamations of equal treatment, regardless of sex, were accompanied by or followed more specific decrees or provisions with protective measures for women. Compare the 1918 constitution and the initial minimum wage and health insurance decrees, for example, with the Eight-Hour Law (establishing an eight-hour working day), promulgated one week after the Revolution (and before all the sex-neutral statutes). The general provisions of the statute are set forth in gender-neutral terms ("1. This law applies to all . . . persons employed in hired labor"). The specific provisions of the statute, however, reflect the concept of "equality *plus*."[20] Women were prohibited from night work (defined as from 9:00 P.M. to 6:00 A.M.), from overtime work, and from underground work.[21] Implicit or explicit in these regulations of conditions for women in the workforce was the assumption that all women are, or will be, mothers. The root of the ban on night work as expressed by the Bolsheviks lay in the belief that it was harmful to the woman's reproductive system,[22] and would interfere with women's ability to care for their children at home.[23]

The early legislation also served to institutionalize the existing sex-segregation of the labor force. Regulations listed professions and sectors of industry prohibited to women,[24] while others detailed professions reserved for women or for which women should be given preference.[25] Numerous studies were commissioned to examine the effects of certain jobs on women's reproductive capacities.[26] The 1918 Labor Code and subsequent legislation in the 1920s further defined maternity leave and special benefits accorded pregnant and nursing women.[27] These regulations, drafted as part of the labor code, were regarded both as labor regulations and as components for securing women's equality. The Bolsheviks declared such "protection" of women necessary to achieve equality. The underlying view of woman, however, saw her not as worker, but as mother. Male workers needed protection as workers. Women workers, in contrast, needed protection as mothers.

Particularly in the early 1920s, when support for the Bolshevik regime was tenuous and women offered a critical constituency to ensure the Bolshevik hold on power, the leadership, especially the women, exhorted the triumph of Soviet power and what it offered women. Instrumental in this period was the *Zhenotdel* (the "Women's Department" of the Communist Party), established in 1919 to advance the cause of women's emancipation. In countless speeches, meetings, and periodical articles, Inessa Armand, Alexandra Kollontai, Sofia Smidovich, Alexandra Artiukhina, and other zhenotdel activists trumpeted the legal achievements of the Bolsheviks, specifically, the establishment of legal equality and the emancipation of Soviet women. Explicitly, they cheered the achievement of legal equality; implicitly, the nature of law itself that brought about this success.[28] The zhenotdel spread this message throughout the country by organizing meetings and conferences which were designed to indoctrinate and to raise women's political consciousness. These meetings could be as small as a neighborhood or factory sewing circle, or as large as an All-Union conference with delegates transported in from all over the Soviet Union. The zhenotdel distributed guidelines, agenda for community and regional meetings, and texts for discussion.

The agenda for these meetings invariably included basic legislation on women's emancipation. The meeting leaders informed the women that these laws would establish their equality and deliver them from the drudgery of housework.[29] They encouraged women to write their local zhenotdel offices with stories of how their lives had improved since the Revolution.[30] Working women were brought in from all over the country to large conferences in Moscow and regional centers, where they spoke about how their lives had changed for the better as a result of Bolshevik rule. They extolled the new legislation that gave them the freedom to divorce, the vote, and a voice in political life. This, no doubt, nurtured the development of a nascent legal consciousness,[31] encouraging working women to believe that the law offered some guarantee of their new rights.

The limitations of Bolshevik legal policy toward women become evident where the myths about law and women converge. The Bolsheviks contended that women would be free only if they entered the wage labor force.[32] Only a monetary wage could offer women economic independence and access to the public arena. For women to be liberated economically and psychologically, they needed to become more like men, or more specifically, more like male workers. The limitations of this policy, however, lay in the fact that the law made this impossible, because it insisted on viewing women as mothers or in reference to their maternal potential. The law made no provision for men as fathers: men were "ordinary"—or the standard—workers.

The Marxist (and Bolshevik) fixation on class and labor was so great that the theorists and leaders failed to see and, therefore, to challenge the gendered nature of the economic system. The images of women in early Marxist and Bolshevik writing reveal the acceptance of a sex-segregated workforce. Engels, for example, recognized that the attainment of legal and political equality alone would not liberate women from their subordinate position in the family; the family itself needed to cease functioning as an economic unit. This proposal, as reformulated by Alexandra Kollontai,[33] posited two conditions for the full liberation of women once private property was abolished. First, women were to have access to productive employment outside the home. Second, unpaid work performed in the home would become publicly funded paid work performed in the socialized sector. But these writers still assumed that women would perform household tasks; the difference was that the tasks would be collectively organized, performed for pay, and outside the home.[34] This transformation of the private household economy through industrialization and socialization and abolition of private ownership of the means of production would provide the foundation for complete gender equality, where both sexes would stand in an equal and identical relationship to the means of production.

Like Engels and Kollontai, the zhenotdel also did not challenge the sex-segregation of the economy, advocating only a change in venue and a paid wage for performing collectivized household tasks. Kollontai and the zhenotdel actively supported this sex-segregation by reinforcing essentialist notions of women's nature as mother, by institutionalizing them through legislation. For example, they promoted the institution of public cafeterias and nurseries to supplant the domestic economy. Their slogans extolled the liberating power of these institutions and called on women—not men—to staff them.[35]

Kollontai made this viewpoint explicit in her articulation of the Party's task regarding the working woman. One prong of the Party's task was to raise the working woman's *aktivnost'*;[36] the second was the defence of women's special interests.[37] The Party cannot simply regard a woman only as a member of the working class, only in her capacity as worker, Kollontai wrote, but as one who

> carried before society an independent, additional obligation—the carrying, birthing, and feeding of a child. Women's second additional social

obligation, peculiar to women, places before the Party the need for additional measures to protect and defend the interests, strength, and health of women, as the fundamental carrier (*nositel'nitsa*) of the family.[38]

This latter obligation obviously echoes the Russian image of the mother as the family's binding force,[39] and the notion that biology has determined that not only childbearing, but also child rearing, be predominantly, if not exclusively, a female activity.[40]

Russian history and culture worked together with the new regime's policies and ideology to reinforce old myths and images of women. These forces influenced women's views of themselves and their definitions of sexual equality. Myths of gender and of law shaped women's legal "strategies" to prod the regime to deliver on its promises in this sphere. Traditional gender roles and images confronted a working woman's nascent conception of equality as women began to challenge what they perceived as unequal treatment in the workforce. By the mid- to late-1920s, the myth of women's legal equality began to conflict with new legislation embodying the myth of the mother. By this time, ordinary Russian women did not view themselves exclusively as mothers, perhaps even as mothers first and foremost. As workers in the first "Workers' State" they could develop new perceptions of themselves and of their contribution to society. Their real-life experiences in the working world—and the desire for recognition as equal workers—clashed with an enduring myth system of "women as mothers," which became embedded in new legislation. Conflict inexorably erupted in dispute resolution proceedings where women seeking to restructure, if not eradicate, old myths and hierarchies faced male defendants and authorities who were socialized to see women in traditional ways, according to a view the regime continued to support. The remainder of this chapter explores how these myths and images influenced both men and women, and the evolution of a nascent legal consciousness, in these cases of discrimination, particularly in cases of sexual harassment. By examining the role of courts and the range and choice of dispute resolution mechanisms, it also considers why women's efforts in these cases were ultimately unavailing.

Litigating Sexual Harassment in the 1920s

Moscow and Leningrad archival materials of the period evidence a surprising number of women petitioning for redress for instances of what we would now characterize as sexual harassment. The list of institutions to which women appealed for relief is extensive. In this section I review the development of the women's causes of action, the range of options and choices they made in deciding to complain, and the procedure and outcome of selected cases.

The Biuro zhalob

A complaint department (*biuro zhalob*) of the Workers' and Peasants' Inspectorate (*Narodnyi Komissariat Raboche-Krest'ianskoi Inspektsii [RKI]* or *Rabkrin*[41]) had been set up in 1919[42] consisting of a central office in Moscow (*Tsentral'noe biuro zhalob*) and local bureaux, generally affiliated with the regional (*guberniia*) branch of the RKI.[43] Its original jurisdiction extended to complaints regarding "abuse" or "improper" or "unlawful" activity on the part of soviet organs.[44] Instructions for the establishment of local biuro zhalob affiliates in 1919 extended their jurisdiction to cases of "*gruboe otnoshenie*,"[45] literally translated as rude or crude behavior. The Instruction offered no definition of the behavioral term. In November 1924, Rabkrin, jointly with the Party's Central Control Commission, issued a seemingly innocuous circular letter[46] aiming to include more women in the work of Rabkrin and to "popularize" the work of the biuro zhalob, in particular, among working and peasant women. Specifically, Rabkrin wanted the biuro zhalob to be seen as a forum for review of complaints of "bureaucratism, red tape," and a disparaging or scornful attitude (*prenebrizhitel'noe otnoshenie*) toward workers.[47] Although the TsKK-RKI circular letter did not further define *prenebrizhitel'noe* or *gruboe otnoshenie*, it reiterated the need for working women in the countryside to keep the biuro zhalob apprised of improprieties in the activities of local state institutions.[48] As such, the biuro zhalob clearly was in part a component of Rabkrin's effort to keep tabs on local officials.[49]

This circular letter was unusual in that the leadership publicized it in the women's press. Its publication in the zhenotdel's journal, *Kommunistka,* was accompanied by a commentary by S. Smidovich, then chair of the zhenotdel.[50] Smidovich charged the local zhenotdel offices with carrying out the directives in the circular letter. (This would be done, for example, at sewing circles and other meetings.) She exhorted them to engage more women in the work of the Rabkrin, to help women understand how their involvement with Rabkrin would improve both the country and their lives in particular.[51] She made no specific reference to complaints for disparaging treatment.

Complainants could write to the biuro zhalob directly, and other agencies (newspapers, the People's Commissariat of Labor, Party offices, etc.) receiving complaints could forward them to the biuro zhalob for review.[52] The biuro could, and did, refuse to conduct investigations if it regarded the allegations as groundless or without sufficient information to justify an investigation.[53] In cases where a complaint involved "an abuse of extraordinary importance, having not only local but state meaning," or when the head of the local biuro could see by the circumstances of the complaint that the local authorities did not have the power to address the problem, he could direct it to the Central Biuro zhalob, which was not under the authority of the *guberniia* (region) or *uezd* (district) in which the problem resided.[54] The local Party or professional organization appointed the head of the local biuro zhalob.[55]

Complaints to the biuro were filed with a docket sheet recording the working status of the complainant, the subject matter area of the complaint, the issue of the complaint, the action taken, and in what period of time the complaint was addressed and closed.[56] The docket sheet did not record the name and gender of the complainant. Neither did reviews of biuro zhalob activity and the complaints received tend to consider the gender of the complainants.[57] A random survey of hundreds of complaints in the Central Biuro zhalob files revealed far more complaints by men than women.[58] While a full study of biuro zhalob cases is beyond the scope of this chapter, within the context of unequal treatment on the job it is striking to note that many more men than women complained about improper dismissals, even though the unemployment rate for women was higher, employers favored male workers, growth was centered in traditionally male sectors of the economy through at least the mid-1920s, and female workers were more likely than male workers to be displaced.[59]

Biuro zhalob instructions outlining case procedure and management for its officials did not contain standards for complaint review,[60] leaving the biuro with considerable discretion. As an example of its arbitrary power of discretion, it is important to note that the biuro itself regularly violated its own procedural regulations. The biuro zhalob procedural *Instruktsii* of 1919 and 1926 plainly state that in no way were anonymous complaints to be accepted.[61] Further instructions state that anonymous complaints were to be destroyed (except if the contents of the complaint indicated some great danger to state security).[62] Irrespective of the prohibition against anonymous complaints, the biuro zhalob files nonetheless contain anonymous complaints that triggered investigations.[63]

There is no doubt that, at least to some degree, granting the biuro jurisdiction over cases involving disparaging behavior toward workers reflected an ideological (Marxist-Leninist) concern among elites with the attitudes of management and other superiors toward their subordinates. Neither the circular nor any accompanying commentary offered a more explicit definition of what *"prenebrizhitel'noe otnoshenie"* encompassed. Moreover, the biuro had the discretionary power to pursue and investigate a defendant beyond the scope of the issue set forth in the complaint. All told, these factors, as well as those mentioned above, facilitated the use of the biuro zhalob as a means of arbitrary and discretionary state control, rather than as an agency ensuring the accountiblity of public officials.

Although the cases discussed below suggest that working women complainants invoking *"gruboe," "gnusnoe,"* and *"prenebrizhitel'noe otnoshenie"* interpreted these terms quite broadly, it is highly unlikely that the Bolshevik leadership intended the biuro zhalob (or any other legal or administrative agency, for that matter) to address what we now view as sexual harassment. Indeed, it is doubtful that their notion of a "disparaging attitude" toward workers encompassed that concept.[64] It is further unlikely that the male Party leadership conceived of the eradication of gender harassment as an element of gender equality. Nor do the writings of prominent women in the Party seem to make that connection, since their conception of equality encompassed only a working wage and deliverance from uncompensated housework. They did not consider the *environment* in which that wage was earned, or demands made for its payment or increase. An examination of factors influencing the average working woman's vision of legal equality and emancipation, in contradistinction to the leaders' views, is necessary to understand how the consciousness of some working women evolved and how these women came to pursue their complaints. It is also instructive to examine how these claims originated, why they increased as the decade progressed, and why they extended beyond the Biuro zhalob into other venues.

The Genesis of Complaints for Disparaging Treatment

First, for several reasons, women began to regard courts and other dispute resolution tribunals as receptive to their concerns. The 1918 Family Code offered women greater opportunities to go to court for divorce, alimony, paternity determination, and support, than had been available under the imperial regime. The 1926 Family Code transferred jurisdiction for these cases to an administrative agency (ZAGS[65]), thereby lessening the role of courts *per se* and increasing the status of administrative agencies in the adjudication of women's "problems." Goldman reports a sharp increase in women's petitioning in court (or ZAGS) by the middle of the decade.[66] Women who had been married, as well as those in brief or temporary unions, successfully sued their partners for support. Women who gave birth after being forced to submit to the sexual advances of their employers or co-workers, or as a result of sexual favors exchanged for promises of employment, also received court-ordered child support.[67] At least through the first half of the 1920s, judges reportedly employed very flexible standards for determining paternity, relying heavily on the petitioning woman's testimony.[68] Women therefore had grounds to regard both the courts and administrative agencies as legal institutions that might afford them relief.

Second, 1927 was the tenth anniversary of the Revolution. The press was filled with articles, and the streets with posters, trumpeting the achievements of Communist power. The zhenotdel organized numerous meetings, congresses, and conferences to extol the virtues of the regime, including the equality bestowed upon them by Soviet law.[69] These meetings also allowed women the opportunity to note the degree to which full "equality" had not yet been achieved.[70] They compared notes about discrimination they experienced at work and the opposition they encountered from managers, foremen, or other male workers who believed women had no place in the workplace.[71] Hearing the offensive treatment of other women may have allowed some women to recognize their own discrimination experiences, helped them articulate these experiences, and motivated them to seek redress. Alternatively, the contradiction between the glorious, liberated present depicted by the anniversary propaganda and the reality of a hostile working environment for women, or of unemployment precipitated or prolonged by refusal to provide sexual services to employers or officials at the labor exchanges,[72] may have impelled some women to petition.

Agendas and transcripts of local zhenotdel meetings after 1924 reflect a more detailed and expanded notion of what equality necessitated: notes for a report to be given at a 1927 Leningrad oblast' zhenotdel meeting, for example, state that speakers at almost all the local and regional meetings noted the inattentive and disparaging attitude toward the work of women on the part of their male leaders.[73] They mention that women are systematically excluded from positions of power, are denied skills training, and that additional benefits are allotted exclusively to men.[74] They complain that men mock zhenotdel activities, have no respect for women or their performance at work, and expect women to fulfill identical quotas as male workers, but with inferior equipment.[75] They then call for the elimination of such disparaging attitudes toward women on the part of men.[76]

Another factor possibly stimulating the increase in claims filed after about 1926 was the growing tendency to complain about insults and other "shortcomings" occurring in the workplace.[77] The Bolsheviks actively promoted this culture of complaint. They touted governmental control (including Rabkrin/Biuro zhalob court oversight[78]) and citizen complaints against red tape, "bureaucratism," and abuses by local officials.[79] Further, they set up legal consultation points (*konsul'tatsii*) throughout the cities to advise workers on legal issues and to assist them in pursuing claims. Leningrad, for example, had two to five consultation points for the six districts (*raiony*) by July 1929.[80]

Public complaining became more popular with the increased frequency of production meetings (*proizvodstvennye soveshchaniia*) from late 1926 through at least 1929, which were designed in part as a forum for workers to publicize shortcomings and "abnormalities" in production, management, and factory life.[81] Although women were less inclined than men to attend production meetings[82]—and once there less inclined than men to speak[83]—press accounts,[84] books intended for working women,[85] and Party documents[86] indicate an official attempt to stimulate female attendance and participation. These meetings promoted the culture of criticism, which, while they may have included the pursuit of personal vendettas,[87] offered an additional venue for complaints of (and learning about) "disparaging," rude, or crass behavior toward women. Emotions, complaints, and the frequency of criticism accelerated in 1928 with the Central Committee appeal "On the Development of Self-Criticism,"[88] along with the official campaign against the bourgeois *spetsy* (specialists), which invited a flood of denunciations by workers. Women were encouraged to use the production meetings and criticism to air and remedy the problems inhibiting their professional advancement and other travails of their lives.[89] Finally, in all of these instances, public posters may have inspired or encouraged some petitions. Women came to believe that their complaints were part of a constructive effort in building the new society that included equality for them.

Archival data reveal that working women had a broader view of the prerequisites of this equality, especially labor equality. Beyond formal legal guarantees, they believed that these guarantees needed to be enforced. Working women repeatedly asserted the desire to be viewed "equally" as a worker (*rabotnitsa*), not just as a woman. Women had to be guaranteed equal opportunities for hiring, training, performance, and promotion, and a work environment free from harassment and abuse. Their notion of equality made violations of these guarantees, including freedom from "disparaging treatment," actionable and held men who violated these standards accountable and punishable for their actions.[90]

Complaints by ordinary female workers indicate how they defined the "disparaging, crass, and rude" behavior meriting legal action.[91] These instances involved the classic *quid pro quo*, an exploitation of power by men in authority—superiors demanded sexual favors in return for employment, promotions, or registration at the labor exchanges.[92] These claims included discriminatory activity in which employers fired only pregnant and nursing women, replacing them with men in a "factory reorganization" in an effort to "rationalize" the factory's operations;[93] or circumstances in which the employer technically complied wth the law, but in such a way as to create an "intolerable environment" for the female employees.[94] In one case in this last category, for example, an employer provided a room for the exclusive use of mothers nursing their children. The nursing station, however, was placed in an area of the factory so distant from the locations in which women worked that it was impossible to get to the station, feed the baby, and return to one's tasks in the time allotted; women inevitably returned late to their posts, for which they would be reprimanded, and were unable to meet their quotas, eliciting further demerits.[95] In other allegations, women complained of working in circumstances of constant ridicule (gendered in content),[96] in which they are taunted that all women are "baby,"[97] or that they are incapable of competent work as miners, engineers, plasterers, or some other profession (usually one that previously had been male-dominated). In some cases, women alleged that they worked with the constant threat of violence by male workers in their factory.[98] Sometimes these cases extended beyond taunting, insults, and threats to actual physical attacks.[99] Women complained about offensive treatment both by male bosses and other male workers.[100] In other cases, women were held to the same standards as men but forced to perform with no training and inferior equipment.[101] They were ostracized and their machinery sabotaged.[102] Appeals to authorities usually fell on deaf ears.

Filing Complaints

Having their complaints ignored did not deter some Soviet women: they simply appealed elsewhere. The absence of any clear jurisdictional and decision-making hierarchy led to the filing of complaints throughout the legal and administrative apparatus; apart from the biuro zhalob, women could and did complain to as many as 32 different offices or agencies for redress. These included Party agencies (the local or central zhenotdel offices, local or national Party committees); governmental agencies (the Commissariat of Justice, or *Narkomiust*; the procuracy for labor cases [*po trudovym delam*], the people's courts; Rabkrin labor inspectors); union or factory committees (*fabkomy*; *zavkomy*; the RKK [rates and disputes commission], foremen or management officials); and the press, where the legal department of a newspaper or journal might investigate and/or forward a complaint to one of these other agencies for complaints of particular merit or Party interest.[103] In some instances, ad hoc committees could be convened to hear these complaints, before or after the petitioner sought judicial recourse.[104] In 1929, yet another forum was established whose jurisdiction included these claims: the industrial-comrades' courts (*proizvodstvenno-tovarishcheskie sudy*).[105] Complainants often filed petitions in several fora at the same time to increase the chances that at least one agency would act, or provoke another agency to investigate and pursue the matter.[106] The plethora of complaints and conflicting dispositions illustrate an absence of clear authority and hierarchy among these agencies relative to one another. The biuro zhalob could be a forum of original or appellate jurisdiction. Any court or Party decision (at least through the guberniia level) could, and often would, be appealed at any time to the biuro zhalob. The biuro could effectively vacate the prior decisions, conduct an investigation *de novo*, then issue its own ruling or transfer the case to another agency for disposition.[107]

Finally, women also sent appeals to individual Party leaders, from the head of the local Party committee to national leaders such as Stalin and Kalinin, a practice reminiscent of the pre-Revolutionary appeals to the tsar for relief. Although these personal appeals were frequently forwarded to the biuro zhalob, their existence reflects one of the major shortcomings of the Soviet system, namely the tendency to go *outside* the established legal or administrative system for relief.

This is not to suggest that women definitively opted not to go to court to pursue sexual harassment claims. The available records of such cases in Soviet Russia during this period do indicate, however, that despite positive judicial reception to cases of paternity and support, women believed that alternative fora might be more receptive to their claims about their working environment. They did so for several reasons. First, as discussed above, women were pressed to pursue other avenues. Zhenotdel leaders and the press encouraged them to appeal to their union committees, factory directors, the press, the local zhenotdel, the biuro zhalob.

Second, the jurisdiction of some of these other committees—often publicized in the press—suggested that these alternatives perhaps were more appropriate fora. Certainly in some cases involving rape, women appealed to prosecutors for the institution of criminal actions. The available evidence on the work of the procurator for labor cases does not indicate any interest or involvement of the procuracy in pursuing such cases. To the contrary, press reports suggest that the procuracy was only involved, and then only reluctantly, when cases developed a "serious nature," such as when harassment resulted in the rapes of several female workers.[108] In cases of clear statutory violations (firing pregnant women, rape), women appealed to the procuracy to file suit,[109] but in cases that pushed the definition of legal equality—indeed, cases of *gruboe otnoshenie*—alternative fora may have appeared more auspicious. The early bolshevik experiment with judge-made law did not appear to extend to these cases.[110]

Third, for women who considered their complaints to have a moral rather than a legal basis, it may have seemed logical to pursue these cases outside the traditional legal system. For example, if the defendant were a Party member, some women chose Party commissions (local control commissions) to make their claims, asserting that such immoral behavior was an internal Party matter that need not be addressed in public, through the court system.[111]

Fourth, some complained in fora with a track record of giving women a hearing. Hence, as women claiming spousal abuse often complained to, and were heard by, the local control commission at a husband's workplace,[112] women themselves at that factory might have considered it a receptive forum for other cases of disparaging treatment or abuse by male against female workers.[113]

Fifth, these complainants sought results. Consequently, they were more likely to appeal to the dispute resolution alternative they perceived as the most powerful, most likely to offer them actual relief. The supremacy of the Party over the unions was increasingly apparent by the end of the decade. Moreover, women may have inferred that the Biuro zhalob and other organs of control were more powerful than the courts, given the Biuro's ability to summarily review and scuttle both trial and appellate court decisions (as in the Tifenbakher case discussed below). The Party's devaluation of legal institutions by making them subservient to Party control organizations also kept courts weak by reducing their prestige and perceived effectiveness.[114]

The Morgunov case highlights several of these procedural issues. A senior volost' Party official defamed and harassed an unnamed female delegate at a conference. The delegate complained both to the local Party and regional Party committees about her experience, but was ignored. Morgunov, who appeared to be on a campaign to expose local abuses, decided to pursue the delegate's claim. He filed three petitions simultaneously with the Central Biuro zhalob, the Central Committee of the Party, and Narkomiust. In response to Morgunov's complaint, both the Biuro zhalob and the Justice Ministry commissioned independent investigations. The Central Committee forwarded the petition to the Biuro zhalob. The Party also charged the regional Control Commission (*GubKK*) with investigating the incident.

Procurator Lunin, who handled the case addressed to Narkomiust, concluded Morgunov had "complaint-itis" and did not pursue the case further. The Biuro zhalob, to the contrary, concluded the complaint was well founded. The local and regional Party committees and the regional control commission, meanwhile, held a series of secret and public meetings at which both the Biuro zhalob and the Control Commission reports were discussed and affirmed, with orders for "corresonding measures to be taken, . . . for legal violations to be identified, and for the offenders to be punished." These last two clauses appear to refer less to the instances of harassment than to internal infractions regarding the various investigations. As for the legal violations, within this maze of complaints and hearings it became apparent that someone was negligent. The regional office of Rabkrin alerted Narkomiust (and a top official of the procuracy of the Republic) to the infractions by the named procurator (Lunin), stressing that greater attention needed to be accorded to citizens' petitions and that drawing conclusions without the adequate foundation was "intolerable." Curiously, the last item in the case file is a brief note from the official stating simply that "Lunin doesn't work here anymore."[115] Perhaps a record of "corresponding measures" taken to hold the offending volost' Party official accountable was never made, or got lost in the bureaucratic morass. But it appears that, even when raised by a man, the woman's grievance mattered less than internal bureaucratic infractions.

The System's Response

How did the system respond to women's complaints? As mentioned earlier, evidence indicates that in the vast majority of instances their cases were ignored. While intially the unions were charged with addressing most worker problems, they were evidently insensitive, uninterested, indifferent, or hostile to women's grievances. Women often turned for assistance to their zhenotdel representatives, but the zhenotdel had neither authority nor power to enforce legislation nor to take direct action against offenders.[116] Although zhenotdel meetings offered an opportunity for consciousness raising where women could compare notes and commiserate about the way in which they were treated unfairly by colleagues and bosses at work,[117] the power of zhenotdel activists was limited to publicizing the issue, at meetings or through the press,[118] in the hope that publicity would prompt action by some truly empowered authority.[119]

If the authorities did not simply ignore complaints, it was more likely than not that an investigation would discard the allegations of harassment and provide no relief to the complainant. The case of one Lidia Sycheva[120] is typical. In mid-1928, Sycheva worked temporarily in a factory accounting department. Her direct superior began to accompany her home at the end of the workday, asking her questions of an increasingly personal nature, ultimately promising her that upon the dispensation of certain personal favors she would be registered as a permanent employee. Sycheva flatly declined and was immediately dismissed. She complained to the local labor exchange and requested a new job, but was unable to find further employment. Upon reporting her own experience and related improprieties committed by this employer (he circumvented the Labor Exchange in recruiting new employees, as was commonly, though unlawfully, done), Sycheva quickly found herself subjected to a series of retaliatory actions and was unable to receive relief (or a job) anywhere else. Complaints to the *zavkom* (factory committee of the union) were ignored. She then tried to complain to the factory rates and disputes commission, but by then she was branded a troublemaker despite an otherwise unblemished work record. She appealed to the Biuro zhalob, citing witnesses to several of her allegations.[121] Her petition included an affidavit delineating her work experience and job skills.[122] The RKI investigator reported that the complainant was dismissed because she was "politically unreliable," and found her assertions unfounded.[123] Curiously, the letter from the deputy director of the Biuro to Sycheva made no mention of this finding, stating simply that she had not been given a job because she lacked experience.[124] No reference was made, of course, to the *quid pro quo* that began Sycheva's travail. Finally, she was told that she could get a job only through the Labor Exchange (not through the Biuro). Sycheva's case illustrates how women's claims of sexual harassment suddenly disappeared even following an investigation, as well as the way in which sexual harassment claims typically became inflected with political accusations and denunciations.

Another illuminating case in which women's complaints were not simply dismissed was the case of the Tifenbakher factory.[125] The Tifenbakher case is most unusual in that the factory union appealed on behalf of the women complainants. The director of the factory had summarily dismissed five workers in an efficiency campaign. All were women with very young children, and some of them were pregnant. The women first went to their *fabkom* rates and disputes commission and the regional department (*gubotdel*) of the union. Both divisions objected to the dismissals but were unable to get the women reinstated. The women then filed an action in the labor court (*trudsessiia*); surprisingly, the court held that the violations were unlawful and ordered the workers reinstated. The factory director appealed the decision to the regional people's court (*gubsud*), which reviewed the case and remanded it to the trial court session for labor cases, with a different bench. At the second sitting, the court ignored the law, which, on its face, prohibited the dismissal of women who were pregnant or who had very young children, and ruled the terminations proper. In late March 1928, the local union then appealed further on behalf of the five women, both to the guberniia union office for assistance, and to the biuro zhalob. The RKI took up an investigation.

The archival evidence reveals that the investigation had little to do with the matter of the dismissed women, but was instead an excuse to harass a factory with foreign (German) connections and a capitalist past.[126] The investigations at the Tifenbakher factory occurred after the Shakhty affair in which several German and 50 Russian engineers were accused of sabotage of the coal industry. Lerkhpfel'd, the factory director, appealed to the SNK Concession Committee that the RKI investigation had been improperly conducted.[127] Internal Biuro zhalob correspondence reflects the Biuro directors' awareness that the investigators acted improperly. The file concludes with a letter to the Sovnarkom Concession Committee from the Biuro indicating that the investigations regarding the Tifenbakher women's dismissals and the subsequent court proceedings had been properly conducted, denying that the investigators were in violation of the concession agreement, but acknowledging that one investigator who exceeded his authority had been relieved of his duties.

There is no indication from the case materials that the court proceedings or their circumstances were investigated.[128] The union itself seemed interested not so much because of the women themselves, but because the women's dismissals were only the most flagrant of a series of collective agreement (*koldogovor*) violations by the factory administration.[129] The biuro zhalob appeared interested only because of a personal appeal made by the union to a senior official at the biuro. The investigator evidently queried the other infractions that the union alleged (save regarding the women) and then carried on with their own agenda—perhaps inspired by their superiors, perhaps by the tenor of the times—in light of the Shakhty trial. In either case, concern for the women was absent, and the women did not get their jobs back.

Although women began to file or lodge complaints with numerous authorities as early as 1925, public acknowledgment of their occurrence did not appear in the press until 1927. More detailed, frequent, and extensive coverage appeared in 1928 and 1929 as the number of complaints increased. The issue of sexual harassment (disparaging treatment, hooliganism, and other abuses of women in the workplace were addressed together) was usually framed within the context of other Party concerns. The substance of women's actual claims was co-opted by zhenotdel leaders in service of higher Party goals to encourage women to participate in production meetings, to engage in criticism and self-criticism, or to promote the new industrial-comrades' courts.[130] The incidence of complaints and discussion of discriminatory treatment fell precipitously after 1930, when the Party Orgburo dissolved the zhenotdel and pronounced the Woman Question "solved."[131] Henceforth, correspondents and workers cast complaints and tales of harassment in the workplace in the past tense: perhaps when women first entered the ranks of trolley-car drivers, for example, they were ridiculed and relegated to the yards, or passengers would not board their cars; but now they have the respect of most and drive regular routes with no problems.[132] If the writer mentioned existing problems, then she might end the article with a rhetorical "Should the situation really be this way?"[133]—or suggest that women raise a ruckus about the problem—but did not propose a specific mechanism to follow or place to lodge a complaint.[134] A story that did not have a neat, happy ending would be followed by one that did.[135] Panegyrics of women's contributions to the Five Year Plan displaced discussion of gender equality and its obstacles.[136]

Given the degree to which the zhenotdel (and indeed the Party itself) co-opted working women's claims, the dispersion of complaints among numerous fora, and the existence of legislation that reinstitutionalized traditional gender myths, it is not surprising these female complainants' efforts were unavailing. But the explanation is more complex. In most, if not all, of the cases surveyed, the arbiter (to the extent he considered the merits of the woman's claims) personalized the incidents, reducing the offensive behavior to the inappropriate or illegal activity of one man or a few individuals. Personalizing the activity ignores that it is happening within a specific context, the workplace, and disregards what could have been an inherently coercive employment relationship. But it also removed the conflict from the only arena in which the state retained a serious interest and placed the controversy outside the jurisdiction of some tribunals. The "Workers' State" was most interested in its population as workers. Reducing the working woman to simply a woman took her outside the workers' movement. Since Soviet Russia denied women a separate women's movement (as their liberation was only to come through workers' liberation), personalizing a woman's dispute—or even the dispute of several women in a single factory—served to keep the claims, and especially the claimants, atomized and with no appropriate forum.

Far from being an odd exception, each of these cases alleging unequal treatment reveals efforts by women to make their voices heard. In pursuit of these efforts, women tried to frame these complaints in a discourse favorable to the regime. This was not likely to be a conscious and strategic "framing" of the issues, as a lawyer frames her client's complaint in a form and discourse so that it will be heard by a court. In other words, these cases do not prove that the mass, much less a majority, of Russian working women developed a Western notion of legal rights, and decided to engage in a campaign of strategic litigation to get these rights recognized. To the contrary, more important was the development of a consciousness of power: rather than recognizing legal institutions, within a specific hierarchy, as reasonably objective, beneficial, and effective dispute-resolution mechanisms, to which one might appeal for relief, the Soviet complainant was more likely to appeal to the authority perceived as the one with the power to provide relief.[137] Personal connections to, and the interests of, potential arbiters carried greater weight than appeals to statutory authority. This priority accorded to the personal appeal over a systematic review of all complaints according to defined standards, with defined routes of appeal, stymied the development of a legal consciousness. Instead, it encouraged citizens to develop their power consciousness. With no clear hierarchy of dispute resolution mechanisms, complaints could, and would, be filed with multiple authorities; receipt of an unfavorable result would only precipitate a reassessment of the power calculus as complainants appealed anew to the authorities—legal, administrative, Party institutions—for reconsideration of their grievance.

The importance of power consciousness further illuminates the earlier discussion of how and why women often selected extra-judicial fora to hear their complaints.[138] In determining where to appeal, women would consider who specifically might be most able to bring them results. In some areas that might be the local Party leader. Others would follow the time-honored Russian tradition of the personal petition to the tsar—or, in these cases, the central Party leaders.

It is worth noting that the attitudes of Russian men, and their response to working women, were not atypical.[139] Russian women were not alone in experiencing or reporting sexual harassment in the 1920s. Evidence exists of sexual harassment in the workplace before and after the Revolution, both inside[140] and outside Russia. For example, until they coined the term "sexual harassment," American women also sought legal redress for the injuries they perceived that did not fall squarely within recognized causes of action.[141] Like Russian women, they attempted to fit their experiences into existing legal definitions and to expand these legal definitions to capture their experiences. American women brought civil claims for rape,[142] trespass,[143] seduction,[144] and assault and battery[145] as they tried through their lawyers to translate their experiences into language—language the authorities would understand and perhaps make into law.[146]

In making their complaints, it is more likely that Russian women came to voice their claims within the context of their recent political socialization. As such, Bolshevik propaganda and rhetoric was the lens through which women came to see their grievances. Of course, once one identifies the issue, it is then strategically expedient to buttress one's argument by placing it within the context of other laws and public policy priorities. Whatever sort of discriminatory treatment they experienced, they petitioned in terms they thought the authorities might recognize. The complaints themselves were not structured with direct reference to statute, but were more likely to parrot slogans and agitprop as to how the offensive behavior violated the new law and morality. Be it "disparaging and rude treatment to workers," behavior "offensive to communist morality," "violative of the defense of the health and safety of women workers," or "unlawful activity in violation of collective labor agreements and the law," women sought to have their claims and injuries recognized, receive some sort of remedy or compensation, and have the offender punished or somehow held accountable.

Women's primary goal in complaining was to hold the perpetrator accountable for his actions. Depending upon the severity of the offense, requested relief ranged from reprimand to criminal sanction. Rarely did the women request their own transfer; more often they simply wanted to remain in their own jobs and work in an environment free from harassment. In this regard it is important to recall that unemployment, especially among women, was a serious problem throughout the 1920s. Further, in the "workers' state" it was politically hazardous to be unemployed, thereby not complying with the new social contract. Women were acutely aware and anxious of their jobs' precarious nature.[147] Fearing that a request for transfer would result in dismissal if the harassment took any form short of rape, complainants preferred to remain with their offending bosses or colleagues and only asked that the offensive behavior be terminated.

Conclusion

Despite the complaints and petitions submitted, and the articles and stories written, Russian working women had little to show for their efforts to expand the notion of legal equality to provide a remedy for sexual harassment in the workforce. The cases and materials discussed in this chapter illuminate some of the characteristics of the Soviet system that foiled these women's efforts to articulate and establish a cognizable legal interest. First, despite the brief employment of common-law methods of legal development in the early years of the regime, by the late 1920s it was not possible to change law through strategic litigation. The complexity of the system, with its overlapping and conflicting jurisdictions and the unclear hierarchy among them, made it impossible for women to achieve any sort of critical mass to provoke change. Control of information kept women isolated and unaware of the activities of other women outside their locality (except to the extent that such information was disseminated by the Party). If appeals were not simply ignored at the outset, the maze of filings, investigations, hearings, and reports made it difficult, if not impossible, for an aggrieved plaintiff to pursue her case (especially when she had lost her job and had no means of support). In some cases the matter got lost in the bureaucracy, or simply dropped once the official responsible for the matter changed employment.[148]

With no *stare decisis*, no fixed and predictable hierarchy among dispute resolution tribunals, and no independent judiciary, it was impossible to expand the law in terms not sanctioned by the Party. Women were able to receive relief in cases for support and alimony because their understanding of the law was concordant with the regime's. Not so with issues regarding women's egalitarian integration into the workforce, especially when they might conflict with or impede more important Party goals such as increased production and accelerated industrialization.[149] Party goals were primary and women's needs ancillary.

Further, encouraging—even allowing—women to seek redress through extrajudicial appeals to individuals places them outside, at best on the periphery, of the legal process. A woman's complaint could be pursued to the extent that it triggered a more important Party interest, or it could be trivialized and dismissed as just another of the innumerable (and presumably frivolous) complaints filed. In addition, the continued use of the individual appeal as a viable "administrative remedy" also retards the development and diminishes the prestige of legal institutions. Appeals to individuals reinforce the notion that all power resides in persons rather than institutions.

Finally, as discussed earlier, there were numerous other factors militating against men—be they coworkers, foremen, managers, or Party leaders—from regarding women in anything other than the traditional way. Official policy, law, and symbols all operated to reinforce traditional notions of women as mothers, as subservient and subordinate. Women believed the official propaganda that they were creating a new, equal society, where women and men did indeed work side by side, standing shoulder to shoulder. Official propaganda aimed at women supported this view and may have encouraged women to file complaints in order to prod the system into according them the respect and status they felt they deserved. Propaganda and official activity directed at men (or to a general audience) did little to dispel traditional notions. Despite the widely acknowledged need for men to be re-educated in terms of proper gender relations, no effort was expended in this regard. Moreover, even when women's claims were given a hearing, and actionable conduct of some sort was found to have occurred, the response of the regime was not to condemn the behavior; the perpetrator was unlikely to be sentenced with more than a slap on the wrist.[150]

For all these reasons, Soviet efforts to use law as a mechanism to integrate women into the workforce to achieve gender equality had limited results. Nor do conditions seem remarkably different in post-Soviet Russia. Since the collapse of the Soviet Union, numerous writers have observed the pervasive and continued sexual harassment and discriminatory treatment of Russian working women. Women workers constitute at least two-thirds of all dismissals;[151] those working do not receive equal pay for equal work; unemployment offices refuse to help women find new employment; women are required to look "sexy" and dress provocatively in interviews and on the job.[152] These reports demonstrate the futility of women's earlier attempts to secure their vision of equality in the workplace and society at large. In 1994, a Moscow woman met with her local procurator for labor issues, alleging that her boss was harassing her, demanding sexual favors, and making sexual comments about her at work. "What do you expect?—Look at how you're dressed," the female prosecutor chided the complainant. "Go home and change your clothes."

Author's note: Support for this research has been generously provided through a Ford Foundation Fellowship in International Law, an International Research and Exchanges Board (IREX) Long-Term Research Grant; and a USIA Research Grant through the American Council of Teachers of Russian (ACTR). This essay would never have been completed without the guidance and brilliance of Professor Leon L. Lipson; I dedicate it to his memory. *Zekher tzaddik livrakha.*

Notes

1. Alessandra Stanley, "Russia's Gross National Legislature," *The New York Times*, 19 January 1977: Section 4, 3.

2. See, for example, Gail W. Lapidus, *Women in Soviet Society: Equality, Development, and Social Change* (Berkeley, CA, 1979); Elizabeth Wood, "Working Women under the New Economic Policy, 1918-1928," unpublished Ph.D. dissertation (University of Michigan, 1991).

3. This study is limited to Soviet Russia (the RSFSR) and predominantly urban areas, unless indicated otherwise. (It might be noted that rural women, or their proxy, did also raise complaints of sexual harassment, but that is beyond the scope of this paper. See, e.g., *Rossiiskii gosudarstvennyi arkhiv ekonomiki* [hereafter, RGAE], *f.* 396, *op.* 10, *d.* 66: 136; *d.* 86: 278-81.)

4. Sex-role assumptions and assignments, especially within a country's national ideology, form part of a society's myth system. Of course, myth systems, especially the sex/gender myth system, are grounded in reality. This partially accounts for their tenacity. As part of a longer work that examines how the dynamic generated among gender, law, and ideology forms a durable, mutually reinforcing system, this chapter explores how the application of laws ostensibly designed to eradicate social hierarchies ironically reinforces old myths and creates a new set of inputs to further support the underlying myth system.

5. See, for example, Vera Dunham, "The Changing Image of Women in Soviet Literature," in Donald Brown, ed., *The Role and Status of Women in the Soviet Union* (New York, 1968), 65. ("Without maternal worship, in whatever form, Russian lyricism would be unrecognizable.")

6. James Billington, *The Icon and the Axe: An Interpretative History of Russian Culture* (New York, 1966), 19.

7. Joanna Hubbs, *Mother Russia: The Feminine Myth in Russian Culture* (Bloomington, IN, 1988), 237.

8. Nadezhda Krupskaia, "About Youth," in *On Education* (1940), 150, cited in Mollie Rosenhan, "Images of Male and Female in Children's Readers," in Dorothy Atkinson, Alexander Dallin, and Gail Warshofsky Lapidus, eds., *Women in Russia* (Stanford, CA, 1977), 301. Krupskaia herself had no children. She also was perhaps the only female Bolshevik aware that the economy remained sharply sex-segregated, expressing concern that women remained predominantly in subordinate, low-paying positions, and that, despite growing political socialization, they were not entering political positions of power.

9. For a discussion of Marxism/Leninism as a religion, see, e.g., Harold Berman, *Justice in the U.S.S.R.: An Interpretation of Soviet Law* (Boston, 1963), 228-32.

10. Hubbs, *Mother Russia*, 203.

11. See Elizabeth Waters, "The Female Form in Soviet Political Iconography, 1917-32," in Barbara Clements, *et al.*, eds., *Russia's Women: Accommodation, Resistance, Transformation* (Berkeley, CA, 1991), 225; Frances Bernstein, "Images of Women during the Sanitary Enlightenment of the 1920s," unpublished paper delivered at the Annual Convention of the American Association for the Advancement of Slavic Studies (17-20 November 1994) (author's files). Waters suggests that the Bolsheviks deliberately excluded the allegorical woman from their iconography: "The Bolsheviks preferred an iconography peopled by men because the revolution was largely a male event and was perceived as such by those" commissioning and designing the new symbols. Waters, "The Female Form," 232.

12. Waters, "The Female Form," 228.

13. The Department of Motherhood and Youth sponsored these posters. In the West, similar child care literature featured the infant alone. *Ibid.*, 236.

14. P. Kaminskaia, *Rabotnitsa v promyshlennosti* (1928).

15. The Institute for Contemporary Art, Museum, Public School No. 1 (Queens, NY), *The Aesthetic Arsenal: Socialist Realism under Stalin*, image 28b (1993).

16. M. Cherermnykh, *Glavpolitprosvet* #232 (July 1921). It could also be argued that the peasant woman and folk healer were regarded as dangerous as well as backward.

17. See O. Voronina, "The Mythology of Women's Emancipation in the USSR as the Foundation for a Policy of Discrimination," in Anastasia Posadskaia, ed., *Women in Russia: A New Era in Russian Feminism* (London, 1994), 37-56.

18. A. Kollontai, "Mezhdunarodnyi den' rabotnits," *Kommunistka*, 1922, No. 2: 1-4.

19. See, for example, S. Kaplun, *Okhraniaite zhenskii trud* (Moscow, 1926); A. Kollontai, "Trudovaia povinnost' i okhrana zhenskogo truda," *Kommunistka*, 1920, No. 1-2: 26-27 ("The mother is the carrier of the future. Therefore our party, and particularly the department of working women, must watch out to be sure that the measures *for the defense of women's labor* are completely implemented . . . for the most expedient use of female power" [emphasis in the original].)

20. "Equality plus" refers to the notion that women are equal, except in certain circumstances they receive additional benefits. See Wendy Williams, "The Equality Crisis: Some Reflections on Culture, Courts, and Feminism," *Women's Rights Law Reporter* VII, no. 3 (Spring 1982): 175-200.

21. "O vos'michasovom trudovom dne," Dekret Sovnarkoma ot 11 noiabria 1917, *Sobranie uzakonenii* (hereafter *SU*), 1917, No. 1, st. 10; st. 16 (underground work), st. 19 (overtime). Implementation of the ban on night work reportedly was never effective, however, primarily because women were needed in the communications services. S. Kaplun, *Zhenskii trud i okhrana ego v Sovetskoi Rossii* (Moscow, 1921); V. Lebedeva, *Okhrana materinstva i mladenchestva v Sovetskoi trudovoi respublike* (Moscow, 1921).

22. A distinction can be made between women's, Marxist/Leninist, and management's opposition to women's night work. Glickman reports that before the Revolution industry's opposition to night work for women and adolescents was rooted in economic competitiveness. (Night work in the Central Economic Region was necessary to compete with more productive areas such as St. Petersburg.) The arguments made by the St. Petersburg textile manufacturers opposing night work were couched in concerns for the morals and health of

the women workers. Rose Glickman, *Russian Factory Women: Workplace and Society, 1880-1914* (Berkeley, CA, 1984). These views were shared in the West. For example, Brief for the State of Oregon at 28-55, Muller *v.* Oregon, 208 U.S. 412 (1908), offers extensive documentation supporting maximum hours regulations for women, stressing the health and morals of women and successive generations; see also "Draft Convention concerning the Employment of Women before and after Childbirth," *International Labour Conference* (1919): 259-60; "Draft Convention Concerning the Employment of Women during the Night," *International Labour Conference* (1919): 260-61. (These draft conventions were in part a response to the Bolshevik Revolution.) See also Permanent Court of International Justice, Interpretation of the Convention of 1919 Concerning Employment of Women during the Night, Advisory Opinion of 15 November 1932, Series A/B, No. 50, at 373. The Russians also believed that lifting and carrying heavy weights would interfere with the menstrual cycle and cause a "confusion" (*smeshenie*) of a woman's sexual organs. Tsentral'nyi gosudarstvennyi arkhiv, Moscow (hereafter TsGA), *f.* 390-A, *op.* 21, *d.* 38: 49.

23.   Kaplun, *Okhraniaite zhenskii trud*; see also TsGA, *f.* 390-A, *op.* 21, *d.* 37: 44 (that women cannot even be retained in the evenings because they must run home to care for their children).

24.   *Kodeks zakonov o trude* (hereafter *KZoT*) (Moscow, 1922) included a special section dealing with women and minors. It prohibited the employment of women, regardless of pregnancy or motherhood, in occupations involving heavy work, work detrimental to health, or underground work. *KZoT* (1922g.) Sec. XIII, Arts. 129-37. The People's Commissariat of Labor, in cooperation with the trade unions, was to compile a list of such occupations. Art. 129. Pregnant and nursing women were "unconditionally" (*bezuslovno*) prohibited from nightwork and overtime work. Art. 131. The Commissariat and the unions also were to set norms for excessive loads and the like. See also Judith Grunfeld, "Women's Work in Russia's Planned Economy," *Social Research* IX, no. 1 (February 1942): 22, 37-38.

25.   Norton Dodge, *Women in the Soviet Economy* (Baltimore, 1966), 63.

26.   See, for example, *Gosudarstvennyi arkhiv Rossiiskoi Federatsii* (hereafter GARF), *f.* 5515, *op.* 13, *d.* 13: 14 (discussing a study done on the effects of carrying heavy loads on a woman's reproductive capacity); TsGA, *f.* 390-A, *op.* 21, *d.* 43: 63.

27.   "Kodeks zakonov o trude" (1918), *SU*, 1918, No. 10, st. 87-88; *KZoT* (1918), Art. 89, *Primechanie*; *KZoT* (1922), Arts. 131-34.

28.   GARF, *f.* 3316, *op.* 49, *d.* 6.

29.   See "Materialy k besede 'Obshchestvenno-pravovoe polozhenie zhenshchiny'," in *Zhenshchina i byt: Materialy po rabote sredi zhenshchin v klube krasnom ugolke, obshchezhitii zhenkruchke i pr.* (Moscow, 1926). "Article 64 of the 1928 Constitution established women's equality with men's. . . ." "Materialy k besede," 41. "The proletarian court defends the rights of the unmarried woman and her child." "Materialy k besede," 44. See also Iu. Esbe, *Chto dala Oktiabr'skaia revoliutsiia zhenshchine* (undated). Presumably housework would be less onerous were it compensated. There was no suggestion that housework would suddenly become *enjoyable* once it was collectivized, except insofar as it developed a new social meaning: women working in this new social sector would be supporting a significant public institution of the socialist enterprise.

30. See *Tsentr khraneniia dokumentov noveishei istorii Iaroslavskoi oblasti* (TsKhDNI IaO), *f.* 1, *op.* 27, *d.* 3220-3221.

31. The notion of what constitutes a legal consciousness remains contested and murky; its analysis is beyond the scope of the present work. An exploration of legal consciousness and how it relates to a power consciousness (as discussed below) will be addressed in another work.

32. Bolshevik feminism differed from Western feminism in that for Western women political emancipation was the goal. For the Bolsheviks, including the women, political emancipation was only the beginning and made sense only within the context of and as an instrument furthering the socialist revolution. Lenin, Bebel, and Kollontai argued that the development of an independent women's movement and the struggle for special rights for women (not for the transformation of society as a whole) was bourgeois, serving to divert the mass of women from the revolutionary struggle. Thus were women's interests subordinated to those of the (male led) "working class."

33. A. Kollontai, *Sotsial'nye osnovy zhenskogo voprosa* (St. Petersburg, 1909).

34. F. Engels, *Der Ursprung*, 77-83, cited in Alfred G. Meyer, "Marxism and the Women's Movement," in Atkinson, *et al.*, eds., *Women in Russia*, 85, 94-95.

35. This extended beyond slogans directed at women. In an article extolling the virtues of socialized upbringing of children, senior Party economist E. Preobrazhenskii clearly evinces the assumption that women would staff the nurseries: "If in an individual family one mother will raise 3-5 of her own children, through socialized upbringing one woman on average will raise 5-10 children that are not her own (*chuzhikh detei*). . . ." E. Preobrazhenskii, "Put' k raskreposhcheniiu zhenshchiny," *Kommunistka*, 1920, No. 7: 20.

36. *Aktivnost'* refers to a person's level of engagement or participation in Party activities.

37. Kollontai, "Mezhdunarodnyi den'," 1.

38. *Ibid.*, 1. See also A. Kollontai, "Rabotnitsa i organizatsiia proizvodstva," *Kommunistka*, 1920, No. 1-2: 23, 26 ("The mother is the carrier of the future . . .").

39. Billington, *The Icon and the Axe*, 19-20.

40. See also Preobrazhenskii, "Put' k raskreposhcheniiu," 19-21. Rosenhan, in her discussion of images of women in Soviet children's literature (note 7 above), notes that only women are represented in nurturing, child rearing roles.

41. *Rabkrin* is a contraction of *Raboche-Krest'ianskaia Inspektsiia*. In 1923, the RKI merged with the Central Control Commission (TsKK) and effectively became one agency (TsKK-RKI). Ostensibly the RKI's jurisdiction included state organs; the TsKK's, the Party.

42. "O gosudarstvennom kontrole," Dekret VTsIKa (*SU*, 1919, No. 12, st. 122); "Instruktsiia biuro zhalob" (*SU*, 1919, No. 23, st. 27); "Instruktsiia iacheikam sodeistviia Raboche-Krest'ianskoi Inspektsii," ch. 5, reprinted in *Chto takoe R.K.I. i ee zadachi* (Moscow, 1919); "Polozhenie o mestnykh otdeleniiakh Tsentral'nogo Biuro zhalob i zaiavlenii," *Izvestiia*, 24 May 1919.

43. "Instruktsiia iacheikam sodeistviia," at V.(1).

44. *Ibid.* at V.

45. TsGA SPb, *f.* 8, *op.* 1, *d.* 3342a: 101.

46. "Narkom RKI SSSR, Tsirkuliarno No. 15 (17 November 1924), Vsem KK i RKI: O formakh privlecheniia zhenshchin-rabotnits k rabote organov RKI," *Kommunistka*, 1924, No. 12: 13 (hereafter TsKK-RKI circular letter).

47. TsKK-RKI circular letter, 14. "Workers" in this context appears in the "gender-inclusive" masculine plural (*prenebrizhitel'noe otnoshenie k trudiashchimsia*), presumably applying to both men and women. Elsewhere the circular is specifically concerned with the increased involvement of working women. One explicit aim of the circular is to encourage female workers and peasants in the work of the biuro zhalob. The language of the circular is silent as to whether it is concerned with a disparaging attitude on the part of employers, coworkers, local officials, or all these groups.

48. *Ibid.*

49. For a broader analysis of the *Rabkrin* and the Central Control Commission, see Robert V. Daniels, *The Conscience of the Revolution: Communist Opposition in Soviet Russia* (Cambridge, MA, 1960); Leonard Schapiro, *The Communist Party of the Soviet Union* (New York, 1960); and S. N. Ikonnikov, *Sozdanie i deiatel'nost' ob"edinennykh organov TsKK-RKI v 1923-1924 gg.* (Moscow, 1971).

50. S. Smidovich, "O privlechenii rabotnits k rabote organov RKI," *Kommunistka*, 1924, No. 12: 13.

51. Smidovich's comments were not the first to appeal for increased female participation in Rabkrin. The Rabkrin labor inspectors were regarded as important watchdogs to ensure the enforcement of protective labor legislation for women. Further, active involvement in Rabkrin was expected to raise the workers' political consciousness and increase their sense of engagement with productive processes. See, e.g., V. Avanesov, "Uchastie rabotnits v Raboche-Krest'ianskoi Inspektsii," *Kommunistka*, 1920, No. 6: 8. For a discussion of how Lenin regarded women's participation in Rabkrin as especially important, and how local branches of the zhenotdel worked to increase female participation in Rabkrin, see G. T. Uvarova, *Zhenotdely partiinykh komitetov Tsentral'nogo Chernozem'ia, 1921-1927 gg.* (1975).

52. See, e.g., GARF, *f.* 374, *op.* 28, *d.* 3502. The newspaper *Pravda* had its own investigation bureau, which would forward materials it had collected or received to Rabkrin (of the relevant jurisdiction), ask that a careful investigation be conducted, that *Pravda* be informed of the results, and that the materials be returned. TsGA SPb, *f.* 8, *op.* 1, *dd.* 3372-3373. *Rabochaia gazeta* had form sheets with which its legal department would send clippings or materials to the offending factory, to the biuro zhalob, or to another local office of the RKI requesting that "corresponding measures" be taken. TsGA SPb, *f.* 8, *op.* 1, *d.* 3369. It was not the women's press that engaged in this triage for the Buiro zhalob, but more general interest newspapers such as *Leningradskaia pravda*, *Trud*, *Krest'ianskaia gazeta*, and *Izvestiia*, among others. See, e.g., TsGA SPb, *f.* 8, *op.* 1, *d.* 3369 (*Izvestiia*), d. 3370 (various papers), and *dd.* 3378-3382 (*Leningradskaia pravda*).

53. TsGA SPb, *f.* 8, *op.* 1, *d.* 3369: 101-103.

54. TsGA SPb, *f.* 8, *op.* 1, *d.* 3342a: 7.

55. *Instruktsiia*, TsGA SPb, *f.* 8, *op.* 1, *d.* 3324a. It is most likely that even if appointed by the local professional organization, it was with Party consent or pursuant to Party suggestion.

56. GARF, *f.* 374, *op.* 28, *d.* 2583. In part, the docket sheet reads as follows: "A. Who is complaining? (underline answer) 1. Worker 2. Peasant . . . 4. Member of the Red Army or veteran 5. Student 6. Invalid 7. Craftsman or person of free profession 8. Non-working element 9. State or social organization 10. Organ of press B. On what question? 11. Land 12. Forest 13. Labor 14. Health and Human Services . . . 17. Tax 18. Judicial-Legal 19. Industrial . . . 21.Transport and communications . . . 24. Soviet democracy C. What is the complaint? 25. Improper decision 26. Red tape 27. Rude-disparaging behavior 28. Mismanagement 29. Organizational defects in the *apparat* . . . D. What was done in regard to the complaint? 31. Transferred to a different agency 32. Reviewed by the Biuro zhalob 33. Investigated and not affirmed 36. Penalty (fine) imposed on offender 37. Matter transferred to court. E. In what time period was the complaint discharged? 38. 5 days 39. 10 days 40. 20 days 41. 30 days 42. 2 months 43. longer than 2 months."

57. See, e.g., "Otchet biuro zhaloba Leningradskoi oblasti za 1924," 1-6, 1924, GARF, *f.* 374, *op.* 21, *d.* 98; also *op.* 28, *d.* 2989: 11-47. One report did note, however, that all those complaining "in the name of Krupskaia" were women. GARF, *f.* 374, *op.* 28, *d.* 2989: 34. While the legal department of the Leningrad oblast' Council of Trade Unions regularly tallied the work of the member unions according to the number of clients, subject matter areas of law (labor, land tax, criminal, administrative, etc.) addressed, number of lawsuits filed, and number of instances in which legal department members appeared in court or before the organs of the *Narkomtruda*, again, the gender of complainants was not considered. TsGA SPb, *f.* 6276, *op.* 266, *d.* 1 (containing quarterly, statistical reports of the legal work of oblast' labor unions from 1925 through 1930). Similarly, a review of the Special Session of the People's Court for Labor Cases for the City of Leningrad considered the social status of the claimant (worker, peasant, *sluzhashchie*, etc.) and the statutory grounds of cases filed, but did not report the gender of the petitioners. TsGA SPb, *f.* 6276, *op.* 266, *d.* 3: 12.

58. While not evident from the docket sheet, review of an entire case file would reveal the complainant's gender, either through the complainant's name or through the Russian language, which is gender sensitive.

59. For an extensive discussion of the reasons for and the structures of female unemployment, see Wood, "Working Women under the New Economic Policy," 197-275.

60. Investigators conducting any investigation pursuant to a complaint, however, were required to prepare an investigative report (*akt*), signed by the investigator and all those present at the investigation. *Instruktsii o poriadke proizvodstva sotrudnikami BZh i zaiavlenii obsledovanii 1-go aprelia 1921 g.* TsGA SPb, *f.* 8, *op.* 1, *d.* 3342a: 125.

61. *Ibid.*: 1, 38.

62. *Ibid.*

63. See, for example, GARF, *f.* 374, *op.* 28, *d.* 2994: 65. A more extensive study of the Biuro zhalob proper would be necessary to determine what sorts of complaints immediately triggered investigations, received speedy hearings, whether this varied among jurisdictions, whether there was any consistent rationale to such decisions, or whether all was subject to the vagaries of individual officials.

64. There can be little doubt, however, that for Russian women, the terms *gruboe* or *prenebrizhitel'noe otnoshenie* have come to signify the American notion of sexual harassment. In researching this paper, I have talked to countless Russian women (and men). Explaining that I was researching legal claims of *gruboe* or *prenebrizhitel'noe otnoshenie k zhenshchinam*—with no elaboration—repeatedly sparked smiles, nods, and comments: "Yes, we know that is now a hotly debated topic in the United States, the creation of a hostile atmosphere for working women"; or "yes, we read about that case of the female law professor and the judge" (alluding to the confirmation hearings of US Supreme Court Justice Clarence Thomas). These conversations of the 1990s contain the same language and concepts used in the materials from the 1920s and 1930s cited in this article.

65. The State Registry Office (*Zapis' aktov grazhdanskogo sostoianiia*).

66. Wendy Goldman, *Women, the State and Revolution* (Cambridge, MA, 1993), 134-35.

67. *Ibid.*, citing A. Stel'makhovich, *Dela ob alimentakh* (Moscow, 1926), 134-35.

68. *Ibid.* There were, however, serious difficulties in collecting support awards.

69. See TsGAIPD, *f.* 81, *op.* 1, *d.* 149: 1-2 (women of Uritskii Tobacco Factory discuss new laws and rights).

70. GARF, *f.* 3316, *op.* 49, *d.* 6.

71. See TsGAIPD, *f.* 81, *op.* 1, *d.* 74: 105; *f.* 16, *op.* 13, *d.* 13171: 3-4; and "Nam ne nado Lentiaev," *Tabachniki Uritskogo*, 26 October 1927: 2 (male metalworkers delay repairing women's machines and women are blamed); *f.* 81, *op.* 1, *d.* 88: 21 (complaints that unskilled men are paid less than skilled women); *d.* 95: 27 (husbands interfering with their wives' educations) (Uritskii Tobacco Factory).

72. Labor exchanges, formally introduced by the government in 1918, were to serve as a state monopoly on hiring workers and employees. Although they fell into desuetude during the Civil War, they were revived with the 1922 Labor Code, which mandated that all employers "without exception" hire through their intermediacy. *KZoT* (1922), Art. 7. All persons desiring employment were to register with their local labor exchange, where they were then to be placed on a first-come-first-served list. Abuses were common. Wood, "Gender and Politics in Soviet Russia," 53, citing M. Nefedov, "Itogi raboty Petrogradskikh Birzhi Truda za 1922," *Voprosy truda*, 1923, No. 3: 71.

73. *Tsentral'nyi gosudarstvennyi arkhiv istoriko-politicheskikh dokumentov Sankt-Peterburga* (hereafter TsGAIPD SPb), *f.* 24, *op.* 8, *d.* 3: 13.

74. *Ibid.*: 15, 20, 27.

75. *Ibid.*

76. *Ibid.*: 13.

77. The distinction between home and the workplace is often less than clear in the United States, but was even more blurred in Soviet Russia, where workers lived in barracks and other complexes affiliated with their place of employment. Disputes arising in the barracks of a particular factory often would be adjudicated by the control commission, people's court, factory, Party, or union committee of that particular enterprise. Indeed, women did appeal to all of these venues for relief in cases of rape, marital abuse, or other harassment by men

living in their same barracks. See, for example, TsGAIPD, *f.* 580, *op.* 1, *d.* 86 (also includes accusations of general insults brought before factory Party cell); *dd.* 310, 311, 312 (complaints of harassment and violence at home and in the workplace brought before control commissions).

78. GARF, *f.* 374, *op.* 28, *d.* 4034: 18 (*V Komissiiu Sovnarkoma RSFSR i VTsIK po karatel'noi politike, 16 IX 1927 g.*).

79. See, for example, *Politsvodka No. 3 Sekretariata SNK SSSR po priemu zaiavlenii i zhalob za period s 1/XII-27 g. Po 1/II-1928 g. (sekretno)*, GARF, *f.* 374, *op.* 28, *d.* 2989: 11; N. Kartel'tseva, "Smelee i uvernee k zavoevaniiu obshchei pechati!," *Rabotnitsa i krest'ianka*, 1928, No. 23: 1 (that all women wishing to participate in the construction of socialism should write in and appeal to the press about abnormalities at work; that socialist construction demands such participation).

80. TsGA SPb, *f.* 6276, *op.* 266, *d.* 6: 2. Official reviews of the activity of these consultation points did not report the gender of clients seeking legal assistance. These reports delineated the number of clients served; the subject matter of the question (land law, labor law, criminal law, family law, etc.); whether the advice given was written or oral; whether a suit was filed; and whether the case necessitated appearance at a court or administrative hearing. TsGA SPb, *f.* 6276, *d.* 1: 9, 22; *d.* 4: 2, 3, 4, 7, 29, 41, 42, 50; *d.* 6: 2, 12; *d.* 9: 2; *d.* 10: 6, 11.

81. For example, TsGAIPD, *f.* 81, *op.* 1, *d.* 88: 25; William J. Chase, *Workers, Society and the Soviet State: Labor and Life in Moscow, 1919-1929* (Urbana, IL, 1990), 270-87.

82. Sometimes women complained that they did not speak at these meetings because they did not feel as though they were equal with men, TsGAIPD, *f.* 1012, *op.* 1, *d.* 621: 63 (general meeting of the women of the Krasnyi Putilovets factory offices, 27 November 1928); or that the meeting organizers did not call on them, or refused to address issues of importance to women. See Rabkorka, "'Na nashi predlozheniia ne obrashchaiut vnimaniia'—Tak li eto?," *Rabotnitsa i krest'ianka*, 1930, No. 1: 5. But see TsGAIPD, *f.* 1012, *op.* 1, *d.* 730: 136 (woman speaking at 1929 Krasnyi Putilovets production meeting asserts that women now have complete equality).

83. One of the countless articles and archival files discussing women's poor participation in production meetings notes that it follows from inattentiveness to women's concerns, and that women are laughed at when they attend and raise questions. Man, "Rabotnitsy v obide," *Rabotnitsa*, 1926, No. 17: 14. Although women did seem to attend with less frequency than men, and despite their inhibitions about complaining, extant press and archival evidence reveals that their cumulative participation was more than negligible.

84. Numerous articles lamented the dearth of women attending production meetings and their disinclination to participate actively. See Rabotnitsa K-aia, "Trud i byt na zavode im. Engel'sa," *Rabotnitsa i krest'ianka* (Leningrad), 1927, No. 9: 16; Rabotnitsa, "Vnimanie proizzvodsoveshchaniiam! S uchastiem rabotnits plokho," *Rabotnitsa i krest'ianka* (Leningrad), 1928, No. 3: 20; L. Kagan, *Ratsionalizatsiia i rabotnitsa* (1928), 60-89.

85. Kagan, *Ratsionalizatsiia*, 60-89.

86. TsGA, *f.* 390-A, *op.* 21, *d.* 40: 8; TsGAIPD, *f.* 24, *op.* 1, *d.* 20: *op.* 8, *d.* 26. At women's meetings in factories, local and regional Party leaders told women that increased participation in production meetings would improve their own material positions and

industry as a whole. TsGAIPD, *f.* 388, *op.* 1, *d.* 76: 2 (women's meeting at Trampark im. Skorokhodova, Leningrad, 4 July 1927). At such all-women's meetings, and to female labor inspectors, women complained that they were not given the chance to speak at meetings, even though they asked to be recognized. TsGAIPD, *f.* 24, *op.* 8, *d.* 4: 131 (zhenotdel labor inspector reporting on women's complaints, 23 July 1928); *d.* 12: 106 (Leningrad zhenotdel meeting, 24 January 1928).

87. Chase, *Workers, Society and the Soviet State*, 281.

88. *Ibid.*

89. See N. Torskaia, "Kritikui smelei," *Rabotnitsa*, 1928, No. 36: 1; A. Artiukhina, "Na bor'bu s nedostatkami v bytu i stroitel'stve," *Kommunistka*, 1928, No. 5: 1; "Vydvigaite reshitel'nee, pomogaite v rabote," *Rabotnitsa*, 1929, No. 7: 1; and "Bol'she smelosti v samokritike," *Rabotnitsa*, 1929, No. 37: 1.

90. The next section considers these complaints and requested relief in greater detail.

91. This researcher found that men complained of "disparaging" or "rude treatment" less frequently, and found no evidence of men complaining of an intolerable atmosphere. Further, when men did complain of insults (*oskorbleniia*) or crass behavior, the offensive behavior was not gendered in content (unless one argued that the worker was presumed to be male). Sometimes these complaints were about annoying neighbors or bosses with unreasonable expectations. But men did not appear to complain that supervisors or authorities insulted their manhood. Men might be incompetent workers; women were incompetent because they were women.

92. GARF, *f.* 374, *op.* 28s, *d.* 2998: 1-13.

93. GARF, *f.* 374, *op.* 28s, *d.* 3512: 30-43. See also TsGAIPD, *f.* 24, *op.* 8, *d.* 12: 55 ("rationalization" used as an excuse to fire women and replace them with men, asserting that men were strong and more efficient).

94. M. G., "Eshche raz o rabotnitse," *Trud*, 9 January 1928: 4; L. Vorontsova, "Zavod ne blagotvoritel'noe uchrezhdenie," *Trud*, 14 January 1928: 3. The Russian texts use the clear terms "intolerable environment" or "atmosphere of persecution." The phrases *tiazhelaia obstanovka* and *atmosfera* also frequently appear. "*Tiazhelaia*" can be translated as "difficult," "burdensome," "trying," and "severe." *Obstanovka* means conditions or environment. This is not an imposition of the American legal term of art "hostile working environment," which consists of unwelcome physical or verbal conduct of a sexual nature that is "sufficiently severe or pervasive to alter the conditions of the victim's employment and create an abusive working environment," *Harris v. Forklift*, 114S.Ct. 367,370 (1993); *Meritor Savings Bank v. Vinson*, 477 U.S. 57, 67, 106 S.Ct. 2399, 2405. The Russians themselves used these very terms.

95. M. G., "Eshche raz," 4.

96. A. Bode, "Tol'ko v kukly igrat'," *Smena*, 8 April 1927: 3. See also *Smena*, 11 June 1927: 2 (cartoon depicts two young men, laughing hysterically, and a girl, covering her ears, running away from them and their taunts).

97. TsGAIPD, *f.* 24, *op.* 1, *d.* 20: 9, 10; *op.* 8, *d.* 35: 23. One commented at a Leningrad oblast' zhenotdel meeting that "it doesn't matter what you do, whether you're a good or bad worker . . . because you're always looked at as a woman (*zhenshchina*) and not as a working

woman (*rabotnitsa*). TsGAIPD, *f.* 24, *op.* 8, *d.* 35: 31.

98. M. G., "Eshche raz," 4; O. Mamaeva, "Vstrechaiut v shtyki," *Kommunistka*, 1929, No. 10: 19; Osipova, "Kapitalisticheskii podkhod na sotsialisticheskoi fabrike," *ibid.*: 22. Literally, the women alleged (and the arbiter found) that the men created a "difficult" or "painful" "atmosphere" in which to work. TsGAIPD, *f.* 80, *op.* 1, *d.* 167: 30.

99. M. G., "Eshche raz," 4.

100. See, for example, *ibid.* (complaints about bosses and male workers); TsGAIPD, *f.* 16, *op.* 13, *d.* 13171: 3, 4, 8 (complaints about male workers), and the cases discussed below in this chapter.

101. N. Serov, "Tramvaishchitsy," *Rabotnitsa*, 1928, No. 35: 13-14. For a spirited discussion of various forms of *gruboe* or *prenebrizhitel'noe otnoshenie k zhenshchinam*, see generally TsGAIPD, *f.* 24, *op.* 8, *d.* 11: 108-122.

102. TsGAIPD, *f.* 24, *op.* 8, *d.* 11: 108-122. The use of the word "sabotage" is to be taken in its traditional sense and not in the politicized sense as used in the Soviet Union during this period.

103. For example, TsGA SPb, *f.* 1027, *op.* 1, *d.* 2504; RGAE, *f.* 396, *op.* 10, *dd.* 66, 86.

104. TsGAIPD, *f.* 24, *op.* 8, *d.* 11: 123-130; *f.* 80, *op.* 1, *d.* 89: 20-30, 89 (ad hoc committee formed at Leningrad Mining Institute to address sexual harassment of female students included representatives from the local city Party organization [*raikom*], the city zhenotdel organization, the local union of metal workers, the Leningrad oblast' *Proletstuda*, and the local Komsomol organization [*raikom*]); see also Osipova, "Kapitalisticheskii podkhod," 22 (harassment at factory led to appeals to management, union, and factory committees yielding no result; alternative union committee convened only after 57 women complained of hostile working environment; committee resolved to transfer matter to court).

105. "O promyshlennykh-tovarishcheskikh sudakh," Postanovlenie VTsIK i SNK ot 30 dekabria 1930 (*SU*, 1930, No. 4, st. 52); "O rabote tovarishcheskikh sudov," Postanovlenie VTsIK i SNK ot 28 avgusta 1928; "Pravila o primiritel'no-treteiskom i sudebnom rassmotrenii trudovykh konfliktov" (*SU*, 1928, No. 56, st. 494); "Instruktsiia o rabote tovarishcheskikh sudov," TsGA SPb, *f.* 6276, *op.* 14, *d.* 298: 4.

106. See, GARF, *f.* 374, *op.* 21, *d.* 127: 7-16 (complaint filed to biuro zhalob, *Narkomiust*, and TsK VKP(b); see discussion below).

107. See GARF, *f.* 374, *op.* 28, *d.* 2583 (intake sheet for recording of substance and disposition of case), see note 55 above.

108. M. G., "Eshche raz"; Mamaeva, "Vstrechaiut v shtyki," 106.

109. Violations of Labor Code provisions regarding "the defense of labor" and labor conditions were subject to criminal proceedings, necessitating participation of the procuracy. *Ugolovnyi kodeks RSFSR (1922)*, Art. 132. This included violations of protective labor legislation for women, *Ugolovnyi kodeks RSFSR (1922)*, Art. 132, Comments 2a, 9g; and violations of legislation regulating the hiring and firing of workers, including circumventing the labor exchanges, *Ugolovnyi kodeks RSFSR (1922)*, Art. 132, Comment 9e. See also "O nakazaniiakh za narusheniia postanovlenii ob okhrana truda," Postanovlenie SNK (27/VII 1922 g.); *KZoT (1922)*, Arts. 168, 169. Involvement of the procuracy was necessary whether

the claim was civil or criminal, as actions for all violations of the Labor Code were handled by the Narkomtruda and the procurator for labor cases, *KZoT (1922)*, Arts. 168, 169. Women had to appeal to these authorities to press their claims in court.

110. John Hazard, *Settling Disputes in Soviet Society: The Formative Years of Legal Institutions* (New York, 1960), 18-19, citing P. Stuchka, "Proletarskaia revoliutsiia i sud," *Proletarskaia revoliutsiia i pravo*, 1918, No. 1: 3; J. Hildebrand, *The Sociology of Soviet Law* (Buffalo, NY, 1972), 48-49.

111. TsGAIPD, *f.* 580, *op.* 1, *d.* 311: 48 (complainant also asserting that the morals of Party members should be different from those of the average citizen, implying that the court system would not take that into account, as it should in cases of this sort).

112. TsGAIPD, *f.* 580, *op.* 1, *d.* 310: 17 (male workers assaulting female workers); 36; *d.* 322: 134, 188, 190, 194, 210 (domestic violence in workers' barracks). These files contain cases of women harrassed by men at home and in the workplace.

113. TsGAIPD, *f.* 580, *op.* 1, *d.* 322: 211 (male workers harassing female employee).

114. A story in *Rabotnitsa* offers another example of how women were guided to seek alternatives to the courts. A friend persuaded a battered woman to go to court for relief. Her husband threatened to kill their children if she did not withdraw her motion. Someone then suggested that she appeal to her *fabkom* (factory committee). The fabkom then organized a boycott of the husband (the couple worked in the same factory but in different jobs). Although several of the husband's drinking buddies at work continued to harass the woman, a boycott of the offender was announced, and posters were put up until he ultimately apologized and promised never to abuse her again. The story concluded with a question in a black box: Have there been similar cases in your factory? N. Stepnogo, "Annushka," *Rabotnitsa*, 1926, No. 7: 6-8.

115. GARF, *f.* 374, *op.* 28, *d.* 127: 7-16.

116. For a broader discussion of the zhenotdel and its weakness, see generally Carol Hayden, "Feminism and Bolshevism: The Zhenotdel and the Politics of Women's Emancipation in Russia, 1917-1930," unpublished Ph.D. dissertation (University of California, Berkeley, 1979); Wood, "Gender and Politics in Soviet Russia"; Michelle Patterson, "The Early Years of the Petrograd-Leningrad Zhenotdel," unpublished Ph.D. dissertation (University of Toronto, forthcoming).

117. TsGAIPD, *f.* 24, *op.* 8, *d.* 11: 105-122, 185-188, 227, 258.

118. *Ibid.*: 227, 258 (Zhenotdel leader exhorts women to write to the press to induce action).

119. *Rossiiskii tsentr khraneniia i izucheniia dokumentov noveishei istorii* (RTsKhIDNI), *f.* 17, *op.* 10, *d.* 490 (speech by zhenotdel leader A. Artiukhina to the Moscow Party Organization about the shameless manner in which women were harassed by employers and "even by Party members" while engaged in Party work).

120. GARF, *f.* 374, *op.* 28s, *d.* 2998: 1-13.

121. *Ibid.*: 7.

122. *Ibid.*: 13.

123. RKI investigators generally conducted Biuro zhalob investigations. *Ibid.*: 5.

124. *Ibid.*: 4.

125. GARF, *f.* 374, *op.* 28, *d.* 3512: 28-43.

126. The Tifenbakher factory operated as a German industrial concession. GARF, f. 374, *op.* 28, *d.* 3512: 43.

127. He complained that the investigators demanded financial records and interrogated factory workers on issues beyond the scope of their search warrant (*lit.* "mandate"). GARF, *f.* 374, *op.* 28, *d.* 3512: 33.

128. The extant case materials pertain to investigations of the factory, but neither the investigators' notes nor the investigators' final reports indicate that there was any inquiry into the facts surrounding the disputed court proceedings.

129. One of the union's appeals cited as many as 21 separate violations of the *koldogovor*, which were also confirmed by a visiting labor inspector. GARF, *f.* 374, *op.* 28, *d.* 3512: 37. It is possible that the dismissals of pregnant women and young mothers were not simply the most flagrant violations, but ones calculated to elicit a response from the higher authorities.

130. This would mirror, or follow from, the argument that the zhenotdel itself was co-opted by the Party to serve the larger Party goals of industrialization, hierarchy, and control, rather than the interests of women. See Wood, "Gender and Politics in Soviet Russia," 367-68, in reference to the co-optation of women organizers.

131. Complaints after 1933 are beyond the scope of this article. Although the biuro zhalob was dismantled, there is evidence that some women did complain throughout the 1930s within the context of other labor unrest. See Jeffrey Rossman, "Workers against the Worker's State: Gender and Class in Ivanovo," unpublished Ph.D. dissertation (University of California, Berkeley, forthcoming). See also William K. Wolf, "Russia's Revolutionary Underground: The Construction of the Moscow Subway, 1931-35," unpublished Ph.D. dissertation (Ohio State University, 1994), 150-57, regarding sexual harassment of female Moscow Metrostroi workers during the mid-1930s.

132. A. Ivanova, "Upravliaiu gruzovikom," *Rabotnitsa i krest'ianka* (Leningrad), 1930, No. 21: 30; Gerasimchuk, "Kak ia stala vagonovozhatym," *ibid.*; Grigor'evna, "Rabotnitsy zhelezno-dorozhnogo transporta," *Rabotnitsa i krest'ianka* (Leningrad), 1930, No. 11: 8.

133. Florinskaia, "Zhenshchina? Ne prinimaem!," *Rabotnitsa i krest'ianka* (Leningrad), 1930, No. 23: 6.

134. Fokina, "Vnimanie transportnitse," *Rabotnitsa i krest'ianka* (Leningrad), 1930, No. 11: 9; "Zhenshchiny-puteitsy," *ibid.*: 10.

135. Naderzhdinskaia, "Kuda tebe v inzhenery," *Rabotnitsa i krest'ianka* (Leningrad), 1930, No. 13: 6 (detailing problems of women in engineering institutes); E. Mirskaia, "Shire dorogu rabotnitse k uchebe," *ibid.* (describing greater educational opportunities for working women).

136. See, for example, A. Artiukhina, "Na vyshuiu stepen'," *Rabotnitsa i krest'ianka*, 1930, No. 4: 4; "Vse rabotnitsy—v riady udarnikov!," *Rabotnitsa i krest'ianka*, 1930, No. 5: 5.

137. Many Russian sociologists and lawyers argue that this has been an endemic problem in Russia, not least during the late 1920s when the fate of law was uncertain and power struggles ongoing. Discussions with N. Lebina, A. Protushinskii, G. Kolubkov.

138. In cases other than rape, archival data were unavailable to assess what impelled women to *court* rather than to alternative dispute forums. Archival conditions in Russia in 1993-1995 only offered access to court materials that would permit an assessment of why women might choose alternative forums over the courts.

139. American male unionists during this period also "viewed women first as women—potential or actual wives and mothers—and secondarily as workers." Nancy Cott, *The Grounding of Modern Feminism* (New Haven, CT, 1987), 126.

140. Glickman, *Russian Factory Women*, 141-43, 205-206, 208.

141. The term "sexual harassment" did not appear as a term of art until 1975, when it was conceived by the Working Women United Institute. Interview with Karen Sauvigné, formerly of WWU (14 Jaunuary 1997). The term first appeared in print in the Alliance Against Sexual Coercion's "Position Paper #1" (September 1976) and Carroll Brodsky's *The Harassed Worker* (Lexington, MA, 1976). Catharine MacKinnon, *Sexual Harassment of Working Women: A Case of Sex Discrimination* (New Haven, CT, 1979), note 13, 250. MacKinnon notes that the unnamed, of course, should not be mistaken for the non-existent. MacKinnon, *Sexual Harassment*, 28.

142. *Bishop v. Liston*, 199 N.W. 825 (Neb. 1924).

143. *Palmer v. Baum*, 111 Ill. App. 584 (1905).

144. *State v. Oakes*, 100 S.W. 434, 202 Mo. 86 (1907); *Easley v. State*, 29 (Ohio Cir. C. R. 568, 1906).

145. *Martin v. Jansen*, 113 Wash. 290, 193 P. 674 (1920); *Skousen v. Nidy*, 90 Ariz. 215, 367 P.2d 248 (1961).

146. Throughout this century, both Russian and American women describe a continuum of behavior and attitudes that extend beyond the legal definitions of discriminatory treatment actionable in their respective countries. Consider the following statement by an American woman welder: "It's a form of harassment every time I pick up a sledgehammer and that prick laughs at me, you know. It's a form of harassment when the journeyman is supposed to be training me and it's real clear to me that he does not want to give me any information whatsoever. . . . It's a form of harassment to me when the working foreman puts me in a dangerous situation and tells me to do something in an improper way and then tells me, Oh, you can't do that! It's a form of harassment when someone takes a tool out of my hand and said, Oh, I'm going to show you . . . and he grabs the sledgehammer from my hand and proceeded to . . . show me how to do this thing . . . you know, straighten up a post . . . it's nothing to it, you just bang it and it gets straight. . . . Ah, you know, it's all a form of harassment to me. It's not right. They don't treat each other that way. They shouldn't treat me that way." Vicki Schultz, "Telling Stories about Women and Work," *Harvard Law Review* CIII, no. 8 (June 1990): 1883, citing Mary L. Walshok, *Blue-Collar Women: Pioneers on the Male Frontier* (Garden City, NY, 1981), 221-22. A more comprehensive comparison of American and Russian attempts to develop sexual harassment law will be addressed in a forthcoming work.

147. TsGA SPb, *f.* 6276, *op.* 11, *d.* 416: 61-63 (women workers complaining about hostile treatment by the chair of production meetings; women state that they have been reduced to silence as they fear dismissal, that they prefer the status quo to being on the street).

148. See, for example, GARF, *f.* 374, *op.* 21, *d.* 127.

149. For a discussion suggesting Bolshevik reluctance to risk male worker stability when economic development was a priority see Wood, "Gender and Politics in Soviet Russia," 232-33.

150. See, for example, TsGAIPD, *f.* 80, *op.* 1, *d.* 167: 30 (students responsible for creating hostile environment and slandering female student "reprimanded").

151. As of this writing, the Moscow Institute for Gender Studies reports that women are 70 percent of the unemployed in rural areas and 80 percent in the major cities. "Cruel cuts," *The Chicago Tribune* (20 August 1995): 10; "Yarmarka vakansii," *Rabotnitsa*, 1992, No. 2: 10, reporting that 75 percent of the recently unemployed are women.

152. See Z. Khotkina, "Women in the Labour Market," in Posadskaia, ed., *Women in Russia*, 85-108; discussion with Professor Kathryn Hendley, July 1993 (regarding unemployment agencies assisting unemployed men, but not women, with great alacrity; unemployment office workers explaining that women "need time to be with their families"). I have elaborated on this issue in J. Hunt-McCool and Lisa Granik, *The Legal Status of Women in the New Independent States of the Former Soviet Union* (Washington, DC, 1994).

8

EXPOSING ILLEGALITY AND ONESELF: COMPLAINT AND RISK IN STALIN'S RUSSIA

Golfo Alexopoulos

In Soviet Russia in the 1920s and 1930s, people were encouraged to complain about local authorities, and complain they did. They wrote complaints (*zhaloby*) in duplicate, signed them personally, and sent them widely. Central authorities touted this form of complaining as the civic duty of all honest citizens who should be quick to report instances of impropriety and abuse by middle and low ranking officials. In response, the state assured its subjects that it would give special attention to their grievances and punish those who were charged with behaving improperly. Implicit in this arrangement was the promise that citizen-complainers who complied with official instruction would be empowered by direct access to the state's coercive apparatus.[1] The subject of their complaint would be punished and they would be vindicated.

Yet those who filed complaints exposing the misconduct of their local officials were not necessarily empowered. For in reporting cases of official misconduct, the writer exposed himself or herself as an accuser and assumed a degree of risk. He or she could face harm in the form of reprisals from the subject of the complaint, as well as reproach from outside investigators. The outcome of a complaint could prove most unpleasant for the writer. One could hope for corrective action, but the act of exposing illegality had other possible consequences.

This chapter looks at complaints of official misconduct that were processed by control commissions and administrative organs, as well as procurators and Party leaders in the 1920s and 1930s. It seeks to demonstrate that, even though the regime encouraged complaints about the misconduct of local officials, complainants could not be confident of being vindicated. I begin by examining the climate of complaint which was officially encouraged, the variety of institutions assigned the task of hearing complaints, and the growing participation of people in the chorus of complaint. I then describe how the treatment and travels of damaging letters in an overburdened, bureaucratic environment had the result of putting the writer at risk. The Soviet writer-warrior who took up his pen in the battle against local corruption was often disarmed.

The Climate of Complaint

In order to increase control over local administration and regulate the implementation of its policies, the Soviet leadership fostered a climate of complaint. From stores and kiosks to the public courts, there was supposed to be a book of complaints (*zhalobnaia kniga*) available for people to comment on how poorly they were being serviced. All Soviet institutions were expected to record and process written and verbal complaints and keep regular hours for hearing them. Grievances were voiced and heard on a range of subjects and by a range of officials, as citizens complained to Joseph Stalin, the Chairman of the Central Executive Committee (TsIK) M. I. Kalinin, Prime Minister V. M. Molotov, the Commissariat of Justice (*Narkomiust*), and the newspaper editors; they complained about their tax rate, their court sentence, their pensions, and their expulsions (from the Party, the collective farm [*kolkhoz*], the university, or trade union).[2] As there were few rules to govern this process of complaint, people sent their letters or marched into offices wherever and whenever they wished.

A Call to Complain

Throughout the 1920s, the Party steadily intensified its appeal to citizens for information on the wrongful actions of state officials and, in particular, cases of bureaucratism and stifling red-tape (*volokita*). Lenin said of the war on bureaucratism that "this war is much more difficult than the civil war."[3] It had to be waged "from below,"[4] as all Soviet citizens were expected to "broadly exercise their right to criticize the work of . . . any organ of Soviet power."[5] The call to complain reached a pitch in 1928, when Stalin declared the need to "call the masses, the millions of workers and peasants, to the task of criticism from below" in order to improve the work of the Soviet bureaucracy.[6] So much of this war on bureaucratism was about improving the treatment (*obsluzhivanie*) of citizens by state officials and enforcing a code of official propriety. The campaign insisted that officials treat people in a way that ceased to be insulting, scornful, arrogant, rude, disgraceful, and callous—such behavior was viewed most severely "as sabotage and a crime against Soviet power."[7]

The benign official language employed in the call to complain was probably intended to neutralize the social unacceptance of negative reporting. Popular complaints and criticism were called "signals" (*signaly*) from below. Complaints "sent signals" (*signaliziruiut*) to Soviet power, exposing "gross violations of revolutionary legality."[8] One district procurator (*raiprokuror*) kept a register of the complaints he received in a notebook he labeled "the signal-maker" (*signalizator*).[9] Although these signals of illegality were sometimes called denunciations (*donosy*), only those who were the unfortunate subjects of complaint were quick to identify damaging charges by this term.[10] Instead of characterizing their complaint as a denunciation, those who wrote claimed that they reported on someone (*na nego pisal*), leveled criticism (*kritika*), or sent a notice to the newspaper or the radio (*pisat' zametku v gazetu, podat' zametku v radiotsentr*). This multiplicity of signifiers, which largely replaced the pejorative term "donos" in the official discourse, illustrates how Soviet officials sought to legitimize the act of informing.

The legitimation of reporting on others is expressed not only by these more neutral or euphemistic terms which emerged to describe the practice, but also by the regime's easing of sanctions against over-zealous complainers, those accused of false denunciation (*lozhnyi donos*)[11] and slander (*kleveta*). Lenin issued what was probably the strongest Bolshevik statement against false denunciation in 1918 when he wrote that persons should be "more severely apprehended and punished by execution for false denunciations."[12] Yet from the 1920s to the 1930s there was a progressive and steady softening of state sanctions against such abuses of complaint. In November 1921, when the government issued its first decree on false denunciation, there was no instruction to execute offenders. The punishment for making spurious allegations against another citizen, whether orally or in writing, was established at "no less than one year's deprivation of freedom."[13] This punishment was reduced to "up to" one year by 1922 with the publication of the first RSFSR Criminal Code.[14] And in the 1926 Criminal Code the punishment for false denunciation was reduced yet again to deprivation of freedom or forced labor for up to three months.[15] Similarly, the punishment for slander became increasingly mild from the 1920s to the 1930s, moving from deprivation of freedom to a fine.[16] Thus, the official call to complain was accompanied by legislation which treated false informers with greater leniency and encouraged complaining by reducing its impediments.

Complaints and Addressees

Although many organs were expected to process and review letters, one institution, the Worker-Peasant Inspectorate (*Rabkrin*), was established and promoted specifically to handle complaints of bureaucratism.[17] Rabkrin was to "wage a battle" against administrative and economic crime and to verify the observance of Soviet laws.[18] It was responsible for exposing behavior that ranged from criminal to non-Soviet to inadmissible, and it often referred criminals to the courts for sentencing or had people deported, fired from their jobs, or admonished in some way.

Rabkrin's Central complaints bureau (*Biuro zhalob*) was specifically assigned the task of processing popular signals of illegality, especially those concerning state officials. To send a complaint about the improper functioning of government, one had only to include "complaints bureau" on the envelope and it would be delivered free, without postage.[19] Before the establishment of the procuracy in 1922, the complaints bureau was involved in a wide range of disputes, but these narrowed in 1924 when Rabkrin's bureau was identified as the organ best suited for the war on bureaucratism. To combat bureaucratic inefficiencies and the abuse of power, the head of Rabkrin, Kuibyshev, urged in 1925 that special attention be paid to worker and peasant petitions and complaints.[20] The complaints bureau was supposed to discover when Party and state directives were not being properly implemented. The major newspapers—*Pravda, Izvestiia, Bednota, Gudok, Rabochii Moskvy*—were urged to direct all notices (*zametki*) and letters from workers and peasants to the complaints bureau when they concerned the improper activities of government officials.[21] In 1933, the Rabkrin complaints bureau was described as "an organ of mass control" which involved workers and collective farm peasants as "the party's helpers" in the fight against bureaucratic distortions in the state structure (*gosapparat*).[22] One of the principal goals of Rabkrin was mass participation—to include "the mass of workers and peasants" in the task of improving government[23]—and its complaints bureau was promoted to serve this purpose.

As the complaints bureau grew in significance by the late 1920s and into the early 1930s, its responsibilities were increasingly described in legalistic terms. The bureau was supposed to "expose the guilty,"[24] organize show trials, and establish a court of worker-assessors. Even those punished by its decisions called it "the court."[25] Indeed, many of the complaints received by the Rabkrin complaints bureau were from people who had had previous complaints rejected by procurators and the courts. These complaints, together with supporting materials, were compiled in a case file resembling

a court dossier. However, complaints were frequently sent without supporting documents and addressees relied heavily on the information presented
in these texts.[26] For example, the Rabkrin complaints bureau encouraged
citizens to include in their complaints "a detailed account of all circumstances which are grounds for issuing the complaint . . . and a list of
evidence and witnesses which can confirm the truth of the complaint."[27]
Since the complaints bureau received reports of wrongdoing in the form of
written complaints (and decided cases largely from the information provided
in these texts), it functioned as a kind of correspondence court.

The complaints bureaux of the All-Union and RSFSR Rabkrin were
combined into one by 1928, and by 1930 complaints bureaux were opened
in larger factories and collective farms. The growing public profile of Rabkrin's complaints bureau is evidenced by the appointment in 1932 of Lenin's
sister as its director. On 9-14 April 1932, M. I. Ulianova initiated a five-day
campaign on the work of complaints bureaux (*piatidnevnik po rabote biuro
zhalob*) which she referred to as "the most important political campaign."[28]
Its purpose was to bring a "new mass" of people (such as women and rural
correspondents) to act on citizen complaints. The campaign also sought to
improve the operations of complaint bureaux throughout the country so that
they would more responsively deal with and investigate complaints of
bureaucratism in all organizations. Ulianova stressed that because the
complaints bureau was Rabkrin's "most mass organ" it had the greatest
potential for including elements from below in the war against distortions of
the Party line and bureaucratism in state institutions.[29]

Rabkrin may have been the most prominent government organ in the
battle against bureaucratism, but it was by no means the only addressee for
citizens filing complaints. Rather, a variety of Soviet institutions were
expected to process complaints on the illegalities of local officials. Party
leaders, including Stalin and Kalinin, as well as the Commissariat of Justice
and the newspapers all received such complaints. There was a great deal of
overlap and duplication, as individuals chose those to whom they wished to
complain. For example, in the Moscow oblast' a man charged the chairman
of the rural soviet (*sel'sovet*) with hiding rich peasants or kulaks, getting
drunk, and overtaxing the village poor. He sent his accusation to the district
(*raion*) procurator and, when no action was taken, he wrote Kalinin, who
was one of the most popular addressees in this period.[30] Just as writers sent
their complaints to various individuals and institutions, the latter circulated
these letters among one another. An individual might send a complaint to
Rabkrin and, after receiving no reply, turn to the Council of People's
Commissars (*Sovnarkom*) or to a newspaper, which would then pass the

letter to the Procuracy for an investigation. The numerous institutions which reviewed citizen letters complained about each other as well and participated in the chorus of complaint. For example, in 1935 the Kalinin oblast' procurator condemned the complaints bureau for making decisions contrary to the law.[31]

Before the mid-1930s, legal institutions played an important, albeit auxiliary, role in the campaign against official misconduct by helping to investigate and sentence local officials who acted improperly. For example, procurators were expected to intervene when citizen complaints to various institutions were being ignored or mishandled. The Procurator of the RSFSR, A. I. Vyshinskii, urged procurators in 1932 to go into the villages and check up on how the rural soviets and district soviet executive committees (*raiispolkomy*) were handling complaints from peasants.[32] Procurators also assisted in the investigation of complaints and were supposed to take special notice when a letter exposed behavior by local officials which was cause for prosecution.[33] Moreover, almost every other organ which received complaints of impropriety passed at least some of their letters to the Procuracy. For example, the peasant newspaper *Krest'ianskaia gazeta* (which employed people to process letters, provide legal consultation, and investigate cases) used to send the Procuracy complaints of illegality with a request for a decision and assessment.[34] Other legal organs also took part in the investigation of complaints and received letters forwarded to them by the complaints bureau and others. The courts reviewed complaints on the wrongful acts of court officials, and in 1932 the complaints office of the Commissariat of Justice received over 200 letters of complaint and over 100 visitors per day.[35] During the campaign initiated by Ulianova, Justice Commissar Nikolai V. Krylenko urged the comrades' court judges and people's assessors to assist Rabkrin in combatting "red tape."[36]

The Rising Chorus of Complaint

The official call to complain and the numerous institutions responsible for handling citizen complaints did not themselves account for the climate of complaint. Most important was the fact that people heeded the call to complain. The leadership not only encouraged criticism of abusive local officials, but during intense economic transformation and harsh political campaigns such criticism came rather easily. People did, in fact, complain because there was good cause to in a period of economic shortages, disenfranchisement, forced collectivization, expropriation, draconian laws, and onerous taxation. One wonders whether the call to complain was due in part to the growing groundswell of grievance and the regime's desire to co-opt these dissenting voices.

The chorus of complaint intensified throughout the 1920s and 1930s as the number of complaints received centrally steadily increased. The Rabkrin central complaints bureau received 4,000 complaints in 1927, 20,000 in 1928, and 43,000 in 1929.[37] The Procuracy received hundreds of complaints per year before 1927, while by 1928 the number of complaints per year had risen to the tens of thousands.[38] By 1930, the center was simply bombarded with demands from peasants,[39] as people sent complaints to higher-level officials and deliberately bypassed their local procurators and complaints bureaux. Krylenko responded to the fact that too many people were flooding the republic, krai, and oblast' procurators with complaints by issuing a circular in 1930 instructing that all complaints concerning the actions of local officials be sent locally, to the raion procurators.[40]

When Rabkrin was abolished in 1934, responsibility over complaints of official misconduct was assumed by the newly created Soviet Control Commission, the courts (particularly after 1936), the procuracy, and the administrative organs. This new responsibility was particularly onerous for the administrative organs. The soviet executive committees (*ispolkomy*) were urged to process, investigate, and decide complaints, inform the complainant and relevant local authority about the decision reached, provide oversight in the enforcement of these decisions, and repeal "illegal decisions" on complaints. Yet local administrative organs were the least prepared to accept that "the role of the executive committees and rural soviets in reviewing workers' complaints [was] increasing."[41] In the Central Volga krai, the new order of things left only one person to sort the mail, which included over 300 complaints, inquiries, and supplemental materials per day. As a result, complaints would accumulate on tables and in boxes, left unattended for six months and more.[42] So burdensome was this onslaught of letters that one official, the head of municipal police, told TsIK: "If I accept complaints from everyone, then there will be no time for other matters."[43]

In the mid-1930s, the procuracy—already emerging as the most powerful legal agency—assumed primary responsibility over complaints of official misconduct. It had little choice, for with the dissolution of Rabkrin, the public directed more and more of its complaints to the procuracy. A 1935 report stated that "the number of complaints to the Supreme Court and the RSFSR Procuracy increases significantly with every year, even every month."[44] Compared with the number of complaints it received in January 1934, the USSR Procuracy received five times as many complaints in October 1935 and twelve times as many in May 1936.[45] The Commissariat of Justice's department of complaints (*otdel zhalob*), which received and registered all complaints addressed to the Supreme Court and the Procuracy, also confronted an increase in letters.[46] The average number of complaints it received per month doubled from 1931 to 1932 and more than doubled between 1932 and 1935.[47] Not all these complaints involved official misconduct. In fact, some of the complaints came from convicts petitioning the Procuracy for reduced sentences.[48] But others related to officials, for when people complained about the confiscation of their property, expulsion from the collective farm, or excessive taxation or punishment, some local official was usually to blame.[49]

Complaints of official misconduct were largely dealt with outside the legal system before 1934, and few rules were established to give structure and regularity to this process of complaint. People wrote to whomever they wished, and addressees acted on complaints as they wished. There was no limit on the number of people one could approach with a complaint, only general guidelines concerning jurisdiction, and no regular procedure for impartial fact-finding or investigation. And so, letters were passed continuously by complainers and addressees alike to various institutions and officials—often with unfortunate results.

The Trail of Damaging Letters

Letters are usually considered private communication between the writer and addressee, but when addressed to Soviet authorities they were often made public, published in the local press, or discussed at meetings. Even if it was not the author's intention, complaints quickly became public documents, traveling from the newspapers and radio stations, to Stalin and Molotov, to various organs of the Party and state apparatus. There was nothing private about a complaint sent to Stalin, even if addressed with a familiar "dear comrade," because Stalin simply sent it elsewhere.

Letters traveled not because they were being expediently processed, but rather diligently avoided. Believing that the poor handling of citizen complaints reflected officials' "bureaucratic attitude," the leadership in Moscow issued its own complaint. Central organs were critical of how complaints were not being promptly handled, recorded, and tracked. The Soviet government's dissatisfaction with the poor handling of complaints persisted through the 1930s, and its litany of grievances was constant and repetitive: those who issued complaints were being ignored; complaints were not being investigated; they were being passed from one institution to another and often to that institution which was the subject of complaint;

upper level organs passed complaints downward and then simply rubber-stamped the lower organs' decision; facts of the complaint were not being investigated.[50] A Commissariat of Justice decree of 1932 condemned the long delays in processing and instances in which complaints were lost.[51] People were even illegally required to pay a fee for issuing a complaint,[52] with some district soviet executive committees charging between one and five rubles per complaint.[53]

Periodically, an attempt would be made to improve the handling of complaints. In 1935, at the urging of the Party committee, all the workers in the Moscow oblast' reception room (*priemnaia*) were fired and replaced.[54] But officials confronted letters largely with indifference and neglect, as complaints were ignored and filed away, lost, even burned. A report noted that "proposals and inquiries by the central organs of justice concerning complaints . . . are being ignored with impunity for 6-10 months and more."[55] In one case, the oblast' issued four "reminders with threats" and still the raion gave no response.[56] Swamped with complaints, local authorities (in particular, the district soviet executive committees and the rural soviets) were "either not accepting complaints at all or rejecting them without grounds."[57] Even the secretary of TsIK, who in 1934 rebuked officials for neglecting complaints, took three months to put his signature to an already prepared decree on the subject.[58] Clearly, citizen complaints failed to generate much enthusiasm from Soviet officials. In 1935, while admitting prosecutors were "swamped" with complaints, Vyshinskii still condemned officials for having the "completely wrong attitude toward complaints," and leaving them largely neglected, "resting on shelves, mingling with rats"[59]

At a meeting of the heads of Rabkrin complaint bureaux in 1933, Kalinin expressed a certain degree of sympathy with the worker who every day faced the drudgery of citizen complaints and petitions. In his view, it was the work itself which hardened the individual and turned one into an insensitive bureaucrat.

> People quickly become hardened in this line of work. When they run into complaints day after day and these complaints are often about mundane, personal things, then a person becomes numb to feeling . . . a worker becomes bureaucratized . . . sending cases from one office to another.[60]

Indeed, when officials did not entirely ignore complaints, they found it easier to pass the buck—relegate the tasks of review and investigation to others or insist that other organs had jurisdiction. Letters moved vertically and horizontally as officials from one institution attempted to unload their complaints onto another. As early as 1921, Lenin sent a memo to the leaders of all central Soviet institutions condemning bureaucratic practices such as automatically passing petitions to other institutions, and warned that those guilty of such practices would be punished.[61] Still, into the 1920s and 1930s letters continued to travel from one prosecutor to another, even to offices and divisions that did not exist.[62] In 1931, the Central Black Earth oblast' and the Central Volga Rabkrin deferred over 60 percent of their complaints to other organs.[63] The Rabkrin complaints bureau of the Moscow oblast' received 52,727 complaints between August 1930 and December 1931 and most of them concerned official misconduct; yet the bureau decided that the majority of these complaints were not within its jurisdiction. Therefore, they were sent elsewhere—for example, to a comrades' court, the Moscow City Soviet, or the city finance office.[64] In the city of Gorkii in September and October of 1934 the prosecutor passed 78 percent of the complaints he received to raion prosecutors and other organizations.[65] In 1937, the Tatar ASSR TsIK distributed over 80 percent of the complaints it received "to the appropriate organizations."[66]

The complaints mechanism functioned such that so-called "signals from below" were often sent below. That is, letters were passed not only from one state organ to another, but down the hierarchy. Complaints tended to travel a circular journey from the complainant to a high-level official and back down again to a local official. For example, nearly 70 percent of all complaints received by the Kalinin regional soviet executive committee (*oblispolkom*) in 1935 "were mechanically passed to lower organs for a decision."[67] In 1933, a man from the Omsk oblast' sent a complaint concerning his disenfranchisement to the district soviet executive committees, which sent it to the rural soviet, which sent it to the collective farm to be discussed at the general meeting.[68] In a 1934 report, Ulianova condemned this tendency to pass complaints from the central and oblast' level to the raion and even further to the rural soviet and collective farm. The result was that Soviet organs on the lowest rung of the hierarchy were deciding cases:

> . . . the rural soviets frequently have to "judge" [complaints] themselves
> and they issue whatever decisions they like. Most often, the raion organs
> decide on individual complaints based solely on the conclusions reached
> by the rural soviets and the collective farms.[69]

It was difficult for those who sent complaints down the hierarchy to then get a response or status report from local officials. Doing damage control as well as asserting their power, local officials often either failed to act on complaints of impropriety or remained silent despite repeated requests from higher level organs for information. This was a persistent problem in Cheliabinsk:

> As a rule, up to half of all complaints that come into the regional soviet executive committee reception room are passed to the district soviet executive committees and the oblast' divisions for review. In several cases, the regional soviet executive committee had to send 7-10 reminders to the district soviet executive committees in order to get a response. . . .[70]

Local officials who "maliciously refused" to execute decisions of higher organs on complaints were supposed to be seriously reprimanded and made the subject of a show trial.[71] In some instances, local silence was not a sign of neglect but of a deliberate intent to conceal. As one commentator noted, it was not surprising to find complaints left unresolved when they fell into the hands of those local officials who were the subject of the complaint.[72]

This was often the destiny of damaging letters—individuals would issue a complaint only to have it sent to that organ whose illegalities they had exposed. Central authorities repeatedly called for a decisive end to this practice. From 1930 to 1937, official decrees issued by the RSFSR Central Executive Committee (VTsIK), Rabkrin, the Soviet Control Commission, the Commissariat of Justice, and others explicitly forbade the passing of complaints to those institutions and persons which were the subject of the complaint.[73] Official exhortations took a form similar to the following from 1931:

> Local rabkrin organs and complaint bureaus must verify and investigate complaints through an involvement of the masses and not through the administrative organs. Complaints cannot be given for investigation to those institutions about which the complainer is complaining.[74]

Despite such condemnations and prohibitions, the practice continued. In 1935, the Soviet Control Commission reported that workers' complaints in the Kursk oblast were being sent "as a rule" to those rural soviets which were the subject of complaint.[75]

To some degree, it made sense to contact persons closest to the source of a dispute for information. Since few institutions had the resources to send independent investigators, they relied instead on local officials who were already on site. For example, when the Procuracy received letters from women whose husbands failed to pay alimony or from persons wrongly deported or criminally sentenced, Vyshinskii would simply contact the local prosecutor to review the case.[76] However, the interests of justice were hardly served when the local prosecutor was either himself the subject of complaint or knew those involved. One man wrote a complaint about the investigator on his case, but the prosecutor passed his complaint right to the accused investigator.[77] While those who complained appealed for outside help, the right of prosecution and sanction was often left to individuals who were close to the dispute, if not themselves involved. The downward flow of complaints meant that too many local officials were being asked to evaluate charges of their own wrongdoing or that of people they knew. Rather than trouble themselves with this determination, some of those accused turned instead to silencing their accusers.

The Writer at Risk

When letters traveled frequently and to places unintended, the writer could find himself confronted by the subject of his complaint. This inspired one writer to send an angry complaint to Stalin about the way the leader was handling his mail. He was especially annoyed by the fact that Stalin was passing complaints which were addressed to him along to others. As a result, the man's complaints were landing in the hands of those local officials, the subjects of his complaint, who disenfranchised him in 1934.

> I asked you in every letter to investigate my case . . . but you send my letter to the oblast', the oblast' sends it to the raion, the raion sends it to the rural soviet and they make my head spin.[78]

Targets of complaint often became aware of who wrote against them when a letter was investigated or passed down the hierarchy. These local officials would then employ various means to silence their accusers. A rural correspondent in Smolensk described how the leaders of the collective farm were persecuting him because he had exposed their criminal actions. He wrote a plea to his sponsoring newspaper, "With tears in my eyes, I beg you for your protection."[79] Those who made charges of official misconduct often complained that as a result of writing they were dekulakized, deported, arrested, disenfranchised, expelled from the collective farm, or fired from work. Local administrative organs threatened to arrest a collective farm peasant after he reported on the drunkenness of the collective farm chairman.[80] A complaint sent to the radio station in Moscow resulted in a rural soviet chairman being fired from his post and a supply manager (*zavkhoz*) expelled from his collective farm and deported; the writer of the complaint was then disenfranchised for "agitation against the collective farm."[81] One peasant described the situation in his raion in 1929:

It was enough to write one notice in a newspaper or send a complaint about someone. Often such innocents were dekulakized or charged with some kind of crime, thrown in prison, and taken to court.[82]

Writers of damaging letters were subject to various threats and some, particularly rural, correspondents, were reportedly murdered.[83] A man from the Western oblast', whose letters of complaint resulted in at least one arrest, claimed that local officials finally disenfranchised him so that he "wouldn't have the right to file petitions about them."[84] A Urals man claimed he was disenfranchised because local officials resented him for a letter he wrote to *Krest'ianskaia gazeta* exposing their "hooliganism."[85] A peasant was dekulakized because he wrote to a newspaper exposing the criminal activity of a local official. In his letter to Kalinin, the peasant described his dekulakization as an effort by the official to eliminate him: "Of course, it serves Smirnov to label me a kulak and get rid of someone who reports on him (*na nego pishet*). . . ."[86]

Letters of complaint were often used to persecute the writers rather than the subjects of the complaint. Still, local officials viewed these documents as dangerously incriminating and made attempts to intercept or seize them en route to their superiors. This, however, did not discourage the janitor from Krasnodar. In 1936, he decided it was time to write Molotov after his school had failed for years to grant its janitors their due raise in pay. The letter which did in fact reach Molotov was the janitor's second; the first had been confiscated by municipal authorities and the janitor threatened with arrest.

When the director of the school, Chudnyi, heard about it, he took the petition away from me and said, "I'll read it over and add some.". . . Within a day, they came from the Municipal Office of Public Education and the Party Committee and started yelling at me for writing. They also interrogated me about who helped me write. Later, the head of the municipal trade unions told me, "You don't have the right to write Molotov; for this I'll have you arrested," and a whole series of other threats.[87]

Exposing another's illegality meant exposing oneself as well—not only to one's enemies, but to the scrutiny of an outside investigator. While investigators might accept allegations concerning the wrongdoing of local officials who were so notorious for their abuses, sympathy for the writer was not a given, even among supposedly disinterested parties. For example, a man who was fined 50 rubles by the police issued a complaint to the city soviet only to have the latter double the fine to 100 rubles.[88]

Often, those who investigated letters determined that the writer himself deserved to be reprimanded. The secretariat of Sovnarkom received a complaint in 1933 from a widow, Novikova, who lived in the Tatar autonomous republic. She charged the rural soviet chairman with acting illegally when he dekulakized her, confiscated all her property, and evicted her and her children from their home. Sovnarkom directed the woman's complaint to the procurator of the Tatar republic for an investigation who in turn passed the complaint to the raion procurator and instructed him to investigate. The complaint's downward journey continued as this procurator then passed the complaint to the people's investigator. Rather than vindicate Novikova, the investigator filed criminal charges against the widow. She was sentenced according to Article 58 of the Criminal Code for counter-revolutionary activity and the raion procurator who saw her original complaint confirmed the sentence.[89] Novikova was actually better off before she wrote.

Another case involving a man from Moscow further illustrates how the involvement of an outside investigator could condemn rather than vindicate the writer. The man claimed in his letters to Stalin, Kaganovich, and Ezhov that he was fired after having exposed criminal activity at the workplace for which several people were tried and convicted. When the Soviet Control Commission investigated the case, it discovered that the man was quite unpleasant, with a long history of making allegations against others on the job. His coworkers, eager to rid themselves of his constant criticism, managed to have him transferred by naming him a shock worker (*udarnik*), insisting he was uniquely qualified for certain positions, and even promising him bonuses. Evidently, they tired of such benevolent tactics and finally had him fired. The Commission reinstated him but only reluctantly after having him rebuked for his "inadmissible behavior" and "groundless accusations."[90]

Third party sympathy with the accused could even go so far as to sanction the deportation of a zealous complainer. A Moscow jurist and member of the College of Defenders claimed in 1925 that he was disenfranchised for having written a damaging letter about the former chairman of the volost' executive committee. The letter, published in the local paper, *Krasnyi put'*, alleged that this official sold materials that had been specifically allocated for the building of a school. According to the jurist, the official and his friends want to "wipe me off the face of the earth for hindering their criminal activity."[91] Representatives from the Moscow Control Commission who came to investigate the case reported that the jurist made "an extremely negative impression." They concluded that he should be deported for his "anti-soviet disposition" which, from the following description, was tantamount to overly-scrupulous informing:

> Aksenov is a petty village spider type, a parasite, an underground lawyer. For years he collects petty evidences of others' blunders, mistakes, etc. He follows everyone, eavesdrops on everything, spies. In a word, he's a typical informer and slanderer.[92]

Those who wrote about local injustices or transgressions, even if their charges were legitimate, were apt to be perceived as "zealous busybodies"[93] or scribblers (*pisaki*).[94] One group of peasants remarked that "the chairmen of the rural soviets and the district soviet executive committees call those who come to them with complaints bandits."[95] Communities did not generally like their informers. An investigator looking into a complaint about local officials by a certain Gershberg went to the writer's town only to find himself confronted by a wall of silence. No one claimed to know Gershberg. In the district soviet executive committee, enterprises, and organizations, everyone denied they knew anyone by that name, although they were not reluctant to voice the opinion that Gershberg's letter was "a provocation."[96] Because the writer was often viewed as a troublemaker, a third party could not be expected to come to his defense.

If those who issued charges of another's wrongdoing could do so with virtual impunity from criminal sanction, they were still vulnerable to other forms of coercion. The outcomes of complaint letters presented here, neither effective nor conclusive for the writer, reveal an element of uncertainty and risk. Yet despite the dangerous conditions, most informers did not show concern for reprisals by concealing their identities. For example, the vast majority of complaints received by the Moscow oblast' complaints bureau in 1930-31 concerned another's wrongful or illegal actions, yet fewer than one percent of these complaints were anonymous.[97] Although complaining posed some risk to the writer, people chose to sign their names to damaging accusations against officials well positioned to retaliate.

When one considers the risks of making charges against others in writing, it is not immediately apparent what motivated Russia's literate critics. Some who acknowledged the possibility of retaliation, such as the janitor from Krasnodar, decided nonetheless to speak out against others more powerful than they. Why did they make this choice? Perhaps those who wrote were more concerned with justice than the potential backlash. On the other hand, their risk-taking may have been motivated instead by frustration over official corruption, indignation, or a desire for revenge.[98]

For some, however, the risk appeared worth taking. There was always the chance that they could reclaim their rights if they managed to discredit those responsible for their own disenfranchisement, dekulakization, arrest, or expulsion from the collective farm. A common strategy of defense and rehabilitation in this period was to denounce one's accusers. Some writers hoped to reverse their fortunes by discrediting those who discredited them. Many had little more to lose and even stood to gain if they could turn a private dispute into one with political importance.[99] This strategy was frequently adopted, yet had the effect of simply reproducing local acts of repression.

Finally, writers may have been motivated by the need to gain favor with the regime, as they demonstrated their loyalty and service to Soviet power by answering the call to complain. For example, in his letter to Kalinin requesting the reinstatement of rights, one man proudly listed his service to the state—he fought in the civil war with the Reds, carried out anti-religious agitation, and wrote a series of notices to various newspapers which resulted in the arrest of several administrators.[100] The informer had an even greater claim to political loyalty when his act of informing put him in harm's way. The persecuted writer, the victim of reprisals, was quick to play the martyr for Soviet power.

Conclusion

Some citizen complaints of official misconduct did result in sanctions against local officials.[101] My purpose here, however, is to emphasize that, given the trail of these damaging letters and the possibility of counter-accusation, complaining often did less to improve the functions of state than to extend and exacerbate local disputes. Complaining failed to generate a predictable outcome because the balance of power between the complainer and his target was indeterminate, thus introducing an element of risk. Although the power relation between the accuser and accused may have been tilted in favor of the former given the regime's call to complain, it was a precarious balance at best. The ability to impose coercive sanctions shifted and it was never clear where this power resided—with the accuser who exposed another's crime, or his target who could issue reprisals and silence him.

Author's note: The author would like to thank those who read various drafts of this chapter and offered valuable comments: Sheila Fitzpatrick, Lisa Harteker, Peter Holquist, Daniel Klerman, Mark Marquardt, Alexis Papadopoulos, Gábor Rittersporn, Peter Solomon, and Michael Warren.

Notes

1. Jan T. Gross, "A Note on the Nature of Soviet Totalitarianism," *Soviet Studies* 34, no. 3 (1982): 375.

2. A number of works treat the subject of popular letters to Russian and Soviet authorities. Among them are: Horace W. Dewey and Ann Marie Kleimola, "The Petition (Chelobitnaja) as an Old Russian Literary Genre," *Slavonic and East European Review* 14, no. 3 (1970): 284-301; Andrew Verner, "Discursive Strategies in the 1905 Revolution: Peasant Petitions from Vladimir Province," *Russian Review* 54, no. 1 (January 1995): 65-91; Sheila Fitzpatrick, "Supplicants and Citizens: Public Letter-Writing in Soviet Russia in the 1930s," *Slavic Review* 55, no. 1 (Spring 1996): 78-106.

3. "Bolshe vnimaniia zhalobshchiku-trudiashchemusia," *Sovetskaia iustitsiia*, 1932, No. 13: 1.

4. V. I. Lenin, *Polnoe sobranie sochinenii*, Vol. XVII (Moscow, 1963), 188.

5. *Tretii s'ezd sovetov SSSR: postanovleniia* (Moscow, 1925), 14-15.

6. "Protiv oposhleniia lozunga samokritiki," *Pravda*, 28 June 1928: 2.

7. "Bolshe vnimaniia zhalobshchiku-trudiashchemusia": 1-2; "Iz rezoliutsii XV s'ezda VKP(b) o rabote TsKK RKI," in *Spravochnik po rassmotrenii krest'ianskikh zhalob* (Voronezh, 1932), 5.

8. "O zhalobakh," *Vlast' sovetov*, 1937, No. 2: 44.

9. "O prokurorskom «signalizatore» i o neuchtennykh «urokakh»," *Vlast' sovetov*, 1932, No. 19: 21-24.

10. On Russian and Soviet denunciations, see A. M. Kleimola, "The Duty to Denounce in Muscovite Russia," *Slavic Review* 31, no. 4 (Winter 1972): 759-79; Merle Fainsod, *Smolensk under Soviet Rule* (Cambridge, MA, 1958); Sheila Fitzpatrick, "Signals from Below: Soviet Letters of Denunciation of the 1930s," in Sheila Fitzpatrick and Robert Gellately, eds., "Practices of Denunciation in Modern Europe," special issue of *The Journal of Modern History* 68, no. 4 (December 1996); Sheila Fitzpatrick, *Stalin's Peasants* (Oxford, 1994).

11. For a general discussion of legislation concerning false denunciation, see *Kurs sovet-skogo ugolovnogo prava* III (Leningrad, 1973), 614-16; M. Kh. Khabibullin, *Otvetstvennost' za zavedemo lozhnyi donos i zavedemo lozhnoe pokazanie po sovetskomu ugolovnomu pravu* (Kazan, 1975).

12. V. I. Lenin, "Predlozheniia o rabote VChK," *Polnoe sobranie sochinenii*, Vol. XXXVII (Moscow, 1963), 535.

13. "Deistviia i rasporiazheniia pravitel'stva," *Izvestiia*, 1 December 1921: 2. The decree also treated certain forms of denunciation more severely. If the denunciation was made for the purpose of profit, included false documents and the charge that another committed a heinous crime, the punishment increased to no less than two years' deprivation of freedom.

14. "Ugolovnyi kodeks RSFSR, 1922," *Sobranie kodeksov RSFSR* (Moscow, 1925), 560. See Article 177.

15. "Ugolovnyi kodeks RSFSR, 1926," in *Sobranie kodeksov RSFSR* (Moscow, 1929), 679. See Article 95. Punishment for the most serious form of denunciation was reduced from "no less" than two years to "up to" two years. Three conditions had to be demonstrated. The most severe penalty could be issued for false denunciation combined with the charge of a heinous crime, profit motives *and* the creation of false evidence. These penalties for false denunciation remained unchanged in the 1937 Criminal Code.

16. The 1922 RSFSR Criminal Code defined slander as: "a false statement made intentionally and to defame another person." The Code, however, made a distinction between two types of slander—that which did and did not appear in print (or was reproduced and distributed). The latter was punished more leniently. Persons charged with slander were sentenced to deprivation of freedom or forced labor for up to six months. Slanderous statements which appeared in print were punishable by deprivation of freedom for up to one year. However, a softening of the official position on slander was reflected in the 1937 Criminal Code. Here, slander which appeared in print was subject to corrective labor (*ispravitel'no-trudovye raboty*) for up to one year or a fine of up to 1000 rubles. Other forms of slander were punishable by up to six months of corrective labor or a fine of up to 500 rubles. Thus, according to the 1937 law, slander might simply result in a minor fine for the writer. See "Ugolovnyi kodeks RSFSR, 1922," 559-560, Articles 174-175; *Ugolovnyi kodeks RSFSR* (Moscow, 1937), 77, Article 161.

17. For a history of Rabkrin, see E. A. Rees, *State Control in Soviet Russia: The Rise and Fall of the Workers' and Peasants' Inspectorate, 1920-1934* (New York, 1987); S. N. Ikonnikov, *Sozdanie i deiatel'nost' ob'edinennykh organov TsKK-RKI v 1923-1934* (Moscow, 1971).

18. *Kuda zhalovat'sia na neporiadki* (Moscow, 1926), 5.

19. *Ibid.*, 16.

20. *Chto nado znat' o biuro zhalob?* (Kzyl-Orda, 1927), 3.

21. Ikonnikov, *Sozdanie i deiatel'nost'*, p. 234.

22. "O zadachakh, formakh i metodakh raboty biuro zhalob," Joint Decree of the Presidium of the Party Central Control Commission and Rabkrin SSSR, 14 July 1933, *Gosudarstvennyi arkhiv Rossiiskoi Federatsii* (hereafter GARF), *f.* 7511, *op.* 1, *d.* 58: 30.

23. *Spravochnik pri rassmotrenii krest'ianskikh zhalob*, 6.

24. *Ibid.*, 7.

25. GARF, *f.* 7511, *op.* 1, *d.* 64: 20.

26. In 1935, the Procurator General, A. I. Vyshinskii, made the point that "complaints often provide enough material for one to decide an issue." He said that it was possible for prosecutors to decide on a complaint from this text alone, without needing to view other documents such as the sentence (*prigovor*) or the case file (*delo*). "Kratkaia stenogramma," GARF, *f.* 8131, *op.* 12, *d.* 3: 28.

27. *Chto nado znat' o biuro zhalob?*, 11.

28. M. Ulianova, "Piatidnevnik—politicheskaia kampaniia," *Pravda*, 4 March 1932: 4.

29. *Tsentral'nyi gosudarstvennyi arkhiv Moskovskoi oblasti* (hereafter TsGAMO), *f.* 807, *op.* 1, *d.* 2431: 13.

30. Kalinin's popular reception room *(priemnaia)* is discussed in "V priemnoi M. I. Kalinina," *Vlast' sovetov*, 1934, No. 6: 34.

31. GARF, *f.* 7511, *op.* 1, *d.* 143: 77.

32. "Ob uporiadochenii rassmotreniia krest'ianskikh zhalob," Tsirkuliar Narkomiusta No. 77 ot 10 maia 1932, in *Sovetskaia iustitsiia*, 1932, No. 15: 32-33.

33. At the time of the complaints bureau campaign in April 1932, Vyshinskii urged prosecutors to improve their processing and investigation of complaints, particularly those concerning bureaucratism. See *ibid.*

34. GARF, *f.* 8131, *op.* 11, *d.* 147: 20.

35. The former *Tsentral'nyi gosudarstvennyi arkhiv RSFSR* (TsGA RSFSR), currently GARF A, *f.* 406, *op.* 13, *d.* 952a: 41.

36. "Ob uchastii organov iustitsii vo Vsesoiuznom piatidnevnike po rabote Biuro zhalob RKI," Tsirkuliar Narkomiusta No. 43 ot 16 marta 1932, in *Sovetskaia iustitsiia*, 1932, No. 8: 26.

37. Ikonnikov, *Sozdanie i deiatel'nost*, 243.

38. *Sovetskaia iustitsiia*, 1930, No. 13: 15.

39. "O meropriiatiiakh po rassmotreniiu krest'ianskikh zhalob," Postanovlenie Prezidiuma VTsIKa ot 20 avgusta 1930, in GARF, *f.* 7511, *op.* 1, *d.* 58: 3.

40. *Sovetskaia iustitsiia*, 1930, No. 28: 33.

41. "Vnimatel'no podoiti k kazhdoi zhalobe," *Vlast' sovetov*, 1934, No. 14: 32. On the growing legal responsibilities of local governments in this period, see Peter H. Solomon, Jr., "Criminalization and Decriminalization in Soviet Criminal Policy, 1917-1941," *Law and Society* 16, no. 1 (1981-82): 9-43.

42. "Rabotu po zhalobam nuzhno perestroit'," *Vlast' sovetov*, 1934, No. 14: 34.

43. "Nuzhny reshitel'nye mery," *Vlast' sovetov*, 1935, No. 24: 35.

44. "Litsom k zhalobshchiku," *Sovetskaia iustitsiia*, 1936, No. 1: 12.

45. GARF, *f.* 7511, *op.* 1, *d.* 143: 47.

46. The Procuracy received 2,204 complaints in January 1934, 11,670 complaints in October 1935, and 26,000 complaints in May 1936. "Kratkaia stenogramma," GARF, *f.* 8131, *op.* 12, *d.* 3: 19; "Reshenie III Plenuma," *Sovetskaia iustitsiia*, 1936, No. 21: 8.

47. In 1935, the Commissariat of Justice established a separate complaints department (*otdel zhalob*) under the Supreme Court and the Procuracy to handle the growing volume of complaints (GARF, *f.* 7511, *op.* 1, *d.* 142: 47, 52), but then abolished the one under the Supreme Court and had all complaints directed to the Procuracy.

48. "Iz deiat'elnosti NKIu," *Sovetskaia iustitsiia*, 1933, No. 1: 21; "Pokonchit' s nedo-otsenkoi zhalob trudiashchikhsia," *Sovetskaia iustitsiia*, 1935, No. 12: 6; "Litsom k zhalobshchiku," *Sovetskaia iustitsiia*, 1936, No. 1: 12.

49. The example of Kalinin's reception room (*priemnaia*) offers a glimpse into the kinds of complaints which people wrote in different periods. Prior to 1928, most of the complaints this priemnaia received concerned unemployment, personal requests for housing, medical care, education, stipends, and other social assistance. The character of complaints later changed, with most people charging that local officials were breaking the law and committing abuses related to over-taxation (*pereoblozhenie*), collectivization, the confiscation of property, and dekulakization. See "Rabotu po zhalobam nuzhno perestroit'," *Vlast' sovetov*, 1934, No. 14: 31, 34. The character of complaints continued to change into the 1930s. By 1934-35, a growing number of complaints concerned exclusion from and non-admission to the collective farm. See "Kak rabotaet Sekretariat M. I. Kalinina," *Vlast' sovetov*, 1935, No. 18: 17.

50. "Poriadok rassmotreniia zhalob," *Vlast' sovetov*, 1934, No. 14: 30-38; "O ras-smotrenii zhalob trudiashchikhsia," Postanovlenie TsIKa ot 30 maia 1936, *Sobranie zakonov i rasporiazhenii*, 1936, No. 31, st. 276: 472-75.

51. GARF A, *f.* 406, *op.* 13, *d.* 952a: 21.

52. Ikonnikov, *Sozdanie i deiatel'nost'*, 255.

53. "O zhalobakh," *Vlast' sovetov*, 1937, No. 4: 29.

54. *Ibid.*, No. 2: 43.

55. GARF, *f.* 7511, *op.* 1, *d.* 143: 54.

56. *Ibid.*: 80.

57. "O meropriiatiiakh po rassmotreniiu krest'ianskikh zhalob," Postanovlenie Prezidi-uma VTsIKa ot 20 avgusta 1930, in GARF, *f.* 7511, *op.* 1, *d.* 58: 3.

58. "Pora pokonchit' s volokitoi i biurokratizmom po razboru zhalob," *Vlast' sovetov*, 1935, No. 10: 20.

59. "Kratkaia stenogramma," GARF, *f.* 8131, *op.* 12, *d.* 3: 3, 28.

60. I. Kutuzov, *Organizatsiia ucheta, rassmotreniia zhalob i khodataistv lits, lishennykh izbiratel'nykh prav* (Moscow, 1935), 22.

61. V. I. Lenin, *Polnoe sobranie sochinenii*, Vol. LIV (Moscow, 1965), 101.

62. "Zhaloby trudiashchikhsia," *Vlast' sovetov*, 1937, No. 11: 21.

63. "O mestnykh biuro zhalob RKI," *Vlast' sovetov*, 1931, No. 23-24: 32.

64. TsGAMO, *f.* 807, *op.* 1, *d.* 2431: 4-8.

65. Nearly a third of the complaints concerned judicial sentences, another third concerned various forms of taxation, and roughly ten percent concerned disenfranchisement. "V Gorkovskoi prokurature plokho postavleno rassmotrenie zhalob," *Sovetskaia iustitsiia*, 1935, No. 4: 13.

66. "Zhaloby trudiashchikhsia," *Vlast' sovetov*, 1937, No. 16: 34.

67. GARF, *f.* 7511, *op.* 1, *d.* 143: 76.

68. *Tsentr khraneniia strakhovogo fonda* (Center for the Preservation of a Reserve Record), located in the Western Siberian town of Ialutorovsk (hereafter TsKhSF), *f.* 5248, *op.* 14, *d.* 10275: 6.

69. GARF, *f.* 7511, *op.* 1, *d.* 58: 6.

70. "O zhalobakh," *Vlast' sovetov*, 1937, No. 4: 29.

71. "Za volokitu o razborom krest'ianskikh zhalob—k otvetstvennosti," *Sovetskaia iustitsiia*, 1933, No. 1: 25.

72. "Zhaloby trudiashchikhsia," *Vlast' sovetov*, 1937, No. 17: 29.

73. "O meropriiatiiakh po rassmotreniiu krest'ianskikh zhalob," Postanovlenie VTsIKa ot 20 avgusta 1930, in GARF, *f.* 7511, *op.* 1, *d.* 58: 3; "Ob uporiadochenii rassmotreniia krest'ianskikh zhalob," Tsirkuliar Narkomiusta No. 77 ot 10 maia 1932, *Sovetskaia iustitsiia*, 1932, No. 15: 32-33; "Za volokitu o razborom krest'ianskikh zhalob—k otvetstvennosti," *Sovetskaia iustitsiia*, 1933, No. 1: 25; "Ob uporiadochenii dela rassmotreniia i razresheniia zhalob," Postanovleniie Prezidiuma VTsIKa ot 1 iiulia 1934, *Vlast' sovetov*, 1934, No. 14: 30-31; "Zhaloby trudiashchikhsia," *Vlast' sovetov*, 1937, No. 5: 12.

74. *Sovetskaia iustitsiia*, 1931, No. 13: 21.

75. GARF, *f.* 7511, *op.* 1, *d.* 143: 60.

76. GARF, *f.* 8131, *op.* 13, *d.* 14: 5, 13-15, 20-32.

77. GARF, *f.* 8131, *op.* 12, *d.* 10: 27.

78. TsKhSF, *f.* 5248, *op.* 2, *d.* 21: 37.

79. Fainsod, *Smolensk under Soviet Rule,* 385.

80. GARF, *f.* 7511, *op.* 1, *d.* 143: 30.

81. TsKhSF, *f.* 5248, *op.* 14, *d.* 9069: 8-9.

82. GARF, *f.* 1235, *op.* 141, *d.* 582: 67.

83. N. Lagovier and A. Rodnianskii, *Dela rabsel'korovskie: ugolovno-sudebnye ocherki* (Moscow, 1929).

84. TsKhSF, *f.* 5248, *op.* 13, *d.* 3799: 36.

85. TsKhSF, *f.* 5248, *op.* 9, *d.* 10170: 13-14.

86. GARF, *f.* 1235, *op.* 64, *d.* 527: 36.

87. GARF, *f.* 7511, *op.* 1, *d.* 193: 108. The one who helped the janitor write his letter to Molotov was expelled from the Party. The petition or damaging document was retained by city authorities, despite the janitor's repeated requests that it be returned. Molotov took a special interest in this case and asked Antipov, head of Sovnarkom's Commission on Soviet Control, to investigate.

88. "Zhaloby trudiashchikhsia," *Vlast' sovetov*, 1937, No. 11: 19.

89. "V prokurature RSFSR," *Sovetskaia iustitsiia*, 1934, No. 22: 19.

90. GARF, *f.* 7511, *op.* 1, *d.* 139: 33-36.

91. GARF, *f.* 1235, *op.* 140, *d.* 284: 19-21.

92. *Ibid.*:16.

93. Fainsod, *Smolensk under Soviet Rule*, 385. Informers were not always popular in the pre-Revolutionary period either. John LeDonne describes how the Manifesto of 1762 abolishing the Secret Chancery condemned those who denounced others as "evil, lowborn and lazy people." See John P. LeDonne, *Ruling Russia* (Princeton, NJ, 1984), 123.

94. Lagovier and Rodnianskii, *Dela rabsel'korovskie*, 21.

95. GARF, *f.* 1235, *op.* 141, *d.* 586: 9-13.

96. GARF, *f.* 1235, *op.* 141, *d.* 428: 44, 48.

97. TsGAMO, *f.* 807, *op.* 1, *d.* 2431: 4.

98. On indignation, revenge, and seemingly irrational behavior, see Jon Elster, "Some Unresolved Problems in the Theory of Rational Behavior," *Acta Sociologica* 36, no. 3 (1993): 179-91. I thank Alexis Papadopoulos for bringing this article to my attention.

99.   Sally Falk Moore, "Legal Liability and Evolutionary Interpretation: Some Aspects of Strict Liability, Self-Help and Collective Responsibility," in Max Gluckman, ed., *The Allocation of Responsibility* (Manchester, 1972), 51-107.

100.   GARF, *f.* 5404, *op.* 2, *d.* 114: 25.

101.   It is difficult to determine the number of complaints which were resolved compared with those which were ignored, passed to others, or resulted in reprisals against the writer. A proportional breakdown of this kind would be necessary in order to determine the degree to which the Soviet complaints mechanism responded to citizen letters. Although a proportional breakdown of the outcome of complaints can sometimes be found in journals and archival documents, one should be skeptical of these figures because they were compiled by local officials responsible for reviewing letters whose interest it was to present a favorable image to their superiors of how they were satisfying citizen complaints.

9

THE POLITBURO, PENAL POLICY, AND "LEGAL REFORMS" IN THE 1930s

Oleg V. Khlevniuk

Throughout several decades of Soviet history, the highest organs of Communist Party power, most notably the Politburo, formulated and implemented the principal state policies. The Politburo initiated not only state terror but also those reforms, from NEP to the "thaw" to perestroika, that ultimately brought about the present changes to the political system in Russia. Contemporary Russian society bears the heavy influence of the old governing style epitomized by the Politburo.

The study of the Politburo's activities, however, has been hindered by the lack of primary sources, for until the late 1980s pertinent documents have constituted a state secret. Recently, the situation has improved. Although a substantial amount of Politburo documents remain in the closed Politburo Archive,[1] researchers have received access to large quantities of sources in the Russian Center for the Preservation and Study of Documents of Recent History (RTsKhIDNI, the former Central Party Archive) and in the State Archive of the Russian Federation (GARF—the former Central State Archive of the October Revolution, Social Construction, and the Highest Organs of State Power of the USSR). In addition, from spring 1994, a part of the collection of Politburo documents has been transferred from the Presidential Archive to RTsKhIDNI. For some time historians have been studying the so-called Politburo "special protocols"—top secret decisions bearing the designation "special folder" (*osobaia papka*). Other Politburo documents from the Presidential Archive, such as the original copies of Politburo protocols and personal collections of Politburo members, will soon also be accessible for research.

In this chapter I sketch the preliminary results of my research in the Politburo archival depositories on the subject of penal policy of the 1930s, and the Politburo's role in the instigation of state terror and in the "reforms" following the terror. Three crucial questions are addressed: (1) what role did the Politburo play in the management of the Soviet judicial system, and what policies did it implement? (2) to what extent did the penal policy of the 1930s experience changes, and what were the purpose and the logistics underlying the "judicial reforms" introduced during the period? and (3) finally, what impact did the penal system established in the 1930s make on Soviet legal culture, particularly with respect to public perceptions of the essence and limits of judicial reforms?

Within the Soviet penal system, the Politburo's basic functions had been established by the early 1930s. The protocols of Politburo meetings confirm that the Politburo initiated and organized all the most important state-terror and dekulakization campaigns, as well as the policies concerning mass deportations from the borderlands and mass arrests of "anti-Soviet elements." It also engineered the key political trials, and decided in advance the punishments, whether execution or specific terms of imprisonment. Questions related to this subject were regularly discussed during Politburo sessions. On 30 December 1930 Stalin proposed holding closed Politburo sessions, for matters relating to the OGPU, defense, and foreign policy, as well as to certain questions of internal Party affairs. These closed sessions were to be held on the 10th, 20th, and 30th of each month.[2]

In order to supervise penal campaigns the Politburo set up special commissions. The bulk of these commissions were occupied with specific issues and functioned only for a limited time; but two—the Commission for *spetspereselentsy* (special settlers) and the Commission for Judicial (later, Political) Cases—operated on a permanent basis. The former was established by Politburo resolutions on 20 February and 11 March 1931 to oversee the "exile and resettlement of the kulaks." Its members were A. A. Andreev (chairman), G. G. Iagoda, and P. P. Postyshev. On 5 October 1931 Ia. E. Rudzutak was designated chairman in Andreev's stead. The Commission for spetspereselentsy terminated its activities by the mid-1930s.

In contrast, the Commission for Political Cases continued to operate for several decades beginning in the late 1920s, and served as the highest branch in the strictly centralized system of court proceedings for political cases. On 23 December 1926 the Politburo approved the statute of the three-member Commission whose activities would encompass the entire territory of the USSR. Local Soviet and Party organs were to transfer to the Commission "indictments in all cases which they [the locals] deemed to be of special sociopolitical importance, or merited hearing in public show trials." Further, the statute stipulated that for these types of cases local Party committees "could not give any directives to courts and investigative organs before consideration by the Political Commission." The Commission, after having examined the proposals of the local authorities, established which cases had "sociopolitical importance" and referred these to the Politburo for discussion, the issuing of the appropriate directive, and the referral to local judicial agencies.[3] On 22 October 1928 the Politburo approved the following membership of the Political Commission: Ianson (chairman), Menzhinskii, and Shkiriatov.[4]

When terror escalated with the onset of collectivization, this complicated sequence of court proceedings for "counter-revolutionary cases" and its coordination with the Politburo was altered. On 5 December 1929, at the suggestion of Ianson, new rules were established. In significant (especially political) cases, after the investigation was concluded, the regional or republican procurator had to check and approve the charge(s) before sending the case to the court. After the trial the court would send a copy of its sentence to the Political Commission of the Politburo, which would give its instructions to the first court of appeal (cassation instance). Those cases in which the death penalty had been assigned and approved in the cassation review would proceed to the republican procuracy for consideration of a further review in supervision, but with the recommendation of the Politburo's Political Commission included in the case record.[5] In the 1930s, the Political Commission under the chair of M. I. Kalinin became the top appellate body for political cases involving the death penalty. Accordingly, in Politburo protocols it was called not only the commission for court or political cases, but also the commission on sentences, the commission on capital punishment, or the commission for the examination of cases of capital punishment.

The Politburo's attempts to control the proceedings in political cases reflected one of the trends in the penal policy of the early 1930s. Faced with the devastating effects of mass repressions, the Party leadership tried to regulate terror and to keep it within controllable limits. Thus, steps in the direction of legal reforms were made for the first time in 1931, after the beginning of collectivization and the struggle against the "bourgeois specialists." The crisis that engulfed the entire country compelled the leadership to control terror with changes in legal procedures and penal policy, which R. W. Davies called "minireforms." From mid-1931, the Politburo issued resolutions limiting the OGPU's powers to arrest engineers and technical personnel.[6] Stalin highlighted the essence of these provisions in June 1931 in his speech to a conference of managers: ". . . the policeman must not become a technical expert in production. . . . It is also impermissible that in the factory an entire OGPU crew sits idly under a signboard and expects to be delivered cases, otherwise they make them up."[7] (When the text of the speech was prepared for publication, Stalin crossed out this passage.)

For an open declaration of the need to restrict terror to the countryside and to continue legal "minireforms" consider the government decree of 25 June 1932, "On Revolutionary Legality." This decree called for criminal prosecution of officials who violated laws relating to the peasantry. At the same time, the decree forbade the dismissal and/or transfer of people's court judges and district procurators without the consent of the regional authorities. (This measure was meant to protect legal officials from local political bosses.) It is important to emphasize that the resolution of 25 June constituted part of the reforms initiated in spring–summer 1932. These reforms are sometimes referred to as the "neo-NEP" because of the government's authorization of a free market, the restitution of confiscated cattle to the peasants, and partial relaxation of centralized control over artisans. However, the whole "neo-NEP" remained mere declaration. Already in the fall of 1932, repression, particularly in the countryside, escalated.

State terror during this period was epitomized by the famous law of 7 August 1932, "On the Defence of Socialist Property," adopted on Stalin's initiative. On 16 September 1932 the Politburo issued a special instruction for the implementation of this law. The main purpose of the instruction was to establish a simplified procedure for the approval of death sentences. For cases prosecuted under the August law, death sentences came into effect after their approval by the Republican Supreme Courts (for cases tried in regular courts in the republics), by the Supreme Court of the USSR (for cases tried by transport courts or military tribunals), or by the OGPU Board (for cases examined by OGPU plenipotentiaries). After receiving a case file for review, these instances were to hand down within 48 hours a decision either approving or setting aside the death penalty. Implementation of death sentences was to follow immediately after approval.[8]

The abrogation of regular legal procedures affected not only cases falling under the Law of 7 August; all of the large-scale punitive actions of 1930-1933 assumed an extraordinary character, reflected in the activity of an assortment of extrajudicial agencies. Along with the OGPU Board, the Presidium of the Central Executive Committee (TsIK) on 3 February 1930 authorized the creation of *troiki* made up of an OGPU plenipotentiary, the procurator of the region, and a regional Party official. During the campaign of "liquidation of kulaks," the OGPU delegated its authority to conduct extrajudicial proceedings to the troiki. According to the data collected by V. P. Popov on OGPU bodies, the troiki convicted more than 179,000 persons in 1930; 152,000 in 1931; and 60,000 in 1932. For their part, the Special Board and the Collegium of the OGPU convicted about 28,000 in 1930, 28,000 in 1931, and 33,000 in 1932.[9]

The terror unleashed in the early 1930s assumed such dimensions that it threatened to destroy all levers of control over penal actions. The OGPU often failed to organize new settlements for the deported peasants, and mass arrests were carried out by functionaries who had no plenary powers, such as chairmen of kolkhozy and rural soviets, the leaders of district soviets, secretaries of Party cells, and all sorts of plenipotentiaries. Detention as a preventive measure was assigned even for the most insignificant infraction. As a result, prisons and jails were overcrowded beyond all limits, resulting in an epidemic of typhus.

This situation forced the government, while continuing repression, to take measures regulating terror. On 10 March 1933 the Council of People's Commissars adopted the resolution "Relieving the Places of Confinement," which called for an inspection of prisons and camps by the procuracy and limited the use of detention as a preventive measure.[10] On 7 May 1933 the Politburo adopted (by survey) the directive "On the OGPU *Troiki*" which prohibited republican, territorial, and regional troiki (excluding the Far East) from passing death sentences. Finally, on the next day, the Politburo issued the well-known "Instruction" to Party and Soviet officials, OGPU, courts, and the procuracy. The Instruction of 8 May forbade mass deportations of the peasantry; it permitted, however, "individual" deportations of active "counter-revolutionaries"—with a limit of 12,000 households for the entire country. Arrests by officials lacking legal authority to make them and the use of detainment as a preventive measure for "unimportant crimes" were also prohibited. The Instruction went on to set a maximum limit for the total number of prisoners in the various prisons and colonies (excluding camps and settlements) under the Commissariat of Justice, OGPU, and the Police—400,000 persons, in contrast to 800,000 held in prison at the time. The Instruction authorized commuting sentences of one and three years' confinement to one year of non-custodial forced labor; the rest of the term was to be considered conditional.[11]

All these measures did not, however, change penal policy in a fundamental way. The arrests and deportations of kulaks and "declassified elements" continued unabated. The Politburo itself violated its own provision to curtail the prerogatives of the troiki. For example, on 11 July 1933, in response to a request of R. I. Eikhe, the Party secretary of the Western Siberian territory, the Politburo granted the territorial troika of the OGPU the right to use the death penalty against "bandits" who terrorized the population and new settlers. On 11 August 1933, upon the entreaty of OGPU chairman Iagoda, the Politburo "temporarily permitted" the troiki in Ukraine, the Volga region, Byelorussia, Kazakhstan, the Ural region, and Western Siberia to use the death penalty against the ringleaders of "armed banditry."[12]

Still, under the threat of growing chaos, the Party leadership realized the need to reinforce "legal order." On 11 August 1933, after a visit to his old village in Kalininskii district of Moscow region, Mikhail Kalinin (among other things head of the Politburo commission on court cases) wrote to Lazar Kaganovich that

> large numbers of convicts, sentenced mainly to forced labor, overcrowded the villages. After a first-hand review of the cases, it is clear that in the overwhelming majority of cases the punishment is largely formal and by far exceeds the level of guilt. A large percentage of the convicts are of "Soviet people [*publiki*]," including communists. It seems to me that it is urgent to elevate seriously the prestige of the court, so that the court's decisions (I refer to the people's court) not only be based on law, but also correspond to all the circumstances of the crime. I think that it would be advisable to enlist as judges old communist-pensioners, kolkhozniks with life experience, and discerning Party workers. The judicial system is crucial in popularizing communism. It would be also beneficial from time to time to send classified directives from the Moscow regional Party committee to procurators and people's judges.[13]

In 1934, the government was forced to relax its penal policies. The "reforms" affected almost all socioeconomic spheres. At the beginning of 1934, the second Five-Year Plan provided for relatively moderate growth of industrial production. The government also made some concessions to the peasantry, particularly with respect to subsidiary private farm-holdings. Rigid ideological control also subsided and the slogan of a "cultured, prosperous life" replaced the promotion of revolutionary asceticism. An important component of this "turn" was the restructuring of the OGPU and the court system.

The particulars of the "reforms" of 1934 are as yet unknown. Historians have argued over the existence within the Politburo of two groups, "moderates" and "radicals," whose rivalry supposedly determined fluctuations in the "general line," such as the moderate policies of 1934. However, judging by the available factual material, it was Stalin who initiated the turn, and the rest of the Politburo merely followed suit. Thus, on 20 February 1934, at Stalin's suggestion, the Politburo decided to organize the "All-Union

People's Commissariat of Internal Affairs [NKVD], including within it a restructured OGPU."[14] The establishment of the NKVD prompted questions about the reorganization of the courts and procuracy and for this issue a special commission was formed under V. V. Kuibyshev.[15] On 10 July 1934, the Politburo approved several resolutions concerning the agencies of punishment and the courts.

The first resolution, which established the new NKVD with the former OGPU as a component part, simultaneously deprived the NKVD of its court functions. The cases investigated by the NKVD's political police, upon the completion of the investigation, were to be directed to the "appropriate courts for regular legal proceedings." The OGPU's Judicial Collegium was abolished; and the prerogatives of the NKVD's new Special Board were also partially restricted.

At the same time, a second resolution "On the Work of Courts and Procuracy" established a new mechanism through which the courts could accommodate the cases transferred to them which previously had been examined by extrajudicial organs. For the examination of state crimes investigated by the NKVD, special judicial collegia were created at the USSR Supreme Court, the supreme courts of the republics, and the territorial and regional courts. Cases of "high treason, espionage, terror, explosions, arson, and other kinds of destructions" were to be transferred to military tribunals and the Military Collegium of the USSR Supreme Court. Cases of crimes on railroads and water transport were to be turned over to the corresponding courts and the Transport Collegium of the USSR Supreme Court. All other cases investigated by the NKVD were to be examined by "people's courts in the regular way."

A Court-Supervision Collegium was formed at the Supreme Court for examining the appeals of decisions from the republican supreme courts and the other collegia of the USSR Supreme Court. Still, the decisions of this new Collegium dealing with death sentences had to be submitted for approval to the Politburo's Commission on Political Cases. All death sentences pronounced by republican supreme courts and not examined by the Court-Supervision Collegium were also to be confirmed by the same commission. Finally, the Politburo resolution "On the Work of the Courts and Procuracy" also authorized the appointment of additional cadres for new court instances and called for strengthening of the regional Colleges of Advocates.[16]

In this way, the reorganization of the court system in 1934 was meant to limit to a degree the activities of extrajudicial and extraordinary bodies. The strengthening of regular court proceedings was theoretically justified by the need to utilize the best achievements of capitalist justice and to retain some "bourgeois" components in socialist civil law.[17]

It is difficult to say how far the regime was willing to carry out these "reforms." Available documents offer a contradictory picture. On the one hand, the Politburo continued numerous repressive actions: for example, on 19 September 1934 the Politburo violated the established order of sanctioning the death penalty. In response to a telegram by V. M. Molotov, who at the time was visiting Siberia, the Politburo authorized the Party secretary of Western Siberia, Eikhe, to sanction death penalties in September and October.[18] On 2 November this term was extended to 15 November. On the other hand, other evidence supports the view that the ongoing reorganization of judicial and penal agencies continued through the fall of 1934. Thus, a commission of the Politburo was investigating wrongdoing on the part of NKVD officials.

This commission was organized in response to two complaints received by the Party leadership. As early as spring 1933, seeking a scapegoat for the famine and the failure of grain procurement, the OGPU fabricated a case about a counter-revolutionary organization within the Commissariat of Agriculture and the Commissariat of Sovkhozy.[19] In this case, the OGPU arrested about a hundred agricultural specialists. At the head of this "organization," the OGPU alleged, were F. M. Konar and A. M. Markevich, two Deputy Commissars of Agriculture, along with M. M. Wolf, a Deputy Commissar of Sovkhozy. Although at the trial fourteen defendants renounced their "confessions," forty defendants were sentenced to death and the rest to various terms in prison. Already in a camp, one of the convicts in the case, Deputy Commissar Markevich, wrote an appeal to Stalin, Molotov, and the Procurator-General Akulov complaining about "incorrect methods of the OGPU investigation." Simultaneously, another convict, A. G. Revis, complained to Mariia Ulianova (also Lenin's sister) of the Party's Control Commission about the OGPU's use of torture during the investigation. Ulianova forwarded the letter to Stalin who decided to take action against the OGPU. In a special memo to Kuibyshev and Zhdanov, Stalin wrote:

> I draw your attention to the enclosed documents, especially Revis's letter. It appears that the content of both documents is accurate. I therefore suggest: a) authorizing a commission consisting of Kaganovich, Kuibyshev, and Akulov to verify the content of the documents; b) releasing any innocent persons in confinement; c) cleansing the OGPU of the fanciers of specific 'investigative methods' and punishing them regardless of rank and post. The case, in my opinion, is serious, and must be pursued to the end.

On 15 September 1934, on Stalin's order, the Politburo adopted a top secret resolution on the "A. P. and A. M." case (designated as a "special folder"). The case was to be examined by the special commission consisting of Kuibyshev, Kaganovich, and Akulov. On 4 October the commission was reinforced by the addition of Zhdanov.[20]

Apparently, the commission examined the matter thoroughly, and, in addition to the case of Revis and Markevich, several similar cases also came to light.[21] For example, a procurator from Saratov region sent a memo to Deputy USSR Procurator General Vyshinskii, who, in turn, forwarded it to Kuibyshev and Zhdanov.[22] In his memorandum dated 31 August 1934, the Saratov procurator Apeter wrote about the unlawful methods of investigation by the Lysogorsk NKVD district. To extract the necessary evidence the interrogators had kept the arrested on a hot stove for several days after having held them in a cold cell. For six to seven days, NKVD henchmen deprived the prisoners of bread, threatened to execute them, forced them to maintain a posture in which they could not breathe, and kept them in overcrowded cells, etc. According to Apeter three police functionaries responsible for these acts had already been arrested.[23]

Having collected similar facts, the commission prepared a draft resolution providing for the "elimination of unlawful investigative methods, punishment of those [police employees] guilty of such offenses, and the reconsideration of the case of Revis and Markevich."[24] However, immediately after Kirov's murder, the re-examination of the case was discontinued. On Stalin's order, Markevich was returned from a Moscow prison, where he awaited a new trial, back to the labor camp.

In the first months after Kirov's assassination, the upsurge of state terror threatened to swallow up all the "moderate" reforms of the previous period. Already within a few hours after learning about the events in Leningrad, Stalin himself prepared a government resolution, which became known as the "Law of 1 December." This extraordinary act went into effect with only Stalin's personal decision; formal ratification by the Politburo came only on 3 December.[25] The Law of 1 December required that in cases of terrorism the investigation be completed within ten days; the indictment was to be handed down to the accused only a day before the trial; the case was to be heard in camera without the accused, defense counsel, or procurator; and the right to cassation appeal and appeal for clemency were eliminated, so that death sentences would be carried out immediately after their announcement. The December decree was to create optimal conditions for the conduct of large-scale repressions and was widely used in 1937 and 1938.

In the beginning of 1935, the NKVD applied the December decree to a large group of former Party oppositionists, who were arrested and charged with complicity in Kirov's murder. At the same time, the NKVD began deportations of "socially-alien elements" from Leningrad and other regions of the country. In spite of this wave of repression, the press of circumstances forced the Stalinist leadership to continue its comparatively moderate policy.

To a degree, Stalin's policy of moderation was connected to the Kremlin's new foreign policy toward the West; but the situation inside the USSR impeded the implementation of repression even more. In the mid-1930s, the five-year terms of exile for hundreds of thousands of peasants-spetspereselentsy (kulaks) were expiring, and, according to the law, they had the right to return to their homes. Besides the former kulaks, there were millions of people who had experienced various kinds of repressions in previous years, and the government regarded all of them as a potential "fifth column." In order to neutralize this "column," the government went to all lengths. On the one hand, it took harsh measures such as prohibiting kulaks from leaving their places of exile. At the same time, the government attempted to make peace with several categories of the "aggrieved" and win them over through concessions and rehabilitations. After all, stability was also needed to promote the country's recovery from profound economic crisis. All of these circumstances helped to restrain the spread of terror and checked the activities of extraordinary extrajudicial agencies.

Already on 31 January 1935—at the height of the repression unleashed by Kirov's assassination—the Politburo at Stalin's suggestion decided to introduce major changes in the constitution concerning in particular the electoral system. The idea was to replace the indirect and unequal elections, with voting in full public view, with direct and equal elections through secret ballot.[26] In the following days this issue became the subject of a mass propaganda campaign. Promises to introduce a new constitution were accompanied by several other "liberal" actions of the government.

On 17 June 1935, the Sovnarkom and Central Committee issued the resolution "On Procedures for Making Arrests," which expanded the rules set out in the Instruction of 8 May 1933. The resolution provided that "the NKVD could make arrests, in all cases, without exception, only with the sanction of a corresponding procurator." It also established an intricate procedure for the clearance of arrests of top officials, specialists, and Party members with the chiefs of the People's commissariats, departments, and Party committees.[27] As this June resolution partially restricted the arbitrary power of the NKVD, it was not accidental that in 1937-1938 the resolution was ignored and in effect set aside.

On 26 July 1935 the Politburo took a decision affecting a large part of the rural population: "On the Remission of Previous Convictions for the Kolkhozniks."[28] This resolution removed the convictions of ". . . kolkhozniks who had been sentenced to prison terms of up to five years, or to non-custodial sanctions, if they had either completed their terms or been assigned early release, as long as they are now working honestly in a kolkhoz (even though at the time of their crimes they had been private farmers)." Although the resolution affected thousands of peasants, it did not embrace those accused of counter-revolutionary crimes, nor those sentenced to terms of more than five years.

The implementation of the resolution dragged out for several years. On 25 April 1936, the Procurator General Vyshinskii, in a memorandum to Stalin, Kalinin, and Molotov, summed up the results of the remission campaign. He informed the government that in the entire USSR, between 29 July 1935 and 1 March 1936, 556,790 kolkhozniks had had their records of conviction cancelled. In addition, another 212,199 kolkhozniks in Ukraine had their convictions removed pursuant to a decision of its republican government. In spite of such high numbers, Vyshinskii suggested an inspection of those regions, where a high percentage of applications for the elimination of criminal records had been refused. The Politburo approved this suggestion.[29]

Simultaneously with the campaign to remove records of conviction among kolkhozniks, the government began the exoneration and release of managerial personnel convicted for economic crimes in 1932-34. On 10 August 1935, the Politburo approved a government resolution on the issue.[30] Further, in early 1936, the Politburo decided to rehabilitate several categories of convicts sentenced under the Law of 7 August 1932, on theft of socialist property. Vyshinskii reported to Stalin, Molotov, and Kalinin that as of 20 July 1936, 115,000 cases had been reviewed, and of these more than 91,000 involved incorrect application of the Law. As a result, 37,425 persons (or 32 percent of the convicts whose cases were reviewed) had been released.[31]

The campaign to review cases was accompanied by noisy propaganda shows focusing on Stalin's pronouncement—"cadres decide every-thing!"—at the May 1935 meeting with graduates of military academies and at the December 1935 conference of combine operators on the necessity of "concern for the welfare of workers," and that "a son is not responsible for his father's deeds." These manifestations reflected the regime's intention to reconcile itself with different social strata which had been earlier subjected to repressions, particularly young people.

Slackening of terror and the government's flirtation with "legality" objectively strengthened the position of the courts and procuracy in their constant rivalry with the NKVD. In 1935-1936, NKVD leadership regularly complained to the Central Committee that local courts and procurators had been denying the NKVD arrest warrants in political cases, acquitting the accused, demanding supplementary investigations, or in a series of cases handing down sentences that the NKVD found too mild.[32] The unwillingness of legal officials to ignore irregularities perpetrated by the NKVD extended beyond local judges. For example, in July 1935, the Chairman of the USSR Supreme Court, Alexander N. Vinokurov, sent out a circular demanding an end to unfounded criminal prosecutions and launched a review of cases in places where the NKVD had violated the law. This circular, however, annoyed some political leaders and was withdrawn several months later.[33]

The courts' insistence on a degree of independence in their relations with the NKVD complicated the conduct of mass repressions. It was for this reason that, during the 1937-1938 terror, the courts were effectively replaced by extrajudicial bodies, the Special Board and the troiki of the NKVD.

On 2 July 1937 the Politburo sent a telegram to local NKVD and Party leaders. The telegram called for "registration of all kulaks who had returned from exile and criminals from confinement, so that the most hostile of them would be quickly arrested and shot under the supervision of the troiki. The rest, that is, the less active but still hostile elements, were to be registered and deported to regions stipulated by the NKVD." Local authorities had five days to submit to Moscow data regarding the composition of the troiki and the number of persons liable to be arrested and executed.[34]

After having received the data furnished by the local officials, the NKVD prepared the order "On the Operations to Repress Former Kulaks, Criminals, and Other Anti-Soviet Elements." Depending on the region, the operation was to begin sometime between 5 August and 15 August and be completed within four months. All those subjected to repressions were divided into two groups: the first category were to be immediately arrested and executed; the rest were to be detained in camps or prisons for eight to ten years. All regions, territories, and republics received quotas for each category, and out of 259,450 persons subjected to arrest, 72,950 were to be shot. These numbers, however, were obviously incomplete, for several regions of the country were not listed. The order also allowed local officials to ask Moscow to increase execution quotas. In addition, the families of convicts were liable to exile or detainment in camps. On 31 July the Politburo confirmed the NKVD order.[35]

As a rule, the regional, territorial, and republican troiki were made up of the head of the relevant NKVD unit (regional chief or republican commissar), the secretary of the corresponding Party organization, and the procurator. The troiki received extraordinary powers: to impose sentences even to death, without supervision, and to oversee the implementation of their decisions.

Beginning in late August, local officials began approaching the Central Committee with requests to increase the quotas on repression. Between 28 August and 15 December, the Politburo extended the quotas for various regions adding 22,500 and 16,800 people in both categories, respectively.[36] Besides the "general" operation to liquidate "anti-Soviet elements," the NKVD began special actions against the German and Polish populations, and, in the Far East, the Koreans.

Plans not withstanding, the operation of "repressing anti-Soviet elements" was not completed within four months. On 31 January 1938, the Politburo approved the NKVD's suggestion that "additional numbers of former kulaks, criminals, and active anti-Soviet elements be subjected to repression." Pursuant to this resolution, by 15 March, and in the Far East 1 April, an additional 57,000 persons were to be arrested and 48,000 of them were to be shot. Accordingly, the powers of the troiki were extended.[37]

After the Politburo had approved the new quotas of repression, the situation of the previous year recurred. Again, local officials started requesting further increases in the numbers and an extension of the terms of the operation. In response, between 1 February and 29 August 1938, the Politburo sanctioned—in addition to the January quotas—the repression of another almost 90,000 persons.[38] This meant that the Politburo disregarded its own April deadline for ending the operation.[39]

According to the data that Khrushchev produced at the July Plenum of 1957, out of more than one-and-a half million people arrested in 1937-1938, more than 680,000 were shot. Even these horrifying numbers, however, are scarcely complete. For one thing, they omit hundreds of thousands of persons who were deported and exiled. For another, it is unclear which categories (if any) accounted for repressed persons who died during their "investigations."

If one uses not only Khrushchev's data but also those elaborated by V. P. Popov, it turns out that the overwhelming majority of persons repressed in 1937 and 1938 were convicted by extrajudicial organs—the troiki and the Special Board. Moreover, the courts and procuracy, so research has shown, were virtually destroyed during the terror.[40]

To stop the terror it was enough for the government to terminate the activities of extrajudicial organs, partially restrict the powers of the NKVD, and declare a return to regular court proceedings. This moment came near the end of 1938. On 15 November 1938, a directive of SNK and TsK forbade the examination of cases by the troiki, and the joint edict of 17 November 1938 stopped mass arrests and deportations.[41] Furthermore, as scholars have noticed, the late 1930s marked a turning point in the development of Soviet law and legal institutions. The struggle against "legal nihilism" was announced; the system of legal education transformed; and the influence of central authority on local justice increased, while the influence of local leaders reduced.[42]

Facts known today confirm that the mass repressions of the Stalinist period as well as their periodic mitigation were actions of the center, as a rule initiated by the Politburo, and above all by Stalin. Certain fluctuations of the "general line" were possible only because of the separation of the realms of terror and law, and the division of the activities of judicial and extrajudicial organs. During the periods of relaxation when extraordinary laws and extrajudicial organs were somewhat restrained, the regular courts and laws played a greater role, acquiring and exercising more authority. Even at these times, law and the courts remained exclusively an instrument of penal policy, but they did help to place limits on the terror. As Stalin wrote to Kaganovich (24 June 1932) proposing a new law defending socialist property, "we must act on the basis of law (the *muzhik* loves legality), and not merely on the basis of the OGPU's inclinations. In these circumstances, the OGPU's prestige will be effectively raised and its role will be 'ennobled,' for [in the people's eyes] the organs will act not arbitrarily but guided by laws."[43]

The reasons for such manipulations and the preservation of justice and law, in spite of the use of terror, have already been addressed in the scholarly literature. The acceptance of such "bourgeois residues" as law and justice was a concession to the realities of socioeconomic development, a necessary condition for the administration of society and for keeping the system in balance. A similar picture could be seen in the economy, where commodity-money relations were introduced and, in order to stimulate productivity, calls for a "cultured and prosperous life" replaced the slogans of revolutionary asceticism. Likewise, the stabilizing role of legal institutions (even in their modified Soviet form) emerged in the effort to overcome the crises caused by mass terror.

The fluctuations of state-terror policy do not by any means indicate that the Soviet leadership ever considered justice and courts as a neutral source of social regulation. Through all the legal "reforms" of the Stalinist period, law and justice remained an instrument of penal policy. These reforms served merely to regulate the terror, so that it did not undermine the system itself.

Well tested during the Stalin era, the principle of the separation of terror and justice was adopted by the Soviet leadership in the post-Stalin period. The familiarity of this principle from the late Stalin years helps to explain the rapid success of the "destalinization" campaign in the months after Stalin's death. Khrushchev's reforms put an end to mass repression and the most abhorrent Stalinist laws, placed the MVD-MGB organs under strict control, and promoted the rehabilitation of the millions of victims. These reforms represented a significant step in the direction of the democratization of Soviet society.

The principal role of law and justice, however, did not change. Having come to political maturity during the Stalinist era, the Soviet leaders of the 1950s-1980s were committed to preserving the foundations of the regime, including the treatment of law and justice as mere institutions of penal policy. The turn away from mass repression was, in the view of post-Stalin leaders, the limit of their "legal reform," the point beyond which they considered it unnecessary to move.

In pursuing this policy, the Soviet leadership found substantial backing in society, the legal culture of which was distorted by Stalin's terror and memories of it. A sense of the law's shakiness and the constant threat of state "exceptionalism" *(chrezvychaishchina)* was firmly rooted in the people's consciousness. These ideas, along with an indifference toward state institutions reflected in the saying "the main thing is that they don't lock us up," limited the social base for legal reforms. A significant part of the population thus considered a law-based and predictable authoritarianism to be a blessing, in comparison to the "extraordinary," terrorist, and absolutely unpredictable Stalinist regime. It is possible to suggest that on this basis government and society reached a compromise to ensure political stability. As a result, even today one can observe in Russian society two peculiar tendencies: a calm and even sympathetic attitude toward authoritarianism and a legal apathy based on profound disbelief about the capacity of law and the courts to defend the interests of ordinary persons.

This chapter was translated by Alexander Prusin and Peter H. Solomon, Jr.

Notes

1. During the Gorbachev era, the archive was renamed the Archive of the President of the USSR, and is now known as the Archive of the President of the Russian Federation, or the Kremlin Archive.

2. O. V. Khlevniuk, *et al.*, eds., *Stalinskoe Politbiuro v 30-e gody: Sbornik dokumentov* (Moscow, 1995), 180-81.

3. *Ibid.*, 58.

4. *Rossiiskii tsentr khraneniia i izucheniia dokumentov noveishei istorii* (hereafter RTsKhIDNI), *f.* 17, *op.* 3, *d.* 710: 3.

5. Khlevniuk, *et al.*, eds., *Stalinskoe Politbiuro*, 59.

6. Hiroaki Kuromiya, *Stalin's Industrial Revolution: Politics and Workers, 1928-1932* (Cambridge, MA, 1988), 272-76.

7. RTsKhIDNI, *f.* 85, *op.* 28, *d.* 8: 160, 192.

8. RTsKhIDNI, *f.* 17, *op.* 162, *d.* 13: 99-100; excerpts published in Khlevniuk, *et al.*, eds., *Stalinskoe Politbiuro*, 61-62.

9. V. P. Popov, "Gosudarstvennyi terror v sovetskoi Rossii, 1923-1953 (Istochniki i ikh interpretatsii)," *Otechestvennye arkhivy*, 1992, No. 2: 20-31; "State Terror in Soviet Russia, 1923-1953," *Russian Politics and Law* 32, no. 3 (May-June 1994): 94.

10. *Gosudarstvennyi arkhiv Rossiiskoi Federatsii* (hereafter GARF), *f.* 5446, *op.* 57, *d.* 23: 141-146.

11. RTsKhIDNI, *f.* 17, *op.* 3, *d.* 922: 58-58.

12. Khlevniuk, *et al.*, eds., *Stalinskoe Politbiuro*, 64-65.

13. *Ibid.*, 132.

14. RTsKhIDNI, *f.* 17, *op.* 3, *d.* 939: 2.

15. GARF, *f.* 5446, *op.* 27, *d.* 57: 1-22.

16. RTsKhIDNI, *f.* 17, *op.* 3, *d.* 948: 95-100.

17. Eugene Huskey, "Vyshynskii, Krylenko, and the Shaping of the Soviet Legal Order," *Slavic Review* 46, no. 3 (Fall 1987): 420-21.

18. RTsKhIDNI, *f.* 17, *op.* 162, *d.* 17: 43.

19. *Pravda*, 5 March 1933.

20. RTsKhIDNI, *f.* 17, *op.* 162, *d.* 17: 57.

21. B. A. Viktorov, *Bez grifa "sekretno"* (Moscow, 1990), 140.

22. The copy of the note has been preserved in the archive of Kuibyshev's secretariat.

23. GARF, *f.* 5446, *op.* 22, *d.* 81: 428-429.

24. Viktorov, *Bez grifa*, 140.

25. RTsKhIDNI, *f.* 17, *op.* 162, *d.* 17: 87.

26. RTsKhIDNI, *f.* 17, *op.* 163, *d.* 515: 152.

27. The entire text of the resolution is in Viktorov, *Bez grifa*, 202-204.

28. RTsKhIDNI, *f.* 17, *op.* 3, *d.* 969: 21. Registered as the resolution of the SNK and TsIK SSSR of 29 July 1935.

29. RTsKhIDNI, *f.* 17, *d.* 569: 135-137.

30. RTsKhIDNI, *f.* 17, *op.* 3, *d.* 970: 144-145.

31. GARF, *f.* 5446, *op.* 12, *d.* 896: 52.

32. For a detailed description, see O. V. Khlevniuk, *1937: Stalin, NKVD i sovetskoe obshchestvo* (Moscow, 1992), 63-66.

33. RTsKhIDNI, *f.* 78, op. 6, *d.* 86: 32-135; GARF, *f.* 8131, op. 37, *d.* 60: 109-116.

34. *Trud*, 4 June 1992.

35. *Ibid.*

36. The data are partially published in *Moskovskie novosti*, 21 June 1992; see also in RTsKhIDNI the protocols of Politburo conferences (marked "special folder").

37. *Moskovskie novosti*, 21 June 1992.

38. Computed on the basis of data in RTsKhIDNI, Politburo protocols ("special folder").

39. For additional details on penal actions in 1937-38, see O. V. Khlevniuk, "The Objectives of the Great Terror, 1937-1938," *Soviet History, 1917-1953: Essays in Honor of R. W. Davies* (London, 1995), 158-76.

40. Peter H. Solomon, Jr., "Soviet Criminal Justice and the Great Terror," *Slavic Review* 46, no. 3 (1987): 395-408; A. Muranov and V. Zviagintsev, *Sud nad sudiami (osobaia papka Ulrikha)* (Kazan, 1993).

41. *Istoricheskii arkhiv*, 1992, No. 1: 125-28.

42. Robert Sharlet, "Stalinism and Soviet Legal Culture," in Robert Tucker, ed., *Stalinism* (New York, 1974), 155-180; Peter H. Solomon, Jr., "Local Political Power and Soviet Criminal Justice, 1922-1941," *Soviet Studies* 37, no. 3 (1985): 305-329.

43. "Pis'mo ot Stalina k Kaganovichu," 24 iiunia 1932.

10

EXTRA-JUDICIAL REPRESSION AND THE COURTS: THEIR RELATIONSHIP IN THE 1930s

Gábor T. Rittersporn

In the 1930s Soviet leaders sought to change the way both the courts and extra-judicial bodies (political police) dealt with what the regime took for infringements of its order. The decade saw a series of reorganizations touching the procuracy, the courts, the People's Commissariat of Justice, and the agencies of the secret police, as well as measures to redistribute powers among these bodies.[1] It also witnessed new draft criminal and civil procedure codes and debates behind the scenes within the judicial establishment, in which advocates of firm legal norms seemed to take the upper hand.[2] However, the impact of these debates and organizational measures on actual judicial and penal practice was limited. The discussions of the mid-1930s about constraining repression through law were followed by a whirlwind of terror in 1937-38, and the most prominent spokesman of the moderate camp, Procurator General A. Ia. Vyshinskii, became closely associated with this proliferation of coercion. To be sure, in early 1936 Vyshinskii did denounce to Stalin some of the practices of the NKVD that had doubled the penal population in less than four years. But the growth in the number of inmates in camps, colonies, and prisons continued, exceeding 2,400,000 in January 1941.[3] Although some leaders saw a need to improve the administration of justice, it proved impossible to achieve real changes before World War II, and in fact until the mid-1950s.

It is a truism that this incapacity to reshape judicial policy resulted from the constraints of the Soviet system itself. One way to evaluate the system's impact is to explore the relationship between the working of the courts and the functioning of extra-judicial tribunals, i.e., between bodies that were supposed to operate according to precise legal standards, and structures whose sheer existence ensued from political considerations.[4] Political expediency had always been an essential ingredient in the administration of Soviet justice, but in the early 1930s (during collectivization) it constituted the basic principle of operation, with an elaborate theoretical foundation and far-reaching consequences for the judiciary.[5] The reign of expediency threatened to blur the distinction between judicial and extra-judicial procedures and to move the working of the former beyond the limits of even Soviet laws. The danger did not go unnoticed at the summit of the regime, where top politicians took measures in 1934 not only to normalize the functioning of the courts, but also to restrict the adjudication and sentencing powers of the political police and strengthen procuratorial supervision over their use.

However, the police quickly recovered and extended its prerogatives, escaping all control and legal regulation in 1937-38. Even when the scope of extra-judicial adjudication was significantly narrowed after 1938, many of its functions were assumed by courts.

Already in the 1920s, Soviet criminal policy was marked by a highly politicized understanding of crime and punishment, as well as contradictions between an educative approach to punishment and limited means to realize it.[6] The dramatic conflicts of collectivization and the chaotic spread of violence in the wake of the attack on the peasantry only increased the weight of political considerations in the administration of justice.[7] Moreover, the campaign produced reactions and effects unanticipated in high places. Open and covert resistance to the drive proved stronger and more widespread than expected.[8] In addition, local authorities tended to overreach when dealing with real and imaginary opponents of collectivization. Even though the secret police and its deputy chief, Genrykh Iagoda, often condemned excesses,[9] the top leadership preferred to tolerate arbitrariness in the administration of repression rather than make concessions to the rural world. After all, when in March 1930 Stalin expressed disapproval of the way the campaign was progressing, peasants reacted with insubordination, mass withdrawal from collective farms, and in some cases even rebellion.[10]

In 1931 the population of the camps under OGPU control grew by almost 27 percent; between January 1931 and mid-1932 the number of inmates in penal institutions of the Russian Federation increased by nearly 30 percent; and in 1931 the 479,065 persons arrested by the political police exceeded the total they had taken in custody between 1924 and 1928. Still, 298,369 of these detainees were never prosecuted, although more than 70 percent of them were alleged counter-revolutionaries.[11] This "slippage" related to the regime's determination in spring 1932 to re-establish "revolutionary legality."[12] Among other things, the Politburo proposed the "strictest" punishment "for the slightest attempt to transgress laws" by Party members, and "categorically" forbade Party bodies to interfere with the administration of justice. Nevertheless, its strictures against arbitrarily removing judges were mitigated through a clause according to which Party instances could do so if their actions were endorsed by higher bodies. Moreover, the Politburo's practice of prescribing sentences in particular cases (especially involving capital punishment) did not convey the impression that Party intervention in court decisions was over.[13] The leadership may well have intended to check arbitrary repression, but in 1932 as a whole 410,433 people were arrested by the secret police, 47.6 percent on political charges, and of those 268,514 would be released without standing trial. While 2,109 persons were executed in these cases in 1929, the number rose to 20,201 in 1930 and dropped back to 10,651 in 1931. In 1932 the number of executions was 2,728.[14]

These high figures were closely related to circumstances beyond the realm of the justice agencies as well as the control of the Party-state. The consequences of the bad harvest of 1931—which had been aggravated by the peasants' unwillingness to cooperate with the regime's rural policy—were by spring 1932 threatening the supply of food in the country. No wonder that assaults on state property by famished people became frequent, and the issue figured more than once on the agenda of the Politburo.[15] This is why the prospect of an even worse harvest did away with the project of protecting "revolutionary legality," shortly after it had been launched, and motivated a merciless attack whose aim was not merely to meet the state's food procurement plans, but also to demonstrate, with every possible means, that peasants could not avoid working in the kolkhoz and shouldering compulsory deliveries.[16]

Beyond climatic conditions or the problems of agriculture, the reaction of officialdom in the wake of the campaigns also had a strong influence on judicial policy and practice. The problem was that excesses similar to those committed during collectivization tended to occur whenever officials were charged with producing quick results, under threat of punishment if they failed to live up to Moscow's expectations.[17] And throughout the decade the top leadership continued to rely upon such high-pressure tactics, repeatedly launching extreme initiatives, correcting them several times, mostly through confidential instructions, coming close to losing control over events, and ultimately stopping the process with directives contrary to the spirit of the original operations. The offensive against the theft of state and kolkhoz property that accompanied the famine of 1932–33 represents a typical example of such an enterprise. Starting with the "Law of 7 August," which called for a mandatory death penalty or, in case of mitigating circumstances, ten years of confinement, this attempt to curtail thefts of the regime's property soon became captive to a series of measures that led in 1934 to its abandonment.[18] Nothing characterizes better the chaotic implementation of this Law than the fact that in 1936, when it was decided to review all sentences pronounced in these cases between 1932 and 1935, legal officials were unable to specify the exact number of convicts still affected by the Law.[19] This was due in part to an earlier revision of a substantial number of the more than 400,000 sentences rendered in 1932-33[20] (which included 16,838 death verdicts).

The campaign against theft constituted a major factor in the doubling of the population of penal institutions between early 1932 and the spring of 1933, and led to the decision to reduce the number of inmates.[21] The secret Instruction of 8 May 1933, in which the Central Committee and the government ordered an end to the "orgy of arrests" and "violent forms of repression on the countryside . . . ," reinforced the control of the procuracy over detention procedures and restricted the right of local authorities to take suspects in custody.[22] Thereafter, the number of criminal convictions declined sharply. Between the first halves of 1933 and 1936, it fell by nearly 40 percent in Russia and 75 percent in Belorussia.[23] Still, although convictions decreased, the number of cases that fell apart remained high and convictions by extra-judicial bodies declined only a little.[24] Moreover, illegal arrests continued to be a problem, and procurators frequently condoned them, despite their duty to prevent this practice.[25] Even when the Central Committee and the government issued another secret instruction in June 1935 stipulating that no one could be taken in custody without procuratorial sanction, officials of the political police did not always comply.[26]

Getting control over arrests was just one of a series of actions on the part of the regime to put repression, both judicial and extra-judicial, under control. These steps included the creation in 1933 of an All-Union Procuracy with enlarged supervisory prerogatives and the reorganization in 1934 of the political police. The regional bodies of the police lost the right to adjudicate and sentence, as most "counter-revolutionary" crimes were passed to the jurisdiction of military tribunals and special collegia of regional courts, and procuratorial supervision of the new NKVD was strengthened.[27] Moreover, the top Party leaders went out of their way to insist upon the elimination of arbitrary repression and the full use of courts and legal procedure even in dealing with "class enemies."[28]

There can be no doubt that the leadership's intention to contain excesses and gain control over the application of coercion was genuine. In the mid-1930s the regime had every reason to want to regulate the application of repression. After all, when, as in 1933–34, mere teachers felt entitled to arrest people, and the highest instance of the state had to remind regional authorities repeatedly that it and not they had the prerogative to decide about the application of the death penalty,[29] it appeared that the state's monopoly on the use of legitimate violence had come under threat. For all this, the limitations on extra-judicial repression did not materialize, because they proved incompatible with other demands and with the regime's political agenda.

It is tempting to hypothesize that the assassination of Sergei Kirov played a crucial role in the decision to revive police adjudication. To be sure, police and courts alike were enjoined to punish persons who even spoke approvingly of terrorists, even with capital punishment.[30] Yet, a closer look at the jurisdiction and actual practice of the restored regional tribunals of the police (known as the *troiki* of the provincial administrations of the NKVD) reveals that they did not deal with allegedly political offenses. The establishment of these new police tribunals less than a year after the dissolution of the earlier troiki indicated that Soviet criminal policy could not be pursued through the courts and regular criminal procedure alone, however flexible it might be.

The regional police troiki were set up in the spring of 1935 and—like the Special Board of the NKVD—they were empowered to pronounce sentences of up to five years of detention. This step represented a return to the routine of the collectivization drive, and although the procuracy was theoretically in a position to control police jurisdiction it did not exert a strong influence on extra-judicial sentencing. Even the Procurator General complained that some of his protests went unheard.[31] In contrast to the Special Board in Moscow, the regional troiki did not hear "counter-revolutionary" cases.[32] Besides "malevolent violators of law" accused of having infringed upon passport regulations and "professional beggars," they were supposed to decide the fate of a vague category of people who had been either sentenced in the past and presumed to maintain relations with the "criminal milieu," or, without previous judgment, did not perform "socially useful work," had no fixed residence, and were suspected to have links with outlaws. In spite of warnings against "superfluous haste" and "campaign-like actions," this "removal of the criminal and déclassé element"[33] tended to overstep even the vague rules governing police conduct. It is characteristic, however, that the procuracy, which repeatedly protested against this state of affairs, did not object to the fact that persons sentenced by regional troiki were not prosecuted for particular offenses or that the courts passed to the police troiki cases in which they found no legal ground for conviction.[34]

Between 1934 and 1936 the share of camp inmates sentenced by courts, as opposed to extrajudicial bodies, rose from 57.8 percent to 69.1 percent.[35] Yet, in this period when the courts were supposed to be assuming almost exclusive handling of criminal cases, the new regional police troiki were responsible for the conviction of 260,477 persons, or about 8.7 percent of all convictions rendered by courts and extra-judicial bodies in the USSR. This contrasted with the Special Board in Moscow which accounted for only 2 percent, and had yielded most "political" cases to the special collegia.[36] Moreover, the number of "socially dangerous and harmful elements" confined in the labor camps (with terms exceeding three years)—a large part of the production of the new troiki—reached 103,513 in 1936, almost equalling the figure for convicted "counter-revolutionaries," which stood at 104,826.[37] Note that the involvement of troiki in cases of "counter-revolutionary crimes" declined between 1935 and 1936 (by 22.5 percent or more than 30,000 inmates).[38] With the release in 1936 of a second wave of prisoners convicted under the Law of 7 August 1932 (discussed above), "socially dangerous persons" became the only group whose share of the camp population was growing.[39]

It was precisely during the campaign against this obscure category of offenders—in 1935-36—that the debate on the need for firm legal norms took place. As the discussion also touched upon the principle of analogy, whose presence in the criminal code legitimated vague terms like "harmful elements," and as Vyshinskii opposed the continuation of this postulate in the criminal code, the controversy may appear to have been a demagogic exercise or at least as futile.[40] However, the dispute did concern the real issue of developing a regular and manageable judiciary—and indirectly also the entire Party and state apparatus. Moreover, this period was marked by efforts to limit arbitrariness on the part of judges as well as of the police. These facts indicate both the seriousness of the debate and the inconsistency of the regime's actions. The problem of the large number of unjustly prosecuted people must have caused concern in high places, because a department of the Central Committee prepared a draft of a confidential letter on this issue,[41] the final version of which was nonetheless never approved or sent to law enforcement agencies. A directive of the Supreme Court that broached the question of the "enormous number of people" who had been groundlessly prosecuted was found by Vyshinskii to be too conciliatory toward "class enemies."[42] But even if the Procurator General shared NKVD chief Iagoda's view that the courts did not always show sufficient "vigilance," he reproached the police for the feeble quality of its investigations. In the last months of 1935 Vyshinskii began to plead for the enlargement of the competencies even of the lowest levels of the judicial hierarchy as well as for the reinforcement of procuratorial control over the work of security bodies.[43]

The consequences of "vigilance" would soon pose problems. Already at the beginning of 1936 Vyshinskii and his main opponent in the analogy discussion, Justice Commissar N. V. Krylenko, found it necessary to alert the highest leaders about the disproportionate growth in accusations and convictions for "anti-Soviet agitation and propaganda." What is more, the Procurator General seized this opportunity to protest against both the growth of the camp population and the jurisdiction of the NKVD.[44] Iagoda did his best to defend his agency and even sought to insinuate that his adversary was trying to create a "tribune for the dissemination of counter-revolutionary calumny" through his proposal to limit the sentencing authority of the Special Board in affairs of "anti-Soviet agitation."[45] But Vyshinskii, who originally had only mentioned this category of cases, enlarged his accusations against the extra-judicial bodies and came close to criticizing almost every law enforcement operation of the NKVD.[46]

Nonetheless, the issue of "harmful individuals" was not brought up in the discussion on the need for solid legal norms and did not become an object of controversy in the heated conflict over police jurisdiction. The proliferation of convicts allegedly endangering the social order did not appear problematic, although the numbers of failed investigations, the increase in the number of prosecutions for "counter-revolutionary agitators," and the growth of the camp population did. This incongruence was closely related to the unexpressed—and in the conceptual framework of the regime's self-understanding, indefinable—sense of danger on the part of the Soviet elite, which put the guiding principles of criminal policy into conflict with the realities of judicial practice. The fact that there was hardly any sphere of agriculture in which judges were not summoned to intervene and often also to detect "political crimes," or that the procuracy and the courts were enjoined to "fight for the non-ferrous metallurgy," to "struggle for the preparedness [of the water transport] for navigation," to answer through "harsh repression . . . criminal attempts on Stakhanovites" or to inflict penalties "for counter-revolutionary expressions in connection with comrade Kirov's assassination"[47] suggest that there was scarcely a walk of life in which the Bolsheviks could feel their claim to undisputed leadership secure. Even new laws could not always be applied according to the current priorities of the rural and industrial economy or in harmony with the political campaigns of the moment—hence the resort to analogy and the enshrinement of this principle in the criminal code.

The doubts about the utility of this fundamental principle (analogy) and the controversies about the mass of groundless criminal proceedings show a rather clear vision of the extent to which the judiciary, the police, and even government administration in general eluded attempts at control. Still, the continuing persecution of "socially dangerous elements" shows that the peril this vague category of people presumably represented was felt more strongly than the need to bring order to the working of the Party and state apparatus, and that leading politicians were ready to tolerate even the uncontrollable functioning of governmental mechanisms in order to deal with this threat. Only extreme insecurity on the part of the top leaders could account for a judicial practice that the legal chiefs found excessive, but still was designed not only to target precisely defined offenses, but also to identify and neutralize every potential deviation from the regime's norms. It was inevitable that, besides the prophylactic criminalization of a wide range of largely indefinable acts and life circumstances, these conditions would sooner or later bring under suspicion a great number of people on the basis of ascribed characteristics and legitimate the principle of collective guilt, even if this had not been an axiom of Bolshevik "class justice." The forcible resettlement of ethnic minorities from border areas (and above all of Poles, Germans, and Koreans), which started in the mid-1930s, showed all the more that entire nationalities were becoming "suspect," since these actions were accompanied by a "cleansing" of these districts of other "unreliable elements," who were sent to distant regions or into exile, regardless of their ethnic origin.[48]

The official discourse of a regime that pretends to be the most popular in the world has no way to conceptualize, let alone explain, how its stability might seem threatened even by vagabonds. Moreover, the self-understanding of an elite that acts without a shadow of bad conscience cannot account for the contradiction between its intentions and administrative practices, that risk transforming actions into excesses and disorganizing the institutions that support its positions. The refusal of the Soviet elite to recognize that its own patterns of conduct and the ensuing failures of administration were part of the normal workings of government—and in fact as system-inherent phenomena—made it inevitable that their manifestations would be ascribed to alleged subversive machinations of persons who, despite their place in the establishment, came to be defined as alien infiltrators. Present in every walk of life, these phenomena appeared to reflect widespread conspiratorial intrigues, and the unpopularity of the regime helped lend credibility among the public to the accusations leveled at purported saboteurs, called "enemies of the people."[49] These conditions led to a hunt for "political criminals," producing murderous conflicts within the Party-state as well as between the regime and the rest of society. The conflicts were hard to grasp for both the participants and the people who became their victims and who were often the same officials pursuing the "fight against enemies."[50]

Between 1936 and 1939, the share of "political" prisoners in hard regime camps rose from 12.8 percent to 34.5 percent and that of "socially dangerous people" from 12.6 percent to 21.7 percent. In these years, while the camp population overall grew at a rate of 1.6, the number of alleged counter-revolutionaries grew by 4.6 and of "socially harmful elements" by 2.8. But if we look at the period between 1934 and 1939, we discover that while the number of "politicals" (which significantly diminished in 1934-36) grew 2.6 times, the number of "dangerous persons" multiplied by 7.[51] While the quantity of arrests and executions in cases initiated or heard by police bodies regularly decreased between 1933 and 1936, from 1936 to 1937 arrests of this kind multiplied by a factor of 7.1 and the ensuing shootings by a factor of 315.8 to reach 681,692 in 1937 and 1938. About 30 percent of the more than 3,840,000 persons sentenced in 1937-38 (including "socially dangerous persons") were condemned by extra-judicial bodies and the share of persons sent to the camps by these bodies reached 59.4 percent in 1939.[52]

Extra-judicial repression was closely related to the search for individuals supposedly responsible for dysfunctions of the Party and state apparatus. Still, the major factor in the wholesale terror of 1937-38 was a Politburo order of 31 July 1937 to shoot or imprison "former kulaks, members of anti-Soviet parties, White Guards, gendarmes and officials of tsarist Russia, bandits, returned emigres, participants of anti-Soviet organizations, churchmen and sectarians [and] recidivist criminals."[53] The launching of these "mass operations" appears to have been decided only in the summer of 1937. There were no earlier plans to increase the camp population. Moveover, the operations lasted four times as long as foreseen at the outset and victimized five times more persons than the number targeted in the initial directive.[54] The agencies spearheading the "mass operations" were new "special *troiki*" established in 1937 in each province and composed of the NKVD chief, the procurator, and the Party secretary of a given region. Their establishment signified a return to the routine prevailing before 1934 when regional troiki (and the Special Board of the OGPU as well) had been empowered to pronounce death sentences.[55] The available sources show that the arrests and shootings spread beyond the categories the original Politburo directive earmarked as objectives of the operation in a chaotic way, in part because of a series of directives targeting mainly ethnic minorities. This spillover was also fueled by the demands of regional authorities who were literally vying for higher "plan indicators" than those originally fixed. The documents also demonstrate that Moscow was ready to accept these demands and that it did not try to restrain the increasingly absurd crusade whose victims were selected on grounds that had little in common even with the fight against supposedly "harmful elements."[56]

One could argue that the operation of the courts was not influenced by these activities on the part of extra-judicial bodies, and to a degree this was so. As in years past, the confidential bulletin of the People's Commissariat of Justice carried items in 1937 that denounced the interference in court decisions by local leaders, and the proportion of people acquitted and cases dismissed by trial court did not differ in 1937 from that of 1935.[57] However, judges on two specialized courts did become involved in the terror. In 1937-38, nearly 180,000 persons were sentenced by military tribunals and the special collegia of regional courts in cases initiated or investigated by the NKVD. Furthermore, central and provincial Party authorities alike called upon the special collegia to stage "demonstration" trials whose outcome was decided in Moscow or by its local representatives.[58] In these ways at least some judges were involved in the terror. Well before the launching of the "mass operations" and obviously under the influence of the widening search for "counter-revolutionaries," the Supreme Court and the People's Commissariat of Justice instructed their subordinate agencies to find "political criminals" at any price.[59] The procuracy showed particular zeal: it anticipated the drive through a proposal to intensify the police clampdown on "dangerous people" and had no objections when the purge campaign began to focus even on beggars.[60] This institutional guardian of legality did not raise questions about the wholesale terror as such, even though it did protest when persons slated to stand trial before a military tribunal were summarily shot on a decision of a "special troika."[61]

Still, the specific place the procuracy occupied in the judicial system made it inevitable that this institution would be placed in charge of moderating the hunt for "enemies," even though the impulse was to come from the political leaders.[62] Beginning in February 1938 the procuracy dispatched a series of directives to the effect that prosecutions of "counter-revolutionary offenses" could not be initiated without sanction from regional procurators, whose preliminary authorization was also needed to arrest the suspects, and that local procurators should strengthen their supervision over the "isolation of socially harmful elements."[63] At the same time, however—and all the while thundering against excesses reported to him—Vyshinskii cautioned his subordinates to make inquiries "only in exceptional cases. . . ." when it came to appeals by victims of the "mass operations,"[64] a stance that discouraged local procurators from delving into these cases. The trouble was that, according to Politburo instructions superseding earlier ones, these campaigns should have been over by April 1938, whereas they were still continuing on such a scale that, as late as mid-September, Procurator General Pankratev had to designate regional procurators to sit in judgment, in the company of provincial NKVD chiefs and Party secretaries, over "arrested counter-revolutionary ethnic contingents."[65] Someone had to decide what to do with the large number of unfortunates already in custody. Nevertheless, it seems that the Politburo resolved to stop the drive following a proposal of the procuracy, two months later, although on the same day it had sanctioned the establishment of two more regional troiki.[66]

The ensuing resolution of the Central Committee and the government (of 17 November 1938) explained that "enemies of the people" had been responsible for the indiscriminate terror, expressed indignation at the demands of the NKVD for the authorization to arrest more and more people (which the regime's summit had not rejected up to this moment), denounced the way that cases were summarily investigated and settled (which did not seem to be a problem even a few days earlier), called off the "mass operations," abolished all the troiki, and placed all detention procedures under the control of the procuracy.[67] Although the follow-up instructions of both the security police and the procuracy went out of their way to stress the need to observe legal norms, the former did not dwell too much on procuratorial controls and devoted space to the necessity of maintaining the sentencing authority of the Special Board, even while recommending "maximal reduction" of its case-load and insisting that it observe the code of criminal procedure.[68]

Problems with legality were far from over. In 1939 the procuracy lodged protests against arrests that it had not been asked to sanction, even detentions of such "enemies" as former leaders of the NKVD, which were no doubt decided by the highest authorities.[69] At the same time, reflecting the momentary political expediency that dictated the legality drive of 1939, Procurator General Pankratev insisted that defense lawyers should not participate at the hearing of "political" cases without careful screening and that procurators should refrain from staging a show trial of fallen officials, on the grounds that this was not ". . . indispensable . . . from the point of view of mobilizing the masses" and that there was no guarantee that the accused would play their parts as expected.[70]

In fact, the detainees under investigation and on trial soon started to retract their confessions which had been extracted under torture and—true to the administration's habit of overreacting whenever a campaign was launched—procurators and judges often made a show of observing the law, in some cases obviously in order to make up for the earlier excesses in which they had taken part or which they had condoned.[71] In view of these excesses it became necessary to review many of the court convictions from 1937-38 and even some cases heard at extra-judicial bodies (although for these latter cases the word of the Special Board remained decisive).[72] However, by the summer of 1940, these reviews came to a virtual halt, after procurators were enjoined to refrain from "indiscriminately appealing" verdicts police troiki had inflicted upon "harmful elements," and instructed "to take decisions [in these matters] independently of the punishment and the article of the penal code on the basis of which the person was sentenced . . . and to proceed through reassessing the social danger of the person and the crime he had committed."[73]

This partial return to the principles of the period prior to late 1938 heralded a general hardening of criminal policy, revealed as well in a new approach to acquittals in cases brought up by the secret police. At the start of 1940, top security officials made vehement protests against the acquittals of alleged counter-revolutionaries, a practice which, at the Moscow city court at least, had purportedly acquired a "mass character."[74] It is against this background that Vyshinskii, in his new role of deputy head of government, suggested in March 1940 issuing a directive according to which people exonerated from "political" charges could not be set free without the sanction of the secret police.[75] Such a directive was drafted within hours and made it mandatory to clarify if the NKVD had "any objections . . . independently from the exculpating sentence. . . ."[76] Later, once again upon the insistence of Vyshinskii, this principle was extended to all cases investigated by the secret police, but not to political cases in which the ordinary police or the procuracy conducted inquiries.[77] The NKVD had a tendency to give an excessively broad interpretation to these directives, so that it refused to release defendants acquitted by the Supreme Court of Russia, even though the original instruction applied only to rulings at the first instance.[78] In contrast, regional court judges found that the new rule violated the code of criminal procedure and infringed upon the constitutionally proclaimed independence of judges. One of them wrote a letter to the Supreme Leader himself to "ask [his] intervention" against this "absolutely incorrect" measure.[79] Yet this measure remained in force until 1953 and symbolized the limits of changes in judicial policy.[80]

For all that, the number of "political" convictions declined sharply after 1937-39, when about 28 percent of the nearly 5 million persons who stood trial were convicted in cases initiated or investigated by the secret police, as opposed to 11 percent of the more than 5.3 million individuals in the period between 1933 and 1935.[81] Between 1940 and late 1952, the proportion of convictions for "counter-revolutionary" crimes stood at 4.4 percent among the more than 33 million convictions overall. Moreover, 78.5 percent of these 1,474,174 persons were tried by courts (especially military tribunals) and not by the Special Board.[82]

At first sight, a major change seems to have occurred in the wake of the wholesale terror of 1937-38, even if the security apparatus managed to gain prerogatives over the judiciary it had not been invested with before 1940. Yet the change did not consist so much in a radical turn in the administration of justice, as in (1) steps to bring under its purview problems that had been previously entrusted mainly to extra-judicial agencies; and (2) the criminalization of conduct, not subject to penal sanctions in the past and not usually treated as crimes elsewhere. In these circumstances, both substantive and procedural norms were more likely to be observed than before, but in a legal framework which penalized acts beyond the usual boundaries of criminal law.

The hardening of policy concerning hooligans represents an example of the first type of changes, namely, the shift of cases from extra-judicial bodies to the courts. Already by the mid-1930s, the courts had been enjoined to clamp down on "hooligan behavior of a counter-revolutionary character" and authoritative statements stressed that this sort of transgression was to be seen as "sabotage" and even "political" crime.[83] About 130,000 people were sentenced each year under the relevant article of the code, although before 1940 they received relatively mild penalties from ordinary courts.[84] Nevertheless, the evidence shows that many victims of the "mass operations" were hooligans who could be condemned by decisions of regional police troiki if they had a criminal record.[85] In 1940 the highest authorities urged application to hooligans of the strictest penalties allowable by the code (up to five years of hard labor), and the organization of "special judicial sessions" in large cities to deal with these sorts of cases indicates that law enforcement bodies once again pursued hooligans in a campaign-like manner.[86] Consequently, the number of sentences meted out to rowdies nearly doubled in this year and by January 1941 this group of convicts exceeded 10 percent of the camp population.[87] Moreover, by this time the share of "socially dangerous elements" had declined to 11.6 percent (from more than one-fifth two years before), suggesting that courts were assuming some functions of extra-legal bodies.[88]

The measures of 26 June 1940 to strengthen labor discipline exemplify the other major change in post-purge judicial policy, namely, the extension of the criminal law into unfamiliar terrain. Through the 1930s high rates of absenteeism and turnover of labor had plagued Soviet industry, and these problems were aggravated by the insubordination of workers encouraged by purges. After the failure of other measures and in the context of a shortage of manpower as war approached,[89] the leadership made criminal offenses out of shirking (missing or being late for work three times in a month) and unauthorized quitting. Convictions for shirking made offenders liable for up to six months of "corrective work" on the job, which entailed up to 25 percent reduction in pay, and two to four months in prison for quitting without permission.[90] To encourage prosecutions for new offenses, Stalin took unusual measures. After discussion at a Plenum in late July, the Central Committee at his behest denounced the allegedly feeble implementation of the June law and went so far as to fire Procurator General Pankratev, on the grounds that his decision to stage demonstration trials in labor discipline cases (taken jointly with Commissar of Justice Rychkov) had proven a mistake. Better to prosecute all offenders (rather than try to deter through the educative effects of a trial). Management and judges alike, the Central Committee opined, should "not be afraid to implant discipline even through repression."[91]

It is no simple matter to figure out the extent to which the procuracy and the courts failed to comply with the new legislation. The records show instances of leniency as well as the usual overreaction that was likely to follow any centrally sponsored drive.[92] At any rate, labor discipline offenses—extended during the war to cover unruly apprentices and peasants who failed to meet the compulsory minimum of work in the kolkhoz—produced 51 percent of court convictions between 1940 and 1953 (for a total of more than 17 million) and featured 3.9 million custodial sentences, mainly for illegal quitting.[93]

Drawing the courts into such a large scale effort to remedy deficiencies in work incentives and the inability of the regime to find means other than threat of punishment to motivate the work force ran the risk of blurring the distinction between authentic crimes and arbitrary extensions of the criminal sanction. This development boded ill for the future of Soviet justice. To be sure, neither an explicitly instrumental understanding of law nor the use of the courts to serve the policy goals of the regime was new. For years, judges had been expected to join in campaigns such as collectivization of the peasantry and the struggle against juvenile crime and to place the achievement of the goals of these campaigns ahead of concern for the niceties of the law.[94] Yet, extra-judicial instances did play the main role in these same offensives. Local soviets and the secret police had taken charge of the mass deportations of the early 1930s, and 55.7 percent of the more than 155,000 minors who received prison terms between April 1935 and 1940 had been sentenced by the NKVD, not the courts.[95] The 1940 criminalization of labor infractions amounted to making the courts assume the logic inherent in the functions of extra-judicial procedures, so pervasive in the pre-war decade as to suggest that ordinary law enforcement agencies could largely escape it.

The difficulties of the Soviet regime in securing regular and controllable law enforcement led more than once to attempts to base state coercion on legal norms, which were meant to be autonomous from the fleeting priorities in other walks of life. But these attempts remained necessarily stillborn, because sooner or later they inhibited the use of the justice agencies to achieve particular goals that circumstances dictated at this or another conjuncture. Heavy reliance on extra-judicial repression demonstrated the elite's inability to come to grips with the system's ideal of order and to translate it into the language of law. The restriction of the scope of extra-judicial adjudication made this ideal somewhat more explicit, in the official discourse as well as in the way Soviet law defined relations of authority. However, the entrusting of core functions of extra-judicial bodies to the court had far-reaching consequences. It perpetuated a highly instrumental vision of justice and legality, which lasted beyond the two generations of policy-makers and judicial officials whose careers were marked by the terror of 1937-38 and by the legislation in its aftermath. In fact, this instrumental vision led to confusion between the functions of criminal justice and other institutions and, what is more, accustomed officialdom and the public alike to the notion that any use of the criminal sanction was lawful as long as it was sanctioned by legal acts.

This state of affairs may account for the remarkable adaptation of judges to the demands of the Soviet regime and their readiness to put their powers in the service of new political leaders in the post-Soviet era. In the same way, the traditional Soviet understanding of legality is likely to overshadow doubts as to the legality of measures taken under Gorbachev and after, catering to the public's wish to see the rising crime rate curbed.[96] It is difficult to avoid the conclusion that extra-judicial procedures of the pre-war years left a lasting legacy to the Soviet system and its heirs.

Author's note: The archival research whose results are discussed here has been made possible by a grant of the French Ministry of Research.

Notes

1. For the first studies exploring changes in judicial policy in the inter-war period see Peter H. Solomon, Jr., "Soviet Penal Policy, 1917-1934: A Reinterpretation," *Slavic Review* 39, no. 2 (Summer 1980): 196-217; "Soviet Criminal Justice and the Great Terror," *Slavic Review* 46, no. 3/4 (Fall-Winter 1987): 391-413; "Local Political Power and Soviet Criminal Justice, 1922-1941," *Soviet Studies* 36, no. 3 (Summer 1985): 305-329.

2. Eugene Huskey, "Vyshinskii, Krylenko and the Shaping of the Soviet Legal Order," *Slavic Review* 46, no. 3/4 (Fall-Winter 1987): 414-28.

3. *Gosudarstvennyi arkhiv Rossiiskoi Federatsii* (hereafter GARF), *f.* 8131, *op.* 37[27s], *d.* 70: 103-106, 134-136; J. Arch Getty, Gábor T. Rittersporn, and V. N. Zemskov, "Victims of the Soviet Penal System in the Pre-war Years: A First Approach on the Basis of Archival Evidence," *American Historical Review* 98, no. 4 (October 1993): 1048.

4. The inaccessibility of state security archives does not facilitate research on this problem. But despite the lack of information on a wide range of questions related to extra-judiciary bodies, our documentation allows us to form a fairly precise picture on their importance, especially in the years extending from 1935 to the war.

5. Robert Sharlet, "Pashukanis and the Withering Away of the Law in the USSR," in Sheila Fitzpatrick, ed., *Cultural Revolution in Russia, 1928-1931* (Bloomington, IN, 1978), 169-88.

6. David Dallin and Boris Nikolaevsky, *Forced Labor in Soviet Russia* (New Haven, CT, 1947), 149-205; E. H. Carr, *A History of Soviet Russia: Socialism in One Country*, Vol. 2 (Harmondsworth, 1970), 447-81; E. H. Carr, *Foundations of a Planned Economy*, Vol. 2 (Harmondsworth, 1976), 356-98.

7. R. W. Davies, *The Socialist Offensive: The Collectivization of Soviet Agriculture, 1929-1930* (London, 1980), 177-80; 182-85; 228-49; 256-60; Lynne Viola, "The Campaign to Eliminate the Kulak as a Class, Winter 1929-1930: A Reevaluation of the Legislation," *Slavic Review* 45, no. 3 (Summer 1986): 503-524.

8. Sheila Fitzpatrick, *Stalin's Peasants* (Oxford, 1994), 51, 62-66.

9. V. P. Danilov and S. A. Krasil'nikov, eds., *Spetspereselentsy v Zapadnoi Sibiri, 1930-vesna 1931 g.* (Novosibirsk, 1992), 60-79, 83-89, 146-48; V. P. Danilov and A. Berelowitch, "Les documents des VČK-OGPU-NKVD sur la campagne soviétique," *Cahiers du monde russe*, 1994, No. 3: 665-67.

10. Lynne Viola, *The Best Sons of the Fatherland: Workers in the Vanguard of Soviet Collectivization* (Oxford, 1987), 123-26.

11. GARF, *f.* 9401, *op.* 1, *d.* 4157: 203,205; *f.* 9414, *op.* 1, *d.* 1155: 1; *f.* 9474, *op.* 1, *d.* 73: 204.

12. *Sovetskaia iustitsiia*, 1932, No. 20: 1. G. M. Safonov, ed., *Spravochnik po zakonodatel'stvu dlia sudebno-prokurorskikh rabotnikov* (Moscow, 1979), Vol. 3, 473-74; GARF, *f.* 3316, *op.* 64[2s], *d.* 1228: 18.

13. *Rossiiskii tsentr khraneniia i izucheniia dokumentov noveishei istorii* (hereafter RTsKhIDNI), *f.* 17, *op.* 3, *d.* 870: 7; *d.* 880: 6; *d.* 890: 11, 40; *d.* 898: 5.

14. GARF, *f.* 9401, *op.* 1, *d.* 4157: 203, 205.

15. S. V. Kul'nitskii, "Nekotorye problemy sploshnoi kollektivizatsii na Ukraine," *Istoriia SSSR*, 1989, No. 5: 27-29; *The Smolensk Party Archive* (hereafter WKP) 221, pp. 20-21, 39, 50-51; RTsKhIDNI, *f.* 17, *op.* 3, *d.* 880: 6; *d.* 881: 17-21; *d.* 886: 11-12; *d.* 881: 14, 37-38; *d.* 891: 12; *d.* 895: 12.

16. I. E. Zelenin, "O nekotorykh 'belykh piatnakh' zavershaiushchego etapa sploshnoi kollektivizatsii," *Istoriia SSSR*, 1989, No. 2: 3-19; M. B. Tauger, "The 1932 Harvest and the Famine of 1933," *Slavic Review* 50, no. 1 (Spring 1991): 70-89; Kul'nitskii, "Nekotorye problemy," 20-36.

17. See, for example, RTsKhIDNI, *f.* 17, *op.* 3, *d.* 911: 42-43; *f.* 558, *op.* 1, *d.* 3054: 1-5, 9, 11. It may be argued that excesses were deliberately tolerated or even encouraged in order to find scapegoats for the failure of such campaigns. Nevertheless, collectivization, Stakhanovism, the terror of 1937-38, and a multitude of other drives brought disasters which were by no means compensated by the hypothetical benefit of furnishing whipping boys. The assumption of deliberately provoked excesses implies that top decision-makers were inclined to push their regime regularly to the brink of catastrophe.

18. Gábor T. Rittersporn, *Stalinist Simplifications and Soviet Complications: Social Tensions and Political Conflicts in the USSR, 1933-1953* (Reading, 1991), 247-49.

19. See, e.g., GARF, *f.* 3316, *op.* 64[2s], *d.* 1254: 6; *d.* 1754: 21, 26; *f.* 9474, *op.* 16, *d.* 79: 16.

20. GARF, *f.* 9474, *op.* 1, *d.* 77: 1; *d.* 85: 22-23; *Sovetskaia iustitsiia*, 1934, No. 24: 2-3; *Sotsialisticheskaia zakonnost'*, 1937, No. 8: 38.

21. GARF, *f.* 8131, *op.* 37[27s], *d.* 70: 104; *f.* 5446, *op.* 15a, *d.* 1073: 29, 31; *f.* 9414, *op.* 1, *d.* 1155: 1; *d.* 2740: 53.

22. WKP 178, p. 134.

23. GARF, *f.* 9474, *op.* 1, *d.* 104: 4; *op.* 16, *d.* 79: 1.

24. RTsKhIDNI, *f.* 17, *op.* 120, *d.* 171: 153; GARF, *f.* 8131, *op.* 37[27s], *d.* 70: 134, 138; *f.* 9401, *op.* 1, *d.* 1457: 203.

25. GARF, *f.* 8131, *op.* 10, *d.* 94: 56-57, 155, 176-178; *op.* 11, *d.* 12: 30-31, *d.* 21i: 15; *op.* 37[27s], *d.* 28: 1-3, 7-8, 12, 14-15; *d.* 58: 194; *d.* 60: 209; *op.* 38[28s], *d.* 3: 37; *d.* 4: 19; *Sotsialisticheskaia zakonnost'*, 1934, No. 1: 35-36; No. 5: 10; *Sovetskaia iustitsiia*, 1934, No. 13: 9-10; 1935, No. 16: 9.

26. GARF, *f.* 8131. *op.* 27, *d.* 22: 1b; *op.* 28, *d.* 5: 53; *d.* 7: 11; *op.* 28, *d.* 5: 82-83, 99; *d.* 8: 16, 42, 51, 54; *d.* 10: 19-20; *d.* 11: 45; *d.* 22: 47-48. For an ambiguous mention of this decree at the time see *Sovetskaia iustitsiia*, 1936, No. 27: 17. The full text is published in B. A. Viktorov, *Bez grifa 'sekretno'* (Moscow, 1990), 202-204.

27. *Sotsialisticheskaia zakonnost'*, 1934, No. 1: 31; *Sovetskaia iustitsiia*, 1934, No. 19: 4; *Sobranie zakonov i rasporiazhenii Raboche-Krest'ianskogo Pravitel'stva SSSR*, Part I, 1935, 139-140; GARF, *f.* 8131, *op.* 37[27s], *d.* 73: 228; *op.* 38[28s], *d.* 3: 30-32; *f.* 9474, *op.* 1, *d.* 84: 183; *d.* 85: 7; RTsKhIDNI, *f.* 17. *op.* 3, *d.* 948: 95-98.

28. Peter H. Solomon, Jr., *Soviet Criminal Justice Under Stalin* (Cambridge and NY, 1996), 165-66.

29. *Sovetskaia iustitsiia*, 1934, No. 13: 9; *Sotsialisticheskaia zakonnost'*, 1934, No. 7: 36; GARF, *f.* 8131, *op.* 28, *d.* 4: 12; *f.* 9474, *op.* 1, *d.* 67: 36, 38.

30. GARF, *f.* 8131, *op.* 38[28s], *d.* 4: 6; *f.* 9474, *op.* 16, *d.* 65: 37-37ob, 1233-123ob, 108-210; *d.* 88: 93-93ob, 97-97ob, 127, 138-138ob.

31. GARF, *f.* 8131, *op.* 37[27s], *d*, 70: 136; *op.* 38[28s], *d.* 6: 61-64; *d.* 12: 14-15; *Izvestiia TsK KPSS*, 1989, No. 10: 81.

32. Almost 50 percent of the 33,000 persons who had been convicted by decisions of the Special Board in 1935 were not considered as "counter-revolutionaries" (GARF, *f.* 8131, *op.* 37[27s], *d.* 70: 138-139).

33. GARF, *f.* 8131, *op.* 38[28s], *d.* 5: 91-92; *d.* 6: 62, 64.

34. GARF, *f.* 8131, *op.* 38[28s], *d.* 5: 91-92; *d.* 8: 7-8. 11-14. 25. 27; *d.* 12: 13a; *f.* 9474, *op.* 1, *d.* 97: 7. It is only at the very end of 1936 that the idea of "specifying the criteria" according to which this group of presumed offenders was to be defined would surface at the procuracy, without any subsequent action (*ibid.*, *f.* 8131, *op.* 37[27s], *d.* 64: 131).

35. GARF, *f.* 9414, *op.* 1, *d.* 1155: 8.

36. GARF, *f.* 9401, *op.* 1, *d.* 1155: 8.

37. GARF, *f.* 9414, *op.* 1, *d.* 1155: 3, 6. We have no data on the sentences under which people had been imprisoned in labor colonies. It is highly probable that the share of this category of purported delinquents was significant in the population of colonies.

38. GARF, *f.* 8131, *op.* 37[27s], *d.* 70: 105, 107; Getty, *et al.*, "Victims of the Soviet Penal System": 1048.

39. GARF, *f.* 3316, *op.* 64[2s], *d.* 1754: 1-3; *d.* 1837: 3..

40. Huskey, "Vyshinskii, Krylenko," 422-23. Analogy was defined as a basic principle of criminal law by Article 16 of the code. See also Peter H. Solomon, Jr., *Soviet Criminologists and Criminal Policy* (New York, 1978), 22-26; Solomon, *Soviet Criminal Justice under Stalin*, 31-32.

41. RTsKhIDNI, *f.* 17, *op.* 120, *d.* 171: 151-167.

42. GARF, *f.* 8131, *op.* 37[27s], *d.* 60: 109-111, 113-116.

43. GARF, *f.* 3316, *op.* 64[2s], *d.* 1620: 2-22, 58-75; *f.* 8131, *op.* 38[28s], *d.* 7: 47, 83-84.

44. GARF, *f.* 8131, *op.* 37[27s], *d.* 70: 103-106; *d.* 71: 127-133; *d.* 73: 228-235.

45. GARF, *f.* 8131, *op.* 37[27s], *d.* 70: 138-142.

46. *Ibid.*: 134-136.

47. *Sotsialisticheskaia zakonnost'*, 1934, No. 4: 36, 39-41; No. 5: 11; No. 7: 37; No. 8: 3, 31-32; No. 9: 44; No. 10: 1-2, 28-30, 34; No. 11: 48-49; No. 12: 48; 1935, No. 2: 59-60, 63; No. 10: 64; *Sovetskaia iustitsiia*, 1934, No. 8: 3; No. 9: 25; No. 17: 22; 1935, No. 4: 17; No. 5: 24-25; No. 11: 33; No. 18: 10; No. 20: 24; No. 27: 2; No. 36: 2.

48. Political Archive of the Foreign Office, Bonn, Botschaft Moskau, A2 Innerpolitische Verhältnisse der Sowjetunion, Vol. 8: The Leningrad Consulate General to the Embassy, 30 June, 20 July, and 3 August 1935, p. 1; Vol. 13: The Vladivostok Consulate to the Embassy, 14 September 1937; Botschaft Moskau, A4 Militär- und Marineangelegenheiten: The Leningrad Consulate General to the Embassy, 28 May 1935; Botschaft Moskau, A21 Kiew, Kurze Meldungen: The Kiev Consulate to the Embassy, 27 May 1936; N. F. Bugai, "O vyselenii koreitsev iz Dal'nevostochnogo kraia," *Otechestvennaia istoriia*, 1992, No. 6: 140-68; GARF, *f.* 8131, *op.* 37[27s], *d.* 59: 187-189.

49. Gábor T. Rittersporn, "The Omnnipresent Conspiracy: On Soviet Imagery of Politics and Social Relations," in N. Lampert and G. T. Rittersporn, eds., *Stalinism: Its Nature and Aftermath. Essays in Honour of Moshe Lewin* (London and Armonk, NY, 1992), 101-120.

50. J. A. Getty, *Origins of the Great Purges: The Soviet Communist Party Reconsidered 1933-1938* (Cambridge, 1985), 113-95; Rittersporn, *Stalinist Simplifications and Soviet Complications*, 64-182.

51. GARF, *f.* 9414, *op.* 1, *d.* 1155: 6; Getty, *et al.*, "Victims of the Soviet Penal System": 1048.

52. GARF, *f.* 9401, *op.* 1, *d.* 1457: 202-203; *f.* 9492, *op.* 6, *d.* 15: 12-13; Getty, *et al.*, "Victims of the Soviet Penal System": 1034. As for ordinary courts, our data relate to decisions at the first instance.

53. *Izvestiia TsK KPSS*, 1989, No. 10: 81-82; *Trud*, 4 June 1992: 4.

54. Getty, *et al.*, "Victims of the Soviet Penal System": 1022, 1036-38.

55. *Izvestiia TsK KPSS*, 1989, No. 10: 81-82; for regional troiki inflicting capital punishment before 1934 see, e.g., GARF, *f.* 8131, *op.* 37[27s], *d.* 22: 1a; *d.* 28: 16-17.

56. See, e.g., GARF, *f.* 8131, *op.* 37[27s], *d.* 86: 138, 147-148, 150; *d.* 140: 25; *d.* 145: 72-73; *op.* 38[28s], *d.* 33: 2; *f.* 9401, *op.* 1a, *d.* 20: 54; *op.* 2, *d.* 1: 3-4; *f.* 9414, *op.* 1, *d.* 1155: 12; *Izvestiia TsK KPSS*, 1990, No. 1: 188; *Moskovskie novosti*, 21 June 1992: 19; Getty, *et al.*, "Victims of the Soviet Penal System": 1037-38.

57. GARF, *f.* 9474. *op.* 1, *d.* 104: 34-45; *f.* 9492, *op.* 1, *d.* 19: 118-127, 165; *d.* 20: 119-120, 142-148; *op.* 6, *d.* 15: 12-13; RTsKhIDNI, *f.* 17, *op.* 120, *d.* 171: 153.

58. WKP 238, p. 213; GARF, *f.* 9401, *op.* 1, *d.* 1457: 202; *Izvestiia*, 10 June 1992: 7; Fitzpatrick, *Stalin's Peasants*, 296-308.

59. See, e.g., GARF, *f.* 9474, *op.* 1, *d.* 112: 3-4; *f.* 9492, *op.* 1a[1s], *d.* 3: 17-22.

60. GARF. *f.* 8131, *op.* 37[27s], *d.* 83: 71, 161.

61. GARF, *f.* 8131, *op.* 37[27s], *d.* 69: 5-7.

62. GARF, *f.* 8131, *op.* 37[27s], *d.* 111: 15.

63. GARF, *f.* 8131, *op.* 38[28s], *d.* 24: 6, 12, 18; *d.* 25: 20, 31; *d.* 33: 1; *d.* 34: 5. See also *Sotsialisticheskaia zakonnost'*, 1938, No. 5: 22; No. 6: 42-43; No. 9: 13.

64. GARF, *f.* 7523, *op.* 65, *d.* 484: 15-16, 18; *d.* 556: 38; *f.* 8131, *op.* 37[27s]; *d.* 113: 50-51; *op.* 38[28s], *d.* 24: 25; *d.* 26: 3-4, 6; *d.* 27: 9; *d.* 33: 2.

65. GARF, *f.* 8131, *op.* 37[27s], *d.* 86: 180, 217; *d.* 87: 49.

66. *Moskovskie novosti*, 21 June 1992: 19.

67. *Istoricheskii arkhiv*, 1992, No. 1: 125-28.

68. GARF, *f.* 8131, *op.* 38[28s], *d.* 34: 6-7; *f.* 9401, *op.*2, *d.* 1: 1-9.

69. GARF, *f.* 8131, *op.* 37[27s], *d.* 143: 29; *d.* 144: 110; *d.* 238: 40-42. Interestingly enough, the protest against the unsanctioned arrest of NKVD "conspirators" was sent to Stalin and Molotov.

70. GARF, *f.* 8131, *op.* 37[27s], *d.* 143: 78-79; *d.* 144: 114. Pankratev recommended that these people be tried by the Military Board of the Supreme Court, behind closed doors.

71. See, e.g., GARF, *f.* 8131, *op.* 37[27s], *d.* 118: 63; *d.* 139: 83-88; *f.* 9474, *op.* 1a, *d.* 7: 137-139; *d.* 8: 21-36.

72. GARF, *f.* 8131, *op.* 37[27s], *d.* 136: 2-2ob, 9-90b; *d.* 541: 130-133; *op.* 38[28s], *d.* 36: 3-9; *d.* 38: 27, 36, 48; *d.* 39: 4.

73. GARF, *f.* 8131, *op.* 38[28s], *d.* 46: 213-215.

74. See, e.g., GARF, *f.* 9474, *op.* 16, *d.* 173: 216-217, 258-265.

75. GARF, *f.* 8131, *op.* 37[27s], *d.* 210: 2.

76. GARF, *f.* 8131, *op.* 37[27s], *d.* 210: 7; *op.* 38[28s], *d.* 46: 57; *f.* 9492, *op.* 1a[1s], *d.* 63: 167.

77. GARF, *f.* 8131, *op.* 37[27s], *d.* 210: 1; *op.* 38[28s], *d.* 43: 119; *f.* 9492, *op.* 1a[1s], *d.* 63: 46.

78. GARF, *f.* 9492, *op.* 1a[1s], *d.* 72: 254.

79. GARF, *f.* 5446, *op.* 24a, *d.* 233: 2; *d.* 234: 2; *f.* 8131, *op.* 37[27s], *d.* 239: 152-153; *f.* 9492, *op.* 1a[1s], *d.* 78: 73-75.

80. See the notices to this effect in GARF, *f.* 8131, *op.* 38[28s], *d.* 46: 57, 357.

81. Getty, *et al.*, "Victims of the Soviet Penal System": 1033.

82. GARF, *f.* 7523sch, *op.* 89, *d.* 4408: 8, 32, 43; *f.* 9401, *op.* 1, *d.* 4157: 205; *f.* 9474, *op.* 16, *d.* 642: 60, Of the "counter-revolutionaries" prosecuted by the court system, 73.2 percent were sentenced by military tribunals, but these affairs represented only 23.8 percent of their case load.

83. Editorial, *Pravda*, 3 May 1934: 1; *Sotsialisticheskaia zakonnost'*, 1935, No. 5: 10; *Sovetskaia iustitsiia*, 1935, No. 10: 3-4; No. 11: 11-12; No. 18: 10.

84. GARF, *f.* 9474, *op.* 10, *d.* 49: 41-42.

85. See, e.g., GARF, *f.* 7523, *op.* 65, *d.* 557: 29-30, 42-45, 49, 53; *f.* 8131, *op.* 38[28s], *d.* 29: 8.

86. *Ugolovnyi kodeks RSFSR* (Moscow, 1947), 154; *Ugolovno-protsessual'nyi kodeks RSFSR* (Moscow, 1947), 196-97.

87. GARF, *f.* 9492, *op.* 6, *d.* 14: 14.

88. GARF, *f.* 9414, *op.* 1, *d.* 1155: 5-6. Before 1940 no detainees of hard regime camps had been convicted as hooligans.

89. Rittersporn, *Stalinist Simplifications and Soviet Complications*, 33-34, 134, 168, 255-57.

90. "O perekhode na vosmichasovoi rabochii den . . .," Ukaz Prezidiuma Verkhovnogo Sovieta ot 26 iiunia 1940. g., *Ugolovnyi kodeks* (1947), 110-11.

91. *Izvestiia TsK KPSS*, 1990, No. 2: 186-90. The hardened legislation concerning hooligans was in fact a consequence of this move, because workers started to provoke small incidents, after the publication of the 1940 labor law, in order to obtain their firing (GARF, *f.* 8131, *op.* 37[27s], *d.* 137: 53-54). For an extended discussion of the 1940 law see Solomon, *Soviet Criminal Justice under Stalin*, chapter 9.

92. See, e.g., GARF, *f.* 8131, *op.* 37[27s], *d.* 241: 39-43; *d.* 540: 13; *op.* 38[28s], *d.* 46: 205-206, 286-286ob; *f.* 9474, *op.* 16, *d.* 162: 160ob-161; *f.* 9492, *op.* 1a[1s], *d.* 62: 113-114.

93. GARF, *f.* 7523sch, *op.* 89, *d.* 4408: 8, 32; *f.* 9401, *op.* 1, *d.* 4157: 201; *f.* 9492, *op.* 6, *d.* 14: 9-10.

94. For the later drive see, e.g., GARF, *f.* 8131, *op.* 37[27s], *d.* 71: 104-105; O. V. Khlevniuk, *et al.*, *Stalinskoe Politbiuro v 30-e gody* (Moscow, 1995), 144-45.

95. Danilov and Krasil'nikov, *Spetspereselentsy*, 22; GARF, *f.* 9414, *op.* 1, *d.* 28: 15. The deportation of entire ethnic groups and other categories of supposedly suspect elements during and after the war did not involve the judiciary or extra-judicial instances: it was decided by the state administration (V. N. Zemskov, "Spetsposelentsy," *Sotsiologicheskie issledovaniia*, 1990, No. 11: 9, 17).

96. Peter H. Solomon, Jr., "Legality in Soviet Culture: A Perspective on Gorbachev's Reforms," in Lampert and Rittersporn, eds., *Stalinism*, 265-71, 276-81.

11

THE BUREAUCRATIZATION OF CRIMINAL JUSTICE UNDER STALIN

Peter H. Solomon, Jr.

Criminal justice under Stalin is best known for severity, shortcuts, and politicization. All of these features did characterize the administration of justice in the 1930s and 1940s at various times and to varying degrees. There was, however, another dimension to the work of the procuracy and the courts under Stalin that not only shaped their work to a remarkable degree but also remained a strong force in criminal justice right up to the collapse of the USSR. This was the bureaucratization of the management of the justice agencies, their personnel, and the administration of justice itself. The bureaucratization of justice under Stalin developed to a degree unusual in the history of criminal justice worldwide and assumed distinctive features that need explaining.

The distinctiveness lay not in the mere development of systems of training, recruitment, promotion, and discipline for prosecutors and judges that encouraged them to comply with the interests of the political elite. Many modern states, including some in Western Europe, achieved this end.[1] But few, if any, of those states relied so heavily upon statistical indicators in assessing the performance of individual legal officials as did the chiefs of the legal agencies in the USSR of the late Stalin and post-Stalin years. Nor—to my knowledge—did those states concentrate attention on "failures" in investigation, prosecution, and adjudication, such as "unjustified prosecutions" (i.e., acquittals), "unjustified convictions" (cases overturned on appeal), or "unjustified arrests" (detention of persons not later sentenced to confinement).

The development of this peculiar system for evaluating the work of legal officials—based on numbers and emphasizing negative incentives—came only in the late Stalin period. Until the mid-1930s, the legal agencies had not achieved sufficient centralization to make such a system possible; and until the late 1940s too few legal officials pursued careers in the administration of justice to enable any form of evaluation to shape the conduct of legal officials. In the post-war years—with a hypercentralized administrative apparatus and compulsory legal education for legal officials—evaluation through statistical assessment became a fetish. It was in the late 1940s that the bureaucratization of justice in the USSR reached its full and lasting expression.

This chapter begins with an account of the history of the management of the careers of legal officials in the USSR and the use of statistical indicators of performance, placing special emphasis on developments after World War II. It goes on to probe the meaning of this system of evaluation, addressing its novelty, origins, and implications—for bias in the criminal process, the autonomy of the legal agencies, and the reform of post-Soviet criminal justice.

Careers, Centralization, and Control

The Bolshevik leaders did not set out to create a bureaucracy of legal officials engaged in careers as procurators and judges and managed from the political center. This classic approach to justice administration was adopted as a goal by Stalin and his circle and only in the second half of the 1930s.[2]

Despite ambivalence about traditional legal institutions, Lenin and the Bolsheviks wanted to make law an effective instrument of rule in the proletarian state. To ensure that the new legal agencies served the interests of the regime, their designers decided to staff the courts and procuracy offices with reliable cadres—*not* lawyers, who were of questionable loyalty and in short supply, but ordinary, largely uneducated persons who had joined the Bolshevik Party. Such political trustees, the Bolsheviks assumed, would have the "revolutionary consciousness" to exercise discretion in the interests of the rulers who claimed to represent the toilers. Naturally, the actual performance of these amateurs left much to be desired, but in the 1920s Soviet political leaders and legal chieftains alike tolerated and tried to improve the flawed administration of justice through remedial education and simplification of the process to match the qualifications of its participants.

A natural, though not necessarily anticipated, consequence of the "experiment" in the use of non-lawyers as legal officials was the weak development of careers in the justice realm. Without legal education to give them an esoteric skill and corporate identity, only a minority of legal officials made administration of justice a career. Many of those who performed well gained promotion up and out of the legal realm into other, better paying, and more prestigious posts in public administration. The weaker performers were sooner or later released from posts in the legal agencies. With high rates of turnover among legal officials and only a small portion pursuing careers as judges, procurators, or investigators, the central legal agencies lacked leverage over their subordinates.[3]

At the same time, the central legal agencies faced a strong competitor for control over the bulk of courts and procuracy officials, namely the local and regional political bosses. To begin, local authorities recruited most legal officials. Moreover, they exercised strong influence over their futures. To receive a new post outside of justice called for the patronage of local politicians, not central legal officials. Only those who sought promotions within the legal agencies needed to satisfy both masters. Moreover, local political authorities offered most of the perks available to judges and procuracy officials; and by the era of collectivization they had also gained control of the budgets of courts and responsibility for the physical mainte-nance of courts and procuracy offices alike. In these circumstances it proved difficult for central legal officials to get their local counterparts to comply with directives that did not suit the interests of the latter or those of their local masters. Finally, the legal agencies themselves were relatively decentralized. They did not exist beyond the republican level and left most decisions about personnel to their regional and local offices.

Nevertheless, the central agencies stood responsible for the overall performance of their subordinates and collected masses of statistical data for monitoring. In fact, Russia had had a long tradition of collecting statistics on crime and punishment, investigations and prosecutions, decisions of courts, and movement of cases, and the Bolshevik officials who took over the new legal agencies continued tsarist practices in data collection, at first barely modifying the forms. Like their tsarist predecessors, the Bolshevik justice chiefs used the data to check and compare the performance of justice agencies in particular geographical districts. Thus, the Russian Commissariat of Justice would compare the "stability of sentences" (that is, the percentage of sentences appealed that were not changed or overturned) of the courts of particular regions; and in like manner the procuracy of Moscow region would compare how groups of investigators in its particular districts fared in their tempos and rates of case completion.[4] Moreover, in discussions and appraisals of the administration of justice among political officials statistics occupied a central place. There was, in short, a fascination with and reliance on statistics. But there were no signs that in the assessment of individual judges or procuracy officials statistical indicators yet played a major role. This would come only later along with the centralization of decision-making about promotion and firing.

In the second half of the 1930s the Stalinist leadership changed in fundamental ways its approach to the administration of justice, committing itself to careers, centralization, and new ways of managing legal officials. This shift stemmed first of all from the frustration of top legal officials over the results of the post-collectivization policy of restoring observance of legal procedures and normal functioning of the courts and procuracy. It derived as well from the rise of Vyshinskii to a leadership role in legal affairs and the conversion of Stalin, Molotov, and others to his vision of a justice adminis-tration, managed from the center and responsive to central direction. This was hardly difficult to achieve, for Stalin himself registered increasing anger over his difficulties in gaining compliance from provincial and local officials, whose power he wanted to subdue.[5]

Already in spring 1935, Vyshinskii began calling for more lawyers to work as judges and procurators, and after a blistering critique of the work of uneducated legal officials prepared for the Soviet Control Commission later that year, the political leadership approved a new approach to the legal cadres. A draft secret resolution of the Central Committee called for a dramatic expansion of legal education, both at university and remedial levels, aimed especially at current and potential legal officials. The same draft authorized measures for encouraging officials to stay on their jobs. To combat the high rates of turnover among legal officials and induce more of them to make careers in the legal agencies, the resolution called for the introduction of differential levels of salary for procuracy and court workers based upon education and years of service. It also suggested the introduction of standard uniforms for judges and procurators and designated members of a commission to develop their design. Although the resolution was never actually issued, its main points became policy all the same—plans for dramatic expansion of legal education were approved, and in 1936 Deputy Procurator General Roginskii announced a plan for career development in the procuracy that included the establishment of eight ranks of investigator and fourteen ranks of procurator, each with different levels of pay. Promo-tion through these ranks would depend upon both seniority and the results of performance reviews (*attestatsii*).[6]

The new policy of seeking legal officials with legal education and getting them to pursue careers in the legal agencies was not realized quickly. To begin, the Great Purge of 1937-1938 claimed so many victims among judges and procurators that a large new recruitment of uneducated political trustees proved necessary. While many of the new legal officials were put through short remedial courses in law, few were ready to start higher legal education before World War II engulfed Soviet society and government.

Only after the war was it possible to start changing the nature of legal officialdom. Likewise, the plans for encouraging careers in the legal agencies received slow implementation. Thus, only in 1943 were ranks and differential pay, with uniforms and insignia, introduced into the procuracy.[7]

The other pillar of the Stalinist leadership's program for gaining control of the administration of justice was centralization. The first, and outwardly visible, phase of centralization came in the restructuring of the legal agencies associated with the drafting of the 1936 constitution. The restructuring featured new, exclusive subordination of republican procuracies to the all-union Procuracy (breaking their ties to republican justice commissariats); the creation of a USSR-level Justice Commissariat with its own regional field administrations to supervise the courts; and the granting to the USSR Supreme Court of new broad powers to hear in supervision any case heard originally in any court, powers that the Court was forced to use when the presidia and plenums of regional courts were eliminated. From these organizational changes followed measures of centralization in such crucial activities of the legal agencies as personnel management and operational decision-making. Already in 1936 the USSR Procuracy assumed responsibility for the appointment of procurators of regions as well as the republics and established that procurators of cities and districts be appointed by republican procurators. In 1938 regulations stipulated that assistant procurators and investigators working in any procuracy office, even those of cities and districts, be appointed by officials of republican procuracies and that they inform the USSR Procuracy. At the same time, decisions on promotions within the procuracy came to rest with officials of the USSR Procuracy, and as of June 1937 no procurator or investigator above the city or district level could be fired without preliminary approval of the Procurator General. Within the USSR Commissariat of Justice the republican commissariats represented the main power centers, exercising direct and exclusive control over the regional justice administrations and appointing their chiefs. At the same time, the chiefs of the USSR Justice Commissariat did not trust their republican subordinates with operational decision-making, requiring them, as of June 1939, to obtain written permission from the all-union body before circulating any of their directives.[8]

Centralization in the justice agencies enhanced the role of statistical indicators. For one thing, central officials became more accountable for the performance of their subordinates and required means for evaluating it. For another, the exercise of decision-making in the center about personnel below—rewards and promotion for some legal officials, censures and firing for others—called for trustworthy information about the performance of individual officials whom the decision-makers did not know. Starting in 1939, legal officials in the center and the provinces found the answer in numbers and became preoccupied with statistical indicators on the performance of *individual* legal officials.

This development suggested new questions: which indicators should be used and in what rank order? Which criteria should take precedence when different ones came into conflict? Avoiding mistakes in investigation and trials and having decisions overturned required careful work, but bureaucratic superiors also wanted efficiency and fast tempos of work.

Still, achieving the right indicators became in the years just prior to World War II a major concern for any legal official trying to please his masters and pursue a career in the agencies. Investigators, procurators, and judges alike had to meet standards of efficiency—getting their tasks accomplished within the prescribed time periods and avoiding backlogs of cases. Beyond this common concern, each official faced his/her own particular targets of performance. Thus, procurators were judged first and foremost on the basis of the number and percentage of appearances in court. Both procurators and investigators faced censure for having a high percentage of cases sent to trial that ended in returns to supplementary investigation. But investigators routinely sent weak cases to court in order to avoid having excessively high rates of cases stopped during the investigation phase. Often, investigators had to deal with weak cases started by the police or "under pressure from district organizations," and did not feel up to stopping them. For their part, judges faced assessment on the basis of the percentage of their decisions (verdicts and sentences) that, when taken to appeal, remained unchanged. To a considerable extent, though, records of "stability of sentence" depended not upon the work of trial judges but the norms of performance for judges of the cassation panels who heard the appeals.[9]

The new preoccupation with the statistical indicators of individual legal officials soon dominated the relationship between central and local legal officials. From central, republican, and regional offices alike came a stream of directives calling for new statistical reports, far more than regional and local procuracy offices and courts could handle. At the same time, visits from the central procuracy, according to a regional procuracy official in 1940, usually consisted of "statistics collection missions," while the inspectors (*revizory*) sent by the justice administrations to check the people's courts also focused upon the gathering of statistics.[10]

In sum, centralized management of the legal agencies and in particular the careers of their officials made quantitative indicators of performance a principal instrument of rule for central legal officials. In the plain words of a top official in the Russian Commissariat of Justice: "without statistics one cannot direct the work of judges."[11] Which statistics mattered most in the appraisal of particular officials would change more than once and the conflict between measures of efficiency and quality of performance remain a constant theme.

Statistical Indicators and the Quest for Perfection

The post-war years of Stalin's rule (1945-1953) saw the completion of the bureaucratization of the administration of justice that had begun just before the war. The political leadership finally succeeded in setting in motion the process of forcing legal officials to acquire legal education, become jurists, and make careers in the legal agencies. Shortly thereafter, the chiefs of the legal agencies began placing new emphasis upon the avoidance of acquittals and verdicts that did not hold on appeal and used the existing system of statistical assessment of legal officials to launch a campaign for perfection.

As we have seen, Stalin and his colleagues had committed themselves to having educated procurators and judges as early as 1936, but as a result of the Great Purge and World War II the educational profile of legal officials in 1945 did not differ from that of 1936. In October 1946 the leadership showed its impatience with this fact by announcing a new program for converting legal officials into jurists. Through a resolution of the Party's Central Committee it obliged all legal officials who lacked higher legal education to enrol in secondary or higher legal education, usually by correspondence. The resolution also provided for an expansion of full-time day legal education, at both levels, to provide a "stream of young specialists" ready for placement in the legal agencies.[12]

The tone of the resolution, in its final form, was sharp. Raising the educational standards of legal officials had become a "top priority" for both the Ministry of Justice and the Ministry of Higher Education. The resolution "obliged" the latter and the legal research institutes to produce textbooks on demand. Moreover, the resolution included a detailed list of positions to which only persons with higher legal education (or, occasionally, secondary legal preparation and long experience in the legal agencies) could be appointed. As well, the resolution supplied concrete targets for the conversion of legal officials into jurists. Within four to five years, all judges, procurators, and investigators working at the regional level and higher, along with district procurators and people's court judges in the capital cities of republics and regions, were to have completed higher legal education. For the chiefs of the Ministry of Justice and the Procuracy, the implementation of the resolution became a major burden. Under constant pressure from Central Committee staff assigned to monitor the resolution's fulfillment, the chiefs of the legal agencies had to contend with resistance from not only some of their subordinates but also local political officials who did not want to release their officials to pursue legal education full-time.[13]

Fulfillment of the planned targets proved difficult, but most legal officials did pursue some kind of education after hours and their educational profile started to change. Whereas in 1948 only 21.4 percent of judges had legal training (6.2 percent higher, 15.2 percent secondary), in 1951 the figure had risen to 57.6 percent (20.2 percent higher; 37.4 percent secondary). An analogous shift took place among procuracy officials, who actually improved their educational profile faster than did the judges. The last years of Stalin marked only the beginning of the process of converting legal officials into jurists that would continue during the 1950s and 1960s.[14] The quality of legal education obtained by correspondence (and in the post-Stalin period at night school) left much to be desired, and most legal officials were not as well educated in law as the advocates and jurisconsults who had attended full-time day faculties. But education by correspondence did give them a grasp, however tenuous, of the technical core of Soviet law; and it gave them a credential that encouraged them to pursue careers in the legal agencies.[15]

Along with the spread of legal education came a steady increase in the proportion of legal officials who did pursue careers. To be sure, rates of turnover among procuracy and court workers would remain high in the post-Stalin years, as one quarter to a third of new appointees, including many of the young specialists who came to the legal agencies with higher legal education, left within a few years. But for those investigators, procurators, and judges who stayed, extended careers became the norm, and the proportion of officials with long tenure increased steadily. Thus, the share of officials in the procuracy whose work experience in the legal agencies exceeded ten years increased from 31.3 percent in 1948 to 48.2 percent in 1954 to 55.4 percent in 1965.[16]

The shift from casual short-term employment in the legal agencies to careers in the procuracy and courts represented an important step in the bureaucratization of Soviet justice. Now working as career officials, investigators, procurators, and judges became more sensitive to the expectations of their superiors and more keen to conform to the standards of evaluation imposed upon them. And those standards were to change in strange ways, serving bureaucratic and political convenience more than the interests of fairness.

Between 1948 and 1951 the chiefs of the legal agencies sponsored a campaign against so-called "groundless" prosecutions, convictions, and arrests that made both acquittals and verdicts cancelled on appeal into the key indicators for legal officials. Achieving favorable, that is, low, rates of these events became necessary for the successful pursuit of careers by legal officials. Here we examine highlights of the story of the campaign for perfection in the work of investigators, procurators, and judges, saving speculation about its origins and implications for the last part of the chapter.[17]

The campaign for perfection in the procuracy and courts began in 1948 with a speech delivered by Deputy Procurator General Konstantin Mokichev at the Second All-Union Conference of Leading Procuracy Officials, convened in April 1948. "In the country of victorious socialism," Mokichev asserted, "legality is the basic factor of state power," and "in such a country there must be no place for unfounded prosecutions. With all decisiveness we must eliminate these cases." Moreover, "with each groundless prosecution and conviction we discredit ourselves, first of all as an agency supervising legality." By unfounded prosecutions and convictions Mokichev meant any cases that ended in an acquittal, either at trial or on appeal, or was stopped by the procuracy after a return to supplementary investigation. To reduce and eventually eliminate these events meant treating "each instance from a political vantage point," that is "as an extraordinary happening of great political import."[18] If Mokichev had merely urged investigators to exercise more care in the choice of cases they sent to trial and the rhetoric mere exaggeration, Molichev's words would have done no harm. But this was not the case.

In the months that followed the speech, the USSR Procuracy seems to have taken no further action on acquittals. But the RSFSR Minister of Justice I. Basavin developed a whole program for confronting "groundless prosecutions and convictions." In a directive to judges and justice officials issued in July 1948 Basavin "suggested" that:

1. with each instance of an acquittal or a return to supplementary investigation in a case that had been investigated by the district procuracy, the *judge* (*sic!*) is to inform the regional procuracy office for a 'determination of responsibility';
2. in each instance of an acquittal or quashing of a conviction on appeal, the regional court inform the regional justice administration, so that it could take 'appropriate measures,' including, when necessary, a review of the trial judge's conduct by a disciplinary college of the Ministry of Justice;

3. the justice administration and regional courts conduct studies of groundless prosecutions and convictions and together with the procuracy hold meetings to plan further measures.[19]

Basavin's directive—though read only by judges and judicial officials in the RSFSR—contained the essential ingredient of the broader campaign against acquittals that unfolded in 1949-1951, namely, the element of personal responsibility. If a trial ended in an acquittal, then those who prepared and approved the case (the investigator and procurator) had made a mistake in sending it to trial. If a conviction was reversed on appeal, then the trial judge must have erred. And, according to the directive, all of these legal officials who made mistakes had to be held to account!

Wherever implemented, the Basavin directive promised to exert pressure on both judges and officials of the procuracy and even pit one against the other. For example, in the Chuvash autonomous republic, a study of "groundless prosecutions and convictions" ordered by the republic's justice ministry revealed substantial numbers of both and put the blame squarely on the shoulders of procuracy officials. To compound the injury, it turned out that the procuracy of the Chuvash republic had falsified the data on acquittals in its reports to the RSFSR procuracy. The Chuvash procurator had allegedly "created the appearance of normality (*blagopoluchie*)" by reporting a mere 32 acquittals in cases investigated by the procuracy during 1948 instead of the more than 300 acquittals registered by justice officials. This scandal came to the attention of the Central Committee, including Secretary Georgii Malenkov.[20]

As the drama in the Chuvash republic unfolded, justice officials in other parts of the USSR began paying attention to acquittals. On 18 February 1949, the USSR Ministry of Justice—reportedly "at the initiative of the USSR Procuracy"—instructed republican ministers of justice to direct all people's court judges "to inform regional procuracy offices about every case reaching trial from the district procuracy that is either stopped in preparatory session or ends in an acquittal," indicating exactly which officials in the police and procuracy had composed the accusation and which had confirmed it. This instruction extended the July 1948 directive of the RSFSR ministry of justice (the Basavin directive) to the other republics of the USSR. Moreover, in March and April the Central Committee received reports on groundless prosecutions and acquittals from the justice ministries of the RSFSR, Ukraine, and Byelorussia, and the supreme courts of Byelorussia, Uzbekistan, and the Mordovian ASSR.[21] What sent the campaign into high gear, however, was the decisive action taken by the Procurator General of the USSR.

In a secret directive (Order No. 61s of 4 April 1949) Procurator General Safonov instructed regional procuracy offices through the USSR to establish "operational control" over every instance of an acquittal or stopped case. District procuracy offices were to mount an inquiry, while the investigatory department or department for supervision of the police in the regional procuracy did the same. If those checking the case from the regional procuracy thought the acquittal justified, they were to identify the person(s) at fault—the investigator and assistant procurator—and raise the question of responsibility. If they found the acquittal unjustified, they were to send the case to the department of supervision of the courts in the regional procuracy for the launching of an appeal and, again, consideration of reprisals for the judge who rendered the decision and the procurator who failed to protest it. For their part, the heads of the departments of courts in the regional procuracy were to keep exact records of all stopped cases and acquittals using special card and statistical forms.[22] Lest any procuracy official fail to recognize the seriousness of the first order on acquittals (of 4 April 1949), Procurator General Safonov issued a follow-up order in December condemning the allegedly high rate of acquittals and stopped cases in the city of Moscow, and punishing those held responsible. Served up as scapegoats were the procurator of the city (who received a censure), some of his subordinates (who were warned), and the procurator of the district within the city that had the highest rate of "unfounded prosecutions." The latter was fired for "anti-governmental practices."[23]

The USSR Procuracy acted in 1949 as if the rate of acquittals in the USSR had reached some new crisis level. But this was not the case. In 1948, courts acquitted just over ten percent of the accused brought before them, the same rate as the average for the past decade. (In the 1920s and early 1930s rates of acquittal had stood even higher, and in the late tsarist period had averaged one third of all cases.[24]) The preoccupation of the Soviet authorities with "unfounded prosecutions and convictions" stemmed not from a change in the practice of the procuracy or courts but from a new intolerance toward imperfections in the administration of justice.

The implementation of the campaign against acquittals assumed high priority in the work of regional procuracy officials. To ensure that these offices did inquire into every acquittal as ordered, they had to submit quarterly reports to higher procuracy authorities (in the RSFSR to the republican procuracy). Although the initial reports in 1949 revealed difficulties in compiling the data, let alone doing the checks, most regional procuracies did produce scorecards on individual procurators and investigators in the districts and delivered censures and warnings to those with the worst records. The pressure from the USSR and RSFSR procuracies to monitor and reduce acquittals continued unabated for three years, long enough to make the avoidance of acquittals a habit.[25] The reports for 1951 showed improvements in the performance of regional procuracy officials in confronting acquittals. The procuracy of Smolensk region had checked the work of twenty-eight out of forty-four district procuracy offices, hearing reports in open sessions from eight district procurators and sixteen investigators from the same district. The department of court supervision of the regional procuracy claimed to have checked every acquittal and sent seventy-nine letters to district procurators concerning particular acquittals. The office also sent three communiqués to the regional justice administration complaining about judges who gave unjustified acquittals. The procurator of Smolensk region gave censures, warnings, or transfers to raion and city procurators with especially high rates of acquittal in 1951, and fired the leader, a district procurator with 13 acquittals (8.7 percent of his cases). The struggle against "unfounded prosecutions" in Smolensk proved especially successful; the rate of acquittal reportedly dropped from 6.6 percent in 1950 to 2.7 percent in 1951.[26]

The procuracy's campaign against acquittals during 1949-51 had considerable support of regional *Party* officials. Thus, in July 1949, the regional Party committee (*obkom*) of Sverdlovsk issued a resolution about procuracy investigations that focused on unfounded prosecutions. Pursuant to this resolution, the head of the administrative organs department of Sverdlovsk prepared a study of unfounded prosecution arrests in the region (December 1950), hosted a meeting of legal officials on the subject (March 1951), and collected further reports during the year from the legal agencies of the region.[27] Moreover, during 1949 and the first part of 1950 a series of regional Party committees (e.g., Gorkii, Irkutsk, Kursk, Orlovskii, Rostov, Mariiskii ASSR) ordered or helped to arrange conferences of procurators and judges, with Party secretaries themselves often in attendance, and in late 1950 and 1951 many other regional Party committees (including Dagestan and Novosibirsk) followed suit.

The involvement of so many regional Party committees in the campaign against unfounded prosecutions suggests direction from the Central Committee of the CPSU. In fact, in May 1950 the Administrative Organs Department prepared for Central Committee Secretary Ponomarenko a draft resolution of the Central Committee "On measures for the elimination of groundless prosecutions and convictions of citizens," which included a "suggestion" to the regional Party committees to increase their supervision of the work of the legal agencies. The draft edict was composed after the receipt by the Central Committee of an anonymous complaint about the failure of the USSR Procuracy to take strong enough measures against groundless prosecutions. The complaint led first to the preparation of a memorandum for Ponomarenko and then to the draft resolution.[28] I do not know whether the resolution was adopted, but it is clear that even before its composition many regional Party committees had taken action.

At the same time, local Party chieftains supported their procurators' concern with acquittals by punishing judges who exceeded the norms. The potential sanctions ranged from censures and deprivation of perks (failure to give apartments, cars, vacations) to firing (recalls and failure to supply renomination). Party bosses joined in the discouraging of acquittals primarily because of their close working relationships with procurators, but also because they too had become accountable to the center for the performance of the justice agencies in their bailiwicks.[29] Without pressure on judges from Party bosses to cooperate in the reduction of acquittals, the attainment of the procurators' goal would have proved difficult. For not all acquittals stemmed from weak investigations or poor prosecutorial decisions regarding which cases to send to court. Those officials could not be expected to achieve perfection and some cases inevitably would unravel in court, if only because a key witness changed his testimony. Once judges were also held "responsible" for acquittals, they began to use substitutes wherever possible. Instead of acquittals, judges favored "returns to supplementary investigation" (which would allow the procurator to drop the case quietly) and "compromise decisions"—conviction for a lesser charge with a sentence to the time already served awaiting trial.[30]

The intense pressure upon investigators, procurators, and judges to avoid acquittals represented only a part of the campaign for perfection in the administration of justice. Each of these officials faced analogous demands, whose fulfillment sometimes required artifice if not distortion. Pressure to achieve high standards of efficacy and productivity remained real, but it took second place to the concerns of top legal officials with the substance of performance. For investigators, not only acquittals but also "returns to supplementary investigation" were taken as a sign of failure. Curtailing returns would prove especially difficult when they emerged as a main substitute for acquittal for cases that fell apart in court. Nonetheless, from 1950 the USSR Procuracy used low rates of return cases as a basis for choosing its "best" investigators in 1950, 1951, 1952, and 1953. Some of these stars had even reduced their personal rates of return to zero, but had benefited from the support of their procuracy offices. They had been given only cases with strong evidence in order for the region to produce "winners" in the all-union competition.[31]

For procurators, who had to sanction all detentions longer than three days, the worst sin, apart from acquittals, was a high rate of bad or "unjustified" arrests, that is, detentions where the accused person was later acquitted or given a non-custodial sanction. In 1933, 1935, and 1938 Stalin had condemned improper and excessive arrests, but his orders had no lasting effect. After the war, authorities gave renewed emphasis to what they now called "unjustified arrests." In 1945 an order of the Procuracy censured procurators for these actions and called for both the collection of data on all releases from detention and the identification of the procurators responsible for each instance of what turned out to be an unjustified arrest. Follow-up orders were issued in 1947 (requiring special reports on each "bad arrest") and in 1949. This final order, coming as part of the campaign for perfection, carried more weight than had the earlier ones. Predictably, some procuracy offices responded by holding fewer persons before trial. But as long as cases came apart in court and ended in acquittals or were stopped by the procurator, there would be "unjustified arrests."[32] Blaming procurators for such detentions only intensified the concern of procuracy officials with avoiding acquittals and returns to supplementary investigation.

Finally, judges also experienced increased pressure to work flawlessly, in their case to avoid verdicts or sentences later changed on appeal (and therefore unjustified) and achieve high rates of sentences that lasted—i.e., "stability of sentences." Starting from 1948 the USSR Ministry of Justice pressed trial judges to aim for perfect records and gave prizes to the "best judges" who had gone months, or as long as a year, without changes in their decisions. To achieve a good record in sentencing required that trial judges not only apply the law correctly (to deter appeals from defense) but also follow the political line in judicial policy. The reason was simple. In the USSR procurators had the right to appeal sentences, and for their own protection many procurators appealed all cases with lenient outcomes. Appellate judges changed some of these verdicts so as to conform to the "line" in their own work. For trial judges, there was no simple way to ensure success. When they harshly punished petty offenders and juveniles they also ran the risk of cancelled sentences. Moreover, some appellate judges proved inconsistent and even arbitrary. Still, most judges found that it was better to err on the side of severity. Giving too many lenient sentences and acquittals could also lead to suspicion of bribe-taking, which, even if unproved, could have dire consequences.[33]

The campaign for perfection in the administration of justice—avoiding unjustified prosecutions, convictions, and arrests—seems to have slackened in 1952, but by this point its concerns had been entrenched permanently into the work of legal officials. The system of evaluating officials with quantitative indicators that stressed the avoidance of acquittals and bad arrests, and the negative experience of legal officials who failed to achieve the desired outcomes, left their mark. Avoiding acquittals and the other discouraged outcomes became a preoccupation for legal officials, and naturally the rates of acquittal declined precipitously. The declines in the early 1950s represented only the start of a long-term process, about which I have written elsewhere. As the pressure to avoid acquittals at trial and on appeal increased during the 1960s and 1970s, the substitutes for acquittals developed in the early 1950s acquired a life of their own. By the 1970s legal officials accepted their use as natural and had for the most part forgotten why they had emerged.[34]

Novelty, Origins, and Implications

The bureaucratization of criminal justice in the late Stalin period raises many questions. How and in what ways was it novel? How can one explain the distinctive aspects? What implications did this process have for such larger issues as the relationship of the justice agencies to politics and the reform of post-Soviet criminal justice?

The practice of organizing judges and prosecutors alike in hierarchical bureaucratic organizations was common to many countries of Western Europe in the twentieth century, and it is those countries' experiences that are most relevant to that of the USSR. In contrast, Anglo-American countries featured recruitment and advancement for both prosecutors and judges that was fragmented and divided among different levels, while lawyers moved in and out of state offices. Systematic evaluation of legal officials even for salary increases, not to speak of promotion, was rare. Only in the 1980s and 1990s did the issue of accountability take on sufficient resonance as to prompt managers of justice systems to consider and in some cases adopt and use methods of evaluation.

As a rule, the evaluation of judges in the United States (e.g., in New Jersey, a pioneer in this enterprise), was based upon questionnaires distributed to the prosecutors, lawyers, court personnel, and others who worked regularly with the judge. The main, if not exclusive, goal of the evaluation was self-improvement of the performance of individual judges.[35] Evaluation of the performance of prosecutors has also been initiated in some places. Thus, in Canada the Ontario Ministry of the Attorney General introduced in 1990 what it called "performance development reviews," which it took into account for salary increases. These involved close monitoring of the work of prosecutors, known as crown counsels, for a period of time through review by superiors of the documents they composed, and observation of their work in court. Quantitative indicators of performance, however, were not used.[36]

In European legal bureaucracies the promotion of judges has traditionally depended upon evaluations by superiors, but in recent years there have been improvements in many countries that have gone a long way toward eliminating undue pressures upon judges. For many years in France high-level prosecutors used to have a crucial say in the promotion of judges, but as of the early 1970s the responsibility for reviewing the work of lower court judges and making decisions about promotion lay exclusively in the hands of a Committee of judges. The Committee reviewed recommendations prepared by the Ministry of Justice. Judges passed over for promotion were still likely to blame their fate on a past verdict disliked by the prosecutor.[37] In Italy, the traditional system of reviewing judges for promotion through a Committee of higher court judges, who took into account "incorrect interpretations of law and opinions that indicated a political persuasion," was abandoned in the 1960s in favor of promotion by strict seniority (which left the Council of Judges with merely disciplinary functions).[38] In Germany into the 1990s, councils of judges evaluated junior judges for possible promotion. In so doing, the councils did make use of an "efficiency rating," based in part upon such objective factors as rates of discharge and reversals (i.e., statistical indicators!). But this was only one part of the evaluation; the superiors also reviewed how well a given judge conducted legal proceedings and the quality of his/her opinions. Moreover, there was no use of indicators relating to the outcomes of cases, and no cult of perfection. The review process was simply, in the words of an admirer, "meritocratic."[39]

The unique features of Soviet management of its prosecutorial and judicial bureaucracies lay in the emphasis placed upon statistical indicators (*protsentomania*) and the treatment of acquittals and reversals on appeal not as natural parts of a self-correcting mechanism but as signs of poor, wasteful, and defective work, and a scourge amenable to conquest. Explaining the first is easier than accounting for the latter.

Although statistics collection had a long history in the USSR and Russia, the tendency to evaluate the performance of legal agencies according to numbers increased during the 1920s and early 1930s. In the late 1930s, with the extreme centralization of the legal agencies and increased accountability of central officials for their performance, statistics emerged as the principal means of evaluation for not only particular geographical units but also individual officials as well. Apart from the impact of centralization, the preoccupation of political officials with administering a state-owned economy seems to have reinforced their inclination toward using statistics. This, combined with the remnants of "scientism" from the 1920s—the belief in the possibility of "scientific management"—helps to explain the dominant position of statistics in the monitoring of performance in the administration of justice. Diffusion of the use of quantitative norms from economic administration occurred not only in the justice realm. From the late 1940s schools and university faculties were assessed in part according to the rates of student completion of particular grades or courses.[40]

How to explain the turn against unfounded prosecutions, convictions, and arrests and the pursuit in the late 1940s of a cult of perfection in the administration of justice? This large and separate question may be broken down into three parts: who instigated this policy innovation—the leaders of the legal agencies, the political leadership (Stalin), or both? Why? And reflecting what larger cultural and institutional processes?

There is no doubting either the active role of the chiefs of the legal agencies (Procuracy and Ministry of Justice) in promoting new standards or the involvement of Stalin and other secretaries of the CPSU. Top leaders had opportunities to know about the campaign: in 1949 Malenkov's office received materials relating to the Chuvash affair; in 1950 Ponomarenko's received an anonymous complaint about unfounded prosecutions that set in motion the drafting of a Central Committee resolution on the question. Earlier, in 1948 the RSFSR minister of justice had written to the Central Committee about unjustified prosecutions and in 1949 the Administrative Organs Department received reports on the issue from republican ministries of justice.[41] Moreover, the unusual length of the campaign, some three years, and the involvement of provincial Party officials suggest some commitment and direction from the top Party leaders. Still unclear, though, is the *extent* of the role of the political leaders. Were they merely complicit in the crackdown on legal officials' performance sponsored by the procuracy or were they its instigators? There is evidence to support both answers.

Although in 1948 the RSFSR ministry of justice introduced the first measures to reduce acquittals, by mid-1949 the policy had become the preserve of the procuracy, promoted by it, and ultimately serving its interests. Once "unfounded prosecutions" had become an issue in justice politics, the leaders of the procuracy were on the spot. Blame for prosecutions that ended in acquittals fell squarely on the shoulders of procuracy officials, and the heads of that agency wanted to minimize harm to its prestige. Under Vyshinskii in the 1930s the Procuracy had emerged as the most powerful of the legal agencies, and his less able and well connected successors still cared about its power and prestige. In 1948 Deputy Procurator General Mokichev focused upon the consequences of groundless prosecutions and convictions for the Procuracy. "With each groundless prosecution and conviction we discredit ourselves, first of all as an agency supervising legality." He repeated the same words about "discrediting the agency" in another speech in 1950.[42] To ensure that the new spotlight on unfounded prosecutions did not harm their agency, the chiefs of the Procuracy may themselves have promoted the intense campaign against acquittals pursued from April 1949.

There are also indirect signs that the political leadership instigated the campaign. One such sign can be found in the rhetoric. Before 1948 the phrases "unfounded prosecution" and "unfounded conviction" were used—as far as I can tell—mainly in Party circles. For example, those terms appeared in a 1935 report (with somewhat different meaning) from the head of the Central Control Commission to Molotov and in a 1940 report to the CCC from three of its "public controllers." The terms reappear in some Party documents in 1946.[43] The terminology did not have deep roots in discourse among justice officials. Another piece of evidence is the draft Central Committee resolution of May 1950. By itself, this document does not resolve our problem. While suggesting high level involvement in the issue, the draft resolution fails to mention any earlier resolutions, a normal practice when a resolution repeats the message of an earlier directive.

Closely connected to the question of agency is the matter of motivation. Without more evidence from archival sources, our exploration of the motivations that lay behind the turn against acquittals has a hypothetical quality. Yet, it is precisely this dimension that reinforces the argument for leadership instigation of the crackdown. To start, one should consider taking the crackdown against "unjustified prosecutions, convictions, and arrests" at face value. It was possible that some members of the leadership wanted to reduce the incidence of Soviet citizens facing the ordeals of confinement, prosecution, and trial because of what turned out to be mistakes in judgment on the part of police and legal officials. No doubt it was easier to pursue this course of action with regard to the legal agencies than to the extralegal agencies of coercion, i.e., police and tribunals of the political police. (It is possible that an analogous crackdown was pursued with police tribunals, although this would have featured the review of convictions registered rather than acquittals, which, one can assume, were rare events.) Of course, the true elimination of unjustified prosecutions from the work of the political police, including contrived and weak cases, could come only after Stalin's death, but the language of "unjustified" measures was used later on, for example by N. S. Khrushchev, to refer to these events.[44]

An equally if not more plausible reason for the political leadership to want a reduction in acquittals and cases reversed on appeal was a desire to enhance the reputation of Soviet criminal justice. The position of the USSR in the world order might well have prompted Stalin, Zhdanov, and/or Malenkov to seek the appearance of an administration of justice that worked flawlessly. Rivalry with the United States in the Cold War and the new role of the USSR as a model system for emulation by its satellites in Eastern Europe made it useful for the Soviet government to put on its best public face. Soviet ideologists of the day described the USSR as having built socialist government, a higher form than that achieved by mere "people's democracies" and one that they were expected to emulate. In this context, the reputation of criminal justice had special import because of the damage already done to the reputation of the Soviet government by the Terror. Abroad, the USSR was known for the "unfounded prosecutions and convictions" delivered in the tribunal of the NKVD. While after the war the political police pursued its work in relative secrecy, the more visible activity of Soviet courts could signal to the outside world that the USSR had now met its standards. Stalin and other leaders might have hoped that a decline in "unfounded prosecutions and convictions" in ordinary criminal cases would enhance the reputation of the Soviet government. There were precedents for this line of thinking. The promulgation of the constitution of 1936 was meant in part to convey the message of normal legal order to the outside world; and the policy of converting legal officials into jurists, especially in its 1946 iteration, also reflected embarrassment of political leaders with the amateurish and sloppy work of the justice agencies.

Whatever the exact role of Stalin and his colleagues, and whatever their motives, the crackdown on acquittals would not have been possible without two underlying, enabling conditions—the use in the USSR of a version of the inquisitorial procedure common to the states of the Civil Law tradition; and what one might call Stalinist political style. Arguably, it was the fatal combination of these two conditions that made the turn against "unfounded prosecutions and convictions" possible.

How, a reader might ask, could Soviet leaders have thought that the virtual elimination of acquittals or verdicts overturned on appeal signalled a well-functioning and fair administration of justice? From the vantage point of the adversarial procedure of the Anglo-American legal tradition, where the trial serves as a locus of conflict between two sides, this proposition sounds strange. But in the Civil Law tradition to which the USSR belonged, the trial represented not the place for a contest but rather the final stage of a common search for truth. If investigators and prosecutors have performed their tasks properly during the pre-trial phase—and have had the legal power to stop cases when the evidence seemed insufficient for conviction—then there should be few acquittals at trial. Unlike the Anglo-American procedures, where different standards of evidence apply to charge, committal to trial, and conviction, in inquisitorial procedure, at least in its Soviet version, the standard of proof did not become more stringent in the later phases of the criminal process. Levels of acquittal in inquisitorial systems of Continental Europe tended to be much lower than in adversarial ones—with the exception of countries where prosecutors could not stop cases during the pre-trial phase.[45] In this context, then, acquittals might plausibly be understood as signs of "mistakes in judgment" by the officials responsible for conducting the pre-trial investigation. The same kind of rhetoric came to be used in the USSR in connection with changes in verdicts introduced at appellate courts. When a higher court reversed the decision of a lower one, this meant that the lower court judge had erred or committed a "judicial mistake." Though strange to Anglo-American ears, this kind of language was used in the USSR of the 1970s by jurists of all political stripes, including reformers.[46]

It is one thing to regard acquittals as reflecting mistakes by investigators and prosecutors and verdicts and sentences overturned as reflecting mistakes by trial judges; but another thing entirely to regard these mistakes as abnormal or subject to significant reduction or elimination. The intolerance of mistakes and the drive for perfection in the administration of justice from the late 1940s was rooted, I would contend, in Stalinist political style. As I use the term, Stalinist political style combined a proto-military approach to public policy with organizations based on the principle of multiple and overlapping accountability. Together these two elements produced a culture of blame.

The proto-military approach to addressing public problems originated in the industrialization, collectivization, and grain collection drives of the 1920s and early 1930s but extended to other areas of life and lasted throughout the Stalin period. The familiar pattern involved: setting high (even unreachable) goals and attempting to achieve those goals through "simulated combat" (the term is Bialer's), that is, organized campaigns (*shturmovshchiny*), with battles on various fronts, tactical retreats, and renewed attacks.[47] The pattern involved more than rhetoric. In this case, discourse reflected an underlying reality, a habit of attacking problems as if concentration of resources and efforts alone could conquer all. This approach entered Soviet criminal justice many times before the crackdown on acquittals, for example in the campaign to get factory and legal officials to enforce the newly criminalized, and unpopular, strictures against shirking and quitting; or in the more long term pressure to force legal officials to acquire legal education.

Multiple and overlapping accountability of officials represented a key feature of Soviet bureaucracy that the centralization of the late 1930s and 1940s did not displace. As of the late Stalin years, the various agencies were highly centralized internally but still lacked important features of Western or Weberian bureaucratic organization. Clear and predictable lines of responsibility and accountability did not enter the Soviet bureaucratic system, and particular officials and agencies stood accountable for matters that were beyond their control.[48] The combination of the pursuit of difficult goals in a military fashion with the system of multiple accountability assured that there would be many candidates for blame when things went awry.

Laying blame became a vital part of government operations. It was used as an instrument for getting a campaign started or wound down. It also served as an instrument for encouraging officials to give priority to a new directive. Scapegoating a few officials for failure to execute a directive properly was a common way for leaders to seek compliance with their demands. As we have seen, this technique was used by the chiefs of the Procuracy and Ministry of Justice in addressing the problems of unjustified prosecutions and arrests. Writ large, this syndrome, itself a product of policy style and institutions, produced "a culture of blame," a world of public administration in which failures were normal and so was posing and answering the question "who is to blame?"

The emphasis on management through blame reflected Joseph Stalin's personal predilections.[49] At the same time, an element in Russian culture provided support for this approach. The question "*kto vinovat*" had an old pedigree, at least in intelligentsia and socialist circles. Perhaps this helps to explain why Soviet officials, like the Soviet public at large, accepted an approach to administration that focused so much on blame, even though it was counterproductive.[50]

Finally, let us shift attention from the sources of the peculiar bureaucratization of criminal justice in Stalin's USSR to its implications—for bias in the criminal process, the autonomy of the legal agencies, and the reform of criminal justice in post-Soviet Russia.

On the one hand, the expectation that legal officials would achieve near perfect indicators, especially regarding rates of conviction, accounted to a large degree for the "accusatorial bias" that infected Soviet criminal process from the late 1940s. Once a charge had been laid against an accused person, it was difficult to gain an acquittal, and difficult to win on appeal. Even when cases fell apart in court, judges relied upon such surrogates for acquittals as returns to supplementary investigation or convictions on lesser charges. Moreover, at the appellate level judges avoided changing verdicts and sentences, especially from 1956 when appellate court judges became responsible for the performance of trial court judges under their supervision (a classic conflict of interest).[51]

On the other hand, the bureaucratization of criminal justice under Stalin may have had a favorable impact on the relationship between the legal agencies and their political masters. As the legal agencies centralized decision-making about personnel and operations and came to rely on statistical methods of evaluation, they succeeded in converting legal officials into conformists, a corps of investigators, procurators, and judges who understood what was expected by their superiors and by and large acted accordingly. Not only was this condition new for Soviet administration of justice (something not present through most of the Stalin era), but it may have given central legal officials an unaccustomed degree of operational autonomy—autonomy, that is, from political officials at the local level and in the center.[52]

To be sure, legal officials in the cities and districts of the USSR still had to please two sets of masters—politicians in the locality and vertical superiors in the agencies. But the vertical masters emerged as the more important ones, making more demands upon legal officials and shaping their conduct. Satisfying the horizontal masters, politicians in the bailiwick, meant first and foremost responding to their occasional requests in particular cases. In contrast, superior officials in the legal agencies defined larger expectations for overall performance, which local masters shared and sometimes reinforced. At the same time, the vigorous pursuit by the central legal agencies of standards of performance understood and endorsed by the top political leaders and the display of a "house in good order" may have led after Stalin's death to a less active and direct involvement by Central Committee officials in the work of the central legal agencies. Archival sources have underscored the degree of petty tutelage exercised by Central Committee secretaries and their subordinates in the late 1940s over the chiefs of the Procuracy, Ministry of Justice, and Supreme Court. Thus, in 1948 the USSR Minister of Justice sought consent from his political superiors to close a branch of the water courts; to change the requirements for admission to the judicial schools; to start two new journals (permission not granted); to reprint a brochure on the selection of judges; to issue a *festschrift* in honor of Andrei Vyshinskii; and even to clear a speech that the Minister was to present to a conference of judges. A scandal erupted when Procurator General Safonov arranged to hold a conference of investigators without prior clearance from the Central Committee and without its officials having a chance to screen the theses of the main presentations well in advance.[53]

The bureaucratization of Stalinist criminal justice continued into the post-Stalin period and its key features lasted right up to the collapse of the USSR. As a result, the system of rule by statistical indicators and discouragement of "failures" in investigation, prosecution, and trial stood as obstacles to the reform of criminal justice in post-Soviet Russia and the achievement of a fairer investigation and adjudication. Initial experience suggests that the chiefs of the legal agencies found it difficult to detach themselves from their customary system of managing subordinates through statistical indicators. Moreover, even without Party bosses to penalize them, judges continued to avoid acquittals, partly out of habit and partly because of the continuation of dependence upon local power without the Communist Party.[54]

What, then, could be done? One possibility was to attempt a decentralization of the management of the Procuracy and Ministry of Justice. Such a course might well undercut the importance of quantitative indicators of performance. At the same time, though, it might also have the unfortunate consequences of reviving an excessive degree of influence in the administration of justice on the part of provincial and local politicians. The battles of 1994-95 over which levels of government would select and monitor judges suggested that this danger was real. Another question is whether the general justice agencies—without decentralization—could find alternative ways of managing their cadres, eliminating if not the use of statistical indicators at least the untoward discouragement of acquittals and overturning of convictions on appeal. Some radical reformers in post-Soviet Russia operated on the assumption that such a change was impossible as long as Russia used a variant of the inquisitorial system of criminal procedure. Only a shift from the inquisitorial to the adversarial, from a system like that of France to one like that of England, would overcome the entrenched opposition to acquittals and the accusatorial bias more generally. At a minimum, they believed, it was necessary to recreate the peculiar and possibly unstable mixture of inquisitorial pre-trial procedures and adversarial procedure at trials that characterized criminal justice in the late tsarist years. Were they right? Was Russia a country so doomed by other elements in its political culture that an inquisitorial system of justice was bound to be warped in practice to the point of imbalance and unfairness to the accused? I leave this question for others to debate.

Author's note: Portions of this chapter appeared in different form in Peter H. Solomon, Jr., *Soviet Criminal Justice under Stalin* (Cambridge and New York, 1996).

Notes

1. Martin Shapiro, *Courts: A Comparative and Political Analysis* (Chicago and London, 1981), esp. 32-35.

2. This section draws upon Peter H. Solomon, Jr., *Soviet Criminal Justice under Stalin* (Cambridge and New York, 1996). For more detailed analysis and references, see chapters 1, 5, and 8. See also Peter H. Solomon, Jr., "Local Political Power and Soviet Criminal Justice, 1922-1941," *Soviet Studies* 36, no. 3 (July 1985): 305-329.

3. See, for example, S. Kostin, "Uravnilovka, i tekuchest rabotnokov v organnakh iustitsii," *Sovetskaia iustitsiia*, 1932, No. 14: 25-26.

4. See, for example, *Otchet Keletskago okruzhnago suda za 1885-1889s.s.* (Keltsakh, 1890); *Svod statisticheskikh svedenii po delam ugolovnym proizvodiamshimsia v 1904 godu v sudebnykh uchrezhdeniiakh* (St. Petersburg, 1907); *Vsepoddanneishii otchet Ministra Iustitsii za 1914* (Petrograd, 1915); and *Sbornik statisticheskikh svedenii Ministerstva Iustitsii*, vyp. 13, "Svedeniia o lichnom sostave i o deiatel'nost'i subednykh ustanovlenii Evropeiski i Aziatskoi Rossii za 1914" (Petrograd, 1916).

For similar data for the Soviet period, see, for example, *Otchet Prokuratury RSFSR Prezidiumu VTsIK za 1926 g.* (Moscow, 1927); N. A. Cherliuchakevich, ed., *Prestupnost' i repressia v RSFSR* (Moscow, 1930). A comprehensive guide to statistical publications in the Soviet period (which by the 1930s became sparse) is Ger P. van den Berg, *The Soviet System of Justice: Figures and Policy* (Dordrecht, 1985).

While legal journals of 1939-1941 contain sustained discussion of statistical assessment of the work of individual legal officials, before then the subject received occasional mention and only in the context of special measures. Thus, a contest for the best investigators in Moscow oblast' in 1934 focused on speed and rates of case completion as well as the percentage of cases returned to supplementary investigation. "V borbe za vysokoe kachestvo sledstviia," *Sovetskaia iustitsiia*, 1935, No. 33: 1-3.

5. Solomon, *Soviet Criminal Justice under Stalin*, chapter 5.

6. A. Ia. Vyshinskii, "Nashi zadachi," *Za sotsialisticheskuiu zakonnost'*, 1935, No. 5: 5-6; *Rossiiskii tsentr khraneniia i izucheniia dokumentov noveishei istorii* (hereafter RTsKhIDNI), *f.* 17, *op.* 120, *d.* 171: 2-20; *d.* 170: 18-21; G. Roginskii, "Organizatsionnye voprosy perestroiki raboty organov Prokuratury v svete proekta Stalinskoi Konstitutsii,"

Sotsialisticheskaia zakonnost', 1936, No. 8: 28-40.

7. *Gosudarstvennyi arkhiv Rossiiskoi Federatsii* (hereafter GARF), *f.* 353, *op.* 13, *d.* 41: 89; "Ob ustanovlenii klassovykh chinov dlia prokurorsko-sledvstvennytkh rabotnikov organov prokuratury," Ukaz Prezidiuma Vertnovnogo Soveta SSSR ot 16 sent.1943, in G. Safonov, ed., *Spravochnik po zakonodatelstvu dlia sudebno-prokurorskikh rabotnikov* (Moscow 1949), I, 81-85.

8. Solomon, *Soviet Criminal Justice under Stalin*, 179-82; 274-77.

9. M. Zolotov, "Zadachi ugolovno-sudebnykh otdelov," *Sotsialisticheskaia zakonnost'*, 1940, No. 6: 9-14; M. Pankratev, "Nazrevshie voprosy sledstviia," *ibid.*, 1939, No. 8-9: 11-17; "Republikanskoe soveshchanie sledstvennykh otdelov prokuratury ASSR, kraev, i oblastei RSFSR," *ibid.* 1940, No. 7: 22-41; "Soveshchanie aktiva NKIu RSFSR," *Sovetskaia iustitsiia*, 1940, No. 23-24: 8-15.

10. "Republikanskoe soveshchanie," 22-29; Sokolov, "Rol i zadachi revizora," *Sovetskaia iustitsiia*, 1941, No. 2: 4-5; "Rol i zadacha revizora: Obsuzhdaem statiu tov. Sokolova," *ibid.*, No. 9: 9-11.

11. "Soveshchanie aktiva," 9.

12. RTsKhIDNI, *f.* 17, *op.* 116, *d.* 227 (O rasshirenii i ulushchenii iuridicheskogo obrazovaniia v strane): 4-8, and *op.* 118, *d.* 644: 98-102. For details on the drafting and implementation of this resolution, see Solomon, *Soviet Criminal Justice under Stalin*, chapter 10.

13. GARF, *f.* 8131, *op.* 28, *d.* 242b: *passim*; *f.* 9396, *op.* 2, *d.* 293; *f.* 9492, *op.* 1, *d.* 198: 347-358.

14. GARF, *f.* 9492, *op.* 1, *d.* 243; *f.* 8131, *op.* 28, *d.* 1092: 112-115.

15. Solomon, *Soviet Criminal Justice under Stalin*, 344-48.

16. From tables compiled by Yoram Gorlizki from GARF, *f.* 8131, *op.* 28, *d.* 1481: 1; *d.* 3941: 2; *d.* 5051: 29.

17. The rest of this section draws on and paraphrases Solomon, *Soviet Criminal Justice under Stalin*, 367-83.

18. "Vsesoiuznoe soveshchanie rukovodiashchikh rabotnikov Prokuratury," part I: *Sotsialisticheskaia zakonnost'*, 1948, No. 6: 38; GARF, *f.* 813lsch, *op.* 27s, *d.* 4034 ("Stenogramma vsesoiuznogo soveshchaniia prokurorskikh rabotnikov, 5-15 apreliia 1948," tom 1): 297-318, esp. 300-302.

19. GARF (TsGA), *f.* 353, *op.* 16s, *d.* 70: 42-47.

20. RTsKhIDNI, *f.* 17, *op.* 136, *d.* 70: 3-20.

21. GARF, *f.* 9492sch, *op.* 1s, *d.* 558: 7; GARF (TsGA), *f.* 353, *op.* 16s, *d.* 713: 13; Zav. sektorom Administrativnogo otdela TsK VKP(b) Lopukhov, "V sekretnyi arkhiv" (24 noiabria 1949 g).

22. GARF, *f.* 813lsch, *op.* 28s, *d.* 597: 31-34 (Prikaz General'nogo Prokurora No. 61s ot 4 apreliia 1949 "Ob usilienii borby s faktami neosnovatel'nogo privlechenii k sudebnoi otvetsvennosti").

23.   GARF, *f.* 8131sch, *op.* 28s, *d.* 597: 133-135.

24.   GARF, *f.* 9492sch, *op.* 6s, *d.* 15: 12-13;

25.   GARF (TsGA), *f.* 461, *op.* 8s, *d.* 1733, *d.* 1953, *d.* 219.

26.   GARF (TsGA), *f.* 461s, *op.* 8s, *d.* 219: 1-18.

27.   *Partiinyi arkhiv Sverdlovksogo obkoma KPSS, f.* 4, *op.* 47, *d.* 259: 115-130; *op.* 49, *d.* 251: 14-20; 105-107; 112-117; 118-127. I am grateful to James Harris for locating and arranging photocopies of these materials.

28.   RTsKhIDNI, *f.* 17, *op.* 136, *d.* 166: 322-329; for the text of the anonymous letter, see *ibid., op.* 118, *d.* 720: 91-95ob.

29.   Solomon, *Soviet Criminal Justice under Stalin*, 383-88.

30.   Peter H. Solomon, Jr., "The Case of the Vanishing Acquittal: Informal Norms and the Practice of Soviet Criminal Justice," *Soviet Studies* 39, no. 4 (October 1987): 531-55.

31.   *Rabota luchshikh sledovatelei. Materialy uchebno-metodicheskoi konferentsii luchshikh sledstvennykh rabotnikov organov prokuratury. Sbornik 1* (Moscow, 1951), 30-26, 49, 57, 60-61.

32.   GARF, *f.* 353, *op.* 13, *d.* 134: 91, 93-93ob; *f.* 8131, *op.* 28s, *d.* 155: 33-36; *d.* 235: 111-1166; *d.* 282: 100-103; *op.* 27s, *d.* 3871: 6-12.

33.   GARF, *f.* 8131, *op.* 26, *d.* 12: 101; *f.* 9492, *op.* 1, *d.* 179: 71-72; *f.* 353; *op.* 13, *d.* 150: 111; V. Krutskikh, "Povysit' kachestvo kassatsionnykh i chastnykh protsessov," *Sotsialisticheskaia zakonnost'*, 1956, No. 2: 26-31; GARF, *f.* 9492, *op.* 1s, *d.* 578: 54; *op.* 2s, *d.* 44: 112-115; *d.* 58: 237; *f.* 8131, *op.* 27s, d. 4044: 7, 173.

34.   Solomon, "The Case of the Vanishing Acquittal."

35.   Manitoba Law Reform Commission, *Report on the Independence of Provincial Judges* (June 28, 1989), chapter 6 (Evaluation); American Bar Association, Special Committee on the Evaluation of Judicial Performance, *Guidelines for the Evaluation of Judicial Performance* (1985); Martin L. Friedland, *A Place Apart: Judicial Independence and Accountability in Canada* (Ottawa, 1995), chapter 8; Randall Rader, "Evaluate Your Own Performance on the Bench: Here's How," *The Judge's Journal* 30, no. 3 (Summer 1991): 33-38.

36.   Ontario, Ministry of the Attorney General, "Performance Planning and Review for Crown Counsel," (n.d., 1990); Interview with Mr. Douglas Hunt, Ministry of the Attorney General, 15 March 1990.

37.   Dallis Rudamaker, "The Courts in France," in Jerome Waldman and Kenneth Holland, eds., *The Political Role of Law Courts in Modern Democracies* (London, 1988), 29-152; Mary L. Volcansek and Jacqueline Lafon, *Judicial Selection. The Cross-Evolution of French and American Practices* (New York, 1988), chapters 5 and 6; John Bell, "Principles and Methods of Judicial Selection in France," *Southern California Law Review* 61, no. 6 (1988): 1757-94.

38. Carlo Guarnieri, "The Courts in Italy," in Waldman and Holland, eds., *The Political Role of Law Courts*, 153-80; Mary Volcansek, "The Judicial Role in Italy: Independence, Impartiality and Legitimacy," *Judicature* 76, no. 6 (April-May 1990): 322-27; Michele Graziadei and Ugo Mattei, "Judicial Responsibility in Italy: A New Statute," *American Journal of Comparative Law* 38, no. 1 (Winter 1990): 103-126.

39. John H. Langbein, "The German Advantage in Civil Procedure," *University of Chicago Law Review* 52, no. 4 (Fall 1985): 823-66, esp. 850-51. See also David S. Clarke, "The Selection and Accountability of Judges in West Germany's Implementation of a *Rechtsstaat*," *Southern California Law Review* 61, no. 6 (1987-88): 1797-1847.

40. On the spread of statistical reports and indicators from economic management to education, culture, science, and cadres management, see G. Gudkov, *et al.,* "Biurokratizm i biurokratiia: neobkhodimost utochnenii," *Kommunist*, 1988, No. 12: 73-84, esp. 75-76.

41. See note 20 above.

42. "Vsesoiuznoe soveshchanie rukovodiashchikh rabotnikov," 38; *Rabota luchshikh sledovatelei*, 6.

43. RTsKhIDNI, *f.* 17, *op.* 120, *d.* 171: 16, 18; *op.* 117, d. 681: 58-65; *d.* 764:104-105; GARF, *f.* 8131, *op.* 27s, *d.* 157: 18.

44. See Yoram Gorlizki, "De-Stalinization and the Politics of Russian Criminal Justice, 1953-1964," unpublished D.Phil.thesis (University of Oxford, 1992).

45. Solomon, "The Case of the Vanishing Acquittal;" see also Mirjan Damaska, *The Faces of Justice and State Authority: A Comparative Approach to the Legal Process* (New Haven, CT, 1986).

46. V. N. Kudriavtsev, ed., *Effektivnost' pravosudiia i problem ustraneniiu sudebnykh oshibok*, 2 vols. (Moscow, 1975).

47. Seweryn Bialer, *Stalin's Successors: Leadership, Stability and Change in the Soviet Union* (Cambridge, 1980), 22-23.

48. *Ibid.*, 16-17.

49. Testimony to this side of Stalin's character is provided in the memoirs of his interpreter Valentin Berezhkov. See *At Stalin's Side: His Interpreter's Memoirs from the October Revolution to the Fall of the Dictator's Empire* (Secaucus, NJ, 1994), 212-14.

50. The pervasive use of scapegoating and blame assured that officials' conduct would be guided more by negative than by positive incentives. Overemphasis on discipline and negative incentives tends to produce, as Charles Rosenberg noted in his study of Prussian bureaucracy, superficial conformity and resort to subterfuge and deceit. Soviet sociologists reflecting on the bureaucratic tendencies that developed under Stalin stressed how the pressures of potential reprisals produced mediocre performance and an unwillingness to take initiatives. See Charles Rosenberg, *Bureaucracy, Aristocracy and Autocracy: The Prussian Experience 1660-1815* (Cambridge, 1958), 94-95; and Gudkov, *et al.*, "Biurokratizm i biurokratiia," 76ff.

51. Solomon, "The Case of the Vanishing Acquittal."

52. Conversation with Yoram Gorlizki.

53. GARF, *f.* 9492, *op.* 1, *d.* 169 (Initsiativnye i informatsionnye pis'ma TsK VKP(b), fev-dek., 1948), *passim; f.* 974sch, *op.* 16s, *d.* 322: 87-97; *d.* 311: 24-29; *f.* 9492sch, *op.* 2s, *d.* 58: 180-182, "Sekretrariam TsK VKP(b) tov. Malenkovu, G. M., tov. Kuznetsovu, A. A., ot zam. zav. Administrativnym Otedelam TsK VKP(b) Bakakina i zav. sektorom Administrativnogo Otdela TsK VKP(b) Lopukhova (16 oktiabriia 1948 g.); "V tekhsekretariata ob TsK VKP(b) ot zav. sektorom Administrativnogo Otdela TsK VKP(b) Lopukhova i instruktora Administrativnogo Otdela TsK VKP(b) Iakimenkov (12 fevralia 1949 g.); "O sozyve t. Safonova, G. N., Vsesoiuznoi metodicheskoi konferentsii luchshikh sledstvennykh rabotnikov organov Prokuratury SSSR," Postanovlenie Sekretariata TsK VKP(b)—na golosovanie.

54. Todd Foglesong, "The Politics of Judicial Independence and Impartiality: Russian Criminal Justice, 1977-1992," unpublished Ph.D. dissertation (University of Toronto, 1995).

12

POLITICAL REFORM AND LOCAL PARTY INTERVENTIONS UNDER KHRUSHCHEV

Yoram Gorlizki

To many scholars the Khrushchev era continues to stand out as a period of reform. Stalin's successors—most notably Khrushchev himself—are credited with curbing repression, rationalizing administration, improving consumer welfare, and subjecting the autocratic methods of the preceding years to searing criticism. Notwithstanding the occasional lurch toward Stalinist orthodoxy, it was the wide sweep of these new programs that marks this out as a period of reform. Whereas other phases in Soviet history may have witnessed reformist shifts in policy, rarely were they sustained along such a broad front.[1]

Behind the front lines there were nevertheless significant tensions among Khrushchev's reforms. In this chapter I survey one of the most important of these tensions. I begin by re-examining Khrushchev's campaigns to stop local Party officials from interfering in the courts. Whereas most observers have viewed these campaigns as consistent with the generally reformist tendencies of the new post-Stalin regime,[2] I see in them a clash between two opposing principles of Khrushchev's rule. On the one hand, as a means of repudiating and correcting abuses committed under Stalin, Khrushchev and his allies placed a fresh emphasis on the legal system. Accordingly, they bolstered the twin principles of procedural justice (the notion that all citizens are treated equally under the law) and judicial independence (the notion that judges reach verdicts free of outside interference). As we shall see, leadership commitment to these principles was openly articulated in the campaigns against Party interventions. On the other hand, however, Khrushchev was also a keen supporter of the Party's leading role in society. This view translated in policy terms into the Party's right to intervene in all areas of social and economic life and in social terms into the superior status of Party members. In his early efforts to revitalize the Party ideologically and to elevate Party-based modes of leadership,

Khrushchev only added to political pressures on the courts. Indeed, Khrushchev's insistence on the Party's leadership role was arguably to prove more corrosive of judicial independence than the reform programs of any of his serious competitors.

For most of his period in office Khrushchev continued to advocate the virtues of Party leadership and political interventionism; it was only toward the end that he finally began to recognize the tension between Party rule and procedural justice, a tension that he had inadvertently accentuated.

In writing about political interventions and the campaigns against them I, as others before me, have had to treat available sources with care. Given their negative associations, interventions were rarely mentioned in the press. Indeed, Party pressures on individual judges were hardly ever committed to paper. Instead, Party officials avoided undue risks by confining themselves to oral instructions, either directly or by telephone, and as such there is limited evidence of them even in the archives. Nevertheless, reports on the practice were compiled by central Party and legal agencies, especially in the wake of a campaign. Similarly, complaints against political interference were voiced at national and regional conferences of legal officials whose proceedings, though unpublished, have recently been opened to scholarly attention in the archives.[3] To complement these empirical findings I also challenge the reasoning of others who have looked at this topic. Although I build on Solomon's arguments about the rationale for interventions in the post-Stalin period, I suggest that the logic of interference was made all the more compelling by Khrushchev's broader political strategies, not less so. In running against the current of Khrushchev's political reforms, the campaigns against interventions were fated to yield only marginal results.

To understand the tension at the heart of Khrushchev's strategy on Party interventions we must first take account of the early post-Stalin emphasis on the leadership role of the Communist Party. An unreserved commitment to Party rule was by no means a foregone conclusion of the leadership contest that ensued after Stalin's death. The last years of Stalin's life had been marked by uncertainty over the Party's relation to an active security police and an increasingly powerful ministerial system. After Stalin's death, the proponents of Party rule led by Khrushchev fought off attempts, most notably by Beria and Malenkov, to narrow the Party's responsibilities. At the Central Committee plenum in summer 1953 which confirmed Beria's removal from office Khrushchev poured scorn above all on Beria's proposal to "dismiss the leading role of the Party and to limit its activities to work with cadres . . . and propaganda."[4] Khrushchev's stand struck a chord with the July plenum which ended with a resolution committing the country to Party leadership in all public affairs. In rejecting Beria's efforts to "limit the activities of the Party" Khrushchev and the Central Committee reaffirmed the traditional Bolshevik claim that only the Party could transcend the narrow departmental perspectives of individual institutions and pursue the interests of society as a whole.[5] While taking care not to substitute for the functions of the state, Khrushchev underlined the Party's right to intervene in all areas of public life. Such a commitment to interventionism was especially strong in the early phase of Khrushchev's rule, as the new leader distinguished himself from his main rival Malenkov by laying particular stress on Party initiatives and Party-based solutions to the main economic and social problems of the day.[6]

As in other areas of public policy the Party leadership regarded guidance over the legal agencies as its prerogative. The rationale for Party involvement in the administration of justice was so compelling that neither Party nor legal officials saw a need to disguise the fact. On the contrary, Party interest in legal affairs was actively welcomed by senior justice officials.[7] Instead of damaging the reputation of the courts, association with the Party would enhance the court's authority and lift its standing in society. As one legal scholar remarked only months after Stalin's death:

> Drawing judges into the Party leadership and into the political life of an area will widen their circle, enrich their experience and strengthen the authority of the court. . . . Regular Party control of the legal organs guarantees the success of the struggle with various efforts to push the courts into the hands of narrow, local and other illegal interests.[8]

Personnel in the legal organs were actively encouraged to discuss their concerns with secretaries of the local Party committees, to participate on Party commissions, to carry out Party assignments, and themselves to seek election onto the local Party committee.[9]

Inevitably, however, the Party's unlimited competence also generated difficulties. Although Party interventions in legal affairs were plainly justified with reference to the Party's leading role in society, they also had consequences which were worrying to the central leadership. First, extensive political interventions threatened to undermine the authority of the justice system. Following the widespread abuses of the Stalin period the new leadership regarded reform of the administration of justice as a priority. To this end the regime launched a campaign for "socialist legality" (*sotsialisticheskaia zakonnost'*) and thoroughly reorganized the main legal agencies.[10] In order to shore up the credibility of the justice system, however, the regime recognized that it needed to go further than the mere instigation of adminis-trative reforms. In most modern societies the legitimacy of law rests on the ideal of procedural justice, that is, the notion that all citizens will enter the legal process bearing equal rights. Evidence of differential treatment under the law will erode the authority of the legal system.[11] Further, if the laws are to be fairly interpreted and impartially applied it is vital that the judiciary be relatively untouched by political pressures, that it should, in other words, enjoy a measure of operational independence. In the Soviet Union in the early 1950s the main danger to procedural justice was posed by the Communist Party.[12] As Safonov, the Procurator General, lamented in a memorandum to the Central Committee before Stalin died, "there are, in essence, two criminal codes [in Russia], one for Communists and another for everyone else. There have been a number of instances where, for one and the same crime, the Party member remains free while the non-Communist languishes in prison."[13] In its bid to shore up the legitimacy of the justice system after Stalin the regime needed to prevent politicians from habitually interfering in criminal cases and overtly deploying the court apparatus as an instrument in their own interest.

For the central leadership a second danger of an overactive Party was that it raised the specter of local political power. Solomon and others have argued that the crackdown on local influence during the Great Purges and the bid to strengthen central control in the years after resulted in a new equilibrium whereby certain limited forms of Party supervision became institutionalized and the frequency of interference by local politicians was reduced.[14] Having gone to the lengths of a general purge of Party officials in order to eliminate rampant interference in the administration of justice in the 1930s, the central authorities were justifiably concerned not to encourage a new round of political interventions. The leadership in Moscow clearly benefited from an administration of justice according to law and were loath to see local politicians once more violating legal norms and turning the courts to their own ends as they had in the early 1930s.

To illustrate the challenge to central authority of recalcitrant local Party officials, consider the following example. On 26 October 1951 criminal proceedings were instituted against a Party member, A. E. Bolshakov, for malicious hooliganism in the Chernovsk district in Kirov province. Bolshakov proceeded to break bail and eloped to the Vokhomsk district in nearby Kostroma province. When the court order summoning Bolshakov reached the authorities in Kostroma, however, a secretary of the local district Party committee, Krasil'nikov, declined to give permission for Bolshakov's arrest. On 26 March, the head of the administrative organs department of the Kostroma obkom, Zhidkov, elaborated:

> The Vokhomsk district committee has now discussed the misdemeanor [sic] of A. S. Bolshakov at a meeting of its bureau. Given that Bolshakov—a permanent resident of this area—has a good record, the bureau considers it inadvisable to draw Bolshakov into criminal accountability. Instead, it has chosen to issue a reprimand and has entered a severe warning on his Party card.[15]

In the event a deal was finally brokered between the court in Chernovsk and the city Party committee in Vokhomsk by the deputy minister of justice, Sukhodrev. Nevertheless, Sukhodrev had to give his assurance to the Kostroma regional committee that he would personally "issue a directive to the court calling for an objective consideration of the case" and that he would "communicate [the court's] decision to the regional Party committee."[16] Although Bolshakov had committed an act of wanton hooliganism in a public space, it had taken nine months and high level interventions from the USSR deputy minister of justice himself to get the case resolved. For justice to be done the USSR Ministry had had to bend over backward to accommodate the local Party authorities.

Even prior to Stalin's death there is evidence that the central Party leadership was concerned about the need to curtail local Party interventions and to maintain the authority of the justice system.[17] Following Stalin's death the regime's new emphasis on legality provided yet further reason for the central authorities to act on these issues. The crux of the problem lay in safeguarding the independence of the courts without subverting the renewed commitment to Party supremacy in all spheres. The most obvious means of negotiating this problem was to resuscitate Vyshinskii's formula of the 1930s, in which "general" Party supervision and guidance was to be distinguished from "interference" in specific cases. According to Vyshinskii, Party officials were expected to check in broad terms on whether legal agents were following the Party line, but they were prohibited from intervening in the "operational work" of judges.[18]

It would not be long before an opportunity arose for a new post-Stalin restatement of the Vyshinskii doctrine. On 26 October 1953 the Zarech'e district Party committee in Tula passed a resolution condemning one of the local judges, N. Ia. Tarakanova, for her court's failure to comply with raikom instructions. Although Tarakanova had obtained ratification of her conduct from the Tula obkom, the raikom insisted that Tarakanova follow its own orders, on pain of a Party reprimand.[19] Tarakanova chose to take on her local

Party bosses by appealing to a yet higher instance and writing to Khrushchev himself. An instructor from the Central Committee's Department of Administrative Organs was duly sent out to Tula to look into the matter. In his report, the Central Committee official substantiated the essence of Tarakanova's claims.[20]

The Tarakanova affair was widely covered in the press. In a celebrated article in *Partiinnaia zhizn'*, the new Procurator General, Roman Rudenko, made much of the unconstitutionality of Party interventions, as well as of the harm they inflicted on public perceptions of Soviet justice. "Such interference," he said, "undermines the authority of the court and disorients judges, forcing them to adopt illegal decisions and to violate the principle, established in the constitution, of the independence of the courts and their subordination solely to the law."[21] The thrust of the Rudenko article was reiterated in a series of publications, all of which repeated the injunction against Party pressure in "specific" cases, and endorsed the distinction between "political guidance" and "interference."[22] The topic was also virtually the first touched on by the Russian minister of justice, A. T. Rubichev, in his opening speech at a conference for legal officials in Moscow in spring 1954.[23]

The Tarakanova affair was accompanied by a full-scale Central Committee resolution of 27 March 1954 which condemned all interventions by local Party committees in specific criminal cases.[24] The effects of this well-known resolution should not be underestimated. In particular, it may have reinforced the outer limits beyond which most Party secretaries dared not tread. Even the boldest thought twice before trying to cover up a crime of violence or one over which local feelings ran high. A good illustration of the risks that attended interventions in such cases comes from the Krasnoarmeiskii district in Stalingrad in 1955. Following the murder of a 17-year-old girl, investigators found strong incriminating evidence against the section head of a Volga shipyard. Despite this, the district first secretary took the suspect under his wing and orchestrated a platform in the suspect's defense. First, the raikom secretary instructed the district procurator to speak in favor of the suspect at a Party meeting devoted to the case; under pressure from its own secretary, the primary Party organization reluctantly decided against expulsion. Second, the head of a department at the local committee telephoned the judge a day before the trial and asked her to take account of various "mitigating circumstances." Third, the procurator chose to indict the defendant on very light charges that patently failed to match the gravity of the crime. On 6 September the people's court of the third ward sat to consider the case. Though they found the defendant guilty of the charges, the judge and the two lay assessors brought in a paltry sentence of one year's correctional labor. This is what followed:

> Those present in the courtroom and others on the street began vociferously to express outrage at the leniency of the punishment. Certain hooligans and others with previous convictions broke into the court and demanded that the defendant be given over for punishment (*dlia raspravy*). [The defendant] got scared and tried to escape through a window in the courtroom, but was hunted down by the mob who set him alight, and killed him.[25]

This embarassing incident caused indignation at the regional Party committee. Within days, the district first secretary was fired and the department head sacked and expelled from the Party. In addition, both the district and Stalingrad city procurators were dismissed, and steps were taken to have the district judge recalled. The bureau of the obkom was spurred, furthermore, to pass a resolution in which all efforts by Party committees to afford protection to Communist criminals was denounced as a "most gross violation of socialist legality."[26]

Cases such as this one, however, were exceptional. Despite the Central Committee resolution of March 1954 and the efforts of Rudenko and others in publicizing it, it appears that the spring campaign to stamp out local Party interference in criminal cases had little effect on the practice of local secretaries. Indeed, within a year of the March resolution a further Central Committee decree of 19 January 1955 made reference to continuing widespread evidence of interventions and drew the attention of Party officials once again to the "unacceptability of interference by Party officials in the resolution of criminal cases."[27]

There are several regional examples which support the claim that the impact of the March 1954 Central Committee resolution on interventions was at best limited. In the spring of 1954 a three-man brigade from the All-Union Ministry of Justice, including the deputy minister, Danilov, was sent on a two-month tour of the Far East. In the course of their inspections, they discovered several instances of interference by politicians in the work of the courts.[28] The problem was especially rife in Komsomol'sk-na-Amure. Judges from both the Lenin and Central districts in that town complained of constant meddling by leading officials in criminal cases. The deputy minister, Danilov, consequently got in contact with the first secretary of the Khabarovsk territorial Party committee, A. B.Aristov, who assured Danilov that the administrative organs department would prepare the matter for discussion at the bureau.[29] Nevertheless, despite the Central Committee resolution, the personal intervention of the deputy minister of justice, and the support of the territorial first secretary, the behavior of local Party officials continued as before into the spring and summer of 1955. Even eighteen months after Danilov's original visit, in the autumn of 1955, reports continued to stream into the Central Committee of unwarranted interferences by Party officials in the area; the situation in Komsomol'sk-na-Amure, one report noted, continued to be acute.[30]

The ineffectiveness of Party edicts in containing overeager politicians was noted also by procurators in the spring of 1955, at a series of republican and regional conferences convened to discuss the progress of the resolution of 19 January. According to the main report summarizing the proceedings of these conferences, many procurators continued to be unhappy about the "incorrect interference of district Party committees in the resolution of specific cases, and about their dilatory handling of cases relating to the prosecution of Communists."[31] Examples abounded of Party committees refusing to allow prosecutions against suspects who were patently guilty of crimes; in one case, in Krasnoiarsk, the secretary of one district committee even ordered police officials not to enforce a verdict that had already been handed down by the court.[32]

A spate of Party interventions in criminal cases was also reported a year later, in March 1956, by the Russian deputy minister of justice, G. Z. Anashkin, following a visit to Kamensk region. In one case highlighted by Anashkin, secretaries from the Millerovo town and Kamensk regional committees prevailed on the town procurator and on the head of the regional justice administration to release from custody three pilots accused of serious assault; the trial itself was repeatedly postponed. In another case, the head of the regional court, on instructions from one of the regional Party secretaries, sent a telegram to the head of the Novoshakhtinsk city police ordering him to suspend the implementation of a sentence pending clarification of the convict's Party status. Perhaps the most blatant intervention concerned a relation of a Shakhty city Party secretary. The accused was charged with forcing his way into a drinking establishment (*chainaia*), biting an attendant, and slashing an interceding bystander in the face. Within five days, the defendant was released from custody after a telephone call from his cousin, the Party secretary. At the trial, the charge was requalified from Article 74, part II, to Article 74, part I, on top of which Article 53 was applied, reducing the punishment still further to a year's suspended sentence. The regional procurator lodged a protest, however, and the verdict was duly overturned by the presidium of the regional court. Under pressure from the city Party secretary the court of first instance disregarded a ruling from the oblast' court to increase the sentence. A merry-go-round ensued in which the regional court returned the case for re-trial on four occasions in eight months. The compromise eventually reached between the two courts was a one-year custodial sentence on the basis of Article 74, part II. This was still, in the eyes of Anashkin, inordinately lenient.[33]

Appalled at these transgressions, Anashkin invited the regional Party secretariat to convene a local seminar on legal matters. The session was well attended, and included among others the Party secretary in charge of legal affairs, the deputy head of the administrative organs department, the chairman of the regional court, and the head of the regional justice administration. Unabashed, Anashkin raised the matter of unwarranted interferences in judicial procedures. Although he conceded that it was not within his jurisdiction to examine questions relating to Party workers, Anashkin invited the secretariat to check on the facts for themselves and to take appropriate measures. Rather than listen to the evidence laid out by the deputy minister, however, Dobrynin, the Party secretary chairing the meeting, in Anashkin's words,

> rudely interrupted me and tried in every way possible to denigrate me and to discredit my evidence. No decision was taken on the matter and no assignments were made out to check the truth of my claims. Furthermore, no mention was made of the inadmissability of illegal interference in resolving specific cases by the courts.[34]

On their return from Kamensk, the brigade from the RSFSR ministry of justice recommended to the collegium that the chairman of the Kamensk regional court be released from his post. As for those Party officials who had behaved illegally, the ministry of justice team knew full well that such questions lay outside their domain. The matter was referred to the Central Committee, but no disciplinary action against the Kamensk Party officials was ever taken.[35]

The March 1954 resolution on interference supplied some kind of rhetorical ammunition to those legal officials who purported to take the notion of procedural justice seriously. Nevertheless, the legal bureaucracies had no recourse to independent legal or disciplinary powers which they could have brought to bear against errant Party officials. Instead, they were forced to apply to Party bodies—usually the Central Committee—for help. Although the Central Committee sounded off about the impropriety of interference, it was usually reluctant to take concrete action on such matters. The main punitive measures it had at its disposal, the local purge, it saved for the grander tasks of building political alliances or forging ahead on the agricultural or industrial fronts. The preferred mechanisms for dealing with the irritation of Party interference were the central and regional Party control committees, which were fairly weak in this period and were usually, in any case, firmly under the thumb of the corresponding Party apparat.[36]

A second reason why Party interference persisted was that the rationales which had led Party officials to intervene in the first place did not somehow vanish with the announcement of the socialist legality campaign; if anything, they became more pronounced. Most Party officials did not intervene in criminal cases merely because they had dissolute or corrupt personalities. Rather they intervened in response to incentives that were firmly rooted in the Soviet political economy, incentives that were usually powerful enough to outweigh the prohibitions against interference. The most persuasive typology of the various purposes served by political interference in criminal cases is that offered by Peter Solomon.[37] Apart from the perpetual practice of "private" interventions—be they to protect relations or to pursue enemies—Solomon outlined two further types, both of which had wider justifications. The first involved protecting leading government and, especially, Party officials, so as to uphold the authority of the regime. As Solomon argues, "The problem for the Party secretary stemmed from the fact that the offender held a position of public responsibility or honor. To reveal to the public at large that certain important officials were unworthy of their positions might arouse suspicions about other officials and politicians." "Party secretaries knew that when a scandal broke in their bailiwick and among their officials, whom they were supposed to have vetted and supervised, they might be held personally responsible."[38]

The second type of intervention which served a wider purpose was that in which Party secretaries protected executives who had broken the law in order to further the interests of a local firm. Thus the executive who bribed suppliers or padded reports so as to deflect pressure from Moscow could often expect some sort of assistance from the raikom.[39] As Solomon observes, "Not only was the factory manager himself judged according to figures on production, but also his superiors in the ministry and the Party authorities in his locality."[40] From all their points of view, the ostensibly illegal action of the executive constituted "business practices rather than crimes"—all "for the good of the cause (v pol'zu dela)."[41]

There are reasons to suppose that these rationales gained rather than lost in salience following Stalin's death. First, in the early years of the new regime Khrushchev vigorously sought to build up the image of the Party. The incipient criticisms of the "cult of personality" were matched by assiduous praise for the leadership role of Communists. Indeed, the reaffirmation of the Leninist creed of Party rule was to be more pronounced in these years than at any time after the war, and was buttressed by fierce pro-Party propaganda.[42] To have allowed the image of the Party to be tarnished by sleaze, corruption, and scandals merely for the sake of "socialist legality" would have been hard to justify, especially now. With the reassertion of the Party's authority in full swing, suppressing public trials of major Party officials was much the easier route. This was all the more so in the early phase of Khrushchev's rule, at a time when the reform program placed much faith on Party dynamism and on the Leninist, Party-based credentials of the leadership.

With regard to corporate crimes, the creation of regional economic councils in 1957 was designed precisely to increase local Party responsibility for industrial production.[43] With the elimination of central ministerial coordination and accountability not only had the pressure on the local enterprise director to forge illegal ties across regions increased. Since his own reputation had become more closely bound to regional economic performance than ever before, the onus on the local Party boss to help out an enterprise manager who had broken the law in the interests of firm and region had also grown. In such circumstances, there was every incentive for a Party secretary to help those who helped him by interceding in criminal cases.

A third reason why conditions had become more conducive to intervention during the 1950s is that this was a period when Party supervision over the legal sector was consolidated through the establishment of administrative organs departments at regional Party committees. Set up in 1948, the administrative organs departments were staffed with specialists and provided a regular basis for monitoring the progress of the justice agencies. Although it was unusual for personnel within these departments to interfere on their own initiative, they were in a position to keep Party secretaries abreast of developments in the courts. In providing a regular current of information and legal expertise, the administrative organs departments brought Party secretaries closer to the legal sector, enhancing their capacity to manipulate it in the process.[44]

In fact, regional committees did not stop at intervening in local legal affairs; they even contrived to take on the central courts in Moscow. One common target for regional disquiet was the RSFSR supreme court which, since the late 1940s, had enjoyed an enduring reputation for leniency. Indeed, as befitted its reputation, the RSFSR court took a lead in implementing the new more liberal criminal policy of the early post-Stalin regime. In so doing, it ran into opposition from a number of provincial Party committees which were inclined toward harsher penalties.

No polls of regional Party secretaries on questions of criminal policy were ever conducted under Khrushchev. Evidence from the archives does nonetheless support the view that provincial Party bosses were generally disposed toward draconian criminal punishments, especially for social order crimes. In this they found common cause with procurators who, in addition to being noted for their "accusatorial bias," were professionally inclined to push for high sentences. Sometimes procurators would turn to their regional Party secretaries for support. In one case referred to in the archives, the Orel procurator approached the regional Party committee at the beginning of 1954 to see whether the Central Committee administrative organs department might do something to discipline those members of the RSFSR court who appeared bent on declining procuratorial protests.[45] But most often the regional committees, it seems, hardly needed pushing. One issue over which many regional Party officials felt especially strongly was the reluctance of the RSFSR court to employ the death penalty more widely. The RSFSR court considered very few first instance cases, usually only the five to ten large scale crimes a year which crossed oblast' jurisdictions. After adoption on 25 April 1954 of the law on aggravated murder, however, many death sentences originally passed at the regional court were appealed and commuted by the RSFSR court. This line angered a number of regional Party bosses who believed the regime was losing a grip on social order, and who saw in executions an effective remedy.

One natural focal point for lobbying by regional Party bosses was the administrative organs department of the new RSFSR bureau of the Central Committee. Shortly after its formation in March 1956, the RSFSR administrative organs department was showered with notes from regional committees complaining of the RSFSR court's laxity on the question of death penalties. According to one bitter secretary at the Kirov regional Party committee, almost half the death sentences passed at the regional court in the three years since the April law had been watered down by the RSFSR court.[46] A similar communiqué from the head of the administrative organs department in Gor'kii region observed that despite the "widespread acclamation" with which the local population had greeted the original death warrants, more than two-fifths had been replaced by custodial sentences at the RSFSR court. "Such a practice does not help in the struggle with serious crimes," the report argued.[47] Similar protests hailed from regional Party committees in Irkutsk and elsewhere.[48]

Certain local Party committees assumed that they could ply the RSFSR court as they did the local courts. One letter, from the Taganrog city Party committee to the secretary of the RSFSR bureau, Beliaev, expressed dismay that the republican court had declined the execution of an alleged murderer of two girls. "The community of Taganrog," it said, "is deeply indignant at such a decision." "The city Party committee considers that the RSFSR supreme court has ruled incorrectly. . . .*We ask you to interfere in this case so that the criminal gets his just deserts.*"[49] Although such appeals rarely brought immediate results, the collected pressures of the regional committees, the provincial procuracies, and, occasionally, the corresponding courts did eventually permeate up the Party hierarchies. Members of the RSFSR court recall that they were regularly invited to the RSFSR administrative organs department and instructed to tighten up their act.[50] Leading RSFSR court officials were, moreover, often forced to fend off hostile audiences at legal conferences.[51] But so long as the leadership of the court retained a liberal gloss it proved difficult for the department to force a direct change in the court's position.

In the years after Stalin's death, two main characters dominated the RSFSR court. The chairman, Bitiukov, a former head of the Gor'kii regional court, was reputed for his sense of balance and his legal skills; the second figure, Arkhangel'skii, the first deputy chairman of the court, was also held in high esteem by his colleagues.[52] Both had strong liberal credentials as well as solid experience, with Bitiukov's tenure as chairman going back to 1948. In March 1957 the terms of judges at the RSFSR supreme court came up for renewal. The new composition of the court was determined in large part by the RSFSR administrative organs department, which felt the need to put the court on a harsher tack. Consequently, two-fifths of the judges were replaced, with many of the new members "possessing experience in the Party and soviet organs."[53] The departure of Arkhangel'skii, who had in any event reached retirement age, opened a space for Kriukov, the arch-conservative from the Moscow regional court, who became the new first deputy chairman. At the highest rung, the expulsion from the court of Bitiukov is remembered to this day for its "unpleasantness."[54] Just prior to the election of the new court at the March session of the RSFSR supreme soviet, the head of the RSFSR administrative organs department, A. Kidin, sent a letter to the secretariat in which the department's animosity toward Bitiukov could hardly have been less veiled.

The department of administrative organs [of the RSFSR bureau] considers it imperative to inform the Central Committee that the chairman of the

RSFSR supreme court, S. P. Bitiukov, has behaved improperly and that his work in improving the performance of the court has been poor. . . . Bitiukov has been warned about serious mistakes in his work and about his incorrect personal conduct in 1955 and 1956 but he has failed to draw the right conclusions. All this seriously impedes the struggle with crime and the further strengthening of socialist legality. Bitiukov is at present incapable of eliminating the mistakes committed by him in leading the supreme court. In connection with this we cannot consider it expedient to recommend his re-election at the forthcoming session of the supreme soviet of the RSFSR to the post of chairman of the republican supreme court.[55]

Bitiukov was replaced at the RSFSR court by A. T. Rubichev, the former RSFSR minister of justice, whose views were more to the liking of Kidin and of regional Party chiefs.[56]

Nevertheless, despite the purge, the Russian court still included a number of independent and liberal minded judges such as Grun, Borodin, and the deputy chairman, F. L. Tokarev.[57] Where a conservative regional court caved in to liberal pressures from these judges, chances were that obkom passions would ignite, just as they had prior to Bitiukov's dismissal. This was the case in the Novosibirsk regional Party headquarters, where the following letter, addressed to Kidin, was penned:

It was disclosed at the obkom bureau that one of the reasons for the unsatisfactory practice of the judicial organs has been the incorrect attitude of the supreme court of the RSFSR. Over the last two years the RSFSR court has systematically revoked punishments in cases that have come its way by means of supervision. Moreover, it has systematically brought hundreds of protests against the verdicts of presidia at the regional courts. These protests have called for reductions in criminal punishments, usually without any grounds. Thus, for example, only in 1957 the deputy chairman of the supreme court of the RSFSR, F. L. Tokarev, addressed 86 protests to the presidium of the Novosibirsk regional court. Of these, 77 called for a reduction in punishment. These included sentences against one murderer, three rapists, three robbers, six thieves, six speculators, and 45 plunderers of socialist property. Tokarev, meanwhile, did not field a single protest against liberal sentences, of which there are many in Novosibirsk.[58]

It is an irony that liberal resistance within the RSFSR court was finally overcome precisely as the central authorities embarked on a campaign against the court's own persecutors in the regions, the Party secretaries. Following a sharp rise in reported levels of crime in the summer of 1960, a joint attack from the administrative organs department and the USSR Supreme Court eventually brought the Russian court to heel. For more than five years judges on the RSFSR supreme court's criminal collegia had managed to withstand complaints from the regional judiciary and the opposition of regional Party committees and procuracy offices; it was to take a general campaign initiated by the central Party leadership and involving a marked reorientation in criminal policy for the RSFSR supreme court to come into line. Having been criticized for watering down harsh sentences the RSFSR court was soon attacked for "careening to the other extreme," for "unprincipled severity," and for a "fixation with maximum sentences."[59]

From the autumn of 1960 regional Party bosses were also treated to a major purge. The immediate trigger was a notorious scandal surrounding the misdemeanors of A. N. Larionov, the first secretary of the Riazan regional Party committee, who was found to have deliberately falsified regional data on meat production. It soon emerged that Larionov was not the only regional first secretary to have responded to Khrushchev's relentless pressures with subterfuge. In the face of overambitious targets from Moscow and enhanced lateral responsibilities for regional production, provincial Party leaders had taken refuge in "padding" production figures, bribing suppliers for additional raw materials, and shielding those involved from the force of the law. Khrushchev's reaction to these revelations was typically robust. In all, one-third of regional first secretaries in the RSFSR were removed within a year of the Larionov affair. In Yanov's words, this was a "purge of regional dictators unprecedented in its proportions in the post-totalitarian era."[60]

In the winter of 1960-61 Khrushchev began to see how local Party interventionism and disregard for central rules were undermining goals to which he and the rest of the central leadership accorded priority. As long as regional Party first secretaries delivered on production goals set by Moscow the central Party leadership seemed willing to let them regulate their own domains, even if this meant occasional interference in the work of the courts. Thus although the sovnarkhoz reforms had fueled local interventions, these had been tolerated as a marginal nuisance. It was only when it emerged that regional economic achievements rested on a fabric of lies that the center turned to its most powerful tool, a general purge, to bring provincial fiefs to heel.

By the autumn of 1961 Khrushchev was also resorting to other means in order to tame the regional Party bureaucracies. At the XXIInd Party congress in October 1961 he sought to "make the purge of the little Stalins permanent" by introducing a new article to the Party statutes limiting the tenure of members of republican and regional Party leaderships to two terms.[61] The following March at a session of the Central Committee he announced that supervision of agricultural production was to be taken out of the hands of the rural Party committees and vested in district production directorates staffed with professional managers.[62] The attack on Party bureaucracies was taken a step further in November 1962 with the division of regional Party hierarchies into agricultural and industrial branches. This resulted, according to Yanov, in fierce battles between the Party's rural and urban prefects and the splitting of regional Party alliances.[63]

The attack on regional and local Party officials also involved a redefinition of their relationship to the law. From the beginning of 1961 Khrushchev for the first time leveled charges of anti-state behavior at local *Party* as well as state officials.[64] The journal *Kommunist* quoted Khrushchev's speech to the January 1961 plenum of the Central Committee in which he criticized, among others, the leaders of the Tula, Kirov, and Riazan Party committees:

> These are not political organizers but careerists, people who wormed their way into the Party; they bring shame on the Party and must be expelled from the Party and *turned over to the law. . . .*[65]

Khrushchev also began to round on Party committees which shielded Party "miscreants" from the full force of the law. This, indeed, was a major theme of Khrushchev's address to the same Central Committee plenum, in November 1962, that divided the regional Party bureaucracies. "It is completely unacceptable," declared Khrushchev,

> that certain Party committees tolerate abuse of office by Communists and, moreover, sometimes even offer them protection and take them under their wing. It is well-known that V. I. Lenin always opposed defending law-breakers solely on account of their being members of the Party. [66]

Khrushchev then recited a memorandum from Lenin in which the Party's founder denounced any Party committee that shielded "Communist-criminals" from the law. "It is the height of infamy and disgrace," Khrushchev quoted Lenin, *"for the party in power to protect 'its own' scoundrels"* and for Party secretaries to "indulge Communist-criminals when, in fact, they should be hanged." Even "the slightest attempt to 'influence' the courts by 'lightening' the burden on Communists" had—Lenin believed—to be met with expulsion from the Party.[67]

Shortly after the November plenum, in December 1962 the presidium of the Central Committee issued a decree establishing new rules relating to the prosecution of Communists. The decree stipulated that criminal proceedings against Communists no longer required permission from local Party committees.[68] By loosening ties between Party committees and legal representatives in criminal cases, the new rules made it harder for Party committees to protect "Communist-criminals."

The new rules were also significant because they signaled a re-evaluation of the status of Party members. The requirement that Party committees "clear" the prosecution of Communists had originally been intended to ensure that members were expelled from the Party before the public humiliation of a trial.[69] To have had Party members appearing in court, laboring in camps, or freely mixing in society while having a criminal record would have been detrimental to the image of the Party. Such a prospect would have been particularly unattractive at a time, such as the early 1950s, when Party membership was regarded as a point of honor and a condition of leadership.[70] By the early 1960s, however, Khrushchev had lost all reservations in his attacks on Party functionaries and had started openly to turn his fire on Party officials as a group. In these circumstances the need to retain procedures protecting Party members from association with criminal prosecutions had become less of a priority. Indeed, Khrushchev himself now insisted that Party members who had committed crimes be turned over to the law. Thus, on 20 December 1962 the leadership finally dispensed with special arrangements for the prosecution of Communists that had existed since the 1930s:

> On the basis of the present resolution all procedures making the arrest of a Party member or candidate conditional upon the agreement of the local Party organs are cancelled . . . and the joint resolution of 1 December 1938 "On sanctioning arrests" is revoked. As a rule, the question of Party status should be resolved before the trial, but in certain cases it may be settled only after the investigation or after the trial itself has been concluded.[71]

For most of the 1950s the regime had remained committed to maintaining the Party's image at all costs. That the leadership could now contemplate Party members appearing in court or laboring in camps *as Party members* reflected a reduced need to distinguish the status of Party members from the rest of society. Other considerations had now come to the fore:

> A number of Party organs have incorrectly held that a Communist can go to court only if he has been expelled from the Party, and on these grounds have often forbidden the organs of the procuracy from instituting criminal

proceedings against members and candidates of the Party who have committed crimes. This has meant that for one and the same criminally punishable act the person without a Party card is drawn into legal accountability, while the Communist is subjected only to Party punishments.[72]

Khrushchev had encountered intractable problems of control over regional Party principals and had turned to the criminal law as a means of discipline and containment. As Stalin had done before, Khrushchev intoned the catechism that neither Party nor state officials were exempt from the law. In order to back up this strategy, however, he and the leadership explicitly appealed to the source of legitimacy that underpinned the legal system, the notion of equality of all before the law. It was wrong and improper, the Presidium conceded, that for "one and the same criminally punishable act" the Party member should go free while others languished in prison. Shortly after the Presidium ruling, in the early months of 1963, this principle of equality before the law was reinforced in the Party press. Thus in an article in the Party's leading theoretical journal Nikolai Mironov, head of the Central Committee's Department of Administrative Organs, condemned the injustice of criminal cases against Party members being dropped while non-Party accomplices landed up in jail, and he reiterated the principle that all citizens, irrespective of their Party status, would be treated equally before the law.[73]

By the last three years of his leadership Khrushchev had come to question some of the tenets of Party rule that had underpinned his earlier reform program. First among these was the status distinction between Party members and others, a distinction that had gone hand in hand with the discourse of Party leadership over society. By the early 1960s Khrushchev's position in this area had changed. As he proclaimed to the XXIInd Party congress: "In our times, non-Party people are actively building Communism arm in arm with the Communists, and the overwhelming majority of them reason like Communists."[74] Toward the end of his rule Khrushchev also began to question the merits of Party interventionism. To the Central Committee plenum in March 1962, for example, Khrushchev lambasted local Party organs for "intervening" in the life of agricultural cooperatives. This, writes Yanov, left the audience "astonished" since "no one until then . . . had seen anything at all wrong in the intervention of Party professionals in the trivial affairs of the kolkhozy."[75]

For most of his period in office, Khrushchev had been very much a Party-based reformer, one who premised the success of his project on the right combination of Party activism and proper Party organization. This reliance had made Party interventions which served the cause more likely. That, however, was a bargain that Khrushchev was willing to make.[76] It was only when Khrushchev realized that this bargain was undermining primary production goals that he began to question the logic of interventionism and to withdraw from the deal he had struck with regional dignitaries. He responded by purging regional Party principals, reorganizing the Party hierarchy, and introducing new rules on tenure and on the prosecution of Communists.

That these responses failed was to be a problem not just for Khrushchev but for the post-Stalin regime as a whole. Impressionistic polls suggest that by the late Brezhnev period the proportion of judges who experienced political interventions was on the rise.[77] By that stage, however, interventions had become detached from their ideological moorings. In particular, the number of interventions to do with private gain, personal vendettas, and the protection of relations and patronage networks had proliferated. These interventions served no wider political purpose and followed no general social logic; they reflected not the policies of the regime, reform or otherwise, but disenchantment with political and legal norms and a decisive shift in the balance between public goals and private ones.

Much of the harm inflicted on the legitimacy of the regime by Party interventions under Brezhnev was a consequence of innovations introduced in the Khrushchev era. Whereas under Stalin legislation and state rules had been shrouded in secrecy, Khrushchev and his colleagues accorded widespread publicity to new legislation and ensured public access to state laws, Party resolutions, and administrative decrees, many of which were serialized or compiled in volumes with large circulations. But this reverence for the external forms of law was to lumber the regime with a new dilemma. For the more open and accessible the state's rules became, the more easily would state officeholders be measured by these standards and the more visibly would the "Party in power" be exposed breaking its own rules and "protecting its 'own' scoundrels." Although the conflict between Party-based political reform and procedural justice achieved a peculiar intensity under Khrushchev, the corrosive effect on regime legitimacy was a long-term one which would carry on into the Brezhnev period and beyond.

Author's note: My thanks are due to the British Academy for the Personal Research Grant and travel awards in 1993-94 which made research for this article possible. I am also grateful to Todd Foglesong, Eugene Huskey, and Peter Solomon for their comments on an earlier version of this paper.

Notes

1. Stephen Cohen, for example, refers to the Khrushchev years as a "decade-long triumph of Soviet reformism" in which "[v]irtually every area of Soviet life was affected (and improved)," Stephen F. Cohen, "The Friends and Foes of Change: Reformism and Conservatism in the Soviet Union," in Stephen F. Cohen, *et al.*, eds., *The Soviet Union Since Stalin* (London, 1980), 16. For works that focus on Khrushchev's reformist leadership see Alexander Yanov, *The Drama of the Soviet 1960s: A Lost Reform* (Berkeley, CA, 1984), 95, 97, 111; *idem,* "In the Grip of the Adversarial Paradigm: The Case of Nikita Sergeevich Khrushchev in Retrospect," in Robert O. Crummey, ed., *Reform in Russia and the USSR* (Urbana, IL, 1989), 160; Carl A. Linden, *Khrushchev and the Soviet Leadership* (Baltimore, 1990), 27; and W. J. Tompson, "Khrushchev and Gorbachev as Reformers: A Comparison," *British Journal of Political Science* 23, no. 1 (1993): 78-79. A singular attempt to show how Khrushchev's reformist bent coexisted alongside what were distinctly non-reformist tendencies is George W. Breslauer, *Khrushchev and Brezhnev as Leaders: Building Authority in Soviet Politics* (London, 1982), 270-72, 281.

2. In one of the earliest commentaries, George Ginsburgs described the original 1954 resolution as a "positive measure [which] represent[s] a long overdue attempt to limit to some extent direct Party interference in court work, almost a standard phenomenon during Stalin's regime." George Ginsburgs, "Structural and Functional Evolution of the Soviet Judiciary since Stalin's Death: 1953-1956," *Soviet Studies* 13, no. 3 (January 1962): 284. Another writer who has looked at the attack on interventions is Peter Solomon. "In 1954," writes Solomon, "Khrushchev launched a personal attack on party interventions in prosecutions" whose message was "reinforced by that leader's campaign in the late 1950s to promote the observance of socialist legality." The attacks on local Party interventions are seen as symptomatic of Khrushchev's "intense concern with legality" as well as of his willingness to take on established local interests. As such, they are presented as an integral part of Khrushchev's effort to reform the Stalinist political system before Brezhnev's stagnation set in: Peter H. Solomon, Jr., "Soviet Politicians and Criminal Prosecutions: The Logic of Party Intervention," in James R. Millar, ed., *Cracks in the Monolith* (Armonk, NY, 1992), 3-34 (esp. 3-4, 8, 9-10, 18, 22). For another discussion of this campaign, see Robert Sharlet's important article, "The Communist Party and the Administration of Justice in the USSR," in Donald D. Barry, *et al.*, eds., *Soviet Law after Stalin* (Alphen aan den Rijn, 1979), Vol. 3, 330, 339.

3. Materials on Party interference in criminal cases in this article are taken from the following archives: *Gosudarstvennyi arkhiv Rossiiskoi Federatsii* (henceforth GARF), *f.* 353 (RSFSR Ministry of Justice), *f.* 8131 (USSR Procuracy), *f.* 9492 (USSR Ministry of Justice); *Tsentral'noe khranenie sovremennoi dokumentatsii* (henceforth TsKhSD), *f.* 4 (Central Committee Secretariat); and *Rossiiskii tsentr khraneniia i izucheniia dokumentov noveishei istorii* (henceforth RTsKhIDNI), *f.* 17 (General Fond), *f.* 556 (RSFSR Bureau of Communist Party).

4.   *Ibid.*, no. 1 (1991), 153. Similarly, Lazar Kaganovich denounced the "scoundrel Beria" for trying to reduce "the functions of the central committee to 'propaganda' and 'cadres' rather than letting it "lead the whole life of . . . the country and of the state." *Ibid.*, 198. For more on Beria's attempts to shift power from the Central Committee to the Council of Ministers (especially for foreign policy), see *ibid.*, 161; and on Beria's efforts to undermine the Party's control over his own ministry, the MVD, see *ibid.*, 174; and *Izvestiia TsK KPSS*, 1991, No. 2: 173.

5.   The July plenum resolved in its final statement that "Party leadership of all organizations is the principal condition of their success." See *Izvestiia TsK KPSS*, 1991, No. 2: 205. For more on the Party's traditional claim that it was uniquely able to take on tasks of "societal" or "overarching significance," see: T. H. Rigby, "Traditional, Market and Organizational Societies," reprinted in T. H. Rigby, *The Changing Soviet System* (Aldershot, 1990), 74; T. H. Rigby, "Stalin and the Mono-organizational Society," in *ibid.*, 83; Zbigniew Brzezinski, "The Soviet Political System," in Z. Brzezinski, *Dilemmas of Change in Soviet Politics* (New York, 1969), 5, 24; Seweryn Bialer, *Stalin's Successors* (Cambridge, 1980), 202-203.

6.   For a more nuanced discussion of this issue see Yoram Gorlizki, "Party Revivalism and the Death of Stalin," *Slavic Review* 54, no. 1 (Spring 1995): 1-22.

7.   Thus, for example, in a letter to Khrushchev of 21 April 1953, Konstantin Gorshenin, the Minister of Justice, pleaded that Party functionaries be pressed into a *more active* role in the selection of future legal officials. GARF, *f.* 9492, *op.* 1 *d.* 290: 14.

8.   V. M. Petrenko, *Nezavisimost' sovetskikh sudei i podchinenie ikh tol'ko zakonu* (Moscow, 1953), 23-25; and see V. M. Petrenko, *Sovetskie sud'i nezavisimy i podchiniaiutsia tol'ko zakonu* (Moscow, 1954), 39.

9.   *Ibid.*, 36, 42; and I. I. Dolbik, *KPSS v bor'be za ukreplenie sotsialisticheskoi zakonnosti v deiatel'nosti sovetskogo gosudarstvennogo apparata (1951-1955 gg.)* (Minsk, 1956), 207.

10.   There is more on this in chapter 3 of my work in progress, "Soviet Politicians and Russian Justice, 1948-1964."

11.   Dennis Lloyd, *The Idea of Law* (Harmondsworth, 1987), 125-28, 256-57.

12.   One of the most serious other threats to the autonomy of the courts in 1953 was posed by the Ministry of Justice, which in the months after Stalin's death issued a number of orders and directives designed, much to the consternation of the USSR Supreme Court, to reorient judicial decisions. In the ensuing battle between the Ministry and the courts, the bias of the new leadership soon became apparent; as the profile of the courts was raised, that of the Ministry declined. Indeed, from summer 1954 the Ministry was decisively weakened, and within two years it had been dismantled. (For more on this see Yoram Gorlizki, "Anti-ministerialism and the USSR Ministry of Justice: A Study in Organizational Decline," *Europe-Asia Studies* 48, no. 8 [December 1996]: 1279-1318.) The potential of other bodies, such as the security organs, to compromise the integrity of judges in ordinary criminal cases had already been limited by the effective separation of political cases from the realm of ordinary criminal law in the late Stalin period; the further efforts to place the secret police under civilian authority after Stalin only added to these limitations.

13.   GARF, *f.* 8131, *op.* 27, *d.* 4668: 126.

14.   Peter H. Solomon, Jr., "Local Political Power and Soviet Criminal Justice, 1922-1941," *Soviet Studies* 37, no. 3 (July 1985): 320-23.

15.   GARF, *f.* 9492, *op.* 2, *d.* 93: 17

16.   *Ibid.*: 17-19.

17.   This is suggested for example by the request in January 1953 from F. K. Iakovlev, the deputy head of the department of trade union and komsomol organs, for the USSR Ministry to supply the Central Committee with a report on recent unfounded interventions by local Party organs in criminal cases. *Ibid.*: 17.

18.   Solomon, "Local Political Power," 322-23.

19.   GARF, *f.* 353, *op.* 13, *d.* 197: 75-76

20.   Interview with N. F. Chistiakov, Moscow, 31 May 1991.

21.   R. A. Rudenko, "Strogo bliusti sotsialisticheskuiu zakonnost," *Partiinaia zhizn'*, 1954, No. 6: 16. Rudenko's reference to the constitution related to Article 112 of the all-union constitution and Article 116 of the RSFSR constitution which had stipulated explicitly that "judges are independent and subordinate only to the law." (Note that these provisions were retained as center-pieces of Khrushchev's court-related legislation [i.e., Article 2 of the 1957 statute on the supreme court; Article 9 of the 1958 Fundamentals of legislation on court structure; and Article 7 of the 1960 law on court structure in the RSFSR]. See *Vedomosti*, 1957, No. 4; 1959, No.1; and *Vedomosti RSFSR*, 1960, No.40.)

22.   Petrenko, "Nezavisimost," 26, 36. The publication most closely inspired by the Central Committeee resolution was Petrenko, *Sovetskie sud'i* , esp. 7, 16, 35. See also *Sovetskoe gosudarstvo i pravo*, 1954, No. 7: 7-9; and Dolbik, *KPSS v bor'be*, 199.

23.   GARF, *f.* 353, *op.* 13, *d.* 197: 75-6.

24.   TsKhSD, 19th session, protocol 54, point 15.

25.   Letter of 14 September 1957 from N. Chmutov, secretary of the Stalingrad obkom, to the Central Committee, in RTsKhIDNI, *f.* 556, *op.* 23, *d.* 32. "Soobscheniia mestnykh partiinykh organov. . ."

26.   *Ibid.*

27.   *Ibid.*, point 19.

28.   For example on 12 March 1954, the East Sakhalinsk Party committee issued a reprimand against a local ward judge for interfering with the system of trade. GARF, *f.* 9492, *op.* 1, *d.* 2869: 119.

29.   *Ibid.*: 116.

30.   Report from head of administrative organs department of Khabarovsk kraikom to administrative organs deparment of RSFSR bureau, January 1957, RTsKhIDNI, *f.* 556, *op.* 23, *d.* 28: 19.

31.   GARF, *f.* 8131, *op.* 28, *d.* 2529: 25.

32.   *Ibid.*

33.   See letter from Anashkin of 3 April 1956 to the RSFSR administrative organs department including a report, dated 16 March 1956, "O faktakh besprintsipnogo otnosheniia otdel'nykh sudei Kamenskoi oblasti k sobliudeniiu trebovanii zakona i nezakonnogo meshatel'stva v deiatel'nost' sudebno-sledstvennykh organov po otdel'nym delam so storony nekotorykh rabotnikov rukovodiashchikh organov;" and note of 8 October 1956 from Zenchenko to the Central Committee. Both in "Proekt UVPS RSFSR . . ." RTsKhIDNI, *f.* 556, *op.* 23, *d.* 10. For additional information on Anashkin, interview with I. L. Petrukhin, Moscow, 13 May 1991.

34.   See report from Anashkin of 16 March 1956, "O faktakh besprintsipnogo otnosheniia," in *ibid.*

35.   *Ibid.*

36.   Paul Cocks, "Politics of Party Control: The Historical and Institutional Role of Control Organs in the CPSU and CPC," unpublished Ph.D. dissertation (Harvard University, 1971), 582, 586.

37.   Solomon, "Soviet Politicians," 13-19.

38.   *Ibid.*, 17-18.

39.   The three main types of crime committed here were bribery, misuse of authority, and padding. *Ibid.*, 13-16.

40.   *Ibid.*, 21.

41.   *Ibid.*, 14.

42.   The rise of the Party in this period has of course long been recognized by scholars. See Merle Fainsod, *How Russia is Ruled* (Cambridge, 1963), 174-75; Leonard Schapiro, *The Communist Party of the Soviet Union*, 2d ed. (London, 1970), 561; Grey Hodnett, "Introduction," in R. H. McNeal, ed., *Resolutions and Decisions of the CPSU, vol.4, 1953-1964* (Toronto, 1974), 3; Mary McAuley, *Politics and the Soviet Union* (Harmondsworth, 1977), 178; Bialer, *Stalin's Successors*, 203; *id., The Soviet Paradox* (New York, 1986), 8, 42; R. F. Miller, "Khrushchev and the Soviet Economy: Management by Reorganization," in R. F. Miller and F. Feher, eds., *Khrushchev and the Communist World* (London, 1984), 113; Peter Hauslohner, "Politics before Gorbachev: De-Stalinization and the Roots of Reform," in Seweryn Bialer, ed., *Inside Gorbachev's Russia* (Boulder, CO, 1989), 51-54.

43.   As Alec Nove has written: "The effect of basing industrial planning on regional economic councils . . . represents a transfer of power towards local and republican Party organs, since these were dominant vis-à-vis any institutions operating within 'their' territories." Alec Nove, "Industry," in Martin McCauley, ed., *Khrushchev and Khrushchevism* (London, 1987), 65; and see Alec Nove, "The Soviet Industrial Reorganization," *Problems of Communism* 6, no. 6 (1957): 21-23.

44.   There are more details of this in my work in progress, "Soviet Politicians and Russian Justice, 1948-1964."

45.   GARF, *f.* 353, *op.* 13, *d.* 197: 35.

46.   Report from A. Pcheliakov, secretary of Kirov obkom, to RSFSR administrative organs department in RTsKhIDNI, *f.* 556, *op.* 23, *d.* 85: 78.

47. Letter from the head of the administrative organs department of Gorkii obkom to A. N. Kidin, head of RSFSR administrative organs department, on implementation of the decree of the Presidium of the Supreme Soviet of 30 April 1954 "Ob usilenii ugolovnoi otvetstvennosti za umyshlennoe ubiistvo" in RTsKhIDNI, *f.* 556, *op.* 23, *d.* 58: 43-44.

48. Report from head of administrative organs department of Khabarovsk kraikom to administrative organs department of RSFSR bureau, January 1957, RTsKhIDNI, *f.* 556, *op.* 23, *d.* 28: 19.

49. Letter from S. Bitkin, secretary of Taganrog gorkom, to N. I. Beliaev, of 8 March 1957, in "Soobscheniia mestnykh partiinykh organov . . ." in RTsKhIDNI, *f.* 556, *op.* 23, *d.* 32.

50. Interview with S. V. Borodin, former member and deputy chairman of the RSFSR supreme court, Moscow, 3 June 1991.

51. See, for example, the account of the conference of 28-30 January 1957, in *Sovetskaia iustitsiia*, 1957, No. 1: 71-72.

52. Interview with S. V. Borodin.

53. "Novyi sostav vysshego sudebnogo organa RSFSR," *Sovetskaia iustitsiia*, 1957, No. 2: 10.

54. Interview with S. V. Borodin.

55. Letter of 2 March 1957 from A. Kidin, head of the RSFSR administrative organs department, to the secretariat in "Zapiski, pis'ma, otchety . . ." RTsKhIDNI, *f.* 556, *op.* 23, *d.* 33.

56. According to his colleague, Stanislav Borodin, Rubichev's principle to his dying day was "the harsher (the punishment), the better (*chem strozhe, tem luchshe*)." Interview with S. V. Borodin.

57. Those regional courts who remained "attached" to these judges continued to suffer downward pressures on sentencing. Such messages from the supreme court provoked protests from some provincial court chairmen. See the report on a legal conference held in June 1957, and especially comments from the heads of the Ivanov, Rostov, Stavropol, Kursk and Belgorod courts. *Sovetskaia iustitsiia*, 1957, No. 6: 50, 52.

58. Letter of 16 April 1958 from B. Kobelev, the secretary of the Novosibirsk obkom, to A. N. Kidin, the head of the RSFSR administrative organs department, in RTsKhIDNI, *f.* 556, *op.* 23, *d.* 165.

59. A. Boiter, "Special Courts in the USSR," unpublished Ph.D. dissertation (Columbia University, 1965), 261, 283; *Izvestiia*, 21 November 1961.

60. Yanov, *The Drama of the Soviet 1960s*, 74.

61. *Ibid.*, 91.

62. *Ibid.*, 86-87.

63. *Ibid.*, 94.

64. Breslauer, *Khrushchev and Brezhnev*, 98, *cf.* 46, 235.

65. Cited in Yanov, *The Drama of the Soviet 1960s*, 74 (italics added).

66. *Pravda*, 20 November 1962: 7.

67. *Ibid.* (italics added).

68. In fact, the authority of Party committees over cases involving Communists had been a matter of some dispute since the 1930s. Party committees were ostensibly guided by rules going back to the months preceding the 1936 constitution. A key document here was the resolution of the third plenum of the committee of Party control, held in March 1936, which ruled that "Party organizations should strictly distinguish *Party* punishments imposed on Communists for breaking *Party* rules and *Party* discipline from those punishments imposed on Communists for violating *soviet law.*" In the latter case, Communists would be "held accountable on *general grounds as are all soviet citizens.*" However, in the wake of the Great Purge a further resolution of 1 December 1938, "On obtaining agreements for arrests," had stipulated that prior to sanctioning the arrest of a Communist procurators would have to obtain permission from the first secretary of the local Party committee. Strictly speaking, the two resolutions applied to different stages of the criminal process. The 1938 resolution applied to decisions on arrests, not to decisions on whether to prosecute a case after the arrest had occurred; it was also understood that permission for an arrest would be granted following any reasonable request from procurators. Nevertheless, regional Party leaders took advantage of the apparent discrepancy between these two edicts, usually making the most of the 1938 resolution. In the late 1940s and early 1950s some seized on the confusion by issuing independent directives instructing justice officials that members and candidates of the Party who had committed crimes could be prosecuted only after they had been expelled from the Party. This in effect transformed the prerogative of Party committees to expel Communists into a right to sanction prosecutions. See "O poriadke nalozhenii partiinykh vzyskanii," in GARF, *f.* 8131, *op.* 27, *d.* 4668: 128, 130 (italics added).

69. These provisions had originally been designed, in the wake of the Great Terror, to secure special rights for Party members against the possibility of arbitrary and illegal arrest. The main item of legislation explicitly revoked by the 20 December Presidium decision was the joint resolution of Sovnarkom and the Central Committee of 1 December 1938, "On sanctioning arrests," which, in the wake of the purges, had introduced special regulations to safeguard the rights of Communists from arbitrary arrest. RTsKhIDNI, *f.* 17, *op.* 93, *d.* 292: 169 .

70. At the height of the campaign to re-establish the prestige of the Party in 1953, for example, the head of the Central Committee's letters section, Gorbunov, had written of the disgrace of "people presently serving in labour camps of the MVD with Party cards in their hands (*s partbiletami na rukakh*)." See "Zapiska t.t. Gorbunova i Nefedova o narusheniiakh mestnymi partiinymi, prokurorskami i sudebnymi organami poriadka privlecheniia kommunistov k sudebnoi otvetstvennosti," of 31 January 1953 in TsKhSD, *f.* 4, *op.* 9, *d.* 646: 52.

71. RTsKhIDNI, *f.* 17, *op.* 93, *d.* 292: 169.

72. *Ibid.*: 167.

73. N. R. Mironov, "Nasushchnye voprosy dal'neishego ukrepleniia sotsialisticheskoi zakonnosti," *Kommunist*, 1963, No. 1: 49-59; also see Sharlet, "The Communist Party and the Administration of Justice," 361-62.

74. Cited by Breslauer, *Khrushchev and Brezhnev*, 104-105. Khrushchev's behavior toward the end, argues Breslauer (103), suggests a recognition that "[t]he political status of local party officials . . . was now an impediment to authentic initiative."

75. Yanov, *The Drama of the Soviet 1960s*, 86. Similarly Breslauer writes that Khrushchev had been wedded to the principle of "political intervention in managerial affairs" "[u]ntil circumstances forced him to rethink his assumptions during his last two years in power." See Breslauer, *Khrushchev and Brezhnev*, 271.

76. As we have seen more recently, this was not the last time a populist Russian leader was willing to strike such a bargain with local executives, except that now, under Yeltsin, it is being done without the benefit of utopian pretensions. See Julia Wishnevsky, "Russians Gripped by 'Court Fever'," *RFE/RL Research Report* 1, no. 10 (6 March 1992).

77. I. L. Petrukhin, "Pravosudie i zakonnost'," *Sovetskoe gosudarstvo i pravo*, 1987, No. 6: 75, cited in Solomon, "Soviet Politicians," 27, note 4; Louise Shelley, "Party Members and the Courts: Exploitation of Privilege," in Dietrich A. Loeber, *et al.*, eds., *Ruling Communist Parties and their Status under Law* (Dordrecht, 1986), 80.

13

THE REFORM OF CRIMINAL JUSTICE AND EVOLUTION OF JUDICIAL DEPENDENCE IN LATE SOVIET RUSSIA

Todd Foglesong

Criminal justice in late Soviet Russia underwent radical change. During the 1980s, the state first curtailed and then stopped altogether prosecuting citizens for "anti-Soviet agitation and propaganda" and "defamation of the Soviet state," the two crimes with which most dissidents were charged.[1] Over the course of the decade, the number of persons punished for vagrancy, begging, and other forms of social "parasitism" was cut virtually in half. The ability of citizens to defend themselves in court for such offenses as "justifiable homicide" and engaging in "entrepreneurial risk" was greatly improved, and people who spat or cursed in public for the first time were no longer subjected to criminal penalties. While some of these changes were prosaic, others were profound, and all constitute parts of a radical liberalization in the administration of justice.[2]

The two clearest manifestations of this liberalization were an increase in the "exactitude" (*trebovatel'nost'*) displayed by trial court judges in their review of the dossier prepared by the police and prosecution, and a decrease in the percentage of convicted defendants who were sent to prison. Simply put, at the end of the 1980s, accused persons were much less likely to be found guilty at trial and, if found guilty, far more likely to receive a non-custodial punishment than they were at the beginning of the decade. The magnitude of these two changes was reflected clearly in the statistical ledgers maintained by the ministry of justice of the RSFSR. Whereas in 1980 approximately 94 percent of criminal defendants in Soviet Russia were found guilty at trial, in 1990 this figure was only 84 percent. And whereas in 1980 almost 60 percent of defendants found guilty were imprisoned, in 1990 fewer than 40 percent were so deprived of their freedom.[3] Such marked shifts in criminal justice occur rarely in legal systems, and none of the many changes in criminal justice in the post-Stalin period was of comparable scale.[4] Their intensity calls for explanation.

Unfortunately, it is easier to describe *how* these changes came about than it is to explain *why*. Much information about the making of criminal policy in the late 1970s and early 1980s remains classified or is simply inaccessible to researchers, and many of the key actors (legal officials, judges, scholars) show either poor recall or reticence in their accounts of events. Still, it is possible on the basis of the record of public debates and interviews with a few of the participants to offer a tentative explanation for these great changes in criminal justice.

In this chapter I demonstrate how radical changes in judging and sentencing emerged in the 1980s. I show how the USSR Supreme Court, especially after 1984 and under the vigorous leadership of its chairman, Vladimir I. Terebilov, ushered in these changes. I focus in particular on the methods used by higher courts and superior judges to reform the practice of criminal justice, and argue that the particular way in which changes in justice were effected altered the nature of judicial dependence in Soviet Russia. Whereas in an earlier era, Soviet judges were supervised, pressured, instructed, and even influenced primarily by officials from the Communist Party and Ministries of Justice, in the 1980s as a result of the campaign to liberalize criminal justice Russian judges' approaches to the application of law and the administration of justice came to be dominated by the views and wishes of their immediate judicial superiors.

My argument about the evolution of judicial dependence in Russia requires both historical background and discussion of the concept of judicial independence. I begin with the problem of defining judicial independence and then turn to the challenge of studying its obverse in Soviet Russia. Only then do I examine the actual reform of criminal justice in the 1980s and its impact upon the situation of judges.

What is Judicial Independence?

Despite its importance for the study of the judicial process and public affairs in general, the term judicial independence has been neither well defined nor rigorously studied. Indeed, there is no widely recognized legal definition of judicial independence; nor is there much case law about it.[5] Political scientists have neither claimed judicial independence as part of their conceptual territory nor examined it carefully.[6] Only fifteen years ago, in one of the few studies by a political scientist to grapple with the concept analytically, Martin Shapiro came to the lamentable conclusion that judicial independence "has been less a rigorously defined concept than a generaliza-tion of Anglo-American experience."[7] Not much has changed since the publication of Shapiro's study. In current textbooks on the judicial process, "judicial independence" still serves as shorthand for the experience of separation of powers and judicial review in the United States.[8] But this understanding of the concept has limited application for the study of courts in general, for in most countries the courts are not conceived as a separate branch of government or endowed with powers of judicial review.

It is possible to develop a definition of judicial independence that captures the conventional understanding of judicial independence, yet is also deployable in comparative research on courts. One way is to boil the term down to its bare essentials:

> the set of arrangements by which a society seeks to protect its judges from external pressures in the course of making decisions and immunize them from these and other inducements to administer the law in a particular or prejudiced manner.[9]

Of course, no society endeavors to insulate its judiciary from "external pressures" absolutely. Some, wisely I think, establish arrangements for the organized channeling of such pressures—for example through elections, the appointment process, judicial discipline or performance review commis-sions, and retraining courses. But while the "set of arrangements" I refer to varies from society to society, almost all countries or states aspire to have laws administered impartially and therefore seek to insulate judges from some kinds of external pressures.

The two most widely recognized sources of pressures on judiciaries are the executive and legislature. A fear of the potentially pernicious conse-quences for justice of pressures from these sources leads most societies to create some barriers between judges and other government actors. In the United States, for example, two provisions in the constitution prohibit the arbitrary and facile removal of federal judges from the bench and any arbitrary reduction of their salaries. American judges sometimes claim that two clauses in the constitution (the so-called "Good Behavior Clause" and "Compensation Clause") secure for them "absolute" judicial independence.[10] But it is common now, among lawyers at least, to perceive the judiciary itself as a potential source of pressure on judges and thus, in my terms as well as theirs, a source of "dependence." This perception stems from a recognition that, almost uniformly, judiciaries have become hierarchical organizations and that, therefore, the exercise of authority by superior judges can have a coercive influence on those at subordinate or inferior levels. As the originator of this argument put it, hierarchical structures have "chilling effects," which, within a judiciary, "give rise to latent pressures on the judges and may result in subservience to judicial superiors."[11]

The main object of concern for those who share this broader understanding of courts and judicial independence is those pressures emanating from the exercise of authority by superior judges in an administrative capacity—such as managing the court's case load (assigning and distributing cases to individual judges), chairing disciplinary hearings, and solving routine administrative matters such as the scheduling of judges' vacations.[12] Actions taken by superior judges in strictly procedural settings—such as the handling of appellate reviews—are not considered threatening to judical independence. For example, while it is readily acknowledged that the prospect of reversal, the obligation to follow higher court rulings, and the principle of *stare decisis* do place pressures on judges to administer the law in a particular manner, these kinds of influence on judges are believed to be both legitimate and benign.[13] They are thus rarely a subject of concern in western writing on judicial politics. A number of peculiar features of court organization and appellate procedure in Soviet Russia, however, force us to be more suspicious about the nature of this influence in that country. I explain below why this dimension of judicial independence cannot be ignored in Russia.

What was Judicial Dependence like in the USSR?

It is axiomatic that the Soviet judiciary was not independent. There was no "set of arrangements" in the USSR by which the independence of the judiciary was secured. In fact, apart from the laconic proclamation of judicial independence in the Soviet constitution ("judges are independent and subordinate only to the law"), the state did nothing to insulate or immunize its judges from pressures to administer the law in a prejudiced or particular manner.[14] To explain the Soviet principle of judicial independence, M. S. Strogovich, perhaps the most influential Soviet scholar of courts and criminal procedure, wrote:

> The principle of the independence of the court . . . cannot be interpreted to mean that the court in its activity stands *outside of politics*, that in being guided in its decisions only by law, the court somehow exempts itself from participating in the resolution of those immediate political tasks which the Party and the government place before the state and all of Soviet society.[15]

Clearly, the goal of the Party was not to insulate and immunize but rather to systematically expose courts and judges to the desires and wishes of political forces. And the CPSU, following Article 6 of the constitution, was the leading conductor of these forces.

There were several administrative incarnations of the Party upon which the judiciary depended. Within Party committee organizations at each territorial unit above the district level, there was a department of administrative organs which was responsible for, among other things, supervising the work of the courts. "Cadres policy" for the people's courts was worked out in the department of the regional Party committee and city Party committee but usually only after consultation with, if not the prompting of, a Party secretary from the district or city in which a judge would work. Since Soviet judges were elected, and thus came to the bench only after passing through a nomination process over which the Party exercised a monopoly, they were exposed to several levels and layers of Party influence. Thus, district, city, and regional Party officials were all rich sources of judicial dependence.

But Soviet judges were dependent not just upon the Party; they also had to contend with the ministries of justice and the higher courts, both of which had at different times in Soviet history been assigned important supervisory functions. As of the 1970s and 1980s, the ministries of justice and their detachments in the regions, the departments of justice, were responsible for "judicial administration" (*sudebnoe upravlenie*), while the higher courts were in charge of "judicial supervision" (*sudebnyi nadzor*). The ministry of justice administered the courts by controlling their budgets, distributing bonuses, handling complaints, monitoring delays, and writing the performance evaluations on which judges' career advancement depended. The higher courts supervised by holding training courses, convening conferences on judicial practice, conducting disciplinary proceedings, and, most importantly, using their considerable appellate power. In other words, in addition to the Party, judges faced two lines of judicial dependence. And while it was not easy to distinguish between "judicial administration" and "judicial supervision," each function kept open an important line of influence on the courts.[16]

How the use of appellate power in Soviet Russia compromised judicial independence needs to be elaborated here. In all judiciaries, the prospect of having a decision reversed by an appellate court is intended and believed to influence trial court judges. In the United States, for example, judges study the rulings of superior courts and readily admit that being reversed is a humbling, sometimes humiliating, experience. Upon retirement from the South Carolina Court of Appeals, a judge recently explained, by way of a parable, "how a judge feels about getting reversed." Confronted by the devil with an offer for an absolute guarantee against reversal in exchange for the eternal damnation of his soul as well as that of his family and friends, the judge responds, "what's the catch?" Judges, he suggests, will go to great lengths to avoid being overruled.[17]

American judges can afford to be sanguine about the influence on judicial behavior of the prospect of reversal since, at least in unelected judiciaries, few political repercussions flow from being reversed. In the USSR, however, there were serious adverse consequences to being reversed on appeal. A judge's performance rating, potential bonus, professional reputation, and future career depended closely on his rate of reversal, or on its obverse, "stability of sentences" (*stabil'nost' prigovorov*). Stability of verdicts and sentences served as the main measure of the "quality" of a judge's work.[18] There was also a host of "organizational conclusions" which might be drawn about judges reversed too often—such as disciplinary proceedings, a "grilling" (*razbor*) at the presidium of the regional court, and occasionally even a recall (*otzyv*). The prospect of reversal in Soviet Russia thus was inherently coercive. It created strong and tangible incentives for trial court judges to both anticipate and abide by the regional court's view of the law.[19]

The unusually broad scope of appellate review in the USSR ensured that these incentives to conform applied even to higher courts' view of the facts. Unlike "cassation" in its classical (i.e., French) conception, where the court evaluates only an alleged error of law in the trial court's decision, cassation proceedings in Soviet Russia were not limited to a review only of the legal issues raised by the appellant.[20] The Soviet concept of cassation was much broader, and followed a "principle of revision" (*revizionnoe nachalo*), according to which the court was entitled and even obligated to search the complete record of the proceedings in the trial court for errors of any kind.[21] Accordingly, a cassation panel was authorized to change the verdict and/or sentence upon finding what amounted to errors of fact—the official grounds for reversal in such instances being "incompleteness or one-sidedness" of the judicial investigation of the evidence and "non-correspondence" of the trial court's conclusions to the factual circumstances of the case.[22] According to official commentaries to the Code of Criminal Procedure cassation courts enjoyed broad discretion in making such rulings. They might overrule when they believed the trial court's findings to be based on evidence that was "insufficiently complete" or "not precisely established."[23] Furthermore, upon finding errors of this kind, a cassation court could issue binding "instructions" (*ukazaniia*) about what needed to be rectified at re-trial.[24] Essentially the same provisions and powers were conferred on courts reviewing cases in supervision, the second level of appeal.

Soviet legal scholars were aware that the broad scope of appellate review gave superior courts considerable influence over the behavior of trial court judges. This in fact was its avowed purpose—to enable higher courts to "shape" (*formirovat'*), "guide" (*napravliat'*), and "orient" (*orientirovat'*) judicial practice. These powers, it was claimed, facilitated "uniformity" in the application of the laws.[25] As we shall see, however, the structure and organization of appellate procedure in the USSR were used not only to achieve uniformity in the administration of the laws, but also to manufacture consent in the courts.[26]

While judges were deeply dependent on many different institutions and officials, not all of the lines or kinds of dependence were equal. By 1982, the Ministry of Justice and higher courts had clearly eclipsed the CPSU in terms of both the amount of supervision and extent of their influence on judges. Local and regional Party officials paid little attention to judicial policy and were aloof even from personnel matters—that is, staffing the courts. The problem of putting judges on and off the bench—recruiting, nominating, electing, and recalling them—had fallen almost entirely into the hands of the regional departments of justice and regional courts.[27] Meetings at the administrative organs departments of regional and city Party bodies, where questions of criminal justice used to be discussed, had become by 1982 infrequent and ritualized. Political interventions in individual cases—the practice of "telephone law"—were rare, and even then usually routed through the appellate courts.[28] Whether or not the decline of Party influence was the result of a deliberate withdrawal from judicial affairs or a general loss of capacity, the practice of criminal justice in the early 1980s was relatively free from the Party's yoke.

This development did not leave judges independent or less vulnerable. Both the ministries of justice and superior courts maintained a tight grip on judges; indeed, the state's hands-on guidance made Party work in this area unnecessary. Judges still had two masters and they sometimes worried about whom to please first. A common refrain captured their predicament: "if you have delays, they chew you out; and if you get reversed, you get beaten [*za sroki pozhuriat, a za otmenu b'iut*]." Judicial dependence, in other words, presented judges with a dilemma. In administering justice they labored under the threat of two onerous reprisals: a verbal lashing from a ministerial official or a professional rebuke from a superior court. Which consequence was more feared and which line of dependence most influenced the minds of judges might depend on many factors, such as the career plans, patronage patterns, and even the personality of a judge. Major reforms in criminal justice in the late Soviet period, however, made the calculus of judicial dependence simpler, elevating the importance of the higher courts.

The Reform of Criminal Justice in Late Soviet Russia

Two major reforms in criminal justice helped change the nature of judicial dependence: a reduction in the use of custodial sentences, especially in cases of minor crimes and first-time offenders; and an increase in the exactingness of trial court judges' review of materials produced by the pre-trial investigation. These changes in judicial practice deeply affected the work of judges, and the campaigns to effect them helped transform the nature of judges' dependence. The entire arsenal of appellate court influence was brought to bear upon judges. In addition to reversing decisions arbitrarily on appeal, superior court judges cajoled, badgered, admonished, and disciplined trial court judges in order to get them to change the way they administered the law.

The Dynamics of Depenalization

In the late 1970s, the Soviet regime introduced a number of changes to the USSR Fundamentals of Criminal Legislation. In February and March 1977, the Presidium of the USSR Supreme Soviet issued decrees that decriminalized second-offense petty hooliganism; made non-custodial penalties possible for a host of negligent offenses previously punishable only by imprisonment; gave courts the right to stay sentences for juvenile offenders; enabled them to assign administrative penalties (fines, or 15 days in jail) to persons charged with crimes punishable by up to one year in prison if by the time of trial the offense or offender in the judge's estimation was no longer "socially dangerous;" and expanded judges' powers to order the conditional early release from prison and compulsory labor assignments to persons serving custodial sentences of not more than three years.[29] In the following year, the Supreme Soviet issued a decree that decriminalized second-time petty speculation, further broadening the category of defendants to whom judges might apply fines and other non-custodial punishments.[30]

There may have been many motives behind this package of changes. For example, the decision to encourage judges to release more residents of penal colonies and assign them compulsory labor may have been linked to an upsurge in demand for labor resources. Placing able-bodied criminals at the "sites of economic construction" (*stroiki narodnogo khoziaistva*)—a punishment established in 1970 and known colloquially as "chemo" (*khimiia*)—had a strong economic as well as rehabilitative rationale. Also, giving judges the power to deal administratively with persons usually punished as criminals was in some respects a repressive maneuver, enabling authorities to deal quickly with vagrants, drunks, and other petty criminals. Under the new rules judges could send to jail for two weeks a larger number of persons without having to engage in full criminal proceedings.[31] But there was a more general reason for the changes. A more liberal criminal and penal policy had emerged, and, according to Igor Karpets, a leading criminologist and, at the time, Director of the All-Union Scientific Research Institute of the MVD, its direction was transparent. The legislative changes, he argued, inaugurated a policy which could be summarized by "three Ds"—Decriminalization, Depenalization, and the Deinstitutionalization of punishment.[32] The essence of this new policy was a call for a "more differentiated approach" to the application of criminal sanctions.[33] This was an elliptical way of saying that judges were to use custodial sentences in cases of minor crime more sparingly and to apply non-custodial alternatives whenever possible.

The new direction in Soviet criminal policy may have reflected in part the influence on policy-makers of Soviet criminologists. Already in the 1960s researchers working under Boris Nikoforov at the All-Union Institute for the Study of the Causes and Prevention of Crime (the Procuracy Institute) called into question the efficacy of short-term imprisonment and urged policy-makers to place more emphasis on non-custodial alternatives.[34] In the 1970s, researchers from different legal institutes completed research that yielded "new" findings about the sources of criminal behavior in the USSR. At a round-table discussion in 1980, Korobeinikov, Director of the Procuracy Institute, reported that the combined research of recent years had uncovered "changes in the very factors" that caused and facilitated criminal behavior.[35] What was discovered, one scholar claimed, was that among other things the "disruption of family and other socially useful ties" was an important source of criminal conduct. Anti-social behavior was fostered by a lack of integration into the vast networks of "mature socialism" and its allegedly growing wealth and benefits.[36] If this was true, it meant that aggravation of a sense of isolation from society through imprisonment would have negative repercussions for the level of crime in the USSR.

The claims made by these criminologists were nicely supported by Foucault-like findings from penological research on the effects of imprisonment. As early as 1976, for example, Karpets contended that there were adverse "social consequences" to putting people in prison, and he insisted that these had to be heeded when deciding the proper "role of this form of punishment in social life in general."[37] In 1979, M. I. Kovalev used similar reasoning to show how short-term prison sentences were "ineffective" in the fight against crime,[38] while A. M. Iakovlev concluded that the "likelihood of a person convicted of a crime acquiring the social role of a prisoner and viewing himself as a criminal" could be reduced if non-custodial punishments were used more often.[39] In other words, several senior and influential scholars suggested that it was prisons that bred criminals, not vice versa.

Although it would be hard to prove that Soviet criminologists had an influence on Party policy-makers, their arguments were compelling, and made in a potentially convincing way. Soviet legal scholars took advantage of the regime's instrumentalist sociological discourse, its preoccupation with the deteriorating economy, and fascination with the "scientific-technical revolution." Criminologists repeatedly emphasized how the legislative changes adopted in 1977 and 1978 would foster a more "rational" use of the (presumably finite) coercive resources of the state and, in the pithy expression of one scholar, "greater economy in the use of the means of repression."[40] Others stressed that the changes would make Soviet criminal law much more "effective" in achieving the regime's policy objectives.[41] Still other criminologists underscored the scientific nature of their findings, thereby reminding the regime that especially during the "scientific technical revolution," policy should be based on science.

Soviet scholars also emphasized that the shift in policy they advocated was based on metaphysics as well as science. One scholar insisted that Marx himself stood behind the changes, noting that Marx claimed that "the unconditional duty of the legislator is not to turn into a crime that which has the character of a misdemeanor, and even that on account of the circumstances" (of its commission).[42] Other scholars wrote new treatises on the goals and meaning of punishment, in which they characterized the recent changes in legislation as a move away from a purely "punitive" (*karatel'naia*) or retributive justification for the imposition of punishment and a step toward a "utilitarian" (*utilitarnaia*) philosophy of criminal law.[43] Moreover, some criminologists insisted that in sentencing the retributive urge to punish criminals for their behavior should take second place to the achievement of the goals of a socialist society. Thus, Boris Nikiforov distinguished the *za* and *dlia* of criminal law.[44]

With the support of Soviet legal scholarship and the blessing of the regime, the USSR Supreme Court took steps to implement the new line in criminal policy. At a plenum in early 1978, the Court affirmed that any appellate court had the right to substitute "corrective labor"—a mild punishment imposing a 20 percent deduction in salary—for more severe penalties such as "chemo," even if the period of corrective labor assigned was longer than that of "chemo."[45] The following year, the Court issued resolutions on "general principles of sentencing," in which it chastized judges for sentencing "solely on the basis of the nature of the crime committed" and established the rule that wherever the law allows a non-custodial measure of punishment, the trial court must consider using one.[46] There was little doubt about which direction the USSR Supreme Court was pushing criminal policy. Evgenii Smolentsev, then the Court's Deputy Chairman, summarized the trend in 1980 by affirming that "all" of the Court's recent rulings and decrees aimed at getting trial court judges to "make wider use of the supplementary opportunities recently provided to achieve a more differentiated approach to criminal sentencing."[47]

Despite the changes in criminal law and policy, vocal support from criminologists, and unambiguous guidance of the USSR Supreme Court, there was little change in judges' sentencing practices between 1978 and 1980. In fact, between 1979 and 1980—that is, after the USSR Supreme Court's admonition to use non-custodial sentences whenever possible—the percent of persons given custodial sentences rose slightly (from 56.6 to 58.3 percent). This led the Court's Deputy Chairman to remark that "on the ground (*na mestakh*) the new legislation has not been properly understood."[48]

In July 1982 the movement for depenalization was accelerated by new legislation. By an edict of the Presidium of the Supreme Soviet of the USSR, the state raised the cap for fines that could be imposed for minor offenses and expanded the number of crimes for which such fines could be applied. The same decree authorized stayed sentences (*otsrochka ispolneniia prigovora* [Article 39[1] of the Criminal Code of the RSFSR]) for adults in certain categories of crime. (Before the decree, stayed sentences could be given only to juveniles and members of the armed forces.[49]) Later in the same year, by edict of the Presidium of the RSFSR Supreme Soviet, the maximum term of "corrective labor" (Article 27) was raised from one to two years.[50] These changes made non-custodial punishments more compelling alternatives for judges accustomed to depriving criminals of their freedom.[51] Judges were also given considerable discretion in applying these more lenient measures of punishment to a larger category of offenders.[52]

Table 13.1 presents data on the sentencing practices of trial courts in Soviet Russia from 1972 to 1990. The table shows that it was not until 1982 that a decrease in the use of custodial punishments became noticeable, followed by a more steady decline after 1983. There was also a gradual increase in the incidence of the most common form of non-custodial punishment—corrective labor.[53] At first glance, these slow but steady changes seem to contrast sharply with the almost immediate and significant increase in the percentage of criminals given stayed sentences after the July

Table 13.1
Sentencing Patterns, RSFSR, 1972-1990

Year	Depriva-tion of Freedom	Correc-tional Labor (art 27)	Compul-sory Labor (art 24²)	Condi-tional Convic-tion	Stayed Sentence
1972	60.9	17.0	7.0	n.a.	n.a.
1973	62.0	14.3	6.5	n.a.	n.a.
1974	58.2	17.2	7.6	n.a.	n.a.
1975-1977	n.a.	n.a.	n.a.	n.a.	n.a.
1978	55.8	15.1	12.8	(10.0	combined)
1979	56.6	16.5	12.6	(9.4	combined)
1980	58.4	15.5	12.6	(8.7	combined)
1981	58.3	16.6	11.6	(9.0	combined)
1982	55.3	17.8	12.0	6.6	2.8
1983	54.8	18.9	9.1	4.1	6.8
1984	50.8	20.5	8.4	4.1	8.8
1985	47.4	21.8	7.5	4.3	9.6
1986	38.3	24.5	6.4	4.3	10.0
1987	34.1	26.1	5.9	5.4	11.2

Source: Department of Statistics, RSFSR Ministry of Justice.

1982 decree. However, much of this increase stems from a reduction in the in the rate of conditional convictions (*uslovnoe osuzhdenie*) and a small rise in the rate at which juveniles were given stayed sentences in that year.

It is not easy to say whether these changes should be interpreted as slow or rapid. Such a judgment depends on, among other things, one's understanding of the wider political environment in the USSR in the early 1980s.[54] But whatever one makes of the pace of change in sentencing practices, there is no doubt that a considerable amount of "guidance" from superior courts was required in order for the new policies to take hold.

In December 1983, in order to facilitate the implementation of these new policies by lower courts, the USSR Supreme Court reissued its 1971 guiding explanation "on the practice of reviewing criminal cases in cassation," this time with the addition of a provision which, in its own words, "significantly expanded the powers of cassation courts to reduce sentences."[55] The Court also reiterated on several occasions over the next few years the main provisions of the 1982 legislative decrees and instructed judges to be bolder in their application of non-custodial punishments. For example, at a plenum in April 1984, the Court discussed a review (*obobshchenie*) of trial court practice that identified the "non-application" of conditional sentences where it was legally possible as the main shortcoming in the conduct of the courts. As a result, the Court "advised" trial court judges of the "necessity" of using non-custodial sentences (especially fines) for persons convicted of minor offenses for the first time.[56] In June 1985, the Court issued a guiding explanation on stayed sentences, requiring that the trial court in every case consider giving them and, if it chose not to do so, justify its decision in writing.[57] While trial judges in Soviet Russia, as in other civil law jurisdictions, were always required to explain in writing the reasoning behind their decisions, the Supreme Court resolutions placed a greater burden of justification on decisions to imprison than on those involving non-custodial sentences.

In theory, guiding explanations of the USSR Supreme Court were "binding" upon lower courts, but in practice their influence was neither immediate nor direct.[58] The cooperation, or compliance, of intermediate appellate and lower trial courts had to be obtained. That the Supreme Court of the USSR was in this respect dependent on the law's administrators at lower levels was acknowledged at the last plenum of the USSR Supreme Court before the appointment of Vladimir I. Terebilov as its chairman.[59] "The further improvement of the administration of justice," the Court announced, "will depend on the level of the organization of the work of the criminal divisions of the courts of union republics."[60]

In an effort to secure the compliance of republican courts, the USSR Supreme Court made more frequent use of its own appellate authority, reviewing and overturning many more decisions of the supreme courts of union republics than it had in preceding years.[61] But it could not rely solely on its power as an appellate tribunal. Without the power of precedent attached to individual rulings, the influence on judicial practice of the Court's appellate work would be marginal. Accordingly, the Court took several quasi- and extra-legal steps to improve the "level of the organization" in the courts of the union republics and thus make more likely the proper fulfillment of its instructions. First, it ordered republican supreme courts to submit for its "review" (*rassmotrenie*) drafts of all their decrees on judicial policy two months prior to consideration at the courts' plenary sessions.[62] Second, the USSR Supreme Court dispatched a number of its own judges together with clerks (*konsul'tanty*) from its Department of Generalization to do "explanatory work" in the supreme courts of the union republics. Third, the Court seconded from the USSR Procuracy Robert G. Tikhomirnov, who had been the Director of its Department for the Supervision of Criminal Cases in the Courts, and shortly thereafter made him one of its judges. Tikhomirnov's transfer, and the deployment of his skills in aid of the Court, expanded the Supreme Court's supervisory repertoire and opened more channels of influence on subordinate legal agencies.[63]

The cooperation of the RSFSR supreme court was quickly obtained, and it soon assumed responsibility for the campaign to reduce the use of custodial punishment. At plenary discussions of the "general principles" of sentencing, regional courts were routinely censured for their failure to toe the new line and ensure its adoption by the people's courts. The Deputy Chairman of the Novosibirsk regional court, for example, was called to task in 1985 for the fact that the people's courts under her supervision were "insufficiently" using non-custodial sentences and "underestimating" their efficacy.[64] When regional courts did not rectify the errant ways of people's courts on their own, the supreme court intervened. Acting on its own authority in supervisory review, it reversed and changed decisions of people's courts when their conclusions about the "impossibility" of using non-custodial punishments were, in its view, "insufficiently justified." Its rulings in such cases often appeared arbitrary. In one case the supreme court ordered the re-trial of a young man sentenced to one year's deprivation of liberty for having falsified his labor record (art. 196) because the trial court, it alleged, "did not to the necessary degree consider" the mitigating circumstances in the case. The trial court in fact had cited these circum-stances to justify what it considered a lenient punishment.[65] More and more, however, the supreme court of the RSFSR moved away from an appellate practice based on identifiable legal error. Between 1983 and 1988, the rate at which it "adjusted" (i.e., reduced) the sentences of regional courts without requalifying the charge increased by more than fourfold.[66]

More often than not, regional courts in the RSFSR followed suit. As Table 13.2 shows, there was a significant increase in these years in the proportion of adjustments of people's court judgments which consisted solely of a reduction in the sentence. Table 13.2 also shows that there was a steady and rather dramatic decline in the rate of reversals of people's court decisions for "leniency."[67]

The practices of appellate courts at all levels made the new line in sentencing policy abundantly clear. But the number of errors that had to be corrected on appeal remained high, and the RSFSR supreme court stated baldly in April 1985 that judges still "frequently assign deprivation of freedom without even discussing" alternative forms of punishment.[68] The USSR Ministry of Justice concluded that some people's court judges were not getting the message. A report it issued in November 1984 decried "the absence of an adequate process through which the decisions of higher courts exert influence on concrete persons, on judges."[69]

Table 13.2

Reversals and Adjustments of Decisions of People's Courts for Leniency and Severity, RSFSR, 1983-1987

Year	Percentage of all reversals of judgment due to "excessive leniency" *In Cassation / In Supervision*	Percentage of all adjustments involving reduction of sentence only: *In Cassation / In Supervision*
1983	20.1 / 20.9	n.a.
1985	15.9 / 18.2	38.7 / 61.5
1986	13.2 / 14.2	38.5 / 57.5
1987	9.7 / 6.3	50.3 / 56.9

Source: Department of Statistics, RSFSR Supreme Court.

This was a curious finding, since all regional courts supplemented their appellate practice with a large amount of organizational work aimed at shaping the decisions reached by people's courts. Regional courts regularly convened conferences (*soveshchaniia*) to discuss new laws and digest for lower court judges the meaning of recent rulings and guiding explanations of the USSR or RSFSR supreme court. They also held training sessions for young judges and refresher courses for senior judges. At these sessions, commonly referred to as a "practicum," judges were given the materials from recently tried cases and asked to solve them in writing. Judges whose answers accorded with the view of the regional court were given high marks.[70] Finally, regional courts conducted "surveys" and "generalizations" of judicial practice, the results of which were distributed to all courts in the region and accompanied by an explanatory note, called an "informational letter," which exposed the courts and individual judges which had made the most common or egregious mistakes.

Nonetheless, the Ministry of Justice sought further means of shaping judicial behavior. One court, the Orenburg regional court, developed a special strategy for doing this that appealed particularly to the Ministry. The account of its technique was distributed to all regional courts in the spring of 1985 as an example of "positive experience" which deserved emulation.[71]

The Orenburg Method

Each member of the Orenburg regional court not employed as a trial court judge was assigned a "zone" usually consisting of one or two people's courts, over which he or she was expected to exercise "judicial supervision." All cases in that zone appealed in cassation were to be first reviewed by and then tried with the participation of that member of the court.[72] This judge, referred to as a "mentor" (*kurator*), was supposed to record in a special journal the mistakes made in his zone, and he was held accountable by the presidium for the performance of the court(s) under his supervision. A kurator was also specifically "attached" to one or more of the younger judges within the courts of his zone and responsible for his education and professional development. The relationship between the kurator and court was described as one of "patronage" and the relationship between the kurator and subordinate judges as one of "tutelage." When such benevolent measures of preventing mistakes failed, judges with poor performance indices were summoned to meetings of the presidium of the regional court, sometimes along with their chairman and kurator, and "subjected to sharp criticism."

"These measures of influence," the Orenburg regional court claimed, "lead, as a rule, to positive results."[73]

"Positive results" in fact were obtained in the RSFSR as a whole as a result of the propagation of the "Orenburg Method." In 1987, the percentage of all criminals who received custodial sentences fell to almost half what it had been in 1973. But there was much variation among regions, as well as significant discrepancies within individual regions, and in 1988 the overall rate of custodial sentences crept upwards slightly (see Table 13.1). The RSFSR supreme court attributed this to a misunderstanding of the Central Committee decree of 2 April 1988 "on the condition of the struggle against crime in the country and supplemental measures for the prevention of legal infractions." According to Smolentsev, its new Chairman, "a number of comrades have raised the question: is the policy we've pursued for so many years now changing?" The answer given by the plenum convened to deliberate this question at the end of April was a resolute "no." As Smolentsev declared, "we have to find other means of struggle and not use deprivation of freedom. And we have to adhere to this line firmly." But as the discussion at the plenum revealed, it was not going to be easy for regional courts to get their subordinates to toe the line.[74]

All speakers at the plenum reported that achieving a reduction in the rate of custodial sentencing had required overcoming numerous obstacles. For example, Lebedev, then Chairman of the Moscow city court, claimed that people's court judges were unable to distinguish between crimes that were premeditated versus those in which criminal intent (*umysel*) had been "suddenly aroused." A judge from the RSFSR supreme court claimed that trial court judges uniformly failed to interpret the confession of the accused as a mitigating factor, which had the effect of inflating sentences. The chairman of the supreme court of the Udmurt Autonomous Republic demonstrated, with the help of statistics, how pre-trial confinement influenced the sentencing disposition of her judges, as prior convictions did in other jurisdictions. And a people's court judge from Gorky region suggested that his colleagues sentenced solely on the basis of the "character" of the accused, which, "to put it mildly," he claimed, "was often not the very best."

While these factors were treated at the plenum as "defects" and "shortcomings" in judges' understanding of the laws, they reflected the judges' real views and beliefs about punishment. Indeed, almost all speakers suggested that the main obstacle to reduction in the rate of custodial sentences was judges' "consciousness" and "attitude" toward deprivation of freedom.[75] Most trial judges, to put it plainly, opposed the new policies. The comments of Vinogradova, the Chairman of the Primorskii territorial court, expressed this best:

> I have to say this work [to reduce sentences] has not been easy. Breaking established patterns of thought (*stereotip myshleniia*) and convincing [judges] of the need for another approach to sentencing turned out to be rather difficult.
>
> The people's court judges responded slowly and with difficulty to the new approach in sentencing and economical use of judicial repression in the form of deprivation of freedom. They reprimanded those in cassation and supervision for interfering with their decisions.
>
> It has to be said that they were not alone in their beliefs. Workers in other law-enforcement agencies held the same views. It seemed to them that they had worked in vain (*v kholostuiu*) if the accused was not deprived of freedom (a view held by a number of responsible officials as well). The fact that in our territory since 1984 custodial sentences have dropped by only 5 percent (from 65.6 to 60.5) shows how difficult it has been to solve this problem. We have had again and again to work at persuading judges that the use of non-custodial sentences was not just a short-term campaign, but the true direction of penal policy.

Vinogradova concluded by saying the problem in fact had not been solved, for there were still a number of people's judges "with considerable professional experience who know how to resolve complex cases, but cannot agree with the new approach in sentencing. Some of them simply do not heed (*ne podchiniaiutsia*) these demands, others reform themselves (*perestraivaiutsia*) with difficulty."[76]

The attitudes of lower court judges described by Vinogradova, and the conflict created by the attempt to overcome them, were not limited to the Primorskii territory. Surveys of judges' opinions conducted in this period suggested that there was opposition to greater leniency in penal policy.[77] And conflict between trial court judges and their superiors was common. At an expanded meeting of the Collegium of the RSFSR ministry of justice held four months after the supreme court plenum on sentencing, Abolentsev, the Minister, treated the two problems as universal, and directly related:

> two quite distinct positions with respect to sentencing policy have emerged: the position of regional courts, which in many cases reduce sentences; and the position of the people's courts, who continue to assign severe measures without regard to the new demands to humanize punishment. It is important now to break down the wall of misunderstanding, and to end the well known competition, as it were, between the

people's and higher courts. There is one way forward. The position of the regional court must become intelligible (*dokhodchivaia*) and understandable to the people's court. Only in this way can the "lessers" (*nizy*) orient themselves to the "higher ups" (*verkhi*).[78]

Abolentsev's proposed remedy for breaking down the "wall of misunderstanding" was to "summon together the cadres more often" and hold "comradely conversations." But his hierarchical conception of the judicial corps and condescending representation of the perspective from below suggests that he did not envision such conversations as equal exchanges. Nor did he believe that propaganda and agitation alone would produce the desired changes in consciousness. His view of the judicial educational process was coercive. Indeed, at the April plenum he had extolled the instructional style of the Novgorod regional court, where, he reported enthusiastically, "a grilling at the presidium is obligatory for every mistake."[79]

Judges' reluctance to change their sentencing styles meant that in order to achieve reductions in the use of custodial sentences, regional courts had to do much more than simply reverse and change decisions of people's courts at an unprecedented rate. They had to use the entire arsenal of their influence. They conducted "analyses," "reviews," and "generalizations" of judicial practice, sent out "informational letters," and held "seminars," "study sessions," and "lessons," many of them "on site" and likely run by heavy-handed instructors. A number of highly placed legal officials nevertheless suspected that even this barrage of education would not be enough to curb judges' impulse to deprive criminals of their freedom. Ironically, it was Emelianov, the Procurator of the RSFSR, who delivered the sternest warning to judges at the April plenum "not to get carried away" by their urges in the future.[80]

The Campaign for More Exactitude

"Exactitude" (*trebovatel'nost'*) was a term used by Soviet legal officials to describe the degree of rigor in trial courts' investigation of the evidence collected by the police and their examination of the materials supporting the procurator's conclusion to indict. There was no precise measure for exactitude. The requirement that courts be exacting was formulated in Soviet law as a vague rule obliging them to conduct a "thorough, complete, and objective" investigation of the circumstances in the case (Article 20 of the Code of Criminal Procedure of the RSFSR). The determination whether a trial court had been sufficiently "thorough, complete, and objective" was, if not arbitrary, at least idiosyncratic, and left to the discretion of appellate courts. Nevertheless, there were a number of approximate indicators of exactitude. For example, the decision of a trial court to send a case back for supplementary investigation was a positive sign that it had been exacting, if not thorough, complete, and objective. A judgment of acquittal, too, was believed to reflect an exacting approach to the materials of the pre-trial investigation, as was the decision to terminate criminal proceedings in a case. A conviction reversed on appeal for "rehabilitative reasons," by contrast, was a clear indicator of "inexactitude."[81]

In the early 1980s, there were strong indications that the people's courts were not exacting in their examination of the materials of the pre-trial investigation. Appellate courts overturned many convictions because the trial court had overlooked violations of the law by the agencies conducting the pre-trial investigation or failed to detect inconsistencies in the evidence supporting the charges.[82] Only 2.5 percent of all criminal prosecutions were terminated by courts at the pre-trial stage and fewer than one-quarter of 1 percent ended in acquittals. And while approximately 4 percent of all criminal cases brought to people's courts were sent back for supplementary investigation, the RSFSR supreme court believed this figure was too small. In its decree of 17 April 1984 on the practice of returning cases for supplementary investigation, it claimed that an "increase in the exactitude of courts toward the quality of criminal inquiry and preliminary investigation" was necessary in order to realize the twin goals, or "tasks" (*zadachi*), of criminal justice—namely, that "every person who commits a crime is subjected to just punishment and that not one innocent person is prosecuted and convicted."[83]

Table 13.3 presents data on rates of acquittal and termination of criminal proceedings in the RSFSR between 1980 and 1984. By distinguishing between acquittals and terminations in cases with and without pre-trial investigations, it reveals how unexacting trial courts were in these years.

Terebilov was vexed by the inexactitude of lower courts and alarmed by its consequences. In 1983 and 1984, as USSR Minister of Justice, he received numerous "assignments" from the Central Committee and Presidium of the USSR Supreme Soviet to investigate the allegations of negligence and wrong-doing by judges which had been raised in letters submitted by relatives of those who claimed to have suffered injustices at the hands of the people's courts. He also came under pressure to take action against judges when the Soviet press began publishing highly critical re-

Table 13.3
**Rates of Acquittal and Termination of Criminal Proceedings,
RSFSR, 1980–1984**

Year	Number / Percentage acquitted	Number / Percentage acquitted in cases with pre-trial investigation	Number / Percentage terminated	Number / Percentage terminated in cases with pre-trial investigation
1980	1521 / .23	562 / .08	15,964 / 2.4	125 / .01
1981	1493 / .21	565 / .08	13,983 / 2.0	158 / .02
1982	1658 / .21	612 / .08	19,849 / 2.0	118 / .01
1983	1419 / .17	593 / .07	23,256 / 2.8	138 / .01
1984	1609 / .18	683 / .07	19,384 / 2.2	177 / .02

Source: Department of Statistics (Generalization), RSFSR Supreme Court.
Note: Rate of Acquittal is calculated as a percent of total number of persons convicted + acquitted + terminated + deemed unfit to stand trial (*nevmeniaemye*).

views of the administration of justice in Soviet courts. According to the reports compiled by the Administration of General Courts of the USSR Ministry of Justice, 54 "critical articles" on the work of courts were published in the central press in 1983, 80 percent of which pertained to the RSFSR. More than half of these articles reported egregious mistakes of law, including ten cases of wrongful convictions.[84] At the end of January 1984, Terebilov convened a meeting to evaluate the response to these publications by the relevant regional departments of justice and courts. In few cases, it was discovered, had any steps been taken either to rectify the harmful impression of Soviet justice created by such publications or to punish those responsible for the errors in the first place. Terebilov thereupon issued a decree ordering both departments and courts to establish "strict control" over such publications, to summon and review the files and the record of each and every case serving as the subject of such publications, and to "initiate disciplinary proceedings where necessary."[85]

Even before Terebilov's decree, there had been a trend toward greater use of disciplinary sanctions against judges who made bad decisions. It appears that the number of judicial disciplinary proceedings began to rise soon after Brezhnev's death.[86] For example, whereas in the USSR as a whole between 1977 and 1981, the average number of judges disciplined per year ranged between 370 and 385, in the RSFSR alone in 1983 and 1984, respectively 372 and 364 judges were disciplined.[87] But Terebilov's decree of January 1984 and another one issued on 30 November 1984 (this time under the signature of Boris Kravtsov, Terebilov's replacement) made mandatory the initiation of disciplinary proceedings against judges who had presided over trials resulting in wrongful convictions, and accelerated the trend.[88] By the end of 1985, eleven percent of all people's judges in the RSFSR had been disciplined—many of them more than once, for among the corps, according to the ministry of justice, there was no small number of "recidivists."[89]

Punishing them for inexactitude was not the only way trial court judges were encouraged to be more thorough, complete, and objective. Another way was for appellate courts themselves to be more exacting of trial court decisions on review. Terebilov encouraged greater and more comprehensive scrutiny of lower court decisions by ordering appellate courts to summon the records of the case from the court of first instance "when doubt about its legality arises in any manner."[90] Appellate courts obliged. Between 1983 and 1987, the percentage of people's court decisions in the RSFSR that were reversed in cassation rose from 3.0 to 7.8. Higher courts were also told to teach lower court judges how to be exacting by trying more cases. A trial held at a superior court, according to Terebilov, would serve as a "school of justice" for all lower court judges.[91] The USSR Supreme Court itself became a veritable university in these years, trying as a court of first instance three times more cases than it had between 1978 and 1983.[92]

These individual lessons in exactitude were supplemented by clear and detailed explications of the rules of criminal procedure in the guiding explanations of the supreme courts. The RSFSR supreme court, for example, discovered that at least one reason why trial courts did not return enough cases for supplementary investigation was vagueness of the legal grounds on which they might do so (Article 232 of the Criminal Procedure Code).[93] At a plenum convened to deliberate this question in 1984, many judges requested a concrete list of the kinds of lacunae in the materials of the pre-trial investigation that were to be considered "unremediable" at trial and thus furnished grounds for a supplementary investigation. Other judges demanded to know the difference between a "substantial" violation of the Code of Criminal Procedure and one that constituted harmless error. Without instruction on these issues, they could not be sure of the legality of their own rulings and, fearing reversal, would continue to be reluctant to send cases for supplementary investigation.[94] The leadership of the RSFSR supreme court responded to these requests and issued what in the words of one of the plenum's participants was a "revolutionary" ruling.[95]

There was an almost immediate and marked rise in the number of cases sent back for supplementary investigation after the adoption of the decree. According to Terebilov, in the USSR as a whole in 1984, courts sent back for supplementary investigation 15 percent more cases than they had in 1983.[96] In 1985 and 1986, this upward trend continued. According to data from the RSFSR ministry of justice, the rate of returns for supplementary investigation in 1985 was 5.4 and in 1986—6.3. There was also, as Table 13.4 shows, a dramatic rise in the number of cases terminated by courts at preliminary hearings—from 19,384 in 1984 to 33,407 in 1985. The rate of acquittals, by contrast, increased only slightly.

Despite these gains, the RSFSR supreme court found that courts continued to examine the materials of the pre-trial investigation only "superficially," and as a result "uncritically convicted" those brought before

Table 13.4
Rates of Acquittal and Termination of Criminal Proceedings, RSFSR, 1984–1986

Year	Number / Percentage acquitted	Number / Percentage acquitted in cases with pre-trial investigation	Number / Percentage terminated	Number / Percentage terminated in cases with pre-trial investigation
1984	1609 / .18	683 / .07	19,384 / 2.2	177 / .02
1985	1684 / .18	728 / .08	33,407 / 3.7	327 / .03
1986	2043 / .24	904 / .11	26,794 / 3.2	328 / .04

Source: Department of Statistics (Generalization), RSFSR Supreme Court.

them. In many cases, their "carelessness" precipitated wrongful convictions. After a slight decline in 1985, the total number of convictions that were reversed and terminated for "rehabilitative reasons" on appeal rose to 599 in 1986.[97] A record number of judges was disciplined in that year, and the perception that judges were guilty of negligence was widespread. Terebilov contemplated introducing drastic measures. In February 1986, when requested to submit "recommendations for improvements in the work of the courts in light of the decisions of the XXVIIth Party Congress," he proposed, among other things, establishing criminal penalties for judges who had issued guilty verdicts to defendants who were subsequently "rehabilitated."[98]

At a plenum in April 1987, the RSFSR supreme court returned again to the problem of inexactitude. Shubin, the First Deputy Chairman, delivered a long report claiming that there had been a "decline" in the exactitude of many courts in the preceding years.[99] Most of the participants at the plenum concurred with his judgment. For example, Belikov, the Chairman of the Berdsk city court in Novosibirsk, said in a somber tone, "we practitioners understand the concern over the present situation in regard to the quality of the administration of justice, for the situation, truly, is very serious (ves'ma ser'eznoe)." N. I. Sidorenko, the Chairman of a district people's court in Leningrad, expressed a similar belief in different language. "It's true," he said, "we've been too indulgent of the mistakes in the preliminary investigation and inquiry. It must be admitted that we take pity on investigators for the fact that they are so overworked and, as a result, we lose our grip (razmagnichivaem), instilling [in them] the confidence that a poorly or carelessly investigated case will make it past us." And all speakers concluded that the caliber of judicial examinations did not meet the demands of the law. The Deputy Chairman of the Perm regional court reported that in most of the convictions overturned by his court, the trial court's "investigation" of material evidence in the case had consisted only of "reading out loud" in the court room the documents collected in the dossier.[100]

A number of the participants at the plenum indicated also that, despite the rule in the RSFSR supreme court's 1984 guiding explanation (paragraph 10) requiring courts to acquit when all efforts to establish the facts in the case had been exhausted, many people's courts still sent cases back for supplementary investigation that should have ended in acquittal, or should never have been committed to trial in the first place. According to the data presented by Taldykina, one of the RSFSR supreme court's senior judges, of the 53,000 persons in respect to whom cases were sent back for supplementary investigation in 1986, 890 had their cases terminated for "rehabilitative reasons" by the organs of criminal investigation or procuracy. In her view, this meant that 1.67 percent of supplementary investigations should have been acquittals. Emelianov, as always, the last speaker, suggested that Taldykina had in fact underestimated the extent of the problem: "I can cite even greater figures," he said impressively, "for the number of people who have had criminal proceedings against them end this way."[101]

The April plenum concluded with the adoption of a new guiding explanation about the "heightened importance" of conducting a thorough, complete, and objective investigation of the circumstances in each case. These explanations reiterated the injunction against avoiding acquittals that had been present in previous rulings. But it was clear from the comments of the participants at the plenum that the court could not afford to leave the implementation of this ruling to the judges in trial courts themselves. It was essential that regional courts assume responsibility for its implementation.

In fact, Terebilov had made it clear early in the campaign for improvements in the administration of justice that regional courts would be instrumental in its success. But his wager on regional courts was in many respects unwise. The responsibility they bore for the performance of lower courts created strong incentives to overlook mistakes. There was an inherent and apparently intractable conflict of interest in the *kurator* system, whose consequences for judicial supervision and appellate practice were well understood by Terebilov.[102] Ministerial studies of cassation panels in the 1980s had uncovered much evidence of a kind of "corporatism" in their work, including the frequent substitution of "private rulings" for reversals and a light touch in matters of discipline.[103] The supreme court of the RSFSR, too, observed how cassation courts sometimes "cover up" (*prikryvaiut*) the mistakes of their subordinates. In its view, this practice was widespread. One-half of all decisions reversed in supervision in 1987 had earlier been the subject of cassation proceedings and yet were left unchanged (an increase from a ratio of two-fifths in 1983).[104]

Especially in matters of acquittals and supplementary investigation, regional courts had not followed the new line consistently. For example, 18 of the 32 acquittals issued by the people's courts of the Komi Autonomous Republic between 1986 and 1987 had been overturned by its supreme court and sent back for supplementary investigation, where all were subsequently terminated. The Moscow city court, too, had adopted what was generously referred to as an "inconsistent" position in these matters. Twice its cassation panel had overturned the decision of the Krasnopresensk district court to return a case for supplementary investigation, and when the latter then issued a guilty verdict in the case the city court returned for supplementary investigation. According to the RSFSR ministry of justice, the city court was guilty of "disorienting" the people's courts, and leading them "astray."[105]

Not always could the presidia of regional courts (whose chairmen were appointed jointly by the USSR Minister of Justice and Chairman of the USSR Supreme Court) be relied on to root out this collusion and confusion. Reports conducted by the RSFSR ministry of justice at the end of 1987 claimed that in many regions the presidia were "inert" and had fostered an "environment of tolerance" toward the mistakes of their colleagues in cassation.[106] According to Abolentsev, the RSFSR minister of justice, who took up this question in a speech presented to judges right after the 19th Party Conference, the organizational work of presidia lacked conviction. He described the efforts of the Primorskii territorial court to analyze the mistakes in its territory: "The plan was good (*zamysel khoroshii*), but its execution could not have been worse. The territorial court paid no attention to the fact that some mistakes run like a rapid and others merely trickle in. It treated all mistakes alike and, as a result, judges are not oriented toward rectifying the most numerous mistakes and continue to commit them." The only way to remedy these problems, he claimed, was to put more pressure on the chairmen of regional courts, "from whom," he concluded pointedly, "we await more effective procedural influence."[107]

In 1988, the time was ripe for a formal resolution on these issues. In August, under the watchful eye of Terebilov, the RSFSR supreme court convened a plenum "on raising the role of cassation courts in ensuring quality in the administration of justice." Natalia Semenko, the head of the Ivanovo regional court, was the first to speak at the plenum and thus the first to withstand his relentless questioning. She reported that of the 30 decisions overturned by her court in cassation in 1987, 18 had been returned for supplementary investigation. In the first half of 1988, five of the twelve decisions that had been reversed were sent back for more investigation—the "majority" of which, she noted, had not been returned back again to the people's courts by the police or procuracy. At the conclusion of Semenko's report, Terebilov requested the floor. He wanted to know why her court had returned cases for supplementary investigation when "this practice has been criticized," and "it is said that judicial organs should not be doing this, but rather correct the problem on their own or exclude part of the charges." He asked, "are you sure that supplementary investigation was the only correct decision here?"

Semenko's reply, and the subsequent exchange between her and Terebilov, conveys something of the nature of the relationship between the different levels of the judicial hierarchy. Their conversation assumed the character of an interrogation.

> *Semenko*: Yes, a certain amount of daring was required in order to take this decision. If there is no element of a crime, one has to reverse the conviction. But this was not the case. Practice shows that in two cases of article 198 [violating passport regulations] a check-up [*proverka*] was in order.

> *Terebilov*: You say two. But earlier, you said five. What were the other three like?

> *Semenko*: A decision could have been made in another two cases. Three cases required supplementary investigation. Besides, one was returned to the people's court.

> *Terebilov*: But did the Procuracy of the RSFSR say that these cases had to be returned for supplementary investigation?

> *Semenko*: No. As a rule, cassation panels say that these things have to be checked again.

> *Terebilov*: Did the cassation panels raise any questions about the groundlessness of the pre-trial confinement, or was this not discussed?

> *Semenko*: No private warnings were issued by cassation courts. But a while back, people's courts were rebuked by the MVD for the fact that the rate of deprivation of freedom was high. So we tried to figure out the source of the problem. We found out that all these persons had been taken into custody in the course of pre-trial investigations. Of course, if the cassation court finds the conviction incorrect and reverses the decision or sends it back for supplementary investigation, it always issues a private warning (*chastnoe opredelenie*).

> *Terebilov*: The main thing is to make sure this doesn't happen often.

> *Semenko*: Yes.

> *Terebilov*: Okay. You analyzed in some detail the mistakes of people's courts. But what about the reversal of the rulings of the cassation courts? How is it possible that such a capable court as yours is unable to cope with its responsibilities and has to be corrected?[108]

Semenko replied to this last question by outlining the details of the cases in question, implying that each case was complicated and had to be judged individually, on its merits. This was a subtle way of alluding to the need to display deference to the trial court. Such a nuanced rebuttal was likely to be lost on Terebilov, however, for, as the tone of his interrogation revealed, he had little patience for such principles, especially when they stood in the way of implementing the campaign to improve justice.

The pressure Terebilov and others put on regional court leaders such as Semenko was reproduced at each successively lower level of the judicial hierarchy, constituting something of a pattern of oppression. The presidia of regional courts exerted pressure on cassation panel judges who, in turn, browbeat lower court judges. The accumulated weight of this pressure was so great that trial court judges began to complain about interference. For example, speaking at a plenum of the RSFSR supreme court in 1987, a people's court judge from Leningrad noted how "striving to avoid being reversed, judges sometimes 'look over their shoulder' while making decisions, and choose the one most likely to hold up on appeal, even though it doesn't always accord with their convictions."[109] In the following year, at an expanded session of the meeting of the Collegium of the RSFSR ministry of justice, Titov, the Chairman of a district people's court in Moscow, charged that higher courts were guilty of "worrying the law" (*dodumyvanie zakona*), and he appealed to them to stop "pressuring the court from above."[110] These were not lone voices. Responding to the discussion of draft legislation on the independence of the judiciary in the journal *Sovetskaia iustitsiia* in the summer of 1989, another people's court judge argued more generally that "above all, judges must be defended legislatively from the judges of higher courts."[111]

Nonetheless, the leaders of the central legal institutions, and Terebilov in particular, remained blithely indifferent to the plight of trial court judges and the various difficulties reforms created for them. At the RSFSR supreme court plenum on cassation courts in 1988, for example, when several judges informed him of the pressures to which they were subjected from local authorities, including threats from Party officials to cut their staffs in half, Terebilov reacted with derision. "Did any of you go to the first secretary and register your opposition?" he asked. Sobolev, the head of the Krasnodar territorial court, responded: "I called the secretary. He told me to put it in writing." Terebilov scoffed: "As if you were a typical petty complainant. If that's what happened, you should have spoken out on local television or radio." At that, there were hoots of "it's not that easy," and what the stenographer registered as "laughter in the audience." Terebilov retorted:

"I'm not saying this so that all of you go out and get yourselves on television and radio. But the position of you, the leadership, is one of simply waiting for someone from Moscow to come and solve it all. The question is, what are *you* doing?"[112]

Terebilov's bullying of regional court judges was characteristic of his reform strategy. He made imperious demands and attempted to realize them by methods which the British would call "bolshie." As Minister of Justice he repeatedly ordered that disciplinary proceedings against judges be initiated in cases of wrongful convictions, and, as Chairman of the USSR Supreme Court, he advocated the criminalization of mistakes made by judges. Flaunting convention, Terebilov aired the dirty laundry of the judiciary in public. From the pulpit of the Plenum of the Supreme Court, he expressed contempt for "certain judges for whom [the basics of evidentiary law] are beyond comprehension" and had his remarks published in the Bulletin of the Supreme Court.[113] Official and public censure of judges were important weapons in Terebilov's campaign to reorient the courts.

The results of this approach to reform, however, were far from clear. An increase in levels of exactitude and a decrease in the percentage of defendants sent to prison were undeniable; justice, at least in the aggregate, was improved. But in carrying out reforms in such a blind and stubborn manner, Terebilov exacerbated the dependence of trial court judges. Most changes in the practice of judges came from pressure, not a change of heart; this more tempered Soviet justice was not administered voluntarily. In the course of improving justice, moreover, Terebilov undermined the integrity of the appellate process and denigrated some fundamental principles of the law. Trial court judges ceased to think of appellate courts as librarians of the law, and they lost respect for the legal norm of impartiality. By the end of the 1980s, Article 20 of the Code of Criminal Procedure, the statutory requirement of objectivity, had acquired the moniker "rubber article" (*rezinovaia stat'ia*), a label which reflected both judges' disdain for its arbitrary use by higher courts and its employment as a truncheon in the campaign to change their behavior.

Conclusion

The campaigns to liberalize Soviet criminal justice described in this chapter ushered in significant changes in the way judges administered the law. By the end of the 1980s fewer people were convicted without good evidence, and fewer convicted of lesser crimes went to prison. These same campaigns also led to an important change in the nature of judicial dependence. The primary agents of change were neither Party nor Ministerial officials, but higher court judges. Higher court judges repeatedly reversed and censured their subordinates for decisions that did not accord with the new lines in sentencing policy and adjudication. And because of the peculiar meaning of adverse appellate rulings in Russia and the professional significance of an administrative rebuke, it became increasingly important for the dispensers of justice at the lower levels to heed their superiors. That these superiors were themselves judges was of little consolation, as the independence of judges trying cases was compromised. In the 1980s, far from being liberated from the bonds of judicial dependence, judges acquired new and more effective masters.

The transformation of judicial dependence in the last decade of Soviet power has important implications for the future of justice and judicial reform in Russia. Judicial dependence in Russia did not end with the demise of communism and collapse of the USSR. Indeed, the intensification of the vertical dimension of judicial dependence in the 1980s kept judges and the administration of justice susceptible to political intervention and manipulation even after the Communist Party was abolished and major changes were made to the processes by which judges came to the bench. Higher courts remained a conduit for the peddling of influence and distortion of justice. "Telephone law," the Chairman of the Moscow regional court reported in 1994, was practiced "primarily through the higher courts."[114] This legacy of Soviet judicial dependence means that efforts to insulate judges from the more conventional sources of outside interference in adjudication will not be enough to secure their independence.

The channel of influence created by the vertical dimension of judicial dependence remains open in 1997. None of the laws on judicial reform passed by the new Russian parliament has addressed this aspect of judicial dependence, and there is no evidence in the various draft codes of criminal procedure of an attempt to reduce the scope of appellate court interference in trial court fact-finding and sentencing. On the contrary, as a result of recent reforms, judges in some respects have been made even *more* dependent on higher courts. For example, higher court personnel play a greater role in the vetting of judicial candidates under the new selection and appointment process than they did in the late Soviet period.[115] In addition, the introduction into the judiciary of formal ranks (*kvalifikatsionnye klassy*) and the delegation of broader disciplinary authority to senior judges have increased both the hierarchical character of and coercive potential in the judicial corps.[116] And regional courts, the central link in the vertical chain of judicial dependence, appear today more susceptible to the demands and wishes of regional governments as a result of the latters' increased political clout and control over local economic resources.[117] Trial court judges today thus face possibly even greater pressures from their colleagues and superiors in appellate courts to administer the law in a particular or prejudiced manner.

Eliminating this kind of dependence and curbing the undue influence of appellate courts in Russia will not be easy. Changes to the law of criminal procedure or institutional architecture of the judiciary may not be sufficient. For in Russia there is no history of deference to the trial court and its findings of fact, little respect for the principle of finality, and considerable reluctance to giving lower judges real discretion. Indeed, the desire to maintain broad appellate powers and preserve for higher judges the right to reverse rulings of their juniors is so strong that it has plagued the introduction of jury trials. The Appellate Chamber of the Supreme Court of Russia, which was created in 1993 in order to review the rulings of judges and verdicts of jurors in jury trials, has frequently reversed decisions on questions of fact, not law—to the great consternation of Russian judges and legal scholars as well as some Western observers.[118] The attempt to establish independent courts in Russia runs against not only institutional inertia, but also a long-standing preference for the prerogative of higher courts to intervene in the administration of criminal justice.

Notes

1.   In a memorandum sent to Gorbachev on 2 February 1987, Rekunkov, the USSR Procurator General, and Chebrikov, Chairman of the Committee for State Security (KGB), reported that in 1986 the total number of persons convicted for these crimes was less than half of what it was in 1981, and that most prisoners had been released from custody in some way. According to statistics kept by the ministry of justice of the RSFSR, in 1987 only one person was convicted for defamation of the Soviet state.

Convictions for Crimes against the Soviet State, 1977–1986

Year	Number of persons convicted for "anti-Soviet agitation and propaganda" (Art 70)	Number of persons convicted for "defamation of the Soviet state" (Art 190¹)
1977	6	54
1978	12	44
1979	4	65
1980	35	67

Year	Number of persons convicted for "anti-Soviet agitation and propaganda" (Art. 70)	Number of persons convicted for "defamation of the Soviet state" (Art. 190^1)
1981	39	88
1982	26	69
1983	n/a	119
1984	25	57
1985	16	57
1986	11	47

Source: Letter from Rekunkov, USSR Procurator General, and Chebrikov, Chairman of the Committee for State Security (KGB) to M. S. Gorbachev, dated 2 February 1987. *Tsentr khraneniia sovremennoi dokumentatsii* (hereafter TsKhSD), *f.* 89, *op.* 18, *d.* 112.

Note: According to data from the RSFSR ministry of justice, only one person was convicted of "defamation of the Soviet state" in 1987 and none in 1988. On 8 April 1989 a decree of the Supreme Soviet repealed Article 190^1.

2.   This argument, and a detailed description of changes in the administration of justice in Russia in the 1980s, is made more thoroughly in Todd Foglesong, "The Politics of Judicial Independence and the Administration of Criminal Justice in Soviet Russia, 1982-1992," unpublished Ph.D. dissertation (University of Toronto, 1995).

3.   The table below contains information on rates of acquittal and termination of criminal proceedings between 1980 and 1990. It shows that whereas in 1980 approximately 2.7 percent of defendants were acquitted or had proceedings against them stopped by a court, in 1990 the percent was 6.5. In 1980, another 3.1 percent of criminal defendants were not found guilty and instead had their cases returned to the procuracy by courts for "supplementary investigation." In 1990, 9.5 percent of defendants had cases returned for supplementary investigation. By adding together these percentages, we get a conviction rate of 94 percent in 1980 and 84 percent in 1990.

Rates of Acquittal and Termination of Criminal Proceedings, RSFSR, 1980-1990

Year	Number / Percentage acquitted	Number / Percentage acquitted in cases with pre-trial investigation	Number / Percentage terminated	Number / Percentage terminated in cases with pre-trial investigation
1980	1521 / .23	562 / .08	15,964 / 2.4	125 / .01
1981	1493 / .21	565 / .08	13,983 / 2.0	158 / .02

Year	Number / Percentage acquitted	Number / Percentage acquitted in cases with pre-trial investigation	Number / Percentage terminated	Number / Percentage terminated in cases with pre-trial investigation
1982	1658 / .21	612 / .08	19,849 / 2.0	118 / .01
1983	1419 / .17	593 / .07	23,256 / 2.8	138 / .01
1984	1609 / .18	683 / .07	19,384 / 2.2	177 / .02
1985	1684 / .18	728 / .08	33,407 / 3.7	327 / .03
1986	2043 / .24	904 / .11	26,794 / 3.2	328 / .04
1987	2618 / .42	1440 / .23	36,960 / 5.9	354 / .05
1988	3034 / .65	1568 / .34	30,461 / 6.5	381 / .08
1989	3098 / .65	1518 / .32	29,840 / 6.3	244 / .05
1990	3080 / .53	1708 / .29	34,490 / 5.9	417 / .07

Source: Department of Statistics (Generalization), RSFSR Court.

4.   See Yoram Gorlizki, "De-Stalinization and the Politics of Russian Criminal Justice, 1953-1964," unpublished D.Phil. dissertation (University of Oxford , 1992).

5.   For the most recent discussion of judicial independence by a legal scholar in North America, see Martin L. Friedland, *A Place Apart: Judicial Independence and Accountability in Canada* (Ottawa, 1995).

6.   Theodore Becker, in *Comparative Judicial Politics: The Political Functionings of Courts* (Boston, 1970), defined judicial independence in explicitly behavioral terms—that is, as the degree to which decisions reached by courts are in fact uninfluenced by and in opposition to the wishes of those with political power. For several methodological reasons, however, it is hard to study judicial independence in these terms. For a sustained critique of this definition, see Foglesong, "The Politics of Judicial Independence," chapters 1-3.

7.   Martin Shapiro, in *Courts: A Comparative and Political Analysis* (Chicago, 1981).

8.   Henry Abrams, *The Judicial Process*, 4th ed. (New York, 1986).

9.   This is the definition I provide in my dissertation on the basis of an analysis of current writing on courts by lawyers and political scientists. See Foglesong, "The Politics of Judicial Independence," chapter 1.

10.   At a meeting between a group of lawyers from Chicago and several senior scholars from the Institute of State and Law of the Russian Academy of Sciences in Moscow, on 22 June 1922, the Chief Justice of the Sixth District Court of Appeals called his own

independence "pretty much absolute."

11. See Shimon Shetreet and Jules Deschenes, eds., *Judicial Independence: The Contemporary Debate* (Dordrecht, 1988).

12. It is now widely accepted that the arbitrary or unregulated exercise of authority in the resolution of such ostensibly mundane administrative matters of the courts can exert significant pressures on judges as well as shape the way in which justice is administered. See, for example, the discussion in Russell Wheeler, *Judicial Administration and its Relationship to Judicial Independence* (Williamsburg, VA, 1988). For two recent examples of the impact on fellow judges of arbitrary decisions on such matters, see "Chief Judges Seen as Too Powerful," *The Globe and Mail*, 9 June 1993, and the discussion of the politics of assigning judges to cases in Los Angeles Superior Court, "The Whole World's Watching," *California Lawyer*, May 1994: 33.

13. This is not true in all jurisdictions. In Germany, for example, trial court judges are free to disregard the decisions of superior courts—in part because of doubts about the value of influence which is obligatory. These doubts furnish at least one of the reasons why judges in almost all jurisdictions insist on the right and freedom to write dissenting and concurring opinions. See the discussion in Shetreet and Deschenes, eds., *Judicial Independence,* esp. 639-40.

14. The affirmation of independence, moreover, extended only to judges, not courts. See, for example, the discussion in V. I. Terebilov, *The Soviet Court* (Moscow, 1986).

15. Quoted in Robert Sharlet, "The Communist Party and the Administration of Justice in the USSR," in Donald D. Barry, *et al.* eds., *Soviet Law After Stalin,* Vol. 3 (Aalphen aan den Rijn, 1979), 324 (emphasis added). It should be noted that Sharlet termed this a "consensual understanding of judicial independence."

16. Soviet legal scholars took great pains to distinguish in theoretical terms the two kinds of activity. See, for example, Oleg Temushkin, *Organizatsionno-pravovye formi proverki zakonnosti i obosnovannosti prigovorov* (Moscow, 1978).

17. See Alex Sanders, "A Judge's Swan Song," *The Judges' Journal* 33, no. 3 (Spring 1994): 25.

18. There were in fact two different ways of measuring the "quality" (*kachestvo*) of judicial performance in the USSR. One way was to divide the number of decisions overturned in cassation by the total number appealed. The other way was add the number of decisions overturned or modified in both cassation and supervision and then divide by the total number of cases tried by the court or judge. See Iu. D. Severin, "Kriterii kachestva pravosudiia trebuiut sovershenstvovaniia," *Sovetskaia iustitsiia,* 1989, No. 15, 1989: 2-4.

19. Yoram Gorlizki describes this problem in great detail in his dissertation, "De-Stalinization and the Politics of Russian Criminal Justice," chapter 4. I have benefited greatly from his insights.

20. For a discussion of the scope of a cassation appeal in France, see G. Kock and R. Frase, *The French Code of Criminal Procedure* (Littleton, CO, 1988), 36-38, and A. V. Sheehan, *Criminal Procedure in Scotland and France* (Edinburgh, 1975), 91-92.

21.   Christopher Osakwe, in "Modern Soviet Criminal Procedure: A Critical Analysis," *Tulane Law Review* 57, no. 3 (1983): 484, suggests that the scope of cassation in the USSR was "narrower than review *de novo* but wider than review for error."

22.   *Ugolovno-protsessual'nyi kodeks RSFSR*, Articles 342-344. See also the discussion in Strogovich's textbook, *Kurs sovetskogo ugolovnogo protsessa*, t. 2 (Moscow, 1970), esp. 385-87.

23.   *Kommentarii k ugolovnomu-protsessual'nomy kodeksu RSFSR* (Moscow, 1976), 480-84. For examples of such rulings, see *Biulleten' verkhovnogo suda RSFSR*, 1981, No. 9; 1985, No. 10; 1987, No. 12. Appellate courts in the US have the right to reverse for "insufficiency of evidence" but rarely do so. See the discussion in Malinda Seymore and Mark Thielman, "Appellate Reversal for Insufficient Evidence in Criminal Cases: The Interaction of the Proof and the Jury Charge," *American Journal of Criminal Law* 16, no. 2 (1989): 161-80, and Jon O. Newmann, "Beyond Reasonable Doubt," *New York University Law Review* 68, no. 5 (November 1993): 979-1002.

24.   Although these instructions were "binding" (*obiazatelny*), most Soviet legal scholars insisted they did not prejudice the outcome of the subsequent trial nor compromise the independence of the trier of fact. See M. S. Strogovich, *Pravovye garantii zakonnosti* (Moscow 1962), 172, 208. V. M. Savitskii, *Konstitutsionnye osnovy sovetskogo pravosudiia* (Moscow, 1981), 231, by contrast, suggested that there was a certain amount of "psychological" dependence upon re-trial. The supreme court of the RSFSR straddled the fence on this question, upholding the rule in principle but acknowledging in its annual reviews of the work of cassation panels that, in practice, trial court decisions "are not infrequently prejudiced" (*neredko predreshaetsia*) by the improper formulation of these instructions. See *Biulleten' Verkhovnogo Suda RSFSR*, 1981, No. 9.

25.   See A. Orlov, "Nadzor Verkhovnogo Suda RSFSR za osushestvleniem pravosudiia," *Sovetskaia iustitsiia*, 1972, No. 24: 4. O. P. Temushkin, *Organizatsionno-pravovye formy proverki obosnovannosti i zakonnosti prigovorov* (Moscow 1978), 111, explains that, etymologically, the meaning of the verb "guide" (*napravliat'*) differs little from "direct" (*upriavliat'*). In exercising their authority, of course, superior courts were not to infringe on the "independence" of trial court judges—that is, not dictate the outcomes of individual cases. In practice, however, this rule was difficult to observe.

26.   This may not have been its original purpose. The broad scope of cassation and supervisory appeals was crafted in the 1920s, a period in which trial court judges were poorly educated. In the 1970s, a number of Soviet legal scholars argued against reducing the scope of appeal for the sake of conferring on criminal defendants the maximum possible protection against erroneous judgments. See I. L. Petrukhin, "Sistemnyi podkhod k izucheniiu effektivnosti pravosudiia," *Sovetskoe gosudarstvo i pravo*, 1976, No. 1: 75-82, and Temushkin, *Organizatsionno-pravovye formi*. For a different interpretation of the purposes of appeal, see Martin Shapiro, "Appeal," *Law and Society Review* 14, no. 3 (Spring 1980): 62-57; and Shapiro, *Courts: A Comparative and Political Perspective* (Chicago, 1981), chapters 1 and 5.

27.   For a comparison of Party and ministerial supervision of the courts based on archival research, see Foglesong, "The Politics of Judicial Independence," chapter 2.

28.   See Peter H. Solomon, Jr., "Soviet Politicians and Criminal Prosecution: The Logic of Party Intervention," in James Millar, ed., *Cracks in the Monolith* (Armonk, NY, 1992), 3-32.

29. *Vedomosti VS SSSR*, 1977, No. 7, articles 116-122, and No. 8, articles 137-138.

30. *Vedomosti VS SSSR*, 1978, No. 35, article 941.

31. S. G. Kelina, Deputy Director of the Institute of State and Law of the USSR Academy of Sciences, worried about the prospect of the arbitrary use of this expansion in the "administrative arrest" power of judges and referred to it as a "debatable step of the legislator." S. G. Kelina, "Mery otvetstvennosti, predusmotrennye ugolovnym zakonom, i osnovaniia ikh primeneniia," *Sovetskoe gosudarstvo i pravo*, 1982, No. 5: 106.

32. See Igor Karpets, "Sootnoshenie kriminologii, ugolovnogo i ispravitel'no-trudovogo prava," *Sovetskoe gosudarstvo i pravo*, 1981, No. 4: 75.

33. See G. A. Zlobin, S. G. Kelina, and A. M. Iakovlev, "Sovetskaia ugolovnaia politika: diffferentsiatsiia otvetstvennosti," *Sovetskoe gosudarstvo i pravo*, 1977, No. 9: 60. See also A. M. Iakovlev, "Sotsial'nye funktsii protsessa kriminalizatsii," *Sovetskoe gosudarstvo i pravo*, 1980, No. 2: 103.

34. Peter H. Solomon, Jr., *Soviet Criminologists and Criminal Policy: Specialists in Policy-Making* (NY and London, 1978), 99-101. B. S. Nikiforov, *Effektivnost' ugolovno-pravovykh mer borby s prestupnostiu* (Moscow, 1968).

35. A. M. Khalilov, "Novyi etap national'nogo gosudarstvennogo stroitel'stva v SSSR," *Sovetskoe gosudarstvo i pravo*, 1980, No. 12: 7; see also the summary of the remarks of leading criminologists made at a July 1979 conference, in "Obsuzhdenie ugolovnogo zakonodatel'stva," *Sovetskoe gosudarstvo i pravo*, 1979, No. 11: 148.

36. I. M. Galperin, "Differentsiatsiia ugolovnoi otvetstvennosti i effektivnost' nakazaniia," *Sovetskoe gosudarstvo i pravo*, 1983, No. 3: 70.

37. I. Karpets, "Sotsial'nye aspekty primeneniia nakazaniia, sviazannogo s lisheniem svobody," *Sovetskaia iustitsiia*, 1976, No. 10: 6. See also I. V. Shmarov, "Preodolenie otritsatel'nykh posledstvii otbyvaniia ugolovnogo nakazaniia," *Sovetskoe gosudarstvo i pravo*, 1977, No. 2: 84-90.

38. M. I. Kovalev, "Sootnoshenie ugolovnoi politiki i ugolovnogo prava," *Sovetskoe gosudarstvo i pravo*, 1979, No. 12: 71.

39. Iakovlev, "Sotsial'nye funktsii protsessa kriminalizatsii": 103.

40. G. V. Drovosekov, "Puti povysheniia effektivnosti nakazanii, ne sviazannykh s lisheniem svobody," *Sovetskoe gosudarstvo i pravo*, 1980, No. 9: 117.

41. The titles of hundreds of articles and books about criminal punishment published in this period began with the word "effectiveness." See, for example, V. N. Iakovlev, ed., *Effektivnost' primeneniia ugolovnogo zakona* (Moscow, 1977).

42. Quoted in G. A. Zlobin, "Osnovanaia i printsipy ugolovono-pravovogo zapreta," *Sovetskoe gosudarstvo i pravo*, 1980, No. 1: 72.

43. See, for examples, Kovalev, "Sootnoshenie ugolovnoi politiki i ugolovnogo prava": 71; and G. Z. Anashkin, "Spravedlivost' naznacheniia ugolovnogo nakazaniia," *Sovetskoe gosudarstvo i pravo*, 1982, No. 7: 59-66.

44. B. S. Nikiforov, "Nakazanie i ego tseli," *Sovetskoe gosudarstvo i pravo*, 1981, No. 9: 66.

45. See *Biulleten' Verkhovnogo Suda SSSR*, 1978, No. 3: 9.

46. See especially paragraph nine of the decree in *Biulleten' Verkhovnogo Suda SSSR*, 1979, No. 4: 17-19.

47. See E. A. Smolentsev, "Zakon o Verkhovnom Sude SSSR," *Sovetskoe gosudarstvo i pravo*, 1980, No. 5: 17.

48. *Ibid.*

49. *Vedomosti Verkhovnogo Soveta SSSR*, 1982, No. 30, article 572. See also the discussion of the practice of giving stayed sentences in I. L. Marogulova, "Otsrochka ispolneniia prigovora," *Kommentarii sudebnoi praktiki za 1986 god* (Moscow, 1987), 95-98.

50. "Corrective labor" was usually carried out at the place of one's employment, the "correction" consisting of a 20 percent deduction in salary, but a person who was sentenced to corrective labor might also be compelled to work at a site designated by the "institutions administering the conduct of correctional labor" (Article 27, RSFSR Criminal Code). The corrective labor in this kind of sentence nevertheless differed greatly from that which typically resulted from a "conditional conviction to deprivation of freedom with compulsory labor" (Article 24^2), which was known colloquially as "chemical treatment" (or *khimiia*), for the toxic nature of the effluents in the factories at which convicts were forced to work.

51. For a discussion of attitudes about crime and punishment among the population and legal officials, see G. Kh. Efremova, *et al.* eds., *Obshchestvennoe mnenie i prestuplenie* (Tbilisi, 1984), and Efremova and A. P. Ratinov, *Izuchenie pravosoznaniia i obshchestvennogo mneniia o prestupnosti i deiatel'nosti pravookhranitel'nykh organov* (Moscow, 1989).

52. The decrees set out loosely the conditions under which such alternatives could be used, and required only that the court raise the question of the possibility of applying noncustodial punishments. It was made plain that the primary consideration in selecting a punishment should be the character of the defendant—especially the prospects for his/her "reform" (*ispravlenie*) without isolation from society. See the discussion of penal policy in the last years of Soviet power in Irina Marogulova, "O gumanizatsii ugolovnogo zakonodatel'stva," *Sovetskaia iustitsiia*, 1992, No. 19-20: 19-20.

53. The second most common non-custodial punishment was the imposition of fines. Unfortunately, the supreme court tabulations I examined did not record these rates until 1985. In that year, 8.7 percent of all convictions were dealt with by fines; in 1986 the figure was 15.6 percent; in 1987— 16.8 percent; in 1988— 12.7 percent ; in 1989— 11.9 percent; and in 1990— 11.6 percent.

54. Louise Shelley, "Criminal Law and Justice Since Brezhnev," in Donald D. Barry, *et al.*, eds., *Law and the Gorbachev Era* (Kluwer, 1988), 184, suggested that in 1983 and 1984 Soviet criminal law was moving "in a more punitive direction." Robert Sharlet's discussion of legal policy in the "interregnum" in *Soviet Constitutional Crisis: From De-Stalinization to Disintegration* (Armonk, NY, 1993) appears to concur with this opinion.

55. See *Biulleten' Verkhovnogo Suda SSSR*, 1984, No. 1: 4-9, for the decree and 1984, No. 6: 24-31, for its own review of recent court practice and commentary.

56. See *Biulleten' Verkhovnogo Suda SSSR*, 1984, No. 4, and the discussion in A. M. Medvedev, "Praktika uslovnogo osuzhdeniia," *Kommentarii sudebnoi praktiki za 1985 god* (Moscow, 1986), esp. 95-99.

57. See *Biulleten' Verkhovnogo Suda SSSR*, 1985, No. 4, and the discussion in Marogulova, "Otsrochka ispolneniia prigovora."

58. See the discussion of the meaning of "guiding explanations" and the Supreme Court's statutory authority more generally in Kh. B. Sheinin, "Rukovodiadshchie raz"iasneniia plenuma Verkhovnogo suda SSSR," *Sovetskoe gosudarstvo i pravo*, 1980, No. 9: 70-78. For an overview of the structure and function of the USSR Supreme Court, see Peter H. Solomon, Jr., "The USSR Supreme Court: History, Rule, and Future Prospects," *American Journal of Comparative Law* 38, no. 1 (1990): 127-42.

59. Terebilov became Chairman of the USSR Supreme Court at some time between March and April 1984. He had been USSR Minister of Justice from 1970 to 1984. See his less than candid and, unfortunately, unrevealing autobiography, *Zapiski iurista* (Moscow, 1993).

60. See "Sovershentsvovat' nadzor sa sudebnoi deiatel'nostiu," *Biulleten' Verkhovnogo Suda SSSR*, 1984, No. 1: 23-24.

61. Terebilov revealed in his "report" to the USSR Supreme Soviet in May 1988 that the amount of the Court's work in supervision during the first years of perestroika was "significantly greater" than in previous periods. *Izvestiia*, 28 May 1988. Because some of this work consisted of the posthumous review of convictions in political trials in the 1930s and 1940s, however, it is impossible to make a precise measure of the increase in the amount of the supervisory work of the Court during this period. Even after the publication in 1991 of more detailed statistical information on the work of the USSR Supreme Court , it is still impossible to assemble a precise portrait of its work in supervision.

62. In the Court's view, these actions were sanctioned by the provision in the new Law on the Supreme Court which for the first time endowed it with the right to "supervise the fulfillment" of its own guiding explanations. See the discussion in Sheinin, "Rukovodiadshchie raz"iasneniia."

63. Interview with S. B. Romazin, 14 April 1992. In 1984, Romazin was Director of the Department of Generalization of the USSR Supreme Court.

64. See, for example, *Biulleten' Verkhovnogo Suda RSFSR*, 1985, No. 7: 2-5.

65. See the reports of its decisions in individual cases on general principles of sentencing and stayed sentences in particular in E. A. Smolentsev, ed., *Postanovleniia i opredeleniia po ugolovnym delam Verkhovnogo Suda RSFSR, 1981-1988 gg.* (Moscow, 1989), 55-64, 78-83.

66. There were three ways in which an appellate court might "change" (*izmeniat'*) the decision of a trial court. The first was to requalify the charge. It did this when it deemed the sentence appropriate but found that the trial court had made an error in the application of material law. The second way was to requalify the charge *and* reduce the sentence. The third way was simply to reduce the sentence. It did this when it found no substantial error in the trial court's application of the law, but believed the sentence too severe. Data from the RSFSR supreme court show it moved away from making changes because of legal error. For

example, in 1985, approximately 15 percent of the changes made to people's courts decisions in cassation by regional courts were of the first kind; in 1988, less than 10 percent. In 1985, 46 percent of the changes were of the second kind; in 1988, 37.6 percent. In 1985, 38.7 percent of the changes were of the third kind; in 1988, 52.9 percent.

67. A number of Soviet scholars insisted that, throughout the 1970s, appellate courts reversed and modified trial court sentences for "superfluous severity" three times more frequently than for "excessive leniency." See Iu. A. Ivanov, "Ugolovno-pravovye osnovaniia otmeny prigovora za miagkost'iu nakazaniia," *Kommentarii sudebnoi praktiki za 1977 god* (Moscow, 1978); Anashkin, "Spravedlivost' naznacheniia ugolovnogo nakazaniia": 62; and Temushkin, *Organizatsionno-pravovye formy*, 132.

68. See Decree no. 4 of the Plenum of the RSFSR Supreme Court from 23 April 1985 in *Sbornik postanovlenii plenumov verkhovnykh sudov SSSR i RSFSR po ugolovnym delam* (Moscow, 1995), 468-69.

69. *Gosudarstvennyi arkhiv Rossiiskoi Federatsii* (hereafter GARF), *f.* 9492, *op.* 8, *d.* 2064: 34.

70. The USSR Ministry of Justice maintained an institute for improving the qualifications of judges and justice officials (The All-Union Institute for the Improvement of Workers of Justice, or VIURIu) and the RSFSR ministry of justice's Institute for the Study of Soviet Legislation held seminars for judges, too, but neither had the capacity to train or instruct judges systematically. On average, a judge would be "commandeered" to Moscow for a two week training session at the All-Union institute only once every five years. Interview with L. S. Khaldeev, former Director of VIURIu, 16 March 1992.

71. See the report on the organization of the Orenburg regional court, GARF, *f.* 9492, *op.* 8, *d.* 2064: 189-199.

72. Some regional courts organized cassation review along functional lines—that is, each member of the court would review a certain category of case, irrespective of its provenance. Most courts, however, arranged their appellate work in a very personalized manner, and were encouraged to do so by the USSR Ministry of Justice.

73. The organization of the Orenburg court was in fact unexceptional. Most judges I interviewed said that the appellate panels of their regional courts worked this way, too. The Chairman of the Leningrad city court confirmed that such practices had been a staple of judicial supervision since at least 1970. Interview, 24 November 1991. For a recent discussion of this question by a former functionary of the USSR Ministry of Justice, see L. S. Simkin, "Obsluzhivanie sudebnoi vlasti: funktsii i struktury," *Trudy pravovoi akademii*, vyp. 1, 1991, 53.

74. Stenograficheskii otchet plenuma Verkhovnogo Suda RSFSR ot 14 aprelia, 1988 goda, 76.

75. Smolentsev and Emelianov, then Procurator of the RSFSR, were the only ones to treat these attitudes as artefacts of the material conditions of Soviet society. Both believed the "weak material base" of the institutes where non-custodial sentences were carried out (especially the Educative-Labor-Prophylactoriia) made judges resort to deprivation of freedom. *Ibid.*, 73, 77.

76. *Ibid.*, 17; 20.

77. For example, L. S. Simkin, who worked closely with judges as a plenipotentiary for the USSR Ministry of Justice, reported that more than 20 percent of appellate court judges opposed the reforms in sentencing policy. See L. S. Simkin, "Ugolovnaia politika i sovershenstvovanie sudebnoi deiatel'nosti," *Sovetskoe gosudarstvo i pravo*, 1986, No. 6: 61-67. See also I. M. Galperin and A. M. Ratinov, "Sotsial'naia spravedlivost' i nakazanie," *Sovetskoe gosudarstvo i pravo*, 1986, No. 10: 71-78.

78. Protokol rasshirennogo zasedaniia kollegii Ministerstva iustitsii RSFSR ot 24 avgusta, 1988 goda.

79. Stenograficheskii otchet plenuma Verkhovnogo Suda RSFSR ot 14 aprelia, 1988 goda, 55-56.

80. *Ibid.*, 72.

81. There were many grounds (*osnovaniia*) on which an appellate court might overturn a conviction and terminate criminal proceedings. These were listed in Articles 5-9 of the Code of Criminal Procedure of the RSFSR. Soviet legal scholars (but not Soviet law) distinguished between grounds which were "rehabilitative"—that is, roughly, "exculpatory"—and those that were "non-rehabilitative." Paragraphs one and two of Article 5 of the Code ("the absence of the event of a crime," and "the absence of the elements of a crime") were considered "rehabilitative," as was point 2 of Article 349 ("if the accusation made against the prisoner is not confirmed by the evidence examined by the trial court and there are no reasons to conduct a supplementary investigation and new judicial examination"). This latter ground was analogous, but not identical, to one of the grounds for which a trial court might itself terminate criminal proceedings prior to trial—that is, if the participation of the accused in the commission of the crime was "not proven" (*nedokazannost'*). See Article 208 of the Code. For a discussion of these differences by Soviet scholars, see A. A. Rzaev, "Problemy prekrashcheniia ugolovnkyh del po nereabilitiruiushchim osnovaniiam v stadii predvaritel'nogo sledstviia," kandidat dissertation (Karaganda, 1985); V. V. Solov'ev, "Nedokazannost' uchastiia obviniaemogo v sovershenii prestupleniia kak osnovanie prekrashcheniia ugolovnogo dela v stadii rassledovaniia," kandidat dissertation (Higher Juridical School of the MVD, Moscow, 1990); and I. A. Popov, "Zakonnost' i obosnovannost' prekrashcheniia ugolovnykh del v stadii predvaritel'nogo rassledovaniia," kandidat dissertation (DSP, Academy of the MVD, Moscow, 1992).

82. According to data compiled by the Department of Generalization of the RSFSR Supreme Court, 421 persons had their convictions overturned and terminated for "rehabilitative reasons" in 1983. For examples of such reversals in the following years, see *Biulleten' Verkhovnogo Suda RSFSR*, 1983, No. 8: 7; 1985, No. 3: 1-2; 1985, No. 7: 11; 1985, No. 9: 6.

83. Article 2 of the Code of Criminal Procedure of the RSFSR.

84. GARF, *f.* 9492, *op.* 8, *d.* 2061: 5-15. For examples of such articles, see *Literaturnaia gazeta*, 11 July 1983, *Pravda*, 16 July 1983, and *Izvestiia*, 27 November 1983. The trend toward greater public criticism of the courts continued in 1984. The USSR Ministry of Justice placed under "strict control" 33 articles in the press published during the course of 1984; 21 pertained to the work of courts in the RSFSR, five of which involved wrongful convictions. See GARF, *f.* 9492, *op.* 8, *d.* 2178: 50-59.

85. GARF, *f.* 9492, *op.* 8, *d.* 2070: 1-4.

86. The increase in the use of discipline may in fact have begun as early as 1981, when, in response to the large number of letters submitted to the 26th Congress of the CPSU by citizens who in one way or another had been aggrieved by the judiciary, the USSR Ministry of Justice commissioned a study of disciplinary proceedings and railed against patterns of "appeasement" *(primirenchestvo)* in the work of disciplinary boards. GARF, *f.* 9492, *op.* 8, also *d.* 1639: 135; also *d.* 1782: 150-180. It is also worth noting that in this period many regional departments lobbied for the right to discipline judges on their own initiative, without having to go through the disciplinary boards. See, for example, GARF, *f.* 9492, *op.* 8, *d.* 1505: 24.

87. The numbers of judges disciplined for the years 1977 and 1978 were reported in GARF, *f.* 9492, *op.* 8, *d.* 1504: 20, those for 1979 through 1981 in *ibid., d.* 1708: 41-2, and those in the RSFSR for 1983 and 1984 in *ibid., d.* 2115: 100-102.

88. See the decree "on measures to ensure the purity of cadres in the organs of justice and to raise the demandingness of leaders in response to instances of carelessness, abuse of office, and conduct unbecoming of workers of the organs and institutions of justice and courts," GARF, *f.* 9492, *op.* 8, *d.* 2160: 112. This trend was furthered in April 1985 by the adoption of detailed "recommendations" on the application of the statute on the discipline of judges.

89. See Protokoly zasedaniia kollegi Ministerstva iustitsii RSFSR ot 24 sentiabria, 29 oktiabria, i 23 dekabria, 1985 goda.

90. See Postanovlenie No. 2 Plenuma Verkhovnogo suda SSSR ot 5 aprelia 1985 g. "O primenenii sudami zakonodatel'stva, reglamentiruiushchego peresmotr v poriadke nadzora prigovorov, opredelenii, postanovlenii ugolovnym delam," *Biulleten' Verkhovnogo Suda SSSR*, 1985, No. 3: 18-22. One Soviet legal scholar claimed that there was a 71 percent increase in the number of appeals in which the case records were summoned by the RSFSR supreme court before a decision to reject or support the appeal was made. See V. I. Vlasov, "Problemy kachestva rassledovaniia prestuplenii i puti ikh resheniia," doctoral dissertation, written under the auspices of the Council of Nationalities of the Supreme Soviet of the RSFSR (Moscow, 1991), 302. See also the Court's own account of its work in supervision in these years in *Biulleten' Verkhovnogo Suda RSFSR*, 1989, No. 1: 5.

91. *Biulleten' Verkhovnogo Suda SSSR*, 1985, No. 3: 11.

92. For a truncated report of the work of the criminal division of the USSR Supreme Court in these years, see *Biulleten' Verkhovnogo Suda SSSR*, 1987, No. 6.

93. This was understood well before the first promulgation of guiding explanations on this question. See the discussion in T. G. Morshchakova, "Napravlenie ugolovnykh del sudom pervoi instantsii dlia dopolnitel'nogo rassledovaniia," *Kommentarii sudebnoi praktiki za 1980 god* (Moscow, 1981).

94. See Stenograficheskii otchet plenuma Verkhovnogo Suda RSFSR ot 17 aprelia, 1984 goda, 26; 25, in the current archive of the RSFSR supreme court, *f.* 423, *op.* 6, *d* . 113.

95. Interview with T. G. Morshchakova, Vice-President of the Russian Constitutional Court, 11 March 1994.

96. *Biulleten' Verkhovnogo Suda SSSR*, 1985, No. 3: 11, 18-23.

97. For examples, see *Biulleten' Verkhovnogo Suda RSFSR*, 1986, No. 8, and 1986, No. 9.

98. A copy of the recommendations submitted to the Central Committee was given to me by the former Chief Clerk of the USSR Supreme Court.

99. Because of its length, Shubin's report was not recorded in the stenogram. However, a synopsis of his report was published in *Biulleten' Verkhovnogo Suda RSFSR*, 1987, No. 7.

100. Stenograficheskii otchet plenuma Verkhovnogo Suda RSFSR ot 21 aprelia, 1987 goda, 26; 25.

101. *Ibid.*, 45; 53.

102. The principle rationale for re-establishing the ministries of justice in 1970 in fact had been the belief that higher courts' responsibility for the performance of their subordinates fostered both indulgence of the mistakes and interference in the work of lower courts. See V. B. Alekseev, "Osnovnye funktsii sistemy sudebnogo upravleniia," *Uchenye zapiski VNIISZ*, vyp. 30 (Moscow, 1974): 72-90, and L. S. Simkin, "Opyt sotsiologi-cheskogo izucheniia obshchestvennogo mneniia rabotnikov iustitsii o funktsional'nykh problemakh sudebnogo upravleniia," in *Problemy sovershenstvovaniia sovetskogo zakonodatel'stva: trudy VNIISZ*, vyp. 7 (1976): 175-80. See also G. P. Baturov, *Organizatsiia sudebnoi deiatel'nosti* (Moscow, 1977).

103. A report of the USSR Ministry of Justice in 1982 revealed that cassation panels often reacted to mistakes in the people's courts not by reversing their decisions but rather by writing a "private ruling" (*chastnoe opredelenie*), which nevertheless chastised the trial judge for some procedural indiscretion and "put under suspicion the legality and justifiability" of the original verdicts. GARF, *f.* 9492, *op.* 8, *d.* 1783: 237. In discussing the practice of disciplinary boards, which were staffed primarily by members of cassation panels in the regional courts, V. A. Bukov, the former Deputy Director of the Administration of Cadres of the USSR Ministry of Justice, claimed that their work was governed by a "corporate approach." Interview, 12 May 1992.

104. See *Biulleten' Verkhovnogo Suda RSFSR*, 1986, No. 3: 7, and *Biulleten' Verkhovnogo Suda SSSR*, 1987, No. 2: 42. Simkin, a long-time worker in the Administration of General Courts of the USSR Ministry of Justice, claimed that "there was an unwritten rule that operated for years in the majority of regional courts according to which every case with the prospect of being overturned in cassation was quietly reported to one of the leaders of the court. He in turn would give advice to the cassation panel based not only on juridical considerations, but also statistical ones as well—so that the oblast's record didn't look worse than others." L. S. Simkin, "Obsluzhivanie sudebnoi vlasti: funktsii i struktury," *Trudy pravovoi akademii*, vyp. 1 (Moscow, 1991), 53. V. P. Poludniakov, the Chairman of the Leningrad city court, confirmed the existence of this practice in his court, but claimed that he personally ordered an end to it in 1985. Interview (24 November 1991).

105. Undated report of the Administration of Judicial Organs of the RSFSR ministry of justice, "O rabote moskovskogo gorodskogo suda v 1987 godu," 6.

106. See the reports discussed at the meetings of the Collegium of the Ministry of Justice on 13 October and 16 December 1987.

107. Abolentsev's speech can be found in the files of the Administration of Judicial Organs of the RSFSR Ministry of Justice, 1988. Abram Move gave a similar portrait of the work of appellate courts in *Pravda,* on 5 July 1988, a day after the "resolution on legal reform" was passed by the 19th Party Conference.

108. Stenograficheskii otchet plenuma Verkhovnogo Suda RSFSR ot 23 avgusta, 1988 goda, 13-16.

109. Stenograficheskii otchet plenuma Verkhovnogo Suda RSFSR ot 21 aprelia, 1987 goda, 31.

110. See the compilation of the remarks made at the expanded session, in Protokol rasshirennogo zasedaniia kollegii Ministerstva iustitsii RSFSR ot 24 avgusta, 1988 goda.

111. See "Slovo prosiat sud'i," *Sovetskaia iustitsiia,* 1989, No. 13: 5.

112. Abolentsev reported at this plenum that as a result of the accounting techniques of Goskomstat (including judges as "administrative personnel") a decision had been made to reduce the staff of union republic courts by 50 percent, and that of regional courts by 30 percent. Stenograficheskii otchet plenuma Verkhovnogo Suda RSFSR ot 23 avgusta, 1988 goda, 25-27.

113. See, for example, the abbreviated version of his speech on the "tasks" of courts in light of the XXVIIth Congress, *Biulleten' Verkhovnogo Suda SSSR,* 1986, No. 3: 4-13.

114. See the comments by Mikhail Bobrov in "Reforma? Da my lish' na podstupkakh," *Iuridicheskii vestnik,* 1994, No. 18-19: 6.

115. See the discussion of the politics of judicial selection in the chapter by Eugene Huskey in this volume.

116. A far greater number of judges have been expelled from the corps in the post-Soviet period than before. See the report in "74 sud'i lisheny polnomochii za porochashchie prostupki," *Rossiiskaia iustitsiia,* 1995, No. 3: 54.

117. See the discussion of the enhanced powers of regional governments in Peter Kirkow, "Regional Warlordism in Russia: The Case of Primorskii Krai," *Europe-Asia Studies* 47, no. 6 (September 1995): 923-47.

118. See the discussion in Stephen C. Thaman, "The Resurrection of Trial By Jury in Russia," *Stanford International Law Journal* 31, no. 1 (Winter 1995): 65-274.

14

RUSSIAN JUDICIAL REFORM AFTER COMMUNISM

Eugene Huskey

After decades of halting, incremental reform, Soviet law seemed on the verge of a revolution in the late 1980s. The ideological and institutional pillars of Soviet legal orthodoxy began to weaken in the face of a campaign for a law-based state (*pravovoe gosudarstvo*).[1] At the level of discourse, this campaign replaced the dominant view of the distinctiveness, and superiority, of Soviet law with an acceptance of what Eugene Kamenka and Alice Erh-Soon Tay have called the "heritability" of Western law. It was an ideological concession as sweeping in its implications for domestic affairs as the "new thinking" was for foreign policy. Philosophically, at least, the way was open for the wholesale incorporation of Western legal principles, such as adversarialness and judicial independence, into Soviet law.

Standing in the path of reform, however, was the institutional self-interest of the dominant agencies of Soviet law. Since the 1930s, a conservative alliance of institutions, including the Ministry of Internal Affairs (MVD), the Committee on State Security (KGB), the Procuracy, and the Communist Party's Administrative Organs Departments, had fiercely defended the legal status quo. This permanent institutional majority was committed to retaining the existing distribution of power among branches of the legal profession and between the individual and the state. But the campaign for a *pravovoe gosudarstvo* began to break down this alliance by mobilizing Party institutions behind legal reform. Once the Party emerged as the institutional patron of change, the "collective responsibility" characteristic of Soviet politics imposed a measure of discipline on state legal institutions. Equally important, the Party's patronage brought out previously muted reformist voices within institutions such as the courts and the procuracy. Moreover, the variety of reform proposals created new lines of institutional conflict that cut across the ruling conservative alliance. In short, a new configuration of institutional power was in the making.

Such was the status of legal reform at the end of the Soviet era. Change was underway, but a new legal order had not yet taken shape, much less taken root. The collapse of communism, then, raised the most fundamental questions about the sustainability of legal reform in Russia. Could the impetus for legal change survive the diffusion of ideas and political power that accompanied the fall of the USSR? Could an initiative designed to restrain state power succeed in an era of state formation? More than five years into the post-Soviet era, the prospects for genuine legal reform remain uncertain at best. To be sure, the normative landscape of Russia has changed dramatically since 1991. Besides a new constitution, Russian lawmakers have introduced an impressive array of market-oriented legislation, including a new civil code. New codes of criminal law and criminal procedure are now under review. But the decisive test is whether Russia can construct a legal regime that offers its population a set of stable, efficient, and just remedies. Only effective institutions can translate rights into remedies, and institutional development is now battling against a rising tide of corruption and legal nihilism.[2]

To assess the depth and direction of legal reform in post-Communist Russia, this chapter examines the institutional centerpiece of the modern legal system, the court. Throughout the Soviet era, the court was little more than an extension of executive power. In theory, judges were independent and subject only to law; in practice, they conformed to the expectations, and occasionally the explicit commands, of the Communist Party, the Procuracy, the Ministry of Justice, and even local soviets. There was, therefore, much to be done to raise the authority of the courts in the new Russian legal system. A reformed judiciary required insulation from direct political and financial pressure, enhanced jurisdiction, and more competent personnel. The efforts since 1991 to effect such changes form the subject of this chapter.

Judicial Reform and Russian Bureaucratic Politics

The collapse of the Soviet Union left legal reform without an institutional patron, an uncomfortable, if not untenable, position for reform movements in Russian history. To fill this vacuum, legal reformists close to Yeltsin began to put in place a new engine of legal reform, this time in the Russian presidency. The driving force behind the revival of an institutional headquarters for legal change was Sergei Shakhrai, the first legal counsellor to Yeltsin and a fellow defender of the White House during the dramatic days of August 1991. In December 1991, at Shakhrai's urging, Yeltsin formed within the presidency a State-Legal Administration (*Gosudarstvenno-pravovoe Upravlenie*, or GPU) of some 300 persons, which had responsibility for the oversight of law and legal institutions. One of the GPU's eight subdivisions, the Department for Court Reform and Court Procedure, had as its explicit mission the transformation of the Russian court system.

The head of the Department for Court Reform, Sergei Pashin, quickly emerged as the most visible, and controversial, advocate of change in the Russian judiciary. Only 29 years old at the time of his appointment, Pashin was part of Shakhrai's growing network of clients in the Russian executive. Indeed, few could claim closer ties to Shakhrai. Pashin had been an associate of Shakhrai's in the law faculty of Moscow State University as well as Shakhrai's electoral agent in the Russian parliamentary elections of 1990. In his new position as department head in the GPU, Pashin had Shakhrai's assurances that they would be able to carry out court reform "under the protection of the very highest spheres."[3]

Pashin is perhaps best known for his authorship of the Conception of Judicial Reform, an agenda for change in the legal system that was adopted by the Russian parliament in October 1991.[4] If the GPU's Department of Court Reform replaced the Party as institutional sponsor of legal change, the Conception of Court Reform served as a substitute for the conception of a *pravovoe gosudarstvo*, which, as Peter Solomon points out, "had disappeared from the rhetoric of politicians and legal reformers alike."[5] In advancing the Conception of Court Reform, Pashin sought to create a new "general line" on law, this time, however, with a more explicit statement of the measures to be taken in pursuit of reform. The Conception has not, of course, been without its critics. A. D. Boikov, an official in the Procuracy Institute, attacked the document—"prepared by a small group of scholars in absence of glasnost'"—for ignoring Russian national traditions and awkwardly combining elements of Anglo-American and Continental law.[6] And according to Mikhail Bobrov, the chair of the Council of Judges of Russia, "opponents of the Conception of Court Reform have managed to enact a number of anti-democratic laws or laws giving only the impression of reform."[7]

The role of the presidency as a surrogate for the Party has also encountered the resistance of conservative forces in Russian politics. According to Anatolii Lukianov, the former speaker of the Soviet parliament, "the President has revived de facto the Central Committee of CPSU in the guise of his executive office [*administratsiia*] . . .", which now contains 2,500 persons, 700 more than the old Central Committee. Drawing unfavorable comparisons to the former Administrative Organs Department, Lukianov complained that "the State-Legal Administration has grown to monstrous proportions and concerns itself with issues of law as well as [the Ministry of] Justice, the Procuracy, and the courts."[8]

Although obviously self-serving, the conservative critique of the GPU and the presidency merits serious attention. Rather than ruling through the Government and its ministries, Yeltsin has insisted on creating a parallel executive to shadow, duplicate, and in some cases replace existing executive agencies. As I have argued elsewhere, this checking mechanism in the presidency not only replicates Party rule but continues an older Russian tradition of institutional redundancy.[9] Unable to insure the loyalty of the bureaucracy through the normal instruments of law and patronage, Russian leaders have turned to parallel structures as a means of coordinating the making and implementation of policy. In the legal sphere, this institutional redundancy has brought the GPU into direct conflict with ministries and agencies that view an ambitious reform of law and the courts as a threat to their power and prerogatives.

The most serious opposition to broad-based judicial reform has been centered in the Ministry of Justice, the Procuracy, and the MVD.[10] Each institution has its own motives for limiting the scope of court reform.[11] For its part, the Ministry of Justice fears losing its last levers of influence over judicial behavior. Through its logistical support, training programs, quantitative measurements of judicial competence, and recommendations for pay and promotions, the Ministry of Justice long served as the primary patron of the courts. This patronage ensured a measure of judicial deference toward the Ministry. Some reform proposals, however, would create a self-governing judiciary, wholly independent of the Ministry of Justice. For Justice officials, such proposals call into question the very raison d'être of the Ministry. After losing most of its supervisory responsibilities over the Bar at the end of the Soviet era, the Ministry has in recent years witnessed the encroachment of the State-Legal Administration on its traditional functions of legislative drafting and the gathering of legal information.[12] The last two ministers of justice, Nikolai Fedorov and Iurii Kalmykov, left office protesting loudly the loss of their institutional prerogatives to the presidency. The new Communist justice minister, Valentin Kovalev, is likely to resist even more vigorously attempts to create a judiciary that is independent of the Ministry of Justice.

Judicial reform presents a more subtle, but no less far-reaching, threat to the procuracy. As George Fletcher argued a quarter century ago, in the Russian tradition the courts and procuracy are natural adversaries.[13] This institutional conflict was evident at the beginning of the 1990s when judges employed newly-granted powers to challenge the arrest orders of procura-tors. The Procuracy responded with "shrieks, threats, and provocations" (*okriki, ugrozi i provokatsii*).[14]

Through its oversight of legality, the procuracy claims to serve as the guarantor of justice in the Russian legal system as well as the prosecutorial arm of the Russian state. It refuses to be bound by the classical concepts of judicial and executive power. In the deeply-held view of Russian procura-tors, the procuracy is an original Russian contribution to law that transcends traditional Western categories.[15] When the December 1993 constitution relegated the procuracy to an article within the section on the judiciary, procurators cried foul.[16] An official in the Moscow regional procuracy argued that "the subordination of the procuracy to the executive or judicial branch would destroy the emerging system of checks and balances and would heighten the danger of legal violations."[17] Procurators have opposed, therefore, any efforts to narrow their functions to prosecution alone, a change that would deny their role as guardian of legality and transform them into merely one "side" in an adversarial process. Yet without such a reform, the Russian judiciary will remain in the shadow of the larger, better-funded, and more prestigious procuracy.[18]

The MVD's opposition to court reform reflects a preference for executive rather than judicial solutions to issues of law and order. Like law enforcement organs everywhere, the MVD views legal reform in terms of changes in policing rather than changes in judicial procedures. Indeed, for the MVD, the courts are viewed as impediments to law enforcement. In the words of the Minister of Internal Affairs, Viktor Erin, "Crime is growing and becoming more brazen, but the judges frequently display liberalism, to put it mildly."[19] To maintain the dominance of executive over judicial power in the legal system, the MVD launched a campaign of intimidation against Russian judges in late 1993. An MVD inspection of the courts purported to reveal a widespread pattern of inappropriate pre-trial release and acquittals in cases involving criminal gangs. On the basis of its statistical analyses, the MVD compiled a list of 111 unreliable judges, "whose verdicts give rise to considerable . . . doubts." Erin then asked, ". . . are not the categories of officials in our country who have legal guarantees of immunity too broad?"[20]

When the MVD places new law enforcement campaigns on the political agenda, they tend to crowd out initiatives designed to enhance the authority of the courts. Such was the case in May 1994, when the MVD convinced Yeltsin to sign a forty-page crime-fighting program which was followed within weeks by a presidential decree that openly violated the constitution and existing law.[21] Responding to liberal criticisms of the decree, the head of the Federal Counter-Intelligence Service (FSK), the successor to the KGB, commented, "I'm all for the violation of human rights if the human is a bandit or criminal."[22] Whatever the nature of the political system, a liberalization of judicial policy is difficult to sustain in the midst of a campaign against crime and terrorism. It has been all the more difficult in Russia because of the proliferation of executive agencies responsible for security. The presidential Security Council now includes heads of the following agencies with internal security portfolios: the MVD, the FSK, the Presidential Guard of Aleksandr Korzhakov, the Main Administration for the Protection of the Russian Federation, and the Federal Agency for Government Communications and Information (FAPSI).

The judiciary is itself divided into several discrete court hierarchies. Besides a Supreme Court of general jurisdiction, there is a Supreme Arbitrazh Court to hear economic cases and a Constitutional Court to interpret the country's basic law. Such a system may produce sound law—Germany, after all, has a similar judicial structure[23]—but it has the potential to dilute the political influence of the judiciary. In contrast to the 1980s, when Vladimir Terebilov served as the champion of the judiciary from his position as Chief Justice of the USSR Supreme Court, the Russian judiciary now has several leaders who have been unable to act in concert. Besides the chairs of the three highest courts, the president of the newly-formed Council of Russian Judges can also claim to represent the interests of the judiciary. This splintering of judicial leadership has almost certainly weakened the courts' voice in the political arena.

Throughout the Soviet era, legal scholars were at the forefront of law reform, both as legal draftsmen and publicists. In this regard, the historical record is unbroken through the mid-1990s. But what is remarkable about the latest wave of reform is the depth of divisions among the advocates of legal change. Ranged against conservative in-house scholars from state legal institutions are two competing groups of reform-oriented jurists. These reformist groups are divided by generation, by their models of legal development (Continental vs. Anglo-American), and by their approach to legal change, which recalls the split between geneticists and teleologists in the USSR of the late 1920s. Where the older generation of reformist scholars tends to work "from the achieved level," building incrementally on the Continental and Soviet traditions, their younger and brasher counterparts envision a series of great reforms in law to rival those of the 1860s.

As this survey of bureaucratic politics suggests, the institutional impediments to court reform in post-Communist Russia are formidable. Despite the efforts of reformists like Pashin, the presidency has not yet succeeded in recreating the Communist Party's coordinating role in the executive. As a result, departmentalism (*vedomstvennost'*) runs rampant. In the institutional free-for-all that has characterized Russian politics since 1991, the traditionally weaker agencies suffer, among them the courts. Further complicating judicial reform has been a lack of unity among the friends of change and an inhospitable political environment, where rising crime and corruption encourage authoritarian rather than liberal approaches to law. Given these structural and environmental barriers to change, it is remarkable that judicial reform remains a subject of vigorous debate in Russian law and politics.

The Ingredients of Russian Judicial Reform

Court Organization

The judicial reform debate engages three sets of issues: court organization, court procedure, and court personnel.[24] On what might be termed the horizontal axis of court organization, there appears to be little sentiment in favor of altering the status quo. Proposals to fuse the constitutional, *arbitrazh*, and general jurisdiction courts into a unified judiciary have failed to gain support in any quarter. The vertical structure of the judiciary, however, has been under serious review. Within the three competing drafts of the Law on the Court System—written by Sergei Pashin, the Ministry of Justice, and the Council of Judges of Russia—were proposals to alter the existing geographical orientation of the courts.[25] The most far-reaching of these envisioned the creation of a new layer of general jurisdiction courts between those in Moscow and the regions, a reform already in place in the system of arbitrazh courts. Primarily designed as courts of cassation and appeal, these courts would lighten the herculean caseload of the Russian Supreme Court, thus paving the way for a reduction in the size of the highest court of general jurisdiction, which had 115 justices at the beginning of 1995.

In the view of its proponents, the formation of the interregional courts would enhance both the independence and centralization of the courts. Instead of locating courts at the regional level, where they would be subject to the influence of regional government, federal court territories would "have boundaries that do not correspond to the boundaries of the administrative-political units of the state."[26] As late as October 1994, Rinat Smakov, the deputy chair of the Russian supreme court, asked, "What kind of judicial power is it if regional courts are directly dependent on the [regional] administration?"[27] In addition to the interregional courts, located in territories such as Western Siberia and the Urals, reformists proposed creating federal courts in precincts (*uchastki*) within regions, presumably embracing several administrative districts (*raiony*). Furthermore, according to the Pashin and Ministry of Justice drafts, at the base of this federal judicial pyramid would be justices of the peace rather than the traditional district, or people's, courts inherited from the Soviet era. Students of Russian legal history will recognize in these proposals an attempt to revive the court organization of the post-1864 period.[28]

By the time the law passed its first reading in the Duma on 21 April 1995, the Pashin draft had emerged as the official version, though not before being revised by a committee that represented varied institutional and policy interests. The bill that passed in a third reading by the Duma on 20 July 1995 retained the Soviet-era structure for courts of general jurisdiction, with a Supreme Court at the apex, federal territorial (*okruzhnye*) courts at the republic and regional level, and lower courts in urban and rural districts.[29] Only the justice of the peace courts survived Duma scrutiny intact. Although designated as courts of Russia's subject territories, the justices of the peace were said to form part of a single federal judiciary—not the first piece of legislative ambiguity used to avoid, or postpone, conflicts between center and periphery.[30] The wording did not have its intended effect, however. The law's provisions restricting the rights of the subject territories over the formation of courts and the selection of judges led to its rejection in October 1995 by the upper house, the Federation Council, which represented the country's regional interests.

To enhance the autonomy of the courts, reformists also proposed measures that would reduce dramatically the judiciary's financial dependence on political authorities. For decades, ministries and local governments had traded financial favors to the penurious courts for influence on judicial behavior. At issue was not just the level of funding for salaries and court buildings but the access of judges to the accoutrements of modern life, whether apartments, transportation, telephones, or daycare for children. Russia's transition toward a market, and moneyed, economy should in theory have freed the judges from their reliance on officials as suppliers of scarce goods. This has not been the case, however. Like all Russians of modest means, judges cannot yet do without the bureaucratic economy.

The condition of court buildings has been a perennial source of embarrassment for the judiciary. Unlike executive and legislative accommodations, court facilities have none of the dignity or grandeur of buildings of state. Indeed, courts are often housed in rundown structures that lack basic amenities. Because the federal budget has failed to provide adequate funding for even the maintenance of existing court facilities, judges have been forced to turn to local authorities as housing patrons. In St. Petersburg, for example, the 1994 federal budget allocated 75 million rubles for the operation of the city's courts, with no funds earmarked for court repair. The local government, for its part, supplied 600 million rubles that year for the operation and repair of courts.[31]

Although full financial independence of the courts must await a deepening of economic reform and further healthy increases in the salaries of judges, reformists have advanced numerous legislative proposals designed to insulate the judiciary against the vagaries of budgetary politics.[32] The rejected Law on the Court System of 1995 guaranteed court officials the opportunity to participate actively in the formation of the budget in both executive and legislative institutions. It also would have ensured that court funding would not be lowered without the permission of judicial leaders and that the judiciary will have a separate line in the federal budget. When the courts were financed from funds credited to the Ministry of Justice, the Ministry at times underpaid the judiciary in order to reward its own officials.[33]

To further reduce the dependence of the judiciary on executive agencies, reformists favored the establishment of a Department of Court Administration (*Departament sudebnogo upravleniia*) or a Court Department (*Sudebnyi departament*). This department would not be an instrument of self-government—that role would remain with the Council of Judges of Russia and the All-Russian Congress of Judges—but rather an institution providing logistical support to the courts. Whether such a department should be a free-standing body within the judiciary or an appendage of the Ministry of Justice has been a source of continuing controversy. Predictably, the draft Law on the Court System prepared by the Ministry of Justice assigned to the Ministry the responsibility for supplying the courts with their "material-technical" needs. The drafts of Pashin and the Council of Judges, on the other hand, provided for an independent department that answers to the judges alone.[34] The latter proposal made its way into the abortive Law on the Court System, which had called for the creation of a Court Department with branches at various levels of the judiciary to handle court administration.[35]

At the end of 1996 a revised version of the Law on the Court System finally gained approval of both houses of the legislature and the President. The Law included endorsement of a Court Department as wel as compromises to satisfy regional interests.[36]

Court Procedure

The introduction of the jury trial has been at the center of attempts to reform court procedure. Reformist legal scholars wrote the jury trial into Gorbachev-era legislation, but it was Sergei Pashin and his colleagues in the Department of Court Reform who ensured the implementation of the jury system in the early 1990s. By the end of 1994, the jury trial was in use in nine of Russia's 89 regions[37]; it was to be extended to four more regions in 1996. Conservatives and even many moderate reformists continue, however, to approach the jury experiment with suspicion, if not disdain. It is, in their view, an expensive distraction that is inappropriate to current Russian conditions. In the words of the former acting Procurator General, Aleksei Il'iushenko,

> We come out against attempts at the unthought out and hurried introduc-
> tion of legal institutions, which work effectively in a developed law-based
> state but for which we have still not developed the necessary conditions
> and real opportunities. . . . [for us] it may have negative consequences.[38]

But despite opposition, the jury trial remains an essential ingredient of judicial reform. All three drafts on the court reform circulating in early 1995 contained detailed sections on jury trials, and the Law on the Court System passed by the Duma—and rejected by the Federation Council—referred to the jury trial in its opening line.

For legal reformers as diverse as Aleksandr Maksimovich Iakovlev and Sergei Pashin, juries were necessary to break up the cozy relationship between judges and procurators, which had sustained for decades the accusatorial bias in Soviet criminal justice. By taking the decision on a verdict out of the hands of the professional judge, jury trials ensured that the court hearing would not be merely a cursory review of the results of the preliminary investigation but a fully adversarial contest between the sides. According to Pashin, "[i]n a jury trial the procurator does not simply press charges; he has to prove the accusation."[39] Relieved of responsibility for the verdict, the judge is insulated from attacks by executive institutions and is therefore more likely to preside impartially over the proceedings. The expectation of the reformists is that the new patterns of behavior developed in jury trials will set a standard for all criminal cases.

In a seeming paradox, Pashin and the GPU have also supported an expansion in the role of the one-man bench in criminal cases where the sanction is five years or less, apparently as a means of eliminating the

Soviet-style bench, with its single professional judge and two lay assessors. This proposal, contained in the Law on the Jury, has provoked a vigorous reaction from jurists of varied political orientations. In the view of a leading procuracy official, such a reform "would create administrative justice."[40] Judges, however, seem to support the measure as a solution to the growing delays in the court docket.[41]

Some reformists are also intent on revising the method of lodging appeals in criminal cases. In Russian, as in Soviet law, the most substantial appeals are those issued by way of supervision (*v poriadke nadzora*). Yet citizens cannot bring these appeals directly; only higher-level offices of the procuracy or court have the right to lodge such protests. According to reformists, this bureaucratization of the appeals process restricts the rights of citizens and exposes those *chinovniki* responsible for appeals to undue political pressure. As the former chair of the Council of Judges, Mikhail Bobrov, noted, in the post-Soviet era telephone law has shifted its focus from the trial to the appellate stage.[42] In the Council of Judges' draft Code of Criminal Procedure, therefore, the parties to suits would themselves acquire full rights of criminal appeal.[43]

There continues to be a vigorous debate about the sources of judicial decision-making. Here again one finds important divisions in the reformist camp. The more traditional reformists, such as Igor Petrukhin of the Institute of State and Law, favor grounding judicial decisions in written norms alone. Radical reformists would allow judges to look beyond the written law (*zakon, Gesetz*) to a broader concept of law (*pravo, Recht*) for inspiration. For the more traditional-minded reformists, such an expansive field for judicial interpretation is inappropriate to a Continental system. Furthermore, it opens the way for an arbitrariness in judicial decision-making that characterized earlier moments of Soviet history, when judges relied on their own revolutionary legal consciousness as a source of law.

Court Personnel

Whatever changes are made in court organization and procedure, judicial reform will not succeed in Russia without competent and independent-minded judges. The Soviet legacy to the Russian legal system was the "leftover principle" of judicial selection: whoever was not taken by other legal institutions wound up in a judgeship. Since the late 1980s, legal reformists have introduced changes in the length of judicial tenure and the method of judicial selection in order to create a more autonomous and professional corps of judges. Current laws provide for tenure until age 65 for judges on the supreme courts and life tenure for lower-court judges.

The method of judicial selection has changed dramatically during the last decade.[44] Originally, the Communist Party placed judges on the bench by nominating them to run unopposed in stage-managed elections. At the end of the 1980s, with the revival of legislative institutions in the USSR, the responsibility for confirming judges shifted from the population at large to the system of soviets. When the Communist Party collapsed at the end of 1991, the Ministry of Justice—along with new judicial nominating commissions comprised of senior judges[45]—began recommending judicial candidates to the soviets. The latest, and most far-reaching, change in the method of judicial selection came in December 1993, with the adoption of a new constitution. In order to reduce the influence of the legislature and local authorities on the courts, the 1993 constitution granted the president extraordinary powers of judicial selection. The president now nominates the members of the supreme courts, who are then confirmed by the Federation Council, the legislative chamber designed as a support base for the presidency. According to the constitution, the president appoints the remaining federal judges directly.

Despite laws to the contrary, in some subject territories executive leaders have begun to assume responsibility for appointing judges to vacancies on district, city, and in some cases even regional, courts. This practice has been particularly widespread in the republics, which enjoy a special—though as yet ambiguous—status in Russian federalism. When the leadership of the 20 republics were asked whether they acknowledged that judges at all levels should be appointed by the President, "thirteen replied with a flat no, six gave evasive answers, and only the Ingush Republic agreed with the constitutional norm."[46] This resistance prompted President Yeltsin to issue a decree in November 1994 that warned local authorities against "investing judges with powers and elaborating normative acts on questions concerning the judiciary."[47]

An established pattern of judicial selection has yet to emerge in Russia. Depending on the level of the court and the region of Russia, any one of the following may be involved: the President of the Russian Federation, central and local judicial nominating commissions,[48] court chairmen, the Council of Judges and its local affiliates, and regional and local executives.[49] In some cases, no selection is taking place at all. Rather than replace judges whose terms of office have expired, the presidency and other executive authorities are simply allowing them to continue on the bench. Two factors are at work here. First, judicial terms are being extended informally until the adoption of new legislation on the court system. Second, there is no pool of qualified replacement jurists anyway. With vacancies in more than 1,500 of the 14,000 judicial posts across Russia, some courts have had to close.[50] Even in cities such as St. Petersburg, local nominating commissions wrestle with whether they should leave judgeships unfilled or recommend jurists to the bench who lack the requisite qualifications.[51] In Murmansk, local authorities attempted to solve the shortage in judges by elevating lay assessors to the professional bench.[52]

The widening gap between salaries and work conditions in the public and private sectors has heightened attrition from the bench to alarming proportions. But the lure of commercial structures is not the only explanation for the exodus of judges. In an atmosphere of increasing lawlessness, many judges fear for their personal safety and that of their families. It is a pattern not unlike that found in countries such as Italy and Colombia. The threats to uncooperative judges can come from corrupt law enforcement officials as well as from criminal gangs. Reporting in August 1994 on the campaign of physical intimidation against judges, *Izvestiia*'s chief legal correspondent, Iurii Feofanov, described

> a bundle of dispatches . . . from Vladivostok, Achinsk, Verkh-Isetsk and Chita. [They contained] threats against judges, assassination attempts, beatings, grenade explosions, murders. They are committed by people who have been sentenced or whose cases are being considered. . . .The result is the same in each case: not one crime against judges has been solved, and no one has incurred a penalty. . . .[53]

At a recent conference of judges, the delegates recommended changing the Law on the Status of Judges to grant judges the right to bear arms.[54]

Not surprisingly, in these conditions it is also difficult to find lay assessors willing to fulfill their civic duty. Because of the shortage of assessors, many courts have had to resort to semi-permanent lay assessors, often retirees or the unemployed, who sit on the bench for months at a time.[55] Under the abortive Law on the Court System, the lay assessors would not have been drawn randomly from the voter rolls, like Russian jurors, but elected by the legislative chamber at the corresponding level of the court. This provision, which resembles the filtering of cadres used in the Soviet era, would almost certainly have produced a pool of conservative assessors given the growing strength of the Communist and Agrarian parties in local and regional assemblies.

Not since the 1930s and 1940s has Russia confronted such a crisis in the stability and quality of its judicial cadres.[56] It is a crisis that will deepen if, as some propose, Russia doubles or trebles the size of the judiciary in order to staff justice of the peace and other new courts.[57] In anticipation of a larger demand for jurists of all sorts, new law faculties have opened throughout the country, though the standard of legal education in these programs is suspect. One may now, for example, receive a higher legal education in the Academy of Oil and Gas and other specialized technical institutes. Although no one has yet proposed a return to the short courses in law used to train many in the replacement generation of Soviet judges in the 1940s, there are recommendations to waive certain requirements as a means of attracting personnel to the court.[58]

Conclusion: Judicial Reform or Judicial Counter-Reform?

In the mid-1990s, 130 years after the country's first judicial reform, Russian legal history was at a new turning point. The movement for legal change launched in the Gorbachev era was reaching its legislative denouement. Parliament and presidency were applying the finishing touches to a new generation of substantive and procedural laws, including laws on a new court system. In May 1995, President Yeltsin signed a presidential decree granting more generous and stable funding for the judiciary. The decree also ordered local officials to provide the courts with dignified facilities for their work.[59] Two months later, on 20 July 1995, the Duma passed in a third reading the "Law on the Court System," a revised version of the bill prepared by Sergei Pashin and submitted to parliament by the presidency. In its provisions on financing, court administration, and judicial selection, the new law promised to enhance the position of the courts as a third branch of government.[60] It did not, however, address the concerns of Russia's powerful regions, and therefore failed to receive the approval of the Federation Council.

Amid these legislative developments, a group of liberal jurists met in Moscow in September 1995 to announce the death of judicial reform in Russia. The fatal blow, in their view, was not the rejection of the Law on the Court System but the elimination of the GPU's Department of Court Reform and the resignation of its head, Sergei Pashin. Ol'ga Chaikovskaia, the conscience of the Russian legal community for more than three decades, warned of the "horrible" (*strashnye*) consequences that Pashin's departure would have for law reform in general.[61] Pashin himself was more circumspect in his assessment of the prospects for reform after the bureaucratic shakeup, though he admitted that "our work ha[s] been rejected." Speaking of the progress made in the 1990s in the field of judicial reform, he noted that "we cannot yet say that it is irreversible. The whole approach can go backward. I have some fears."[62]

The immediate future for judicial reform in Russia depends in part on the reasons for Pashin's resignation. If his superiors in the presidency gutted Pashin's office in response to rising pressure from his traditional enemies in the Procuracy, the Ministry of Justice, and the power ministries, then one may conclude that the prospects for legal change in Russia are indeed grim. But it appears more likely that the decisive pressure to undercut Pashin's authority and institutional resources came from senior officials in the presidency who resented Pashin's attempts to elevate the status of his department. Thus, issues of bureaucratic power rather than legal policy may explain the departure of Russia's architect of judicial reform. Circumventing the established lines of bureaucratic authority in the presidency, Pashin made a direct, and successful, appeal to Yeltsin in March 1995 to officially designate his office as the "head agency" (*golovnoi otdel*) for judicial reform. In Pashin's own words, "at a certain stage our work outgrew the confines of a 'department'." The concession from the President provoked "furious resistance" from Pashin's immediate superior, Ruslan Orekhov, the head of the GPU, who then raised the matter with Sergei Filatov, the leader of the Executive Office of the President. On 21 April, while Pashin was on vacation, Filatov fired five of Pashin's 18 subordinates and relabeled his office the Department of Criminal Law and Procedure.[63]

Whatever precipitated Pashin's downfall, a more troubling question is whether the Russian political system can sustain judicial reform without an institutional engine of change akin to the Department of Court Reform. As in 1991, judicial reform is again without an institutional patron. Russia's dramatic transition from communism owes much to a small, and dwindling, group of reform-minded officials. Linking their institutions to the authority of the President, these officials have maneuvered around the barricades protecting entrenched bureaucratic interests. Because there is still little demand for fundamental court reform in the population, in the state bureaucracies, and even in the judicial corps itself, the impetus for change must continue to come from above, from the commanding heights of Russian politics.

Who will now provide this leadership? The obvious candidate would appear to be the presidency's Council on Judicial Reform, created in November 1994.[64] However, this 30-person body, chaired by a second-tier figure in the Russian legal community, Sergei Vitsin, is deeply divided along ideological and institutional lines. Furthermore, it is merely a consultative organ that meets infrequently and lacks a sizable permanent support staff. In

Vitsin's own words: "I want to warn against excessive expectations for our Council. The ministries and agencies [*vedomstva*] will stand to the death to defend their positions."[65] Other potential candidates in the presidency, such as Mikhail Krasnov, Yeltsin's counsellor for legal affairs, and Ruslan Orekhov, are technocrats weighed down by bureaucratic tasks. They lack the political commitment and skills to champion broad-based legal change.[66] Without political patronage, the continuing efforts of reform-oriented legal scholars in Russia will come to naught.

One may argue, of course, that, four years into the post-Soviet era, judicial reform is self-sustaining. The laws necessary to support a new court system are already in place or appear destined for imminent adoption. But Russian history illustrates that the decisive phase for law reform occurs after the normative foundations of a new legal order are in place. It is then that the conservative state bureaucracies seek their revenge on reformers by ignoring, delaying, or distorting the implementation of new laws. At times, such as in the 1970s, this revenge takes the form of a quiet erosion of provisions of reform legislation. At other times, such as in the 1880s, reactionary forces exploit a crisis of authority to mount a full-fledged counter-reform, during which the philosophical underpinnings of reform procedures and institutions come under attack.

As Russia approaches the new century, one can expect a vigorous struggle between the friends and foes of judicial reform as they seek to support—or obstruct—the implementation of new laws governing the courts. Where the passage of reform legislation requires only a momentary political victory, its faithful execution demands the continuing political hegemony of progressive forces or a respect for the spirit of the law among state officials. Russian reformists can rely on neither, at least over the short term. They must prepare themselves, therefore, for a protracted battle to be fought step by step, issue by issue, over the expansion of the jury experiment, the deepening of adversarialness in criminal proceedings, and the extension of the courts' independence and authority. At stake in this contest of ideas and interests is the shape of Russian law and politics in the next century.

Notes

1. On the course of the campaign for a law-based state, see Donald D. Barry, ed., *Toward the "Rule of Law" in Russia? Political and Legal Reform in the Transition Period* (Armonk, NY, 1992), especially 257-75.

2. As Valerii Savitskii noted at the end of the Soviet era, a measure of the absence of judicial remedies was the huge number of complaints addressed to state and Party institutions as well as prominent individuals. In 1990, Savitskii had personally received

4,000 complaints from citizens who hoped that he would intervene on their behalf. V. Savitskii, "Aspects of Judicial Reform in the USSR," *Coexistence* 28 (1991): 119-31. Sergei Stankevich put the matter even more pointedly. "Russia's problem is its tendency to complain to everyone but the court." "Slozhnye problemy segodniashnego dnia," *Sovetskaia iustitsiia*, 1991, No. 4: 4.

3. "Sergei Pashin: Chinovnik, dalekii ot chinovnichestva," *Stolitsa*, 1993, No. 9: 8.

4. "O Kontseptsii sudebnoi reformy v RSFSR," *Vedomosti S"ezda narodnykh deputatov i Verkhovnogo Soveta RSFSR*, 1991, No. 44: 1435.

5. Peter H. Solomon, Jr., "The Limits of Legal Order in Post-Soviet Russia," *Post-Soviet Affairs* 11, no. 2 (April-June 1995): 107.

6. A. D. Boikov, "Sudebnaia reforma: obreteniia i proschety," *Gosudarstvo i pravo*, 1994, No. 6: 14. In Boikov's comments are echoes of slavophile objections to the judicial reform of the last century. Writing in the 1860s, S. I. Zarudnyi noted that "[t]o adopt as a whole any foreign legislation is to separate yourself from your national identity [*ot narodnoi samobytnosti*], from the conditions of daily life, and to subordinate yourself to another nation [*narod*] in the matter of the judiciary. It is to create by means of a theory new and unknown beginnings; in other words, it is to deny unconditionally the historical development of the nation and to replace the experience of centuries with the musings of a philosopher. . . ." Quoted in Iurii Feofanov, "Rossiia vsegda spotykalas' na sudebnoi reforme," *Izvestiia*, 15 September 1992: 3.

7. M. Bobrov, "Zigzagi sudebnoi reformy," *Zakonnost'*, 1993, No. 10: 22.

8. "A nachinali s razrusheniia komandno-biurokraticheskoi sistemy . . . ," *Rossiiskaia federatsiia*, 1994, Nos. 22-24: 11.

9. Eugene Huskey, "The State-Legal Administration and the Politics of Redundancy," *Post-Soviet Affairs* 11, no. 2 (April-June 1995): 115-43.

10. For an assessment of the institutional barriers to judicial reform at the end of the Soviet era, see Eugene Huskey, "The Administration of Justice: Courts, Procuracy, and Ministry of Justice," in Huskey, ed., *Executive Power and Soviet Politics* (Armonk, NY, 1992): 221-246.

11. For a perceptive assessment of the relations between courts and their institutional overseers in the Soviet era, see Todd Foglesong, "The Politics of Judicial Independence and the Administration of Criminal Justice in Soviet Russia, 1982-1992," unpublished Ph.D. dissertation (University of Toronto, 1995).

12. The passage of the Law on the Status of Judges in June 1992 limited the dependence of the courts on the Ministry of Justice.

13. George P. Fletcher, "The Presumption of Innocence in the Soviet Union," *UCLA Law Review* 15 (1968): 1201-1225. As V. Rudnev has argued, "court reform goes against the interests of the Procuracy of the Stalinist-Brezhnev type." "General'nyi prokuror protiv suda prisiazhnykh," *Izvestiia*, 10 March 1993, quoted in A. D. Boikov, "Sudebnaia reforma: obreteniia i proschety," *Gosudarstvo i pravo*, 1994, No. 6: 21. Likewise, the liberal jurist, Valerii Savitskii, has labeled the procuracy "a rudiment of the totalitarian system of the Soviet period." *Rossiiskaia iustitsiia*, 1994, No. 10: 24. It was outspoken comments such as this that contributed to the defeat of Savitskii's nomination for a place on the Constitutional Court.

In a perceptive analysis of the procuracy written in the mid-1980s, George Ginsburgs argued that "the party, for various motives, desires a strong procuracy in order to ensure a built-in check on the judiciary's official performance and, to do so, has to portray the procuracy as more than just the 'voice of the state,' or it would be tilting the balance in the courtroom in such a way as to destroy the credibility of the judicial proceedings." George Ginsburgs, "The Soviet Judicial Elite: Is It?" *Review of Socialist Law*, 1985, No. 2: 304. It may now be asked, in the absence of the Communist Party, whose interests the procuracy is serving.

14. Valerii Rudnev, "Sudy narashchivaiut vlast': obshchestvo ot etogo luchshe," *Izvestiia*, 30 May 1995: 4. Procurators have worked themselves into a fury against the efforts of reformers to create an independent judiciary. In a recent letter, a district procurator complained that "the attempts of the courts to become independent not only of everyone and everything [*vsekh i vsia*] but of the law itself are alarming." "U prokurora i sud'i raznye funktsii," *Rossiiskaia iustitsiia*, 1995, No. 9: 51.

15. Never mind that Peter the Great borrowed the institution of the procuracy from Sweden in 1722.

16. Adding to the insult was a last-minute decision of personnel close to Yeltsin to drop wording acceptable to the procuracy from the final version of the constitution. Personal interview with Ivan Kliver, Head of Department, Procuracy Institute of the Russian Federation, Washington, DC, 21 February 1995.

17. N. Kostenko, "Prokuratura - opora prezidentskoi vlasti," *Rossiiskaia iustitsiia*, 1994, No. 11: 25-27. Responding to the shift of institutional power in Russia after October 1993, this same procurator sought to defend the procuracy by linking its fate to that of the presidency. "[T]he procuracy," in his view, ". . . should become an important and necessary support [*opora*] for presidential power, which is particularly necessary in the developing conditions of unstable legal relations in society." *Ibid.* : 26. Andrei Vyshinskii employed a similar tactic in the mid-1930s as a means of promoting the institutional interests of the procuracy against the Ministry of Justice and the NKVD.

18. If the judiciary is independent, why do representatives from executive legal institutions, such as the Procuracy, the MVD, and the Ministry of Justice, continue to attend plenums of the Supreme Court? Is the chair of the Supreme Court present at the meetings of the MVD Collegium? That questions such as these have not traditionally been posed in Russia reveals much about the assumptions underlying the relationship between executive and judicial power.

19. "MVD Minister's List of 'Unreliable Judges' Scored," *Izvestiia*, 18 November 1993: 1, in *Foreign Broadcast Information Service* [hereafter *FBIS*], 22 November 1993: 18.

20. *Ibid.* "Judiciary's Role in Anticrime Work Studied," *Literaturnaia gazeta*, 3 August 1994: 13, in *FBIS*, 21 August 1994: 23-25. As Iurii Feofanov has argued, law enforcement officials have been frustrated by article 16 of the Law on the Status of Judges, which states that "under no circumstances may a judge be detained, or forcibly taken to any state agency during proceedings involving cases of administrative law-breaking. . . . [A] judge who is detained and taken to an internal affairs agency . . . must be released immediately after his identity has been established." "Revamped Judicial System Suffers Birth Pangs," *Izvestiia*, 25 August 1994: 5, in *Current Digest of the Post-Soviet Press*, 1994, No. 34: 10.

21. "O neotlozhnykh merakh po realizatsii Federal'noi programmy Rossiiskoi Federatsii po usileniiu bor'by s prestupnost'iu na 1994-1995 gody," *Sobranie zakonodatel'stva*, 1994, No. 5: 403; "O neotlozhnykh merakh po zashchite naseleniia ot banditizma i inykh proiavlenii organizovannoi prestupnosti," Ukaz Prezidenta Rossiiskoi Federatsii ot 14 iiunia 1994, *Rossiiskaia gazeta*, 17 June 1994: 1. For reaction to the decree, see the selections in "Yeltsin's Anticrime Decree Draws Flood of Protests," *Current Digest of the Post-Soviet Press*, 1994, No. 24: 1-7.

22. John Lloyd, "Anti-crime measures split Russians," *Financial Times*, 27 June 1994:   3.

23. For an excellent account of the German judiciary, see David P. Currie, "Separation of Powers in the Federal Republic of Germany," *American Journal of Comparative Law* 41 (1993): 239-59.

24. For an excellent analysis of policy and practice in these three areas as of the end of 1994, see Peter H. Solomon, Jr., "The Limits of Legal Order in Post-Soviet Russia," *Post-Soviet Affairs*, no. 2 (1995): 89-114.

25. The analysis that follows is based largely on "Kak nam ustroit' sudebnuiu sistemu," *Rossiiskaia iustitsiia*, 1994, No. 5: 2-5, and the Ministry of Justice and Council of Judges drafts on the court system. My thanks to Peter Solomon for providing copies of these drafts.

26. "Kak nam ustroit' sudebnuiu sistemu," 2-5.

27. "Podvedeny pervye itogi," *Rossiiskaia iustitsiia*, 1994, No. 12: 5.

28. For a brief history of the justice of the peace courts in late imperial Russia, see V. Vlasov, "Mirovoi sud kak forma narodnogo samoupravleniia," *Rossiiskaia iustitsiia*, 1995, No. 7: 19-21.

29. "O sudebnoi sisteme Rossiiskoi Federatsii," adopted by the Duma in a third reading on 20 July 1995 (copy in possession of the author).

30. According to Articles 10 and 16 of the 1993 constitution, each of Russia's 89 republics and regions has the right to form its own judicial system and, within limits, its own substantive law. Indeed, V. V. Ershov argues that the wording of the constitution opens the way for three systems of courts: federal, subject territory, and local. For his analysis of the constitution's contradictory and ambiguous provisions on court organization, see "Konstitutsionnye problemy sudoustroistva i sudoproizvodstva," *Gosudarstvo i pravo*, 1994, No. 12: 46-48.
    One of the more peculiar, and dangerous, provisions of the Law on the Court System (Art. 39) authorizes subject territories to create their own constitutional, or charter, courts outside of the federal court system. As of late 1995, no subject territory had yet created its own courts. Given the centripetal currents now at work in Russian politics and the enormous complexity and expense of establishing parallel legal systems on Russian territory, it is unlikely that regional governments will soon test their constitutional powers on the courts. Should they do so, they could expect to face the resistance of Jacobins as well as reformists in Moscow.

31. Iuliia Kantor, "Sudebnaia sistema v Rossii rushitsia," *Nezavisimaia gazeta*, 6 December 1994: 6.

32. See, for example, "Kak nam ustroit' sudebnuiu sistemu," 4. According to A. Borin, at the end of the 1980s the courts brought in 800 million rubles annually to the Soviet budget, whereas only 160 million was expended on the courts, 40 million less than on the procuracy. "Nishchaia iustitsiia, ili skol'ko stoit pravovoe gosudarstvo?" *Literaturnaia gazeta*, 23 August 1989: 10. However, the failure of Government officials to raise fees has led to a literal "undervaluing of justice" in a period of high inflation. In 1995, it cost only 5 rubles (a tenth of a penny) to get a copy of a court judgement and 200 rubles (5 cents) to get a divorce. Vladimir Somov, "'Spasaites' sami, Vasha chest'!'" *Iuridicheskii vestnik*, 1995, Nos. 11-12: 26.

33. The scale of this ministerial "embezzlement" was substantial in 1994. See Anatolii Babenko, "Sudy okazalis' 'na zadvorkakh' finansirovaniia," *Rossiiskaia iustitsiia*, 1995, No. 9: 13-14.

34. It is a measure of the gap between the judicial leadership and the more conservative rank-and-file judges that the III (Extraordinary) All-Russian Congress of Judges supported the establishment of a Court Department within the Ministry of Justice. Tamara Gromova, "Femida Rossii. Kakoi ei byt'?" *Iuridicheskii vestnik*, 1994, No. 24-25:   3. See also "Sudebnyi departament - kakim emu byt'?" *Rossiiskaia iustitsiia*, 1995, No. 2: 1.

35. Unlike the first reading of the Law on the Court System, the version passed in the third reading by the Duma stipulated that the General Director of the Court Department would be hired and fired by the Chair of the Supreme Court with the agreement of the Council of Judges of Russia. The earlier version had granted to the President the right to hire and fire the General Director, based on the approval of the All Russian Congress of Judges (Art. 32).

36. To win the support of the Federation Council, which represented the interests of the subjects of the Federation, the 1996 Law on the Court System included: the right of republics and regions to establish their own constitutional or charter courts; a promise of federal funding for the new justice of the peace courts (which would still be considered courts of the subjects of the Federation); and a voice for regional and republican governments in the selection of most judges. Although the President will make the actual appointments, nominations of candidates for positions on district, regional, and republican supreme courts will have to gain the consent of regional or republican legislatures before being forwarded to the President. See "O sudebnoi sisteme Rossiiskoi Federatsii," *Rossiiskaia gazeta*, 6 January 1997: 3.

37. In one of those regions, Ulianovsk, the resistance of local officials, most notably procurators, has effectively scuttled the experiment.

38. "Podvedeny pervye itogi," *Rossiiskaia iustitsiia*, 1994, No. 12: 4.

39. "State Legal Directorate Chief on Significance of Jury Court," *Obshchaia gazeta*, 29 April 1994: 6, in *FBIS*, 18 May 1994: 12.

40. A. D. Boikov, "Sudebnaia reforma: obreteniia i proschety," *Gosudarstvo i pravo*, 1994, No. 6: 20.

41. At the III (Extraordinary) All-Russian Congress of Judges, 83 percent of the delegates surveyed favored this reform. "Sotsiologicheskii opros," *Rossiiskaia iustitsiia*, 1994, No. 6: 5. In the Cheliabinsk region in 1993, the average monthly caseload per judge was 6.8 criminal cases, 19.5 civil cases, and 12.1 administrative cases. V. Shaburnikov, "Formiro-

vanie sudeiskogo korpusa v oblasti," *Rossiiskaia iustitsiia*, 1994, No. 8: 12.

42. "Reforma? Da my lish' na podstupakh," *Iuridicheskii vestnik*, 1994, No. 18-19: 6.

43. *Ibid.* Recent reforms have also enhanced the role of the courts in pre-trial proceedings, which at the end of the Soviet era were dominated by the investigative organs of the MVD, the KGB, and the Procuracy. For a useful survey of these reforms, which are among the most important in Russian law, see Peter H. Solomon, Jr., "The Limits of Legal Order in Post-Soviet Russia," *Post-Soviet Affairs*, no. 2 (1995), pp. 99-103.

44. For a fuller discussion of recent changes in judicial selection, see Solomon, "The Limits of Legal Order," 95-97.

45. These commissions, known in Russian as *kvalifikatsionnye kollegii*, do more than vet judicial candidates. They also hear ethical complaints against judges and review proposals to remove judges from office for malfeasance. In at least one instance, the highest-level judicial nominating commission resisted attempts by executive officials to remove a judge in Rostov. "Polozhenie o kvalifikatsionnykh kollegiiakh sudei trebuet utochneniia," *Rossiiskaia iustitsiia*, 1994, No. 2: 1.

46. Yury Feofanov, "Neither the Police nor the State likes Independent Judges," *Izvestiia*, 25 August 1994: 5, in *FBIS* 46, no. 34 (1994): 10-11.

47. "Text of Yeltsin's Letter on Powers of Judges," *Rossiiskie vesti*, 9 November 1994: 1, in *FBIS*, 9 November 1994: 8.

48. The Supreme Qualification Commission, based in Moscow, consists of 32 members who review candidates for appointment and disciplinary cases at the regional level. In 1993 and the first half of 1994, it removed 74 judges from the Bench for improper conduct. "74 sud'i lisheny polnomochii za porochashchie prostupki," *Rossiiskaia iustitsiia*, 1995, No. 3: 54. The President also selects the chairs and deputy chairs of courts. The leaders of the highest courts of the Russian Federation must then be confirmed by the upper house, the Federation Council.

The Law on the Court System passed by the Duma but rejected by the Federation Council in October 1995 stipulated that all candidates for the Bench had to have a positive recommendation from a judicial nominating commission.

49. See the description, for example, of judicial selection in the Kurgan region in V. Verbenko, "Bezvlastie 'tret'ei vlasti'," *Rossiiskaia iustitsiia*, 1994, No. 6: 3. According to Peter Solomon, "[a]lready in May 1994 the President was appointing judges to regional level courts (including *arbitrazh* courts) and by November had reportedly appointed 600 judges to these courts. He had also made some 130 appointments to district or people's courts and was considering another 300 nominations." Solomon, "The Limits of Legal Order," 96.

50. The vacancies, it should be noted, are caused in part by an increase in the number of judgeships. The *shtatnaia chislennost'* of the Russian judiciary increased in 1993 from 10,465 to 11,623 in the people's courts and from 2,330 to 2,472 in higher-level courts. "Sudebnaia statistika," *Rossiiskaia iustitsiia*, 1994, No. 7: 46. In the first half of 1994, there were 11,675 judges and 9,236 court executors in Russia's 2,459 district and city courts, 2,624 judges in 85 regional courts, and 115 judges on the Supreme Court. A. Gagarskii, "O rabote sudov Rossiiskoi Federatsii za 1-e polugodie 1994 goda," *Rossiiskaia iustitsiia*, 1995, No. 1: 41.

51. Kantor, "Sudebnaia sistema v Rossii rushitsia," 6.

52. A presidential directive annulled this action by the Murmansk regional administration. "Yeltsin Removes Illegally Appointed Judges," *RFE/RL Daily Report*, 10 August 1994.

53. "Revamped Judicial System Suffers Birth Pangs," *Izvestiia*, 25 August 1994: 5, in *Current Digest of the Post-Soviet Press*, no. 34 (1994): 10.

54. "Sud'i idut k nezavisimosti," *Rossiiskaia iustitsiia*, 1994, No. 5: 1.

55. "Predlagaet iustitsiia Rossii," *Rossiiskaia iustitsiia*, 1994, No. 4: 4.

56. The formation of a Soviet judicial corps is a central theme of Peter H. Solomon, Jr., *Soviet Criminal Justice under Stalin* (Cambridge, 1996).

57. See the proposal of former Justice Minister Kalmykov in "Glavnaia problema - kadry," *Rossiiskaia iustitsiia*, 1994, No. 4: 2-4.

58. V. Ershov and L. Khaldeev, "O professional'noi podgotovke kandidatov v sud'i," *Rossiiskaia iustitsiia*, 1994, No. 8: 11.

59. "O nekotorykh organizatsionnykh merakh po uskoreniiu provedeniia sudebnoi reformy v RF," *Sobranie zakonodatel'stva*, 1995, No. 22: 2033. [ukaz no. 521, 23 May 1995] See also Aleksei Kirpichnikov, "Boris El'tsin nasleduet eshche odno delo tsaria-osvoboditelia," *Segodnia*, 24 May 1995: 2. Yeltsin issued a subsequent decree calling for an increase in the pay and status of judges in the country's supreme courts. "O dopolnitel'nykh garantiiakh sotsial'noi zashchishchennosti rabotnikov organov sudebnoi vlasti," *Sobranie zakonodatel'stva*, 1995, No. 23: 2205.

60. "O sudebnoi sisteme Rossiiskoi Federatsii," adopted by the Duma in a third reading on 20 July 1995 (copy in possession of the author).

61. Comments made during press conference of Sergei Pashin, Radisson-Slavianskaia Hotel, Moscow, 27 September 1995, attended by the author. One liberal jurist noted, only half in jest, that Russia was again in a time of troubles, with a real Kovalev (Sergei, the human rights advocate) and a false Kovalev (Valentin the Pretender, the new Minister of Justice).

62. David Hoffman, "Jury Experiment Slow, Incomplete," *The Washington Post*, 8 October 1995: A45. Pashin's pessimism reflected his lack of faith in democratic politicians, especially those in the Duma. With large numbers of democrats absent from the assembly when the law on the jury trial came up for a vote, it was left to Sergei Baburin, the Russian nationalist, to play the unlikely role of champion of the new law. Press conference of Sergei Pashin, Radisson-Slavianskaia Hotel, Moscow, 27 September 1995.

63. Press conference of Sergei Pashin, Radisson-Slavianskaia Hotel, Moscow, 27 September 1995, and edited remarks of Pashin printed in "Sudy prisiazhnykh i sudebnaia reforma 130 let spustia" (copy in possession of the author). Pashin noted that "the leadership of the GPU, which before [March] had not taken an active interest in our work, began to take measures to halt it." He recognized that his success with Yeltsin had attracted attention to his department that proved destructive [*gubitel'nym*].

64. On the formation of this Council, see "O merakh po realizatsii Kontsepsii sudebnoi reformy v Rossiiskoi Federatsii" [ukaz Prezidenta no. 2100 ot 22 noiabria 1994]," *Rossiiskaia iustitsiia*, 1995, No. 1: 1. The Council at inception had 26 jurists, who were drawn from various institutions and political camps. Four more members were added at the end of December 1994. "Ob izmeneniiakh v sostave Soveta po sudebnoi reforme pri Prezidente RF," *Rossiiskaia iustitsiia*, 1995, No. 3: 5. The chair, S. E. Vitsin, is a scholar and department chair at the Moscow Higher School for Militsia. His deputy is Sergei Pashin. *Ibid.*: 3. For accounts of the Council's first meetings, see "Sovet po sudebnoi reformy: pervye shagi," *Iuridicheskii vestnik*, 1994, Nos. 38-39: 2, and Vasilii Kononenko, "Sud'i vse eshche v sil'noi zavisimosti," *Izvestiia*, 24 March 1995: 1.

65. Vladimir Somov, "'Spasaites' sami, Vasha chest'!'" *Iuridicheskii vestnik*, 1995, Nos. 11-12: 26. For a description of the work of the Council in early 1995, see "Ne vremia revoliutsii, no vremia sudebnoi reformy," *Rossiiskaia iustitsiia*, 1995, No. 5: 3-6.

66. For interviews with Krasnov, see "Molodogo konia - v staruiu telegu," *Rossiiskie vesti*, 6 October 1995: 1, and "Mikhail Krasnov: Kreml' sudami ne komanduet," *Iuridicheskii vestnik*, 1995, Nos. 23-24: 3.

15

THE STRUGGLE OVER THE PROCURACY

Gordon B. Smith

The procuracy stands at the heart of the debate surrounding legal reform in post-Soviet Russia. As the Gorbachev-era legal reforms unfolded, the procuracy became a focal point of reformist criticism. With the collapse of the USSR, the outlawing of the CPSU, the dismantling of Gosplan, and the reorganization of the KGB, the major coercive bureaucracies of the former Soviet state were disarmed or destroyed—all except the procuracy. The procuracy managed to survive and continues to play a central, if not predominant, role in the Russian legal system today. This chapter analyzes the late and post-Soviet debate over the procuracy, the reasons behind the liberal attack on it, how the onslaught of criticism escalated, and how the procuracy dealt with it. The chapter concludes with some observations on the likely course of developments affecting the procuracy in the immediate future and suggests ways in which its mission could be redefined to satisfy the needs of law enforcement, while still placating liberal reformers.

This chapter draws heavily on data acquired from more than 40 interviews with 29 leading figures in the Russian legal system, especially procurators and legal scholars. The interviews were conducted in Moscow and St. Petersburg, as well as Nizhnyi Novgorod, Kazan, Petrozavodsk, and Vladimir, between 1991 and mid-1995. In several cases, follow-up interviews were conducted to uncover changes in attitudes and positions toward legal reform proposals.

Devil in a Uniform:
The Origins of the Negative Image of the Procurator

The negative image of the procuracy lies in roots going back to Lenin and even Peter the Great. Peter the Great created the post of Procurator General, subordinate to the Imperial Senate, in 1722. The procuracy was charged with the functions of (1) supervising the activities of the Senate (to protect against abrogation of its decrees and regulations), and (2) executing the Tsar's edicts promptly and fully. The introduction of the procuracy was an attempt, in a single stroke, to incorporate in Russia a public law system similar to those that had developed in Western Europe over the course of centuries. Peter's attempt to introduce public law norms into Russia ultimately failed due to the absolutist and personal nature of power of the Russian monarchy and the absence of a workable foundation of private law in Russian society.

Catherine II extended procuratorial supervision to regional and local levels where procurators served as the "eyes of the tsar" in monitoring the activity of provincial governors and other officials. Procurators attended meetings of various administrative and executive bodies to insure that their actions conformed to law. When a breach of the law was discovered, it was reported to a superior procurator as well as to the provincial governor and, in some cases, to the Minister of Justice. As Sergei Kazantsev notes, "reinforcement of the power of Russian Procurators General was not accompanied with the rising level of legality in the country."[1] Rather, procuratorial action came to be dictated not by the law, but by political expediency.

Procuratorial supervision of regional and local administration was resented by the provincial governors and was eliminated by the legal reforms of 1864. Those reforms confined the procuracy to the prosecution of criminal cases, supervision of legality in the courts, and appealing criminal and civil court actions. Formal responsibility for criminal investigations was also taken away and given to pre-trial investigators who were supposed to function as independent judicial officers, but became in reality partially subordinate to the procurators.[2] At the same time, the procuracy's responsibility to combat crime, especially activities of revolutionary movements, was increased. Thus, the procuracy after 1864 resembled somewhat its French counterpart and its functions remained largely unchanged until the Bolshevik Revolution in 1917.

A decree of the Council of People's Commissars of 24 November 1917 abolished the procuracy along with other tsarist legal institutions. Initially, the Bolshevik leaders tried to use informal bodies, such as worker tribunals, to monitor the legality of public administration. However, just as Peter the Great had discovered two hundred years earlier, Lenin found that the tribunals were inadequate to stem the rise of crime and abuses of power by local and regional officials. In 1922 the Bolshevik Government re-established the procuracy and invested it with not only prosecutorial functions, but also the power to supervise the legality of administrative officials, agencies, and citizens. In his famous letter on "Dual Subordination and Legality" Lenin insisted that the procuracy had to be a single, unified, hierarchical   organization, wholly independent of local and regional authorities. Thus, from 1922 onward, the procuracy resumed its pre-1864 character, as the "eyes of the State" to ensure full and complete cooperation of officialdom in executing the policies of the rulers.

The procuracy's central position in the administration of justice after 1922 derived not only from its hierarchical and centralized organizational structure but also from the wide range of functions it performed. To begin, the procurator was involved at every stage in the criminal process. The arrest of a suspect and the search for evidence required his written authorization. In Soviet criminal procedure, the prosecution of cases proceeded through two stages, preliminary investigation and trial, and the procurator partici-pated in both. By 1928, the investigators for serious cases had become procuratorial officials. Also falling within the realm of procuratorial action were the review or appeal of criminal and civil cases, the supervision of prisons, prisoner complaints, parole, and the release of prisoners; supervision of the actions of the police and secret police; supervision of juvenile commissions; supervision of the courts. Finally, and most important, the procuracy assumed responsibility for supervising the legality of the activities of all government bodies, enterprises, public organizations, and officials. This latter function, the supervision of administrative and economic officials and bodies, is referred to as general supervision.

In the early 1930s, the procuracy was drawn into participating in Stalin's industrialization and collectivization campaigns. Procurators undertook investigations of not only legal infractions and violations, but also the execution of the Party's policies. According to one Soviet jurist,

> The view that the basic content of the work of the procurator in general supervision must be his direct "organizational-political" participation in carrying out economic campaigns was widely disseminated. In practice, this vague arrangement often led to converting the procurator into the authorized representative in sowing, harvesting, procurement and other economic campaigns.[3]

Some local procurators went so far as to prescribe the times and manner in which grain should be harvested or the manner in which production should be organized in a factory.[4] This economic focus of procuratorial supervision would continue throughout the Stalin years, and to a lesser extent until the late 1980s.

Later in the 1930s, with Stalin's prosecutor Andrei Vyshinskii at the helm, the procuracy came to emphasize its prosecutorial role—with regard to both ordinary and political charges—and for a time was drawn into the terror through its approval of arrests and involvement in the mock trials conducted by the *troiki* of the NKVD. In this context, both general supervision and the handling of citizen complaints declined, but these activities would begin to make a revival after World War II.[5]

Following Stalin's death in 1953 and Khrushchev's denunciation of Stalin's abuses, discussions flourished concerning the need for legal reforms. Stalin's successors moved quickly to dismantle the apparatus of terror, including the NKVD's Special Board. At the same time, they sought to strengthen the procuracy and further revive its supervisory role and the rights of citizens to complain against officials. An editorial in *Pravda* in April 1955 criticized the procuracy for "serious shortcomings" in failing to stop the "anti-State activities of individual officials."[6]

Soon thereafter, the Statute on Procuratorial Supervision in the USSR of 24 May 1955 expanded the procuracy's terms of reference relative to general supervision. The Statute spelled out for the first time procuratorial powers of protest, representation, and proposal. It also empowered procurators to demand official documents, records, and information concerning possible violations of laws.[7]

Meanwhile, in criminal justice the procuracy held a dominant position. It supervised the preliminary investigation, approved search warrants, reviewed the findings of the investigation before formulating an indictment, and then prosecuted the case in court. By the 1970s rates of acquittal had fallen below one percent, and even so the procurator had the right to appeal acquittals. Furthermore, the procuracy retained the responsibility to supervise the proper functioning of the courts, making the judges accountable to the procurators that appeared before them and giving those procurators a status superior to defense counsel.

The origins of the procuracy's later unpopularity was multifaceted. For one thing, with the resumption of general supervision in 1955 factory managers, farm directors, and other officials resented what they considered to be procuratorial interference in administrative matters. Nevertheless, officials had little choice but to comply with procuratorial protests and representations, given the procuracy's close ties to the CPSU. After 1968 the majority of procuratorial actions addressed economic problems—theft of state property, padding of plan fulfillment reports, and substandard production.[8] For example, in 1972, 73.8 percent of all procuratorial investigations undertaken by the RSFSR procuracy concerned actions by industrial enterprise or collective farm officials.[9] In addition to these formal actions, procurators routinely telephoned factory managers and state farm directors "to express concerns" over timely plan fulfillment on behalf of local and regional Party bosses. The implied threat was clear. Brow-beating factory directors was the least favorite activity of procurators and when the Party began to lose its influence on the procuracy in 1990 this practice stopped, allowing prosecutors to concentrate on real legal violations rather than matters of economic management.[10] Yet the image continued after 1990, at least in the perceptions of many, that the procuracy was simply a tool of the Party.

Moreover, in 1990 the extension of the procuracy's general supervision over local and regional soviets heightened resentment of it, especially among pro-reform forces. The quasi-open and free elections of 1990 resulted in many new and inexperienced deputies coming into office, sometimes with a naive or exaggerated sense of their own mandate. No longer under the strict tutelage of the centralized Party apparat, these deputies began to pass legislation and issue ordinances on a host of complex issues. Not infrequently, local or regional soviets undertook actions that directly conflicted with all-union or republic legislation, or overstepped their legal authority. When procurators did issue protests against such actions, deputies often responded angrily. Furthermore, procuratorial protests suspended the execution of protested decisions. Thus, the procuracy was acting in effect like a court, ruling on the illegality or legality of a body's actions.

Finally, throughout the post-Stalin period, and especially under Gorbachev, defense attorneys resented the privileged position that procurators and procuracy investigators enjoyed in criminal cases. They advocated for equal rights to defend their clients during the preliminary investigation, the transfer of responsibility for supervision of preliminary investigations from the procuracy to an independent investigatory agency, and changes that would introduce a more adversarial quality to criminal procedure.

Resentment aside, the procuracy played a useful role in responding to infringements of the rights of citizens by bureaucrats. From 1955 until 1968 the vast majority of procuratorial actions consisted of protests against the illegal imposition of administrative fines, infringements of citizens' labor rights, or complaints regarding housing, pensions, and other social services. In the absence of adequate judicial review of administrative acts, general supervision of the procuracy, much like the activity of the Swedish Ombudsman, offered an effective way for citizens to redress grievances. In the early 1970s procurators handled between 150,000 and 200,000 complaints annually, and provided satisfaction to nearly half of the complainants.[11]

Although Article 48 of the 1977 constitution confirmed the right of citizens to appeal to the court matters arising from the actions of officials, the first broad legislation realizing this provision did not come into force until 1987, and even so the procuracy remained the principal legal agency handling complaints. Yet, despite its good record with complaints, many legal scholars found procuratorial supervision to be inferior to court review. First, once a citizen lodged a complaint with the procurator, the investigation of the complaint shifted to the procuracy and its officials. The procurator had absolute discretion to pursue or drop the matter. As a result, the citizen lost all control over the process. Second, procuratorial supervision seemed to reinforce the citizen's role as a subject or supplicant, seeking redress from the state. Judicial review, on the other hand, would encourage citizens to become more assertive in protecting their rights and interests. Third, given the close ties between the procuracy and the Party at all levels, it was unlikely that citizens could obtain redress in cases that would materially harm powerful interests. Fourth, there was a tendency for the procuracy to respond mainly to complaints whose satisfaction served state interests, including economic ones. There was no clear commitment on the part of the procuracy to protecting individual rights for their own sake.

The supporters of general supervision by the procuracy answered these charges with the argument that procuratorial supervision of citizens' grievances was free, faster than judicial review (unlike use of the courts), and more likely to result in satisfaction. Since many Soviet citizens did not know how to lodge a complaint in court, the availability of procuracy review made sense, even if it recognized their real status as subjects rather than citizens. Moreover, the Soviet public had no reason to assume that their courts were more free from political influence than was the procuracy.

At the same time, most procuracy officials had developed during the perestroika years an agenda of their own, which involved strengthening rather than weakening their supervisory role. Upset at the increasing discrepancy between their powers in law and the demands placed upon them to enforce legality (including protection of human rights), many procurators—surveyed in 1989—wanted a formal extension of the agencies coming under their supervision to include the KGB and the CPSU. They also sought the additional power to impose fines upon persons who failed to comply with their orders. Beyond this, procurators agreed that their institution needed increased resources and a revival of its prestige.[12]

These concerns of the procuracy and its supporters mattered little to its critics. On another level of discourse, they insisted that the whole system of procuratorial supervision was unique to Russia. Under the influence of Gorbachev's policies of perestroika and democratization, legal reformers were seeking to bring the Russian legal system into closer alignment with

West European legal systems. Eliminating the procuracy or at least limiting its role to prosecuting criminal cases in court would, in their view, facilitate the conversion of the Russian legal system into a more "modern," European system. Naturally, supporters of the procuracy would counter that the procuracy was authentically Russian.

The Conception of Judicial Reform

The reformist attack on the procuracy was most fully embodied in a remarkable document "The Conception of Judicial Reform in the USSR," which was drafted by a group of leading Russian scholars and jurists in mid-1991 and approved by the RSFSR Supreme Soviet on 24 October 1991. Overall, the Conception is a detailed, discursive, and at times pedantic analysis of the state of the Russian legal system. Although it proposes various specific measures to remedy the "crisis" in the legal system, the bulk of the document is restricted to a broad brush assessment of the need for reform, especially judicial reforms.

Why it was necessary (or strategic) to bring the Conception before the Supreme Soviet for approval is unclear. While the Soviet's endorsement of the document was not binding, Sergei Pashin, one of its drafters, states in the Preface that "the legal significance of 'The Conception of Judicial Reform in the RSFSR' consists in the fact that its main ideas are obligatory as a criterion of evaluation of any draft legislation or legislative initiative that touches upon questions" related to its substance.[13]

The first line of the Conception clearly reveals the priority of its drafters. "One of the main tasks of the reform is the establishment of judicial power in the state mechanism as an autonomous influential force, independent in its activity of the legislative and executive powers."[14] Pashin also proposes "seeing in the person of the procurator above all the representation of prosecutorial power and a party in the process enjoying equal rights . . ."[15] This implies that the drafters wished to end the prosecutorial bias that favored the procuracy during virtually every phase of the criminal process. The document contends that during the preliminary investigation the investigator, the procurator, and sometimes even the judge performed an accusatory function. Although procurators were always required to assess evidence that would exonerate as well as incriminate, research conducted by the Institute of State and Law showed that in 95 percent of the cases where evidence was inadequate to support the accused's guilt, charges were pursued regardless.[16]

The drafters of the Conception targeted for special criticism the general supervision powers of the procuracy, especially procuratorial investigations into wrongdoing by administrative agencies and local governmental bodies. The authors argued that, as under the tsars, general supervision served as a powerful instrument of coercion, and made the procuracy "the eye of the state" (*oko tsaria*). Consequently, they recommended:

(a) Prohibiting procuratorial supervision where no "signal" of a violation of law has been received. The authors would grant exceptions for "voiceless interests," that is, persons who because of age or incapacity are not able to protect their own interests by bringing their grievances to the procurator. The Conception also recognizes issues affecting the "nonpersonified interests of society" and acknowledges the propriety of procuratorial supervision in such cases. These exceptions constitute, perhaps unwittingly, an admission by the authors of the Conception that the procuracy does play a valuable and legitimate role in protecting citizens' and society's rights and interests and implies that such actions should not be restricted to judicial consideration.

(b) Restricting "procuratorial interference" to cases of presumed criminal violations, or where particular societal interests are at stake, or where recourse through the courts or other channels of dispute resolution is not viable or applicable.

(c) That procuratorial action no longer be permitted to suspend execution of the protested action. Rather it is proposed that the procuratorial action consist of notification of an intent to pursue judicial enforcement if the violation is not eliminated voluntarily.

(d) Eliminating procuratorial warnings and the practice of issuing compulsory prescriptions to correct actions the procuracy considers to be illegal.

(e) Restricting the power of the procuracy to summon citizens and officials to make statements except in the context of criminal investigations.

The Conception proposes the retention of the procuracy's powers to oversee criminal investigations, but favors transferring the responsibility for the actual conduct of the investigation from the procuracy and Ministry of Internal Affairs to an independent investigatory agency, except for special cases, such as the investigation of criminal wrongdoing by investigators, procurators, or other law enforcement officials. (This exception is curious since it would put the procuracy in the position of investigating its own employees where conflicts of interest would arguably be the most likely to distort the investigation.)

The Conception is unambiguous in condemning procuratorial supervision of the courts, arguing that this form of supervision, reintroduced in 1933, violates judicial independence and leads "to the oppression of justice."[17] The drafters of the Conception also advocate restricting the procurators' right to intervene in civil cases except to protect the rights of minors, the elderly, the incapacitated, and the general interests of society. Finally, the Conception advocates that procuratorial supervision of prisons and other correctional facilities be supplemented with court oversight.

Although the Conception has been characterized as a broadside attack on the procuracy, a careful reading reveals that it would leave in place many of the procuracy's broad-reaching powers and responsibilities.

The Conception merely opened the issue for debate. In the wake of the abortive August 1991 coup d'état the positions of supporters and opponents of the procuracy alike became more entrenched. Some reformers wanted the procuracy to be abolished entirely or its functions limited to the prosecution of criminal cases. Especially critical of the procuracy was a group of academic jurists many of whom were affiliated with the Institute of State and Law and the Institute on Soviet Legislation. Included in this group were such noted scholars as Aleksandr M. Larin, Igor L. Petrukhin, Tamara B. Morshchakova, and Inga B. Mikhailovskaia. (Morshchakova would eventually be named to the Constitutional Court, while Mikhailovskaia would work with various human rights organizations and maintain extensive contacts with Western advocates of legal reform.) The prime organizers of the opposition to the procuracy and principal drafters of the Conception were Boris A. Zolotukhin and Sergei Pashin. Once an advocate disbarred for his defense of dissidents, Zolotukhin was a deputy and chair of the Supreme Soviet Committee on Legislation. A much younger jurist, Pashin worked with Zolotukhin before moving to the State Legal Administration to head up its judicial reform programs, including the introduction of jury trials. As we have noted earlier, these scholars favored the creation of strong courts and argued that such a court system could not develop as long as the procuracy occupied a dominant position in the legal system. According to high-level officials in the central procuracy, these scholars greatly admired Western judicial systems and wished to emulate them in Russia, regardless of whether those systems were appropriate for Russia.[18]

The status of the procuracy also became embroiled in the controversies surrounding the adoption of a new constitution and the delineation of powers between the President and the Parliament. The draft of a new Russian federation constitution, published on 11 October 1991, called for limiting the procuracy solely to the prosecution of criminal matters in courts. The procurator's power of general supervision would be assumed by a newly established People's Ombudsman (*pravozashchitnik*), appointed by the Russian Parliament to investigate actions of government agencies, enterprises, local organs, and officials when those actions violated the rights of citizens. The investigatory powers of the procuracy were to be taken away and vested in a special agency for criminal investigation. Supervision of the courts—a power long resented by judges—was to be confined to the Supreme Court of the Russian Republic.

The drastically scaled-back procuracy envisioned in the 1991 draft constitution of the Russian Republic coincided with the views of Russian Minister of Justice Nikolai Fedorov. In a speech before Russian judges in late October 1991, Fedorov noted that the procuracy as a higher supervisory body of state power was a uniquely Soviet institution, a "sacred cow" created by Stalin and Vyshinskii. He denounced procuratorial supervision of the performance of the courts as a "legal atavism" and general supervision as a totalitarian "snoop" (*zagliadyvanie*).[19] He argued that the only proper role of the procuracy is to prosecute criminal cases in court. Limiting the role of the procuracy would, in his view, strengthen the court system and bring the Republic's legal system into closer conformity with established European norms and legal experience.

Not surprisingly, the Procurator General of Russia Stepankov disagreed with the Justice Minister and the authors of the Conception and was determined to protect the procuracy from attack. Valentin Stepankov had already proven his mettle as a political fighter. Appointed by Boris Yeltsin in February 1991, the then 39-year-old former procurator of Sverdlovsk region[20] (Yeltsin's own) had fought hard and well against USSR Procurator General Nikolai Trubin to shift power from the central procuracy to those of the republics. Thus, Stepankov signed a separate protocol on 28 May 1991 recognizing the independent procuracy of the Latvian republic.[21] Stepankov also took the initiative to draft a new RSFSR Law on the Procuracy that granted the republican procuracy sole authority to supervise the execution of laws of the Republic and limited the USSR Procuracy to enforcing all-union laws "in coordination with the Procurator General of the RSFSR."[22] Even personnel, training, and budget were removed from central determination. With the collapse of the USSR, the central Procuracy was disbanded and Stepankov and associates from the RSFSR Procuracy took over its buildings and promptly fired those procurators who had taken the wrong side in the attempted coup of August 1991.

Although Stepankov was identified as Yeltsin's procurator, who promised to use the procuracy to eliminate opposition to reforms such as privatization, Stepankov remained a staunch defender of his institution. Rather than wait for a resolution of the constitutional questions surrounding the status and powers of the procuracy, Stepankov pushed through the Supreme Soviet a new "Law on the Procuracy of the Russian Federation" in January 1992. Passage of this law was justified by the fact that the USSR Procuracy ceased to exist as of 31 December 1991. More important, Stepankov hoped to shore up the position of the procuracy in a new law *before* opponents could mount a crippling attack on the agency.

The 1992 Law on the Procuracy preserved the institution as a single, unified, and centralized institution charged with "supervising the implementation of laws by local legislative and executive bodies, administrative control organs, legal entities, public organizations, and officials, as well as the lawfulness of their acts."[23] Article 2 specified that the procuratorial supervision extended to investigatory agencies, prisons and places of detention, and military units and their administrative offices. In each instance, the procuracy was not meant to supplant the authority of the given agency, but was charged with overseeing that proper procedures and laws were followed.

While the new law retained many of the broad supervisory powers of the procuracy, provisions were introduced to depoliticize the institution. Article 4 stated that no political party organizations are permitted within the procuracy. Procurators could not serve as members of elected or other governmental bodies the legality of whose acts they would have to supervise. In practice, however, many prosecutors who had been elected to national, regional, and local soviets did not resign their posts. Even Procurator General Stepankov, who was elected to the Council of Nationalities of the Russian Supreme Soviet, continued to serve as a deputy until the October 1993 disbanding of the parliament by Yeltsin.

Article 7 gave the Procurator General and his subordinate procurators the right to attend sessions of the Congress of People's Deputies and the Supreme Soviet and their counterpart bodies at subordinate levels. Thus, procurators at the city level had the right to attend sessions of the city soviet. The Procurator General and procurators of the constituent republics also had the right of legislative initiative and could address parliamentary bodies at corresponding levels concerning their interpretations of laws. Finally, the Procurator General and procurators of the constituent republics retained the right to ask the courts at their respective levels to look into the constitutionality of various normative acts and to represent the procuracy's interpretation of such acts in court.

The most important change in Stepankov's 1992 "Law on the Procuracy" was the elimination of procuratorial supervision over the activities of the courts. In this respect the law was consistent with the draft constitution of the Russian Federation and the position of the Justice Minister Fedorov, who favored enhancing judicial independence by limiting the subordination of courts only to higher courts. Article 9, however, granted the procuracy the right to investigate citizens' complaints arising from court decisions as long as those cases were not under appeal or otherwise *sub judice*. The procuracy also retained its longstanding power to submit cassation protests (appeals) against "unlawful or unfounded court decisions," including acquittals.

The 1992 "Law on the Procuracy of the Russian Federation" also retained the full gamut of the procuracy's powers of general supervision over the legality of activities of local administrative agencies, ministries, departments, economic and control agencies, enterprises, institutions, organizations and associations, military administrative organs, political organizations and movements, and officials, as well as local soviets. Heavy lobbying by Stepankov and his deputies in the Russian Procuracy apparently led the deputies to ignore the provision in the draft constitution for the creation of a People's Ombudsman.

The "Law on the Procuracy of the Russian Federation" was an attempt to balance the demands for greater judicial independence with the tradition of a centralized, unified, and powerful procuracy with broad-ranging authority to supervise compliance with the laws of the central government. While procuratorial authority over the courts and the conduct of criminal investigations was substantially reduced, the procuracy retained much of its earlier scope and power. However, passage of the new "Law on the Procuracy of the Russian Federation" did not resolve the conflict over the proper position of the procuracy within the Russian legal system. In the course of drafting a new constitution in 1992 and 1993, that question was revisited and once again resulted in sharp differences of opinion within the legal community.

The Debate Intensifies

As the debate over the role of the procuracy unfolded throughout 1992 and 1993, two dominant positions emerged—one favoring the maintenance of a strong, centralized, and hierarchical procuracy with a wide array of functions, and the other continuing to support the emasculation of the procuracy and the corresponding strengthening of the courts. The latter group argued that as long as the procuracy dominated the legal system, the courts could never develop the legitimacy and independence nor receive the resources they needed to become strong. Consequently, proponents of expanding the role of the courts, such as Minister of Justice Fedorov, usually favored stripping the procuracy of all of its functions except the prosecution of cases in court.

While proponents of judicial reform have stressed the need to subdue the procuracy for the sake of the courts, the procuracy chiefs have urged the preservation of its central place in the Russian legal system and the importance of its retaining broad-ranging powers. In April 1993 when a draft law was circulated calling for the creation of an independent investigatory agency, officials of the Procuracy, the Ministry of Internal Affairs, and the Ministry for Security (former KGB) quickly convened a press conference to voice their opposition.[24] The same day they filed a case with the Constitutional Court, challenging the legality of the proposed reduction of their investigatory authority. Eventually the Parliament did pass a law creating the State Committee on Investigations, but as of 1996 the Committee had not been established. One reason is that the Parliament failed to provide any appropriations or staff for the agency to function. Another is the still pending constitutional challenge to the establishment of the State Committee on Investigations.

The procuracy marshaled even greater resistance to attempts to abolish or curtail its powers of general supervision, and this debate goes to the heart of the future of the Russian legal system. Both Stepankov and numerous other procurators have argued that court review of individual grievances is too complicated and costly for average citizens. Deputy Procurator General N. A. Karavaev insisted that at present the courts lack the necessary personnel and resources to handle large numbers of cases.[25] In many districts of Russia today there is only one judge, and in some remote places one judge must hear the entire caseload (criminal, civil, and family matters) of three districts.[26] Furthermore, Karavaev observed that many of the newly-elected judges are young and inexperienced. He estimated that the development of an adequate court system prepared to replace the procuracy in handling cases against officials would take at least 15 to 20 years.[27]

The procuracy chiefs have a point. Currently the procuracy receives and reviews more than 100,000 complaints from citizens, relating in the main to environmental pollution, housing disputes, pension rights, labor conflicts, and the imposition of administrative fines.[28] The review of these complaints results in approximately 13,000 formal protests every year, and many thousands more cases find resolution in "informal protests" by prosecutors.

Permitting all these complaints to be heard by the courts would further overload the courts, which already are experiencing a seven-month back-log of cases.[29] In contrast to judicial review of citizens' complaints, general supervision by the procuracy has the advantages of being free, fast, and familiar.

Although in 1992-93 the procuracy fended off attacks on its supervisory powers, it did reluctantly acquiesce in 1993 to one of the reformers' dreams, the introduction of jury trials. Deputy Procurator General Orlov characterized prosecutors as "uniformly opposed" to them. According to Orlov, jury trials lacked an established tradition in Russian legal history, 1864 to 1917 notwithstanding. Moreover, Orlov insisted, jury trials would lengthen the hearing of court cases and have the potential for introducing biases and non-professional attitudes of citizens in serious cases. Orlov criticized especially the introduction of jury trials on an "experimental" basis in nine regions of Russia. "They say they are just an experiment, but how can you experiment with someone's life in a murder trial? If the court releases a murderer it is bad, and if the court convicts an innocent man, it is bad, too. The decision of the court must be professional."[30] When Karelia was added to the list of regions to be included in the jury trial experiment in 1995, that republic's procurator, Vladimir M. Bogdanov, indicated a desire to decline participation in the program, but felt pressured to cooperate.[31]

In contrast, judges and defense attorneys have enthusiastically embraced the jury trial program because it offers the possibility of strengthening the independence of the courts and places advocates on an equal footing with prosecutors.[32]

The Politicization of the Procuracy

Having been compelled to cooperate with the jury trial experiment despite reservations, Russian procurators in 1993 were anxious to protect, as much as possible, the procuracy's political clout and powers in other spheres. The principal strategy for furthering these goals was to seek broad political support by capitalizing on the disturbing increase in crime, especially organized crime. Repeatedly during 1992 procurators had argued that the crisis conditions in the country required a strong, centralized agency to insure legality—a role traditionally played by the procuracy. The procuracy's law-and-order agenda, however, tended to align the organization with conservative forces in the Russian Parliament opposed to President Yeltsin. Thus, throughout 1992 and 1993 the procuracy found itself pulled into the stand-off between the President and the Parliament.

Despite Procurator General Stepankov's earlier reputation as a pro-reform supporter of Yeltsin, after the 1991 coup he gravitated to a more status quo or conservative position. Rather than promoting reforms, he used procuratorial powers more often to block reformist policies of Yeltsin and others when those policies lacked proper legislative foundation. This law-and-order orientation of the procuracy found allies among conservative deputies in the Russian Parliament, notably Parliamentary Speaker Ruslan Khasbulatov and Vice President Aleksandr Rutskoi.

In Nizhnyi Novgorod (Gorky), St. Petersburg, Moscow, and Kazan, regional and district procurators successfully protested actions of provincial governors, mayors, or other prominent political officials. Even high-level policies were reversed by procuratorial protests. For example, Stepankov's office issued a protest against the order of the State Bank calling in all ruble notes issued prior to 1993.[33]

Perhaps because it used its powers to challenge the legality (and even the constitutionality) of the acts of executive officers (most of whom were Yeltsin appointees), the procuracy earned the reputation as a fundamentally conservative, anti-reform institution with close links to the Russian Parliament. This characterization is only partly correct. To be sure, procurators did protest against actions related to reform, but they had a valid reason. Procurators from Stepankov down to the provincial and local levels repeatedly objected to the way that political and policy changes outstripped the pace of enacting new legislation. Thus, in the case of Boris Nemtsov's grand scheme for privatizing state property in Nizhnyi Novgorod, the procurator's office correctly protested on the grounds that as yet there was no *legal* basis for him to undertake such a program. Legislation on privatizing most large enterprises in Russia languished in the Russian Parliament. As long as procurators were charged with seeing that all legislative and executive decrees and actions conformed to the law and as long as that law lagged behind political developments, the procuracy inevitably acted as a conservative force blunting the reform process. Deputy Procurator General Karavaev succinctly summarized the dilemma:

> It may be true that the Constitution and laws lag behind public opinion and that resolving the Constitutional dilemma may be impossible without first resolving the gridlock between the President and Parliament. However, to conclude that this Constitution is no longer valid and not to defend it and other laws of the country would lead to anarchy and that is not a viable answer.[34]

On the other hand, this conservative orientation coupled with Stepankov's desire to preserve the status and power of the procuracy also resulted in the forging of close ties to Yeltsin's opponents in the Russian Parliament. In November 1992 Stepankov convened a special emergency conference of procurators to express serious concerns over the ongoing confrontation between the legislative and executive branches of the Russian Government. In his opening remarks Stepankov decried the rapid rise in violent crime. He went on to argue for the maintenance of a centralized, strong, and independent procurator's office, calling it "the backbone of the Russian Federation."[35] He denounced attempts by some deputies and members of the President's office to limit the powers of the procuracy and reduce its functions to simply prosecuting cases in court. He complained that the procuracy had become so marginalized that it was not even mentioned in the latest draft constitution worked out by the Supreme Soviet's Constitutional Commission:

> Given the unstable political situation, the incipient market, the upsurge in crime, and the aggravation of relations between nationalities, only the procurator's office can be a reliable guarantor of law and order and legality. It follows from this that procurators' powers must be broadened and that they must be given real assistance in material-technical and personnel support.[36]

Ruslan Khasbulatov, Speaker of the Russian Parliament and leading opponent of President Yeltsin, also spoke at the conference, echoing Stepankov's sentiments.

As the dispute between President Yeltsin and the Russian Parliament worsened in 1993, Stepankov and the Russian Procuracy sided increasingly with the legislative branch. On 22 April the Prosecutor's office announced that it had brought criminal charges against two of Yeltsin's top associates, State Secretary Gennadi Burbulis and Defense Minister Pavel Grachev. The charges accused the two of illegally selling military property abroad.[37] Less than one week later, Stepankov urged the Russian Parliament to create a special commission to investigate corruption among government officials. Although the commission was made accountable to both the Procuracy and the Parliament, it received special powers to conduct inquiries, interrogations, searches of and the removal of documents from government offices, including those of the staff of the President and the Council of Ministers. Stepankov admitted that the legislative branch was not immune to corruption, but acknowledged that the commission's attention would focus on the President's office and other executive branch agencies.[38] The principal targets of the probe were two Yeltsin aides: First Deputy Prime Minister

Vladimir Shumeiko and head of the Federal Information Center, Mikhail Poltoranin. Shumeiko was the chief architect of Yeltsin's defense conversion program, while Poltoranin was widely blamed by conservative parliamentary deputies for supposedly biased television reporting prior to the presidential referendum of 25 April 1993.

The increasingly partisan role of the procuracy in the confrontation between President Yeltsin and his adversaries in the Russian Parliament seriously undermined the agency's credibility and jeopardized its chances for survival under the Presidential constitution. In fact, the first presidential draft constitution, circulated during the summer of 1993, limited the procuracy to three functions: the supervision of the legality of criminal investigations (but not the actual conduct of those investigations); the prosecution of cases in court; and the challenging in court of illegal acts of state bodies.[39] In other words, the procuracy would be stripped of its power of general supervision. Furthermore, the presidential draft constitution granted to courts the power and responsibility to supervise the legality of procuratorial activity, a reversal of the earlier situation where the procuracy supervised the courts.

Perhaps the biggest blow to the status of the procuracy occurred in late May 1993 when the Military Collegium of the Russian Federation Supreme Court ruled that Procurator General Stepankov and Deputy Procurator General Evgeni Lisov committed "flagrant violations of the law while investigating the criminal case involving the Committee for the State of Emergency."[40] The court indefinitely suspended the trial of the August 1991 coup plotters, pending the assignment of new prosecutors in the case. Stepankov and Lisov had published a book, *The Kremlin Conspiracy: The Investigation's Version*, that appeared prior to the trial and which, according to the court, violated the constitutional principle of presumption of innocence. The court's ruling was called courageous by political commentators,[41] and, according to the *Izvestiia* commentator, it boded well for the future of Russian justice overall, if not for the procuracy specifically:

> One is surprised at the scrupulousness with which the military judges are following procedural rules governing the hearing of a criminal case. And it is even more striking that, for perhaps the first time, we are seeing a court ruling that makes direct references to the Constitution, human rights, the presumption of innocence, and judicial independence. It is an impressive example of Russian justice.[42]

This court ruling, together with Stepankov's siding with the Russian Parliament against Yeltsin in September and October 1993, led the President to insist on Stepankov's resignation, and within days Aleksei I. Kazannik, a law professor from Omsk University, was named Procurator General. Kazannik had no prior experience in the procuracy; his expertise was in environmental and administrative law. He did, however, have strong ties to Boris Yeltsin. In 1990, in the elections to the Russian Supreme Soviet, Boris Yeltsin narrowly missed being elected. Kazannik volunteered to relinquish his seat to the veteran politician, who was soon chosen chairman of the legislature. Not surprisingly, Kazannik's appointment as Procurator General was widely viewed by procurators and legal scholars as a "reward" for his display of loyalty, and they expected him to be a figurehead.

In fact, Kazannik surprised many within the procuracy. During his first month in office he called for the resignation of half of Stepankov's top assistants. Lisov was reassigned deputy procurator of the city of Moscow.[43] Kazannik also ordered a review of all procuratorial employees, even down to the local level, to assess how well they were performing their jobs.

Although he had no previous experience in the procuracy, Kazannik was outspoken in supporting the preservation of the procuracy's central role in the legal system. Deputy Procurator General Orlov reported on Kazannik's first speech to the staff of the procuracy upon assuming office:

> I have never been a defender of bureaucratic interests. I have always considered the general interests of society. But now, for the first time, I will act to protect and defend the interests of the procuracy because those interests are the interests of the general population.[44]

The Deputy Procurator added his own voice to the defense of the institution. According to him, the "radical reformers" saw the procuracy as an instrument of repression from the former totalitarian regime. His response: "Who then did not serve the totalitarian system?"[45]

During the fall of 1993, Kazannik mounted a strenuous campaign to preserve the procuracy's status in various drafts of a new constitution that were circulating in the capital. When the final presidential draft of the constitution was set to limit the procuracy's powers to prosecuting criminals, Kazannik lobbied Yeltsin directly and within one day the section delineating (and cutting) the procuracy's powers was dropped. Kazannik had argued successfully for the ommission of any listing of procuratorial powers in the Constitution, which meant that the procuracy would continue to be governed by the 1992 "Law on the Procuracy."[46] When asked whether they anticipated the need for a new law on the procuracy in light of the approval of Yeltsin's constitution, procurators replied that the newly-elected parliament would be presented with the urgent need to draft and ratify many new pieces of legislation and that a new law on the procuracy would be relatively low priority. This suited the interests of the procuracy, since its chiefs feared that any re-opening of the question of the procuracy's jurisdiction and powers would result in a constriction of those powers.[47]

The Procuracy in the Second Russian Republic

From the break-up of the USSR in 1991, the procuracy was engaged in a two-level game. In the realm of "high politics" the procuracy became embroiled in political struggles between the Duma and President Yeltsin, the murder of Listiev, the dismissal of Moscow police chief Ponomarev, and the Mavrodi corruption scandal. According to its accusers, the procuracy has been engaged in politically motivated criminal investigations of Vice President Aleksandr Rutskoi, Yeltsin aide Gennadi Burbulis, and even the producers of the satirical television show "*Kukli*" ("Puppets"). The effect of these political involvements was to undermine much of the legitimacy that the procuracy possessed. In several instances, it appears, President Yeltsin used the procuracy to further his political interests. Yeltsin's misuse of the procuracy became clearest with the forced resignation of Kazannik in 1994.

At a lower level, the procuracy remained at the center of controversy surrounding the future configuration of the Russian legal system. Advocates of judicial reform have tended to champion the cause of the courts—expanding their jurisdiction, guaranteeing their independence, and increasing their competence and funding. These same scholars and jurists often view the procuracy as a retrograde institution of coercion, with deep roots in the Stalinist system, and as the central, domineering institution in the legal system.

The procuracy again entered a high-level political squabble in early 1994. The State Duma passed a bill of amnesty that stopped prosecutions against and released from custody the organizers of the October 1993 violence in Moscow even before trial. President Yeltsin maintained that the action constituted a pardon, a power that only he enjoyed, and ordered Kazannik "to continue the detention" of the persons charged with organizing the coup. Kazannik responded that the Procurator General's office had no right to interpret legal acts, but must carry them out.[48] Kazannik resigned on 28 February 1994 rather than accede to President Yeltsin's wishes. He was replaced as Acting Procurator General by 36-year-old Aleksei Iliushenko. Iliushenko's 15-year career in the procuracy had begun in Krasnoiarsk territory, and he had been elevated to the RSFSR Procuracy under Stepankov before being appointed to the President's Oversight Administration. For a long time, the Federal Assembly refused to accept Kazannik's resignation and twice the body refused to confirm Iliushenko's nomination. During the stormy confirmation debate, it was repeatedly noted that Iliushenko had served as the head of the Interdepartmental Commission on Combating Corruption, the body that had investigated charges against former Vice President Rutskoi.

Faced with lack of confirmation of Iliushenko's appointment, Yeltsin had two options: either appoint someone else or permit Iliushenko to serve indefinitely as Acting Procurator General. He chose the latter option. In this reduced capacity, Iliushenko was prohibited from appointing local and regional procurators. In other respects, however, he undertook an active role in restructuring the procuracy and mobilizing forces in the war on crime.

Meanwhile in late 1994 discussion resumed over two new draft laws on the procuracy.[49] The first was an official draft law, composed in the President's office with considerable input from the procuracy. Not surprisingly, it retained the institution's broad powers and even strengthened the role of the procuracy in enforcing presidential decrees. Article 23 obliged the procuracy to report to the President any action by a governing body that contradicts the constitution or laws of the Russian federation. The draft also gave procurators the power to supervise the implementation of laws, presidential decrees, and the normative acts of various legislative and executive bodies. The draft keeps for the procuracy the power to supervise criminal investigations and places of detention. Procurators were still permitted to participate in civil cases and could appeal either civil or criminal decisions of the court. The presidential draft, like its predecessor, empowered procurators to attend sessions of either chamber of the Federal Assembly and lower collective bodies—both executive and legislative.

One innovation in the draft (Article 7) assigned the procuracy responsibility for coordinating the activities of the Ministry of Internal Affairs, the counterintelligence service, tax police, customs service, and other law enforcement agencies in combating crime. Just what this would entail was not elucidated. (This responsibility had belonged in the 1960s-1980s to the USSR Procuracy.)

The official draft split the procuracy's traditional function of general supervision between Article 9 (which empowers procurators to look into complaints and suggestions from citizens that may signal violations of laws) and Article 22 (empowering the procuracy to protest illegal actions by officials to the responsible agency or official or to pursue the matter in court).

The other, or alternative, draft federal law "On the Procuracy of the Russian Federation," written by two senior legal scholars, both reformers, based at the Institute of State and Law, Valerii M. Savitskii and Aleksandr M. Larin, was also circulated in early 1995, and in March was sent to the Committee on Legislation and Judicial-Legal Reform of the State Duma for its comments and revisions before presentation to the full assembly. In an explanatory note to the draft the authors argued that a new law was necessitated by the adoption of a new constitution and the ratification of "The Conception of Judicial Reform in the USSR."

Reacting to the surge in violent crime and in particular the murder of the journalist Vladislav Litsev and other noted figures, the authors proposed refocusing the procuracy on combating crime. The procuracy would retain responsibility for guidance (*rukovodstvo*) of investigators, but would not conduct investigations except in a few specified types of cases. The principal function of the procurator would be to prosecute criminal cases in court.

Larin and Savitskii contended that in recent years the procuracy has moved further and further away from the fight against crime. In the majority of criminal cases procurators no longer appeared at trial, on the assumption that the incriminating evidence contained in the report of the preliminary investigation would secure a conviction.

In particular, the authors objected—as one might anticipate—to the large share of the procuracy's time and resources devoted to general supervision. Larin and Savitskii depicted that old *bête noir* of judicial reformers as an intrusion by the procuracy into the work of legislative and executive bodies. Accordingly, Article 3 of their draft law, on the purposes of the procuracy, omitted any mention of general supervision and confined the main thrust of the procuracy to matters related to criminal prosecution. To be sure, Article 48 of the draft law did retain for the procuracy on a temporary basis the power to receive complaints from citizens and issue binding protests against normative acts and individual decisions of governmental bodies or officials deemed to violate the rights and freedoms of citizens. But this power was to last only until an office of the Ombudsman *(Upolnomochennyi po pravo-zasheshcha)* was created. The implication was that if this office were not established, the procuracy would continue the reactive side of general supervision, that is, the processing of citizen complaints against officials. However, the Larin-Savistskii draft left no place at all for the procuracy to undertake any supervision on its own initiative. No longer would the procuracy serve as the enforcer who verified "the full, complete, and unswerving compliance with and implementation of law."[50]

Savitskii and Larin also denounced as an "atavism" the practice of the procurator's reviewing civil cases, especially where the interests of the State are not directly affected.

Finally, in the Larin and Savitskii draft the procuracy would retain responsibility to review complaints and petitions of prisoners and others held in confinement. Operational supervision of prisons and other correctional facilities would fall to other bodies.

Both the alternative and the official drafts assign to the procuracy the responsibility for coordinating the work of the Ministry of Internal Affairs, counter-intelligence agency, tax police, customs service, and other law enforcement agencies in combating crime.

Apart from the big issue of the retention of full supervisory powers of the procuracy, the drafts differed on two further points. The presidential draft sought to extend procuratorial supervision to presidential decrees of normative significance, of which the Larin-Savitskii draft made no mention. And the Larin-Savitskii draft sought to remove from the procuracy its existing right to launch or take part in civil cases.[51]

Although the principals may not have realized it, the two adversaries in the latest phase of the debate over the role of the procuracy had gravitated closer together. At least Larin, if not the other drafters of the "Conception of Judicial Reform," recognized the propriety for the time being of procuratorial review of citizens' complaints against government agencies and officials. For their part, the chiefs of the procuracy accepted the need to focus more attention and resources on crime, as long as they retained most of their supervisory powers.

In November 1995, after a tortuous course in the legislature, a revised verison of the official draft law on the procuracy finally became law. Once again, the procuracy had fended off a challenge to its distinctive role and powers. In the law the procuracy retained its full supervisory powers, and its right to take part in civil cases, but it did not gain the duty to supervise implementation of presidential decrees.[52]

The decision to preserve most of the functions of the procuracy made sense for the short run, but, in my view, the most workable model for the future might be that of the American attorney general. Attorneys general are normally the highest-ranking law enforcement officials in a given jurisdiction with primary responsibility for supervising the prosecution of criminal cases at all levels. The powers of attorneys general are, however, not restricted to criminal prosecution. Attorneys general routinely consult on legislation, issue advisory opinions on normative acts and decisions of subordinate legislative and executive bodies, look into complaints arising from the decisions or actions of government officials and agencies, including those dealing with the detention and incarceration of offenders. Attorneys general also represent the state in civil suits where the interests of the state pertain.

Finally, I would emphasize that the Russian Procuracy does incorporate the valuable role of ombudsman as an official to whom citizens may turn for redressing grievances arising from administrative actions. Advocates of the court argue that all such grievances should be pursued in the courts, and if the procuracy is removed from its dominant position in the Russian legal system it will fall to the courts to fill this void. It remains uncertain, however, whether the courts are up to the task, given the absence of a history of courts with the power and independence to constrain the state and the low level of public awareness of the law and willingness of citizens to seek judicial protection of their rights and interests.

The recent disputes and partisan wrangling over the functions of the procuracy and its place in the emerging Russian legal system illustrate ways in which the procuracy and the rest of the Russian legal system have become politicized. The politicization has complicated the process of reaching a consensus on the future role, powers, and functions of the procuracy. For radical judicial reformers of the mid-1990s the supervisory powers of the procuracy represented a *bête noir* and key obstacle to the development of strong and independent courts, and it was unlikely that they would give up completely their efforts to strip the procuracy of at least part of its supervisory role.

Still, the gradual convergence in views among the protagonists in the long debate over the procuracy may prove more important than the remaining differences. The acknowledgment by the procuracy of the need to devote more attention to combating crime and the recognition by the judicial reformers of the need for some procuratorial supervision suggest that a compromise might result someday. I can envisage a convergence between the two sides to a point not dissimilar to that of the attorney general with the additional powers of a state ombudsman. Such a position is highly desirable because it would leave much of the procuracy intact to fight crime, while not undermining the courts. It would present citizens with a choice whether to seek redress of their grievances through the courts or procuratorial protests. Finally, such a compromise would end the partisan wrangling that has characterized the past decade of legal reform, enabling the procuracy and the courts to get on with the business of law enforcement and justice in Russia.

Author's note: The author wishes to acknowledge support from the National Council for Soviet and East European Research and the University of South Carolina that made this research possible.

Notes

1. See Sergei Kazantsev, "The Judicial Reform of 1864 and the Procuracy in Russia," chapter 3 in this volume.

2. *Ibid.*

3. Cited in S. G. Berezovskaia, "Proshloe i nastoiashchee obshchego nadzora," *Sotsialisticheskaia zakonnost'*, 1937, No. 6: 24-27.

4. M. Braginskii and N. Lagovier, *Revoliutsionnaia zakonnost' i prokurorskii nadzor v selskokhoziaistvennykh politicheskikh kampaniiakh* (Moscow, 1933).

5. On the procuracy's role in the terror see Peter H. Solomon, Jr., *Soviet Criminal Justice under Stalin* (New York and London, 1996), chapter 7. On the attempt to restore general supervision, see Glenn Morgan, *Soviet Administrative Legality* (Stanford, CA, 1962), chapter 7.

6. *Pravda*, 12 April 1955: 1.

7. See Gordon B. Smith, *The Soviet Procuracy and the Supervision of Administration* (Alphen aan den Rijn, 1978).

8. *Ibid.*, 88-109.

9. L. A. Nikolaeva, "Teoreticheskie i prakticheskie problemy obespecheniia zakonnosti v sovetskom gosudarstvennom upravlenii organami prokuratury i suda," unpublished doctoral dissertation (Leningrad State University, 1974), 181.

10. This opinion was expressed by virtually all local and regional procurators interviewed for this research project.

11. Nikolaeva, "Teoreticheskie i prakticheskie problemy," 181.

12. A key source on the attitudes and aspirations of procurators was a survey of 200 procurators in eight regions of northwestern Russia conducted in late 1989 under the auspices of the Laboratory for the Study of Procuracy Supervision, St. Petersburg Law Faculty, and directed by Prof. Lidiia Nikolaeva. Confirmation was provided, *inter alia*, in the following consultations: with Vladimir I. Eremenko, Procurator of St. Petersburg (12 October 1992); Aleksandr I. Bastrykin, Director of the Institute for the Training of Procuratorial Investigators, Leningrad (11 June 1991); Saifkhan Kh. Nafeev, Procurator of Tatarstan, Kazan (6 April 1993); Aleksandr I. Fedotov, Procurator of Nizhnyi Novgorod (7 April 1993); N. A. Karavaev, Head of the Administration of Legal Security, Procuracy of the Russian Federation (9 April 1993). According to Eremenko, in 1990 procuratorial supervision was broadened *de facto* to include the KGB. In Leningrad an official was assigned to this task but he lacked to powers to do it effectively (consultation with Eremenko, 12 October 1992). For further analysis of the procuracy in the perestroika period,

see Gordon B. Smith, *Reforming the Russian Legal System* (Cambridge, 1996), 109-115.

13. Sergei Pashin, Preface to "The Conception of Judicial Reform in the RSFSR," *Statutes and Decisions* 30, no. 2 (March-April 1994): 8.

14. *Ibid.*: 7.

15. *Ibid.*: 8.

16. *Ibid.*: 30.

17. *Ibid.*: 52.

18. For example, consultation with Deputy Procurator General Marat M. Orlov, Moscow, 23 November 1993; and K. F. Skvortsov, Deputy Director, Institute of the Procuracy, Moscow, 22 November 1993.

19. *Rossiiskaia gazeta*, 11 October 1992: 3.

20. Boris Yeltsin's career prior to 1985 was spent in the Communist Party apparatus of Sverdlovsk where he worked closely with Stepankov.

21. Order No. 12 of the Procuracy of the RSFSR, 27 May 1991.

22. "Proekt zakon o prokurature RSFSR" (1991), 2-3.

23. Zakon RSFSR, "O prokurature Rossiiskoi Federatsii," (1992), *Rossiiskaia gazeta*, 18 fevraliia 1992, 3-5, Article 1.

24. ITAR-TASS, 29 April 1993.

25. Consultation with N. A. Karavaev, Deputy Procurator General of Russia, Moscow, 9 April 1993.

26. *Ibid.*

27. *Ibid.*

28. Consultation with Konstantin F. Skvortsov, Deputy Director, Institute of the Procuracy, Moscow, 11 November 1993.

29. *Ibid.*

30. Consultation with Deputy Procurator General Marat M. Orlov, Moscow, 23 November 1993.

31. Consultation with Vladimir M. Bogdanov, Procurator of the Karelian Republic, Petrozavodsk, 29 July 1994.

32. This impression was obtained from numerous interviews with judges and advocates participating in training sessions as the Law Academy of the Ministry of Justice in Moscow (November 1993).

33. Reported on ITAR-TASS, 26 July 1993.

34. Consultation with N. A. Karavaev, Deputy Procurator General, Moscow, 4 April 1993.

35. Cited in *Izvestiia*, 25 November 1992: 2.

36. *Ibid.*

37. ITAR-TASS, 22 April 1993.

38. Reported in *Izvestiia*, 29 April 1993: 2.

39. *Izvestiia*, 30 April 1993: 3-5.

40. *Izvestiia*, 20 May 1993: 5.

41. Igor Achildiev, "Three Against All the Prosecutor's Men," *Megapolis-Express*, 26 May 1993: 5; and Fiodor Burlatskii, "Konstitutsionnyi protsess: nachalo reform," in *Nezavisimaia gazeta*, 30 June 1993: 5.

42. *Izvestiia*, 20 May 1993: 5.

43. Consultation with Deputy Procurator General Marat M. Orlov, Moscow, 24 November 1993.

44. *Ibid.*

45. *Ibid.*

46. This account came from a consultation with Professor Aleksandr M. Larin, Institute of State and Law, Moscow, 25 November 1993.

47. For example, consultation with Deputy Procurator General Marat M. Orlov, Moscow, 23 November 1993.

48. *Izvestiia*, 1 March 1994: 2.

49. For texts of the draft laws, see "Proekt Federal'nyi zakon 'O Prokurature Rossiiskoi Federatsii," n.d. (1995), official draft in two editorial versions; "Proekt federal'nyi zakon 'O Prokurature Rossiiskoi Federatsii: vnbositsia deputatami Gosudarstvennoi Dumy B. A. Zolotuzhinym i V. V. Pokhmelkinym," (1995); "Vypiska iz protokola No. 121 zasedaniia soveta gosudarstvennoi dumy Federalnogo Sobraniia Rossiiskoi Federatsii ot 13 marta 1993, item 59 "O Proekte federalnogo zakona 'O Prokurature . . .'"; "Poiasnitel'naia zapiska k proekty Federal'nogo zakona 'O Prokurature Rossiiskoi Federatsii'." For an interview with Boris Zolotukhin explaining the alternative draft, see "Kakaia prokuratura nuzhna Rossii?" *Iuridicheskii vestnik*, 1995, No. 15-16: 6.

50. The phrase was part of the traditional description of general supervision under the 1955 law on the Procuracy.

51. "O vnesenii i zmenenii i dopolnenii v zakon R. F. 'O prokurature R. F.'," Federalnyi zakon ot 17 noiabria 1995, *Sobranie zakonodatelstva RF*, No. 47 (20 noiabria 1995), st. 4472, 8330-8353.

52. *Ibid.*

16

DRAWING UPON THE PAST: JURY TRIALS IN MODERN RUSSIA

Sarah J. Reynolds

In examining the many legal reforms currently underway in the Russian Federation, the temptation to draw comparisons and look for parallels with the reform efforts of the past is almost irresistible. In part, this is occasioned by a general assumption that a society learns from and responds to its past experiences and that an evaluation of reform efforts must, therefore, include some consideration of the relevant history. With regard to Russia's current legal reforms, concern for the historical context is heightened by a history of sweeping reforms of the law, involving not only change in substantive and procedural legal rules but also wholesale replacement of existing legal institutions within very short time frames.[1] Moreover, the references to the need for Russia to "return" to former principles and "rejoin" the international community that were common at the start of the current reform, as well as the constant debate over the importance of Russia's own unique history and requirements, would suggest a strong focus in reform efforts on the interpretation and adaptation of the past.

In particular, since allusions to such "return" and "rejoinder" are not generally made in reference to Soviet-era legal policies, the expected focus would be on pre-Revolutionary patterns and reform experiences, especially those of the 1860s. One might thus expect to find in the mirror of present discourse on legal reform an interesting and important image of the past and its influence on modern Russian concepts, attitudes, and policy choices. And yet, across a broad spectrum of current law reform activity, the pursuit of a clear reflection of the pre-Revolutionary reform history and its lasting effects—in the form of open comparisons and explicit borrowing or rejection of prior practices—does not meet with easy success. Beyond the level of broad statements and political rhetoric, direct reference to pre-Revolutionary experience is relatively rare. The explanation for this may lie, in part, in the subject matter of the most prominent areas of legal reform, as well as in the conception of law that informs the process. A large proportion of recent law reform activity has been directed either toward the wholesale re-creation of the Russian government along the broad lines of Western constitutionalism or toward the reformation of the Russian economy to approximate the model of the modern regulated market. In these processes, references to the past are more likely to concern the more recent Soviet patterns and models from which the reform must build. The common paradigms of internal governance of the nation-state and the standard structures and institutions of the regulated market economy, the duplication or approximation of which have been widely perceived as compulsory for Russia's survival, have altered so substantially in the intervening century that the details of pre-Revolutionary models of economic regulation and state structure are generally seen as being of limited relevance to the creation of modern systems.[2] Comparisons with historical experience may also be discouraged by a prevailing view of the role of law in society as primarily that of a tool for the production of desired objects and results (e.g., an efficiently functioning legislature, an active capital market) rather than as an expression of the fundamental values of Russian society.

The recent introduction, or re-introduction, of jury trials in Russian criminal procedure is an exception.[3] The influence of the 1864 judicial reform in the post-Soviet re-creation of trial by jury appears to go well beyond its impact on the broader development of Russian legal concepts or a loose reliance on the pre-Revolutionary experience. The drafters of the jury legislation in 1991-93 used the 1864 judicial reform consciously and deliberately as a model for the structure of the post-Soviet jury, the mode of its introduction, and the details of its procedures. In some instances, the drafters cited the pre-Revolutionary provisions and experience in answer to criticism of the draft legislation, and advocates of the legislation made repeated reference to this historical experience, especially in the course of the debates surrounding its passage. Some apparent differences appear to be the result of alterations of the model made in order to avoid problems experienced in the implementation of jury procedures in the tsarist period. In other words, the Judicial Reform of 1864 served as a source both for the model of the jury in post-Soviet Russia and for practical lessons that might help to improve that model. In fact, the very idea of re-introducing the jury and its central place in plans for judicial reform may have stemmed from the reformers' awareness and evaluation of the experience of 1864. The strong and explicit focus on the historical record in the development of the modern Russian jury trial provides an opportunity to examine how history can enter into and affect the reform of law in a later period.

The Jury as the Key to Reform

Already in 1989 the idea of reviving the jury entered discussions among reform-minded jurists in the USSR, and in November a provision was added to the new USSR Fundamental Principles on Court Organization authorizing governments of the republics to introduce some kind of trial by jury for the most serious crimes. The only republic to act on this window of opportunity was the Russian Federation, but it started to do so only as the USSR itself was in full disintegration.[4]

The first official approval of the idea of including jury trial as a significant part of Russian judicial reform came in October 1991, when the Supreme Soviet of the Russian Federation approved the "Conception of Judicial Reform." The Conception, a general blueprint for the reform of the judicial system, was submitted by the President of the RSFSR to the Supreme Soviet and confirmed by that body.[5] The Conception was written between summer 1990 and summer 1991 by a group of experts composed primarily of specialists in criminal law and particularly criminal procedure, and headed by noted criminal defense lawyer Boris A. Zolotukhin, then a deputy of the RSFSR Supreme Soviet and the deputy chair of its Committee on Legislation.[6] The apparent task of the document is to address the reform of the courts and judiciary. But it comments as well on the reform of the entire legal system, from legislative drafting to the execution of court judgments.

The authors diagnose the primary ills of Soviet justice as overly severe laws that fail to reflect the values and morals of the public, use of the judicial system by the state for political ends and social control, excessive power in the hands of the procuracy with respect to criminal investigations and preliminary proceedings, and an alienation of the general public from the justice system. Although some separate comment is provided on civil disputes and other aspects of judicial reform, the main critique focuses on criminal justice and applies only by analogy to the resolution of civil disputes. Moreover, the remedies proposed for these shortcomings—remodeling of the procurator's role on that of a prosecutor, judicial control of preliminary process, and especially the institution of jury trials—would affect civil procedure only tangentially. The composition of the group of experts who wrote the Conception assured that the reform of criminal law and procedure would stand at the center of the discussion of judicial reform as a whole.[7]

Perhaps in part due to its special concern with the criminal process, the Conception shows a distinct perspective on the political and philosophical sources of judicial problems. Although the main text of the Conception avoids explicit mention of the Revolution, communism, socialism, or particular political figures, the association of the problems of the justice system with the Soviet regime is plain. Many of the standard critiques of the Soviet legal system, which had previously been voiced in both Western and unofficial East European/Soviet sources, and which were increasingly in vogue at the time in Russian political circles, are repeated in the Conception. While direct references to "Soviet" state power or political ideologies is absent, there is no doubt about the thrust of the critique. For example, the document places the blame for the deformation of the courts directly on the misconception and misuse of judicial power by a state that was "a hostile force in relation to civil society and the individual"[8]—a reference to a common critique of the Soviet system overall. This identification of the problems of the Russian judicial system as the result of fundamentally flawed concepts of the state, law, and justice prevailing in the Soviet period encouraged the search for alternative institutions and practices not associated with that era, rather than for ways of altering or improving existing institutions and practices, which were in this analysis flawed in their very conception.

Even without the Conception's association of the problems of the judicial system with Soviet power, the actual content of its diagnosis of the system's flaws would have invited comparison with pre-Revolutionary judicial reform. The Conception describes the "deformation" of the judicial system in the Soviet Union as characterized, *inter alia*, by: extreme alienation of the citizenry from the bodies of the judicial system and the law-issuing authorities; perversion of the judicial system into an organ of state control over the populace, reflecting the values and desires of the state alone; an excessively and exclusively punitive character of the system, including extreme punishment for offenses not considered criminal by the public in general; corruption and a lack of professionalism and ethics among those performing legal functions; and lack of independence of the judiciary and poor conception of its proper role, reflected in the requirement that judges bear responsibility for the proper investigation of cases and the determination of fact as well as for the application of the law in individual cases.[9] Having so characterized the problem, the authors could hardly have avoided reference to the pre-Revolutionary situation and the 1864 Judicial Reform for possible alternatives and solutions. The description of the problems faced by the system bears such a strong resemblance to the standard description of the problems facing the tsarist system of justice in the middle of the nineteenth century that no Russian jurist could fail to make the connection.

The authors of the Conception, however, go further than mere reference or comparison. In prescribing a cure for the ills of the modern Russian judicial system, they suggest that the goal is something very near to a return to the system created by the 1864 Reform:

> By proposing ways to renew judicial power in Russia, by defending the idea of judicial control of preliminary proceedings, by proclaiming the principle of adversariality, by seeing in the person of the procurator above all the representative of prosecutorial power and a party in the process enjoying equal rights, and by coming out in favor of the differentiation of forms of court proceedings and the creation of a jury court, the Conception of Judicial Reform in the RSFSR restores us to the achievements of judicial culture that were reflected in the Judicial Statutes of 1864.[10]

Although the Conception advocates a wide variety of changes in the law, to achieve this goal its authors give special prominence to the re-institution of the jury. This follows both from the work's identification of the alienated, anti-democratic nature of Soviet justice as its key defect and its adoption of the 1864 Reform as a model for change.

The provision for juries in the 1864 Reform not only instituted jury trials but involved in jury service many citizens formerly without voice or representation in civic affairs. Trial by jury represented a dramatic inclusion in public life of formerly excluded and alienated persons and was widely discussed in terms of the "democratization" of the process. To be sure, commentators expressed serious concerns about the ability of many potential jurors to perform their obligations and the effect that their previous exclusion from participation in state functions might have on that performance. Due in part to this concern, the jury was a subject of great controversy and public interest. Broad reporting of trials and an apparent tendency for juries to acquit significantly more often than judges trying cases alone concentrated public attention on the workings of the legal system and fostered continued debate on the equity of the criminal laws—both of which were already the subject of public concern and political pressure at the time the Reform was enacted. In addition, several trials with strong political content attracted extensive coverage in the press, and made the jury trial a vehicle for debates over pressing political issues.[11]

Drawing from this experience, the authors of the 1991 Conception of Judicial Reform saw in the re-institution of the jury a means for involving citizens once again in the administration of justice, concentrating public attention on law reform and the actions of the state's agents, illustrating and shaping a humane and equitable public philosophy for the new Russia, and ensuring that adjudication reflected the moral convictions of the public rather than the interests of the state. The jury was characterized as the democratic conscience that would animate the machinery created by other prescribed changes in criminal procedure, maintain pressure on the legal agencies and their officials for positive change, and guide the further process of reform. The risk in such a strategy is clear. The centrality of the jury in the plan for judicial reform made the success of the jury trial in inspiring the reform essential for the grand design to work. Should the public react with apathy or even distaste to the jury experience, should the results of public participation not produce the expected spur to further reform of the law (in the form of leniency, nullifications, and rejection of evidence produced by questionable methods of investigation), or should governmental funding and support not be sufficient to develop and protect the new innovation from its critics until its effects could be felt, the expected benefits would not materialize and doubt would be cast upon the analysis underlying the plan, placing not only the jury but the remainder of the judicial reform program in question.

Historical Influence on Specific Legislative Choices

The influence of the pre-Revolutionary experience was not limited to the conception of the jury's role in judicial reform. Drafts of legislation defining a jury trial "experiment"[12] began to be developed almost immediately after the Conception was confirmed. Especially the early drafts, but also the final version of the legislation, contained many provisions that were strikingly similar to those of the pre-Revolutionary statutes in their content, construction, and language.[13] The draft legislation could not repeat verbatim all of the provisions of tsarist law, as some would have no relevance in post-Soviet Russia. Thus, pre-Revolutionary provisions allowing persons to be found unfit for jury service by a decision of a church institution or of the governing body of their social class (*soslovie*) and other provisions that exempted from jury obligations all those in service to a private person were obsolete and omitted from the new draft laws. Otherwise, categories of persons excluded from service as a juror under the draft legislation of 1991-1992 mimicked the 1864 provisions, even though there would seem to be little reason then to exclude teachers or persons serving some religious functions from modern juries.

Likewise, the procedures for the in-court jury selection process replicated many of the pre-Revolutionary provisions. In response to questioning by the judge, potential jurors are removed from the pool at the beginning of the process for reasons of a legal bar to service, knowledge of the case or relationship to participants, particular reasons for bias in the case, or (with the judge's permission) due to hardship. Thereafter, the law envisions the exercise by the parties only of peremptory challenges and these only within numerical bounds that do not threaten empanelling of a full jury out of the remaining pool.[14] This portion of the modern legislation reproduces the pre-Revolutionary provisions in order and wording to the details of instructing the judge to place the names of the jurors remaining after the parties have used their challenges "into an urn" and to select from that urn the first twelve names as jurors and the next two as alternates.[15]

Another interesting, if more complicated, reflection of the past appears in the design of the jury's task in reaching a verdict. Following the lead of the pre-Revolutionary provisions, the legislation envisioned the presentation to the jury of a set of specific questions regarding the elements of the crime alleged, including whether the alleged crime occurred at all and whether the defendant committed the actions described in the indictment.[16] In addition, the jury must also answer the separate question of whether the defendant is found to be guilty of committing the crime. This combination of questions rarely occurs in the jury rules of other states. As a rule, juries are asked either to determine whether the defendant is guilty of the crime charged or merely to answer the factual questions related to the elements of the crime under the law. The combination of the two tasks creates a situation in which the jury may state that the defendant is not "guilty" in law—that is, not deserving of criminal punishment—even concluding that he or she committed the actions described in the relevant portion of the criminal code. In other words, the set of questions posed is an invitation to jury nullification.

Even the use of more traditional forms of verdict in other countries permits jury nullification, either by a jury finding of "not guilty" or by a jury finding that an essential element of the crime is not proved. In neither of these situations, however, is the nullification revealed to observers, since neither involves a clear statement that the jury found the defendant not guilty despite satisfaction of all of the elements of the crime. The requirement in Russia that they answer the specific questions concerning the defendant's actions and intent before deciding whether to hold him to account enables the jury, if it chooses, to make its acts of nullification public knowledge.[17]

In creating the opportunity for open statements of a jury's unwillingness to apply the law in a particular case, the drafters appeared to have in mind some well-known instances in which pre-Revolutionary juries refused to convict an admittedly or clearly guilty defendant due to an unwillingness to have him or her criminally punished.[18] The results in these cases have been attributed by both Russian and foreign historians alike not only to revolutionary sentiments or resentment of authority among jurors, but also to their reaction to criminal laws that seemed unreasonable or unduly harsh. The drafters of the modern legislation hoped that it, too, would permit jurors to send a clear message to the state when they considered the criminal law too broad or severe and that jury nullifications would signal the need for changes in the criminal law.[19]

A similar use and modification of the pre-Revolutionary experience is evident in the provisions concerning leniency. As in the tsarist law, so the modern legislation gives the jury the right to decide not only whether the defendant is guilty of the crime charged, but also whether the defendant should be treated with leniency. This determination places binding restrictions on the judge's choice of punishment for defendants found guilty.[20] However, the drafters of the modern legislation refined pre-Revolutionary practice by giving the jury greater capacity to use leniency provisions to control the choice of sentence. A finding by a pre-Revolutionary jury that a defendant deserved leniency required the judge to reduce the measure of punishment assigned to the defendant by at least one "level" and permitted a reduction by two levels at the judge's discretion.[21] The jury, however, was not provided with information about the range of sentences available under the law, and a strict distinction was made between the jury's function in determining the guilt of the defendant and the judge's function in applying the law and assigning punishment.[22] In contrast, a finding by a modern jury that the defendant deserves leniency requires the judge to assign a punishment not greater than the average of the maximum and the minimum provided for the crime (often a rather limited range),[23] while a finding that the defendant deserves "special leniency" (an option not open to the pre-Revolutionary jury) requires the judge to assign a punishment lower than the minimum envisioned by the law for the relevant crime or to apply a less severe form of punishment than that envisioned by the code. Anecdotal evidence indicates that modern juries are routinely given information on the sentencing ranges envisioned by the relevant articles of the criminal code and thus have a significant amount of control over the sentencing of the defendant.[24]

The provisions empowering juries to require leniency for some convicted persons may have been intended not only to encourage fair outcomes in individual cases, but also to provide evidence—in the form of heavy use of leniency provisions—that the public found the punishments set out in criminal law to be extreme. This expectation, like the expectation that jury nullification might serve this purpose, rests in turn upon a perception of the effect of the use of similar provisions by pre-Revolutionary juries. There was a widely shared belief among pre-Revolutionary commentators and historians of the period (reflected to a varying degree in different accounts) that tsarist juries were notably more lenient than professional judges and that their decisions extending leniency to defendants served not only as a measure of compassion in individual cases but also as a demonstration that the provisions of the criminal code were not in accord with the moral sensibilities of the population.[25]

Finally, some provisions of the 1992-93 legislation departed from tsarist predecessors in what might be interpreted as an attempt to avoid problems experienced in the pre-Revolutionary use of juries. Examples of this include the provisions concerning payment of jurors and reimbursement of their expenses during their service.[26] Before the Revolution, avoidance of jury duty was commonplace, and those with sufficient money or political connections, or who were occupied with other business, were routinely able to evade their obligation to serve.[27] As a result, the bench was sometimes difficult to fill and juries were frequently composed primarily of peasants and laborers who lacked connections and were too poor to buy their release. The absence in juries of representatives of the upper and middle classes, and sometimes of any educated or even literate person, caused serious concern about the fairness and representativeness of juries and fed critics' claims that juries were incapable of evaluating the evidence presented to them. The inability of some pre-Revolutionary jurors to afford the costs of housing and food during a trial and their consequent need to beg, take handouts from strangers with unclear intentions, or spend the night on the street or in court damaged the prestige of the court and the jury, and left jurors vulnerable to corruption and outside influences.

Contemporary concerns about avoidance of jury service and the quality of jurors generated by a knowledge of the pre-Revolutionary problems were aggravated by awareness of an analogous problem in the late Soviet courts. In the 1980s and early 1990s, courts at the lower levels encountered increasing difficulty in recruiting citizens to serve as people's assessors in criminal cases. Since many cases required two assessors to sit with the judge at trial, the shortage of assessors caused some courts to delay the hearing of criminal cases for extended periods. Moreover, complaints were increasingly heard that assessors had come to comprise only persons with no other diversion or an unhealthy interest in crime and law enforcement. Not surprisingly, one of the more serious sources of opposition within the legal profession to the re-introduction of trial by jury came from those who questioned the ability of courts to secure a sufficient number of jurors on a regular basis. Citing the problems experienced with the assessors, some asked how courts unable to secure two assessors for criminal cases could be expected instead to secure fourteen jurors. This argument raised the specter of the blow to the reform process and to the judicial system in general that would be caused by the creation of a legal, or even a constitutional, right to jury trial which was followed by mass violations of the right due to an inability to fill the jury bench.

As a response to these concerns, early drafts of the current jury trial legislation required that each juror be paid two thirds of the salary of a judge on the corresponding court, calculated on a per diem basis, during the period of their service.[28] The legislation as passed reduced this amount due to budgetary concerns, but still provides jurors with one half of a judge's per diem salary for each day of their service, including time expended in jury selection procedures. Jurors who are able to show that this amount is less than their own average earnings at their regular place of work for the same period are to be paid an amount equal to their own average daily rate of pay. In addition, the juror must be reimbursed for all expenses of travel (including hotel and meals) at the same rate as a judge and reimbursed for the costs of daily travel to and from the court. When discussing the provisions for payment to jurors, the drafters of the legislation and advocates of the jury emphasized the intent to raise the status and prestige of jury service and to provide for jurors' comfort. Less publicly acknowledged were concerns about the broad geographical area served by some courts, the lack of suitable lodging and public catering facilities in many cities and towns, and the difficult financial circumstances of a significant portion of potential jurors. Both the recent experience with absent assessors and the pre-Revolutionary experiences with unrepresentative jury composition and the embarrassment of unsupported jurors could well be repeated unless adequate inducements were offered and provisions made.

A different option for addressing the problem of sufficient jurors would have been that used in most countries where jury trials are a standard feature—the institution of penalties for failure to serve when called. Jury service could have been conceptualized as a public duty, which would distinguish it from voluntary service as an elected people's assessor and would in theory allow for some measure of compulsion to be used, perhaps in addition to a small payment in recognition of the juror's service. Such a system, with its substantially reduced cost, would appear more practical for a state in economic crisis, in which the available budgetary resources were contracting while expenditure demands for reform measures increased. However, although a reliance primarily on compulsion might make budgetary sense, it could not have been considered by the drafters of the legislation in light of their view of the jury as the primary engine of renewal of the judicial system. Unwilling and resentful jurors would be poor sources of "spiritual" renewal for the law, and the public spectacle of compulsion of service would turn the hoped-for lesson in participation of citizens in the affairs of government into another lesson in the state's ability (or if unsuccessful its inability) to impose on its subjects burdens under threat. The analysis of the genesis of judicial problems contained in the Conception of Judicial Reform and the role in curing the system that reformers assigned to juries may have left the drafters with no acceptable option other than to "bribe" the public into participation through attractive payments.[29]

History in Practice: Early Experiences with the Modern Jury Trial

Nine regions were selected for the implementation of jury trials under the new legislation in the first year, beginning in late 1993 or early 1994.[30] Although the number of regions implementing such procedures was originally planned to expand quickly, budgetary problems have consistently delayed the expansion, and as of late 1996 only a few additional regions have begun jury trials. The limitation of the cases eligible for jury trial to only very serious crimes heard at regional courts (or republican supreme courts) and the small percentage of eligible defendants who request juries has resulted in a relatively small number of trials over the ensuing period. It is thus somewhat early to evaluate the effects of the jury on broad reform of the legal system or even to assess particular provisions, including those with clear historical antecedents. Nonetheless, some limited observations may be made and some tentative conclusions drawn.

Many of the specific provisions borrowed from or modeled on the nineteenth century Reform legislation seem to be functioning effectively, or at least to be occasioning no reported complaints. For example, the inclusion of historically based criteria for juror exclusion does not seem to have caused serious question and there are no records of complaint from disqualified teachers or religious functionaries. While this might indicate a continuing view of the inappropriate nature of jury service by these persons, it is more likely that there has been no party that has felt sufficiently aggrieved by their exclusion to complain. The jury selection procedure, up to and including the use of the "urn" (in practice often a dish or a wooden box), also seems to function well, occasioning little complaint and seating juries expeditiously. Likewise, the restriction of exclusion of jurors by the prosecution and defense to peremptory challenges in a number that does not threaten the attainment of the necessary number of jurors has not led to recorded complaint, and has allowed the court to seat a jury on the basis of nearly every jury pool, despite the sometimes limited number of potential jurors who actually appear.[31]

However, the procedures added to the historical model to address possible bias appear to have been used only rarely, if at all, and this may suggest a poor fit between the two. While voluntary recusals of jurors on the basis of the judge's initial questioning of jurors do sometimes occur (for example, due to the potential juror's experience of a similar crime), the open questioning of potential jurors rarely produces information concerning biases based on nationality or other sensitive factors.[32] The right of a party in a case to challenge the entire composition of the bench on the grounds of probable bias (literally "tendentiousness"), new to the modern legislation, would be difficult to exercise on the basis of the limited information that the parties gain about the attitudes of the jurors during the selection process. The only grounds for a suggestion of bias on the part of the jury overall might be the presence of persons of only a single nationality hostile to that of the defendant, of only one gender, or of only a restricted professional group likely be hostile to the defendant.[33] These types of challenges have not been reported.[34] At present, the absence of an effective means to address sources of bias, such as nationality, that are not readily revealed by jurors does not appear to be causing a serious problem, but it may become more of an issue when jury trials move into regions with high tensions and resentments among ethnic groups.

Early evidence concerning the use and effect of provisions allowing for open nullification and for jury-imposed leniency in sentencing is mixed. So far, there has not been a single reported instance of a jury openly nullifying—i.e., answering all factual questions related to the charge in the affirmative, but nonetheless finding the defendant "not guilty." According to anecdotal reports, requests for leniency are not uncommon, but are not seen in the majority of cases.[35] Requests for "special leniency," which forces the judge to assign a punishment below that envisioned in the code, are rare. The statistics in this regard have not given rise to serious complaint or question, and the provisions on jury verdicts might be considered a relative success. However, the hopes of the reformers that juries would use their power of nullification to "send messages" to law makers have not been fulfilled as yet.

The lack of any use by juries of their power to nullify may be a result of the way in which the modern leniency provisions work. Unlike most pre-Revolutionary juries, which had only a right to require simple leniency without knowledge of the range of potential punishments,[36] modern juries have the right to require either simple or "special" leniency and are generally made aware of precisely what the available range of punishment is for each offense charged. Therefore, in judging the defendant the modern Russian jury has the capacity to calculate the range of punishments which might result from any particular verdict and to shape its judgment to ensure the sentence that it deems appropriate. If jurors in the nineteenth century used nullifications in order to avoid the application of punishments that they imagined would be too harsh, jurors in the twentieth century can control sentencing directly and do not need to resort to such drastic methods as nullification (despite the invitation to do so) to avoid a possible injustice in sentencing.[37]

The lack of direct nullifications and limited use of special leniency findings in verdicts might also result from the nature of the cases that juries can hear. The restriction of the introduction of jury trials to the regional courts, justified on budgetary grounds as well as the absence of physical space capacity in the lower courts, limited trial by jury to the small group of serious charges for which the regional court serves as the court of first instance.[38] Most of the charges on the list comprise serious violent crimes. Even a case of murder is eligible only if the charge is intentional murder with aggravating circumstances and only aggravated rape charges (e.g., of a minor, or resulting in severe injury) qualify. While there are a few charges which do not fall into this category (e.g., treason, counterfeiting on an especially large scale), the vast majority of cases actually heard by juries concern violent crimes, especially aggravated murder. While the jury considering such a case might find that a defendant acted in self defense or that the case was not sufficiently proved, these are not the type of cases in which juries are likely to be tempted to nullify—to acquit a clearly guilty defendant—out of conviction that the act should not be punished or in order to send a message to the state about the undue severity of criminal punishments. Similarly, these are not cases in which the jury is likely to strongly identify with a guilty defendant and on this basis decide for special leniency. Although the rarity of special leniency findings (which require sentencing outside the range envisioned by the code) may indicate that jurors have not found the sentencing range offered for the crime committed to be unreasonable, this cannot be taken as juror comment on the severity of the criminal law as a whole or the punishments assigned to lesser offenses.[39] As long as eligibility for jury trial remains limited to the most serious crimes and the jury case load continues to be dominated by aggravated murder charges, it cannot be expected that jury verdicts will produce the broader critique envisioned by the drafters.[40]

The evidence concerning the effect of high juror payments is also mixed. Despite dire predictions based on difficulties with assessors, courts have not been reporting difficulty in obtaining a sufficient number of potential jurors to seat a bench. Some of the willingness to appear for jury duty despite the inconvenience it entails and the lack of public experience with such procedures must be attributed to the high rate of pay. A survey of jurors serving in Saratov over the course of a year shows overall rates of juror satisfaction with their experiences that are extremely high,[41] and while the jurors do not identify payment as a source of their satisfaction it is hard to believe that the high rate of pay does not influence the result.[42] Anecdotal reports do, however, indicate that to attract potential jurors courts must undertake a significant amount of follow-up work through personal visits or telephone calls, explaining the meaning of jury service notices and what service entails.[43] These reports also suggest that courts, in this early stage of implementation of the legislation, are drawing jury pools primarily from residents of the city where the court is located, avoiding the issue of the provision of accommodation and meals (other than lunch) for jurors and the possibility that jurors located farther away from the court would not respond to a call for service.

The high rate of pay for jurors should also be examined in terms of its effect on the diffusion of the institution. Payments made to jurors are not the only cost associated with the re-institution of the jury. The re-equipment of court facilities, the creation and maintenance of juror lists, and the additional staff required for the clerical burden and for direct work with jurors are all costly. The additional cost for juror payments, however, is very significant—amounting to more than it would cost to pay seven judges for each day of trial.[44] Budgetary concerns have been one of the most frequently cited reasons for opposition to the re-institution of jury trials, and they are regularly raised by those in judicial and governmental circles who state that they otherwise support the practice. Problems with financing have continued to hamper the extension of the jury trial option even to regions eager to start it, and at the time of this writing there is little to indicate that this problem will be solved in the near future.

The cost of payment for jurors influenced the restriction of juries to the regional court[45] and the consequent limitation of eligibility for jury trial primarily to serious violent crimes. This limitation, in turn, may have had important consequences for the ability of the jury to play the central role in judicial and legal reform envisioned for it by its creators. The limitation of the right to jury trial to such serious crimes would, even if all eligible cases were tried by jury, ensure a relatively small number of such trials in relation to the total number of criminal cases and thereby reduce the potential for the habits, principles, and processes of jury trial to influence the system's values and conduct overall. Moreover, the effect of the type of case heard on juror willingness to extend leniency or nullify nearly guarantees that verdicts will not serve the drafters' desired function of commentary on the content of the criminal law.

All this suggests that the adoption of features of the jury trial that increased its cost, and particularly large scale payments to jurors, while improving the early performance of the institution, has been a primary factor in limiting its development and broader influence. This would be an ironic conclusion, as it was in large part the drafters' vision of the jury as the spirit and motive force of the reform that prevented reduction of juror payments and the use of measures of compulsion. In other words, the grand vision of the jury as the soul of the reform may have led to policy and drafting choices that ultimately will prevent that grand vision from being realized. There are, however, indications that large juror payments and the restriction of the use of juries are not solely responsible for any failure of the process to become the central motor of broad reform.

In practice, only a minority of the defendants eligible for jury trial request the process.[46] Concerns about the more limited appellate review available following a jury trial (about which defendants are formally warned) and about the skills of defense counsel, as well as other factors,[47] may be influential in producing this result. Nonetheless, the limited use of the procedure raises questions about the degree to which accused persons believe that jury trials are more fair or less repressive than the traditional criminal process. Further, neither the trials in general nor any individual trial has captured and focused the attention of the public and the press in the way that the emblematic trials of political or religious dissidents did in the pre-Revolutionary period. This may be due in part to the repetitive nature of their subject matter and to the small number of trials. However, it may also be the case that the legal and social environment of Russia in the 1990s simply does not resemble that of the 1860s so closely that a policy change can be expected to have similar results.

While the changes in Russian society engendered by the reforms of the late nineteenth century were substantial—including the abolishment of serfdom and significant changes in governmental structures as well as the major judicial reform—the same autocratic dynasty remained in place. Anger over past abuses of the law by this same dynasty could not easily be deflected by a sense that the entity responsible for them had disappeared or been deposed. By contrast, the root cause of the abuses that is identified by the drafters of the Conception of Judicial Reform—the Soviet state and its hostile attitude toward civil society and subordination of the judiciary to political ends—has literally disappeared. Its successors profess abhorrence of all of its organizing principles and have been engaged in an effort to replace much of its law since before the enactment of the jury trial legislation. This being the case, the degree of public concern over abuse of the criminal law and the level of public hostility toward the central state power that made jury trials so important to late nineteenth-century observers may be absent in the modern period. Jury trials and the crimes they concern are far less likely in their modern incarnation to be widely discussed as illustrations of social theory or examples of the continuing abuses of the same resented power and far more likely to be seen as discrete processes concerning primarily those directly involved. In the midst of a disintegration of the previous state structure, hyperinflation and economic collapse, and a general perception of rising lawlessness, the public's concerns about the law and the legal system may be directed more toward access to justice, protection from crime, and the effect of the policies expressed in substantive laws on their communities and economic prospects. In these conditions, the jury—even if it were available for a much broader spectrum of criminal charges—might not serve as a vehicle through which the public could express its current political concerns.

All things considered, the Russian jury of the 1990s may simply be incapable of generating the level of attention and support that would be needed for it to serve as the engine for further judicial and legal reform.

Notes

1. The broad similarity is, of course, not solely in the scale of the proposed change in the legal system. As is the current reform process, the periodic attempts at the wholesale re-creation of the Russian legal system over the last several centuries have often been integral parts of an even broader attempt to completely restructure the state and, sometimes, society. Moreover, many of these attempts, like the current reform, have been undertaken with the stated goal of bringing Russia into line with the practices and theories of other states. Peter the Great, Catherine II, and Alexander II all undertook their substantial reforms of the legal system in the name of correcting Russia's "backwardness" and adopting the best practices of her European neighbors. The outstanding exception to this would be the changes undertaken in the early Soviet period which, although originally conceived as an application of then current European political and social theories, went well beyond the practices of

other states.

2. An exception to this is discussion of the reform of land tenure and the civil-law rules relating to the use and transfer of real property, in which reference back to pre-Revolutionary models and reform attempts (on which, in turn, Soviet models were very consciously based) is quite common and is an important part of political and legal debate on the issue.

3. The reform of judicial institutions as a whole, of which the reintroduction of the jury is a part, is an area in which reference to past practices is more common. This is not surprising, as many of the same individuals were involved in the creation of conceptual documents and the drafting of legislation for both jury trial procedures and the general reform of the structures and processes in the courts of general jurisdiction.

4. "Osnovy zakonodatelstva Soiuza SSR i soiuznykh respublik o sudoustroistve," *Vedomosti Verkhovnogo Soveta SSSR*, 1989, No. 23, item 441, article 11. On discussions of the jury in the perestroika years, see Stephen C. Thaman, "The Resurrection of Trial by Jury in Russia," *Stanford Journal of International Law* 31, no. 1 (1995): 68-72.

5. The Supreme Soviet's confirmation of the Conception, although without the text of the Conception itself, is recorded in *Vedomosti Verkhovnogo Soveta*, 1991, No. 44, item 1435. The full text of the Conception, which occupies just over 100 closely printed pages, along with the Supreme Soviet's confirmation and an introduction by one of the group of authors, was later printed and distributed by the Editorial and Publishing Division of the Presidium of the Supreme Soviet of the Russian Federation and "Respublika" publishers. See *Kontseptsiia sudebnoi reformy v Rossiiskoi Federatsii* (Moscow, 1992). A translation of the entire publication can be found in *Statutes and Decisions: The Laws of the USSR and its Successor States* 30, no. 2 (March-April 1994). It is not clear what legal significance the various actors in this unusual process attached to the "confirmation" of a "concept" for a broad area of legislative and institutional reform. See the Editor's Introduction to the translation in *Statutes and Decisions* 30, no.2 (March-April 1994): 3-6 (S. J. Reynolds, ed.).

6. The other members of the group listed in the published text of the Conception were S. E. Vitsin, A. M. Larin, I. B. Mikhailovskaia, T. G. Morshchakova, R. V. Nazarov, S. A. Pashin, I. L. Petrukhin, and Iu. I. Stetsovskii. S. A. Pashin would later serve as the primary drafter of the legislation establishing jury trials.

7. This is by no means to suggest that a concern with the possibilities for abuse of criminal law and process was inappropriate for a group addressing judicial reform or that a differently composed group would have ignored the issue. The problems identified by the authors of the Conception were (are) serious and some of them would almost certainly have been given prominence in any serious consideration of the needs of judicial reform. However, a group less focused on criminal law and procedure might have been somewhat less attracted to the equation of historical periods and somewhat less convinced concerning the centrality of jury trials to the entire reform, both of which are discussed below.

8. Conception, Part II, section 6, paragraph 1.

9. These ideas appear repeatedly throughout the Conception, but are particularly clearly expressed in Part II.

10. The quoted language appears as the fifth paragraph of the Preface to the Conception.

11. The obvious examples in this category are the Vera Zasulich and Mendel Beilis trials. In the Zasulich trial, a young woman had made an attempt on the life of a tsarist official in response to his alleged abuse of a young man who was detained for illegal political activities. The jury acquitted her despite her admission of the attempt. The trial provided a focus for debate on the permissibility and proper forms of political activity and dissent and the use of the criminal law to suppress them, and also on the broad powers of tsarist officials and the widespread abuse of prisoners, all of which were already issues of serious concern in society at large. In the Beilis trial, a Jewish man was accused of the ritual murder of a child and acquitted by the jury only after a lengthy trial and an intense effort by the prosecuting authorities for a conviction. The trial revealed the extent of state-sponsored anti-Semitism and provided a focus for public anger concerning the ability of state officials to abuse their powers and to pursue groundless prosecutions.

12. In the initial stages, the procedural changes that included the institution of the jury were openly referred to as "experimental." Its proponents have never accepted this designation. They argued that the approval of the Conception of Judicial Reform, which included reference to the need to institute jury trials, occurred prior to the drafting and passage of the new criminal procedure legislation, and that therefore the decision to institute this form of criminal proceeding was final. The inclusion of a right to jury trial in the instances specified by legislation in the 1993 constitution of the Russian Federation strengthened the perception that the matter had been decided and the focus of later discussion turned more toward definition of the boundaries of the right. *Konstitutsiia Rossiiskoi Federatsii* (Moscow, 1994), Article 47.2. Nonetheless, jury trials have been instituted in only a few areas of the country and many continue to refer to the procedure as "experimental."

13. The pre-Revolutionary provisions concerning the use of juries were themselves amended frequently during the period of their effect, making direct comparisons of the legislative provisions somewhat more complicated. For a sense of the pace of legislative amendment in the field of criminal process during that period see the chronicle provided in I. Ya. Foinitskii's *Kurs' ugolovnogo sudoproizvodstva* [Course on Criminal Procedure], 2d ed, Vol. I, Section 22 (53-55)(St. Petersburg, 1896). References to the draft(s) of the jury trial legislation refer to several drafts on file with the author. Additional drafts with slightly different provisions in some of the areas discussed herein may also have been circulated during the preparation and passage process.

14. See Articles 438 and 439 of *Ugolovno-protsessual'nyi kodeks* (Moscow, 1995), referred to hereafter as the Criminal Procedure Code of the RSFSR. This system for jury selection is not unique in its broad outlines to Russia, and has much in common with systems used now or in the past by some European countries.

These and other articles in the code relating to jury trials were introduced in *Zakon Rossiiskoi Federatsii ot iiuliia 1993 g.,* "O vnesenii izmenenii i dopolnenii v Zakone RSFSR 'O sudoustroistve RSFSR', Ugolovno-protsessualnyi kodeks RSFSR, Ugolovnyi kodeks RSFSR, i Kodeks RSFSR ob administrativnykh pravonarushenniiakh," *Vedomosti Verkhovnogo Soveta Rossiiskoi Federatsii,* 1993, No. 33, item 1313, referred to hereafter as Jury Law of 16 July 1993.

15. Compare Article 656 of the 1864 *Ustav ugolovnogo sudoproizvodstva* (hereafter, Statute on Criminal Procedure), to Article 440 of the Criminal Procedure Code of the RSFSR.

16. See Article 449 of the Criminal Procedure Code of the RSFSR.

17. Of course, the modern Russian jury could in answering the relevant questions still hide a nullification by finding that an essential element of the crime was not proved rather than by finding the defendant not to be guilty despite positive findings on all of the factual elements.

18. The most famous instance of this is the case of Vera Zasulich, mentioned above, in which a young woman who admitted to making an attempt on the life of a tsarist official because of his treatment of a prisoner not personally known to her was acquitted.

19. This specific intent was stated by Sergei Anatolevich Pashin during an organized discussion of a draft of the legislation at Harvard Law School in December 1991, in response to questions regarding the nullification issue.

A provision was inserted at the time of passage of the legislation allowing the judge to combine the questions concerning the specific actions and intent of the defendant and the final question of guilt or innocence into a single question concerning the defendant's guilt or innocence. See paragraph 2 of Article 449 of the Criminal Procedure Code. In practice, however, this provision will be difficult to use in any but the simplest of cases. The use of a single question as to the guilt or innocence of the accused would make the clear formulation of questions that are often required concerning mitigating or aggravating factors and positive defenses extremely difficult. Since the legislation as passed makes only a particular set of very serious crimes eligible for jury consideration, there are a limited number of cases in which the simple form of verdict is likely to be acceptable.

20. The provisions concerning jury findings on leniency can be found in paragraph 2 of Article 449 and Article 460 of the Criminal Procedure Code.

21. These rules were contained in Articles 814 and 828 of the Statute on Criminal Procedure. The reform also introduced provisions allowing judges hearing cases alone, upon recognition of certain specific circumstances, to assign the minimum punishment envisioned by law or to reduce the punishment one or two levels.

22. See the discussion in V. M. Palauzov, *Postanovlenie voprosov prisiazhnym po Russkomu pravu*, Part I (Odessa, 1885).

23. Where the law envisions the possibility of the death penalty, a jury finding for leniency prevents its application but does not otherwise limit the judge in assigning punishment over the remaining range of sentences provided in the relevant part of the code. See paragraph 2 of Article 460 of the Criminal Procedure Code.

24. Some factors which are not within the jury's control or knowledge may also affect sentencing under the law, reducing the jury's ability to exercise such specific control. The most prominent of these are possible classification of the defendant as a recidivist or a finding that the defendant has committed the same crime previously, both of which may result in the application of a different range of sentences under the provisions of the criminal code. Because the recognition of the defendant as a recidivist is outside the authority of the jury (under Articles 435, paragraph 1 and 3, and 449, paragraph 5, of the Code of Criminal Procedure of the RSFSR), and juries are not permitted to hear evidence concerning the defendant's prior convictions (see, e.g., Article 446 of the same code), such determinations are made by the judge as a part of the sentencing process following the jury's verdict.

25. The validity of these common perceptions of the results of jury trials during the pre-Revolutionary period may be open to some doubt. While cases like that of Vera Zasulich are sometimes seen as emblems of the era, the impression that pre-Revolutionary juries had a strong tendency to nullify rather than have a law they disliked be applied and to extend leniency to defendants seems to be based heavily on a small number of high profile cases. There is some evidence that juries were not, overall, more lenient than the professional courts. For example, a study conducted in 1894 under the guidance of A. F. Koni found that juries did not produce an exaggerated number of acquittals, and were even more repressive in their verdicts than non-jury courts. See A. F. Koni, "Sud prisiazhnykh," *Entsiklopedicheskii slovar Brokgauza i Efrona*, Vol. 63, cited in Samuel Kucherov, "The Jury as Part of the Russian Judicial Reform of 1864," *American Slavic and East European Review* 9, no. 2 (1950): 88. Doubt has also been cast on the general impression that tsarist courts outside the jury system were uniformly punitive. See, e.g., V. A. Bukov, *V tupikakh revoliutsionnogo pravosoznaniia* [The Dead-Ends of Revolutionary Legal Consciousness] (Moscow, 1994), 61-64. There is a reference to the Koni study in the Conception of Judicial Reform, Part III, section 12 (jury trials), supporting a claim that juries are not overall more lenient than other forms of courts. The evaluation of the competing evidence on the behavior of pre-Revolutionary juries is, however, made complicated by the possible motives of those responsible for the studies. Koni was himself a strong proponent of the jury and issued the results of his study at a time when the use of juries was under strong attack due to their alleged leniency.

26. All of the provisions of the law as passed on this issue appear in Article 86 of Zakon RSFSR "O sudoustroistve RSFSR," as revised by the Jury Law of 16 July 1993 (cited hereafter as RF Law on Court Organization.)

27. On the composition and difficulties of pre-Revolutionary juries, see generally J. W. Atwell, Jr., "The Jury System and Its Role in Russia's Legal, Social and Political Development from 1857 to 1914," unpublished Ph.D. dissertation (Princeton University, 1970), 79-90, and sources cited therein.

28. December 1991 draft, on file with the author.

29. In this connection it is interesting to note that the legislation creating jury procedures, while it refers to the performance of jury service as an obligation, provides no specific penalty for the avoidance of jury service. Administrative penalties are specifically envisioned by the legislation only for the failure to provide information necessary for the creation of jury lists (or the provision of false information) and for interference with the performance by a juror of his or her duty. See Articles 83 and 88 of the RF Law on Court Organization, as revised by the Jury Law of 16 July 1993.

30. The regions were selected on the basis of available court facilities, absence of serious problems between racial, national, or social groups, and interest on the part of both the court and the regional authorities in facilitating the introduction of juries. The very first trial under the new legislation took place in Saratov in November 1993.

31. During a period of observation of jury trials in Saratov from June 1994 through March 1995, jury pools appearing in court for jury selection generally contained between 25 and 35 potential jurors, although more had usually been summoned. Notes on file with the author.

32. During one Saratov trial concerning accusations of homosexual rape, the jurors were asked by the judge during the selection process to indicate if they had a bias concerning homosexuals. A significant portion of the jury pool immediately so indicated, and the remaining potential jurors, having glanced at their fellows, also so indicated within the course of the few minutes allowed by the judge for consideration and answer. The judge rephrased the question to ask the candidates to indicate if they had such a significant animus toward homosexuals that they felt unable to judge the case objectively on the basis of the evidence. No potential juror indicated such a bias and the jury selection process continued. Defendant's counsel made no objection and no attempt to have a new pool called or to strike those jurors who had first indicated their distaste for his client's sexual inclination. A. Feindehl observation notes (on file with the author).

33. An exception would be the case described in the previous note, in which a general question asked by the judge elicited a statement of bias from a substantial number of the potential jurors. This is likely to be a rare occurrence.

34. Another case observed in Saratov concerned a defendant of Chechen heritage accused of the rape and murder of a woman in the same village. The jury pool, judging by the names and appearances of those appearing, did not contain others of Chechen nationality or of another nationality from the "trans-caucasus" regions. Although bias against all of the "trans-caucasian" nationalities is very common among those of Russian and other Slavic heritage and bias against Chechens particularly strong during the past several years of discord and threats, the judge did not ask the pool about their possible biases. The defense attorney did not request that such a question be asked nor did she challenge the composition of the jury on the basis of "tendentiousness." Observation notes on file with the author.

35. There is some public perception that juries are more lenient than judges sitting alone or a court in the traditional composition of a judge and two assessors. Information on the rates with which jurors request leniency is, however, not widely discussed and this perception is more likely due to the fact that juries are believed to doubt evidence and refuse to convict defendants in a higher number of cases. There have been a number of cases in which juries found defendants guilty only of a much lesser included offense or (more rarely) acquitted them altogether. The very first jury trial involved a rejection by the procurator of part of the aggravated murder charge at the start of the trial (on the grounds of insufficient evidence), and the final conviction of the defendants only of a much lesser charge. This was widely publicized as evidence of the positive effect of the jury on evidentiary standards, but also served (along with later cases in which only a far lesser charge has been proven to the jury's satisfaction) to foster a general impression that a conviction is harder to get from a jury.

36. A change in the law some 35 years after the passage of the initial reform legislation did give pre-Revolutionary juries information on the range of sentences envisioned by the law for the crime charged. The study conducted by A. F. Koni which found that juries were not more lenient than other courts pre-dated this change in the law and may have been influential in producing it. See note 26 above and accompanying text. It is interesting to speculate whether Koni's findings might, in fact, have been produced in part by the jury's ignorance of the probable sentence. Although I am aware of no such study, a comparison of jury results in similar cases prior to and following the passage of the amendment might provide interesting results.

37. A questionnaire distributed to legal professionals (judges, procurators, and defense counsel) in Saratov in 1994 concerning their attitudes toward the jury produced a number of expressions of concern about jury sentence selection. In particular, several respondents noted that judges are expected to ensure that defendants who have committed the same types of crime are not sentenced to widely differing punishments. In order to do this, judges must draw upon their experience and knowledge of the kinds of sentences usually imposed in similar cases—experience and knowledge that a jury cannot, by definition, possess. The jury's ability to "tie the hands" of the judge in sentencing, especially if significant evidence that might affect leniency decisions had been excluded from the jury, may have been influential in causing these respondents to worry about an unfair divergence of sentences among similarly situated defendants. Survey materials on file with the author. Results of the survey will appear, along with the results of a concurrent survey of jurors, in M. Findlay and S. Reynolds, "Juror Experiences in Russia" (forthcoming, 1997).

38. It had been originally suggested by the drafters that all cases for which punishment of more than one year's imprisonment was possible should be eligible for jury trial. This would have required jury trials to be held in local people's courts and those courts to be equipped with the staff and processing capacity for summons and selection, as well as the physical space for accommodation of the jury in the courtroom. For a significant number of such courts, in which several judges share office space and there is insufficient funding for paper and other basic supplies, new buildings and staff and budgets in multiples of current allocations would have been required.

39. It should be noted that, at least in recent years, issues of undue severity have most often been raised with respect to lesser crimes. Questions have been raised particularly about the range of punishment for such offenses as petty theft and the possible decriminalization of such offenses as "hooliganism" and consensual homosexual activity.

40. It is interesting to note that the use of leniency findings in early jury trials does not seen to have been cited by the drafters of the jury trial legislation or proponents of criminal law reform as evidence that the jurors found the upper range of code sanctions too harsh, at least in a significant number of instances. The use of such findings was not, perhaps, sufficiently common to support an argument for change. (If crimes and criminals are roughly evenly distributed along a severity spectrum corresponding to the range of available punishments, one would expect the portion of the range from the midway point and lower to be appropriate in roughly half of the cases over time.) Moreover, given rising overall concern about crime and continuing budgetary concerns about jury trials, the use of any argument that suggested that juries were systematically more lenient would be a two-edged sword—possibly useful to a criminal law reform effort but just as possibly fatal to the jury itself.

41. Findlay and Reynolds (forthcoming, 1997), reporting overall levels of satisfaction in the upper 90 percent range for all jurors. Survey materials on file with the author.

42. The figures obtained in the Saratov survey exceed the satisfaction rates reported in almost all foreign jurisdictions conducting similar surveys, despite the fact that the foreign jurors should have been better informed about what to expect and the nature of the process than those in Saratov. Novelty and the intrinsic interest of the new process may account for some of the discrepancy, but the other notable difference between the Saratov jurors and others surveyed in other jurisdictions is the size of the payment made to jurors for service in comparison to average wages in the region.

43. Interviews conducted with jurors appearing for service and with court chancellery personnel in connection with the Saratov survey indicate that many of those who receive notices to appear for jury selection did not initially understand the meaning of the notice. Court personnel were often called upon to calm fears that the notice indicated that the summoned party or a family member was to be accused of some type of wrongdoing. Once this misunderstanding is straightened out, however, the promise of a not insignificant payment for service was reported by court personnel to be a useful inducement to appearance. Interview notes of A. Feindehl, on file with the author.

44. Fourteen jurors, each receiving one half of a judge's per diem salary for each day of service, plus the additional payments made to those who show up for selection.

45. Again, juror payment was not the sole factor in the decision to limit jury trials to the regional courts. Serious facilities limitations were also present for some local courts. It is conceivable, however, that a significant number of local courts could have offered jury trials for at least some offenses, perhaps with the transfer of cases from those local courts not yet able to accommodate a jury.

46. At a session of the Plenum of the Supreme Court of the Russian Federation held in December 1994 to discuss, among other things, a draft decree concerning jury trial practice, it was stated by the reporting judge that jury trials were requested by one out of every five eligible defendants. Attendance notes on file with the author.

47. It is widely believed that procurators, as well as some judges, actively discourage defendants from choosing jury trials. Such advice may also come from defense attorneys who are either lacking in confidence that they can conduct a jury trial or are lacking in enthusiasm for a longer and more difficult trial procedure if appointed by the court and poorly paid.

INDEX